FIFTH GENERATION COMPUTER SYSTEMS 1988

Proceedings of the International Conference on
Fifth Generation Computer Systems 1988
Tokyo, Japan
November 28-December 2, 1988

Edited by
Institute for New Generation
Computer Technology (ICOT)
Tokyo, Japan

Volume 1

 OHM    Springer-Verlag

FIFTH GENERATION COMPUTER SYSTEMS 1988

Proceedings of the International Conference on Fifth Generation Computer Systems 1988

Distribution
Sole distribution rights outside Japan granted to Springer-Verlag
All orders should be sent to the following addresses:

Japan:
OHMSHA LTD., 3-1 Kanda Nishiki-cho, Chiyoda-ku, Tokyo 101, Japan

North America:
Springer-Verlag NY Inc., 175 Fifth Avenue, New York, NY 10010

Rest of the world:
SPRINGER-VERLAG, Heidelberger Platz 3, 1000 Berlin 33, FRG

British Library Cataloguing in Publication Data
International Conference on Fifth Generation Computers: 1988
  International Conference on Fifth Generation Computer Systems (FGCS '88).
  1, Computer systems
  I. Title
  004

Library of Congress Cataloging-in-Publication Data
International Conference on Fifth Generation Computer systems (1988: Tokyo, Japan)
    Proceedings of the International Conference on Fifth Generation Computer Systems 1988:
    Nov. 28 – Dec. 2, 1988, Tokyo Prince Hotel, Tokyo Japan/
    Institute for New Generation Computer Technology.
    p. cm.
    Bibliography: p.
    Includes indexes,

    1. Fifth generation computers — Congresses. I. Shin Sedai Konpyūta Gijutsu Kaihatsu Kikō (Japan) II. Title.
    QA76.85.I58, 1988
    004 — dc20   89-11366
                                                                       CIP

ISBN-13: 978-1-4471-3158-8   e-ISBN-13: 978-1-4471-3156-4
DOI: 10.1007/978-1-4471-3156-4

GREETINGS

Looking back on the history of fifth generation computer research, it was seven years ago, in October of 1981, that research themes and plans aiming at the realization of a fifth generation computer by Japanese scientists were first announced, and the International Conference on Fifth Generation Computer Systems 1981 was held.

In April of 1982, the ten-year Fifth Generation Computer Systems Project was initiated by MITI with the enthusiastic support and cooperation of numerous individuals and organizations in government, academia, and industry. It was this Institute which assumed responsibility for execution of the project.

In November 1984, the International Conference on Fifth Generation Computer Systems 1984 was held, for the purpose of reporting the results of basic research achieved in the initial three-year stage.

This conference is the third of its kind, and coincides with the fourth and last year of the intermediate stage of the project.

The central aim of the intermediate stage of research and development was to lay the foundations for full-fledged parallel processing systems, something never before attempted on a large scale. Another important goal of our work was the accumulation of software resources and expertise for the development of intelligent software programs based on inference mechanisms. For the parallel processing hardware, an experimental parallel inference machine has been completed, incorporating 64 processors, and a demonstration parallel operating system which will serve as the core of the parallel processing software resources has begun to run on this hardware system.

Work is now underway to trial-fabricate a parallel inference machine, consisting of 128 more powerful processors; and our initial goals have nearly been achieved.

Research on intelligent software has culminated in the development of a system for natural language understanding, various expert systems, and a system for theorem-proving and other mathematical operations.

The final stage of research, to begin next year, will aim at the development of a fifth generation computer prototype comprising approximately 1000 processors, a fully functional parallel operating system running on this hardware, and a knowledge programming system and other tools.

ICOT has performed research and development under commission by MITI with a budget of 8.2 billion yen for the initial three-year stage.

In the intermediate stage, ICOT has carried out R&D with a budget of 4.7 billion yen in 1985, 5.5 billion yen in 1986, 5.6 billion yen in 1987, and 5.7 billion yen in 1988, for a total of 21.5 billion in the four years of the intermediate stage.

Overseas as well, countries in Europe and America are vigorously promoting projects, under government direction, for the establishment of fifth generation computer technology. ICOT also emphasizes international exchanges, and makes every effort to facilitate such intercourse, including admission for foreign researchers for extended periods.

At this international conference, we intend to introduce the results of research in the intermediate stage, including more than thirty separate demonstrations, as well as provide a forum both for presentations by researchers from Japan and abroad and for exchange of opinions.

It is my fervent hope that through the synergy and lively exchange of information between the many participants, this international conference will prove a fruitful exercise for all concerned, and will contribute greatly to further advances in information processing in other countries as well.

Katsushige Mita
President of ICOT

CHAIRMAN'S GREETINGS

On behalf of the Organizing Committee, it is my great pleasure to welcome you to this International Conference on Fifth Generation Computer Systems 1988.

This is the third international conference on Fifth Generation Computer Systems, following the first conference in October of 1981 and the second conference in November of 1984. At the 1981 conference, we introduced our country's plans for research and development of Fifth Generation Computer Systems, and called for cooperation from other countries in this endeavor. That conference appears to have had a considerable impact, and became the impetus for the initiation of similar projects in several other countries. The 1984 conference was primarily devoted to explanations of the Fifth Generation Computer Systems Project, and to presentations of research results for the initial stage of two and one-half years at the Institute for New Generation Computer Technology (ICOT), which is responsible for the actual research and development. At this conference, there were also reports of the latest research results, both from within Japan and from abroad. There is no doubt that this conference held great significance, both in confirming the importance of research on Fifth Generation Computers, and in indicating concrete directions for future research efforts.

Professor Tohru Moto-oka of the Department of Electrical Engineering at the University of Tokyo had supervised research at ICOT during the initial three-year stage, and had also overseen preparations for the last two international conferences; unfortunately, Professor Moto-oka passed away in November of 1985, with the work only half completed. Thereafter, I have strived in my humble way to fill the gap left by Professor Moto-oka, and have also done my best to keep alive at ICOT the same positive spirit in which research and development is carried out.

Reflecting on the experiences of '81 and '84, I have noticed that these FGCS conferences are quite unique in several ways. First, an extremely large numbers of outstanding papers have been submitted; second, highest-quality scientists and engineers from around the world cooperated to make the conferences successful, with many persons attending; third, participants from various fields were present, including government officials, journalists and managers involved in R&D projects; fourth, there were animated exchanges of opinion which transcended the perspectives of individuals; and fifth, the conferences ranked as international events commanding worldwide attention. These facts attest to the crucially important role in store for research on Fifth Generation Computer Systems, both for the field of information science, and as a means of resolving the problems faced by information-oriented societies.

At this conference, we would hope that the participants would evaluate the accumulated results of basic research at ICOT over the past six and one-half years, and would also appreciate any comments or criticism of research plans for the final stage of the project. And, we hope for and expect that presentations of technical papers by researchers from Japan and abroad will lead to an understanding of advanced research on Fifth Generation Computer Systems, and will facilitate exchange of opinions. To this end, we have arranged for participants to view a demonstration indicating the major results of research at ICOT. Such a demonstration of advanced technology has not until now been attempted at an international conference; we are confident that it will aid understanding of the fruits of our work. Also, we have planned invited lectures and panel discussions by distinguished researchers active in the 'front lines' of the field, so that participants can better grasp the state of research on an international level, and to aid in estimations of themes for future research. Finally, we have scheduled a reception and banquet so that participants may mingle in an informal atmosphere.

As the late Professor Moto-oka once observed, this is the "age of competition and cooperation." Now is the time for us to pool our most important resource — human ingenuity — to prove what we can achieve, and to aim at a more plentiful society.

It is my fervent hope that this conference will serve as an occasion for vigorous debate and fruitful exchange of opinions and information.

Once more, in my capacity as Chairman of the Organizing Committee I wish to express my heartfelt gratitude to all participants. I would also like to extend warm thanks to those persons on the Program Committee who made great efforts to create such an attractive program of events for this conference, to the many persons from this country and others who agreed to review papers, to the Organizing Committee members for their selfless efforts to ensure that all conference events come off as planned, to the ICOT personnel who labored day and night to make a demonstration of their research results possible, and to the various individuals and institutions who lent their generous support to enable this conference.

Hideo Aiso
Conference Chairman

PREFACE

It has been seven years since the first International Conference on the Fifth Generation Computer Systems. A great deal of research effort has been made toward the goal of FGCS throughout the world and produced many excellent results. Evidence of this progress is that we received 355 papers of very high quality from 29 countries for the third International Conference on FGCS.

These proceedings consist of three volumes. The first volume includes the plenary session and portions of the technical sessions. It contains reports on the current status of the FGCS project research carried out over the past four years at ICOT, as well as future planning along this line. The other two volumes are collections of technical literature. Because the quality of papers we received was very high, we faced difficulty in making the final selections. However, limitation in length of the conference as well as size of this proceedings forced us to select only 95 submissions and four invited papers. Papers were selected according to their relevance, technical content, originality, and clarity by at least four referees: one from Program Committee, one from Japan, and two from other countries.

It is our sincere hope that the conference program itself will prove rewarding and enjoyable to all who are able to participate in FGCS'88 and that the Proceedings will serve as a valuable reference source for years to come.

As Program Chairman, it is my great pleasure to acknowledge the support of a number of people. First of all, I would like to single out the program committee members, who made great efforts to arrange an attractive conference program. They are the Program Vicechairman, Dr. Koichi Furukawa, and the four chairmen of subcommittees, Professors Setsuo Arikawa, Akinori Yonezawa, Makoto Amamiya and Hozumi Tanaka. I would also like to thank the 483 referees from 17 countries who worked hard to evaluate the submitted papers within so limited a schedule. A list of the referees is provided on pages ix to xii for our acknowledgment.

Finally, I would like to thank the many people at ICOT who provided excellent administrative services to the program committee.

Hidehiko Tanaka
Program Chairman

CONFERENCE COMMITTEES

Organizing Committee

Conference Chairman:
Hideo Aiso — Keio University
Vice-Chairman:
Kazuhiro Fuchi — ICOT
Committee:

Makoto Amamiya	Kyushu University
Ken Hirose	Waseda University
Mitsuru Ishizuka	The University of Tokyo
Takayasu Itoh	Tohoku University
Hajime Karatsu	Tokai University
Hiroshi Kashiwagi	ETL
Kazukiyo Kawanobe	NTT
Akira Kikuchi	JEIDA
Shigenobu Kobayashi	Tokyo Institute of Technology
Tetsuya Kurata	ICOT (Chairman, Management Committee)
Fumio Mizoguchi	Science University of Tokyo
Makoto Nagao	Kyoto University
Setsuo Ohsuga	The University of Tokyo
Shigeru Sato	ICOT (Chairman, Technology Committee)
Hidehiko Tanaka	The University of Tokyo
Hozumi Tanaka	Tokyo Institute of Technology
Mario Tokoro	Keio University
Kinko Yamamoto	JIPDEC
Toshio Yokoi	Japan Electronic Dictionary Research Institute
Akinori Yonezawa	Tokyo Institute of Technology

Program Committee

Chairman:
Hidehiko Tanaka — The University of Tokyo
Vice-Chairman:
Koichi Furukawa — ICOT
Committee:

Makoto Amamiya	Kyushu University
Setsuo Arikawa	Kyushu University
Arvind	MIT
Keith L. Clark	Imperial College
Yuichi Fujii	ICOT
Kokichi Futatsugi	ETL
Hervé Gallaire	ECRC
Randy Goebel	University of Alberta
Atsuhiro Goto	ICOT
Satoshi Goto	NEC
Shigeki Goto	NTT
Masami Hagiya	Kyoto University
Seif Haridi	SICS
Gérard Huet	INRIA
Tetsuo Ida	University of Tsukuba
Shun Ishizaki	ETL
Mitsuru Ishizuka	The University of Tokyo
Hidenori Itoh	ICOT
Masaru Kitsuregawa	The University of Tokyo
Susumu Kunifuji	Fujitsu
Toshiaki Kurokawa	IBM Japan
Jean-Louis Lassez	IBM
Douglas B. Lenat	MCC

Giorgio Levi	University of Pisa
John W. Lloyd	University of Bristol
Fumihiro Maruyama	Fujitsu Laboratories
Yuji Matsumoto	Kyoto University
Fumio Mizoguchi	Science University of Tokyo
Kuniaki Mukai	ICOT
Reiji Nakajima	Kyoto University
Katsumi Nitta	ETL
Satoshi Ono	NTT
Fernando Pereira	SRI International
J.A. Robinson	Syracuse University
Masahiko Satoh	Tohoku University
Taisuke Satoh	ETL
Heinz Schweppe	FU Berlin
Ehud Shapiro	The Weizmann Institute of Science
Kiyoshi Shibayama	Kyoto University
Leon Sterling	Case Western Reserve University
Akikazu Takeuchi	Mitsubishi
Kazuo Taki	ICOT
Hisao Tamaki	Ibaraki University
Hozumi Tanaka	Tokyo Institute of Technology
Jiro Tanaka	Fujitsu
Yuzuru Tanaka	Hokkaido University
Sten-Åke Tärnlund	Uppsala University
Mario Tokoro	Keio University
Philip Treleaven	University College London
Kazunori Ueda	ICOT
M.H. van Emden	University of Victoria
David H.D. Warren	University of Bristol
Yoshinori Yamaguchi	ETL
Minoru Yokota	NEC
Akinori Yonezawa	Tokyo Institute of Technology

Publicity Committee

Chairman:
| Kinko Yamamoto | JIPDEC |

Vice-Chairman:
| Fumio Mizoguchi | Science University of Tokyo |

Committee:
Takashi Chikayama	ICOT
Akira Kikuchi	JEIDA
Tsutomu Yoshioka	ICOT

Demonstration Committee

Chairman:
| Takashi Kurozumi | ICOT |

Vice-Chairman:
| Shun-ichi Uchida | ICOT |

Committee:
| Susumu Taba | ICOT |
| Takasumi Ueda | Mitsubishi |

REFEREES

Abadi, M.	U.S.A.	Dahl, V.	Canada
Abramson, H.	U.K.	Davidson, A.	U.K.
Agrawal, R.	U.S.A.	Debray, S.K.	U.S.A.
Aiba, A.	Japan	DeGroot, D.	U.S.A.
Aida, H.	U.S.A.	Demoen, B.	Belgium
Akama, K.	Japan	Demurjian, S.	U.S.A.
Alshawi, H.	U.K.	Deransart, P.	France
Amamiya, M.	Japan	De Schreye, D.	Belgium
Amano, H.	Japan	Despain, A.M.	U.S.A.
Amano, S.	Japan	Deutsch, P.	U.S.A.
Angluin, D.	U.S.A.	di Primio, F.	F.R.G.
Anzai, Y.	Japan	Dincbas, M.	F.R.G.
Appelt, D.E.	U.S.A.	Doshita, S.	Japan
Arbab, B.	U.S.A.	Dubois, M.	U.S.A.
Arikawa, S.	Japan	Eggenhuisen, H.	Netherlands
Arima, J.	Japan	Enomoto, H.	Japan
Asakawa, Y.	Japan	Fahlman, S.E.	U.S.A.
Asirelli, P.	Italy	Falaschi, M.	Italy
Babb II, R.G.	U.S.A.	Farinas del Cerro, L.	France
Balbin, I.	Australia	Feld, M.	Japan
Barklund, J.	Sweden	Ferrand, G.	France
Barstow, D.	U.S.A.	Ferrari, G.L.	Italy
Bawach, R.	U.K.	Feusen, L.	Sweden
Beckman, L.	Sweden	Filgueiras, M.	Portugal
Beer, R.D.	U.S.A.	Fisher, A.L.	U.S.A.
Bellegarde, F.	France	Fitting, M.	U.S.A.
Bellia, M.	Italy	Flannagan, T.	U.K.
Benker, H.	F.R.G.	Forgy, C.	U.S.A.
Bibel, W.	Canada	Foster, I.	U.K.
Bohm, W.	U.K.	Fox, M.	U.S.A.
Bonacina, M.P.	Italy	Fribourg, L.	France
Bose, S.	U.S.A.	Fujii, Y.	Japan
Bowen, D.	U.S.A.	Fujisaki, T.	U.S.A.
Brewka, G.	F.R.G.	Fujita, H.	Japan
Briot, J-P	France	Fukunaga, K.	Japan
Brock, J.D.	U.S.A.	Fuller, D.A.	U.K.
Bruynooghe, M.	Belgium	Furukawa, K.	Japan
Bush, W.	U.S.A.	Fushimi, S.	Japan
Carlsson, M.	Sweden	Futatsugi, K.	Japan
Carlton, M.	U.S.A.	Gallagher, J.	Israel
Chang, C-L	U.S.A.	Gallaire, H.	F.R.G.
Chen, C.	U.S.A.	Gazdar, G.	U.K.
Chen, T.Y.	Hong Kong	Georgeff, M.	Australia
Chigira, E.	Japan	Gero, J.	Australia
Chikayama, T.	Japan	Giandonato, G.	Italy
Chung, S.M.	U.S.A.	Goebel, R.	Canada
Ciancarini, P.	Italy	Gonzalez-Rubio, R.	France
Ciepielewski, A.	Sweden	Goodwin, S.	Canada
Clark, K. L.	U.K.	Goto, A.	Japan
Clarke, E.M.	U.S.A.	Goto, S.	Japan
Codish, M.	Israel	Goto, S.	Japan
Coelho, H.	Portugal	Gregory, S.	U.K.
Cohen, J.	U.S.A.	Gunji, T.	Japan
Colmerauer, A.	France	Gurd, J.R.	U.K.
Conery, J.	U.S.A.	Gustavsson, R.	Sweden
Cooper, R.	U.K.	Gust, H.	F.R.G.
Coquand, T.	France	Hagert, G.	Sweden
Courcelle, B.	France	Hagihara, K.	Japan
Cox, P.T.	Canada	Hagiya, M.	Japan
Crammond, J.	U.K.	Hammond, P.	U.K.

Handa, K.	Japan	Kanamori, T.	Japan
Haraguchi, M.	Japan	Kanbayashi, Y.	Japan
Haraldsson, A.	Sweden	Kaneda, Y.	Japan
Harao, M.	Japan	Kaplan, R.M.	U.S.A.
Hardy, S.	U.S.A.	Katagiri, Y.	Japan
Harel, D.	Israel	Katsuno, H.	Japan
Haridi, S.	Sweden	Kawahara, Y.	Japan
Harland, J.	U.K.	Kawakami, K.	Japan
Hart, P.E.	U.S.A.	Kawasaki, H.	Japan
Hascoet, L.	France	Keller, R.M.	U.S.A.
Hasida, K.	Japan	Kerisit, J-M	France
Haug, D.	U.S.A.	Kimura, Y.	Japan
Hayashi, H.	Japan	Kirchner, C.	France
Haynes, C.T.	U.S.A.	Kishimoto, M.	Japan
Hendler, J.A.	U.S.A.	Kitakami, H.	Japan
Hermenegildo, M.	U.S.A.	Kitsuregawa, M.	Japan
Hertzberger, L.O.	Netherlands	Kiyoki, Y.	Japan
Hibino, Y.	Japan	Klop, J.W.	Netherlands
Hickey, T.	U.S.A.	Kluge, W.	F.R.G.
Higashida, M.	Japan	Kobayashi, S.	Japan
Higuchi, T.	Japan	Kohata, M.	U.S.A.
Hikita, S.	Japan	Kohda, Y.	Japan
Hiraga, Y.	Japan	Koike, N.	Japan
Hirakawa, H.	Japan	Kok, J.N.	Netherlands
Hiraki, K.	Japan	Konagaya, A.	Japan
Hirata, K.	Japan	Konishi, K.	Japan
Hirose, K.	Japan	Kono, S.	Japan
Hirschman, L.	U.S.A.	Koyama, T.	Japan
Hong, S.J.	U.S.A.	Kubono, H.	Japan
Hori, K.	Japan	Kumar, V.	U.S.A.
Horita, E.	Japan	Kumon, K.	Japan
Hosoi, A.	Japan	Kunen, K.	U.S.A.
Hsiang, J.	U.S.A.	Kunifuji, S.	Japan
Huet, G.	France	Kurfess, F.	F.R.G.
Iannucci, R.A.	U.S.A.	Kurokawa, T.	Japan
Ichiyoshi, N.	Japan	Kursawe, P.	F.R.G.
Ida, M.	Japan	Kusalik, A.	Canada
Ida, T.	Japan	Lafue, G.M.E.	U.S.A.
Iizuka, H.	Japan	Lakhotia, A.	U.S.A.
Ikeuchi, K.	U.S.A.	Lang, B.	France
Imai, M.	Japan	Lassez, J-L	U.S.A.
Inagaki, Y.	Japan	Lay, D.E.	U.S.A.
Inoue, K.	Japan	Lee, M.	U.K.
Isahara, H.	Japan	Lehnert, W.G.	U.S.A.
Ishikawa, Y.	Japan	Leinwand, S.	U.S.A.
Ishizaki, S.	Japan	Lescanne, P.	France
Ishizuka, M.	Japan	Levy, J-J	France
Ito, N.	Japan	Lieberman, H.	U.S.A.
Itoh, F.	Japan	Linden, T.	U.S.A.
Itoh, H.	Japan	Lindstrom, G.	U.S.A.
Itoh, M.	Japan	Lipovski, G.J.	U.S.A.
Iwasaki, Y.	U.S.A.	Litcher, C.	U.S.A.
Jaakkola, H.	Finland	Liu, Y.	U.S.A.
Jaffar, J.	U.S.A.	Lloyd, J.W.	U.K.
Janson, S.	Sweden	Lobo, J.	U.S.A.
Johnson, D.S.	U.S.A.	Lytinen, S.	U.S.A.
Jones, N.D.	Denmark	McAloon, K.	U.S.A.
Josephson, A.	U.S.A.	Maeda, A.	Japan
Joshi, A.K.	U.S.A.	Maes, P.	Belgium
Kahn, G.	France	Maher, M.J.	U.S.A.
Kahn, K.M.	U.S.A.	Makowsky, J.A.	Switzerland
Kameyama, Y.	Japan	Maluszynski, J.	Sweden
Kamimura, T.	Japan	Martelli, M.	Italy
Kanada, Y.	Japan	Maruyama, F.	Japan

Mathieu, P.	Sweden	Ohsuga, S.	Japan
Matsumoto, Y.	Japan	Ohta, K.	Japan
Matsuo, F.	Japan	Ohwada, H.	Japan
McCord, M.C.	U.S.A.	Okumura, A.	Japan
McDermott, J.	U.S.A.	Onai, R.	Japan
Menju, S.	Japan	O'Neill, D.	U.S.A.
Meyer, D.	U.S.A.	Ono, S.	Japan
Miller, D.	U.S.A.	Overbeek, R.	U.S.A.
Mills, J.W.	U.S.A.	Ozawa, T.	Japan
Milner, R.	U.K.	Paass, G.	F.R.G.
Minami, T.	Japan	Palamidessi, C.	Italy
Minker, J.	U.S.A.	Patt, Y.N.	U.S.A.
Miranker, D.	U.S.A.	Pedreschi, D.	Italy
Miyachi, T.	Japan	Penttonen, M.	Finland
Miyano, S.	Japan	Pereira, F.	U.S.A.
Miyazaki, N.	Japan	Pereira, L.M.	Portugal
Mizoguchi, F.	Japan	Peters, S.	U.S.A.
Mizoguchi, R.	Japan	Peyton-Jones, S.L.	U.K.
Mizoguchi, T.	Japan	Plaisted, D.A.	U.S.A.
Monien, B.	F.R.G.	Poole, D.	Canada
Monoi, H.	Japan	Port, G.	Australia
Montanari, U.	Italy	Porto, A.	Portugal
Morishita, S.	Japan	Proskurowski, A.	U.S.A.
Morita, Y.	Japan	Pujin, J.M.	France
Moschovakis, Y.N.	U.S.A.	Pylyshyn, Z.W.	Canada
Motoda, H.	Japan	Quiton, P.	France
Motoyoshi, F.	Japan	Raatz, S.	U.S.A.
Moucerella, P.	Italy	Rabinov, A.	U.S.A.
Mukai, K.	Japan	Ramamohanarao, K.	Australia
Müller-Schloer, C.	F.R.G.	Reeve, M.	U.K.
Murakami, M.	Japan	Refenes, P.	U.K.
Muraki, K.	Japan	Revesz, G.	U.S.A.
Muraoka, Y.	Japan	Reyle, U.	F.R.G.
Mycroft, A.	U.K.	Ridoux, O.	France
Nagao, K.	Japan	Ringwood, G.A.	U.K.
Nagashima, S.	Japan	Rohmer, J.	France
Nagata, M	Japan	Rokusawa, K.	Japan
Naish, L.	Australia	Rusinowitch, M.	France
Najjar, W.	U.S.A.	Sabbah, D.	U.S.A.
Nakajima, K.	Japan	Saint-Dizier, P.	France
Nakamura, J.	Japan	Saito, N.	Japan
Nakamura, K.	Japan	Sakai, K.	Japan
Nakanishi, M.	Japan	Sakama, C.	Japan
Nakashima, H.	Japan	Sakurai, A.	Japan
Nakashima, H.	Japan	Sakurai, T.	Japan
Narain, S.	U.S.A.	Sannella, D.	U.K.
Narishima, H.	Japan	Sato, M.	Japan
Nilsson, M.	Japan	Satoh, K.	Japan
Nilsson, U.	Sweden	Satoh, M.	Japan
Nishida, K.	Japan	Satoh, T.	Japan
Nishio, S.	Japan	Sawamura, H.	Japan
Nitta, K.	Japan	Schweppe, H.	F.R.G.
Nitta, Y.	Japan	Seki, H.	Japan
Noye, J.	F.R.G.	Sergot, M.J.	U.K.
Numao, M.	Japan	Sestoft, P.	Denmark
Numao, M.	Japan	Shapiro, E.	Israel
Oba, M.	Japan	Sharma, M.	U.S.A.
Odijk, E.A.M.	Netherlands	Shepherdson, J.C.	U.K.
Ogata, I.	Japan	Shibayama, E.	Japan
Ogawa, H.	Japan	Shibayama, K.	Japan
Ogawa, Y.	Japan	Shibayama, S.	Japan
Ohki, M.	Japan	Shimada, T.	Japan
Ohmori, T.	Japan	Shinohara, T.	Japan
Ohsuga, A.	Japan	Shin, D.	U.S.A.

Shirai, H.	Japan	Toyama, Y.	Japan
Shirai, K.	Japan	Treleaven, P.	U.K.
Shoham, Y.	U.S.A.	Tsujii, J.	Japan
Shoji, I.	Japan	Udagawa, Y.	Japan
Shultz, J.	Australia	Ueda, K.	Japan
Singh, V.	U.S.A.	Ueno, H.	Japan
Sjoland, T.	Sweden	Unemi, T.	Japan
Sleep, R.	U.K.	van Emden, M.H.	Canada
Sonenberg, E.A.	Australia	Van Hentenryck, P.	F.R.G.
Srini, V.P.	U.S.A.	Vardi, M.Y.	U.S.A.
Stalmarck, G.	Sweden	Vieille, L.	F.R.G.
Steels, L.	Belgium	Vree, W.	Netherlands
Sterling, L.	U.S.A.	Wada, K.	Japan
Stickel, M.E.	U.S.A.	Waern, A.	Sweden
Stolfo, S.J.	U.S.A.	Walker, A.	U.S.A.
Su, S.	U.S.A.	Waltz, D.L.	U.S.A.
Sugie, M.	Japan	Waning, E.	Netherlands
Sugimoto, M.	Japan	Warren, D.H.D.	U.K.
Sugimura, R.	Japan	Warren, D.S.	U.S.A.
Sugino, E.	Japan	Watanabe, O.	U.S.A.
Suwa, M.	Japan	Watson, I.	U.K.
Syre, J.C.	F.R.G.	Watson, P.	U.K.
Takagi, S.	Japan	Webb, J.	U.S.A.
Takahashi, K.	Japan	Wilcox, B.	U.S.A.
Takahashi, N.	Japan	Wilk, P.F.	U.K.
Takahashi, Y.	Japan	Wilks, Y.	U.S.A.
Takano, A.	Japan	Yamaguchi, J.	Japan
Takayama, Y.	Japan	Yamaguchi, T.	Japan
Takeda, M.	Japan	Yamaguchi, Y.	Japan
Takeuchi, A.	Japan	Yamamoto, A.	Japan
Taki, K.	Japan	Yamamoto, M.	Japan
Tamai, T.	Japan	Yamasaki, S.	Japan
Tamaki, H.	Japan	Yamashita, M.	Japan
Tamura, H.	Japan	Yamauchi, N.	Japan
Tamura, K.	Japan	Yang, R.	U.K.
Tamura, N.	Japan	Yasukawa, H.	Japan
Tanaka, H.	Japan	Yasumura, M.	Japan
Tanaka, J.	Japan	Yasuura, H.	Japan
Tanaka, K.	Japan	Yokomori, T.	Japan
Tanaka, Y.	Japan	Yokota, H.	Japan
Tanimoto, S.	U.S.A.	Yokota, K.	Japan
Tärnlund, S-Å	Sweden	Yokota, M.	Japan
Terada, H.	Japan	Yokota, M.	Japan
Terano, T.	Japan	Yokouchi, H.	Japan
Thrift, P.	U.S.A.	Yokoyama, S.	Japan
Tick, E.	Japan	Yonezawa, A.	Japan
Togashi, A.	Japan	Yoshida, H.	Japan
Tokoro, M.	Japan	Yoshida, K.	Japan
Tomita, M.	U.S.A.	Yoshida, N.	Japan
Tomita, S.	Japan	Yoshizumi, S.	Japan
Tomura, S.	Japan	You, J-H	Canada
Tonssen, B.	Sweden	Yuba, T.	Japan
Topor, R.W.	Australia	Zeidler, H.Ch.	F.R.G.
Touati, H.	U.S.A.		

TABLE OF CONTENTS

Volume 1

Volume 2

FOUNDATION

SOFTWARE

Volume 3

ARCHITECTURE

Scheduling for Parallel Machines

SPECIAL SESSION

Parallelism in AI

SUBMITTED PAPERS

Implementation Model for Parallel Logic Languages

APPLICATIONS

SUBMITTED PAPERS

Graphics and Music

INVITED PAPER

SUBMITTED PAPERS

Natural Language (1)

KEYNOTE SPEECH

COMPUTER SURGERY

PROCEEDINGS OF THE INTERNATIONAL CONFERENCE
ON FIFTH GENERATION COMPUTER SYSTEMS 1988,
edited by ICOT. © ICOT, 1988

HOP, STEP, and JUMP

Kazuhiro Fuchi

Director
ICOT Research Center
Tokyo, Japan

One of the objectives of FGCS'88 is for us at ICOT to present the results of the middle stage of research being conducted in the fifth generation computer project.

Another objective of this conference is for researchers from all over the world to exchange the results of their research, aiming towards a new generation of computers.

Our fifth-generation project started in 1982. This year is its seventh year, and the end of the middle stage. The previous FGCS conference, FGCS'84, was held at the end of the project's third year, four years ago. The three stages of the project can be represented as three stages of movement : hop, step, and jump. We have already hopped and stepped, and now we are about to jump into the final stage of the project.

I would like to outline the FGCS project briefly. It is proceeding according to plan, along the lines that I envisaged at the beginning of the project, and research is yielding results at the pace expected at the beginning of the project.

It goes without saying that these results could never have been obtained without the concerted efforts of the researchers involved in this project, and without the support and cooperation of the many people around ICOT.

The efforts and cooperation of all these people are bound up with the results, but the excellent project set-up and basic policies have made it possible for everyone to do their best.

I am sure that I have said this many times before, but the key words that express the technological features of this project are parallel inference. I will go into these key words in more detail later, but, briefly, parallel inference was the objective of the project from the start. This objective was not changed in the initial or middle stages. This research has formed a base for the final three years of this project, and the last stage will see the establishment of a basic parallel inference technology, as envisaged when the project was set up.

The initial stage, or "hop" stage, was from 1982 to 1984. It can be thought of as the personal sequential inference machine, or PSI, stage. The research results can be seen in the technical reports and papers of this period, but it is easier to understand by looking at examples.

The PSI is a sequential computer that uses a logic language as the machine language. It was designed as a tool and workstation for software research in the middle and final stages.

In addition to the hardware, the sequential inference machine programming and operating system, or SIMPOS, was being developed as the operating system on the PSI. It was the first operating system and the first large-scale software built using a logic language.

The PSI and SIMPOS are representative results of the initial stage.

In the initial stage, research tools were developed, fundamental software problems were researched based on the concept of logic programming, and progress was made in research on natural languages. Other basic research was also conducted. The initial stage can be roughly thought of as such age.

The middle stage, from 1985 to this year, was the "step" stage. One of the features of research during this period was the start of research on parallelization. On the language side, Guarded Horn Clauses, or GHC, was proposed. It acted as a springboard for research on parallelization. GHC is a logic language with parallel operation added.

The problem of how to add parallel control to a logic language has been a major item in logic programming research worldwide over the last few years. ICOT has contributed greatly to this field by proposing GHC, which formed the base for fundamental research on parallel programming.

With GHC as the base, KL1 was decided on as

the kernel language in the first plans. The kernel language is the software base, and is also the starting point for machine architecture. Research on parallel architecture started, based on KL1.

One of the results of the middle stage was the Multi-PSI. The Multi-PSI uses an upgraded version of the PSI developed in the initial stage. Sixty-four PSIs form one Multi-PSI system. The purpose of developing it was to provide an environment for research on parallel software as quickly as possible. To achieve this purpose, a prototype of the PIMOS, the operating system for parallel inference machines, are being developed on the Multi-PSI.

In parallel with the Multi-PSI, a 100 processor element parallel inference machine, or PIM, system is being developed. This PIM is the middle stage version of the target parallel inference machine, and is expected to be completed during the first half of next year. It will be linked with research in the final stage.

Another feature of the middle stage is research on software based on the PSI and SIMPOS developed in the initial stage. The PSI and SIMPOS have been upgraded. There are now more than 300 PSIs, which are being used as workstations for software research in this project.

One of the main themes in this project is researching logic programming in depth. Parallel programming and constraint programming are major research themes all over the world. ICOT is also researching constraint programming, with the aim of integrating it with parallel programming.

In the framework of logic programming, the development of meta-programming, program transformation, and partial evaluation have been in progress since the initial stage. In the middle stage, parallelization has also been emphasized, based on GHC.

Research on natural language understanding is part of core research on artificial intelligence. It will be essential in future man-machine communication. It has been a major part of research at ICOT since the initial stage. Research on models based on situation semantics theory is also under way.

One result of natural language research in the middle stage is DUALS3, Discourse Understanding Aimed at Logic-based System, a language understanding system that has been upgraded from the system developed in the initial stage. The logic programming library developed through research during this period is the language tool box, or LTB,

for language processing.

Another part of core research on artificial intelligence is knowledge processing. Testing expert systems in various areas is another feature of the middle stage. ICOT is researching knowledge processing not for immediate practical application, but in order to pioneer high-level techniques and to prepare for parallelization. This research will help us to work on knowledge acquisition, induction, learning, hypothetical reasoning, and non-monotonic reasoning.

Compared to the initial stage, research in the middle stage has been more active, and results have diversified. In a broad sense, this is a preparation for integrating and developing the basic concepts held from the beginning in the final stage.

Next year will see the beginning of the final stage, the "jump" stage. This will be the period for in-depth research on parallel inference software. Until now, parallel software has been researched by simulation, but now that a new and powerful research environment has appeared in the form of the Multi-PSI, we hope that research will move faster.

On the hardware side, the target is to build a 1000 processor element parallel inference machine, integrating a knowledge base machine architecture.

By using this machine to the full, the abstract and theoretical research that has been done until now, such as research on resource management, will give birth to specific problems.

The parallelization of knowledge processing, natural language processing, and application programs of a reasonable scale will be a major area of research in the final stage. This is an area on which almost no work has been done as yet.

To realize this research, systemization is necessary, along with research that returns to the basics. At the same time, it is essential to set up a parallel programming environment.

One of the software targets of the final stage is to group parallel programming techniques in the form of knowledge programming, using the environmental conditions provided up to the middle stage.

As I have shown, the project has been developing with parallel inference as the warp of its material, because we expect parallel inference to be the core of future information processing, and because we believe that it will lead to a new type of computer.

One of the assumptions in planning this project was the prediction that the future of information processing and the basic direction of its progress lie in knowledge information processing, usually thought of as artificial intelligence. The situation in 1982, when the project started, and the situation now are completely different, because artificial intelligence is becoming popular all over the world, and is becoming an integral part of society.

However, we have emphasized from the beginning that this project is not an AI project as such. To put it more accurately, the aim of the project is new computers for future AI. The aim of this project is not AI systems that can be used in the near future, nor is it computers that are an extension of present computers.

To diverge, I believe that AI should be viewed as at least three dimensions. Like height, width, and depth in space, AI should also be the volume obtained by multiplying these three dimensions.

The present AI boom is mainly width. The width has been increased as applications for solving problems have been found. Not long ago, there was almost no width in AI, but as AI became more popular, it broadened.

Depth is the depth of research. Research on artificial intelligence has been going on for 30 years, but how far have we managed to clarify what intelligence is? How good are our models of intelligence? This is the scientific side of artificial intelligence.

An example of the height of artificial intelligence is the realization of AI functions and the system with which to realize them. This is the technical dimension.

If obtaining a good volume is a problem, it is necessary to increase each dimension. The width of applications has increased, which is valuable, but is that all that is necessary? It is said increasingly often that the importance of basic research on AI lies in the overall, healthy growth of AI in the dimension of width.

We also believe that the third dimension, height, is as important as the other dimensions. Our project emphasizes the third dimension.

Artificial intelligence systems are multi-layer structures, where the computer, or hardware, is the base, and there are many layers of software. Is the present system form suitable? It is said that knowledge is important, and so is software. This is true, but this does not mean that hardware is not important.

There is still room for growth in present computer technology, and it is certainly nearing maturity. The world of information processing, however, is expected to keep on growing. This poses the question of whether an extension of present computer technology can support growth.

The progress of electronics technology, supporting computers, is truly remarkable. It shows that electronics technology is starting to have enough power even if computers cast off their current form.

If we review computers from the viewpoint that AI and knowledge information processing are the future direction of information processing, it is evident that the structure of today's computers is not ideal. We must therefore review the principles of making computers from a new viewpoint. The starting point of our project was to show that the time for this is coming.

Taking the view that a healthy body houses a healthy mind, we need new types of computers to form a stronger base for future, more advanced information processing. The technical potential is now apparent.

From the point of view of hardware, the guiding principle of parallelization to give more powerful, higher performance has appeared in ultra VLSI.

On the software side, from the viewpoint of high-performance software such as AI, logic programming comes to mind. The basic operation is the inference in logic.

There is an internal relationship between hardware and software by taking parallelization as the form in which inference will be realized. The phrase "parallel inference" is the guiding principle and the key words for new computers.

However, I am not claiming that parallel inference is the only research required for future information processing.

Research on artificial intelligence is spreading throughout society. It is impossible to handle all artificial intelligence in a single project, and, indeed, the time has come when it is better to spread it over many projects. Each project should be formed by placing its strong points on some place in the three dimensional space : height, width, and depth. Our national project has tried to do this, and one of the features of our project is the establishment of basic technology for new computers, not the extension of existing technology.

This is one of the reasons why I have emphasized a little while ago that this project is not an AI project as such.

I said that the increase of artificial intelligence will be a major pointer of the future direction of information processing. This is not the whole story. It is an important trend, but it is more reasonable to consider that the world of information processing is wider than that. There are, however, some areas that are not yet considered as artificial intelligence, particularly in the narrow sense. Systems with more advanced functions and better performance are also essential in these areas.

One major problem that comes to mind here is how to create large-scale, complex, advanced software. It can be said that the desire to use scientific methodology in creating software is the mainstream of computer science.

The concept of logic programming can be looked at from this point of view. Automatic programming is a dream. To realize this dream, we need to identify the logical properties of programs. To develop program transformation and other techniques, however, we should build programming methodology and programming languages on clearer logic. This means rebuilding computer science. Logic programming can be viewed as a possible approach.

Based on this, inference can be taken as the basic concept in building software. If we view parallelization as a method of high-speed realization, parallel inference is necessary to advance future information processing and to give it meaning.

I keep on talking about parallel inference because it's the main theme of our project.

As I said at FGCS'84, it is vital to have simple, clear basic concepts in major long-term research projects, and to keep them in mind right through the project. In the period of transition between the initial stage and the middle stage, we planned development this way.

Even basic concepts must be reviewed periodically. We take great care in doing this, and, so far, have not had to change our basic concepts. In the seven years that research has been developing in this project, I feel that we have verified the initial basic concepts again and again. Of course, we now have many more ideas than we did at the start, and these have been reinforced. As time has passed, we have gained more confidence in our approach.

This afternoon, there will be a more detailed report on plans for the final stage. Our basic approach to these plans has been to re-verify and clarify the basic concepts since the initiation of the project. We have been working on a central theme and improving our plans. We are trying to simplify our plans for the final stage.

To digress again, I believe that there are several things we must take note of if we want a national research project like this to succeed.

The first is the temptation to compromise.

All over the world there is a tendency to lean towards practical topics in order to establish support for a project or to show its success. If the project is set up for practical topics or the research goes much better than expected, this is all right, but in many cases, this tendency means that the initial ideals and targets must be lowered. This in turn lowers the researchers' morale, and means that results that could be attained with a little more hard work are not achieved.

Topics that show a likelihood of practical application are usually best left to the spontaneity and creativity of a private company. Of course, this depends on the nature and scale of the research theme.

In a national project, especially in an industrialized country, not the extension of existing technology, but the creation of new technology, that is, work with risks, is proper.

Another temptation is to set targets too high. There is a natural limit on targets, imposed by time and human resources. There have been cases where the target was too high, or was misinterpreted as being too high, causing an adverse reaction, and damping research.

Targets that are too high are often caused by the naive optimism of researchers. There are cases where dreams or things that seem good are popular, and, whether consciously or unconsciously, the researchers go along with those ideas. These cases are good examples of disguised compromise.

Another problem is the danger of fearing danger. Fear of danger is the biggest incitement to compromise. Fearing danger, compromising time and again, and trying to create new things are certainly contradictory, and may be unattainable targets. However, it is no exaggeration to say that the greatest danger in creative research is compromise.

Considering that many people follow the principle of safety today, surely it is better to follow the principle of adventure.

As our project nears its final stage, we are often asked about its conclusion. Of course, we would like a secure conclusion, but it is not easy to wind up, using the remaining time well.

Rather, we must work on the problem of parallel inference. I like to think of the last seven years as a preparation period for the next three years, in which we start a new project.

This may provoke criticism or questions as to whether we are trying to deal with an impossible problem or trying to deal with the problem in too short a time.

This problem is a huge challenge, even if we limit it to parallel inference. The words are simple, but they embody high-level, diverse research themes. It may be impossible to solve all the problems in that time, but I believe that we are very likely to break through at a basic point.

My basic, optimistic view is that if the problem is correctly set and a good environment is given, researchers can be stimulated far more than expected. The past seven years are the preparation and efforts towards doing that.

The nature of our project is not such that the second half will end in total success, nor that we are embracing impossible challenges.

I have talked mainly about our project today, but research towards a new age of computers and a new age of information processing is going on all over the world. Our project is one of many, and can only be one of many, in this worldwide movement. This is not an expression of Japanese modesty.

We want to contribute to making new history, and are working very hard to do so. Our efforts are part of the vast flow of history, in fact, part of historical inevitability.

Research must take many approaches. In this field, these approaches will bear fruit not by simple diffusion, but when unity can be seen in their diversity. The simultaneous pursuit of diversity and unity is vital for the development of research, and the desirability of open exchange of research by various groups is bound up with it.

We have stressed international exchange and co-operation from the beginning of our project, because we believe that there are people all over the world working towards making history in research in this field, that their numbers are increasing, and that history will be made by the joint efforts of all these researchers. We believe that this is necessary for the future of all mankind.

To realize this, not rivalry between researchers, but co-operation founded on understanding of different approaches is needed. At no time have we needed this as much as now.

This conference is a link in the chain of activities aiming towards the future. We will hear both the interim report of FGCS activities and reports of the research activities of our colleagues all over the world. I would like to thank you all for attending the FGCS'88 conference, and to express my hope that your research will bear fruit through this exchange, and that this conference will be a stepping-stone whereby history can advance towards a new age.

ICOT RESEARCH AND DEVELOPMENT

PROCEEDINGS OF THE INTERNATIONAL CONFERENCE
ON FIFTH GENERATION COMPUTER SYSTEMS 1988,
edited by ICOT. © ICOT, 1988

PRESENT STATUS AND PLANS FOR RESEARCH AND DEVELOPMENT

Takashi Kurozumi

Deputy Director, Research Center
Institute for New Generation Computer Technology
4-28, Mita 1-chome, Minato-ku, Tokyo 108, Japan

ABSTRACT

The Fifth Generation Computer Systems Project was launched in 1982 as part of the information-related policy of the Ministry of International Trade and Industry (MITI). Its purpose is to research and develop a new computer technology that will provide the basis for the creation of knowledge information processing systems (KIPS) needed in the 1990s.

ICOT has been entrusted by MITI to promote this national project in cooperation with manufacturers, national and public research organizations, and universities.

The project has been proceeding according to a ten-year plan, which is divided into an initial three-year stage, an intermediate four-year stage and a final three-year stage. This year, 1988, is the last year of the intermediate stage.

This report describes the R&D status of the intermediate stage and the R&D plan for the final stage.

1   OUTLINE OF THE FIFTH GENERATION COMPUTER SYSTEMS PROJECT

The R&D programs of this project aim at creating prototypes of fifth generation computer systems. The basic framework of fifth generation computers, an outline of the general R&D plan, and the organization to promote this project are described below.

1.1 Basic Framework of Fifth Generation Computers

1.1.1 Concept of Fifth Generation Computers

Conventional computers have been classified into generations according to their constituent hardware elements: vacuum tubes, transistors, IC, LSI and VLSI. But they are all based on the same Von Neumann architecture, which is characterized by sequential processing and stored-program schemes.

In present-day computers, the characteristics of the architecture determines the type of machine language and software based on machine language is procedural. Present-day computers are limited because there is an enormous gap between the way that they work and the way that human beings think, knowledge-based inference. Computers must follow pre-defined procedures; they cannot do processing that depends on the circumstances.

There are basic needs that future computers must satisfy. They should be intelligent, easy to use and readily available; their software must be productive. Although conventional computers have the architectural limitation explained previously, there are technical seeds such as research into artificial intelligent technology, architecture technology and software engineering technology. These technologies have been developed independently.

The objective of the Fifth Generation Computer Systems Project is to overcome the technical restrictions of conventional computers and develop innovative computers capable of intelligent information processing. Such machines will be essential in the information-oriented society of the 1990s.

The concept of the fifth generation computer system stemmed from the idea that meeting future needs would be possible by selecting the existing R&D results that can be used to further development and by combining these results in a completely new framework.

The new framework can be built by specifying a predicate logic language as a new machine language, by creating a hardware system that performs highly parallel inference processing based on the new language, and by creating a software system that performs a new type of processing, a combination of the basic inference processings provided by the hardware system.

1.1.2 Basic Structure of Fifth Generation Computer Systems

A fundamental characteristic of intelligent activity is inference that uses every piece of stored knowledge, whether it is conscious or unconscious. Inference based on predicate logic is a procedure to extract unknown information using existing knowledge.

In fifth generation computers, hardware and software are based on a programming method called logic programming in which programs are described in the form of a logic and executed as inference. The predicate logic languages assigned to do this are called the kernel language.

Based on the findings of previous artificial intelligence research, we estimate that fifth generation computers will require an inference speed 1000 times greater than conventional computers. The high-level integration provided by advanced VLSIs enable us to make a reasonably compact and inexpensive computer with more than a thousand processors working in parallel. In this project, we aim at an inference execution speed of 100M LIPS to 1G LIPS, using prototype hardware consisting of one thousand processing elements.

In the logic programming framework, a knowledge base for inference will also be represented in a form based on predicate logic. A relational expression in a current relational database can correspond to a predicate logic form as its extended form. For the knowledge base function, we will start working from current relational database techniques, and proceed to processing knowledge data that is represented in a variety of ways in the logic programming framework.

We think that fifth generation computers must have a basic software system with the following basic functions for the knowledge information processing system. The functions needed in the future include an intelligent interaction function and an inference function that uses knowledge bases.

(1) Problem-solving and inference function: A function to perform meta-level inference such as inductive inference, used to control hardware effectively and solve given problems.

(2) Knowledge base management function: A function to acquire, store and use various types of knowledge needed in the course of inference. It has advanced database management capability, a knowledge acquisition capability that collects knowledge by judging whether it is meaningful, and the ability to retrieve and use knowledge effectively.

(3) Intelligent interface function: A function to make computers easy to use, enabling humans and computers to communicate with each other in a flexible and natural way through natural language.

(4) Intelligent programming function: A function to lighten the user's workload in the processes from writing programs to maintenance. It supports program development, converts given problems to more efficient programs, and verifies the accuracy of the programs.

Our aim is to realize the above four basic functions with fifth generation computers. Although the interface between the basic software system and hardware will be implemented in the kernel language, user languages and other languages will be defined as high-layer languages that have a modularization function and various types of knowledge representation functions.

1.2 Research and Development Plan of the Fifth Generation Computer Systems Project

1.2.1 Initiation of the Project

The history of fifth generation computers began when a survey committee was founded by MITI in 1979. In that year, the survey was undertaken on the prospects of fifth generation computers. In 1980, the survey focused on the goals and subjects of R&D. During these two years, the vision of a fifth generation computer for large-scale knowledge information processing took clear shape.

In 1981, MITI established an R&D plan for fifth generation computer systems, which was presented at an international conference held by MITI in October 1981 (FGCS '81). In 1982, ICOT (Institute for New Generation Computer Technology) was founded as the central organization for promoting R&D, and it began R&D work on fifth generation computers, under the auspices of MITI.

1.2.2 R&D Stages

This is a national project that spans 10 years. It is divided into three stages: an initial three-year stage, an intermediate four-year stage, and a final three-year stage.

(1) Initial stage (1982 to 1984)

R&D in the initial stage was aimed at developing the basic technology required for fifth generation computers. Within the framework of this project, the R&D results concerning knowledge information processing were analyzed and selected results were restructured to achieve the goals of the initial stage.

The specific subjects of R&D included an inference subsystem, knowledge base subsystem, basic software system and pilot models for software development. Goals were specified independently for each subject.

To sum up the results of R&D in the initial stage, we evaluated the basic technology needed to develop fifth generation computers by reviewing and testing various experimental systems. We became convinced that the basic framework described in section 1.1 was not mere hypothesis, but was viable and effective. The major results of each R&D subject are as follows.

(a) Inference subsystem: We experimentally reviewed and evaluated various inference methods, including data flow and reduction, by implementing software simulators and hardware simulators.

(b) Knowledge base subsystem: We reviewed and evaluated the relational database scheme as the basis of the knowledge base function by making an experimental parallel relational database machine (Delta).

(c) Basic software system: We proposed GHC as the parallel logic programming language and verified the effectiveness of the logic programming method by implementing experimental software systems such as an experimental relational database management system (KAISER) and a discourse understanding experimental system (DUALS V.0).

(d) Pilot models for software development: We showed that systems based on logic languages were viable and could be effective by developing sequential inference machines (PSI, CHI), sequential logic programming languages (KLO, ESP), and a sequential inference machine operating and programming system (SIMPOS), although all of them were sequential.

(2) Intermediate stage (1985 to 1988)

The objective of the intermediate stage is to create small- to medium-scale subsystems that will provide a basis for the fifth generation computers, while considering development of the individual research subjects and the integration of the subsystems in the final stage.

The focus of the first half of this stage was on the specifications of models, algorithms and the basic architecture on which software and hardware were to be built, based on the results of the initial stage. In the second half of this stage, experimental subsystems were implemented and evaluated using the specifications.

R&D activities of each subsystem are performed in the following way.

(a) Basic software: Research on the use of parallel logic languages as the kernel language is conducted, and experimental software is implemented and basic technology is developed for each of the following functions ; problem-solving and inference, knowledge base management, intelligent interface, and intelligent programming.

(b) Hardware system: Part of the system (Inference/knowledge base subsystem), whose scale is 1/10 that of the prototype, has been developed, and its functions verified.

(c) Development support system: An infrastructure has been completed by developing a parallel software environment and equipping it with a network system.

(3) Final stage (1989 to 1991)

In the final stage, the results of R&D activities in hardware and basic software in the initial and intermediate stages will be integrated, and a prototype system of a fifth generation computer will be implemented. The prototype system will demonstrate that the framework and functions described in section 1.1 can be achieved in a system in which software and hardware are integrated, and that the system is fit for knowledge information processing.

1.3 Organization of the Research and Development of the Fifth Generation Computer Systems Project

The Fifth Generation Computer Systems Project is being carried out by ICOT, under the auspices of MITI. The ICOT organization consists of a general affairs office and a research center. In the initial stage, the research center consisted of a research planning department and three laboratories. In the intermediate stage, it has a research planning department and five laboratories. The responsibilities of each laboratory sometimes change in the middle of a stage, depending on the progress that is made. The laboratories' subjects in 1988 are as follows.

(1) First Research Laboratory: The kernel language (extended version), problem-solving and inference software (including meta-level inference), and intelligent programming software for the basic software.

(2) Second Research Laboratory: Intelligent interface software for the basic software.

(3) Third Research Laboratory: Knowledge base subsystem

(4) Fourth Research Laboratory: Inference subsystem, which includes the first version of the kernel language and parallel inference machine OS (PIMOS); development support system; and knowledge base management software (knowledge base management basic software) for the basic software.

(5) Fifth Research Laboratory: Knowledge base management software (acquisition and use of knowledge base) and experimental demonstration software for the basic software.

The research staff at ICOT is made up of researchers on loan from the Electro-technical Laboratory, Mechanical Engineering Laboratory, NTT, KDD, computer manufacturers and others.

There were 50 staff at the beginning of the intermediate stage, and their number has increased every year. At the beginning of 1988, there were about 90, and soon there will be about 100.

This project has been executed in an R&D organization which formed with the idea that the minds of the first-class researchers in related fields in Japan should be brought together.

(1) MITI has set up an advisory committee to provide overall guidance concerning plan and R&D status of this project. The chairman is professor H. Aiso (Keio University), and members are authorities on this area from universities, research institutes and companies.

(2) The researchers at ICOT conduct the core R&D activities, and ICOT entrusts other R&D work that needs experimental manufacturing and development to manufacturers. We are promoting the project as a single structure.

(3) Experts from universities and institutes have been participating in the Project Promotion Committee (PPC) and Working Groups (WGs). PPC supplies us with general advice about the project. WGs facilitate the exchange of information about each research subject. In

1988, we have 12 WGs that are organized according to the status of the R&D.

We consider it important that ICOT researchers, other researchers in Japan, and scientists abroad stimulate each other, present their results, and exchange information. That is why ICOT is actively promoting the following research meetings and information exchange activities with foreign research institutes.

(1) ICOT researchers make presentations at international conferences. We publish the ICOT technical reports and technical memorandums. We also exchange papers with foreign research institutes.

(2) We welcome researchers from other countries as visitors and our researchers visit research institutes and universities abroad to exchange information.

(3) Every year we invite several renowned researchers from abroad for a short period.

(4) Based on the memorandums with NSF in the United States and INRIA in France, we receive researchers from both countries for a long period.

(5) To disseminate the result of the R&D activities, we sponsor symposiums and logic programming conferences every year, as well as this international conference ('81, '84, '88). In addition, we have held a Japan-Sweden workshop four times, a Japan-France AI symposium twice, and a Japan-U.S.A. AI symposium once.

All the R&D expenses for this project are covered by the national budget, and the amount is determined each year according to the government's budgeting system. The budget was 8.3 billion yen for the three-year initial stage and about 21.5 billion yen for the four-year intermediate stage (4.7 billion for '84, 5.5 billion for '85, 5.6 billion for '86, 5.7 billion for '87).

The results of the R&D of this project are reported to the government each year. Intellectual property such as patents are administered by the Agency of Industrial Science and Technology, and any corporate entity that desires to use one of them can obtain permission by paying a fee. PSI, SIMPOS, and other technologies that have already been developed as development support systems are permitted by the government to be used commercially. The spread of these technologies is the start of the distribution of fifth generation computer technology.

2 RESEARCH AND DEVELOPMENT STATUS OF THE INTERMEDIATE STAGE

The objective of the intermediate stage is the development of subsystems. The major R&D subjects are the basic software system, hardware systems, and development support systems. The basic software system further breaks down into the 5G kernel languages, problem-solving and inference software, knowledge base management software, intelligent interface software, and intelligent programming software. The hardware systems are divided into the inference subsystem and the knowledge base subsystem. Three and a half years of the intermediate stage have passed, and as a whole it is proceeding smoothly, as planned, toward the goal.

2.1 Basic Software System

2.1.1 5G Kernel Languages

The 5G Kernel languages play an important role in bridging hardware research and software research. There are two types of 5G kernel languages, sequential processing logic language (kernel language version 0 (KL0)) and parallel processing logic language (kernel language version 1 (KL1)). The goals of the intermediate stage are to perform design, experimental implementation, and feasibility testing of KL1, and to define the conceptual specifications of the parallel logic language (refined kernel language) for the prototype machine.

In the initial stage, we designed Extended Self-contained Prolog (ESP), a system description language, by adding the modularization function and the macro expansion function to KL0 created by improving a logic language Prolog. ESP has been used to describe a number of systems including the sequential inference machine operating programming system in the initial and intermediate stages.

Research into parallel logic languages has resulted in the presentation of Guarded Horn Clauses (GHC) in the initial stage. Since Concurrent Prolog and other existing languages, as well as OR parallel Prolog needed multiple environments, the way that they computed was too complex. GHC is a viable and efficient parallel logic language that is suitable for implementing hardware efficiently.

Also, in the intermediate stage, we developed Flat GHC (FGHC) as a subset of GHC that prohibits the use of user-defined predicates in guarded parts.

We decided to base development of KL1 on FGHC. KL1 consists of the following four languages according to the design of the parallel inference machine and its OS.

(1) KL1-b (base): An abstract machine language which will be the basis of the design of the parallel inference machine.

(2) KL1-c (core): The core language of KL1, designed from FGHC as the base with an additional meta-call function.

(3) KL1-p (pragma): The language for priority control and process allocation for an efficient execution on the parallel machine.

(4) KL1-u (user): KL1-c plus the modularization function.

Regarding KL1-b/c/p, we have experimentally implemented and evaluated the processing system on the sequential inference machine (PSI) and have developed a development support system. We are now working on the design of KL1-b/c/p and their experimental implementation on an experimental parallel inference hardware machine (Multi-PSI). For KL1-u, we designed A'UN, a parallel object-oriented language and implemented an experimental processing system to examine the modularization and stream processing functions.

To develop the refined kernel language for the prototype machine in the final stage, we are studying the possibility of supporting the meta-function, functions for program transformation and partial evaluation, and database and knowledge base function, in addition to the functions of KL1. We have done the following.

* We have made meta-programming more efficient and implemented self-appliable partial evaluation programs that can derive a compiler from an interpreter or a compiler from a compiler.

* We have implemented a constraint solver used for constraint logic programming.

* We have experimented to discover whether GHC, a committed-choice language, can be used to search problems by means of a layered stream structure.

2.1.2 Problem-Solving and Inference Software

The goal of the intermediate stage is being approached in two ways with regard to problem-solving and inference software. One way is to implement the core of the OS that is to control and manage the parallel inference machine (PIM). The other way is to study, from a long range view, meta-level inference methods such as inductive inference

8

and analogy, and cooperative problem-solving methods by complement of knowledge.

The OS for PIM (PIMOS) is an integrated logic OS described in KL1. Its basic scheme is to have sufficient functions for parallel software development, and to achieve high-level user facilities.

PIMOS is to be used on KL1 machines such as Multi-PSI and PIM, and I/Os are processed virtually by the front-end processor. We are now evaluating its design by implementing part of it experimentally, while development is proceeding toward the completion of the core at the end of the intermediate stage. At the same time, we are studying parallel programming techniques and program paradigms.

We have proposed ascription for meta-level inference methods. Ascription is a type of non-monotonic reasonings that offers a technique for a common sense reasoning mechanism to integrate default reasoning, analogy, and induction. We are studying it by implementing experimental systems.

2.1.3 Knowledge Base Management Software

The goal of the intermediate stage is being approached in two ways with regard to knowledge base management software. One way is to study knowledge representation methods, inference methods using knowledge, and knowledge acquisition methods. The other way is to develop basic knowledge base management software that represents various types of knowledge in an integrated manner.

The study of knowledge representation, and acquisition and use of knowledge is related to other themes of the basic software system. To study knowledge representation languages, we designed and applied a specific language for each of the fields, including natural language processing and proof support. Regarding the meta-level inference methods, we are studying common sense reasoning mechanisms in the framework of non-monotonic reasoning. In addition, R&D is being performed on the next generation tools for expert systems, in order to verify the effectiveness of the basic software. The next generation tools for expert systems are planned to be developed throughout the intermediate and final stages. In the intermediate stage, we implemented and evaluated an experimental second generation tool for the current generation level, PROTON. As a result, we are studying hypothetical reasoning, qualitative reasoning using deep knowledge, and knowledge acquisition support as element technologies for the next generation tools. We are implementing an

experimental hypothetical reasoning module, APRICOT, qualitative reasoning module, Qupras, and knowledge acquisition support module, EPSILON/EM. We are developing an experimental system that incorporates several application areas, while considering their relations to the element technologies. We are also studying knowledge representation and search method by implementing computer GO playing as a research subject of inference using knowledge.

R&D of knowledge base management basic software (Kappa) is being done to provide a DBMS/KBMS for knowledge information processing systems. Kappa provides a constructing function to build a large DB/KB that can be used for natural language processing, theorem proving support, and various types of expert systems. It also can be used as a tool for a number of knowledge application systems running on PSI/SIMPOS. We aim at a knowledge base function composed of a deductive DB plus an object-oriented DB. We have already developed Kappa-I, experimental DB software based on a nested relational DB model, and have confirmed that terms and networktype structure data can be efficiently stored on it. We also developed an enhanced nested relational DB software and designed CRL as the internal knowledge representation language. To store and manage real knowledge, we are now implementing Kappa-II, which is to have the knowledge conversion function, knowledge management function and user interface function. We have begun to create a Japanese-language dictionary consisting of dozens of thousands of words in the nested relational DB software of Kappa-II for a research of natural language processing.

2.1.4 Intelligent Interface Software

In the intelligent interface software, we aim at the establishment of discourse understanding techniques required for natural language processing for the Japanese language. R&D activities have two goals. One goal is to study grammar, dictionaries and execution analysis required for the processings at the syntactic level, and to experimentally implement them as general-purpose tools. The processings just mentioned include morphological analysis and syntax analysis that are commonly needed for high-level natural language processings. The other goal is to develop high-level techniques such as semantic analysis and context analysis that are essential for discourse understanding, and construct discourse models. More specifically, we are conducting this research by implementing an experimental discourse understanding system, specifying various targets and applications.

For the study of syntactic level processing, based on the unification-based grammar, we performed R&D on grammar and parser for morphologic analysis and syntactic analysis, R&D on grammar and processing system for Japanese sentence generation, development of a dictionary, formulation of semantic descriptions and study on the syntactic theory about the Japanese phrase structure grammar (JPSG). We developed a semantic analysis description language (CIL) for describing meanings and discourse structure. CIL features data notation by partially specialized terms and delayed execution control function by constraint solver and stream processing. These software modules are the group of software that will provide the basis for the study of context processing. We have made a library of these software modules as a general-purpose Japanese processing system (LTB) and are using it as our common tool for experimentally implementing discourse understanding systems. LTB includes the CIL processing system and its programming environment, morphological analysis and syntactic analysis system, sentence generation system and grammar, Japanese dictionary and KWIC, and LTB-Shell which is used to integrate and use the other modules.

Various types of experimental discourse understanding systems have been implemented to establish the syntactic/semantic analysis and sentence generation processing method and to promote the study of element technologies such as discourse models, context processing, and deep semantic understanding, while verifying their operation in the system. One of the experimental systems is the discourse understanding system being developed at ICOT (DUALS). We began to test the first version of DUALS in the last year of the initial stage. The first version used Prolog descriptions, on short texts (18 sentences). In 1986, the second version, to which CIL and parallel syntactic analysis method were adopted, was completed. We are now developing the third version, which will use LTB and will be able to understand the meaning of text consisting of 100 sentences, or 2000 words. In addition to these three versions of DUALS, we are developing several experimental systems to study the element technologies for understanding meaning and discourse.

2.1.5 Intelligent Programming Software

The purpose of the intelligent programming software is to study, based on logic programming, various problems in software engineering. We have

two themes in the intermediate stage. One is the study of theorem proving support and transformation/synthesis/ verification of programs, based on the similarity between programming and mathematical proof, and the implementation of an experimental system. The other theme is the implementation of pilot models that manage and support the software life cycle from development to maintenance, and the development, as a software knowledge management system, of development support tools that will be put into practice at ICOT as a programming environment.

We are studying intelligent programming software from the point of view of mathematics and logic programming. Based on the similarity between mathematical theorem and program specification (theorem proving and programming), we are investigating a computer aided proof system (CAP) to support mathematical proof as an element technology, and we are building an experimental system. The CAP system consists of a structure editor for proof description, a proof checker, an equation checker, and a proof compiler that creates programs from proofs.

From a logic programming point of view, we are developing an experimental system for program transformation, analysis and verification (Argus). Argus is an experimental system for performing the following operations uniformly on the program with high-level description by using the characteristics of logic programming languages. The operations are transformation and synthesis of the program, extraction and analysis of the basic features of the program, and modification of the program.

As pilot models for the processes from development to maintenance of software, we implemented a prototyping support system that combines programs as modules, and an experimental system that supports consistency verification of design and program by graphically displaying the operation of programs.

As the software knowledge management system, which provides a logic type program development environment for the sequential inference machine OS (SIMPOS), we enhanced library management, program/document generation and management support, and other functions.

2.2 Hardware Systems and Development Support Systems

2.2.1 Inference Subsystem

The goals for inference subsystem R&D in the intermediate stage are to establish a parallel inference machine architecture based on the results of the initial stage R&D on parallel inference machine simulators and sequential inference machines, and to build pilot systems. The parallel inference machine consists of about 100 processing elements. This machine is for parallel inference languages and can efficiently execute the kernel language version 1 (KL1).

The basic concept of R&D for inference subsystem in the intermediate stage is described below.

* To integrate research on hardware and software, the R&D are performed under an integrated organization.

* Regarding the development of the machine, hardware technologies must be accumulated so that they can be used in the final stage. The hardware needs to be used as a software development tool for a wide range of purposes, including the R&D of the final stage.

Regarding the parallel inference machine (PIM), as a pilot system, the performance goal was set at 2 to 5 MLIPS with about 100 processing elements in the planning stage. In the course of R&D in the intermediate stage, we decided to develop a Multi-PSI (V1) as an R&D tool for parallel software such as PIMOS in the development support system, and, by using the results, to develop an experimental parallel inference hardware (Multi-PSI (V2)). Because we determined that we could reach the initial performance goal with the Multi-PSI (V2), we changed the operating performance goal of PIM with 100 processing elements to 10 to 20 MLIPS. This is how the R&D work on inference machines has proceeded during the intermediate stage. The kernel language version 1 (KL1) processing system, parallel software including PIMOS, software development support system and inference system can enhance each other and be combined.

The configuration of the PIM system consists of sixteen clusters, each with eight processing elements (PE), and an inter-cluster network. The PEs adopt tag architecture, high-speed process switching and pipeline processing to realize high-speed processing. PEs support KL1-b as a machine language that can be optimized by compiler, and also support real time GC function using the MRB method. We expect the performance to be 200 to 500 KLIPS per PE. In a cluster, eight PEs are tightly coupled by a shared bus, and the coherency of the cache memory of each PE and shared memory are ensured by parallel caching. Clusters are linked by a message passing network.

The specification design of the intermediate stage version of PIM has almost been completed. Now we are working on the manufacturing designs including VLSI and others. PIM will have one PE for each board, 64 PEs for each cabinet, and clusters connected by networks such as hypercubes.

The Multi-PSI (V2) is also KL1 machine for parallel software development. It uses the CPUs of the small version PSI as processing elements and connects them by a two-dimensional mesh network. Its hardware was completed in F.Y. 1987. The Multi-PSI (V2) provides a basis for R&D on the KL1 processing system and PIMOS. It is also used for the research on the load distribution method and parallel algorithms for the parallel software described in KL1, the debugging method for parallel software, and the program development environment.

2.2.2 Knowledge Base Subsystem

The intermediate stage research and development goal for the knowledge base subsystem is to research the basic technologies needed to implement the knowledge operation mechanism essential for the establishment of a knowledge base machine, and to establish the requisite architecture. Concretely, we established two basic models of the knowledge base for parallel processing and distributed processing, studied mechanisms and architectures to support these models and implemented experimental machines.

We did experiments on a knowledge base operation mechanism by connecting a relational database machine (Delta) developed in the initial stage and a sequential inference machine as the host to each other. They proved the affinity of logic programming language and relational databases, and the high-speed processing of sorting and relational algebra operations by relational database engine. As a result, it was recognized that the knowledge base machine required the following funcitons.

(a) Integrated processing of diverse knowledge representations, broad applicability to multiple fields.

(b) Efficient handling of search, retrieval and knowledge processing using inference for mass volumes of knowledge.

An experiment in the knowledge base function by actively introducing inference function was carried out on sequential inference machine (CHI).

The theme for the distributed processing was to research technologies to integrate and manage multiple knowledge base systems connected through a network in such a way that they became logically one knowledge base system. The experimental system used here consisted of multiple knowledge base systems (PHI) and a host (PSI). The interface between the host and the PHI units was a Horn clause, and the PHI was used as a simulator for deductive database. The PHI consisted of software to manage knowledge and control distribution in the PSI, and an operation processing module with an accelerator to speed up comparisons and searches.

The design and implementation of a knowledge base hardware simulator to research knowledge base parallel control technologies were carried out. This experimental machine consisted of eight element processors and a Multi-port page memory (MPPM) that held the knowledge base. The element processors were connected to the knowledge base operation engine through co-processor interfaces. The knowledge base operation engine was a unification engine for performing operations such as unification join and unification restriction on relational knowledge set. This experimental machine was connected to the PSI and connection tests with the inference machine were performed. As a basic experiment to interface these machines with GHC, the knowledge compiler was implemented and a GHC description of the knowledge retrieval management function was created.

2.2.3 Development Support System

This project is being promoted based on a new type of logic programming language unlike conventional languages. In the intermediate stage, a development environment including a parallel logic language was essential, and therefore one goal was to develop a tool for the development of parallel software. Another goal was to establish a network for the interconnection of development support machines, and an international network for the exchange of information with overseas universities and research institutions by means of electronic mail.

The parallel software development tool began with the first-step development of the Multi-PSI(V1) in 1986 through the networking of six PSI units developed in the initial stage. The KL1 distributed processing system was implemented in ESP, and the characteristics of parallel programs were evaluated. Next, the Multi-PSI (V2) was developed as an experimental machine for the PIM in an inference subsystem. As part of the development of the Multi-PSI(V2), we developed a compact CPU of the PSI for use as a processing element

(PE), and developed the front-end processor (FEP) for the Multi- PSI(V2) using this PE. This PE was also used in the small-sized PSI (PSI-II). The KL1 processing system was developed as firmware for the PE to enhance the execution of parallel logic language on the Multi -PSI (V2) and the FEP, and at the same time the pseudo-parallel processing development environment was refined on the PSI-II.

In the development of the sequential inference machine, we also improved the size and performance of the high-speed, large-memory type machine called CHI, in the first half of the intermediate stage.

We organized the software development environment by the development of the in-house network system in which sequential inference machines were connected to LAN and DDX to transfer mails and files to each other. We connected our in-house network to CSnet, UUCP and JUNET in order to build an international and domestic network system. This network system played an important role in improving the efficiency of our information exchange with universities and research institutions.

3 OUTLINE OF THE RESEARCH AND DEVELOPMENT PLAN FOR THE FINAL STAGE

The objectives of the R&D in the final stage are to implement prototype hardware that has a parallel architecture and that can perform high-speed inference and knowledge retrieval, and to develop prototype software that can program efficiently in a parallel logic language for knowledge information processing.

To achieve these objectives, we will determine the organization of the project in the final stage according to the state of the R&D at that time, on the basis of that at the end of the intermediate stage. In other words, the R&D in the final stage will be geared to making a prototype system, using the results that have been obtained up until the end of the intermediate stage. Research will also be conducted into the basic technologies that are needed to realize the final objectives and that may be needed in the future.

The concrete plan of the R&D in the final stage is now being planned; it still open to alteration.

The R&D themes in the final stage can be divided into the three prototype systems: hardware, basic software, and basic application. The prototype basic software system can be further divided into basic software and knowledge programming software.

In the prototype basic application system, prototypes of some application software systems will be developed to verify the effectiveness of various kinds of basic functions of the fifth generation computer and to clarify the actual application, but the actual field of application is still under consideration. For this reason, the R&D plan for the final stage concerning the prototype hardware system and the basic software system are discussed below.

3.1 Prototype Hardware System

The objective of the R&D for the fifth generation computer prototype hardware system is to implement a hardware system into which the following two hardware mechanisms will be integrated through a hierarchical structure network. They are dedicated hardwares for realizing high-speed inference function and knowledge base function on a vast amount of knowledge base in parallel hardware architecture.

This hardware system will be able to execute basic software (parallel OS) and high-speed execution of application software for large-scale knowledge information processing written in parallel logic programming language.

Concretely, the hardware will be implemented by the connection of about 1,000 processing elements to provide the various functions. For the hardware performance of inference operation we aim at is 100M to 1G LIPS.

To realize the functions, performance and scale of the prototype hardware system, the inference function theme will consist of the evaluation of the intermediate stage R&D results by large-scale parallel software. The R&D results will be: the parallel logic language, the execution mechanism, the parallel inference machine architecture and processing mechanism. We will also carry out research into high-speed data transfer between processing elements, mechanisms of parallel inference execution and control, and mechanisms of parallel software execution management and communication control. The knowledge base function theme will consist of the evaluation of the intermediate stage R&D results such as mechanisms and storage schemes suited to knowledge base processing, and research into mechanisms required for the management and operation of large-volume knowledge bases. Both functions will be implemented and integrated through parallel architecture based on parallel logic languages.

Hardware design will take all functions required by basic software into account, and will be based on the language specifications for the parallel kernel language and the execution models. The results of the intermediate stage will be used to develop new techniques and implementation technologies as required.

The prototype hardware system will be constructed to have both the inference function and the knowledge base function. To implement inference function in hardware, we will use a processing element (PE) that has all the functions needed for high-speed parallel inference processing and a cluster of about 10 PEs tightly coupled, as basic elements. In the system constructed by connecting these clusters by means of a cluster network, we will develop the following modules: inference processing module to perform low granularity parallel processing, connection control module to control the connection and manage communications, parallel execution control module to handle load balancing control and interface functions for hierarchical networking, and communication management module to handle I/O processing on the man-machine and machine-machine levels.

We will develop a knowledge operation management module for the knowledge base function. The module contains knowledge operation functions such as knowledge base retrieval processing and knowledge set operation, and knowledge base management function such as storing and updating of knowledge.

3.2 Prototype Basic Software System

The objectives of the R&D of the fifth generation computer prototype basic software system are to provide the following functions: OS functions for an efficient parallel software execution environment by controlling and managing the hardware system, functions for the description of knowledge forming the core in the development of application softwares in knowledge information processing as programs, functions such as cooperative problem-solving and meta-level inference to support the above activities intelligently, functions to construct, manage and use knowledge bases through the structural formation of described knowledge, and functions for natural language interfaces required essentially for interactive human interfaces.

This configuration consists of the prototype hardware system OS functions, basic software to provide the system programming environment, and knowledge programming software to provide the environment for natural language processing, and the description, management and use of knowledge.

3.2.1 Basic Software

The basic software will handle prototype hardware control and management. It takes as its goal the provision of OS functions, and consists of an inference control module for high-speed parallel inference execution control, and a knowledge base management module for knowledge base operation and management.

The essential functions contain resource management and execution management of the prototype hardware system with an inference function and a knowledge base processing function, efficient execution management of parallel software described in parallel kernel language, and efficient operation management for storing and retrieving large-scale knowledge bases.

(1) Inference control module

The inference control module is software primarily designed to handle execution management and resource management for parallel type inference execution. It is described in parallel logic language. The essential function is the load distribution control function, which divides the parallel program run on the hardware module and assigns the load efficiently to multiple processing elements. It also manages memory and I/O.

To bring about these functions, we will conduct research into new methods in the following ways using the parallel inference software developed in the intermediate stage: evaluation and investigation of algorithms for resource management and execution management, and implementation of technologies by evaluation software. Based on this work, resource management and execution management software design and prototyping will be advanced.

For parallel kernel language processing system, object-oriented models and constraint models will be investigated, and the research results of the intermediate stage will be used for the design and implementation of a language and a processing system suited to system programming. The design and implementation of a system programming environment including debugging function and execution monitoring function for the

parallel execution environment will also be carried out during the basic investigation.

In this design and implementation, basic research will be conducted into a number of remaining problems, such as load distribution specification function for the system programming language, load distribution control for multiple processing elements and the method of implementation, and a variety of parallel algorithms and programming methods.

(2) Knowledge base management module

The knowledge base management module is software designed to manage the storing, search, and update of large-scale knowledge bases on the prototype hardware. It will include the basic database management functions and the knowledge base management functions built upon them.

On data base management function, we will conduct basic research into efficient resource management schemes for memory and processors, internal data representation and management methods suited to store knowledge, and parallel execution models for set operation and nested relational models. For efficient use of the parallel architecture prototype hardware, research will be conducted into relational operators, extension methods, and implementation methods, with attention paid to parallel processing. Research will also be conducted into database management techniques and implementation methods to process distributed knowledge. Software will be designed and implemented according to the results obtained.

On knowledge base management function, we will investigate deductive database models and conduct research into the internal representation form of knowledge suitable for various knowledge representations, a knowledge base description language for program interface function, and query languages for users. This research will be carried out through the implementation of software.

3.2.2 Knowledge Programming Software

Knowledge programming software is a group of utility softwares developed using basic software. To develop application softwares for knowledge information processing, we aim to provide a range of knowledge programming functions, a development support system, and a user interface.

Research will be performed into the development of a cooperative problem-solving technique to process input problems while avoiding the conflicts and contradictions between knowledge processing softwares developed for different application fields. Research will also be conducted into meta-level inference functions such as common sense decision that approach human intelligence, and into meta-level inference techniques for the learning mechanism.

This software provides the following functions as a step to facilitate the construction of knowledge information processing systems: knowledge programming languages, various programming functions, an intelligent programming support function, a knowledge base construction function by the extraction and arrangement of expert knowledge, a function for using knowledge base efficiently according to the application, a function for reconstructing knowledge base, and all the functions required for the construction of an interactive interface that uses natural language to provide a flexible man-machine interface.

This software will consist of the following three modules.

(1) Problem-solving and programming software module

R&D on the parallel logic languages will include work to find methods that can uniformly embody meta-functions and constraint functions, work on semantics of parallel logic language, and work on a constraint logic programming system that integrates multiple constraint solvers as one of the frameworks for cooperative problem-solving.

Concerning parallel knowledge programming languages, a language function needed in order to represent knowledge will be researched from a number of fields including the search problem field, along with research into the basic concepts, programming techniques, and support functions for knowledge programming based on a parallel logic language.

We will also cover basic research into partial evaluation, equivalent transformation (unfold/fold transformation) and verification for parallel logic programs, as well as research into software for interactive conversion, synthesis and verification functions offering parallel partial evaluation, flexibility and expandability.

Software will also be developed to provide expert support for fields that require precise mathematical assistance, such as theorem proving and algorithm design.

(2) Software module to construct and use knowledge base

To simplify the construction and use of application systems for knowledge information processing, a function to extract expert knowledge, organize it, put it in a data base and refine it, as well as an intelligent inference control function that uses deep knowledge, constraints and hypotheses, will be researched. The software to provide these functions will be researched and developed.

Research will be conducted into knowledge models that represent knowledge about structures and relations in the events that will be handled by experts. Ways to use this knowledge to represent problem-solving techniques will also be researched. Technology will be established for a knowledge acquisition support technique to assist in the extraction, and organization of knowledge from the association recalled to experts by the knowledge model, and for a technique for refining knowledge models to alter knowledge bases to suit specific applications. Software will be designed and implemented.

To implement an intelligent inference control function, research will be performed into use, focusing on element technologies such as the use of deep knowledge, cooperative problem-solving, inference control based on hypotheses, and constraint-oriented problem-solving. Along with research into these element technologies, work on the system will also be advanced, and software designed and implemented.

3.2.3 Natural Language Interface Software

In a variety of application systems of knowledge information processing systems, this module will provide the basic functions essential for the establishment of an interactive interface that uses natural language.

To construct an interactive interface that can understand discourse, we will conduct research into implementation of basic functions for semantic processing, clarification of introductive methods for contextual processing functions, and the theory and modeling of functions at the basic level.

This module will be composed of functions for the analysis and generation of Japanese at the syntactic level, functions for semantic description, dictionaries needed to implement the application system, and support functions for developing a lexical database, in a software set forming a general-purpose Japanese-language processing system.

The function for analysis and generation at the syntactic level is designed for application fields with a range of several thousand to several tens of thousands of words. Basic investigation will be performed into software configuration techniques and processing techniques for efficient partial semantic processing, and software will be designed and implemented.

On semantic description function, we will investigate situation theory, type theory and constraint satisfaction method for the semantic description language and processing system. We will take parallel execution models into account in order to research into an expanded version or an refined version of the semantic description language CIL that was developed in the intermediate stage. The language specifications and processing system implementation techniques will be designed and software created.

Appropriate fields for the dictionaries and lexical database forming the basis for these functions will be identified, and thesauri, concept structure and system modeling will be researched, as will techniques for their structure and management. Software will be designed and implemented.

High-level processing functions such as semantic and context processing for discourse understanding will require research into semantic description language, techniques of semantic description and systematic analysis of sentences based on engineering principles. All the above are based on situation theory. Appropriate fields will be identified, an experimental system for evaluation implemented, and the general-purpose Japanese language processing system refined and expanded.

4 CONCLUSION

This project is researching new computer hardware and software technologies using parallel architecture based on logic programming language, with the goal of producing a working prototype. The use of over 300 sequential inference machines as a software research and development tool in the intermediate stage proved that the sequential logic language can be effectively applied to a wide range of subjects. Concerning the parallel logic language, we are advancing with hardware research and development, small-scale test software and PIMOS description, but actual utilization of parallel inference machines as parallel software research and development tools is planned in the final stage. The final stage plan will be carried out along the broad lines outlined in this paper, and the details of the concrete plan will be presented in the ICOT Journal and other sources as completed.

Technical information generated by this project is being publicly released through technical reports, technical memorandums and other publications, and has been the subject of international exchange. We will continue to actively participate in such international information exchange programs in the hope that we can pool our knowledge to everyone's benefit.

ACKNOWLEDGEMENTS

This project has been carried out through the efforts of the researchers at ICOT, and with the support of MITI and many others outside ICOT proper. We wish to extend our appreciation to them all for the direct and indirect assistance and cooperation they have provided.

REFERENCE

Kurozumi: Fifth Generation Computer Systems Project, 1987, ICOT, TM-0303

PROCEEDINGS OF THE INTERNATIONAL CONFERENCE
ON FIFTH GENERATION COMPUTER SYSTEMS 1988,
edited by ICOT. © ICOT, 1988

RESEARCH AND DEVELOPMENT
OF THE PARALLEL INFERENCE SYSTEM
IN THE INTERMEDIATE STAGE OF THE FGCS PROJECT

Shunichi Uchida   Kazuo Taki   Katsuto Nakajima
Atsuhiro Goto   Takashi Chikayama

Institute for New Generation Computer Technology
4-28, Mita-1, Minato-ku, Tokyo 108, Japan

ABSTRACT

This paper introduces the research and development of the inference system in the FGCS project. Research on the parallel inference system in the intermediate stage included the parallel hardware system (PIM) and the parallel software system. It started with the adoption of a new language, GHC, as the base of the parallel kernel language KL1. At the same time, it was determined to develop the multi-PSI system in order to encourage parallel software research. A distributed language processor for KL1 was developed on the multi-PSI system.

The development of the KL1 language processor and also the development of a parallel operating system for the PIM (PIMOS) was considered to include many unknown problems. However, the goal of the research and development for the intermediate stage was set to include the experimental building of the PIMOS on the multi-PSI system and to run some small scale application software systems on it.

The development of a parallel hardware system aimed at the experimental building of a PIM having about 100 processing elements (PEs), making the best use of experiences gained in the development of the smaller version of the PSI CPU.

Another aim was to develop a cross programming environment of KL1 on the smaller version of the PSI, PSI-II, so as to prepare for the wider and larger scale parallel software development to be done in the final stage.

This paper contains not only the research and development results but also the background in which important technical decisions were made.

1   INTRODUCTION

The research of the parallel inference system in the intermediate stage included a parallel hardware system and software system. It started with planning aiming at the experimental building of a parallel inference machine (PIM) having about 100 processing elements (PEs) and also its parallel software system, the PIM operating system (PIMOS). This planning made full use of the development in the initial stage such as the parallel architectures and models proposed in the research on the dataflow machine and the reduction machine, and also the PSI hardware system and its operating system, SIMPOS.

A unique feature of the intermediate stage research and development is the coupling of the research on the parallel hardware with one type of parallel software, the parallel operating system, PIMOS, newly adopted as an important research target.

The research and development of parallel software has never been conducted in as a large project anywhere in the world. This meant that very little pragmatic software had been developed. The main reason was the lack of suitable parallel hardware.

On the other hand, parallel hardware which was worth building parallel operating systems for had never been built, although special purpose parallel hardware systems such as image processors had been built. This was because the design of general purpose parallel hardware needed the characteristics of the behavior of the parallel software running on it. This implies that the parallel software must exist before parallel hardware can exist. Thus, the relation of parallel hardware and software is something like the chicken and egg problem.

To solve this problem, a stepwise development strategy was introduced which used two successive versions of the multi-PSI systems, the multi-PSI-V1 which contained six PSI-I machines as its PEs and the multi-PSI-V2 which contained up to 64 PSI-II CPUs.

These multi-PSI systems enabled software researchers to confirm their ideas on parallel programs by writing and running them in a real parallel hardware environment. Then, their ideas reflected in the design of the next version of the hardware.

Using the multi-PSI-V1, the experimental distributed language processor of the parallel logic programming language, Guarded Horn Clause (GHC), was built to study the communication mechanism between PEs. This work thoroughly analyzed how to extend the GHC language to design the parallel kernel language, KL1, and the kind of functions required for the PIMOS. The experimental distributed language processor of GHC had its debugging functions augmented and extended to a pseudo parallel programming environment of GHC on PSI-I and PSI-II. It was used for parallel algorithm research running many small scale benchmark programs.

This made it possible to start the development of the multi-PSI-V2, followed by the development of the practical KL1 distributed language processor and PIMOS. These research results were reflected in the design of the PIM hardware.

The stepwise development strategy in which the software and hardware development grew little by little worked more effectively than had been expected.

Thus, most of the technical aims included in the intermediate stage goal were achieved by the development of the multi-PSI-V2 with the practical KL1 distributed language processor and the kernel part of the PIMOS running on it.

The contribution of the research of the multi-PSI-V2 and PIMOS to the design of the PIM hardware enabled us to set the research goal of the experimental implementation of the PIM hardware a higher level in terms of its processing speed and the size of its PEs. Thus, the research and development of the PIM in the latter half of the intermediate stage considered not only the intermediate stage goals but also the goal of the final stage which aims at a parallel hardware system having about 1000 PEs.

The flow of the important research activities is shown in Figure 1

This paper describes how we set up the goals and how we made many important technical decisions in the research and development of the PIM and PIMOS in the intermediate stage. Technical details of KL1 language processors, multi-PSI systems, PIMOS and PIM will be described in other papers also presented at the FGCS'88 conference [5] [3].

2 INTERMEDIATE STAGE PLAN

2.1 Evaluation of The Inference Machine Research in The Initial Stage

Research on the PIM and KL1:
The research and development of the inference machine in the initial stage included research on PIM architectures and the development of the sequential inference machines.

Research on the PIM architectures was conducted to find hardware mechanisms that could efficiently execute logic programming languages in parallel using such computational models as dataflow, reduction and Kabuwake.

The languages used for this research were Pure Prolog and Concurrent Prolog, (CP) [14]. Several software and hardware simulators for these languages were built to analyze the algorithms and implementation methods of their interpreters [6].

This research showed us such problems as the insufficiency of OR-parallel Prolog in describing communicating processes and the difficulty of implementing the hardware for the dataflow model. This research made us realized that the scarce accumulation of parallel software would cause a problem in benchmarking the architectures.

Research on the parallel logic programming languages investigated and evaluated such parallel logic programming languages as CP and PARLOG [4] and also, an abstract machine language for Prolog, WAM [21]. Consideration of implementing these languages in hardware motivated us to design a simpler language and GHC was born at the end of the initial stage [20].

Development of sequential inference machines:
In the development of PSI-I [18]and CHI-I [11], the architectures to execute sequential logic programming languages efficiently and their hardware implementation techniques were developed with the KL0 firmware interpreter and the operating system, SIMPOS. This made us decide on the development of the multi-PSI system and start the design of a smaller version of the PSI, PSI-II [19].

The development of PSI-II and also CHI-II [7] established such important techniques as the architecture design based on the WAM instruction set and the code optimization technique in compilers. The development of a new logic programming language, ESP [1] which combined logic programming and object oriented programming features to describe SIMPOS impressed us by its advantages in terms of software productivity, program readability and maintainability. This led us to describe the PIMOS with a single high-level language, KL1, and to make the PIMOS a single language system.

Summary of the research in initial stage:
Considering the goal of the intermediate stage, PIM having about 100 PEs, the research achievements of the initial stage are summarized as follows:

1. Logic programming is appropriate for parallel processing and also for description of operating systems.

2. Current VLSI technology, including CAD tools is not sufficient to confine all the functions required by logic programming in one chip. Thus, the functions implemented in the PE must be restricted. The code optimization technique in compilers is impor-

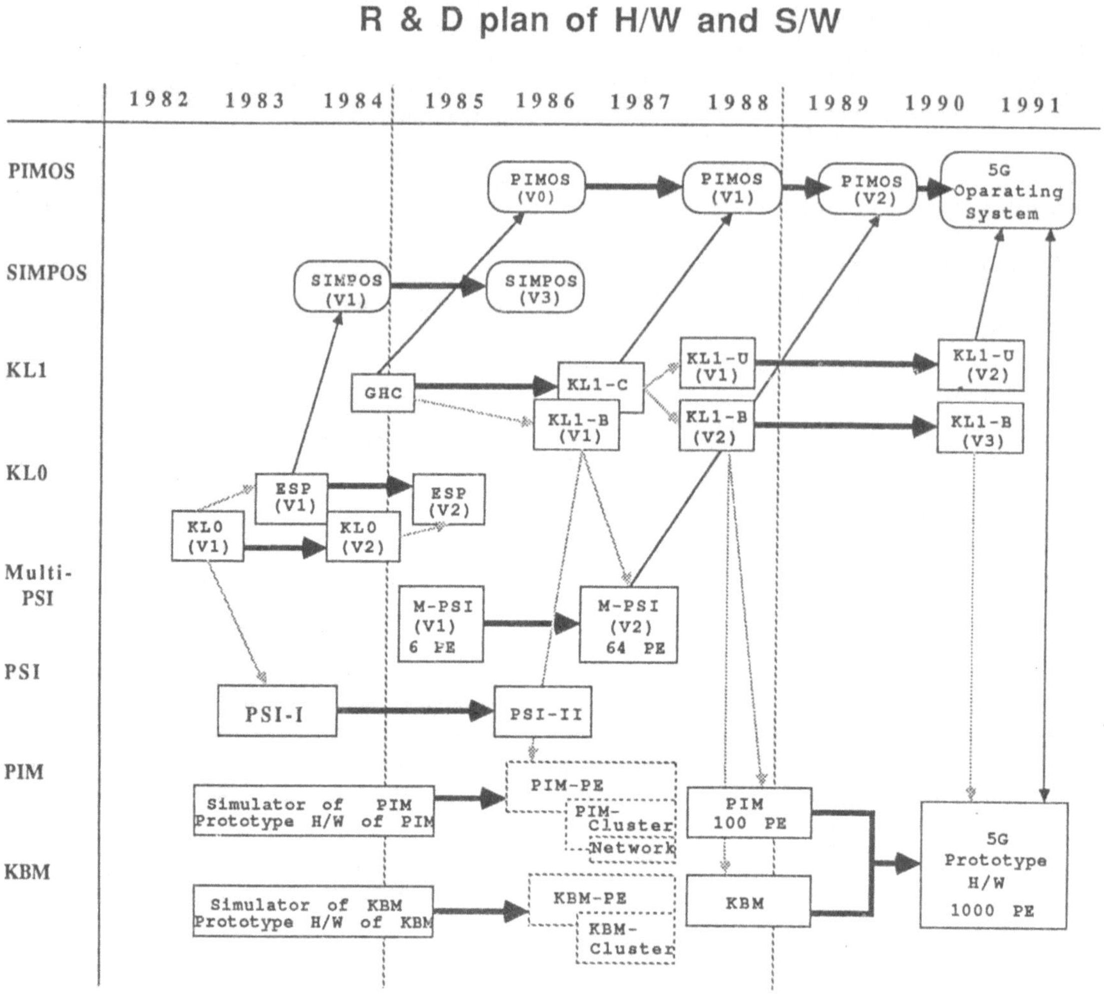

18

Figure 1: Flow of Important Items

tant to reduce the complexity of the PE hardware and attain the high performance and reliability of the PIM.

3. The lack of practical parallel programs makes the architecture design difficult. It is an urgent matter to encourage parallel software research providing software researchers with practical parallel hardware environments.

2.2 The Intermediate Stage Plan and Its Implementation

Before the details of the intermediate stage goal were fixed, the following policies were confirmed:

1. The research of the parallel software systems, specifically, the KL1 language processor and PIMOS, must be closely linked to research on parallel hardware systems, that is, the multi-PSI systems and PIM. They must proceed concurrently and stimulate each other.

2. The parallel hardware systems must be designed to support software research and development. This means that hardware research must not be isolated from software research.

3. Information on the behavior of parallel software systems is essential for practical hardware design although little work had been done it. Then, the tools and the environments to encourage parallel software research must have the highest priority in the investment of human and financial resources.

In line with the above policies, the following goals were defined at the beginning of the intermediate stage, in April 1985. However, the level of these goals had to be set higher in the middle of the intermediate stage.

1. Experimental building of a PIM having about 100 PEs which efficiently supports KL1.

2. Target processing speed of 2M to 5M LIPS.

3. Experimental building of the PIMOS which is described in KL1.

As the PIMOS was considered to be the most difficult of these items, the development of the multi-PSI system which played a role of the PIMOS research tool was begun quickly to stimulate the development of the KL1 language processor. It was decided to develop the multi-PSI system in two consecutive steps: the development of the multi-PSI-V1 using PSI-I and the development of the multi-PSI-V2, making smaller version of the PSI CPUs be its PE.

In the spring of 1986, the detailed design of the PE of the multi-PSI-V2, that is the CPU of PSI-II, was completed and the execution speed of GHC by the multi-PSI-V2 was estimated by small sample programs. The estimated performance of the firmware interpreter of GHC on the PE was very impressive. This also indicated that the performance goal defined at the beginning of the intermediate stage would be attained by the multi-PSI-V2 having 64 PEs although the overhead caused by the PIMOS was uncertain.

Then, the level of the intermediate stage goals were set higher and defined in more detail, taking the final stage goals aiming at a PIM of 1000 PEs into account.

1. The performance goal is 10M to 20M LIPS for a PIM of 100 PEs and 200K to 500K LIPS for one PE.

2. To reduce the communication overhead between PEs, a cluster should be introduced to connect about eight PEs with a shared memory. Then, a PIM with 100 PEs can use several clusters connected by a hierarchical network.

3. The PIMOS should be developed on the multi-PSI-V2. A KL1 distributed language processor should be implemented in firmware. After the PIM hardware is completed, the PIMOS is moved from the multi-PSI-V2 to the PIM.

4. A KL1 cross programming environment should be developed on PSI-II using a KL1 pseudo parallel language processor.

With these goals, the development of the PIM and PIMOS could proceed independently. This enabled us to avoid the problem where one step of development has to wait for the completion of another.

From late 1987, the study of larger scale network mechanisms was started to determine the important technical problems in connecting around 1000 PEs or around 100 clusters. The technical problems were divided among the PIM research groups of the cooperating manufacturers so that they could be further studied through software simulation and by building experimental hardware.

This division of the jobs related to the design and implementation of the PIM among cooperating manufacturers was considered to be essential in the final stage to build a larger scale experimental system. Thus, the preparation for the job division was begun from the latter half of the intermediate stage.

The research and development items described above are summarized in Figure 2.

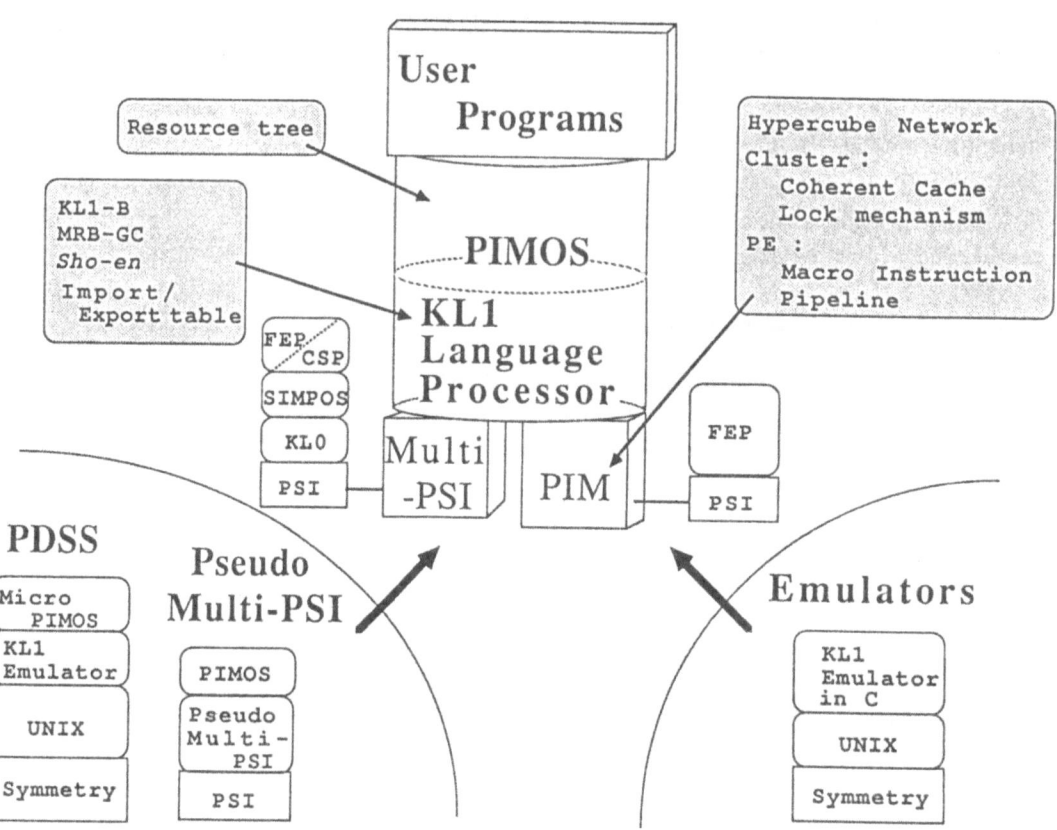

Figure 2: Main Research Items

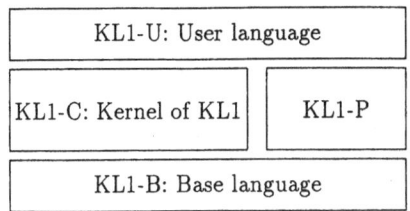

KL1-U: User language	
KL1-C: Kernel of KL1	KL1-P
KL1-B: Base language	

Figure 3: The KL1 Language System

3 KL1 LANGUAGE PROCESSORS

3.1 KL1 Language System

In the design of the language for the PIM, there were two choices: an OR-parallel logic programming language or a stream-based AND-parallel logic programming language. Considerations of the description of the PIMOS which required the description of message passing among many processes and also the simplicity of their hardware support resulted in the adoption of the latter, GHC was decided on.

We believe that this choice was appropriate because we had to make a great effort to develop its distributed language processor although we designed KL1 not fully based on GHC but on a subset of GHC, called Flat GHC (FGHC).

GHC is not a practical language but defines the computational model. A system description language and a machine language has to be designed based on this model. The language system of KL1 was defined at the beginning of the intermediate stage. It had the language layers shown in Figure 3.

KL1-C is a system description language which is the kernel of this language system. It has such functions as modularization and macro-expansion, and many practical built-in predicates in addition to the FGHC functions. KL1-C is used to describe the PIMOS and application systems. KL1-C is compiled to KL1-B.

KL1-B is an abstract machine instruction set used in the same way as WAM is for Prolog. It is used as the common machine language for both the multi-PSI-V2 and PIM.

KL1-P is a notation used with KL1-C to specify how to divide jobs into sub-jobs that can be processed in parallel or how to distribute jobs.

KL1-U is a user defined language which will be designed to fulfill the requirements in a variety of application systems. Some examples are an object-oriented parallel language $\mathcal{A'UM}$ [22] and constraint logic programming languages.

3.2 Distributed Language Processors of KL1

The design of PIM primarily needs information on the specifications of KL1-C and KL1-B and the control

mechanism and behavior of the PIMOS. This means that the characteristics of the total system with layers spanning from application software to hardware must be estimated.

As the estimation of the characteristics of application software was almost impossible, the study was begun from the possible configurations of the PIM hardware system, considering a PIM of 1000 PEs. To connect many PEs, the connection mechanism had to use a loosely coupled mechanism such as a packet switching network.

On the other hand, it was expected that the size of parallel processes, that is, the granularity, would be small in most application software written in KL1. For small granularity, a tightly coupled mechanism such as a common bus with a parallel cache system and a shared memory was adequate to reduce the communication delay.

Both of these are important mechanisms for large scale parallel systems. The PIM of the final stage was expected to use a hierarchical network combining both mechanisms. However, a loosely coupled network could have different structures such as two-dimensional mesh, hypercube, or cross bar, depending on the characteristics of application software in terms of structures of programs and algorithms.

Then, the KL1 language processor had to be designed independently from the details of the hardware structures. Before the design started, we decided to build three experimental KL1 language processors.

1. An intra-PE language processor.

2. A tightly distributed language processor for the PIM cluster.

3. A loosely distributed language processor for the multi-PSI-V2.

The development of the language processors (LPs) began with the design of an intra-PE language processor (LP) of which the key issues were the design of the KL1-B instruction set, optimization techniques in the compiler, the implementation method of the process management, and the garbage collection (GC) technique.

The tightly distributed LP uses a shared memory, and thus, a single address space. The key issues were the communication method between PEs, including the lock mechanism used for PEs to share the common data structure and the cache protocol, and the implementation of GC.

The loosely distributed LP needs communications among multiple address spaces. It contained many difficult research problems not confined to the LP but related to the PIMOS functions. For example, a communication between two different address spaces usually takes much more time than the tightly distributed LP. It requires optimization in its implementation such as the caching of the transferred data. The resource management of both local and global address spaces needs complex mechanisms including global GC. The observation of the behavior of the LP needs also special mechanisms as well as the mechanism for the resource management.

The experimental intra-PE LPs for FGHC had been written in Prolog and the language C in the initial stage. Based on these, the loosely distributed LP was implemented for FGHC on the multi-PSI-V1 to determine the problems in the design of KL1-C and KL1-B.

In the latter half of the intermediate stage, the loosely distributed LP for KL1-B was designed and implemented in firmware on the multi-PSI-V2. KL1-C was designed concurrently followed by the design of the PIMOS. The design of the tightly distributed LP for PIM was started in the middle of 1987 [13].

4   MULTI-PSI SYSTEM

4.1   Outline of A Research and Development

The purpose of the multi-PSI system was to provide software researchers with the parallel hardware environment very quickly; however, its development contained many research problems. The reasons for this development are summarized as follows.

1. The development of KL1 language processors and PIMOS needs many new ideas. Effectiveness of the ideas must be quickly evaluated by making experiments. The research and development of PSI has developed many skillful researchers and engineers and has improved software and firmware tools. It is the most suitable environment in which to make many experiments in a short period.

2. It is not easy to make an experimental parallel hardware system reliable and maintainable enough for use as a software development tool. Using the PSI as its PE greatly reduces this problem.

Before the intermediate stage, discussions were held on the specifications of the multi-PSI system, especially on its network mechanism and the architecture of the smaller version of the PSI.

Their design and implementation started just after the intermediate stage began. The multi-PSI-V1 was completed in the middle of 1986. The CPU of the smaller version of the PSI was completed in early 1987 and built up as the front end machine of the multi-PSI-V2. This front end machine was also used as a stand-alone workstation, PSI-II.

PSI-II employed the instruction set based on WAM and made full use of the code optimization technique

Table 1: Main Features of PSI-I and PSI-II

	PSI-I	PSI-II
Device	TTL (Fast)	CMOS-G.A., TTL
Cycle time	200 ns	200 ns
Word width	40 bits	40 bits
WCS	64b x 16KW	53b x 16KW
Cache memory	4KW x 2	4KW x 1
Main memory	16MW (Max)	64MW (Max)
Memory chip	256 Kbit	1 Mbit
Max. No. of Process	64	S/W defined
Machine code	Table type	WAM type
Structure data	Sharing	Copying
Exe. speed(Average)	30 KLIPS	150 KLIPS
Exe. speed(Append)	35 KLIPS	333 KLIPS

with its compiler. For compactness, its hardware used nine newly developed 8k-gate CMOS gate-array LSIs. PSI-II attained a threefold to fivefold improvement in ESP execution speed.

The network of the multi-PSI system has a two-dimensional mesh structure. Each node of the network has a function to relay the packets from one node to another. The routing control mechanism in the node was extended and implemented in two 20k-gate LSIs for the multi-PSI-V2. Development was completed in the spring of 1988, but the inspection of the hardware consisting of 64 PEs took a long time because of the connection of the front end machine, and preparation of test programs and observation programs. The preparation of the inspection was much more complicated than had been anticipated. The total hardware system began operation in the summer of 1988.

The design of the loosely distributed language processor of KL1-B was started in 1986. Its specification was so complex that its verification had to be made by writing it in the language C. The firmware implementation of the language processor was begun in late 1987 and partially completed in the summer of 1988. It was hurriedly provided to develop the PIMOS on PSI-II.

On PSI-II, the KL1-B firmware resides with the KL0 firmware which runs the SIMPOS. Programs written in KL1 are run as processes under the SIMPOS as well as the programs written in KL0 (or ESP). The SIMPOS switches the firmware depending on whether the process is written in KL0 or KL1-B.

In 1988, the hardware of the multi-PSI-V2 is being reproduced to distribute it to many software research groups so that they can start parallel software research from the beginning of the final stage.

The development of the multi-PSI system made full use of experience and item that had already been developed, such as microprogramming tools, evaluation tools and the SIMPOS.

Without these, we could not cope with the scale and complexity of each part of the system, for example, the large and complex hardware, complex firmware for KL1-B, and observation and diagnosis functions of the front end machine.

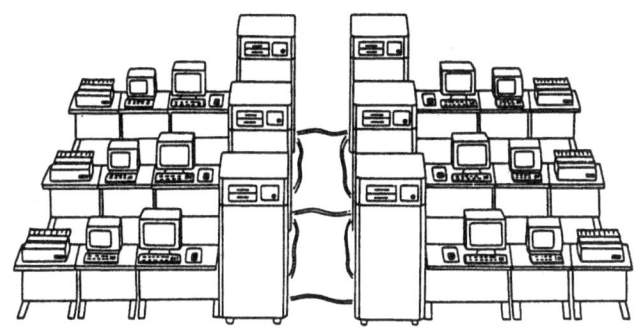

Figure 4: Multi-PSI-V1

4.2 Multi-PSI-V1

4.2.1 Functions and Organization of The System

The multi-PSI-V1 consists of six PSI-Is as its PEs which are connected by a two-dimensional mesh network. The reason why a two-dimensional mesh network was adopted was that it was considered to be appropriate as the first step in studying the load balancing of application software systems.

To solve the load balancing or load distribution problem, we first adopted the policy that programmers must explicitly specify how to divide their jobs into sub-jobs that can be processed in parallel at the system programming level.

This was different from most past proposals on this problem made after past parallel architecture research which tried to provide automatic mechanisms to exploit parallelism in users' programs. We concluded that this method was ideal but too difficult to attain, especially for the PIM and PIMOS.

Our proposal is that one job written in KL1-C be divided into many sub-jobs specified by the programmers using KL1-P. Furthermore, the programmer should be able to specify explicitly the amount of computational resources and the priority given to each sub-job. This specification, however, may not be accurate, something like a first order approximation. The actual loads of sub-jobs on PEs will accordingly be unbalanced among PEs. Thus, the PIMOS tries to compensate dynamically for this imbalance as much as possible.

We examined a model in which computational resources were uniformly distributed on a two-dimensional plane. When a programmer tried to specify the how jobs are divided and the amount of resources of each sub-job, the position and the amount of space were used as the parameters. An overhead caused by a communication between PEs was proportional to the distance between

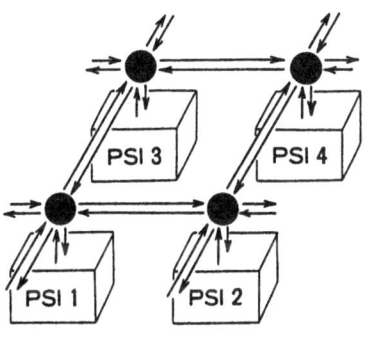

Figure 5: Network of Multi-PSI System

two points on the plane. Thus, the locality of communications is represented. This model was named the Processor Power Plane model [2].

A dynamic job reallocation method based on this model was created. As this method was considered to cause too much overhead if implemented only by the PIMOS, its hardware support mechanism was designed and implemented in the network node of the multi-PSI-V2 [16].

The network of the multi-PSI system was designed based on the above. The appearance of the multi-PSI-V1 is shown in Figure 4. The structure of the network is shown in Figure 5.

Each node of the network has five channels. One of them is connected to the PE of its node and the other four are connected to four neighbors. Each channel has independent input and output circuits, each of which contains 10bit data and signal lines and 4k-byte FIFO buffers, so that multiple communication paths can be opened. Each node also has a simple routing mechanism controlled by a table in which control instructions are kept. The data transfer rate of each channel is 500 Kbytes/sec.

Packet transfer is controlled by the PSI microprogram and the SIMPOS device handler. The FGHC distributed language processor implements inter-PE communications using this handler.

4.2.2 Research on The KL1 Language Processor

The purpose of the multi-PSI-V1 was to develop a loosely distributed LP for FGHC to study the implementation of distributed unification between PEs, the control method of the load distribution, the observation mechanism to watch the behavior of the PEs, and the debugging support mechanism.

The development of this LP started with the development of a pseudo parallel LP for FGHC on a single PSI-I. This pseudo parallel LP simulated the parallel execution of FGHC programs under the control of the SIMPOS. It had a simple tracer and debugger and also some measurement functions for computation time, number of reductions, and communication delay.

After the multi-PSI-V1 hardware was completed, this pseudo parallel LP was moved on to it and extended to execute the programs in parallel among six PEs. As this LP was built to evaluate the implementation methods of the mechanisms described above, the execution speed was about 1K LIPS. However, it ran several small scale programs such as the eight queen problem and the best path problem and contributed to the study of job distribution and the parallel algorithms [17].

Among the achievements of this experiment, the most valuable was the method to implement the observation and maintenance mechanisms to control and measure the distributed execution of programs. This experience was reflected in the design of the multi-PSI-V2.

4.3 Multi-PSI-V2

4.3.1 Functions and Organization of The System

The multi-PSI-V2 contains up to 64 PEs. Its appearance is shown in Figure 6. The organization of the system is as follows.

1. Each PE consists of three CPU boards, one network board and four memory boards containing 80M bytes.

2. Its network has the same structure as the multi-PSI-V1. The functions of each node are augmented using two 20k-gate LSIs to attain the data transfer rate of 5 Mbytes/sec and to contain the circuit to support the load balancing mechanism described in 4.2.1.

3. The main part of the system consists of eight cabinets, each of which contains eight PEs. The minimum configuration of the system is one cabinet.

4. The front end machine, PSI-II, has such functions as input and output, observation and maintenance for the main part. Up to four front end machines can be connected to the 64 PE system.

5. The front end machine has two logically independent functions which are called the front end processor (FEP) and the console processor (CSP). The FEP performs input and output operations for the PIMOS, the CSP performs the functions for observation and maintenance.

6. The front end machine is connected to each PE of the main part with a 10-bit-wide common bus. Using this bus, the front end machine loads firmware and software and monitors and diagnoses all the PEs.

The scale of the hardware of the main part is very large. The hardware contains 512 printed circuit boards and a 5G byte memory. Its testing and debugging required many firmware and software tools. Many of them were prepared as CSP functions. Most of the test programs were written in ESP. In its hardware debugging, the KL0 firmware and the kernel part of the SIMPOS were loaded in each PE to run the test programs written in ESP. This made the debugging very efficient and helped us to keep to the development schedule.

4.3.2 Loosely Distributed KL1 Language Processor

The development of the loosely distributed KL1 LP began with the design of the KL1-B specification. The design of the KL1-C specification was also started by extending the specification of FGHC.

At the beginning of the design, the level of KL1-B was roughly set to the level of WAM and then extended to cover distributed implementation. The architecture of the PE based on this level can be seen in Figure 7. [9]

The execution of KL1-B is performed using several queues such as a ready-queue, suspension records and a goal queue. The PE takes one goal (process) from the ready-queue and prepares the environment in registers to execute the goal. The execution produces new ready goals. They are put in the ready queue again. If some variable is not instantiated, the new goal is added to the suspension record. This is a very rough sketch of basic KL1-B execution.

In addition to the basic execution functions based on FGHC, many important functions to make KL1-B practical were added, as described below.

Incremental garbage collection (GC):
One of the major problems in executing KL1-B in a PE

Figure 6: Multi-PSI-V2

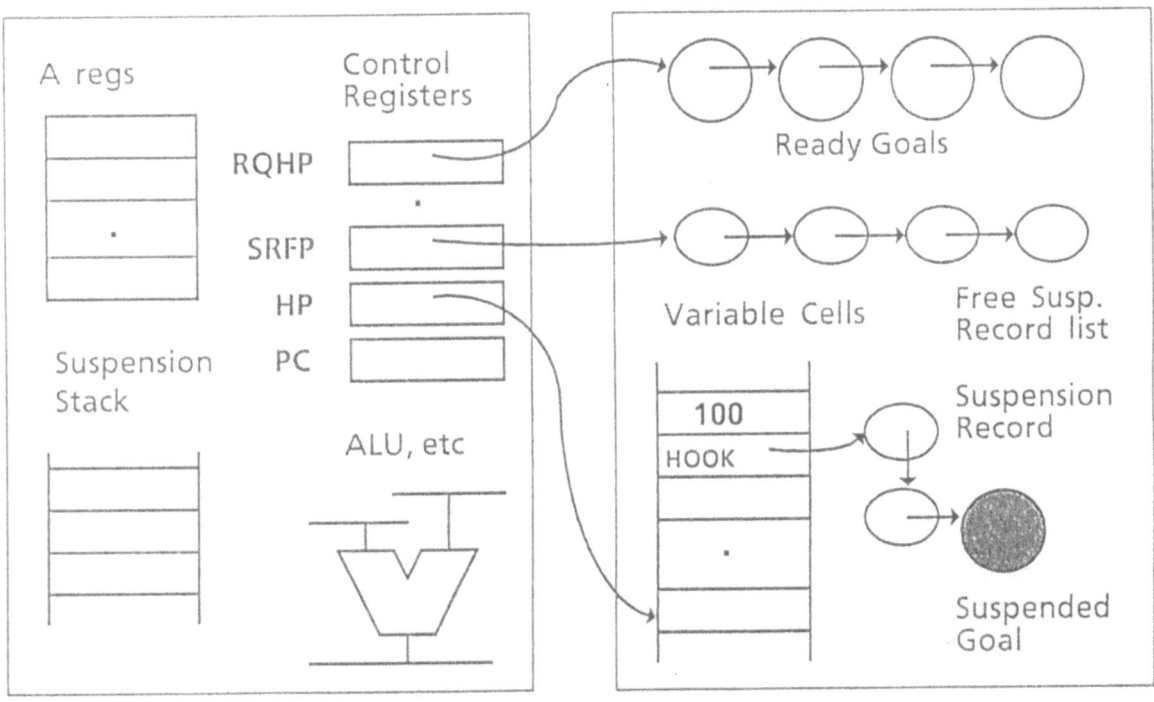

Figure 7: Abstract Architecture of PE

is GC. In executing KL1-B, data areas are made for variables, lists and so on. These areas are made in the heap area in the memory. Some parts of these areas are referred to by several parallel processes.

Languages like KL1 need a method to reclaim the data areas after they become unnecessary. In Prolog, two different methods are used to reclaim unnecessary used areas. One is a stack mechanism which reclaims them on the way of program execution. Another is GC, which usually stops the execution during the GC process.

KL1-B also needs a method to reclaim used memory areas. However, it cannot employ an efficient method like a stack mechanism because the areas can be referred to by several processes. If no such mechanism is employed, reclamation of the used areas relies solely on GC. If usual non-incremental GC is used, the execution will stop very often. Furthermore, non-incremental GC accesses memory almost randomly. Thus, it causes cache mis-hit often and degrades the execution performance.

Incremental GC can be used to solve this problem. However, its naive implementation is very heavy and greatly degrades the performance. We found a method to reduce the heavy overhead of incremental GC. This method was named multiple reference bit (MRB)-GC. MRB-GC uses one additional bit in the tag field of each memory word to indicate whether there are one or more than one references to the word. This made it possible to use the tag handling hardware so as to attain reasonable execution speed.

In the execution of KL1 programs, one memory word is referred to by only one process in many cases. Thus, MRB-GC works very effectively and reduces cache mis-hit ratio and the occurrence of non-incremental GC.

Inter-process communication for distributed unification:

Control of communication among parallel processes is hidden under the KL1-B level. This is useful to make the KL1 language processors common to the multi-PSI-V2 and the PIM.

Unifications among the PEs on the multi-PSI-V2 and the clusters of the PIM are implemented using global packet communication. Implementation of this global communication needs some memory areas in the PE or the cluster. These memory areas should also be reclaimed. A naive solution for this is global GC which must stop all the PEs or the clusters at one time.

To perform GC separately in each PE or cluster, different address spaces have to be provided for each PE or cluster to make a distributed environment. A packet transferred among the different address spaces needs its identifier. A memory address cannot be used for this purpose because the data address is changed by GC. Then, a table is used to convert local addresses to global addresses or vice versa. This table is called an import/export table. This method is often used for high-level language parallel processors.

As the number of entries of this table is limited, used entries have to be reclaimed by GC. The naive solution of this is again global GC. Incremental GC can be applied; however, its ordinary implementation in a distributed environment causes a problem called racing. Racing is caused by delay in packet transfer. If racing occurs, an entry is reclaimed eventhough a packet which refers to that entry still exists.

To solve this problem, we designed a new method called weighted export count (WEC), in which a weight is given to each entry of the table and referenced data [8].

PIMOS support functions:

Many functions were added for supporting the PIMOS. Some examples are functions for program execution management, computational resource management, debugging and maintenance.

Including the functions described above, a KL1-B interpreter which is the kernel of a loosely distributed KL1-B LP was implemented in firmware. To avoid low productivity of firmware development, the interpreter was primarily written in the language C to verify its specification and algorithm of implementation. This interpreter was next used as a specification of the firmware interpreter.

The size of the firmware interpreter is shown below.

Basic instructions	3.8 K
Basic built-in predicates	1.6 K
Memory management, network control, etc.	4.4 K
Hardware control	4.2 K
Total microprogram steps	14 K

Observing this table, the size of the memory management and network control part is larger than that of the basic instruction part which controls the execution of KL1-B in one PE. The basic instructions have been studied in detail in the past. However, the memory management and network control has not. Its instruction design, especially its assignment of required functions to each of the instructions is not optimum. This makes the structure of its firmware implementation complex. This part is most closely related to the control of distributed unification, thus , requiring further study in the future.

A PSI-II which is used as the front end machine of the multi-PSI-V2 or a KL1 cross programming environment must have both KL0 and KL1-B firmware systems. As the total capacity of both firmware systems exceeds the capacity of PSI-II microprogram memory, a firmware overlay function was added. The execution speed of the KL1-B interpreter was 50K to 100K LIPS.

In the development of this interpreter, firmware debugging tools which had been developed for the KL0 firmware were used very effectively. The kernel part of the PIMOS which was being built concurrently was used as a test program for this interpreter.

Experience in the design and implementation of this interpreter is now used as the solid base for the development of the tightly distributed KL1 LP used in a PIM cluster and also the loosely distributed KL1 LP used for communication among the clusters.

5 PARALLEL INFERENCE MACHINE: PIM

5.1 Outline of Research and Development

5.1.1 Design of The Basic PIM Structure

The PIM intermediate stage research began substantially from 1986 after its intermediate stage goals were defined based on the evaluation of the research results attained in the initial stage.

Discussions on the basic design policy of the PIM covered many aspects such as target performance, basic architecture, available device technology, CAD design tools, development period and development cost.

One important discussion was held on circuit density of the device and development period. It proposed two alternative policies on PIM hardware building.

1. To reduce risks, the design of PIM hardware should limit its scale up to 100 PEs. Low density devices which have well prepared CAD tools should be used so as to make the development period short and certain.

2. Although the risk is high, high density devices should be used to confine one PE to one printed board. The PE should have continuity to a PIM in the final stage, which should have about 1000 PEs. The PE should be superiority in performance to the technical standard in the final stage.

Being influenced by the estimated performance of the multi-PSI-V2, the natural conclusion of the discussion was to choose 2. The research goals based on this policy were considered to be very difficult to attain. However, this choice was thought to be more suited to the philosophy of this project.

The basic architecture of the intermediate stage PIM was determined in order to employ a tag architecture which could maintain continuity from the multi-PSI-V2. The performance goal was defined to be 200K to 500K LIPS for one PE, including the overhead caused by incremental GC. This performance goal implies that if this PE is used for Prolog, it will attain more than 1M LIPS.

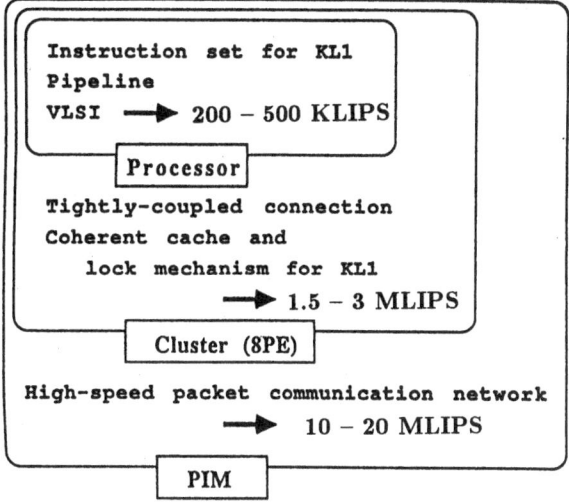

Figure 8: Target execution speed of PIM

To implement one PE on a single board and attain 200K to 500K LIPS, the PE needed not only high density chips and a highly optimized architecture to make its cycle time short but also a sophisticated code optimization technique with its compiler.

The connection mechanism of the PE needed to realize a short response delay for communication between PEs. This delay was considered to determine substantially the lower limit of process's granularity. If the delay is made shorter, the size of processes can be smaller. Then, the number of processes that can be processed in parallel will increase.

The connection mechanism which made this delay shortest was considered to be a common bus with a parallel cache and a shared memory. Then, a cluster was introduced in the PIM. The performance goals of the PE, the cluster and the total system are shown in Figure 8.

5.1.2 Simulators for PIM Design

The design of the PE began with an analysis of the KL1 program's behavior. The primary intention was design of a cache mechanism including its protocol design. This was made through software simulations.

The first simulation was made on VAX 11/785 using a KL1-B interpreter and a parallel cache simulator, both of which were written in the language C. The KL1-B interpreter generated address patterns, by executing small benchmark programs such as the N-queen program. The cache simulator analyzed the address patterns and evaluated the cache mis-hit ratio and traffic on the common bus.

In late 1986, Sequent's Symmetry system was introduced to extend the scale of simulation and to make the simulations more precise. The Symmetry system is a multi processor using conventional microprocessors. On this system, the KL1-B simulator ran at 2K to 5 K LIPS.

Through the simulations, the characteristics of KL1 programs gradually became clear. For example, execution of KL1 programs consumes a heap area very quickly. The locality of its memory accesses was worse than that of usual Prolog. Many memory cells are written and read only once. These facts motivated us to create the MRB-GC method.

For communication among PEs, the communication rate between PEs for KL1 programs is higher than that for conventional language programs. PEs lock memory words before they write them. These write operations, in most cases, do not cause access contention for KL1 programs.

With these results, the number of PEs in the cluster was determined to be eight. The KL1-B simulator was extended to have MRB-GC and then modified to run in parallel using several processors of the Symmetry system. It is now used as a base for designing tightly distributed language processors [13], [10].

5.1.3 Design of The PIM hardware System

PE Design:
The design of PE hardware began with the design of an instruction set. This instruction set may be called a concrete machine instruction set, by contrast with an abstract instruction set like KL1-B. It can approximately be one of two different types as follows:

1. A high-level instruction set which is similar to KL1-B is employed and is implemented in firmware. This instruction set has characteristics like CISC.

2. A low-level instruction set which is directly implemented in hardware. This instruction set has characteristics like RISC. In this case, KL1-B instructions are interpreted by run-time routines written in these low-level instructions.

Each of these choices had both advantages and disadvantages. As described in 4.3.2, the basic instructions of KL1-B had been studied in detail and well optimized. However, instructions for memory management and network control needed further study and were possibly to be changed for better optimization in their implementation.

The advantage of the high-level instruction set with firmware implementation is its flexibility of changing the instruction design and thus, suitable for experimental machines. Its disadvantage is obvious in chip design. It tends to need a long cycle time and large chip area to implement its microprogram memory.

The advantage of low-level instruction set, however, is its simplicity of instructions which results in a short cycle time and small amount of hardware. This feature enables us to improve the execution time if code optimization by compilers works effectively. If the code optimization does not work well, result is drastic, long chains of instructions and slow execution time.

Roughly speaking, the high-level instruction set is suitable for a flexible control oriented design, and the low-level instruction set is for a fast execution oriented design. Both of these are worth further study and evaluation totally in the framework of the PIMOS implementation.

Inter-cluster network design:
The network hardware design has many problems. Most of them are derived from the fact that its performance requirements are very vague. This is because no large scale parallel software has ever run anywhere in the world. Thus, no one can imagine how it will behave and what performance requirements are.

We are trying to design the network hardware bottom up and are holding discussions on the following issues.

1. Control methods and their hardware support of the inter-cluster network

2. Structures (or topology) of the inter-cluster network

On the first item, the target of the design is to attain fast response time or shortest delay for message transfer between two clusters. One idea is hardware support for management of the import/export table and caching of transferred data.

On the second item, several important network structures have been proposed. Some examples are the two-dimensional mesh of the multi-PSI-V2, hypercube and cross-bar.

However, no detailed discussion has been held on the structures in connection with a module structure of parallel programs, distribution of parallel jobs and locality of communication among parallel processes, because the characteristics of large scale parallel programs are not known yet. At this level, software simulation is not as reliable as the simulation of a KL1 program's behavior inside the cluster. No appropriate benchmark program is available. This is something like outer space in the research of parallel processing.

We expect that the PIMOS and some parallel application software running on the multi-PSI-V2 will give us some new knowledge on the above issues.

Current plan of the PIM implementation:
After the design of the PIM cluster was completed in the spring of 1988, the design of the PIM total system which included 16 clusters began in parallel the chip design and production.

The design of the PIM total system made us realize that it would contain many difficult problems and several technical alternatives to be further studied, as described above.

We have decided to deal with these problems including many alternative choices by dividing them among research groups at ICOT and cooperating manufacturers.

First of all, the PIM for the intermediate stage goals adopted the low-level instruction set for its PE and a hypercube network for its inter-cluster network. It was designed to be extensible up to about 500 PEs. An attempt was made to construct a hardware system having 128 PEs around the end of the intermediate stage. As this development will be continued in the final stage, we named it PIM/p to distinguish it from other PIM models to be developed also in the final stage.

We now plan to develop several experimental hardware systems based on different models such as the PIM/c which will adopt the high-level instruction set for its PE and a cross-bar network, and the PIM/m which will be an improved and extended version of the multi-PSI-V2. All of these will use the PIMOS as their common operating system and many software experiments will be made on them.

5.2 Functions and Organization of The PIM/p

5.2.1 Configuration of The Hardware System

The PIM/p, whose hardware system will be constructed around the end of the intermediate stage, consists of a main part which contains 16 clusters, a front end machine, PSI-II, and an SVP which performs maintenance of the main part as shown in Figure 9.

Eight PEs are connected in a cluster. Eight clusters are contained in one cabinet. Then, a PIM/p having 128 PEs consists of two cabinets.

5.2.2 PE and Cluster Architecture

The design of the PE started with the employment of a low-level instruction set and a four stage pipeline hardware for instruction execution. However, it was realized that the complexity of some KL1-B instructions needed too many low-level instructions to be described. Then, some macro instructions were added to the PE's instruction set. A macro instruction is interpreted by dedicated low-level instructions stored in a special internal memory which contains about 8K instructions. The instructions stored in this memory are called internal instructions. Ordinary instructions are read from an instruction cache and called external instructions. Internal instructions can be regarded as a kind of microprogram [15].

The width of the external instruction is either four, six or eight bytes. The function of each of these instructions is much more sophisticated than the usual RISC instruction of a conventional microprocessor. KL1-B instructions are too complicated to be interpreted only by the external instructions. Thus, macro instructions have to be added.

In execution of KL1-B instructions, a conditional branch operation depending on data types appears very often. To perform this operation quickly, delayed branch instructions are provided to reduce useless execution cycles by augmenting the instruction execution pipeline.

A CPU of the PE has thirty-two 40-bit general registers and other dedicated registers for tag checking, floating point numbers and so on. The contents of these registers must be saved for process switching. In execution of KL1-B, process switching happens very frequently. To perform process switching quickly, a special instruction called slit-check is introduced using the characteristics of KL1-B instructions. The slit-check instruction is a kind of optimized interrupt checking instruction. It can be executed in one cycle.

A PE cache is a coherent cache with a write-back mechanism. It has two independent buffers for data and instructions. The size of each buffer is 64K bytes. The block size of the data buffer is four words.

In addition to the functions described above, the PE has functions for connecting it to the front end machine and the inter-cluster network.

The PE is implemented on a single printed board using five 80k-gate LSIs. The cycle time of the CPU is 50 ns. The execution speed of an append operation which is written in KL1-B as high as about 600K LIPS. The structure of the PE is shown in Figure 10.

In a cluster, eight PEs and a shared memory are connected via a 64-bit wide common bus. Its address space is 4G bytes. The current implementation of the cluster includes 256M bytes for the shared memory.

One unit of the PIM network system is a four dimensional hypercube network. Each node of the network has four channels. Each channel has a one-byte data line. Its throughput is 20 Mbyte/sec.

The current implementation uses two units of the network systems to increase the throughput. Each cluster is connected to four other clusters using two channels per cluster.

5.2.3 Program Execution in The Cluster

The tightly distributed KL1-B language processor uses the cluster described above. This language processor implements inter-PE communication using the shared memory. Thus, it can make the communication delay much smaller than that of the multi-PSI-V2. It is expected that the time for one transfer of message from one PE to another can be reduced to a few microseconds or less.

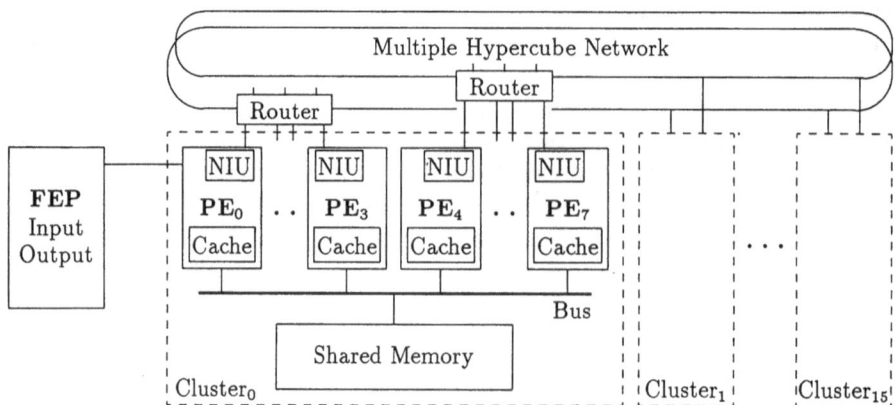

Figure 9: Configuration of PIM/p

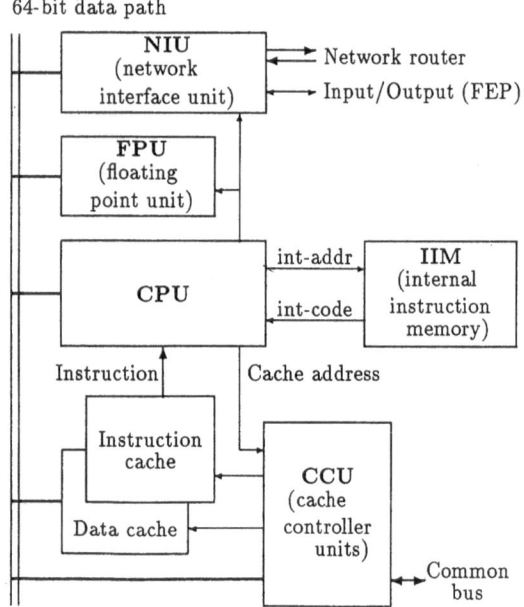

Figure 10: Structure of PE

KL1-B programs are executed in the environment described in 4.3.2, using such data structures as queues and trees. Ready queues and goal records are important data structures. The goal records which are a tree structure contain the history of program execution and are shared by all PEs in a cluster.

If one PE throws one goal to another and this goal is ready to be executed, it is put in a ready queue attached to the PE. Each PE has its own ready queue. As each goal has its own priority for its execution, each ready queue is divided into many subqueues according to the priority. There are several other data structures used for execution.

Some of these data structures are shared among PEs in a cluster. If one data structure is accessed by many PEs very often, it needs to be duplicated and allocated in separate memory areas to avoid access contentions.

Allocation of these data structures is very important to reduce bus traffic and cache mis-hit ratio. An important design criterion is to raise the locality of accesses by the optimized allocation. This enables us to make full use of the cache mechanism.

The language processor for a cluster currently has the following data structure allocation:

1. A total memory area in the shared memory is divided into several local memory areas and a common memory area. Each local memory area is assigned to each PE. The common memory area is shared by all the PEs.

2. A separate ready queue is attached to each PE and put in its local memory area because ready queues are most frequently accessed.

3. The goal records are connected by pointers and from a tree structure. This tree structure extends its branches (subtrees) according to program execution. If one goal is dispatched form one PE to another, a

new subroot is made and a new subtree grows up. In the current design, the goal record subtree is attached to each PE as shown in Figure 11.

Goals are distributed when a busy PE throws a goal when it receives a request from a non-busy PE.

The tightly distributed KL1-B language processor is under detailed design. The design is evaluated using the simulators described in 5.1.2.

6 PIM OPERATING SYSTEM: PIMOS

6.1 Outline of Research and Development

From the intermediate stage, the PIMOS was included in the plan as an important research target of this project. Before that, its role and position in the project were not clear.

Generally speaking, many researchers of parallel processing had realized that management of computational resources in connection with job distribution and load balancing was an indispensable function of parallel machines.

However, it was difficult to tell which layer of parallel machines should mainly perform this function: machine architectures, language processors, operating systems, or application programs. In research of dataflow machines for scientific computing, this function was mainly treated as a problem of machine architectures. Some hardware mechanisms were proposed for this.

In research of parallel inference machines for knowledge information processing, it seemed that machine architectures could play only a subsidiary role for this problem. Furthermore, considering the difficulty in the use of parallelism from application programs by compilers, language processors did not seem to be appropriate to embed this function in themselves. This made us decide to develop a parallel operating system for the PIM, namely, the PIMOS, although we did not have any concrete idea of embedding this function in the PIMOS. Even now, this situation has not yet changed greatly.

To start the research and development of the PIMOS, the following design policies were made:

1. A practical operating system used for large scale software experiments.

2. A stand-alone self-contained operating system.

3. A single operating system showing a parallel machine as one system.

4. To be described in KL1 and be independent from architectural details.

The PIMOS research goal in the intermediate stage was defined to have two basic management functions. One was a function for program execution management, which introduced a layered structure in program execution using meta-programming. This function is called "Sho-en". Another was a function for resource management, which manages such computational resources as CPUs, memories and input/output devices.

Before the PIMOS starts to run, it is loaded from the front end machine using the CSP functions. After it starts, it controls the entire hardware system. The front end machine is regarded as a special PE which controls input/output devices (FEP functions). The PIMOS may imagine that FEP is also running as a part of PIMOS.

To make the scope of its development as small as possible, it was decided to buid its programming environment on a PSI-II. A pseudo parallel KL1 language processor and PIMOS were built on PSI-II; however, most input/output operations including man-machine interface were performed by the SIMPOS.

This programming environment including the PIMOS built on the SIMPOS is called the PIMOS-S (PIMOS on a single processor). It is not easy for us to make many copies of the multi-PSI-V2 to distribute them to software researchers. The PIMOS-S on PSI-II will be the most popular parallel programming tool in the beginning of the final stage.

The PIMOS-S has a debugging tool that can change the order of process scheduling by random numbers so that programmers can detect bugs caused by a different execution order. The development of the programming environment described above was also included in the research goals.

Research on the PIMOS began with the design of its functional specification. As the functions of the PIMOS were closely related to that of KL1-C, the design of KL1-C was carried out concurrently. In the spring of 1987, their conceptual design was completed.

The functional design of the PIMOS and KL1-C proceeded with experimental software building so that the design could be verified. This software was built on Sequent's Symmetry system using the language C and organized into another KL1-C programming environment called the PIMOS development support system (PDSS). The PDSS has a KL1-C language processor including the Sho-en function and micro-PIMOS, both written in the language C. The functional design was completed in the spring of 1988.

In the summer of 1988, the kernel part of a KL1-B firmware interpreter began operation on a PSI-II as described in 4.3.2. The PIMOS-S also started running on the PSI-II for debugging and also for development of demonstration programs for the coming FGCS'88 conference. The PIMOS-M (The PIMOS on the Multi-

Processing Elements in A Cluster

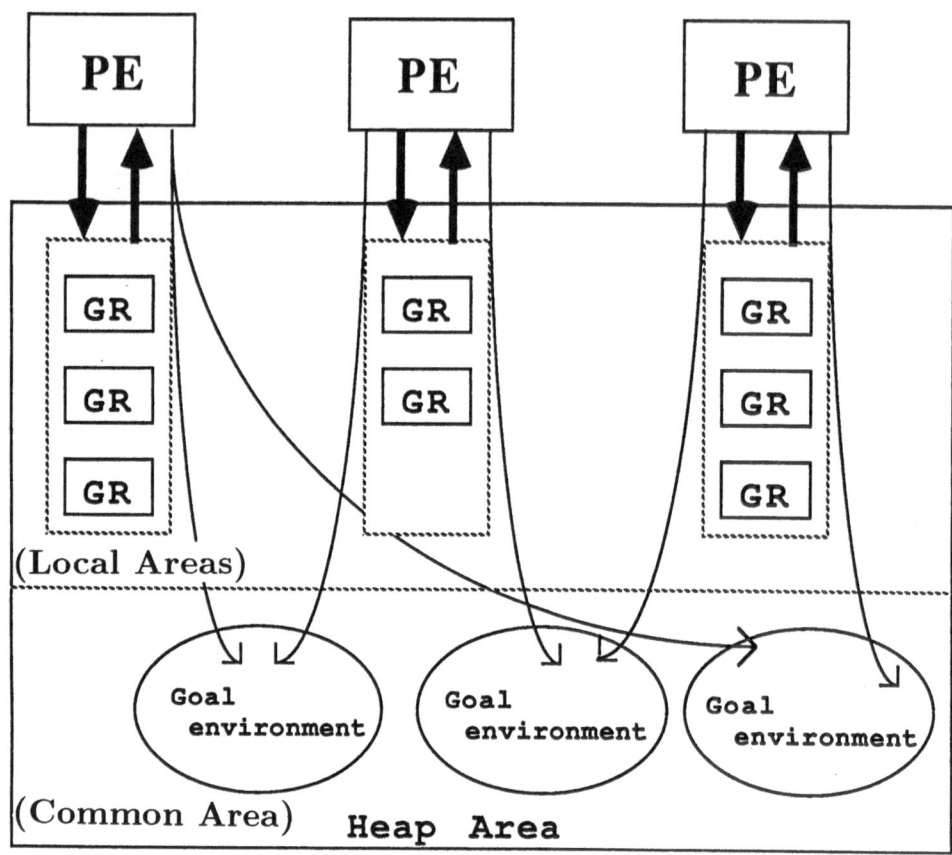

GR: Goal Record

Figure 11: Execution of a KL1 program

PSI-V2) is still under development. The PIMOS-M and PIMOS-S are almost the same except that the PIMOS-M runs on a real parallel environment and will produce more bugs than the PIMOS-S because of real parallel execution of its program. These two versions of the PIMOS are planned to be released in the summer of 1989. The PIMOS-M and PIMOS-S are shown in Figure 12.

6.2 Function and Organization

6.2.1 Main Features of The PIMOS

The main role of the PIMOS is to provide its users with an efficient and safe program execution environment by managing a variety of computational resources such as computing resources, memory resources and input/output devices.

The most basic and important function of management is protection of the operating system against user program bugs. Reflecting on this function, user programs are also protected. To implement the management, structuring of program execution is indispensable. For instance, some conventional operating systems use a layered ring structure for program execution management to protect themselves from user program bugs.

In the PIMOS, this structuring mechanism was implemented as one of the program execution control functions. It was named "Sho-en". Using this function, resource management functions were implemented.

Functions for program execution control:
PIMOS needed the structuring of program execution to implement management mechanisms as described above.

However, FGHC, which was the base of KL1-C, lacked any structuring mechanism. Its execution structure is flat. Then, this mechanism was added as an execution mechanism of KL1-C using meta programming . Meta-programming separates program execution into two levels, a meta level and an object level, using a special program call called a meta-call.

In KL1-C, this call was named a "Sho-en"call. "Sho-en" in Japanese corresponds to "manor" in English. Execution of KL1-C programs repeats a call of a goal which is something like a subroutine call. The Sho-en call is a special goal call. Program execution being expanded under this call is treated as a unit of computation being managed separately. This unit is called a Sho-en. A Sho-en call seems like the entrance to a Sho-en.

A Sho-en call can be made in any Sho-en recursively. Thus, this call makes a tree-like structure in program execution. In this case, Sho-ens are nested making a parent Sho-en, children Sho-en and grandchildren Sho-en. Using this structure, program execution control functions of the PIMOS are implemented.

If a program executed in a Sho-en fails or encounters an unexpected event, it is reported to its parent Sho-

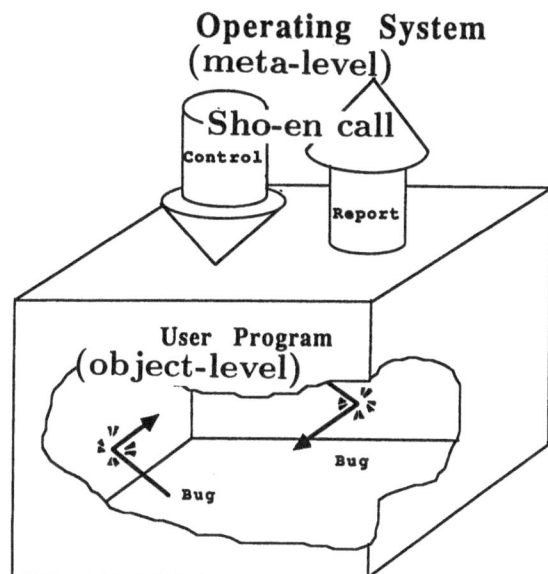

Figure 13: An image of Sho-en

en. The parent Sho-en can control the execution of the children Sho-en in many ways such as continuing and aborting. With this mechanism, protection function is realized in the PIMOS. A Sho-en is shown in Figure 13.

Another important function of the program execution management is priority control. In the PIMOS, each parallel process made by goal calls is given some priority in execution. This priority is used to control the order of execution. It is given to each process in two ways. One is to give it to each goal call using KL1-P. This is fine-grained control. Another is to give it to each Sho-en using a Sho-en call. This is coarse-grained control.

Functions for resource management:
The purpose of resource management of the PIMOS is to prevent unnecessary consumption of computational resources, for example, caused by program bugs such as an endless loop.

This management is performed for the following resources. One is the management of computing resources and memory resources. This is implemented using the Sho-en mechanism. Another is the management of input/output devices. They are managed by the PIMOS using a resouce tree.

A Sho-en or usage of a device is treated as a unit of management and called a task. A Sho-en is a task. For a Sho-en, the resources are managed as follows. When a Sho-en call is made, the amount of computing resources and memory resources can be specified by the parameters in the call. If this amount is used up in the Sho-en, it is reported to its parent Sho-en. Then, the program of the parent Sho-en can make it start, suspend, resume or abort.

Current implementation of the PIMOS:

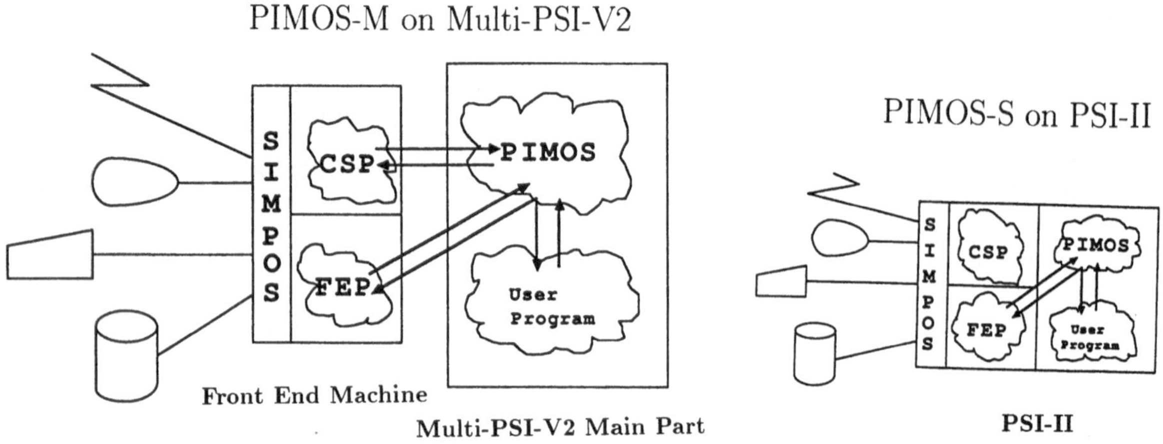

34

Figure 12: Organization of PIMOS

A total PIMOS system consists of a PIMOS main module, an FEP module and a CSP module.

When the PIMOS is used on the multi-PSI-V2, the main module is loaded to all the PEs before the PIMOS starts. Users programs can be loaded in two ways. One is to load a program which has been linked statically beforehand. Another is to dynamically link programs in a module database and load it to specified PEs. The contents of the module database are dynamically changed. Thus, efficient implementation is used for this.

While a user program is being executed, many Sho-ens are made. Some Sho-ens are made spanning two or more PEs. In this case, a foster parent is made in each PE in which a descendant Sho-en is made. When the program terminates, its Sho-ens also disappear. Because of the delay in packet transfer, racing will occur just as the case of reclaiming of the import/export table entries in 4.3.2. This problem is solved by a method called weighted throw count (WTC) [12].

Currently, the PIMOS is designed as a single-user multi-task operating system. To extend it to a multi-user system, additional functions must be added for appropriate distribution of computational resources among users, resolution of resource access conflict, and so on. This needs further study.

However, the current PIMOS has a function to divide PEs logically into several groups and assign them to multiple users. This function is currently sufficient to use the multi-PSI-V2 for software experiments.

7   CONCLUSION

This paper describes the research activities of the parallel inference system in the intermediate stage. They include the multi-PSI system, the PIM, KL1 language

processors and the PIMOS.

The problems to be solved to develop these hardware and software systems were not clear at the beginning of the intermediate stage. As they appeared, we solved them one by one, repeating many experiments.

In this problem solving, the multi-PSI system played a much more important role than had been expected. This meant that the development of the loosely distributed KL1 language processor was much more difficult than had been anticipated.

As we tried to make the hardware systems tools for software development, their specifications had to be conservative. However, we had many difficult problems in building the hardware, especially in chip design and hardware inspection.

Finally, the PIMOS-S has partialy begun operation on a PSI-II with many bugs. Although we are still doing our best to make the PIMOS-M start on the multi-PSI-V2 before the FGCS'88 conference, we are quite sure that it will be completed and released to our users at the beginning of the final stage.

The PIM/p is now under production. It is a very complex hardware system although it consists of only two cabinets. No serious technical problems are left; however, we have to create efficient methods for its debugging and testing. Then, we shall have the fastest and the most sophisticated inference machine in the world.

The multi-PSI-V2 and the PIM/p will enable us to make much larger scale parallel software experiments in the final stage.

ACKNOWLEDGMENT

This research was conducted jointly by many researchers at ICOT and cooperating manufacturers. We would like to express our gratitude to Dr. K. Fuchi, the director of the ICOT research center, Dr. K. Furukawa, the vice director of the ICOT research center, and Prof. H. Tanaka of the University of Tokyo, who is also the chairman of the PIM working group of ICOT, for their support and encouragement. We would also like to thank all the members of the fourth research laboratory of ICOT including Dr. E. Tick and many people at the cooperating manufacturers in charge of joint research work: Mr. Ueda and Mr. Hiratsuka at Mitsubishi Electric Co., Mr. Hattori at Fujitsu Limited., Mr. Sugie at Hitachi, Limited., Mr. Hayashi and Yamamoto at Oki Electric Industry Co., and many others.

REFERENCES

[1] T. Chikayama. Unique features of ESP. In *Proc. of the International Conference on Fifth Generation Computer Systems*, pages 292–298, Tokyo, 1984.

[2] T. Chikayama. Load balancing in a very large scale multi-processor system. In *Proceedings of Fourth Japanese-Swedish Workshop on Fifth Generation Computer Systems*. SICS, 1986.

[3] T. Chikayama, H. Sato, and T. Miyazaki. Overview of the Parallel Inference Machine Operating System (PIMOS). In *Proc. of the International Conference On Fifth Generation Computing Systems 1988*, Tokyo, Japan, November 1988.

[4] Keith L. Clark and Steve Gregory. Parlog: A parallel logic programming language. Research Report TR-83-5, Imperial College, March 1983.

[5] A. Goto, M. Sato, K. Nakajima, K. Taki, and A. Matsumoto. Overview of the Parallel Inference Machine Architecture (PIM). In *Proc. of the International Conference On Fifth Generation Computing Systems 1988*, Tokyo, Japan, November 1988.

[6] A. Goto and S. Uchida. Current Research Status of PIM: Parallel Inference Machine. TM 140, ICOT, 1985. (Third Japan-Sweden workshop on Logic Programming, Tokyo).

[7] S. Habata, R. Nakazaki, A. Konagaya, A. Atarashi, and M. Umemura. Co-operative High Performance Sequential Inference Machine: CHI. In *Proc. of IEEE International Conference on Computer Design: VLSI in Computer and Processors*, Oct 1987.

[8] N. Ichiyoshi and K. Rokusawa. A New External Reference Management and Distributed Unification for KL1. TR 390, ICOT, 1988. (Also submitted to the FGCS'88).

[9] Y. Kimura and T. Chikayama. An Abstract KL1 Machine and its Instruction Set. In *Proceedings of the 1987 Symposium on Logic Programming*, pages 468–477, 1987.

[10] A. Matsumoto et al. Locally Parallel Cache Designed Based on KL1 Memory Access Characterestics. TR 327, ICOT, 1987.

[11] R. Nakazaki, A. Konagaya, S. Habata, H. Shimizu, M. Umemura, M. Yamamoto, M. Yokota, and T. Chikayama. Design of A High-speed Prolog Machie (HPM). In *Proc. of the 12th Annual International Symposium on Computer Architecture*, pages 191–197, June 1985.

[12] K. Rokusawa, N. Ichiyoshi, T. Chikayama, and H. Nakashima. An Efficient Termination Detection and Abortion Algorithm for Distributed Processing Systems. In *Proceedings of the 1988 International Conference on Parallel Processing*, volume 1 Architecture, pages 18–22, August 1988.

[13] M. Sato, A. Goto, et al. KL1 Execution Model for PIM Cluster with Shared Memory. In *Proceedings of the Fourth International Conference on Logic Programming*, pages 338–355, 1987.

[14] E.Y. Shapiro. A subset of Concurrent Prolog and Its Interpreter. TR 003, ICOT, 1983.

[15] T. Shinogi, K. Kumon, A. Hattori, A. Goto, Y. Kimura, and T. Chikayama. Macro-call Instruction for the Efficient KL1 Implementation on PIM. In *Proc. of the International Conference On Fifth Generation Computing Systems 1988*, Tokyo, Japan, November 1988.

[16] Y. Takeda, H. Nakashima, K. Masuda, T. Chikayama, and K. Taki. A Load Balancing Mechanism for Large Scale Multiprocessor Systems and its Implementation. In *Proc. of the International Conference On Fifth Generation Computing Systems 1988*, Tokyo, Japan, November 1988.

[17] K. Taki. The parallel software research and development tool : Multi-PSI system. In *France-Japan Artificial Intelligence and Computer Science Symposium 86*, pages 365–381, October 1986.

[18] K. Taki et al. Hardware Design and Implementation of the Personal Sequential Inference Machine (PSI). In *Proc. of the International Conference on Fifth Generation Computer Systems*, pages 398–409, Tokyo, 1984.

[19] S. Uchida. Inference Machines in FGCS Project. TR 278, ICOT, 1987.

[20] K. Ueda. Introduction to Guarded Horn Clauses. TR 209, ICOT, 1986.

36

[21] D.H.D. Warren. An Abstract Prolog Instruction Set. Technical Note 309, Artificial Intelligence Center, SRI, 1983.

[22] K. Yoshida and T. Chikayama. A'UM–a atream -based concurrent object-oriented language. In *Proc. of the International Conference On Fifth Generation Computing Systems 1988*, Tokyo, Japan, November 1988.

Knowledge Base System
in Logic Programming Paradigm

Hidenori ITOH, Hidetoshi MONOI (ICOT)

Shigeki SHIBAYAMA (Toshiba Corp.)

Nobuyoshi MIYAZAKI (Oki Electric Industry Co. Ltd.)

Haruo YOKOTA (Fujitsu Ltd.)

Akihiko KONAGAYA (NEC Corp.)

ABSTRACT

This paper describes the current research and development status of the knowledge base subsystem being investigated in Japan's Fifth Generation Computer Systems (FGCS) project. Our aim is to realize the subsystem in the logic programming paradigm to manage large knowledge bases shared by AI application systems. In the intermediate stage of the project, several approaches are being taken to realize the knowledge base subsystem. Experimental systems are being developed in order to study the technical aspects. These systems will be integrated into the prototype of the FGCS in the final stage.

1   INTRODUCTION

The Fifth Generation Computer Systems (FGCS) project aims to develop a prototype system for a knowledge information processing system. The prototype system processes knowledge in the logic programming and parallel processing paradigms. To realize the prototype system, we have developed parallel inference subsystems and knowledge base subsystems in the intermediate stage. These subsystems are integrated into the prototype of the FGCS by the parallel logic programming language Guarded Horn Clauses (GHC) in the final stage [Itoh 88].

The knowledge base subsystem provides convenient environments in which to construct, retrieve, and manipulate large, shared knowledge bases for AI applications on the inference subsystems. The subsystem inherits most of the traditional database functions, such as access path selection and transaction control. However, knowledge base systems must have richer functions and interfaces for manipulating knowledge than traditional database systems. In other words, because the AI application programs use knowledge-representing data that has a more complex structure, the knowledge base subsystems must have high-level functions so that they can handle a large amount of knowledge and high-level interfaces between the knowledge bases and application programs.

In the initial (three-year) stage of the project, we developed a relational database experimental system *Delta* as the first step to research the knowledge base subsystem [Murakami 83] [Kakuta 85]. By doing this, we accumulated architectural experience about systems that must process large amounts of knowledge efficiently [Itoh 87]. We also developed an interface between the logic programming language Prolog and the relational database on it so that we could study the technical problems regarding their integration [Kunifuji 82] [Yokota 84] [Yokota 86a].

We are in the intermediate four-year stage, and aim to develop a prototype of the knowledge base subsystem. The subsystem can handle more complex knowledge-representing data directly and provide friendly interfaces for the knowledge processing programs based on logic programming paradigms. To develop the prototype, we have defined and developed four models of the subsystem using the sequential inference machines that were developed in the initial stage. To research the knowledge base subsystem efficiently, we employed the following approaches:

- The first approach is to extend a logic programming language that supports knowledge base functions. We have developed a practical knowledge base system with a large amount of knowledge in order to prove the effectiveness of the functions.

  The entire system is developed on the *CHI* machine with a high-performance sequential inference processor and a large-capacity memory. The memory capacity is sufficient for realizing a practical memory-based knowledge base.

- The second approach is to perform distributed knowledge base processing: the efficient retrieval and management of knowledge bases in the distributed environment. The system is developed on *PSI* machines connected by a local area network.

  In this approach, knowledge bases are realized in the context of deductive databases. We have developed software and hardware systems to manage distributed knowledge bases and to process queries.

- The third approach is to realize parallel knowledge base processing. We have developed an experimental knowledge base subsystem with multiple processing elements and a large-scale multiport memory. We have also developed the control software for the parallel processing. The experimental system is made accessible from *PSI* through a logic-based query language.

  In this approach, we adopted a relational knowledge model, an extension of the relational data model. The architecture of the experimental system follows the ideas behind database machines.

- The last approach is to research interfaces between parallel logic programming languages and knowledge bases.

  In this approach, we selected applications to study the interfaces in the parallel processing environment. We adopted the parallel logic programming language GHC and embedded knowledge-base handling functions in it.

Technologies obtained in these approaches have been integrated into the parallel knowledge base processing model.

This paper describes each system with related research topics. Section 2 describes the knowledge base system on the *CHI* machine. Section 3 describes the distributed knowledge base system using the *PSIs*. Section 4 describes the parallel knowledge base processing model. Section 5 describes the knowledge base interface system for parallel logic programming languages. Lastly, Section 6 is a summary of this paper.

2 KNOWLEDGE BASE SUBSYSTEM ON A SEQUENTIAL INFERENCE MACHINE

This section describes the high performance knowledge base system developed on the *CHI* machine [Habata 87]. We developed this system in order to investigate mechanisms for the efficient retrieval and management of knowledge bases. The novelties of the system are its practicability in terms of performance and memory capacity, and its extension of multiple name space in a multi-process environment.

2.1 Overview of the System

CHI is one of the inference machines developed in the FGCS project, designed for high performance execution of large practical logic programming programs. Figure 1 shows the *CHI* hardware configuration. The hardware consists of a high performance processor (500k LIPS for benchmark programs) and a large main memory (320

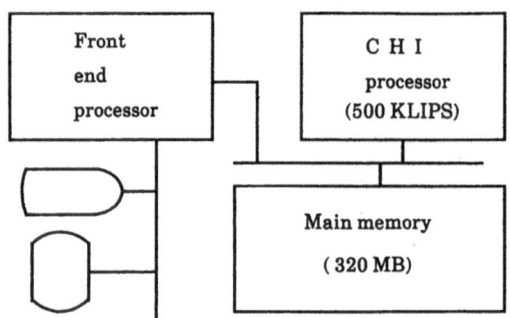

Figure 1. *CHI* hardware system configuration

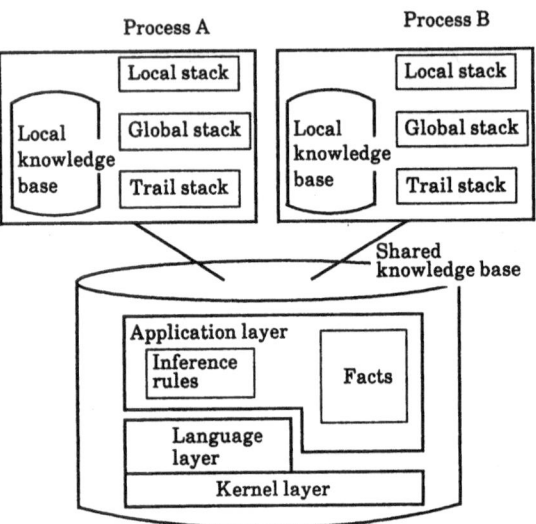

Figure 2. *CHI* software system configuration

MB) connected to a front-end processor for input-output operations.

The knowledge base system is composed of three layers: a kernel layer, a language-processing layer and an application layer (Figure 2). The kernel layer provides basic functions for multi-processing and remote input/output operations [Konagaya 87]. The language-processing layer provides a full interactive programming environment for SUPLOG [Atarashi 88], a Prolog dialect with multiple name space. The application layer provides special inference rules and facts for specific areas, such as DNA sequence matching [Doolittle 86] and machine translation systems. All processes share the knowledge base systems and execute logic programs with their own execution environment: local, global and trail stacks and a local knowledge base. From the user's point of view, *CHI* acts like a domain-oriented knowledge-base machine rather than like a Prolog machine, if application layer programs are loaded with system programs.

The high performance comes from special hardware for unification, backtracking, clause indexing and sophisticated compiler optimization [Habata 87]. To make use of compiler optimization, we divided predicates into dynamic predicates (predicates that can change their definition dynamically) and static predicates (predicates that cannot change their definition dynamically). This division distinction is very effective because we can eliminate the overhead of predicate calling for most predicates (static ones). We also endeavored to implement high-performance dynamic predicates, since the dynamic predicates tend to form a bottleneck if they are executed by an interpreter. We introduced a "dynamic compilation" or "incremental compiling" technique that compiles a clause when asserted [Konagaya 88]. As a result, the *CHI* machine can execute dynamic predicates only three times slower than it executes static predicates.

The large memory capacity (320 MB) makes it possible to realize a memory-based knowledge base system. Knowledge base systems require a large knowledge data as well as a number of inference rules. For example, a DNA sequence matching system requires DNA data (20 million residues), and a machine translation system requires a language translation dictionary (50,000 words). From a practical point of view, large knowledge data retrieval is the most time-consuming process in the implementation of practical knowledge base systems. The memory-based knowledge base system solves this problem, since it eliminates disk access time, which occupies a large proportion of the data retrieval process in conventional computer systems.

A multiple-multiple name space has been introduced to avoid interprocess name conflict and to represent a hierarchical knowledge database. To solve the interprocess name conflict, the multiple-multiple name space facility copies name spaces when a process is created. The name space copying scheme enables processes to access name spaces independently while sharing clauses.

The hierarchical knowledge database can be obtained by the encapsulation, inheritance and shadowing mechanisms of the multiple-multiple name space. The encapsulation mechanism enables the use of the same name in a different way in the knowledge base. The inheritance mechanism provides an efficient way of defining shared clauses. The shadowing mechanism is used for solving name conflicts that occur in inheritance. The mechanism is also useful for representing non-monotonic logic.

The following sections give further details about the multiple-multiple name spaces that play an essential role in knowledge base systems.

2.2 Multiple-Multiple Name Spaces

Multiple-multiple name spaces provide an elegant way of implementing a shared knowledge database in a multi-process environment. The shared knowledge base is very important, especially in the field of co-operative problem solving. The problems that have to be solved are

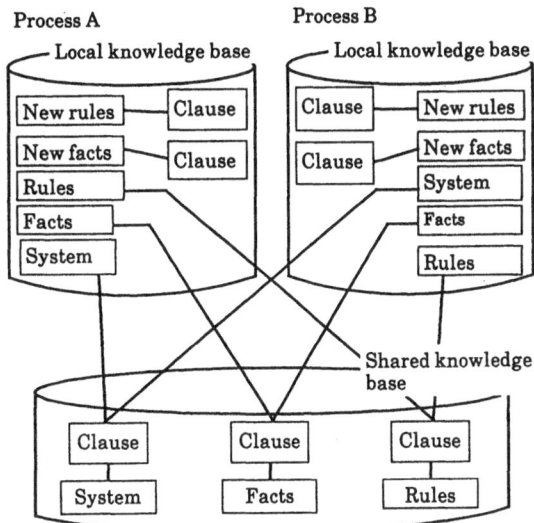

Figure 3. Multiple-multiple name spaces

name consistency and name conflict between processes. The inter-process name conflict results from the inherited nature of a knowledge base that permits it to update its component (clause) dynamically. A lock mechanism may save this problem, but would still leave a scheduling problem; the results of the program might change depending on the process scheduling. Our observations about knowledge bases lead us to conclude that most knowledge bases are static data. We solved the problem by dividing a knowledge base into two parts: a shared knowledge base and a local knowledge base. The shared knowledge base contains all system programs and the static knowledge. The local knowledge base contains the process' own programs and dynamic knowledge. To realize interprocess communication, we chose a mail box, a message based communication, rather than the shared knowledge base, since updating the shared knowledge base causes nondeterminacy of knowledge base access.

The inter-process name conflict may occur when processes share a name space. To solve the problem, we adopted the following name space copying scheme. In the scheme, each process copies the name tables of the shared clause database, if one has been created. The point is that the copied name tables are in the local clause database, so each process can change any name space without affecting other processes. Figure 3 shows an example of this scheme. In this example, each process has three shared-name spaces: "system", "rules" and "facts", and two local name spaces: "new_rules" and "new_facts".

Process scheduling does not affect program execution, no matter how the program changes a clause database dynamically. Local clause database can be removed when a process is terminated or killed.

2.3 Hierarchical Knowledge Base

Multiple-multiple name spaces also give us an elegant way of representing a hierarchical knowledge base that supports encapsulation, inheritance and shadowing of predicates. These facilities make it possible to represent frame-like hierarchical knowledge naturally in logic programming paradigms.

Encapsulation The encapsulation facility reduces name-conflict and increases reliability by hiding internally used predicates from outer-worlds. For example, the knowledge about Mr. Konagaya's account may be written in the following way.

```
:- in_package(konagaya).
:- export withdraw/2, deposit/2.
:- dynamic current_account/1.

   withdraw(Amount,New_balance) :-
       retract(account(Balance)),
       New_balance is Balance - Amount,
       (New_balance >= 0
           -> assert(account(New_balance));
       print("Not enough balance!"),
       assert(account(Balance))).

   deposit(Amount,New_balance) :-
       retract(account(Balance)),
       New_balance is Balance + Amount,
       assert(account(New_balance)).
```

In the above case, the predicate account/1 is used only for keeping Konagaya's current balance. So it should be hidden so that no one can access the balance directly.

Inheritance The inheritance facility enhances hierarchical knowledge representation such as frame theory [Minsky 74] and scripts. One of the great advantages of the name-based inheritance in a clause database is that we can construct both rule hierarchy and data hierarchy in the same way. That is, we can provide more flexible and powerful ways of mixing rule sets and data sets than conventional AI-tools can.

For example, a class of bird may have a general property of birds, such as that a bird has two wings, or a bird can fly. These rules can be described as follows.

```
:- in_package(bird).
:- external wings/1, canfly/1.

   wings(2).
   canfly.
```

A class of sparrow can be defined inheriting a class of bird.

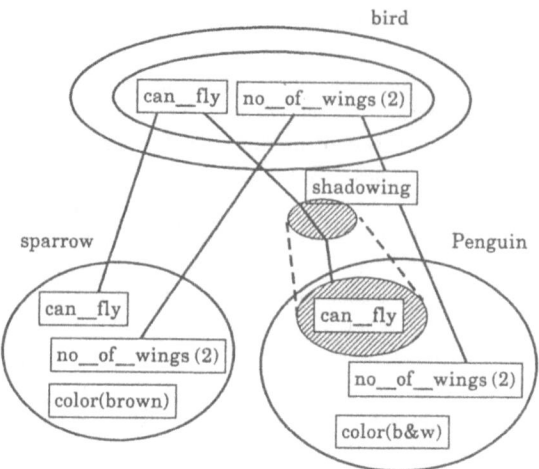

Figure 4. Inheritance in knowledge bases

```
:- in_package(sparrow,[$use(bird)]).
:- external color/1.

   color(brown).
```

Shadowing The shadowing facility makes it possible to hide some predicates so that they are not inherited from the super class. A kind of non-monotonic knowledge can be represented by using the facility. For example, a class of penguin can be defined inheriting a class of bird, but the predicate canfly/0 can be shadowed.

```
:- in_package(penguin,[$use(bird)]).
:- external color/1.
:- shadowing canfly/0.

   color(b & w).
   canfly :- fail.
```

2.4 Summary and Future Works

A clause database can be extended to a knowledge base by means of a multiple-multiple name space. The multiple-multiple name space also gives an elegant way of sharing a knowledge base among processes.

The knowledge base system can be extended to an object-oriented base by introducing a history-dependent data structure, that is, objects. In the system, a clause may be used to define constraints between objects.

3 DISTRIBUTED KNOWLEDGE BASE SUBSYSTEM

Coordination of various knowledge bases and processing knowledge bases in a distributed environment is im-

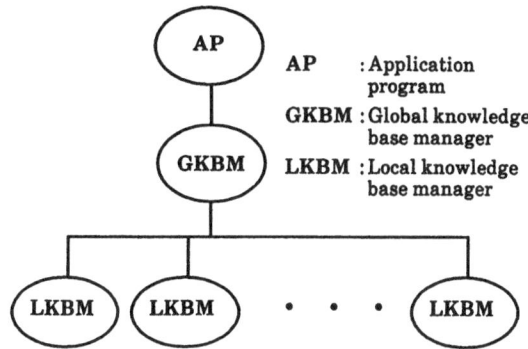

Figure 5. Logical configuration of the *PHI* system

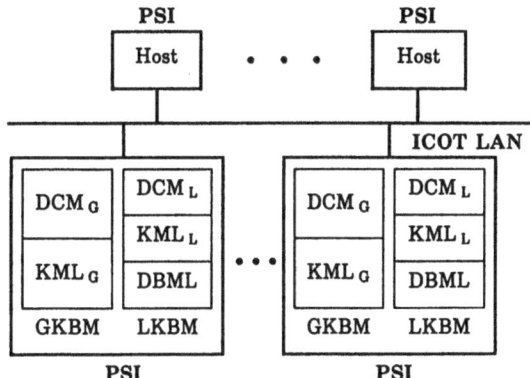

DCM : Distributed control module
KML : Knowledge management layer
DBML : Data base management layer

Figure 6. Physical configuration of the *PHI* system

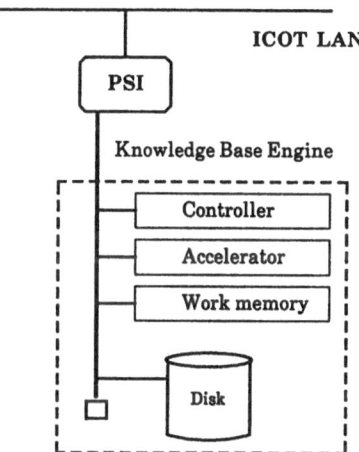

Figure 7. Knowledge base engine

portant for future knowledge information processing systems. One of the most fundamental issues in the study of the knowledge base is the knowledge base model as a framework. We have selected a deductive database as a fundamental platform to study knowledge bases in distributed environment. We call this system a distributed deductive database (DDDB) system.

3.1 Overview of the System

A deductive database consists of an intensional database (IDB), a set of rules, and an extensional database (EDB), a set of facts. The EDB is assumed to be much larger than the IDB. There is a well known one-to-one correspondence between a ground unit clause of the EDB and a tuple of a relational database. We have adopted a two-layered configuration: the lower layer, a relational database management system, handles the EDB and the upper layer handles the IDB.

In order to support a distributed environment, we gave the deductive database system global knowledge managers and local knowledge base managers. An experimental system, the Predicate logic based HIerarchical knowledge management (*PHI*) system, is being developed to study technical issues. In this system, one global manager and one or more local managers are dynamically assigned to each user or application program as shown in Figure 5.

The principal technical issues being investigated in the research of the DDDB system are as follows.

- Distributed query processing.

- Distributed database updating and management.

- Interface between logic programming languages and the DDDB system.

- Architecture of a dedicated processor for efficient handling of the deductive database.

The *PHI* physically consists of a number of personal sequential inference machines (*PSI*s) as shown in Figure 6. Each site has a global manager and a local manager. A dedicated processor is designed as an attached processor of a *PSI*. The processor adopts a superimposed code scheme, and has an accelerator for processing indexes based on the scheme illustrated in Figure 7. An experimental application program for software development is also being developed to investigate the functionality and performance of the system.

3.2 Distributed Deductive Database

Principal Features A DDDB consists of a deductive database distributed over a number of sites. A set of ground unit clauses (facts) having the same predicate symbol corresponds to a relation. IDB is regarded as an extension of views in relational database. A query is denoted by a goal atom or a set of clauses. The answer is a set of ground instances of the query that are "logical consequences" of the set of clauses in the deductive database and of the sets of clauses in the query.

Principal features of the *PHI* are as follows.

- The database is a set of function-free clauses which may have negative literals in their bodies.

- Data manipulations are performed by means of a logic data language that includes extended definite clauses.

- The query processing strategy is a bottom-up strategy with query transformation and dynamic optimization.

- Concurrency control is performed by a two-phase lock method.

- Recovery is performed by a two-phase commitment method.

- Security management is provided using password and data catalogs.

Algorithms used for the last three features above are similar to those developed for traditional distributed relational databases.

The interface of the *PHI* is designed to be embedded in sequential logic programming languages such as Prolog and ESP (Self-contained Extended Prolog). The *PHI* computes the answer to a query as a set, and returns the answer piece by piece to the user program by instantiating values to variables in order to adjust to the sequential execution of the host languages. If a backtrack occurs in the user program, the system returns an alternative answer.

Distributed Query Processing Strategy In DDDB system, it is important to reduce the communication cost to transfer intermediate results by determining appropriate transfer directions. For instance, when the system joins two intermediate results, transferring the smaller one is better. There are two ways to determine transfer direction. One is a static optimization strategy that determines the directions by predicting the sizes of intermediate results before the actual processing. The other is a dynamic optimization strategy that determines the directions by comparing sizes of actual intermediate results during the processing. The *PHI* uses the dynamic optimization strategy because it is difficult to predict sizes of intermediate results for recursive queries. This decision reduces the management overhead of statistical information necessary to predict the size of intermediate results, but increases communication overhead to compare sizes of intermediate results [Takasugi 87]. The latter problem is not serious in the *PHI* because of the broadcast communication capability of *ICOT-LAN* [Taguchi 84].

Recursive Query Processing Strategy Recursive query processing strategies are classified into top-down strategies and bottom-up strategies. A top-down strategy computes the answer to a query by generating subqueries in a similar way to that of Prolog. A bottom-up strategy computes the answer by generating intermediate results from relations in the EDB. We have adopted a bottom-up strategy in the *PHI*, because a top-down strategy results in large communication overhead with frequent interactions between sites. Bottom-up strategies have two problems:

1. They compute unnecessary results because they compute all elements of the least fixpoint (least Herbrand model) of the database.

2. The iterative procedure which computes the least fixpoint involves a lot of redundant computations.

To solve the first problem, query transformation procedures are used. They transform queries to other forms that have smaller least fixpoints while preserving the equivalence of answers. To solve the second problem, a differential computation technique [Balbin 87] is used.

Query Transformations Query transformation procedures called Horn clause transformations (HCTs) are used to transform a set of clauses to an equivalent set of clauses [Miyazaki 88a] [Miyazaki 88b] [Sakama 87]. Three kinds of HCTs have been proposed for the system. They are all based on a fundamental procedure called "clause replacement". Because unnecessary information is removed from the database, the resultant database has a smaller least Herbrand model than the original database. Adding logical consequences preserves the equivalence of the transformed result for a given goal. HCTs are briefly described below.

HCT/P (HCT by Partial evaluation) :
This is a procedure that uses resolution to obtain logical consequences. It is regarded as a generalization of a procedure that substitutes the relational algebra expression of a (derived) relation for the relation symbol. It is called HCT/P because it is based on the partial evaluation technique developed for program transformation.

HCT/R (HCT by Restrictor) :
This is a procedure that uses new predicates called restrictors in order to construct clauses that are logical consequences of original clauses based on the subsumption. HCT/R results in a similar transformed database to the magic set transformation [Bancilhon 86].

HCT/S (HCT by ground Substitution) :

This is a procedure that substitutes ground terms for variables of a clause to obtain logical consequences. This procedure is a generalization of procedures that move the constant in transitive closure operation.

3.3 Handling Negations

The *PHI* allows negative literals in bodies of clauses. This extension introduces some difficulties to the system:

- The semantics of such a database is difficult to define without some syntactical restrictions.

- Efficient query processing for such database is more difficult than for definite databases.

The *PHI* restricts the database to a "stratified" database [Apt 88]. A stratified database is a set of extended clauses that has no recursive paths involving negations. The stratified database can be partitioned into layers, and the semantics of the database are defined layer by layer from the lowest layer. The semantics of stratified databases has been extensively studied by many researchers [Apt 88] [Van Gelder 86] [Gelfond].

For instance, let us consider the following extended clause.

$$r(X,Y) :- p(X,Y), \neg q(X,Z)$$

This clause has a variable, Z, which appears only in a negative literal. This Z is attached by an implicit universal quantifier according to the standard logical interpretation of clauses. It is inefficient to process this kind of clause by a bottom-up procedure, because it is necessary to check all instances of q(X,Z) or actually obtain ground instances of ¬q(X,Z). So the *PHI* handles these kinds of variables as if they are attached by existential quantifiers instead of universal quantifiers. With this convention, the above clause is equivalent to the following clauses.

$$r(X,Y) :- p(X,Y), \neg q1(X).$$
$$q1(X) :- q(X,Z).$$

This convention enables us to compile negative literals to difference operations in relational algebra. It is also used in many Prolog processors.

Query evaluation methods for stratified databases have been also investigated by several researchers. As in the case of definite databases, these methods are classified into either top-down computation or bottom-up computation. As for top-down computation, several query evaluation methods for stratified databases have been recently proposed [Seki 88] [Kemp-Topor 88].

Since the usual SLDNF-resolution is obviously insufficient, these methods have incorporated some bottom-up computation features into a top-down algorithm. In [Seki 88], for example, a query evaluation method called OLDTNF-resolution has been proposed, which is based on OLDT resolution (Ordered Linear Resolution with Tabulation) [Tamaki 86], augmented with negation as failure rule. OLDTNF-resolution was shown to be sound and complete with respect to the standard model semantics for a class of stratified programs under reasonable assumptions for database applications.

The bottom-up query processing of stratified database in the *PHI* is basically same as the query processing of definite database. The *PHI* first transforms a query to an equivalent form using HCTs, and then computes the results layer by layer. However, unconditional usage of HCTs may result in unstratification. HCT/P and HCT/S can be used in stratified database without limitation, because they preserve layered structure of the database. HCT/R may transform a stratified database to an unstratified database, and it is difficult to handle unstratified database in general.

3.4 Superimposed Code Scheme for Deductive Databases

In a deductive database system that adopts a bottom-up strategy, operations such as selections, joins, set operations and set comparisons are frequently performed. The frequent usage of set operations and set comparisons is a major difference between a deductive database and a relational database. The concept of superimposed codes, which originally was proposed for text processing, possibly provides a unified approach that will realize efficient processing of both EDB and IDB [Wada 88] [Morita 88]. Superimposed code schemes have been studied for the knowledge base engine.

Superimposed Code Scheme for the EDB In relational database, indexes to attributes are used for efficient access to tuples in an EDB. If only a few attributes are frequently used in conditions of queries, the design of the indexes is easy. This is usually the case in business applications. We consider that more uniform treatment of attributes is necessary in deductive database. An index scheme based on superimposed codes is a good candidate for such a purpose. The index is obtained as follows (Figure 8).

1. The value of each key attribute is hashed to a code called a binary coded word (BCW)

2. All BCWs for a tuple are ORed together to obtain a superimposed code word (SCW)

The SCWs are much smaller than the original tuples.

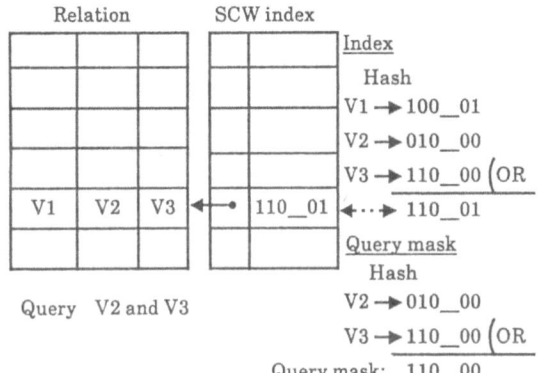

Figure 8. Example of SCW

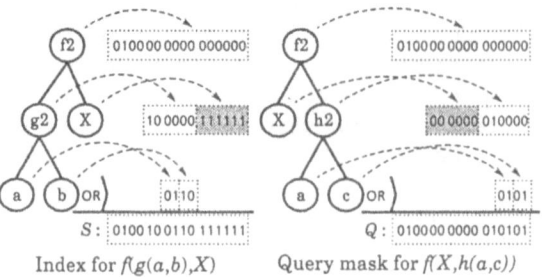

Figure 9. Example of SSCW

Retrieval using this index is performed as follows.

1. The value of each key attribute in the query is hashed to obtain *BCW*.

2. *BCW*s are ORed together to obtain a query mask *Q*.

3. Check the *SCW* index if each *SCW* satisfies (*Q* 'and' *SCW* = *Q*). If a tuple corresponding to the index satisfies the query condition, the SCW satisfies this condition.

Set operations and set comparisons necessary to process recursive queries can also be performed with SCW indexing. The SCW indexes are used to make pairs of indexes whose corresponding pairs of tuples may be the same. Because the SCWs are much smaller than the original tuples, we can improve performance by preprocessing with the SCW index.

The advantages of the superimposed code scheme are as follows.

- The total size of the indexes is smaller than in other index schemes if there are many key attributes. In deductive databases, all attributes might be keys.

- Performance is better if more than one key attribute is specified in a query.

- Index processing can be easily performed in parallel, because the structure of the index is simple.

The disadvantages of the superimposed code scheme are as follows.

- A whole index scan is usually necessary. Although the index may be small, the index scan is still time consuming.

- Retrieval cannot be efficiently handled with range conditions.

Dedicated hardware, a parallel processing architecture, or a combination of both can solve the first problem. Dedicated hardware is used in the experimental system for index processing.

The superimposed code scheme can be extended for structures (functions) and rules. Structures and rules can be handled by a superimposed code scheme for terms. The extended scheme uses structured superimposed code words (SSCW) an example of which is illustrated in Figure 9 [Morita 88].

4   PARALLEL KNOWLEDGE BASE SUBSYSTEM

This section describes the knowledge base system based on the parallel knowledge base model. The distributed model mentioned in the previous section assumes an environment where inference machines (*PSIs*) are connected by a local area network. In that sense it investigates a knowledge base processing scheme among the distributed processing powers. The parallel model, however, is a processing scheme to enhance the processing power of a network site.

4.1   Overview of the System

This system aims at implementing an experimental parallel knowledge base system (*Mu-X*) as the backend of the *PSI* machines. In this approach, dedicated hardware with multiple processors and a large-scale multiport shared memory is implemented.

The *Mu-X* adopted the term-relational model proposed in [Yokota 86b]. The term-relational model was used as a candidate for bridging the gap between logic programming languages and databases. The model could be considered to be a basic mechanism to implement deductive database systems. However, in this research, more attention was paid to providing primitives of term-relational model manipulation. The term relations can naturally store basic logic programming constituents (terms) and provide retrieval capabilities, based on unification, for terms. As a concrete example, a unification-based query language has been implemented [Monoi 88b] on the model. It is based on relational calculus and interfaces *PSI* programming environment and the experimental machine. A set of classes were written in ESP [Chikayama 84] and added in the *PSI* programming environment. These classes provide methods (predicates) which interface with the user in the *PSI*'s programming environment and the *Mu-X*. The classes are activated by the method call from user programs. It forwards the message specified by the method call (typically, a "retrieve" predicate) to the *Mu-X* using network facilities for execution.

Put simply, the *Mu-X*'s role in this context is to be a backend machine for execution of the queries denoted by the retrieve predicates of ESP. Parallel processing was adopted to accelerate the retrieval. This will be described in later chapters. This experimental machine shares many research issues with parallel database machines [Shibayama 87].

4.2 Hardware Considerations

Mu-X has a shared memory multiprocessor architecture (Figure 10). There are two types of shared memories. One is conventional word-granularity shared memory for control information storage and can be regarded as an interconnection structure for multiple processing elements. The other is page-granularity conflict-free multiport page-memory for working knowledge base storage [Tanaka 84b]. The multiport page-memory consists of a set of ordinary memory banks, a switching network for interchanging the multiple ports and memory banks, port controllers attached to each port and a main controller. By cyclically interchanging the network and appropriately reading/writing the proper part of memory banks, simultaneous access from each port to arbitrary memory pages is realized. The multiport page-memory was incorporated so that several idle processing elements (PEs) could participate in the processing of a query without any memory access interference. From another point of view, the multiport page-memory can enhance the memory bandwidth to the multiple of memory banks (usually, number of ports).

The I/O bandwidth enhancement is achieved by providing a disk system to each of the PE. Term relations are horizontally partitioned and stored across the disk systems.

This architecture follows that of the knowledge base machine architecture given in [Yokota 86b] and [Morita 86]. However, simulation study of the architecture [Sakai 88] [Monoi 88a] revealed that even multiple brute-force hardware engines did not provide a performance improvement proportional to the number of PEs. This is because of the input-length dependency of the processing times. If a join processes the area of a rectangle that has sides whose lengths are the cardinalities

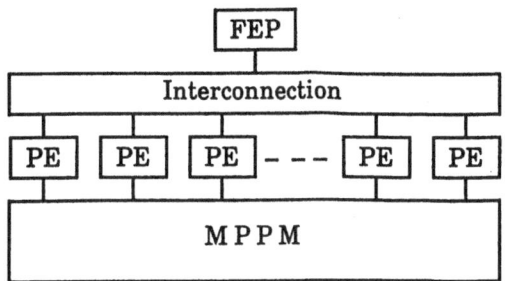

Figure 10. Hardware configuration of the parallel knowledge base system

Table 1. Hardware specifications

Number of PE	8
PE core	MC68020 at 12.5MHz
PE memory	2MB
Multiport page-memory	8 ports
	64MB with 512-byte pages
	5MB/sec/port transfer speed

of the relations, division of the area increases the total input data that must be read to be processed.

So even using a lot of engines that can process join with only the data input time will not reduce the processing time. It was also recognized that a hardware-oriented engine could only perform a limited class of operations. At the time the hardware design of this experimental machine began, it was not clear what operations should be supported by the processing element core.

For these reasons it was decided that the *Mu-X* would not incorporate hardware engines. Instead, it incorporated general-purpose microprocessors in place of the hardware engines. The effort to implement a more flexible unification engine is carried out separately. The multiport page-memory was implemented with eight ports and has a capacity of 64MB. The specification of the hardware is shown in Table 1.

4.3 Software Considerations

The software's aim in this system is to pursue parallel processing technology in the field of knowledge base processing. This aim shares much with database systems research. There are numerous researches belonging to this category, for example, *GAMMA* [DeWitt 86], *Grace* [Kitsure 82], *MPDC* [Tanaka 84a], and *MDBS* [Demurjian 86]. The characteristics of this research are as follows:

- Moderate size of experimental machine.

  Grace and *MPDC*, for example, are systems that require enormous effort to implement because of the variety of hardware components and the complexity of the software. The *Mu-X* falls into a simpler category of parallel processing. There are two kinds of hardware components that must be programmed. One is the processing element (PE), the core of the processing, and the other is the front end processor (FEP). Since the FEP's functions are very simple, the PE is the only component that needs intensive programming.

- Incorporation of terms as the basic data representation scheme

    This system manipulates terms in much the same way that inference machines do. We not only provided an additional data type (term) but also adopted it as the basic data representation scheme in the system. For example, in the interface between *PSI* and the FEP, term representation is used to denote the query language.

- Flexibility of the software

    The system is experimental, so later modification or addition of operations is quite probable. The system software has been designed to cope with those changes.

Parallel Processing

(a) Consideration of hybrid memory systems

The parallel processing in this system is strongly influenced by the two types of memory system: a conventional shared memory and the multiport page-memory. The software is designed to make the best use of the characteristics of the memory systems.

The conventional shared memory has the following characteristics.

- The unit of access is typically a word.

- There is potential access conflict among multiple PEs.

- Access (when there is no memory access conflict) is quick, typically within a few microseconds.

The multiport page-memory is a page-based memory system activated by means of a control block (page transfer control block, PTCB for short). It has the following characteristics.

- The unit of access is a page.

- There is no access conflict among PEs (PE ports).

- Access is associated with overheads.

The overheads are of three types. The first is the overhead similar to the latency of disk access. This is the time that it takes for the asynchronous memory page access request (through the PTCB) to be recognized by the port controller that polls for the request. In this implementation, the polling interval is equal to the page transfer time, so on average there is half the page transfer time latency. The second type is the overhead of one-page transfer. This is the time that it takes for the requested page to be transferred to a buffer space. The last one is software overhead required to prepare a PTCB for the multiport page-memory. It consists of searching the multiport page-memory directory for the proper page number, assigning a destination buffer, making up a PTCB and so on. In the current implementation, four physical pages of 512 bytes constitute a logical page of 2 KB. As physical page transfer time is 100 microseconds and is the interval of request polling, one logical page transfer requires $4 \times 100 + 100/2$ or 450 microseconds on average. The software typically requires about 500 microseconds. To sum up, the transfer time for one logical page is about one millisecond. Both the hardware speed and software speed could be improved using faster technology for the former and a faster processor with cache memory for the latter.

Considering these characteristics, using the multiport page-memory as a buffer memory for the database pages was a natural choice. We also decided to place the system directory in the multiport page-memory. Initially it is stored in the disk and at startup time is loaded into the multiport page-memory so that the PEs can access the shared information quickly. The directory related to a PE is further copied in the local memory of the PE. Other control information, such as command queues, is placed in the conventional shared memory. Locking is done using the conventional shared memory by means of atomic read-modify-write instructions.

(b) Scalability consideration

The multiport page-memory is a hardware component that has a scalable property. We tried to keep the hardware's scalability within the tolerance of the conventional shared memory's bandwidth. For example, the control software is not placed on a special (centralized) control processor. Instead, any processing element can become the control processor in a unit of a transaction. When a transaction is received from a *PSI* machine, an idle PE is assigned to be the master of that transaction. The transaction master takes care of the compilation, parallel command generation, and response generation of that transaction. Parallel command execution is a task for multiple PEs (possibly including the transaction master PE). In that sense, parallel processing is applied toward (1) inter-transaction and (2) parallel command execu-

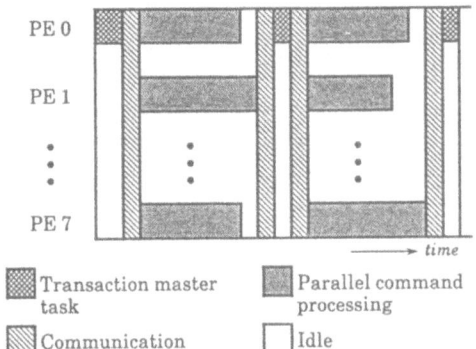

Figure 11. A parallel processing timing diagram

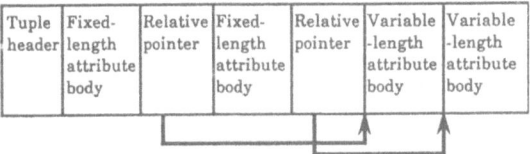

Figure 12. Representation of variable-length records

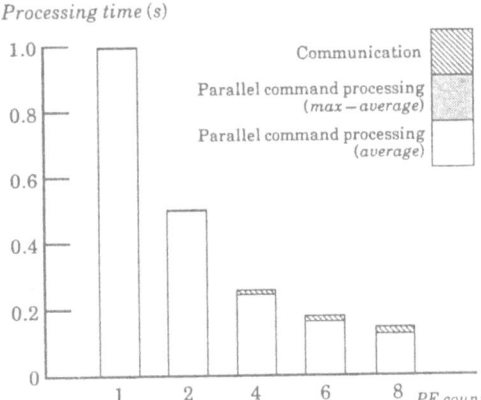

Figure 13. Performance of the selection operation

tion levels. Figure 11 shows a timing diagram of query processing where parallelism in the command execution level is realized. In this figure, PE0 is the transaction master and takes care of the master's tasks. This is a set of serialized operations performed intermittently between parallel command executions. The parallel command execution is done by idle processors as shown in Figure 11.

Term Data Type Support From software's point of view, relational knowledge base support is (1) the addition of a data type (term) and (2) the addition of a set of operations to relational database enhanced with the term data type. To do these, the basic data structure supports tagged data and variable length records, which is required because the term relational model allows variance of atomic and structured data as in Prolog. The structure of a record that supports variable-length record is shown in Figure 12.

Efficiency Consideration In database machine research, the importance of elimination of software overheads is often stressed. The software system has been designed and coded with this clearly in mind. The system owes the file system and the software development environment to the residing operating system. However, the rest of the software was made from scratch. To develop so much new software was expensive, but helped to make a specialized, compact and efficient system. For example, the control software of the PE is a single-process program and there is little overhead in switching between transac-

tion master tasks and parallel command execution tasks. Considering the nature of the system and preliminary evaluation results, we are convinced that this has been a good choice. We note that there are numerous decisions we took that have to undergo further evaluation.

4.4 Evaluation

So far, we have made a preliminary performance evaluation. This evaluation was to obtain the basic speed of the hardware and the efficiency of the parallel processing method, not to discover the final performance values.

The queries we took were selection and join operations. The selection query selects 111 tuples from 1600-tuple relation, the size of which is 500 KB. The join is performed between a 15 KB, 111-tuple relation, the result of the previous selection, and a 20K-byte, 215-tuple relation. A nested-loop algorithm is used. The result is 37 tuples. Note that the tuples are variable-length and, according to the parallel processing scheme, the query is processed as shown in Figure 11.

Figure 13 shows the result of the selection. The total processing time is almost identical to the time for parallel command execution. The overhead of parallel execution (in this case, communication time) is not recognized until the number of participating processors reaches six. Still the overhead is quite low. The effect of parallel processing is thus satisfactory, at least within the machine's degree of parallelism.

Figure 14 shows the result of the join. In contrast to the selection case, the total processing time of the join saturates at the processor count of six. In this case also, the effect of parallel command execution is good. However, the overhead increases as the number of processors increases. The source of overhead is the variance in the processing times of PEs. The communication time is hidden because the absolute processing time is about ten times greater than in the case of selection.

This phenomenon is clearly illustrated by comparing

Processing time (s)

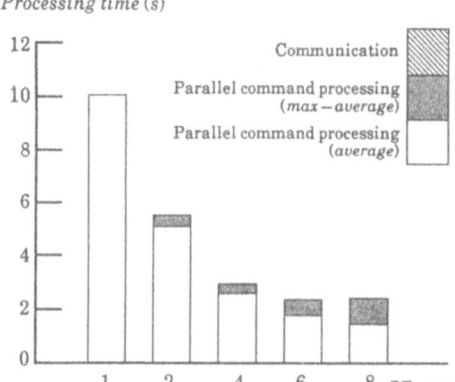

Figure 14. Performance of the join operation

Processing times of PEs

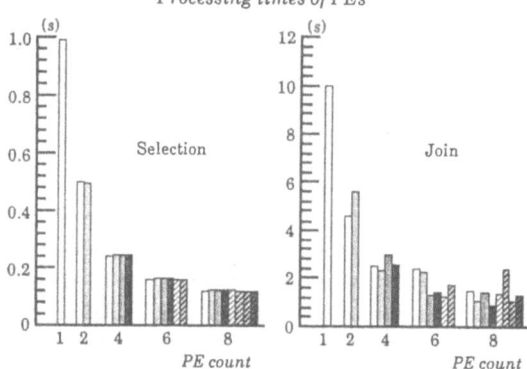

Figure 15. Comparison of processing times

the processing times of PEs in selection and join cases (Figure 15). The reason why there is variance in the join is because the size of the source relation is not large enough to be evenly shared by the PEs. The 20 KB relation (ten 2K pages) is divided by eight PEs, so two PEs have to process two pages while the remaining six only have to process one page each.

This evaluation is done using the first version of software where there are neither indexing schemes nor clustering schemes. The hashing based indexing scheme and, for join operation, bucket-wise hash-join method [Kitsure 83a] is being implemented. We leave more detailed evaluations for the future.

5 INTERFACE BETWEEN GHC AND PARALLEL KNOWLEDGE BASE SUBSYSTEM

The knowledge base subsystem should retrieve information quickly from a large amount of knowledge and treat a variety of knowledge objects uniformly. Then, it should manipulate the retrieved knowledge elements efficiently. The goal of the FGCS project is to build a knowledge information processing system using logic programming paradigms. Combining a parallel logic programming language and a dedicated system for operating a knowledge base seems to be one possible way to implement applications of FGCS project.

This section describes interfaces that combine a parallel logic programming language and a knowledge base system.

5.1 Overview of the System

Retrieval-by-unification (RBU) operations have been proposed [Yokota 86b] as the dedicated system for operating a knowledge base. RBU operations are an extension of relational database operations for manipulating the variety of knowledge objects. A knowledge element is represented by a term, a well-defined structure capable of handling variables. A knowledge base consists of sets of terms called term relations. The RBU system searches the term relations for desired terms, those unifiable with a search condition. We have implemented two extended relational algebra operations: unification restriction stream (urs) and unification join stream (ujs). Other conventional retrieval operations, such as union, projection, join, and selection, and updating operations, such as insert and delete, have also been implemented.

Guarded Horn Clauses (GHC) [Ueda 85], a parallel logic programming language with committed choice semantics, is the kernel language of the FGCS. It handles parallel processes and streams for communication among processes efficiently, but is inadequate in searching for alternative knowledge elements, since a variable of GHC can be assigned only once. GHC also has trouble handling global information such as that in knowledge bases. GHC has no appropriate means of guaranteeing the consistency of knowledge bases during parallel updating.

RBU enables GHC to process knowledge bases. RBU commands for retrieving and updating term relations are issued from parallel problem-solving systems written in GHC. A term relation is used to control consistency in parallel operation. The combination of GHC and RBU is useful in many types of knowledge information processing system for the FGCS project.

5.2 Parallel Retrieval

Now, consider production (rule-based) systems checking for feasibility of the combination of GHC and RBU. The basic concept of a production system involves applying state transition production rules from an initial state to reach a goal state that satisfies termination conditions. Several states can be generated from a single state by applying the production rules, and the state transitions make a search tree. The goal of a production system is to derive a path from the initial state to a goal state by traversing the search tree.

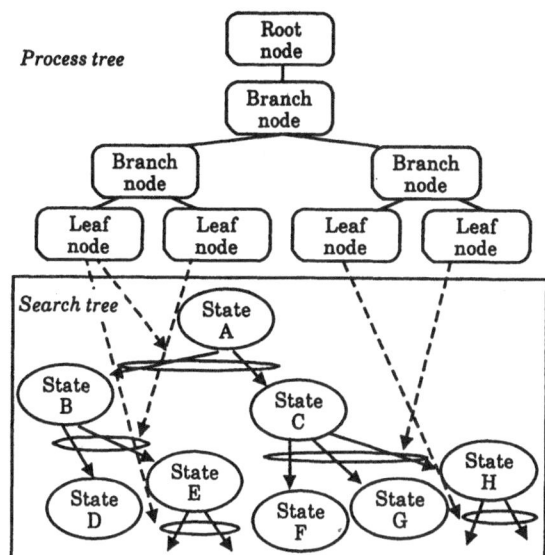

Figure 16. Process configuration and a search tree

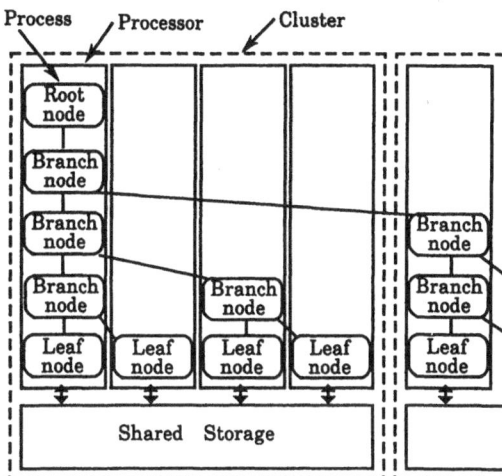

Figure 17. Implementation on the parallel model

Parallel processing is viewed as a way of reducing the large amounts of time consumed by production systems [Gupta 87]. One implementation is the parallel traversal of a search tree in which new states are generated from different states in parallel. Limits on memory and the number of processors require the use of special search strategies. The best first search [Barr 81] is one such strategy. It selects a state from a search tree using state evaluation of the current state to generate new states. The state selected has the best evaluation value in the tree at a given time. The centralized control of this strategy makes finding the best value a bottleneck, however. Control must be localized for efficient parallel processing. We propose a new search strategy called the Better First Search. The strategy looks only in a subtree of the search tree for the state that has the best evaluation value. Although this value is good, it may not be the best in the entire tree; we call it a "better" value.

We use a tree structure as the process configuration to implement the Better First Search in parallel. The tree configuration is not directly related to the search tree traversed by the production system. The three types of nodes (processes) in the process tree are the root node, leaf nodes, and other branch nodes. Productions are performed at the leaf nodes. Production priorities are controlled at the branch nodes based on their evaluation values. System control such as that of the user interface is performed at the root node. Figure 16 shows the process configuration and a search tree.

Nodes in the process tree are implemented using perpetual processes generated from recursively called GHC clauses. Process behavior is controlled by streams bound to variables in arguments in the clauses. The streams are treated as messages for the process. This configuration

is suitable for the parallel model of knowledge base machine mentioned in Section 4. A number of processors and shared storage compose a cluster in this machine, making it important to localize processor communications. We plan to locate each leaf process in a processor (Figure 17).

5.3 GHC Interface

A production is performed by retrieving knowledge elements from a knowledge base and updating the knowledge base based on production rules. The knowledge base is a global state for parallel production processes. GHC cannot handle global states among perpetual processes, nor effectively retrieve and update the knowledge base, even if a common stream is prepared as an argument of every clause to implement a global state in GHC. The unification implemented in GHC cannot be used to search for multiple knowledge elements, because a GHC variable can only be assigned a value once. Once bound to a knowledge element, the GHC variable's binding cannot be changed.

Connecting GHC to a dedicated system that processes knowledge bases enables a parallel production system to be built. RBU knowledge elements are terms defined in the same first-order logic as GHC, thus eliminating syntactical transformation. RBU stores a set of terms as a term relation which is used to guarantee the consistency in knowledge bases during parallel updating.

The special predicate rbu(C) is provided in GHC to enable the use of RBU. Commands for retrieving and updating knowledge bases are bound to the stream argument C.

For example:

$$C = [\mathtt{urs(tr1,[1],p(a,\$(1)),[1],X,}$$

$$ujs(tr1, [2], tr2, [1], [3], Y), \cdots].$$

The first command sentence, urs(tr1, [1], p(a,$(1)), [1], X), dictates a search of the first attribute of the term relation tr1 for terms unifiable with the condition p(a,$(1)), yielding the derivation of the first attribute as a result. Results are returned as a stream bound to the variable X in the command sentence:

$$X = [p(a, g($(2))), p(a, g(b)), \cdots].$$

The second command sentence, ujs(tr1, [2], tr2, [1], [3], Y), is used to derive the third attribute of a result relation generated by a unification join operation which searches the second attribute of tr1 and the first attribute of tr2 for unifiable terms. Results are returned bound to the variable Y.

$$Y = [q($(10), c), \cdots]$$

The special function symbol $ is used to indicate a variable in command sentences and in results. GHC variables cannot be used for knowledge retrieval, so other symbols are needed to indicate variables for retrieval. These variables are bound to knowledge elements in RBU, but unbound in GHC. This corresponds to unbound variables appearing in a template predicate of the setof predicate in Prolog systems.

5.4 Implementation of RBU

Different approaches have been proposed to improve retrieval speed. One approach was to use dedicated hardware: for example, a unification engine was proposed by [Morita 86] [Yokota 86b]. [Ohmori 87] proposed a hash vector for indexing clauses. Superimposed code words for terms and a dedicated engine for manipulating the words were proposed by [Wada 88]. We use indexing that retrieves a set of terms by unification and backtracking. Retrieved terms resemble each other somewhat because they are unifiable with the search condition. For efficient backtracking, these terms must be located near an index. The trie is a type of tree structure that shares identical elements [Knuth 73] and meets this requirement. Figure 18 gives an example of a trie for a set of terms.

The costs of unification are proportional to the count of comparisons between components of the object terms. A trie reduces the number of comparisons when unification is performed. For example, consider what happens when the set of terms in Figure 18 is searched for terms that can be unified with the condition p(f(a,b),h(c)). Using the trie structure, the component p is compared only once, whereas four comparisons are necessary if the trie structure is not used. Using the trie structure, 10 comparisons are needed to search for all terms unifiable with the condition; 18 comparisons are needed if the trie structure is not used.

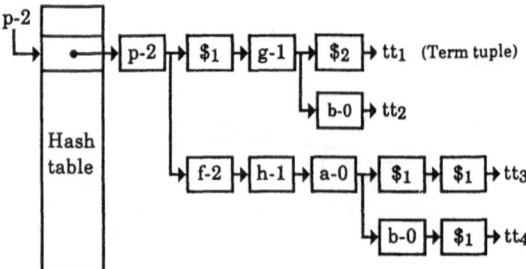

p($(1),g($(2)))   p($(1),g(b))   p(f(a,$(1)),h($(1)))   p(f(a,b),h($(1)))

Figure 18. Tuple index with hashing and trie structure

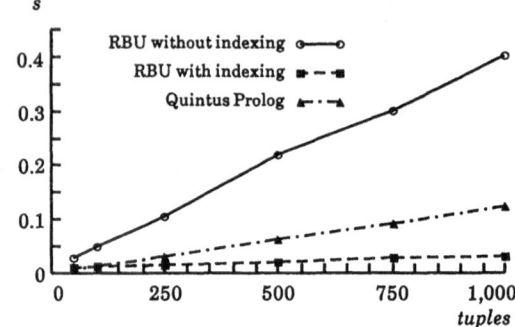

Figure 19. Comparison of search speeds

A hash table is used before the trie structure when storing many types of terms in a term relation (Figure 18). The first components of terms are used as hash entries. The trie structure is combined with hash collision resolution.

We compared the search and updating speeds of the RBU prototype with those of the Quintus-Prolog interpreter. Prolog compilers do not support assert and retrace predicates, (they cannot update knowledge bases), so the compiler has not been examined. Figure 19 compares the search speeds of the Prolog interpreter and *urs* with and without indexing. The *urs* without indexing is about four times slower than the Prolog clause search. This search time increases with tuple count in both Prolog and *urs* without indexing. However, the search time of *urs* with indexing scarcely increases regardless of the number of tuples. For 1000 tuples, it is about one-fourth of the time that a Prolog clause search would take. This is a result of the indexing.

Figure 20 compares the tuple insertion speeds of the two systems. Tuple insertion using RBU takes only about one-sixth the time of a Prolog *consult* operation. The overhead for making an index for a term relation is about one tenth of the insertion time.

6   CONCLUSION

In this paper, we have described the current status of research and development concerning the knowledge base

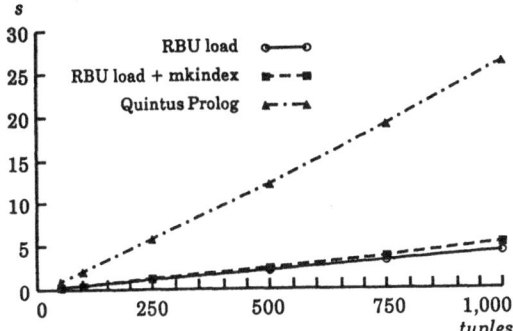

s
30
25
20
15
10
5
0

RBU load o——o
RBU load + mkindex ■- - -■
Quintus Prolog ▲-·-▲

0   250   500   750   1,000
tuples

Figure 20. Insert speed comparison

subsystem in FGCS project. In the intermediate stage, we have investigated and experimented on the following four knowledge base mechanisms required for constructing the prototype of the FGCS.

(1) The knowledge base system developed on the *CHI* machine.

The knowledge base system on the *CHI* machine provides a very high performance knowledge-retrieval mechanism, a practical memory-based knowledge database, and a hierarchical clause database for a multi-process environment. In the system, multiple-multiple name spaces play an essential role in avoiding interprocess name conflicts and in hierarchical knowledge representation. The system will be a good vehicle for the next knowledge base research project.

(2) The distributed knowledge base system based on deductive databases.

A distributed deductive database system has been developed. It uses *PSI* machines connected by *ICOT-LAN*. The query processing strategy of the system is based on a bottom-up approach combined with query transformation procedures. A dynamic optimization method is used to process distributed queries. Dedicated hardware for processing indices has also been designed based on a superimposed code scheme for efficient knowledge base processing.

(3) The parallel knowledge base system.

The total system with the experimental hardware and knowledge base management software has been developed. The system can manipulate sets of terms efficiently in parallel. The hardware configuration proved useful for knowledge base purposes. The system connects to *PSI* machines, and a powerful unification-based query language has been developed as an interface.

(4) The knowledge base interface system for parallel logic programming languages.

We proposed to introduce a parallel logic programming language interface into a dedicated knowledge base system. We considered a parallel production system to check the feasibility of the combination of RBU and GHC. Parallel processes for the production system are implemented by perpetual processes written in GHC. Each process issues RBU commands for retrieving knowledge. We also outlined the concept for interfacing RBU with GHC using streams, and evaluated the search and updating speed of our RBU prototype.

The various kinds of technology developed in this stage will be incorporated into the FGCS prototype.

ACKNOWLEDGMENT

We would like to express our gratitude to the other members of the third laboratory of the ICOT Research Center. Each system described in this paper has been developed with the close co-operation of manufacturers. Thanks goes also to the manufacturers' people who were engaged in the implementations. We are indebted to the members of the KBM Working Group for their fruitful discussions.

References

[Apt 88] Apt, K.R., Blair, H.A. and Walker, A., "Toward A Theory of Declarative Knowledge", Minker (ed.), in *Foundations of Deductive Databases and Logic Programming*, Morgan Kaufmann Publishers, 1988

[Atarashi 88] Atarashi, A., Yanagida, S. and Konagaya, A., "SUPLOG Reference Manual", 1988 (In Japanese)

[Balbin 87] Balbin, I. and Ramamohanarao, K., "A Generalization of the Differential Approach to Recursive Query Evaluation", J. Logic Programming, Vol.4 No.3, 1987

[Bancilhon 86] Bancilhon, F., Maier, D., Sagiv, Y. and Ullman, J.D., "Magic Sets and Other Strange Ways to Implement Logic Programs" 5th ACM PODS, 1986

[Barr 81] Barr, A. and Feigenbaum, E. A., in *The Handbook of Artificial Intelligence*, 1, William Kaufmann, Inc. 1981

[Chikayama 84] Chikayama, T., "Unique Features of ESP", in *Proc. Int. Conf. Fifth Generation Computer Systems*, pp.292-298, 1984

52

[Demurjian 86] Demurjian, S.A. and Hsiao D.K., "A Multibackend Database System for Performance Gains, Capacity Growth and Hardware Upgrade", in *Proc. Int. Conf. on Data Engineering*, pp.542-554, 1986

[DeWitt 86] DeWitt, D.J., Gerber, R.H., Graefe, G., Heytens, M.L., Kumar, K.B. and Muralikrishna, M., "GAMMA - A High Performance Dataflow Database Machine", in *Proc. 12th Int. Conf. Very Large Databases*, pp.228-237, 1986

[Doolittle 86] Doolittle, R. F., "Of Urfs and Orfs, A Primer on How to Analyze Derived Amino Acid Sequences", University Science Books, Mill Valley, CA, 1986

[Gelfond] Gelfond, M. and Przymusinska, H. and Przymusinski, T., "On the Relationship between Circumscription and Negation as Failure", to appear in *Journal of Artificial Intelligence*

[Goto 87] Goto, A., "Parallel Inference Machine Research in FGCS Project", in *Proc. of the US-Japan AI Symposium 87*, pp. 21-36, 1987

[Gupta 87] Gupta, A., in *Parallelism in Production Systems*, Morgan Kaufmann Publishers, Inc.,1987

[Habata 87] Habata, S., Nakazaki, R., Konagaya, A., Atarashi, A. and Umemura, M., "Co-operative High Performance Sequential Inference Machine: CHI", in *Proc. ICCD'87*, New York, 1987

[Itoh 87] Itoh, H., Sakama, C. and Mitomo, Y., "Parallel Control Techniques for Dedicated Relational Database Engines", in *Proc. 3rd Int. Conf. Data Engineering*, pp.208-215, 1987

[Itoh 88] Itoh, H., Takewaki, T. and Yokota, H., "Knowledge Base Machine Based in Parallel Kernel Language", in eds. Kitsuregawa and Tanaka, in *Database Machines and Knowledge Base Machines*, Kluwer Academic Publishers, 1988

[Kakuta 85] Kakuta, T., Miyazaki, N., Shibayama, S., Yokota, H. and Murakami, K., "The Design and Implementation of Relational Database Machine Delta", in *Proc. Int. Workshop on Database machines '85*, 1985

[Kemp-Topor 88] Kemp, B.D. and Topor, W.R., "Completeness of a Top-down Query Evaluation Procedure for Stratified Databases", Dept. of Computer Science, Univ. of Melbourne, Technical Report, 1988, also in *Proc. 5th Int. Conf. and Symp. on Logic Programming*

[Kitsure 82] Kitsuregawa, M., Tanaka, M. and Motooka, T., "Relational Algebra Machine GRACE", *Lecture Notes in Computer Science*, Springer-Werlag, pp.191-214, 1982

[Kitsure 83a] Kitsuregawa, M.,Tanaka, M. and Motooka, T., "Application of Hash to a Data Base Machine and Its Architecture", in *New Generation Computing*, OHMSHA, 1, 1983

[Knuth 73] Knuth, D. E., "The Art of Computer Programming", 3, Sorting and Searching, Addison-Wesley, 1973

[Konagaya 87] Konagaya, A., Nakazaki, R. and Umemura, M., "A Co-operative Programming Environment for a Back-end Type Sequential Inference Machine CHI", in *Proc. Int. Workshop on Parallel Algorithms and Architectures*, East Germany, pp.25-30, 1987

[Konagaya 88] Konagaya, A., "Implementation and Evaluation of a Fast Prolog Interpreter", in IPS Japan SIG-SYM 46-4, 1988 (in Japanese)

[Kunifuji 82] Kunifuji, S. and Yokota, H., "Prolog and Relational Database for Fifth Generation Computer Systems", in *Proc. Workshop on Logical Bases for Data Bases*, Gallaire, et al.(eds.), ONERA-CERT, 1982

[Minsky 74] Minsky, M., "A Framework for Representing Knowledge", MIT AI Memo No.306, 1974

[Miyazaki 88a] Miyazaki, N., Haniuda, H. and Itoh, H., "Horn Clause Transformation: An Application of Partial Evaluation to Deductive Databases", in *Trans. IPSJ*, Vol.29, No.1, 1988 (in Japanese)

[Miyazaki 88b] Miyazaki, N., Haniuda, H., Yokota, K. and Itoh, H., "Query Transformations in Deductive Databases", ICOT-TR 377, 1988

[Monoi 88a] Monoi, H., Morita, Y., Itoh, H., Sakai, H. and Shibayama, S., "Parallel Control Technique and Performance of an MPPM Knowledge Base Machine Architecture", in *Proc. 4th Int. Conf. Data Engineering*, pp.210-217, 1988

[Monoi 88b] Monoi, H., Morita, Y., Itoh, H., Takewaki, T., Sakai, H. and Shibayama, S., "Unification-Based Query Language for Relational Knowledge Bases and its Parallel Execution", in *Proc. Int. Conf. Fifth Generation Computer Systems*, 1988

[Morita 86] Morita, Y., Yokota, H., Nishida, K. and Itoh, H., "Retrieval-By-Unification Operation on a Relational Knowledge Base", in *Proc. of 12th Int. Conf. on Very Large Databases*, pp. 52-59, 1986

[Morita 88] Morita, Y., Itoh, H. and Nakase, A., "An Indexing Scheme for Terms using Structural Superimposed Code Words", ICOT TR-383, 1988

[Murakami 83] Murakami, K., Kakuta, T., Miyazaki, N., Shibayama, S. and Yokota, H., "Relational Database Machine: First Step to a Knowledge Base Machine", in *Proc. 10th int. symp. Computer Architecture*, pp.423-426, 1983

[Ohmori 87] Ohmori, T. and Tanaka, H. "An Algebraic Deductive Database Managing a Mass of Rule Clauses", in *Proc. of 5th Int. Workshop on Database Machines*, pp. 291-304, 1987

[Sakai 88] Sakai, H., Shibayama, S., Monoi, H., Morita, Y. and Itoh, H., "A Simulation Study of a Knowledge Base Machine Architecture", in *Database Machines and Knowledge Base Machines*, Kluwer Academic Publishers, pp.585-598, 1988

[Sakama 87] Sakama, C. and Itoh, H., "Partial Evaluation of Queries in Deductive Databases", Workshop on Partial Evaluation and Mixed Computation, 1987

[Seki 88] Seki, H. and Itoh, H., "A Query Evaluation Method for Stratified Programs under the Extended CWA", ICOT Technical Report TR-337, 1988, also in *Proc. 5th Int. Conf. and Symp. Logic Programming*

[Shibayama 87] Shibayama, S., Sakai, H., Monoi, H., Morita, Y. and Itoh, H., "*Mu-X*: An Experimental Knowledge Base Machine with Unification-Based Retrieval Capability", in *Proc. France-Japan Artificial Intelligence and Computer Science Symposium 87*, pp.343-357, 1987

[Taguchi 84] Taguchi, A., Miyazaki, N., Yamamoto, A., Kitakami, H., Kaneko, K. and Murakami, K., "INI: Internal Network in the ICOT Programming Laboratory and its Future", in *Proc. of 7th ICCC*, 1984

[Takasugi 87] Takasugi, T., Haniuda, H., Miyazaki, N. and Itoh, H., "Distributed Query Processing in KBMS PHI", in *IPS Japan SIG-MDP*, 34-9, 1987 (in Japanese)

[Tamaki 86] Tamaki, H. and Sato, T., "OLD Resolution with Tabulation", in *Proc. of 3rd ICLP*, 1986

[Tanaka 84a] Tanaka, Y., "MPDC: Massive Parallel Architecture for Very Large Databases", in *Proc. Int. Conf. Fifth Generation Computer Systems*, pp.113-137, 1984

[Tanaka 84b] Tanaka, Y., "A Multiport Page-Memory Architecture and A Multiport Disk-Cache System", in *New Generation Computing*, OHMSHA, 2, pp.241-260, 1984

[Ueda 85] Ueda, K., "Guarded Horn Clauses", in *Logic Programming '85*, E. Wada (ed)., Lecture Notes in Computer Science 221, Springer-Verlag, 1986

[Van Gelder 86] Van Gelder, A., "Negation as Failure Using Tight Derivations for General Logic Programs", in *Proc. 1986 Symp. on Logic Programming*, IEEE Computer Society, pp. 127-138, 1986, also to appear in *Journal of Logic Programming*

[Wada 88] Wada, M., Morita, Y., Yamazaki, H., Yamashita, S., Miyazaki, N. and Itoh, H., "A Superimposed Code Scheme for Deductive Databases", in eds. Kitsuregawa and Tanaka, in *Database Machines and Knowledge Base Machines*, Kluwer Academic Publishers, 1988

[Yokota 84] Yokota, H., Kunifuji, S., Kakuta, T., Miyazaki, N., Shibayama, S. and Murakami, K., "An Enhanced Inference Mechanism for Generating Relational Algebra Queries", in *Proc. 3rd ACM SIGACT-SIGMOD Symp. Principles of Database Systems*, pp.229-238, 1984

[Yokota 86a] Yokota, H., Sakai, K. and Itoh, H., "Deductive Database System Based on Unit Resolution", in *Proc. 2nd Int. Conf. Data Engineering*, pp.228-235, 1986

[Yokota 86b] Yokota, H. and Itoh, H., "A Model and an Architecture for a Relational Knowledge Base", in *Proc. 13th Int. Symp. Computer Architecture*, pp.2-9, 1986

PROCEEDINGS OF THE INTERNATIONAL CONFERENCE
ON FIFTH GENERATION COMPUTER SYSTEMS 1988,
edited by ICOT. © ICOT, 1988

PROBLEM-SOLVING AND INFERENCE SOFTWARE

Ryuzo HASEGAWA and Researchers of the First Research Laboratory

Institute for New Generation Computer Technology
4-28, Mita 1-chome, Minato-ku, Tokyo 108, Japan

ABSTRACT

Problem-solving and inference software is basic software which mediates between kernel software (parallel OS) for parallel inference machines and application software. It provides a wide variety of support functions to construct application software.

The final goal of research on problem-solving and inference software is to realize cooperative problem-solving systems. With the main theme in the intermediate stage being the establishment of basic techniques for cooperative problem-solving systems, we proceeded with research and development of parallel logic programming languages, parallel programming techniques, an intelligent programming support environment, and advanced inference mechanisms and learning mechanisms.

Through this research, we developed programming techniques such as meta-programming and constraint programming which give an effective framework for cooperative problem-solving systems and a program transformation technique for the construction of efficient parallel programs.

This paper outlines the research and development of problem-solving and inference software, focusing on the work being done at ICOT.

1 INTRODUCTION

The final goal of the Fifth Generation Computer Systems (FGCS) project is to realize knowledge information processing on parallel inference machines.

In order to construct various kinds of application software for knowledge information processing using the functions provided by kernel software (parallel OS) for parallel inference machines, such as inference control and knowledge base management, we need basic software which mediates between the kernel software and application software.

Problem-solving and inference software, as well as knowledge base management software and natural language interface software, form the basic software. This software gives a wide variety of support functions necessary for the construction of application software. It also plays the role of a knowledge information processing prototype.

One basic framework required for the problem-solving and inference software is a framework for cooperative problem-solving where several agents with knowledge of different areas cooperate to solve a problem by performing their inference independently.

The framework for cooperative problem-solving is the most important base when we construct parallel application software. To establish the foundations of this framework, we need to study a model and mechanism for cooperative problem-solving and its theory. Their investigation is a research theme in problem-solving and inference software.

In order to realize this kind of framework for cooperative problem-solving, research and development of the following is required:

- A parallel computation model and parallel logic programming language which should form the basis of cooperative problem-solving;

- Programming techniques and a programming support environment for the construction of efficient programs using a parallel inference machine and the low-level function of its parallel OS;

- Advanced inference mechanisms and learning mechanisms such as induction and analogy necessary for the achievement of high-level knowledge information processing.

Taking these into consideration, we established the following three themes as the principal areas of research into problem-solving inference software in the intermediate stage:

(1) Kernel language and basic software for cooperative problem-solving

(2) Intelligent programming software

(3) Basic software for advanced inference and learning

The goal of the research on the kernel language and basic software for cooperative problem-solving is to design and develop a parallel logic programming language coordinated with problem-solving, then to establish several parallel programming techniques using it.

Through the research and development of the first version of the kernel language (KL1) [Chikayama et al. 1988], which is based on a parallel logic programming language, GHC [Ueda 1986a, Ueda 1986b], we obtained some practical knowledge of parallel inference control and implementation. At the same time, we found that some desirable functionality could not be provided in the framework of KL1, that is, the meta-function, constraint function and knowledge representation function.

Our final goal of the research on the kernel language is to develop a simple universal language with these functionalities. To achieve this goal, however, we have to delve into each function. Thus, we decided to conduct research on each of them independently for the time being, and then put them together after we have made enough progress in each one of them.

At present, we are researching how to implement the meta-function based on a reflection concept and are also researching a constraint logic programming language, CAL.

Another important area of research is to develop a program transformation technique and a partial evaluation technique, in order to implement user-level language functions and application software efficiently on the KL1 base. In the intermediate stage, we first planned to determine the foundation of these techniques based on Prolog, since the theoretical foundation, for example its program semantics, has already been established. We obtained satisfying results in this plan. We are now researching program transformation and partial evaluation systems based on GHC, and the semantics of GHC.

The research goal of intelligent programming software is to construct an intelligent programming support environment which supports the whole process all the way through, from development to maintenance of the fifth generation computer software.

Here, we aim to research software engineering based on logic programming languages. The main subject of software engineering is not coding but how to design software efficiently around coding, maintenance, and improvement.

From this point of view, we started research on a proof support system which supports mathematical proof as the research core, together with research on a prototyping support system, a Prolog programming (verification, transformation, analysis, and modification) support system, and a design visualization system giving a picture of the structure and the behavior of a program.

The main purpose of the research on the proof support system is to investigate the applicability of theorem proving techniques to programming support by researching support techniques necessary for mathematical proof. Subjects in this research are studies on a term rewriting system generator which supports inference, especially concerning equalities, and a proof compiler which generates programs from given proofs.

The research goal of the basic software for advanced inference and learning is to realize advanced inference functions used in the same way as human problem-solving and to apply them to the development of application software for knowledge information processing.

Logical deductive inference is not enough to provide computers with commonsense judgment and to make them acquire knowledge and learn in the same way as humans. We therefore need to realize inductive inference or advanced inference such as analogy. There are also many areas of human knowledge information processing which logic cannot handle. We need another approach from cognitive science which is different from logic. Therefore, we approached this theme from the angles of both logic and cognitive science.

In order to handle advanced inference in the framework of logic, we need mathematically clear formalization. From this point of view, in the approach from logic, we first tried to formalize commonsense inference using non-monotonic inference, and studied a framework to handle induction and analogy uniformly. Based on it, we are now researching the acquisition and revision of commonsense knowledge. We also researching how to make an automated generator which derives Prolog programs from examples by using a predicate generator and how to make the grammar inference algorithm efficient.

In the approach from cognitive science, we think that there are two parts of human knowledge information processing; conscious and unconscious. We are studying a cognitive model which makes inference and learning efficient based on this characterization.

The following sections describe these three themes of problem-solving and inference software in more detail, focusing on the research and development in ICOT in the intermediate stage.

2 KERNEL LANGUAGE AND BASIC SOFTWARE FOR COOPERATIVE PROBLEM-SOLVING

Research and development of the kernel language and basic software for cooperative problem-solving software is being conducted based on a parallel logic programming language, GHC. There are three goals:

(1) To investigate the provision of language functionality such as the meta-function and constraint function necessary for the construction of a high-level problem-solving system, and to clarify how to realize them, then applying these results to research the expansion of the language function of KL1 in the final stage.

(2) To establish parallel programming paradigms and parallel programming techniques, through the experimental description in GHC of typical algorithms used in various application domains.

(3) To establish program transformation techniques for constructing efficient programs and to give a formal semantics of GHC.

This section outlines research on reflection in GHC, layered-stream programming, partial evaluation, program transformation, formal semantics of GHC, and on a constraint logic programming language (CAL).

2.1 Parallel Logic Language and Reflection

Assume that we are describing an operating system for parallel computers, that is, a parallel programming system, in GHC. Such a programming system needs to input user goals, execute them as GHC processes and output the execution results. It also needs to handle meta-level concepts, such as success or failure of goal execution.

However, the current GHC does not distinguish meta-level phenomena clearly from object-level ones. This makes it difficult to describe an operating system concisely. Therefore, it is important to consider how to handle meta-level concepts which cannot fit into the current language framework of GHC. If we implement these concepts as system-defined predicates or realize them as side effects, the language may become inconsistent and the code size of the implementation may increase enormously. Therefore, we have started to study reflection as a way of handling the meta-level notion consistently.

Reflection can be considered as a function to sense the system itself and modify it dynamically. If a system or a programming language has this reflective ability, it is possible to describe a powerful operating system or problem-solving system which can flexibly perform tasks corresponding to the remaining resources and the current load.

An example of a reflective computation system is shown in Figure 1. Normally, a computation system consists of a program, data, and an executor. A computation system computes something in a certain problem domain, whereas a meta-computation system takes "another computation system" as its problem domain. A reflective system can be considered as a meta-computation system which takes itself as its problem domain and is causally connected to its data.

The concept of reflection has been proposed in FOL [Weyhrauch 1980] and 3-Lisp [Smith 1984]. In 3-Lisp, a reflective system has been realized by providing a reflective mechanism to obtain the current continuation and environment. Smith has also described the meta-circular interpreter of 3-Lisp.

The study of reflection at ICOT examines various reflective operations in GHC and, at the same time, tries to propose the new language specifications of GHC based on those arguments [Tanaka 1988]. Since we have obtained hints from Smith's approach, the basic mechanism of implementing reflection is principally the same.

Since GHC has parallelism, and meta-level phenomena are always invoked during goal execution, the implementation method becomes more complicated. Like 3-Lisp, using reflective operations to describe the GHC meta-interpreter induces the problem of a reflective tower. However, we are concentrating more on the realization of reflective operations rather than considering the problem of a reflective tower. The current status of our research is summarized below:

(1) **Stepwise enhancement of the GHC meta-interpreter**
The simplest GHC meta-interpreter can be described as a four-line program, similar to the four-line interpreter of Prolog. However, this four-line program only simulates the top-level execution of programs and cannot obtain much information from the interpreter. Therefore, we have enhanced this four-line program stepwise, and confirmed that various enhanced meta-interpreters, such as fail-safe, interruptible, scheduling and controlled meta-interpreters, are obtained from this interpreter.

- A failsafe meta-interpreter prevents the system from failing, even if a goal fails during execution;

- An interruptible meta-interpreter can suspend, resume or abort the execution of the given goal;

- A scheduling meta-interpreter enqueues the reduced goals and processes these goal sequentially

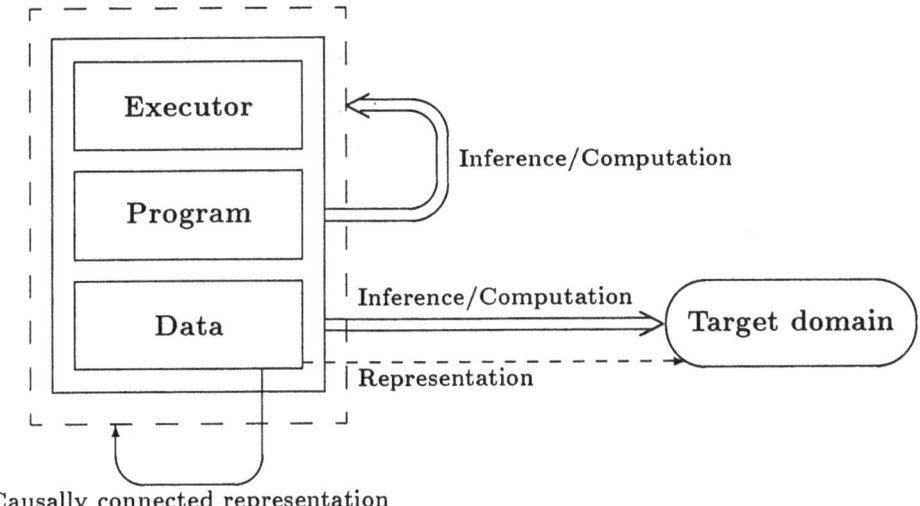

Figure 1: Reflective system

using a scheduling queue;

- A controlled meta-interpreter controls the total reduction time of a given goal using a reduction count.

(2) **Description of a variable management meta-interpreter**

To increase the expressive power of meta-interpreters further, we have developed a variable management interpreter which has the facility to manage its own local variables. In (1), we have assumed a continuation or reduction count as resources which can be controlled. Variable bindings have been added to this interpreter as resources which can be controlled by the user. We confirmed that this interpreter can run at a practical speed by running several sample programs.

(3) **Application of reflection in GHC**

We have examined the distributed computation system of GHC as an application of reflection. We assumed a system where several GHC machines are connected to each other via network managers. We are not interested in simulating the physical structures of distributed computers. Instead, our objective is to provide an abstract model of computation. We have examined the description method of a distributed computation system from the viewpoints of network managers, GHC machines and meta-interpreters. We showed that various reflective operations, such as dynamic reduction count control and load balancing, are performed on this distributed computation system.

However, the approach we have adopted so far is still very primitive. We can freely access meta-level informa-tion or resources which we would like to control. Since this seems to be very dangerous, we are currently working on the language design of Reflective GHC (RGHC) which allows more sophisticated handling of reflections.

We still have many problems as to where to position reflection in logic and how establish it in logic programming. We are planning to work on those problems and consider the semantics of reflective operations.

2.2 Constraint Logic Programming Language CAL

Constraint programming is one of the most important programming paradigms and gives a promising framework for cooperative problem solving as well as for the concept of reflection we discussed in the previous section. The most outstanding feature of constraint programming is that it allows the declarative description of problems. That is, a problem is solved by indicating a goal without reference to the method by which it should be established.

ICOT has been researching and developing a constraint logic programming language, CAL, as an element of basic software research. This subsection outlines the research and development of constraint programming languages, focusing on CAL.

Constraint logic programming languages, proposed by Colmerauer [Colmerauer 1987], and Jaffar and Lassez [Jaffar and Lassez 1987], incorporate the problem solving paradigm of constraint programming into the logic programming paradigm.

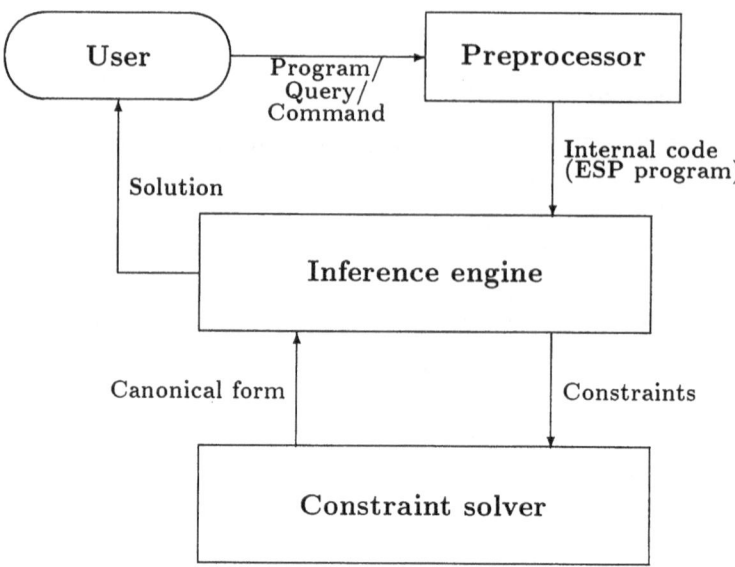

Figure 2: Organization of the CAL system

CAL aims at increasing the descriptive power of logic programming languages by replacing unification with a more powerful computation mechanism: constraints solving. Problems are described in the form of constraints, that is, relations on objects, not only of the Herbrand universe but also of other fields, and are solved by a built-in mechanism. For example, if a system of equations on real numbers occurs in a program, it is solved automatically.

CAL is a constraint logic programming language which allows users to write several types of constraints. The first prototype was implemented in 1987 on DEC2060, and, now, three systems are available on PSI, the Personal Sequential Inference machine: "Algebraic CAL" which handles linear and non-linear algebraic equations, "Boolean CAL" which handles Boolean equations, and "Typed CAL" that handles several types of constraints, including algebraic and Boolean equations, at the same time.

In Algebraic CAL, the Buchberger algorithm for computing Gröbner bases of polynomials, which has been used in recent years in computer algebra and geometry theorem proving, is utilized as the constraint solving algorithm. CAL is the first language to adopt the Buchberger algorithm as its constraint solver. This enables the system to handle non-linear equations and wield its power over a lot of algebraic problems, such as the programming for geometry theorem provers or the computation of conditional extrema by the Lagrange multiplier method.

In Boolean CAL, we use the Gröbner-base approach again. Boolean Gröbner bases can be computed by slightly modifying the Buchberger algorithm.

In Typed CAL, users can use constraints on several types of objects simultaneously. Typing is introduced to indicate the type of constraint. In the execution of a program, a suitable solver is selected automatically according to the type of each constraint.

Each of the PSI's CAL described above consists of a "preprocessor", an "inference engine," and a "constraint solver" as shown in Figure 2. The preprocessor transforms CAL programs and CAL goals (queries) to ESP programs and ESP goals. The inference engine executes ESP programs obtained by the transformation. When a constraint is detected during execution, the constraint solver is invoked to solve it. More precisely, the constraint solver collects constraints passed by the inference engine and computes the canonical form of the set of constraints.

For the final stage of the FGCS project, the geometry theorem prover has been selected as a typical application of constraint logic programming. A constraint solver that handles equations and inequations over real numbers will be investigated through this application. The hierarchical use of constraint solvers will also be investigated concurrently. A preliminary study has begun on research on parallel constraint logic programming. We intend to design a parallel constraint logic programming language with a powerful constraint solver, which will be called PCAL, based on the result of these studies.

2.3 Parallel Programming with Layered Streams

We have been studying how to write search programs in committed-choice languages (CCLs). Prolog, a sequential logic programming language, embodies unification and backtracking as its basic mechanisms, and is suitable for search problems.

Since CCLs do not have a backtracking mechanism, it is not easy to write search programs in CCLs. Solutions may be obtained by replacing some part of other solutions through backtracking. In a CCL, a process should be forked for every candidate instead of backtracking. However, structure copying is necessary for each parallel environment, which is not efficient. We have therefore proposed a data structure, called a layered stream, and a programming style based on them, called layered stream programming, for parallel processing of search problems in CCLs [Okumura and Matsumoto 1987].

The basic idea behind layered streams is to improve communication between processes by sharing some of the data structures and to achieve high parallelism. It is a generalization of the idea which is employed in the PAX parsing system [Matsumoto 1987]. In other words, PAX is a derivative variant of the method.

We have studied a way of programming search problems directly in a CCL. However, there is another way of obtaining search programs by a transformation from some specification of problems. An appropriate description language for search problems would help us to obtain such programs. We have analyzed the property of search problems and aim to devise a compiler which generates efficient codes as directly programmed.

2.4 Partial Evaluation System

The purpose of a partial evaluation system is to derive a more efficient special purpose program from a given general purpose program and its partial input, by partially performing computation on as many parts as possible using the partial input.

One of the most important applications of partial evaluation is its use in compilation, which is well known as the theory of Futamura's projection [Futamura 1971]. There has been a great deal of research on partial evaluation for this application within conventional imperative and functional languages. In particular, within Lisp, results have been obtained in compiling, compiler generation, and compiler-compiler generation by partial evaluation [Jones et al. 1985].

In logic languages such as Prolog, however, partial evaluation has recently attracted many researchers by its use in optimizing meta-programming [Levi 1986, Safra and Shapiro 1986, Takeuchi and Furukawa 1986]. Results have been reported concerning only compiling meta-programs. However, compiler generation and compiler-compiler generation remained as open problems.

The main problems to be solved for partial evaluation system are:

- Automation of the partial evaluation process;
- Making partial evaluation programs self-applicable.

By automating the partial evaluation system, we aim at making the partial evaluation process performable with less human assistance. By making the partial evaluation algorithm self-applicable, we aim at realizing compiler generation and compiler-compiler generation.

Although the implemented system has not yet succeeded in solving the automation problem, it has succeeded in making it self-applicable. Using the system, we have achieved results in compilation, compiler generation, and compiler-compiler generation. We have also succeeded in using it for incremental compilation [Fujita and Furukawa 1988].

The keys to this success are:

- Easy and sufficient use of the given partial input;
- Compactness of the partial evaluation program.

In Prolog, unification makes it very easy to utilize partial information. More concretely, due to the bi-directional nature of unification, information retained in variable bindings can be propagated both top-down and bottom-up. Secondly, it is easy to write meta-interpreters for Prolog concisely (only three lines in its simplest form). Since a partial evaluation program itself is a kind of meta-interpreter, this compactness is a great advantage in realizing self-applicability.

We shall conduct further research for the following purposes:

- Automating the above system;
- Enhancing the partial evaluation ability;
- Constructing a partial evaluation system for parallel logic languages.

In order to automate partial evaluation process, the most important problem to be solved is how to detect termination conditions for recursive user predicates. Since the problem is undecidable in general, we more or less need an indication from programmers.

However, for a limited class of programs, it may be possible to derive determination conditions by performing sophisticated program analyses. Moreover, using mode and type information obtained by the program analyses, partial evaluation process may be made more effective. For these analyses, the abstract interpretation technique will provide a useful method.

As for improvement of the partial evaluation ability, Futamura has recently introduced the notion of generalized partial computation within a functional language [Futamura 1988]. Generalized partial computation extends the task of partial computation from mere propagation of constants and evaluation of constant expressions to propagation and stepwise reduction of constraints. This idea can be reformulated in logic programming languages. We have already obtained some results by implementing this idea.

Finally, in research on partial evaluation in parallel logic languages, we are confronted with the rather serious theoretical problem that there is no established semantics for parallel logic languages or program transformation rules that are proven to be correct.

However, we have defined a set of transformation rules called the UR-set which is rather restricted but sound in the sense that the rules never introduce a deadlock condition [Furukawa et al. 1988]. We have implemented a partial evaluation system based on the UR-set [Fujita et al. 1988]. Further research on semantics and transformation rules is in progress [Ueda 1988]. We expect that this research will contribute to a more practical partial evaluation system.

2.5 Transformation and Formal Semantics of GHC Programs

We have developed a program transformation scheme to improve the efficiency of GHC programs, and also investigated the semantics of GHC programs from the model theoretical point of view, giving an extension of the approach taken by [Apt and van Emden 1982, Lloyd 1984]. The following briefly describes this research.

2.5.1 Transformation of GHC Programs

Unfolding is a basic operation for partial evaluation and program transformation. The unfolding of Prolog programs is straightforward, and has no problem. However, it is not the case when synchronization among goals is considered. Thoughtless unfolding can cause a deadlock.

We have proposed a set of unfolding rules which does not introduce such a deadlock. The basic idea is to prohibit the unfolding of a clause with unification goals in its body if the unfolding changes the guard condition. There are four rules including auxiliary rules. The set of rules is called the UR-set.

The first rule of the UR-set is "Unification Execution/Elimination". The effect of a unification goal in the body or the guard of a clause is applied to some variables in the body. Thus, the variables may be further instantiated.

The second is "Unfolding at an Immediately Executable Goal". A clause is unfolded at a body goal if the set of candidate clauses to which the goal can commit is fixed statically.

The third is an auxiliary "Predicate Introduction and Folding". A new predicate is defined by introducing a clause whose body consists of the non-unification goals of the clause which we want to unfold. The original clause is folded by the new clause. This rule is for enabling application of the last rule.

The last rule is "Unfolding across Guard". A clause is replaced by a set of clauses if it has no unification goal. Each clause is made by unfolding the original clause at some body goal using some program clause.

The UR-set seems to be powerful enough for various applications. Recently, it was restated more formally and the folding rule was generalized [Ueda 1988]. To evaluate its effectiveness, we need to perform further experiments such as process fusion [Furukawa and Ueda 1985], the leveling of the meta-interpreter and its object program, and program synthesis from a naive definition.

To build an automatic partial evaluation system, we must find a valid control strategy to apply the UR-set. We are interested in implementing such a system in GHC. We believe it will take the form of cooperation of several unfolding processes.

2.5.2 Formal Semantics of GHC Programs

In languages such as GHC, the notion of processes which execute infinite computations controlled by guard-commit mechanisms communicating with other processes using input/output streams can be represented naturally.

In pure Horn logic programming languages, the result for declarative semantics based on the least fixpoint has been reported in [Apt and van Emden 1982,

Lloyd 1984].

In this approach, the denotation of a program is given as the minimum model of the set of Horn clauses, in other words, the set of unit clauses which is equivalent to the program. The set of unit clauses is characterized as the least fixpoint of the function obtained from the set of definite clauses. In this approach, we can characterize the set of solutions as the logical consequences of the program independently from the execution mechanism. This approach is one of the best ways of appreciating the clarity of logic programs.

We have investigated an extension of this approach to GHC programs, and presented a declarative semantics of a parallel programming language based on Horn logic such as Flat GHC [Murakami 1988]. The domain of input/output (I/O) histories has been introduced. Intuitively, an I/O history denotes an example of a computation path of a program which is generated when the program is executed without any failure or deadlock. The denotation of a program is defined as a set of I/O histories. The notion of truth is redefined for goal clauses and sets of guarded clauses. The semantics of a program is defined as the maximum model of the program.

We have also shown that the semantics is characterized as the greatest fixpoint of the function obtained from the program. Using the semantics, the solutions of programs which contain perpetual processes controlled by guard commit mechanisms can be characterized as the logical consequence of the programs.

The properties of programs which contain perpetual computation controlled by guard-commit mechanisms can be discussed using the semantics.

3 INTELLIGENT PROGRAMMING SOFTWARE

Research on intelligent programming software aims at high-level facilities from the software engineering point of view, which enables us to automate basic functions needed in each process of software development and maintenance, and to support all the processes in a uniform framework.

In the intermediate stage of the FGCS project, we have been researching basic technology, focusing on mathematical techniques such as the application of automated theorem proving, constructive mathematics, and term rewriting. An outline of this research is given below.

3.1 Computer-Aided Proof System CAP

Research and development of the computer-aided proof system (CAP) aims at technological elements such as program transformation, verification, and synthesis based on methods of automated mathematical reasoning and, thus, construction of a programming support system.

CAP will finally evolve to a cooperative problem solving system equipped with general mathematical reasoning facilities, for example, wide and deep mathematical knowledge, various utilities such as a proof editor, two-dimensional input/output, and symbolic computation.

Figure 3 shows the configuration of the CAP. It consists of a proof editor, proof checker, and proof compiler. For these components, we have been investigating the following facilities in the intermediate stage:

- A general-purpose structure editor based on user-defined grammar with various intelligent proof editing functions;

- An intelligent proof checker enabling users to write proofs easily;

- A proof compiler to construct programs from proofs with optimization functions, and an interpreter which executes constructed programs.

This subsection describes the status of each component.

3.1.1 Proof Editor

The proof editor is an intelligent editor to support description of proofs based on mathematical knowledge. It needs a user-friendly interface. We have developed a structure editor (SEMACS) with general-purpose functions which can be used by not only the CAP but also other intelligent modules such as the knowledge base system (Kappa), computer algebra system, and programming system.

SEMACS has the following features:

- Smooth interface with the text editor;

- General-purpose editor independent of grammar in the sense that it allows users to define grammar;

- Easy extension and customization;

- Guidance functions for users unfamiliar with formal grammar;

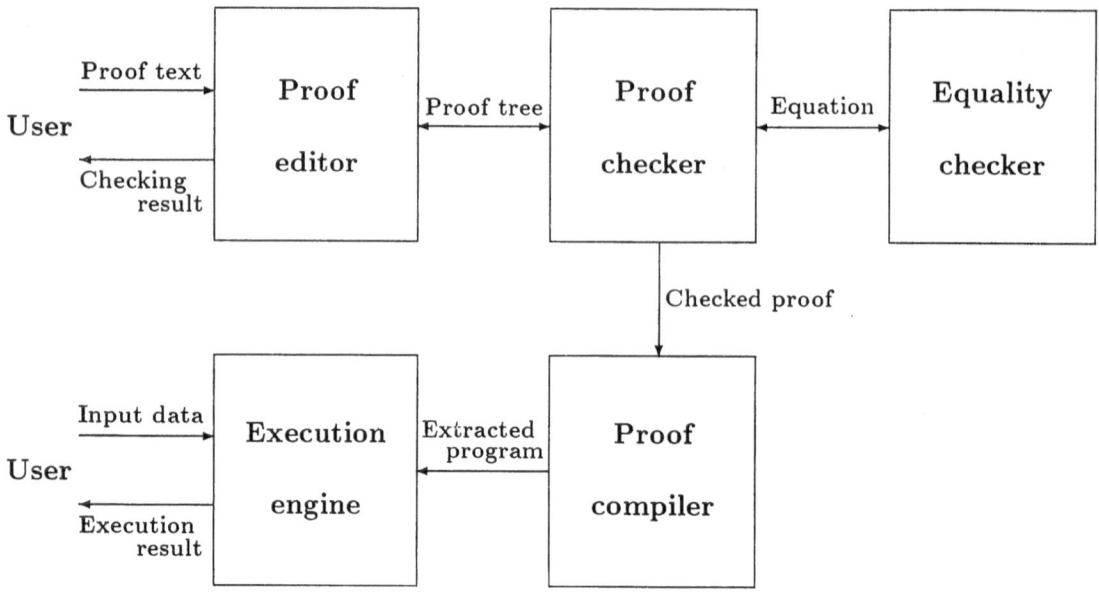

Figure 3: Configuration of the CAP system

- Natural definition and editing of list structure;

- Facility of holophrasting;

- Pretty print function which can be defined by the user;

- Editing a text containing non-terminal symbols.

Using this general-purpose structure editor, we have developed a front end for the CAP. It shows where the proof checker is currently checking in a proof text. In addition to the facility, we are now developing proof editing functions supporting interactive proof writing and checking.

3.1.2 Proof Checker

The proof checker is a kernel component of the CAP. We planned to develop a checker which can check a proof in a natural form enabling the user to write a proof easily. A prototype system, CAP-LA [Sakai 1988], has been designed and implemented according to this policy.

The current system is tuned to linear algebra for first-year university students. It checks proofs written fairly freely by users who do not know the mechanism of the proof checker, although such proofs sometimes need to be rewritten to some extent. These two features of CAP-LA — the limited target field and functions required for checking freely written proofs — accord with research

and development policies. The policies are intended to develop a practical system rather than promote pure research. Other research and development policies on the system are to confirm the latest technologies such as term rewriting, automated theorem proving, logic programming, and intelligent editing, incorporating them the system.

CAP-LA checks proofs constructing the proof tree, which is based on the inference rules of natural deduction (NK), from the proofs written by the user. Generally speaking, proofs which are easily understood by the user have a lot of logical gaps. Therefore, a facility to complement them is necessary. We call this facility a proof finding facility. For first order logic, we use the Prolog theorem proving techniques. For the equations, we use the term rewriting techniques. CAP-LA has the following features:

- Separation of mathematical knowledge from the checking mechanism, providing a facility to add a checking mechanism and strategy easily;

- Environment for modifying grammar and for adding and modifying knowledge for checking;

- Ability to complete proofs through interaction with the user;

- Inference mechanism for equations using term rewriting techniques (described later);

- Automatic type checking to free the user from concern over types.

3.1.3 Proof Compiler

The proof compiler is the system which translates proofs verified by the proof checker system into programs [Takayama 1987]. This is based on the idea that a special kind of proof, called a *constructive proof* [Beeson 1985, Bishop 1967], can be seen as the description of algorithms and their verification information.

The system uses the notion of realizability interpretation [Kleene 1945, Beeson 1985, McCarty 1984], and generates executable codes from the constructive proofs of theorems. It is necessary to implement a variety of constructive logic on the proof assistant system to realize the facility. The QPC [Takayama 1988a], which is a sugared subset of QJ [Sato 1985, Sato 1986], is used as the constructive logic. QPC is the logic in which the specification, algorithms, and justification of algorithms on natural numbers and natural number lists can be described uniformly, and it is simple enough to make the research on the proof finding facilities and the extraction of efficient codes easier than other varieties of constructive logic. Tiny Quty is used as the target language of the proof compiler. The language is a subset of Quty [Sato 1987] which is also the target language of QJ.

The theoretical issues of proof compilation have been investigated, and the core part of the system has been implemented. A feasibility study has been also performed through the extraction of simple programs by the prototype system such as a gcd program for natural numbers. The following are the main research issues:

- Proof compilation algorithm based on the notion of realizability;

- Optimization of the extracted code;

- Operational semantics of Tiny Quty, that is, development of the interpreter of the language.

The first is almost completed. In the second issue, the first problem is the elimination of redundant codes. The verification information of algorithms, which is the redundant code, is extracted by the straightforward application of realizability. It causes a heavy runtime overhead, particularly on the code extracted from proofs in induction, which is generally in the form of multivalued recursive call programs. The extended projection method (EPM), is a technique developed to eliminate the redundant code [Takayama 1988b]. The idea of the EPM is to analyze and eliminate the redundancy at each step of the proof which makes the procedure easier and more effective than the traditional syntactic optimization technique. For higher level optimization of algorithms, proof normalization, which is a well-known notion in the field of proof theory [Prawitz 1965], proved to be effective to some extent. In the last issue, the interpreter was implemented experimentally [Takayama 1987, Takayama 1988a, Takayama 1988b].

The next stage of research will deal with a more general-purpose proof assistant environment. The following themes have been set for this goal:

- Development of an interactive proof assistant environment, and the improvement of the proof editor;

- Introducing higher order features to the proof description language to describe a larger area of mathematics than linear algebra, and enhancing the proof checking facilities;

- Development of the mathematics knowledge base for the improvement of proof assistant facilities.

The main research themes in the final stage of the FGCS project will be as follows: the first is the improvement of the proof assistant system to make it practical. This research which will be along the same lines as current research. Another research theme is to develop an advanced parallel programming environment by using techniques developed for the proof assistant system.

3.2 Term Rewriting System Metis

Metis [Ohsuga and Sakai 1986] supports specific mathematical reasoning, that is, inference associated with the equal sign (=). Such inference is, in general, intricate and complicated, thus invoking an urgent need for machine support. Metis provides an experimental environment for studying practical techniques of equational reasoning. The policy of developing Metis enables implementation, testing, and evaluation of the latest techniques for inference as rapidly and freely as possible. Therefore, we decided to develop a system separate from CAP and intended to incorporate only practical techniques established on Metis in CAP whenever necessary.

We adopted the term rewriting system (TRS) as a basic technique to handle equations. The TRS is a set of oriented equations, called rewrite rules, and rewrites a term replacing the left-hand side by the right-hand side of a rewrite rule. There are main two reasons for our selection of TRS: (1) it is easy to handle by machine and can be efficient, and (2) there are quite a few studies of TRSs from the theoretical point of view, especially studies of termination and confluence property, which is important for the computation mechanism.

The kernel function of Metis is the *Knuth-Bendix* (KB) *completion procedure* [Knuth and Bendix 1970]. Roughly speaking, the KB procedure consists of two processes: (1) the orientation process of equations to assure the termination of rewriting using the semantic ordering or syntactical ordering method, and (2) the superposition process to make TRS confluent generating critical pairs (CPs) as new equations which represent ambiguity between rewrite rules. By iterating these two processes, a complete (terminating and confluent) TRS can be obtained.

However, two major problems are encountered during the KB process. One is the emergence of unorientable CPs in the superposition process. The other is the generation of infinitely many CPs. In neither case can we obtain a complete TRS. We solved the first problem by converting unorientable equations to orientation-free rewrite rules which can be applied either left to right or right to left. This extended procedure, that is, the KB procedure with orientation-free rewrite rules, is called *unfailing KB*. To solve the second problem, we adopted an extension of the KB procedure, called the *S-strategy* [Hsiang and Rusinowitch 1987]. The S-strategy determines whether a given equation is a theorem of the equational theory instead of obtaining a complete TRS and is complete in the sense of refutational theorem proving.

Research and development of Metis on how equational inference can become more efficient without loss of completeness is a long-range project. We are considering this from several points of view: implementation techniques [Ohsuga and Sakai 1988], theoretical view point, and user interface. We are planning to associate Metis with a knowledge base such as Kappa to handle the enormous number of rewrite rules which may be required in the future.

4 BASIC SOFTWARE FOR ADVANCED INFERENCE AND LEARNING

The aims of the study on the basic software for advanced inference and learning are to provide an advanced inference mechanism such as commonsense reasoning, which cannot be achieved by ordinary deductive inference, and knowledge acquisition and learning mechanisms which are essential for building large knowledge information systems. In the intermediate stage, we have been conducting basic research to achieve the above goal and have taken two approaches: logical and cognitive.

In the logical approach, we have been investigating three themes: (1) general formalization of commonsense reasoning, (2) a method for the revision and acquisition of commonsense knowledge, and (3) inductive inference based on the model theory.

In (1), we have developed a unified framework for advanced inference methods such as induction and analogy. In (2), we have been doing research focused on default reasoning, which is a subclass of commonsense reasoning, on formalized revision, and on acquisition of commonsense knowledge. In (3), we have investigated the problem of how to generate new predicates.

In the cognitive approach, we have constructed a cognitive model of conscious/unconscious processing, and simulated the model in a parallel logic programming language. The model consists of two closely interactive parts: symbol processing and pattern processing. One of the parallel symbol processes is executed consciously (conscious processing), and all the other processes are executed automatically (unconscious processing). The following subsections briefly describe these studies.

4.1 General Formalization of Commonsense Reasoning

We believe that human commonsense reasoning is supported by advanced inference mechanisms such as induction, analogy, and default reasoning. We have been studying formalization of commonsense reasoning for mathematical discussion and have developed a unified framework for various advanced inferences.

The unified framework is possible by regarding advanced inference as nonmonotonic reasoning. One of the formalizations of the advanced inference is circumscription by J. McCarthy [McCarthy 1980, McCarthy 1986]. Circumscription formalizes the notion of closed world assumption, that is, "A property is satisfied by only those entities which are explicitly stated so ". However, circumscription does not successfully formalize those inferences which generalize knowledge, such as induction and analogy.

Therefore, we have formalized the following notion: "When all the demonstrated instances of predicate P are positive instances of ψ, we can assume that all instances of P satisfy ψ (When all the instances that proved to have a property P have a property Ψ, all instances having a property P have a property ψ [Arima 1988b].)" This formalization is called *ascription* and is a formalization of induction and analogy.

Advanced inference can be formalized as inferring on the *most preferred models* by introducing a *preference* order over models. Unlike circumscription, ascription has a discrete preference order, and performs radical belief revision. Therefore, ascription is also suitable for representing management mechanisms for hypotheses which are produced by the intelligent system itself.

4.2 Acquisition and Revision of Commonsense Knowledge

In realizing ascription which is a unified framework for commonsense reasoning, how to provide a concrete preference order is a problem. We have studied the human preference order in default reasoning. Default reasoning infers the most plausible result from the commonsense knowledge which is regarded as usually correct knowledge even though there are a few exceptions. The following subsection looks at acquisition and revision methods for default reasoning.

4.2.1 Acquisition of Commonsense Knowledge

Since commonsense varies with historical, geographical, social and individual background, intelligent systems need the ability to acquire commonsense corresponding to different contexts. For example, if they can acquire individual commonsense that users have, they provide user-friendly environments which interpret the users' intention appropriately. From this point of view, we have taken the first step forward away from current research, which assumes that commonsense is provided in advance, towards the future research on acquiring commonsense knowledge.

The idea of the research [Arima 1988a] is intuitively explained as follows: "If entities in a class which are shown to have a property are much more numerous than entities which are shown not to have that property, we can acquire commonsense that the property is usually satisfied in the class."

We have two theoretical problems to perform such commonsense acquisition. They are:

(1) Representation of commonsense knowledge varying with classes;

(2) Representation of an overwhelming majority.

For (1), we have proposed *partially directional circumscription*, a specialized version of *formula circumscription* [McCarthy 1986] which is a general form of circumscription. For (2), we have introduced the *surpassing relation*, a binary relation over predicates.

We now plan to clarify problems for this approach and investigate application and cooperation with ascription.

4.2.2 Revision of Commonsense Knowledge

The idea of the revision method of commonsense knowledge is related to the study on the famous exam-ple of default reasoning called the *Yale Shooting Problem* [Hanks and McDermott 1986].

Hanks and McDermott evaluated the current formalization of the default reasoning on the temporal projection and showed that no current formalization captures human commonsense.

We have taken an approach based on *minimal change* for the Yale Shooting Problem. The formalization of minimal change states that humans infer by commonsense that a set of facts in a new situation is changed minimally from the set of facts in the previous one to preserve consistency. We have given approximate solutions for the Yale Shooting Problem and a similar problem in the inheritance system [Satoh 1987].

We have applied this formalization to the revision method of commonsense knowledge. We have developed a formalization of revision strategy which performs minimal revision, that is, to treat contradictory knowledge as exceptions when it is added to current commonsense knowledge [Satoh 1988].

4.3 Inductive Inference Based on the Model Theory

Shapiro's model inference [Shapiro 1982] gives a very important strategy for inductive inference based on the model theory for logic programs. In the model inference, however, there are very strong assumptions, as follows. Finitely many predicates, which are sufficient for describing a target program, are given in advance. Furthermore, it is assumed that an oracle which gives input/output examples of the program knows the intended interpretation of all the predicates. This means that the ability of the inference system very much depends on the user's programming knowledge.

Recently, several approaches to the problem have been made, in which an inference system generates new predicates by itself [Muggleton and Buntine 1988]. In such approaches, it is important to handle the following problems:

(1) When will be a predicate generated?

(2) What is the meaning of the new predicate?

To deal with these problems, we consider a class of logic programs, which are sufficiently and syntactically restricted, as a target of inference. Ishizaka [Ishizaka 1988] gives an efficient algorithm for inferring one such class, DRLP, which is equivalent to the class of finite state acceptor. We will try to extend this class to deal with more general logic programs.

66

4.4 Cognitive Model of Conscious and Unconscious Processing

We understand that the basic problems in realizing artificial intelligence are knowledge acquisition (or learning) and efficient extraction of acquired knowledge. Realizing their importance, we proposed a cognitive model of conscious/unconscious processing (C/U model) [Oka 1987, Oka 1988].

The model consists of two closely interactive parts: symbol processing and pattern processing. In symbol processing, at most one of the parallel processes is executed consciously (conscious processing) and the others are executed automatically (unconscious symbol processing). Although symbol processing proceeds deterministically, pseudo-backtracking is available in conscious processing using recent memory. Pattern processing is spreading activation in a network, which is executed unconsciously (unconscious pattern processing).

We simulated the model in a parallel logic programming language GHC utilizing the characteristics of the language. That is, we noticed the correspondence between the basic characteristics of the model and that of the language: AND-parallelism, choice nondeterminism, and the suspension rule. Utilizing these characteristics of the language as it is, we added the following functions:

(1) Narrowing down OR candidates with pattern processing;

(2) Enabling pseudo-backtracking with recent memory.

Pattern processing is simulated using the language as a process description language.

We started simulation from the part of interaction between conscious processing and unconscious pattern processing. As an example for simulation, we took up the process of doing a task of selecting a disparate one of a few items, for example, {run, write, pick, eat}.

The process of doing this kind of task consists of conscious processing and unconscious pattern processing. That is, firstly, a property for a classification occurs unconsciously, according to the problem, context, and the solver's explicit and implicit knowledge which reflects his experience. Secondly, the property of each item is checked consciously. If exactly one item is disparate on the property, it is the answer. If not, another property occurs and it is checked. Conscious processing is efficient because it deals only with properties that have occurred; that is, knowledge which can be accessed from conscious processing is narrowed down by unconscious processing.

In the model, tasks can be shared between symbol processing and pattern processing, making the best use of each part; moreover, inference and learning in each part are expected to become more efficient through the interaction of each part.

5 CONCLUSION

Our final goal of the research and development of problem-solving and inference software is to develop a cooperative problem-solving system which supports the construction of many kinds of application software. One of the main themes in the intermediate stage is parallelization which is essential to the development of such a system. We obtained fundamental results in this area.

Meta-programming by reflection and constraint logic programming will be important paradigms to make schemes of knowledge representing languages which should be developed using the kernel language KL1. We believe that the meta-function and constraint-function realized by these paradigms gives a common base for the cooperative problem-solving system.

Program transformation techniques and partial evaluation techniques based on a parallel logic programming language GHC are almost completely developed. In the research on the proof support system, CAP, we developed a good amount of theoretical background and implemented many tools.

Advanced inference and learning is one of the most important themes of the FGCS project. To achieve progress in these areas, however, it is necessary to make it clear what human knowledge information processing is, which is a very difficult problem. There is no world-wide approved standard method to study it yet. At present, we are investigating this theme based on its mathematical model.

Although this paper did not discuss other related research conducted by the First Research Laboratory because of limited space, much has been done. Related research includes ARGUS [Kanamori et al. 1986, Kanamori and Horiuchi 1984, Kanamori and Horiuchi 1986], a program verification, transformation, synthesis and analysis system; ANDOR [Takeuchi et al. 1987a, Takeuchi et al. 1987b], a parallel problem-solving language for concurrent systems; EUODHILOS [Sawamura and Minami 1988, Sawamura et al. 1988], a computer aided reasoning system; and MENDEL [Honiden et al. 1985, Honiden et al. 1986, Uchihira et al. 1987], a prototyping support system.

In the final stage, we will concentrate on parallelization. As part of the research on intelligent programming software, we are planning to develop (1) a parallel knowledge programming language submodule, (2) a parallel intelligent programming support submodule, (3) a proof support submodule and (4) advanced inference and learning mechanisms.

For the parallel knowledge programming language submodule, we will conduct further research on meta-programming, constraint logic programming and semantics based on a parallel logic programming language. Considering these results, we plan to extend and improve KL1.

For the parallel intelligent programming support submodule, we will continue basic research on program transformation and verification of parallel logic programs, then develop a practical partial evaluation system and an interactive transformation, synthesis and verification system considering flexibility and extensibility.

For the proof support submodule, we will enrich the practicality of the proof support system (CAP) developed in the intermediate stage, then expand it to a parallel algorithm design support system to develop an intelligent support environment for parallel programming.

For the advanced inference and learning mechanisms, we plan to proceed with research on the formalization of commonsense reasoning, a predicate generator based on inductive inference, and a model of cognition. Then, cooperating with research on natural language processing and expert systems in the other laboratories, we will develop them as integrated research on learning from the viewpoints of both theory and application.

ACKNOWLEDGMENTS

The research on the problem-solving and inference software was carried out by the first research laboratory at ICOT in tight cooperation with six manufactures. Thanks are firstly due to who have given support and helpful comments, including Dr. Fuchi, the director of the research laboratories at ICOT, Mr. Yokoi, the former chief of the second research laboratory at ICOT and the current director of EDR, and Dr. Furukawa, the deputy director of the research laboratories at ICOT. Many fruitful discussions were done at the meetings of Working Groups: PPS, SYC, and FAI. Special thanks go to many people at the cooperating manufacturers in charge of the joint research programs.

REFERENCES

[Apt and van Emden 1982] Apt, K. and van Emden, M. H., Contributions to the theory of logic programming, *J. ACM*, 29, 1982

[Arima 1988a] Arima, J., Generating Rules with Exceptions, in this volume, 1988

[Arima 1988b] Arima, J., Formalization of Advanced Inference Processing as Nonmonotonic Reasoning (in preparation)

[Beeson 1985] Beeson, M. J., *Foundations of constructive mathematics*, Springer-Verlag, 1985

[Bishop 1967] Bishop, E., *Foundation of constructive analysis*, McGraw-Hill, New York, 1967

[Chikayama et al. 1988] Chikayama, T. et al., Overview of the Parallel Inference Machine Operating System (PIMOS), in this volume, 1988

[Colmerauer 1987] Colmerauer, A., Introduction to Prolog-III, in *ESPRIT'87, Achievements and Impact, Proc. 4th Annual ESPRIT Conference*, pp.28–29, Brussels, North-Holland, 1987

[Fujita and Furukawa 1988] Fujita, H. and Furukawa, K., A Self-Applicable Partial Evaluator and Its Use in Incremental Compilation, *New Generation Computing*, 6(2,3), June 1988

[Fujita et al. 1988] Fujita, H. Okumura, A. and Furukawa, K., Partial Evaluation of GHC Programs Based on the UR-set with Constraints, in *Proc. Fifth International Conference and Symposium on Logic Programming*, Seattle, 1988

[Furukawa and Ueda 1985] Furukawa, K. and Ueda, K., GHC Process Fusion by Program Transformation, in *2nd Conf. Proc. Japan Soc. Softw. Sc. Tech.*, Tokyo, 1985

[Furukawa et al. 1988] Furukawa, K., Okumura, A., and Murakami, M., Unfolding Rules for GHC Programs, *New Generation Computing*, 6(2,3), June 1988

[Futamura 1971] Futamura, Y., Partial Evaluation of Computation Process – An Approach to a Compiler-Compiler, *Systems, Computers, Controls*, 2(5):45–50, 1971

[Futamura 1988] Futamura, Y., Generalized Partial Computation, in D. Bjørner, A. P. Ershov, and N. D. Jones, editors, *Partial Evaluation and Mixed Computation*, North-Holland, 1988

[Hanks and McDermott 1986] Hanks, S. and McDermott, D., Default reasoning, nonmonotonic logics, and the frame problem, in *Proc. AAAI86*, pp.328–333, 1986

[Honiden et al. 1985] Honiden, S., Uchihira, N., and Kasuya, T., Software Prototyping with *MENDEL*, in *Proc. Logic Programming 85*, LNCS-221, pp.108–116, Springer-Verlag, 1985

68

[Honiden et al. 1986] Honiden, S., Uchihira, N., and Kasuya, T., MENDEL: Prolog based concurrent object oriented language, in *Proc. COMPCON 86*, pp.230–234, 1986

[Hsiang and Rusinowitch 1987] Hsiang, J. and Rusinowitch, M., On Word Problems in Equational Theories, in *ICALP, 14th International Colloquium Automata, Languages and Programming*, pp.54–71, 1987

[Ishizaka 1988] Ishizaka, H., Inductive inference of regular languages based on model inference, in *Proc. Logic Programming Conference '87*, LNCS-315, pp.178–184, Springer-Verlag, 1988

[Jaffar and Lassez 1987] Jaffar, J. and Lassez, J-L., Constraint Logic Programming, in *Proc. 4th IEEE Symposium on Logic Programming*, 1987

[Jones et al. 1985] Jones, N. D., Sestoft, P., and Søndergaard, H., An Experiment in Partial Evaluation: The Generation of a Compiler Generator, in J.-P. Jouannaud, editor, *Rewriting Techniques and Applications*, LNCS-202, pp.124–140, Springer-Verlag, 1985

[Kanamori and Horiuchi 1984] Kanamori, T. and Horiuchi, K., Type Inference in Prolog and Its Applications, Tech. Report TR-095, ICOT, 1984, also in *Proc. 9th International Joint Conference on Artificial Intelligence*, pp.704–707, 1985

[Kanamori and Horiuchi 1986] Kanamori, T. and Horiuchi, K., Construction of Logic Programs Based on Generalized Unfold/Fold Rules, Tech. Report TR-177, ICOT, 1986, also in *Proc. 4th International Conference on Logic Programming*, pp.744–768, 1987

[Kanamori et al. 1986] Kanamori, T., Fujita, H., Seki, H., Horiuchi, K., and Maeji, M., Argus/V: A System for Verification of Prolog Programs, in *Proc. FJCC*, Dallas, Texas, IEEE Computer Society Press, 1986

[Kleene 1945] Kleene, S. C., On the interpretation of intuitionistic number theory, *J. of Symbolic Logic*, 10:109–124, 1945

[Knuth and Bendix 1970] Knuth, D. E. and Bendix, P. B., Simple word problems in universal algebras, in J. Leech, editor, *Computational problems in abstract algebra*, pp.263–297, Pergamon Press, Oxford, 1970, also in Siekmann and Wrightson, editors, *Automation of Reasoning 2*, pp.342-376, Springer-Verlag, 1983

[Levi 1986] Levi, G., Object Level Reflection of Inference Rules by Partial Evaluation (extended abstract), in P. Maes and D. Nardi, editors, *Workshop on Meta-Level Architectures and Reflection*, Sardinia, North-Holland, 1986

[Lloyd 1984] Lloyd, J. W., *Foundations of logic programming*, Springer-Verlag, 1984

[Matsumoto 1987] Matsumoto, Y., A Parallel Parsing System for Natural Language Analysis, *New Generation Computing*, 5(1):63–78, 1987

[McCarthy 1980] McCarthy, J., Circumscription — a form of non-monotonic reasoning, *Artif. Intell.*, 13:27–39, 1980

[McCarthy 1986] McCarthy, J., Application of Circumscription to Formalizing Common-sense Knowledge, *Artif. Intell.*, 28:89–116, 1986

[McCarty 1984] McCarty, D. C., *Realizability and Recursive Mathematics*, Ph.D thesis, Oxford, 1984

[Muggleton and Buntine 1988] Muggleton, S. and Buntine, W., Towards Constructive Induction in First-order Predicate Calculus, TIRM 88-031, The Turing Institute, 1988

[Murakami 1988] Murakami, M., A New Declarative Semantics of Parallel Logic Programs with Perpetual Processes, in this volume, 1988

[Ohsuga and Sakai 1986] Ohsuga, A. and Sakai, K., Metis: A Term Rewriting System Generator, in *Symposium on Software Science and Engineering (SSE)*, RIMS, 1986, also Tech. Memorandum TM-0226, ICOT

[Ohsuga and Sakai 1988] Ohsuga, A. and Sakai, K., An efficient implementation method of reduction and narrowing in Metis, in *International Workshop of Unification (UNIF) '88*, 1988 also Tech. Report (to appear), ICOT

[Oka 1987] Oka, N., A Cognitive Model of Conscious/Unconscious Processing. in *4th Conf. Proc. Japan Soc. for Softw. Sc. Tech.*, pages 459–462, 1987 (in Japanese)

[Oka 1988] Oka, N., Cognitive Model of Conscious/Unconscious Processing and Its Simulation in a Parallel Logic Programming Language, Tech. Report TR-415, ICOT, 1988

[Okumura and Matsumoto 1987] Okumura, A. and Matsumoto, Y., Parallel Programming with Layered Streams, in *Proc. Fourth Symposium on Logic Programming*, San Francisco, 1987

[Prawitz 1965] Prawitz, D., *Natural Deduction*, Almquist and Wiksell, Stockholm, 1965

[Safra and Shapiro 1986] Safra, S. and Shapiro, E., Meta Interpreters for Real, in H.-J. Kugler, editor, *Information Processing 86*, pages 271–278, Dublin, Ireland, North-Holland, 1986

[Sakai 1988] Sakai, K., Toward Mechanization of Mathematics, in K. Fuchi and M. Nivat, editors, *Programming of Future Generation Computers*, pp.335–390, North-Holland, 1988

[Sato 1985] Sato, M., Typed Logical Calculus, Tech. Report 85-13, Department of Information Science, Faculty of Science, University of Tokyo, 1985

[Sato 1986] Sato, M., QJ: A Constructive Logical System with Types, in *France-Japan Artificial Intelligence and Computer Science Symposium 86*, Tokyo, 1986

[Sato 1987] Sato, M., Quty: A Concurrent Language Based on Logic and Function, in *Proc. Fourth International Conference on Logic Programming*, pp.1034–1056, MIT Press, 1987

[Satoh 1987] Satoh, K., Minimal change — A criterion for choosing between competing models —, Tech. Report TR-316, ICOT, 1987

[Satoh 1988] Satoh, K., Nonmonotonic reasoning by minimal belief revision, in this volume, 1988

[Sawamura and Minami 1988] Sawamura, H. and Minami, T., General-Purpose Reasoning Assistant System EUODHILOS and Its Applications, Tech. Memorandum TM-0576, ICOT, 1988

[Sawamura et al. 1988] Sawamura, H., Minami, T., Sato, K., and Tsuchiya, K., Potentials of General-Purpose Reasoning Assistant System EUODHILOS, in *Symposium on Software Science and Engineering (SSE)*, RIMS, 1988

[Shapiro 1982] Shapiro, E., *Algorithmic program debugging*, Ph.d thesis, Yale University Computer Science Dept., 1982, Published by MIT Press, 1983

[Smith 1984] Smith, B. C., Reflection and Semantics in Lisp, in *Proc. 11th Annual ACM Symp. on the Principles of Programming Languages*, pp.23–35, ACM, 1984

[Takayama 1987] Takayama, Y., Writing Programs as QJ-Proofs and Compiling into PROLOG Programs, in *Proc. 4th Symposium on Logic Programming*, San Francisco, 1987

[Takayama 1988a] Takayama, Y., QPC: QJ-based Proof Compiler —Simple Examples and Analysis, in *European Symposium on Programming '88*, Nancy, France, 1988

[Takayama 1988b] Takayama, Y., Proof Theoretic Approach to the Extraction of Redundancy-free Realizer Codes, (to appear), 1988

[Takeuchi and Furukawa 1986] Takeuchi, A. and Furukawa, K., Partial Evaluation of Prolog Programs and Its Application to Meta Programming, in H.-J. Kugler, editor, *Information Processing 86*, pages 415–420, Dublin, Ireland, North-Holland, 1986

[Takeuchi et al. 1987a] Takeuchi, A., Takahashi, K., and Shimizu, H., A Description Language with AND/OR Parallelism for Concurrent Systems and Its Stream-Based Realization, Tech. Report TR-229, ICOT, 1987

[Takeuchi et al. 1987b] Takeuchi, A., Takahashi, K., and Shimizu, H., A Parallel Problem Solving Language for Concurrent Systems, in *Proc. IFIP WG10.1*, 1987, (to appear)

[Tanaka 1988] Tanaka, J., Meta-Interpreters and Reflective Operations in GHC, in this volume, 1988

[Uchihira et al. 1987] Uchihira, N., Kasuya, T., Matsumoto, K., and Honiden, S., Concept Program Synthesis with Reusable Components Using Temporal Logic, Tech. Report TR-271, ICOT, 1987

[Ueda 1986a] Ueda, K., Introduction to Guarded Horn Clauses, Tech. Report TR-209, ICOT, 1986

[Ueda 1986b] Ueda, K., Guarded Horn Clauses: A Parallel Logic Programming Language with the Concept of a Guard, Tech. Report TR-208, ICOT, 1986 (revised 1987), also in K. Fuchi and M. Nivat, editors, *Programming of Future Generation Computers*, pp.441–456, North-Holland, 1988

[Ueda 1988] Ueda, K. and Furukawa, K., Transformation Rules for GHC Programs, in this volume, 1988

[Weyhrauch 1980] Weyhrauch, R. W., Prolegomena to a Theory of Mechanized Formal Reasoning, *Artif. Intell.*, 13(1–2):133–170, 1980

PROCEEDINGS OF THE INTERNATIONAL CONFERENCE
ON FIFTH GENERATION COMPUTER SYSTEMS 1988,
edited by ICOT. © ICOT, 1988

The Research and Development
of Natural Language Processing Systems
in The Intermediate Stage of The FGCS Project

UCHIDA Shunichi, YOSHIOKA Tsutomu, SUGIMURA Ryôichi,
TANAKA Yûiti, HASIDA Kôiti, and MUKAI Kuniaki

The Second Research Laboratory, ICOT

ABSTRACT

This paper is an introduction to the research activities on natural language processing (NLP) in the Fifth Generation Computer Systems (FGCS) project. Aiming at a verbal interface of computers, the NLP research in this project concerns itself mainly with discourse understanding.

The intermediate stage of the project has been devoted both to the improvement of the existing methods of syntactic processing as a basis for dealing with contextual aspects such as ellipsis and anaphora, and to the establishment of fundamental methods for representing and processing the structure of discourse and context. These activities are accommodated in the development of an experimental discourse understanding system called **DUALS**.

The methods of processing syntactic aspects have been compiled into a general-purpose software library, called the **Language Tool Box** (**LTB**). The methods in the library can be used, for example, to provide a verbal interface between the user and both expert systems and database systems. In addition to such research as DUALS and LTB, which are conducted on the initiative of ICOT, research conducted by the NLP research groups at the manufacturers cooperating with the FGCS project is outlined.

1 Introduction

The research on natural language processing (NLP) in the FGCS project aims at the implementation of a discourse understanding system. This system should be able to participate in Japanese discourse, and is to serve as a basis for verbal communication between human and computer.

The research in the initial stage attempted to recast in terms of logic programming the current methods for NLP, such as for parsing, to unravel the problems arising there, and to figure out the possibilities of further advancement. In this way, an experimental discourse understanding system called **DUALS-I** was developed in Prolog running on a DEC2060 computer, and was demonstrated at the last FGCS conference, held in November 1984. This system was able to comprehend and answer questions about a small passage which was extracted from a 3rd-grade primary school textbook of Japanese. The passage consisted of 18 sentences/200 words, and included dialogue.

DUALS-I could answer the prepared questions, but its parser, grammar, dictionary, and problem-solving method were quite immature and obviously needed a lot of further development. Nevertheless, a discourse understanding system was compiled into a system on Prolog, which demonstrated the merits of implementing an NLP system in terms of a logic programming paradigm. This not only gave a concrete understanding of the clear view that a logic paradigm provides for software development, but also brought up several new ideas about how to construct a parser and about semantic representation. The research subject was determined in this way in the first half of the intermediate stage.

The initial task of the intermediate stage was a total reconsideration of DUALS-I. The morphological analyzer, the parser, the simplistic context analyzer, the generator, and the dictionary were all to be revised to be more general versions.

As for the underlying hardware, DEC2060, whose memory size and interface functions were very limited, was replaced by PSI-I, a logic-programming machine newly developed at ICOT. A programming language, **CIL**, was developed and employed. It is an extension of Prolog and is more suitable for describing meaning and situation. This new system, called **DUALS-II** was completed at the end of 1986. The adoption of PSI, which provided a large memory and a multi-window environment with Japanese characters, and the employment of CIL as the programming language meant that the syntactic aspects of the system, such as in the parsing module and the sentence generation module, acquired advanced functions and a clear perspective in the software structures. The semantic aspect of the system was put in order as well, along the line of the development of Situation Theory and Situation Semantics.

Through the development of DUALS-II and the accumulation of software thereby, it became possible to shift the focus of research up to processing of context. The next research target towards the end of the intermediate stage, therefore, is to deal with a larger text with 200 sentences/2000 words, and to accept a much less restricted variety of questions. This means that we face the problem of dealing with a wide range of context. We will attack this problem with **DUALS-III**.

In DUALS-III, with a far greater number of sentences, software that just deals with one sentence at at time no longer works. A systematic design method must be engaged. The functions and knowledge of the syntactic aspects of the system, including the parser, the generator, and their dictionaries, were completely rebuilt from the basic methods, in order to achieve greater generality. Also, realistic contextual processing necessitated a thesaurus or a concept dictionary. For these tasks altogether, it was essential to have plenty of tools and adequate environments for developing each function module

Syntactic processing has matured to the extent that the software products can also be used for Japanese language processing in domains other than discourse understanding. We decided to extract those software modules for syntactic processing and put them together to make a library of common software tools called **LTB** (**the Language Tool Box**), a general Japanese processor.

Context processing is a field that is still wide open from a world-wide perspective. Various methods must thus be investigated upon materials that contain a variety of linguistic phenomena. In the FGCS project, the research group at ICOT and those at cooperating manufacturers are working together in seeking adequate methods for context processing, dividing up the whole work into various subtasks. LTB, a common software tool among these groups, has also been developed through the group's joint efforts.

The research on NLP in the FGCS project is described below. The central topic will be the work concerning DUALS, but the research by the groups at cooperating manufacturers will also be mentioned.

2 The Research Plan of the Intermediate Stage

2.1 The Research Topics and Goal

Regarding discourse understanding, the research goal of the intermediate stage was the experimental develop-

ment of a software system that could process semantics and contexts. **DUALS-I**, the pilot system in the initial stage, dealt with a sample text containing 18 sentences/200 words, and the new experimental version towards the end of the intermediate stage was to handle a text containing 100 sentences/1000 words.

Many technical tasks must be completed to achieve this goal, including the following research topics.

(1) The analysis functions for handling morphological, syntactic, and semantic information should be improved so as to cover a larger sample text. Processing speed must be increased enough to carry out efficient experiments. The generation and analysis functions ought to fit each other, and share the same syntactic rules.

(2) A dictionary containing morphological, syntactic, and semantic information needed for sentence analysis should be tailored to work efficiently with the functions provided by the analysis modules. This dictionary will become very large, so peripheral software tools must be prepared that can check the consistency of the its contents of the dictionary.

(3) A high-level programming language should be developed to write the analysis module and to describe the intermediate semantic or pragmatic information, so as to avoid cumbersome coding in Prolog or ESP.

(4) A theoretical model both to represent the structures of meaning and discourse and to carry out inferences on them should be devised on the basis of Situation Theory and Situation Semantics.

(5) Practical schemata and methods for system building should be developed to implement discourse processing methods such as those that resolve anaphora and ellipsis.

(6) The method to construct the thesaurus and the concept dictionary should be considered mainly in connection with the given sample text. Words and concepts appearing in the text must be analyzed, classified, and then compiled into a dictionary. The world-knowledge base should also be prepared for understanding the domain talked about in the sample text.

2.2 Implementation of the Research and Development Plan

2.2.1 Policy on Structuring the System

Every one of the above is a very tough research task. The first half of the four-year intermediate stage was devoted to reconsidering each part of DUALS-I, as well as to extending the functions and improving the processing speed of the syntactic aspect of the whole system. Also, a new language **CIL** needed to be developed; it allows **partially specified terms** (terms represented as bundles of attribute-value pairs) and provides a lazy evaluation function. The development of **DUALS-II** included a total revision of the foregoing system, in terms of CIL.

DUALS-II is a re-implementation of DUALS-I, but it is based on more general methods and has a more consistent software structure throughout the entire system. This was the starting point for the research on **DUALS-III**, a system that will handle a sample text ten times larger than that of DUALS-II. The structure of such a discourse understanding system was expected to be something like Fig. 1.

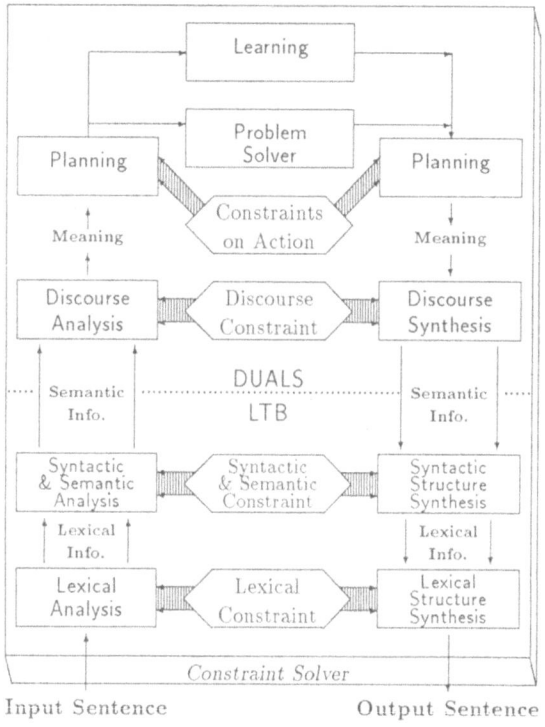

Fig. 1: The Mechanism of DUALS.

The whole system involves the analysis module and the generation module; the former analyzes input sentences, understands them, and produces corresponding discourse structures, and the latter generates response sentences based on the result of problem solving. The processing in each of these modules can be roughly divided into two layers: syntactic and pragmatic. Accordingly, the dictionary and knowledge base for analysis and generation were each regarded as divided into the syntactic part and the pragmatic part.

2.2.2 Syntactic Processing and the General Japanese Processor

Syntactic processing functions, in particular analysis functions, have so far been studied thoroughly not only in the NLP research at ICOT in the initial stage, but also in research and development of machine translation systems all over the world. Since the methods for implementing these functions are comparatively well-known, our main research goal in the syntactic domain was to achieve a higher processing speed. The generation functions have not been studied so well, and hence we planned to implement a software that can generate sentences from an intermediate semantic structure similar to surface sentences. Since the syntactic modules constitute a foundation upon which higher-level functions are piled, and since they can be employed in various types of research on NLP, those modules should be supplemented with, for instance, debugging environments for design and expansion of grammars, so as to form a consistent functional module.

The dictionary was developed in parallel with the lexical analysis of the sample text. The morphological part of the grammar was tailored along the line of a finer-grained approach so as to deal with deep discourse understanding in the future as well. The syntactic part was made so as to cover the sample sentences. For semantic processing, it is important to have a semantic dictionary which contains rules for composing the meaning of words out of morphemes (For example, 'dict' in 'dictionary', 'dictator', and 'contradict' is a morpheme.), lexical property about case-marking, and so forth. The dictionary, the grammar, and those software modules were developed in parallel in order that they could be kept consistent with each other.

It is difficult to maintain consistency between dictionary and grammar, so ours were developed together with their debugging environments. Also the preparation of a corpus of sample sentences and KWIC (key words in context) was considered by which to improve the generality of the description in the dictionary and the grammar. CIL, the language for describing NLP systems, was equipped with a programming environment including a debugger and a compiler, both on a multi-window basis.

The software modules for analysis mentioned so far provide fundamental input-output functions for NLP. They could therefore commonly be employed not only in research on discourse processing, but also in developing natural-language interfaces of expert systems and database systems. We intended to compile those modules into a general Japanese processor (which we call **LTB**: the

Language Tool Box) that would be available not solely in discourse understanding but in a wider domain of research and development.

2.2.3 Contextual Processing

Contextual processing is largely an immature field, and has very little accumulation of achievements in engineering scrutiny. A practical approach must begin by extracting and classifying meaning of words and background knowledge necessary to analyze the subject text and expected questions, and then forming them into a thesaurus and a concept dictionary. Such knowledge is described as 'constraints,' along the line of Situation Semantics.

The research was also intended to cover how to resolve anaphora and ellipsis, how to handle scopes of quantifiers and negation, how to represent the structure of discourse, and so on. This research should be the basis upon which to seek efficient ways to create a system that can understand sentences by using world knowledge and answer questions by problem solving.

Research on this aspect of NLP could be regarded as an attempt to figure out how to cast 'meaning' onto an engineering mechanism. One obstacle is that there is no ready-made structure if we embark on the domain of semantics, and so we are obliged to crawl nearly on a trial-and-error basis, catching at straws scattered by linguistic inquiries. This is totally unlike morphological or syntactic processing, where you can begin with far more refined structures in hand.

Substantial research work on semantics and context must deal with a subject text of a certain degree of complexity, in terms of both the superficial length and the discourse structure. This is because the types of context are practically inexhaustible. Methods for context processing should be examined in a variety of ways upon a variety of sample texts. Research on context processing yields fruits only through comparison across such a wide range of investigation. For this reason we intended to have many groups investigate various texts.

2.3 Organizational Structure of Research and Development

In the FGCS project, the second research laboratory at ICOT and the research groups at cooperating manufacturers are supposed to study various systems for various usages in various situations.

Syntactic processing should meet more strict requirements in terms of both the functional inventory and the processing efficiency. Both the development and the use of LTB, the general Japanese processor, were shared by all these groups. Such sharing of software is easy, because the computer system for research has been unified to PSI/SIMPOS since the beginning of the intermediate stage. LTB is supposed to include also the modules for semantic and contextual processing whose specification has been established clearly enough to share. This is a way to publish successively the concrete achievements of the research; a particularly appropriate way to publish basic research like that of NLP.

DUALS is the central subject of the research at ICOT. ICOT is also supposed to work with research groups at the cooperating manufacturers in the research and development of the common software tools such as LTB. Several research groups at these manufacturers are requested to study semantic processing and contextual processing in dealing with their own sample texts and problem domains.

3   Research at ICOT

3.1   DUALS-II

The research on discourse understanding at ICOT has revolved around the experimental development and extension of DUALS since the initial stage. Fig. 2 illustrates the history of the component methods that have been investigated during this research.

Both DUALS-I and DUALS-II dealt with a sample text extracted from a third-grade elementary school textbook of Japanese. This text, given in Fig. 3, consists of 18 sentences, or about 100 words. There is a great difference in the engaged processing methods and the schemata for software implementation, between DUALS-I, developed in the initial stage, and DUALS-II, developed in the first half of the intermediate stage.

The development of DUALS-I suffered from the shortage of the memory capacity and the poor programming environment available in Prolog on DEC2060. We also had to discover a way to construct syntactic processing along the line of logic programming. The goal to be achieved at that time was to put together the existing methods into a coherent software system, rather than organizing new theories or methods. DUALS-I allows the accumulation of discourse structure through the progress of contextual analysis, and the exploitation of this accumulated knowledge for question-answering.

DUALS-II, though sharing the same basic structure with DUALS-I, engages a largely different set of methods. Between these two versions of DUALS, the grammar was extended from a simple version written in terms of LFG to DCG-representation of Watanabe grammar,

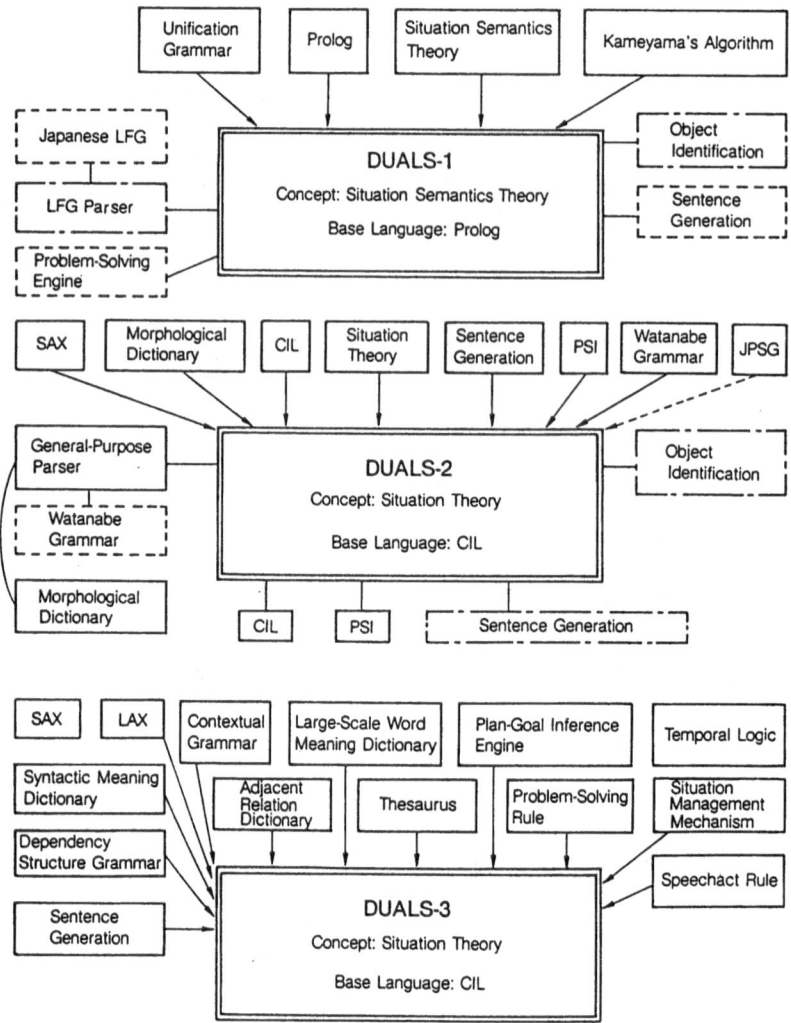

Fig. 2: Progress in DUALS R&D.

while the number of rules increased from 200 to 300. The parser was also revised from BUP, a bottom-up depth-first version, to SAX, a bottom-up breadth-first one. SAX had more functions and worked better. The central parts of semantic processing were improved, being rewritten in terms of **CIL**, a language for semantic description.

As Fig. 4 shows, CIL is a sort of Prolog, extended to allow partially specified terms (terms as bundles of attribute-value pairs) and a lazy evaluation control (in which an instantiation of a variable triggers the evaluation of the subprograms previously attached to that variable). The partially specified terms of CIL greatly reduce the restriction on the numbers and the locations

of arguments in Prolog terms, thus providing a clear view in the description of the system and in the representation of the intermediate semantic data.

The central part of these two versions of DUALS was anaphora resolution, which employed Kameyama's algorithm to find the candidates of antecedents of noun phrases by reference to postpositions. The knowledge representation scheme focused on situations, based on Situation Theory. This representation was referred to by an inference mechanism for problem solving. With the small size of the sample text, however, this mechanism ended up to be a patchwork of ad hoc rules and representations specific to the text. Capturing generality about this aspect of processing was shelved until DUALS-III.

あと一時間でマニラに着こうと言う時、どうしたことか、急にエンジンから白いけむりが吹きだしました。
これを発見したき長のロールさんは、はっとしました。
もしも火でも吹こうものなら、ひこうきは、ばく発してしまいます。
下は、広広と広がる太平洋です。
そうしたら、五十人の乗客のいのちはどうなることでしょう。
ロールさんは、急いで、スチュワーデスのふちがみさんをよびました。
そして、いざというときの用意をするようにめいじました。
ふちがみさんの顔がひきしまりました。
「お客様にお知らせするんですか。」
「いや、何とかこのままとんでみる。お客様には、知らせないほうがいい。」
ふちがみさんは、そうじゅう室を出ると、にっこりとほほえみながら、「みなさん、これから、きゅうめいぐをつけるくんれんをいたします。」と言いました。

Only an hour before arriving Manila, suddenly white smoke began to billow from an engine.
Seeing this, Captain Roll was alarmed.

If the fire spreads, the plane could explode.

Below lies the broad expanse of the Pacific Ocean.

What will become of the 50 passengers?

Captain Roll hurriedly called a flight attendant, Ms. Hutigami.

He instructed her to prepare for an emergency.

A tension showed up on Ms. Hutigami's face.
"Shall I tell the passengers?"
"No, I'll try to keep on flying." said the captain, "Do not let the passengers know."
Ms. Hutigami came out of the cabin and said with a smile, "Ladies and gentlemen, it's time to conduct the life jacket drill."

Fig. 3: The Text for DUALS-I and -II.

$$< PST > ::= \{\alpha_1/\beta_1, \ldots, \alpha_n/\beta_n \}$$
$$\text{where } n \geq 0, \alpha_i \neq \alpha_j \ (i \neq j)$$

```
Example :  {relation/lend,
            who/taro,}
           to_whom/hanako,
           what/{ object/car,
                  owner/taro},
           fee/{$/10},
           date/{ year/1988,
                  month/dec,
                  day/1},
           Period/{month/1}}
```

PST is an expansion of Herbrand Term:

$$P (X , Y , Z) \Rightarrow \{ arg_0/P, arg_1/X, arg_2/Y, arg_3/Z\}$$

$$arg_0 \quad arg_1 \quad arg_2 \quad arg_3$$

Fig. 4: Partially Specified Term.

DUALS-II makes good use of the window system provided by SIMPOS, the operating system of PSI, and provides an efficient interactive interface that supports the Japanese language. Fig. 5 shows the result of a syntactic analysis, and Fig. 6 the internal representation of syntactic and semantic information obtained from this analysis.

The algorithm and dictionary for syntactic processing in DUALS-II work much faster than those of DUALS-I. They repond to a question with a delay of only a few seconds. For each sentence in Fig. 3, parsing takes 1 to 2 seconds, problem solving 2 to 5 seconds, and generation less than 0.5 seconds.

The program of DUALS-II is about 11,000 lines long. Approximately half of it is written in CIL, of which about 4,000 lines are for morphological, syntactic and semantic analysis, about 500 lines are for handling ellipsis and anaphora, and about 500 lines are for problem solving. The other half of the program is written in ESP, the language which describes the underlying PSI/SIMPOS system. This half consists of about 2,000 lines for sentence generation, about 2,300 lines for CIL interpreter, and miscellaneous utility subroutines. Besides DUALS-II itself, there are peripheral software tools for building grammars and dictionaries. This as a whole constitutes a very large software system.

3.2 DUALS-III

The research on DUALS-III aims at a more proper treatment of verbal context, based upon the methods of processing and software implementation accumulated through the development of the first two versions of DUALS. DUALS-III is expected to deal with a sample text containing about 200 sentences/2000 words, and to answer questions of a much greater variety. Part of the sample text and some of the expected questions are given in Fig. 7.

This enlargement of the system necessitated a new pe-

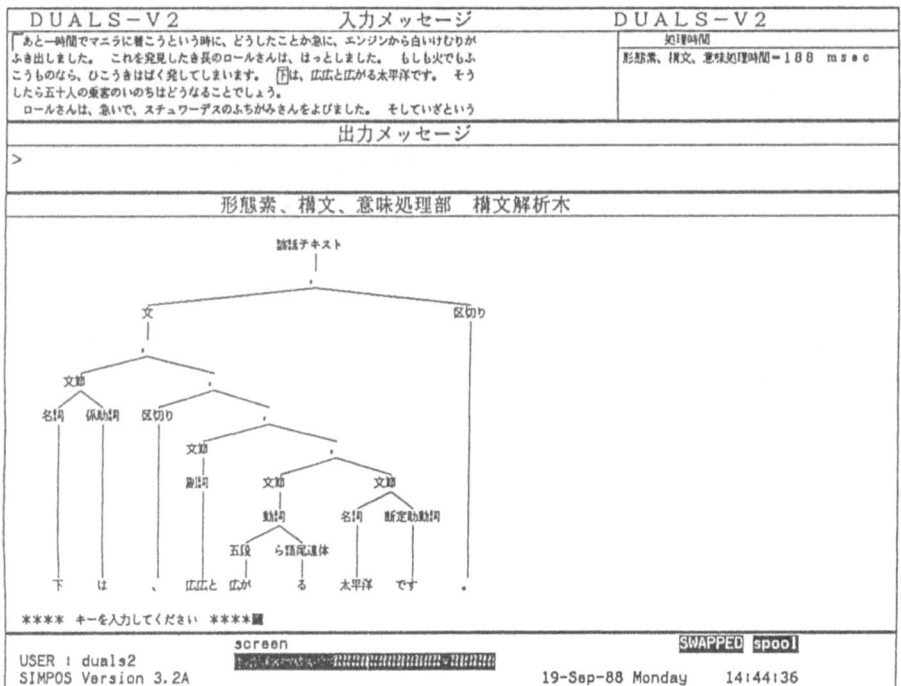

Fig. 5: The Result of a Syntactic Analysis.

Fig. 6: The Internal Structure of a Sentence.

ここで、考えてみなければならないのは、自然界には、さまざまな種類の生物たちが、それぞれの環境に応じて生きているということである。そして、これらの生物たちは、互いに影響を与え合い、複雑に絡み合った関係を保ちながら、生活しているということである。

森という環境を例にとってみよう。

森には、いろいろな動物が住んでいる。獣も鳥も虫も、もっと小さな微生物もいる。彼らは、そこに森があるから生活しているといっていい。

森の植物は、動物たちに食物を提供している。昆虫たちは、木や草の葉を食べたり、花の蜜や、木の幹から出る樹液を吸ったりして生活している。小鳥たちのあるものは、木の実や新芽を盛んについばむ。シカやサルは、木の葉や実を好んで餌にする。

What should be considered here is that a variety of creatures live in nature, adapting themselves to their own environments, and that these creatures make their lives influencing each other and keeping complicated relationships.

Let us take forest as an example of the environment.

In a forest, many kinds of animals live, including beasts, birds, insects and much smaller ones. We can say that they can keep their lives because the forest is there.

Plants in the wood feed animals. Insects live by eating leaves of trees and grasses, and sipping honey of flowers and sap coming out of tree stems. Some small birds peck nuts and sprouts vigorously. Deers and monkeys like to eat leaves and nuts of trees.

Fig. 7a: Sample Text for DUALS-III (part).

rusal of syntactic processing. With a problem domain of this scale, it is impossible for one person to capture the entirety of a grammar and a semantic dictionary all through their developmental stages. The maintenance of consistency across the whole system, therefore, requires not only appropriate schemata for classification and arrangement of the relevant knowledge, but also efficient debugging environments for the systems under construction. CIL, which is used in parsing and semantic processing, should run more efficiently and should be equipped with more powerful debugging tools.

We needed to develop new, properly-arranged versions of the thesaurus, concept dictionary, and so on, and to extend the morphological dictionary and semantic dictionary, in order to implement a more powerful semantic processing and to apply methods for context processing to the longer text. The former rules for handling ellipsis and anaphora should be reorganized into a more systematic structure. We need a proper problem-solving mechanism which can work in cooperation with those rules. An appropriate knowledge base must be developed which will be exploited by this problem solver. The corresponding parts of DUALS-II ware very simplistic, for instance with ad hoc inclusion of contextual processing into sentence analysis and generation. The difference between these two versions of DUALS could be looked upon as a typical example of quantity requiring quality.

The most important feature of DUALS-III is the accommodation of ideas from constraint programming and Situation Semantics. A major reason for believing that these theories can cope with contexts is that they are theories that handle partial information particularly well. The most stubborn problems blocking the way to the proper treatment of discourse include context sensitiv-

ity, ambiguity, and non-monotonicity, all of which follow from the partiality of information. The approach of DUALS-III and its successor versions, therefore, is an attempt to grasp the root of these ubiquitous problems.

In particular, the constraint-based approach poses an interesting but radical view of a NLP system in which analysis and generation share everything, including not only grammar and dictionary tableware, but even processing software. In other words, such an ultimate constraint-based system has no particular program module for parsing, generation, problem solving, or anything else. Nor does it have, for instance, any grammar strictly for analysis or strictly for generation. Instead it has only one general constraint solver to deal with all the types of constraints, morphological, syntactic, semantic, and pragmatic, along a variety of processing directions including those of analysis and generation. Such a unification between analysis and generation and across the types of constraints gives us a new extended view of the NLP system and is quite beneficial in many respects. To mention only a few of many engineering aspects, first, it would make the inference mechanism smart. Second, it would also bring about a sophisticated classification and structuring of the behavior of the constraint management system, which can process various sorts of constraints (such as a morphological constraint and a pragmatic constraint) simultaneously.

This ultimate constraint-based system is somewhat beyond the scope of DUALS-III, however, and should be reserved for its successors. The alternative intermediate goal of DUALS-III is to apply the constraint paradigm to semantic and pragmatic processing. This goal is to be reflected in the problem-solving module, which is a general constraint solver rather than a procedural description of

78

誰が考えてみるのですか。	Who should consider?
自然界の生物たちの生活の様子はどうであると言っていますか。	What is said about the lives of creatures in nature?
環境の例として何をとりあげていますか。	What is taken as an example of environment?
動物たちは、なぜ、森に住んでいるのですか。	Why animals live in the forest?

Fig. 7b: Sample Questions for DUALS-III.

how to deal with individual constraints. This problem solver therefore encompasses not only inferences for the comprehension of input sentences, but also inferences for the preparation of the answers to questions. The above ultimate goal is expected to be implemented in the future by extending and improving this problem solver.

Needless to say, to what extent such a constraint-based approach and Situation Semantics could really fit and contribute to practical software construction should become clear only through the experimental development of DUALS-III and the evaluation of its performance. But at any rate, DUALS-III, facing a number of novel problems, is regarded as the real first step of proper scrutiny into discourse understanding. Fig. 8 presents the structure of DUALS-III and component methods employed therein.

3.3 LTB: a General Japanese Processor

LTB consists of a syntactic analyzer, a sentence generator, dictionaries and grammars referred to by them, and a system of CIL, a language for semantic description. LTB is written in CIL and ESP, and runs on PSI-II/SIMPOS.

LTB is a collection of software modules that not only are in charge of syntactic processing for DUALS-III, but also are intended to serve for a wider variety of usage. Many aspects such as the classification of vocabulary and semantic representation, however, do not yet have established methods. Those parts of LTB are being devised, both the linguistic generality and the specific requirements raised by DUALS-III being taken into consideration.

Since the dictionaries and grammars are to be improved and extended iteratively in the course of their development, systems relating to them also include debugging environments. However, the debugging environments of the processing modules of LTB, having been developed separately, are different in the module interfaces and the ways they operate. Besides, they are rather insufficiently documented. Both the standardization of them and the documentation are currently in progress. A unified operative environment called **LTB-Shell** is also being developed, which provides the user with facilities

for combining the processes of LTB modules in a variety of ways. The present structure of LTB is illustrated in Fig. 9.

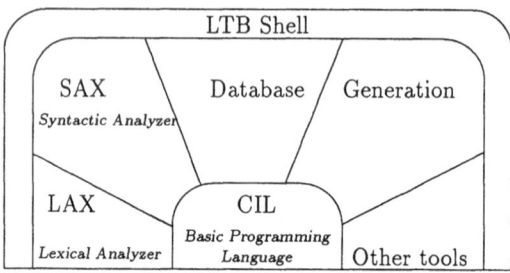

Fig. 9: The Structure of LTB

The major components of LTB are described below.

3.3.1 Dictionary

The dictionary is required to have as wide a coverage of vocabulary as possible, and at the same time to contain deep knowledge. The dictionary in LTB, called the master dictionary, is currently limited to a vocabulary of about 4,000 words, and the emphasis is placed on the description of deep knowledge relating to the sample text that DUALS-III is to work on.

The content of the master dictionary includes syntactic information of words and phrases such as the parts of speech and the types of inflection, and semantic information such as thesaurus codes and semantic constraints. The semantic properties of words are divided into three types. The first type concerns several hundreds of function words, for which the semantic properties are specified in a direct correspondence to the syntactic functions those words perform. The second type concerns those words whose semantic properties are defined in terms of primitive concepts: approximately 2,000 verbs and adjectives of Japanese origin. The words dealt with in the third type of description have their meaning specified in relation to the concepts of the other words.

The master dictionary is to be improved in terms of both the vocabulary and the depth or precision. This extension is planned to be based upon a knowledge-base

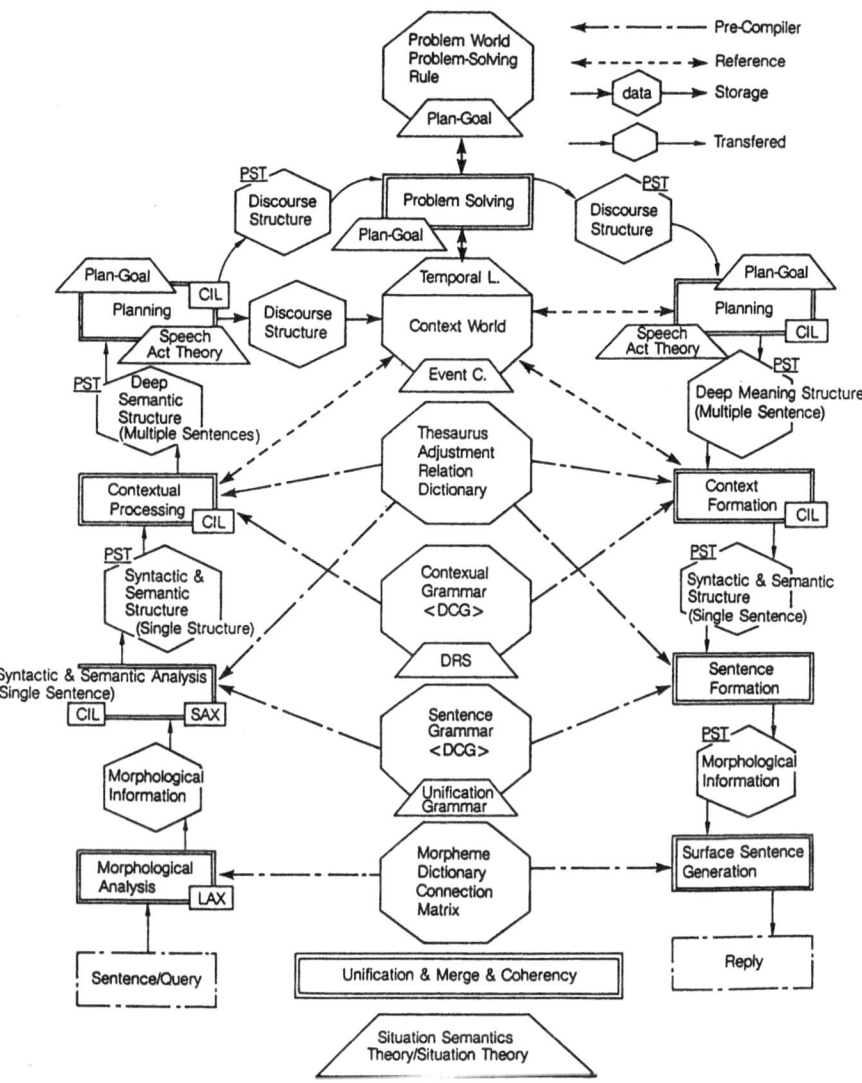

Fig. 8: The Structure of DUALS-III.

management system called Kappa, which is being developed separately from LTB.

3.3.2 Grammar

The morphology grammar is formulated according to Morioka grammar. The purely morphological part of the grammar is described by a regular language, and the semantic part is formulated so that semantic composition should be carried out by unification. The version for analysis includes about 1,000 entries of dependent words, about 3,000 lines of coding in extended DCG plus CIL, and about 1,000 entries, amounting to about 30,000 lines, of independent words. The version for generation is expected to have approximately 4,000 entries.

The syntax grammar is described in DCG, and the corresponding semantic composition is again supposed to be processed by unification. Its version for analysis has about 200 rules and about 1,000 lines of extended DCG program. The version for generation is supposed to include about 100 rules, although the number of rules depends on the format of internal semantic representation.

Obviously, both the analysis version and the generation version of a grammar should preferably be derived from one and the same description, as pointed out earlier. In this respect, a master grammar of morphology is currently being developed that will unify information about part of speech, inflection, connection between words, and so on.

3.3.3 Programming Language

CIL may be considered to be a general-purpose knowledge representation language, because of the special data structure and the lazy evaluation control it provides.

As already described, CIL deals with **partially specified terms (PSTs)** as a basic data structure, and allows successive augmentation of attribute-value pairs in PSTs through unifications. Thanks to this feature, programmers do not have to worry about the positions and the numbers of arguments as they have to in the case of Prolog. PSTs are appropriate for representing parse trees and semantic structures, since they permit recursive occurrences of PSTs as values for attributes.

Another important feature of CIL is a sort of daemon mechanism which invokes the previously specified subprograms upon the instantiation of the variable to which the program was associated. This lazy evaluation mechanism allows declarative description, thus providing a better perspective of programming. It renders debugging much more difficult, however, and debugging functions must hence be enriched accordingly.

CIL is executed after being compiled down to ESP. Speeding up the execution requires some invention. The current system has acquired a practical efficiency, through iterative optimization of the compiler and improvements to the implementation of execution-time routines. This system includes a debugger, and provides the top-level programming interface of LTB.

3.3.4 Morphological and Syntactic Analysis

The module for morphological analysis is called **LAX**. This module consists of a grammar editor to tailor a regular grammar, a transducer which transforms this grammar into an execution form, and an analyzer which executes the analysis based on it. The analyzer looks up a dictionary organized in TRIE structure. The analyzer uses a breadth-first method called the layered stream, to search for the solution. This method is consistent with parallel processing.

The parsing module, which is called **SAX**, consists of a grammar editor to write a grammar in terms of DCG, a transducer to transform this into an execution form, and an analyzer to execute parsing. The DCG format employed here allows CIL programs in extraconditions. As in LAX, the search of the solution exploits the layered stream method.

Both the morphological analysis system and the syntactic analysis system are equipped with their own de-

bugger, which enables easy revision of grammars.

3.3.5 Text Generation

The generation module includes an editor to handle a grammar containing tree-rewriting rules, a transducer of this grammar, a tree-rewriting system, and a morphological processor. Given an intermediate representation of the syntactic structure of a Japanese sentence to be generated, this module produces a surface sentence. Just like the analysis module, the generation module has its own debugger, which makes the grammar easy to revise.

4 Research at Cooperating Manufacturers

As has been mentioned, several groups at the cooperating manufacturers are also conducting related research at the request of ICOT. This research is briefly described below.

4.1 An Intelligent Text-information Retrieval System [21 to 25]

This research aims verify and advance methods for natural language understanding and for inference using the result of understanding texts. For this purpose, an intelligent text-information retrieval system is being developed which will retrieve parts of a text that semantically match against the query. The system accepts a Japanese sentence as a query, and analyzes its semantic structure. Next, it infers a keyword retrieval command on the semantic level to get the passages in the given text which have similar semantic structure to that of the query. Then, the system analyzes the meaning of the retrieved parts of the text, compares them with the meaning of the query, and judges the relatedness between them. Finally, the system shows the retrieved parts of the text in the order of decreasing relatedness. Inference on the semantic level makes it possible to achieve better retrieval than using only the lexical connection such as in a word-thesaurus.

4.2 A Knowledge Representation System for Understanding Discourse and Meaning [26, 27]

This project studies ways to represent and use world knowledge for understanding conversational contexts. The world knowledge is represented in terms of "frames" and "rules." Input sentences are processed by the inference mechanisms. As a specific problem of understanding utterances, that of resolving ambiguities for anaphoric references is being studied.

To understand input sentences, the system extracts candidates for referents of the input expressions from the preceding context, and selects consistent candidates. It then examines their preference by observing causal relations among events in the task domain. The algorithm has been implemented as an experimental system on PSI, with "guidance for VTR operation" as a tentative task.

4.3 A Dialogue Model based on Situation Semantics [28 to 31]

Through the development of a dialogue model, the key technologies to establish man-machine dialogue using natural language (Japanese in this case) are being investigated. They are the utterance recognition and the cooperative response functions, both based on a planning mechanism. A principle in cooperative dialogue has also been studied and tailored into rules. By this strategy, some mechanisms are expected to be designed which will extract meaning from the utterances in a daily conversation (particularly the meaning related to indirect speech acts), and also for cooperative response generation in a dialogue focusing upon the user's final goal.

The current stage is that of software development in CIL on PSI-II. In parallel with this task, modelling of dialogue scenes in connection with the situation semantics is also studied.

4.4 A Task-Oriented Dialogue Understanding System [32 to 34]

This project aims to develop a theory of task-oriented dialog understanding and to design and implement intelligent natural language interface systems. The work focuses on the representation and management of contextual information in discourse and its use for purposes including the following.

- Understanding anaphoric expressions
- Interpreting the semantic contents of user's utterances
- Planning responses to the user
- Controlling and guiding the dialog (including the selection of the topics)

The work has strong connections with Situation Theory. The situation to represent the contextual information about an utterance is called "utterance situation," which contains:

- Who the addressor is
- Sho the adressee is
- What the uttered expression is
- What the situation described by the utterance is
- What the background of the utterance is

A knowledge representation language called **LAST** provides the facilities to represent situations and to make inferences on situations. Another important work is the research on identifying a "user model."

4.5 A Summarization Support System based on World Knowledge [35 to 38]

To realize intelligent communication facilities, context processing and inference based on knowledge are important. This research focuses on a semantic representation model and a summarization support system. The semantic representation model uses an intermediate language to represent contextual information. The summarization support system uses the following four components.

- World knowledge compiled as a thesaurus, a hierarchical structure of frames, is exploited for anaphora resolution.
- The context processing creates frames of contents which embeds the resulting anaphoric relations.
- A contextual structure is constructed out of the relationships among simple sentences.
- The summarizing process applies evaluation rules to the created representations, and abstracts the parts that are regarded as important.

The resultant summary is presented to the user in the form of a text, a summary-table or a picture.

4.6 A Support System for Generating Controlled Japanese Texts [39]

Natural language, Japanese in particular, accompanies a great degree of ambiguity. In order to resolve ambiguities in texts, a prototype system, "A Support System for Generating Controlled Japanese Texts." has been developed.

This system consists of a morphological processing module, a syntactic processing module and a semantic processing module. Each such module presents existing ambiguities to the user in the form of internal representation displayed on a CRT.

Syntactic analysis is based on KAKARIUKE relation, in which sentences are analyzed in terms of relationships between modifiers and heads. One of the KAKARIUKE rules says that a modifier should modify the nearest head.

A unique and the most plausible sentence structure could be generated by exploiting the knowledge-base and user's instructions. The semantic processing module is currently being installed.

5 Final Remarks

We decided to use NLP as a way to create an intelligent interface. In the initial stage of the FGCS project, we intended to integrate NLP with phonetic, visual, and other types of processing. A re-examination of the plan at the beginning of the intermediate stage of the project, however, showed us that this integration was difficult to implement. As for NLP itself, we recognized that there were too many problems to be solved before we could use an NLP system to create a practical interface. The intermediate stage thus restricted itself to research on discourse understanding in Japanese.

The development of a large-scale dictionary was entrusted to Electronic Dictionary Research Laboratory (EDR), which was established at the beginning of the intermediate stage. EDR is thus in charge of the research and development of dictionaries of Japanese, English, technical terms, and so on, consisting of several hundred thousand entries. ICOT decided not to pursue such a wide coverage of vocabulary, but instead to focus on semantic and contextual processing. The contribution of ICOT in the joint research with EDR should be to elucidate the problems the users of the dictionary face. Problems that relate, for example, to the representation schemata and concept classification for building the concept dictionary and thesaurus.

The research on discourse understanding enjoys little heritage of achievements from the foregoing engineering inquiries. For instance, the research on machine translation has not so far regarded discourse as the central subject of study. We were thus obliged to accumulate by ourselves research achievements concerning semantic representation based on Situation Semantics, compilation of dictionaries reflecting linguistic studies on vocabulary classification, systematic software for syntactic processing, and so on. This is how we have come to be ready for a proper study on contextual processing, and how concrete outcomes such as LTB have been brought about.

Starting with a reorganization of DUALS-III, the research of its descendant versions in the final stage will be aimed at establishing more sophisticated methods of processing ellipsis and anaphora, of knowledge representation and problem solving for deeper semantic processing, and particularly of handling verbal communication in terms of speech acts. All of these methods should be accommodated in a declarative format of constraints, rather than procedures. The constraint-based implementation should yield an exponential augmentation of the coverage of DUALS. Besides, the coverage of the system will be augmented by increasing the computational efficiency by means of parallel processing on PIM/PIMOS, a parallel inference machine. Kappa, a knowledge-base management system, might also be employed in order to cope with the greater amount of knowledge accompanying the extension of the grammar, dictionary, and knowledge-base of the domain world.

The software of LTB will also be revised in terms of KL1, a parallel logic programming language, to cope with increasing computational complexity. In order for LTB to handle a greater amount of knowledge, a knowledge-base management system should be used on a PSI machine for the time being. It is planned that LTB should eventually engage a knowledge-base management system to be developed on the parallel inference machine.

Our NLP research is in a sense an integration of all the research about knowledge information processing. It exploits as tools the software and hardware products of the FGCS project, in order to replicate the human linguistic behavior with the greatest possible precision. This research will therefore be a comprehensive benchmark test for the FGCS project.

Acknowledgements

The NLP research in the FGCS project is being conducted jointly by many researchers at ICOT, the cooperating manufacturers, and universities, among others. Thanks are firstly due to those who have given support and helpful comments, including Dr. Fuchi, the director of the research laboratories at ICOT, Mr. Yokoi, the former chief of the second research laboratory at ICOT and the current director of EDR, Prof. Tanaka at Tokyo Institute of Technology, who is also the chairman of the natural language working group at ICOT, and Mr. Takizuka, a former researcher at the second research laboratory at ICOT and presently a researcher at KDD Kamifukuoka R&D Laboratories. Special thanks go to many people at the cooperating manufacturers in charge of the joint research works: Dr. Amano and Mr. Ukita at Toshiba Co., Mr. Sugiyama and Mr. Akiyama at Fujitsu Limited, Mr. Dazai and Mr. Kondoh at Mitsubishi Electric Co., Mr. Komorida and Mr. Yasukawa at Matusita Electric Industrial Co., Mr. Obuchi and Mr. Miyoshi at Sharp Co., and others.

References

[1] Yokoi, T., Mukai, K., Miyoshi, H., and Tanaka, Y. "Research Activities on Natural Language Processing of the FGCS," *Proc. of FJCC'86*, 1986.

[2] Kimura, K., Sugimura, R., Takizuka, T. and Mukai, K. "Danwa Rikai Jikken System DUALS dai 2-han no Sekkei to Jissou (Design and Implementation of Discourse Understanding System DUALS-V2 *in Japanese*), *Proc. of the 3rd National Conference of Japan Society for Software Science and Technology*, pp.33-36, Tokyo, 1986

[3] Matsumoto, Y. and Sugimura, R. "A parsing system based on Logic Programming," *Proc. of the 10th IJCAI*, 1987.

[4] Mukai, K. and Yasukawa, H. "Complex Indeterminates in Prolog and their Application to Discourse Models," *New Generation Computing, 3*, OHMUSHA, Ltd. and Spring Verlag, 1985.

[5] Mukai, K. "A system of Logic Programming for Linguistic Analysis Based on Situation Semantics," *Proc. of the Workshop on Semantic Issues in Human and Computer Languages.*, CSLI, 1987.

[6] Mukai, K. " Partially Specified Term in Logic Programming for Linguistic Analysis," *Proc. of FGCS'88*, 1988.

[7] Okunishi, T., Sugimura, R., Matsumoto, Y., Tamura, N., Kamiwaki, T., and Tanaka, H. "Comparison of Logic Programming Based Natural Language Parsing Systems," *Natural Language Understanding and Logic Programming, II*, Dahl, V. (ed.), North-Holland, pp. 1-14, 1988.

[8] Sugimura, R. "Japanese Honorifics and Situation Semantics," *Proc. of the 11th COLING*, pp. 507-510, 1986.

[9] Sugimura, R., Miyoshi, H., and Mukai, K. "Constraint Analysis on Japanese Modifying Relations", *Natural Language Understanding and Logic Programming,II*, North-Holland, pp. 93-106, 1988.

[10] Hasida, K. "Dependency Propagation: A Unified Theory of Sentence Comprehension and Generation," *Proc. of the 10th IJCAI*, pp. 664-670, 1987

[11] Hasida, K. "Izondenpa (Dependency Propagation, *in Japanese*)," *Proc. of the 29th Programming Symposium*, pp. 147-158, 1988.

[12] Sakai, K. and Sato, Y. "Boolean Gröbner Bases," *ICOT Technical Memo No.488*, 1988.

[13] Yamasaki, S., Sugimura, R., Akasaka, K., and Matsumoto, Y. "Koubun Kaiseki System SAX no Debug Kankyou (Debugging environment of SAX system, *in Japanese*)," *Proc. of the 2nd Annual Conference of Japanese Society for Artificial Intelligence*, pp. 411-414, 1988.

[14] Sugimura, R., Akasaka, K., Kubo, Y., Sano, H., and Matsumoto, Y. "Ronri-gata Keitaiso Kaiseki LAX (Logic Based Lexical Analyzer LAX, *in Japanese*),"

Proc. of the Logic Programming Conference '88, ICOT, pp. 213-222, 1988. (English version will appear in *The Lecture Notes on Computer Science*.)

[15] Ikeda, T. et. al, "Sentence Generation in LTB (*in Japanese*)," *Proc. of the 5th National Conference of Japan Society for Software Science and Technology*, 1988.

[16] Tanaka, Y. and Yoshioka, T. "Overview of the development of dictionary and Lexical Database," *Proc. of FGCS'88*, ICOT, 1988.

[17] Takizuka, T. and Sugimura, R. "LTB Shell no Kousei (Configuration of LTB Shell *in Japanese*)," *Proc. of the 37th National Conference of Information Processing Society of Japan*, pp. 1074-1075, 1988.

[18] Uchida, S. (ed.) *ESP Guide*, ICOT TM-338, Aug. 1987.

[19] Uchida, S. "Inference Machines in FGCS Project," *Proc. of International Conference IFIP TC-10, VLSI'87*, Aug. 1987, also ICOT TR-278.

[20] Yokota, K. Kawamura, M., and Kanaegami, A., "Overview of the Knowledge Base Management System KAPPA," *Proc. of FGCS'88*, ICOT, 1988.

[21] Sugiyama, K., Akiyama, K., Ibuki, K., Kawasaki, M. "IRIS: An Intelligent Information Retrieval System based on Natural Language Understanding" (in Japanese), *IPS Research Report of Natural Language Research Group*, Information Processing Society of Japan, Nov. 1986.

[22] Akiyama, K., Sugiyama, K., Itoh, H. and Onodera, H. "Initial study on transportability of IRIS (An intelligent information retrieval system)" (in Japanese), *Proc. of the 35th National Conference of Information Processing Society of Japan*, pp. 1429-1430, Sep. 1987.

[23] Ibuki, J., Sugiyama, K., Tamada, I. and Kawasaki, M. "Natural Language for Content Retrieval" (in Japanese), *Proc. of the 4th National Conference of Japan Society for Software Science and Technology*, pp. 347-350, 1987.

[24] Kiyama, K. "The Issue of Intelligent Information Retrieval to Textbase," (in Japanese), *IPS Research Report of Database Systems Research Group*, Information Processing Society of Japan, Mar. 1988.

[25] Akiyama, K. "Generation Method Keyword Retrieval Commands in IRIS" (in Japanese), *Proc. of the 37th National Conference of Information Processing Society of Japan*, Sep. 1988.

[26] Kinoshita, Sano, Ukita, Sumita, and Amano "Knowledge Representation and Reasoning for Discourse Understanding," *Proc. of the Logic Programming Conference 1988*, pp. 205-212.

[27] Ukita, Sumita, Kinoshita, Sano, and Amano "Preference Judgement in Comprehending Conversational Sentences with Multi-Paradigm World Knowledge," *Proc. of the FGCS'88*, 1988.

[28] Shimada, H., Kondoh, S., Dazai, T. "A Dialogue Mechanism in IDS (Intelligent Dialogue System)" (in Japanese), The Institute of Electronics Information and Communication Engineers, 1986.

[29] Kondoh, S., Shimada, H., and Dazai, T. "Planning Mechanism based on Dialogue Model (in Japanese)," *Proc. of the 33th National Conference of Information Processing Society of Japan*, pp. 1207-1208, 1986.

[30] Kondoh, S., Imamura, M. "Cooperative Responses based on Dialogue Model" (in Japanese), Information Processing Society of Japan, 1988.

[31] Imamura, M., Kondoh, S., Dazai, T. "A Dialogue Model based on Means-Ends Analysis" (in Japanese), *Proc. of the 36th National Conference of Information Processing Society of Japan*, pp. 1201-1202, 1988.

[32] Motoike, S., Noguchi, N., Yasukawa, H. "The Use of Circumstantial Information in a Task-Oriented Dialogue" (in Japanese), *Proc. of the 5th National Conference of Japan Society for Software Science and Technology*, 1988.

[33] Noguchi, N., Takahashi, M., Yasukawa, H. "Generating Natural Language Responses Appropriate to Conversational Situations — In the Case of Japanese," in Furukawa, K. et al. (Eds.) *Logic Programming '87: Proceedings of the 6th Conference (LNCS Vol. 315)*, Springer Verlag, 1988.

[34] Yasukawa, H., Suzuki, H., Noguchi, N. "Knowledge Representation Language based on Situation Theory," *Proceedings of France-Japan Artificial Intelligence and Computer Science*.

[35] Kita, Komatu, Yasuhara "Summarization support system COGITO" (in Japanese), *IPS Research Report of Natural Language Group*, Information Processing Society of Japan, 1986.

[36] Komatu, Katoh, Yasuhara, Shiino "Summarization support system COGITO — Structural analysis of text" (in Japanese), *IPS Research Report of Natural Language Group*, Information Processing Society of Japan, 1987.

[37] Komatu, Katoh, Yasuhara, Shiino "Summarization Support System COGITO — Summarizing Module" (in Japanese), *Proc. of the 36th National Conference of Information Processing Society of Japan*, 1988.

[38] Katoh, Komatu, Yasuhara, Shiino "Summarization Support System COGITO — Man-machine Interface module" (in Japanese), *Proc. of the 36th National Conference of Information Processing Society of Japan*, 1988.

[39] Obuchi, Y., Hamada, A., Miyoshi, H., and Akiyama, H. "Standardizing Japanese Grammar and its Support System" (in Japanese), *Proceedings of the 36th National Conference of Information Processing Society of Japan*, 1988

PROCEEDINGS OF THE INTERNATIONAL CONFERENCE
ON FIFTH GENERATION COMPUTER SYSTEMS 1988,
edited by ICOT. © ICOT, 1988

EXPERIMENTAL KNOWLEDGE PROCESSING SYSTEM

Yuichi Fujii, Hirokazu Taki and
other researchers of the Fifth Research Laboratory

ICOT Research Center, Institute for New Generation Computer Technology

1-4-28, Mita, Minato-ku, Tokyo 108, Japan

ABSTRACT

This paper describes the research activities of the fifth research laboratory at ICOT. In order to verify ICOT developments such as the PSI and PIM, we are developing next generation expert tool technologies for real application systems on them. We selected the following technologies as basic elements of the new generation expert tools: hypothetical reasoning, knowledge acquisition, constraint problem solving, object modeling, qualitative reasoning, and distributed cooperative problem solving. This paper discusses these technologies and some experimental expert systems.

1 INTRODUCTION

Experimental knowledge processing systems are an objective of research and development started in the first year of the intermediate stage of the FGCS project. The primary motives are to probe and verify hierarchical interfaces between application systems and ICOT development such as the PIM and PIMOS. To develop knowledge system building technologies, we have been researching expert systems as application systems. During the first half of the intermediate stage, we studied and surveyed next-generation tools and knowledge acquisition support and developed a prototype tool, called PROTON. During the second half of the intermediate stage, we are striving to develop element technologies based on the surveys. We also organized academic and industrial experts into working group and subgroups to join our surveys and discussions. To verify element technologies, we developed experimental expert systems for a number of applications, for example, VLSI logic design and machinery design.

2 NEXT-GENERATION TOOLS

Conventional tools for building an expert system have a prominent feature: rapid prototyping. Although such tools are effective for some applications, they are not suitable for building large-scale application systems because a building methodology has not been established. An ideal expert system ought to provide a vocabulary matching the scope of its tasks. Conventional tools, based mainly on rule of thumb, provide only an inference engine common to knowledge representations such as rules and frames, and thus require uniformity of tasks. Under this constraint of the tools, users must state their problems. This may make the building of complicated large-scale application systems difficult. To help build knowledge systems, next-generation tools ought to be organized into problem solving frameworks matching an application domain. In other words, we think that a next-generation expert system will be realized by a set of generic tasks [Chandrasekaran 86] or a set of building blocks. From the perspective of problem solving frameworks, the research and development trend of expert systems is shifting from analytical to synthetic problems. Analytical problems infer the characteristics of a whole system from a given system structure and subsystem characteristics. Diagnostic and control problems are typical examples of this type of problem. Synthetic problems showever involve the determination of the system structure and subsystem features which would result in a set of system characteristics. Examples of synthetic problems are design and planning problems [Kobayashi 86]. Synthetic problems are basically combinatorial problems. The number of solutions in a synthetic problem may be infinite. That is, the problem may result in combinatorial explosion. In order to avoid combinational explosion, next-generation tools are expected to incorporate technologies for intelligent inference control.

Taking these trends into account, we are now researching the following five technological elements.

(1) Tool architecture for design tasks
    (Constraint-based problem solving and object modeling)
(2) Hypothetical reasoning
(3) Distributed cooperative problem solving
(4) Utilization of deep knowledge and qualitative reasoning
(5) Knowledge acquisition support system

3 TOOL ARCHITECTURE FOR DESIGN TASKS

As already explained, existing expert systems are broadly classified into systems for analytical problems and systems for synthetic problems. Analytical problems are, like diagnostic problems, regarded as problems of selecting hypotheses in a limited solution space, because a set of hypothetical solutions and a set of rules for selecting hypotheses can be predetermined. Synthetic problems, however, need efficient problem solving, since solution spaces are so large that fabricating candidate solutions as hypotheses beforehand is difficult. Design problems are typical examples of synthetic problems. The development of a design expert system requires a large amount of knowledge that depends on a design object. Representation of the design knowledge and a problem solving mechanism are important for research on a design expert system. Our objectives are to clarify the architecture of design expert systems and to develop tools for building them.

3.1 Required Functions

Different groups of designers use different kinds of standard such as design methods, parts, and component units. Thus, building tools, enabling designers to build and maintain expert systems by themselves, are required. This section overviews the design knowledge representation and the problem solving mechanism in the tools needed to satisfy this requirment.

3.1.1 Knowledge Representation

To realize a design expert system building tool, knowledge representation requires two facilities: one is that knowledge must be represented suitably for the tool, and the other is that designers must be able to represent them easily. Design knowledge is broadly classified into knowledge about design objects themselves and knowledge about problem solving. Knowledge about design objects consists of the structures, shapes, and attributes of the design objects. A set of items of knowledge about a design object is called an object model. Knowledge about problem solving, however, is composed of methods to analyze object models, to evaluate and modify solutions, and plans to design the object and search from candidate solutions. According to the above classification, a design process can be regarded as a design requirement satisfaction process [Tomiyama 85, Ohsuga 85]; operations such as selection, modification and refinement with knowledge about problem solving are repeatedly applied to an object model. Furthermore, to enable designers to build an expert system by themselves, an environment is required where a design expert system can be built only by declaratively representing an object model and knowledge about problem solving. To realize the environment, we propose a building tool that generates a design plan from separate inputs of an object model and knowledge about problem solving, and that provides an interface between design knowledge and the problem solver. We used a constraint analyzer, similer to knowledge compiler [Araya 87] and constraint compiler [Feldman 88], to obtain these tool facilities.

3.1.2 Problem Solver

If a design plan is given explicitly, a design problem can be solved according to it. There are often cases where a design plan cannot given explicitly, but only constraints can be given. An effective way of solving these cases is to employ constraint problem solving, regarding a design process as a constraint satisfaction process. In addition to this, the whole of a design process can be captured from the single concept of a constraint satisfaction process; an object model represents constraints on the structures of the design objects, and design requirements and knowledge about problem solving also represent constraints. These constraints are given priorities and changed dynamically according to the designer's intention and preference, and to trade off between performance, due dates and cost. Therefore, a constraint solver suitable for a design problem is required.

3.2 Object Model

3.2.1 Object Model in Design Problems

Design objects in design systems are represented in the form of model descriptions. A design object model represents information and knowledge about design objects, such as their attributes, shapes, and structures. During a design process, a model that satisfies requirements is constructed; it represents a solution.

Models used in conventional design systems consist of data structures that are merely static. They need to be interpreted and manipulated in terms of design tasks or procedures. Only knowledge about design methods is important. Knowledge about design objects is embedded in model manipulation procedures or design methods. In conventional design systems, it is difficult to make effective use of the knowledge about design objects. Also, high performance design and the establishment of a general methodology by which to build design expert systems will be hindered because knowledge about design object and knowledge about problem solving are not distinguished between.

Thus, to solve design problems effectively, it is important to represent the knowledge about design objects as object models and to put those models to practical use in the design process.

3.2.2 Use of the Object Model

A frame system has been used to represent structures and attributes of objects in knowledge systems. Recently, an object oriented paradigm whose concept is similar to the frame system has been generally used and also applied to design problems. Although conventional object oriented languages are suitable for representing structures, attributes and behavior, they do not provide facilities for representing or using constraints on design objects. Therefore, introducing constraints to an object oriented paradigm provides efficient formalism for knowledge representation in terms of declarative description. In representation of a design object, however, functions are required that can describe and use not only constraints on numerical attributes (instance variables), but also constraints on the structures. We are examining two ways of using design object models. One is to generate a design plan by analyzing and compiling knowledge about the design object and about problem solving [Nagai 88a]. It is suitable for parametric design. The second way is to provide a system for supporting the design process interpreting knowledge described on object models. This system makes it possible to construct not only models that satisfy the constraints, but also support their effective construction. This second way is suitable for a problem in which the structure of the design object is not given or is not fixed. In such a case, the problem must be solved by trial and error or by interaction with users. This system is briefly explained in the next section.

3.2.3 Design Object Representation System

Currently, a knowledge representation system for design object modeling, FREEDOM [Yokoyama 88], is being developed. To support design tasks, FREEDOM provides the facilities that keep the status of the model for constraint satisfaction by interpreting constraints that are described in the object model and are dynamically added during the design process. Knowledge representation provided in the FREEDOM system, based on the object oriented paradigm, makes it possible to describe constraints about attribute values and structures. The attributes of the design object model are represented numerically or symbolically, and their values can be obtained by solving constraints derived from them. In conventional object oriented systems, the relation between a class and an instance is a static one, whereas·in FREEDOM, the search for a

class that satisfies design requirements is realized using a constraint satisfaction mechanism. Thus, when a structure or an attribute of an instance is modified, if constraint satisfaction cannot be executed in the class to which it belongs, the class may be changed automatically to another class to satisfy the constraints. In this way, it is possible to search for a class that satisfies design requirements not by describing the search procedure explicitly, but by using constraints about the design object. As described above, FREEDOM provides facilities for supporting design processes by using constraints described in the object model, and helps to build advanced design expert systems.

3.3 Design Plan Generation Using a Constraint Analyzer

This section first describes representation of design knowledge about problem solving. Second, design plan generation using a constraint analyzer that enables desiners themselves to build design expert systems is described.

3.3.1 Knowledge about Problem Solving

Knowledge about problem solving consists of methods to analyze object models, to evaluate and modify solutions, and plans to design the object and search from candidate solutions. The characteristics of design knowledge about problem solving are various representation types: there is knowledge, such as design formulas, where solving procedures are represented explicitly, and knowledge, such as that expressed by inequalities, where solving procedures are not represented explicitly. In

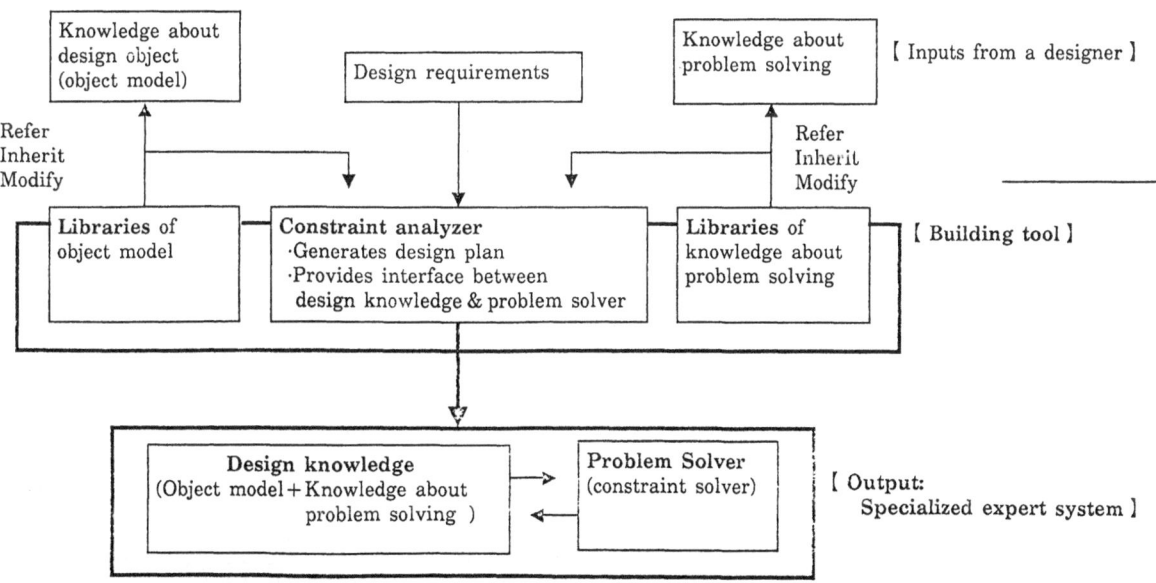

Fig. 3.1 Architecture for an expert system building tool

addition, knowledge that is independent of a design object and heuristics that is closely dependent on a certain design object are mixed. For example, design formulas and searching from catalogues in design knowledge about problem solving, and basic parts and function units in object models are independent of a design object. Therefore, with the aim of enabling designers to represent this knowledge easily, we employed an approach where those independent kinds of knowledge are prepared as system libraries; we prepared sets of design formulas and catalogues in knowledge about problem solving, and sets of basic parts and function units in object models. These types of knowledge must be expressed in a form that designers can easily refer to and modify. Consequently, designers' heuristics can be expressed explicitly, by referring to or by inheriting and modifying libraries.

3.3.2 Design Plan Generation Using a Constraint Analyzer

A constraint analyzer can handle various types of knowledge and can specialize knowledge by combining knowledge independent of a certain design object and designers' heuristics which depend on a certain design object. Since the constraint analyzer can generate a design plan by analyzing dependencies among constraints, design knowledge can be also represent declaratively. Inputs to the tool are design requirements, object models, and knowledge about problem solving. They are given by specifying system libraries, or by modifying libraries with referring or inheriting libraries. Reference to results of previous design and designers' heuristics about searching from alternatives are also represented as knowledge about problem solving. From these inputs, the tool analyzes dependencies among constraints and parameters, generates a design plan, and provides an interface between the design knowledge and the constraint solver. The output from the tool is a specialized expert system including designers' heuristics. Therefore, a flexible environment in which build an expert system can be built by designers themselves is obtained by dividing design knowledge into object models and knowledge about problem solving, and by employing design plan generation using a constraint analyzer.

3.4 Constraints in Design Problems

The structural information derived from the object model is constraints expressed explicitly. In addition, design knowledge such as methods to analyze object models and design requirements such as cost performance are also regarded as constraints, from the single view of the constraint concept. However, not many of the existing tools that support the construction of expert systems provide an environment that makes it easy to express the constraint concept explicitly; the person constructing the system must use the language depending on the tool to realize mechanisms for applying constraint representations which depend on the design object. This section discusses the characteristics of constraints in design problems [Nagai 88b].

(1) Static and dynamic constraints
Many existing constraint solvers consider constraints as static entities. In design problems, however, not all constraints are given in the initial stages of a design process; many are added or deleted during the design process. Furthermore, there are suggestive constraints as described below; constraints are dynamically changed in design problems.

(2) Obligatory and suggestive constraints
Not all the constraints are selected and executed on an equal basis in design problems. In other words, priorities are assigned to constraints, and the priorities are based on design requirements and designers' intentions. All obligatory constraints must be satisfied, and these are generally given explicitly. Suggestive constraints, however, are used as guides in choosing the optimum branch at a node in the search tree, and they are given lower priorities than obligatory constraints. Thus, if an obligatory constraint cannot be satisfied, suggestive constraints may be changed so that the obligatory constraints are satisfied.

(3) Local and global constraints
Many design problems are divided into subproblems when an attempt is made to solve the problems. Thus, it is necessary to distinguish whether the applicable scope of a constraint closes locally within a subproblem or is globally related to other subproblems. In addition, interactions among local constraints within a subproblem and interactions between local and global constraints must be considered.

(4) Propagation of values and interval bounds
Some constraints in design problems are represented by inequalities. Therefore, not only do constraints propagate values, they also propagate over interval bounds in which variables that can take certain values must be considered.

When considering practical design problems, one constraint may belong to multiple types of these characteristics.

3.5 Architecture of the Building Tool

As stated above, we divide design knowledge into object models and knowledge about problem solving. This enables us to maintain knowledge and to modify knowledge flexibly. Viewing knowledge and requirements as constraints, constraint based problem solving is employed. To help designers to build an expert system suitable for a design problem, we propose a building tool that regards inputs of design knowledge as constraints, generates design plans by analyzing their dependencies, and provides an interface between design knowledge and a constraint solver. We used a constraint analyzer to obtain facilities for this building tool. The expert system which is the output of the tool can efficiently obtain solutions that satisfy the design requirements, according to the design plan generated by the tool. Fig. 3.1 shows the architecture of the building tool. An expert system building tool, MECHANICOT [Terasaki 88], is being developed now. MECHANICOT is a tool for a mechanical parametric design. It analyzes dependencies between structures of a design object and parameters, produces a design plan, and builds a specialized design expert system.

4 HYPOTHETICAL REASONING

4.1 Problem Solving with Hypothetical Reasoning [Inoue 88c]

Hypothetical reasoning [Inoue, ed. 88] is a type of inference which is desirable to have when dealing with alternatives among knowledge, or incomplete knowledge (knowledge that may not always be true) in problem solving. It assumes that unclear or insufficient knowledge is true (establishes hypotheses), and attempts to have the inference proceed based on the hypotheses. Because the hypotheses and formulas derived from the knowledge and hypotheses are not guaranteed to be true, it is necessary to check consistency through constraints or other means. If a contradiction occurs in the reasoning process, we must remove the original hypotheses and select other ones instead. For this reason, hypothetical reasoning can be interpreted as a kind of *non-monotonic reasoning*, and belief revision technology is required. Hypothetical reasoning is in fact inference as practiced by humans, and is one key to implementing advanced inference mechanisms such as commonsense reasoning and learning. Conventional research into hypothetical reasoning, however, has concentrated on establishing the basic inferential mechanisms, and there has been little work done *from the viewpoint of application* in problem solving. This section discusses a prototype system called APRICOT/0 of the APRICOT project [Inoue 88c] as a basic software tool for next-generation knowledge-based systems.

A variety of frameworks for handling hypotheses and incomplete knowledge has been proposed [Doyle 79, de Kleer 86a, Poole 88, Reiter 80], but from the viewpoint of application, they have been faced with major problems in that (1) there has been no integrated handling of the generation, selection, and verification of hypotheses, and (2) architecture has not taken problem solving into account. As the basic standpoint for the construction of APRICOT, we stressed the following two points :

(1) By using domain-dependent knowledge, especially deep knowledge (such as structure and function knowledge), commonsense knowledge (knowledge of physical laws, etc.) and constraints, APRICOT will automatically generate and enumerate hypotheses. It will be more intelligent than the conventional approach stressing heuristic rules.

(2) Positioning the inferential control mechanism between the hypothetical reasoning mechanism

and a domain-dependent problem solver will enhance efficiency [Inoue 88a].

There are two points to be considered in the use of hypotheses. The first is a dependency of what knowledge is established on the basis of what hypotheses. *Truth maintenance systems* (TMSs) manage dynamically contradiction-free characteristics in a database (working memory) including the hypotheses, and have been proposed by [Doyle 79] and in the *assumption-based TMS (ATMS)* [de Kleer 86a]. The second is called *abductive reasoning*, where hypotheses that do not contradict the database explaining the observed events are selected. A hypothetical reasoning system of this type has been proposed in [Poole 88]. Both have in common management of *consistency*, however, and can be unified model-thoretically [Inoue 88b]. In other words, the former maintains the contradiction-free style of the database from the input hypotheses, and the latter determines goal hypotheses from the input observations.

APRICOT provides a basic framework for using hypothetical reasoning in problem solving, but as the problem solver is dependent on the problem domain, only one of the above approaches may be stressed, depending on the problem domain. For example, the inferential strategies for *diagnosis* and *constraint satisfaction* would be as outlined below.

4.1.1 Problem Solver for Diagnosis

If components are assumed to be working correctly, and predictions from those assumptions are inconsistent with behavioral observations, the conflict set (the set of disjunctions of negated literals of assumptions) are determined, and possible combinations of faulty components can be calculated theoretically by converting the conjunctive normal form (conflict set) into the disjunctive normal form. This means that it is sufficient to find a consistent set of assumptions that explain the observations and goals through backward reasoning.

4.1.2 Problem Solver for Constraint Satisfaction

Assumptions are regarded as assignments of values to some variables, and so when results derived from them through forward reasoning are inconsistent with the specifications, the combinations of assumptions that support the observations or their negations are determined. In planning, a set of parameter values satisfying various kinds of constraints is collected as a context. In design, multiple design models are maintained, structured with hierarchical contexts so that the upper layers are the design model assumptions and the lower layers the parameter assumptions.

4.2 Hypothetical Reasoning System APRICOT/0

The APRICOT/0 system for hypothetical reasoning consists of the ATMS [de Kleer 86a], which maintains consistency based on combinations of assumptions (called *environments*), and a rule-based problem solver. APRICOT/0 is implemented in ESP [Iijima & Inoue 88, Fujiwara & Inoue 88].

APRICOT/0 treats the ATMS and a rule-based problem solver called the assumption-based

90

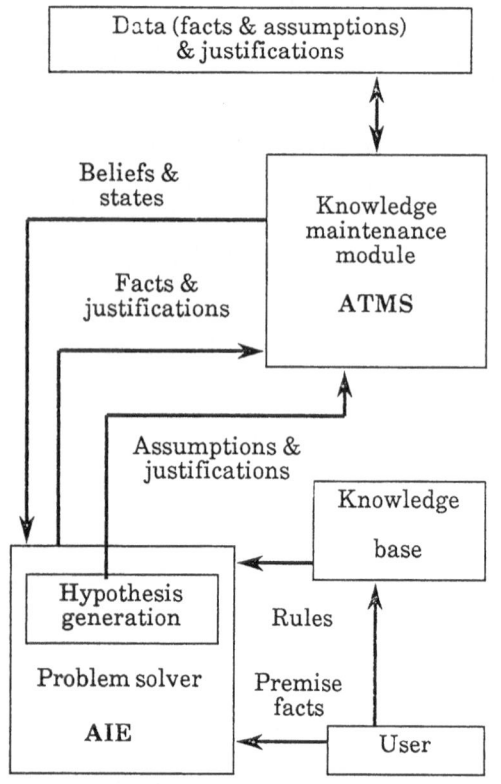

Data (facts & assumptions)
& justifications

Beliefs &
states

Knowledge
maintenance
module

ATMS

Facts &
justifications

Assumptions &
justifications

Knowledge
base

Hypothesis
generation

Problem solver

AIE

Rules

Premise
facts

User

Fig 4.1 Configuration of APRICOT/0

inference engine (AIE) as independent modules. As shown in Fig. 4.1, AIE provides the ATMS with *data* (*facts* and *assumptions*) and their *justifications*, and the ATMS efficiently determines all *contexts* (sets of all data which hold in each consistent environment). AIE proceeds with inferential processing while checking whether the ATMS data holds in some contexts.

In multiple worlds of the ATMS, each time a new fact is inserted it causes other events such as the addition of a justification and the occurrence of a contradiction. To express these activities accurately, APRICOT/0 expresses components such as assumptions, justifications and contradictions as ESP objects. Attribute information for each is contained in the object slot, and the truth maintenance algorithm is implemented through inter-object message passing.

AIE is the actual problem solving mechanism, operating within the hypothetical reasoning system to link the user-input premise facts and rules from the knowledge base with the belief states from the ATMS. To avoid firing unnecessary rules and generate only the minimum essential number of justifications, an inference control mechanism

similar to the Rete algorithm is used. The ESP unification function is used in matching assumptions and facts to rule conditions. A *rule* consists of the *condition* part, which is matched with obtained facts and assumptions taking all contexts into account, and the *action* part, which provides additional facts and assumptions, and their justifications to the ATMS. Each condition of the condition part is an ESP predicate, variable or atom, whose valuation is true if the ATMS node corresponding to the object fact or assumption is believed (called *IN*), that is, the ATMS node holds in some environments, or, a method call or ESP built-in, whose valuation is true if its ESP execution, such as a numerical calculation, succeeds. If all conditions of the condition part are true, a justification of the form : <condition part> ⇒ <action part> is passed to the ATMS. Rules without an action part indicate that they generate contradictions if they are executed, and they will be executed with maximum priority within the same environment in action part queue scheduling. Several AIE rule examples are given below.

Example 4.1

1) `rule91:: temperature (X,Y), {Y>=25} -> cooler_ON (X).`
   %If the temperature Y of room X is 25° or higher, turn on cooler X.

2) `birdfly:: bird(A) -> assume(fly(A)).`
   %If A is a bird, assume it can fly.

3) `contradiction:: not(X), X -> [].`
   %If both affirmative and negative of X exist at the same time, it is contradictory.

4.3 Knowledge Compiling on APRICOT/0

As discussed in 4.1, the basic concept of APRICOT is to utilize various kinds of knowledge, including incomplete knowledge, linked together functionally, to solve problems effectively. Model knowledge expressing principles (called deep knowledge) is combined with constraints and heuristics to generate powerful knowledge that is directly helpful in the domain task; this is called *knowledge compiling*. While the problem solver of APRICOT/0, namely, AIE, is a rule engine and handles AIE rules only, APRICOT/0 can simulate the function implementation of knowledge compiling, only if all knowledge such as default knowledge, logical inference rules and constraints are converted into AIE rules, and are passed through a sophisticated scheduler.

4.3.1 Dynamic Hypothesis Generation and Default Reasoning

When humans solve problems, they perform inference as establishing a succession of assumptions depending on their circumstances. In this process, all possible hypotheses are not listed beforehand; rather, hypotheses can be generated or deleted as required. To implement this process, in APRICOT/0, a function is provided that *dynamically* introduces hypotheses.

Use of this function allows *default rules* to be represented that produce results as long as no evidence contradicts them. For example, a normal default "a(x) : Mb(x)/b(x)" [Reiter 80] can be expressed as an AIE rule "a(x) -> assume(b(x))". Internally, an assumption $\Gamma_{b(\lambda)}$ (λ is a ground term) is introduced, and $b(\lambda)$ is expressed as an assumed node supported by $\Gamma_{b(\lambda)}$. The justification "$a(\lambda) \wedge \Gamma_{b(\lambda)} \Rightarrow b(\lambda)$" [de Kleer 86b] is passed to the ATMS. This allows inference to proceed using $\Gamma_{b(\lambda)}$ as a default assumption.

Example 4.2

When Tom Sawyer met Huckleberry Finn, who watched movies on a weekday, he wondered if Huck was a delinquent. He then remembered that Huck's friend (himself) was not that type of person, and thought that therefore Huck could not be, and denied the belief that "that day was a school day". (See Fig. 4.2)

```
rule1:: not(X), X ->[]. %Logical contradiction.

rule2:: day(weekday) ->
          assume(not(close(school)))).
          %Typically, go to school, school not closed
          on weekdays.

rule3:: not(close(school)), see(X,movie)
          -> go_slow(X,school).
          %School not closed, so people watching
          movies are skipping school.
```

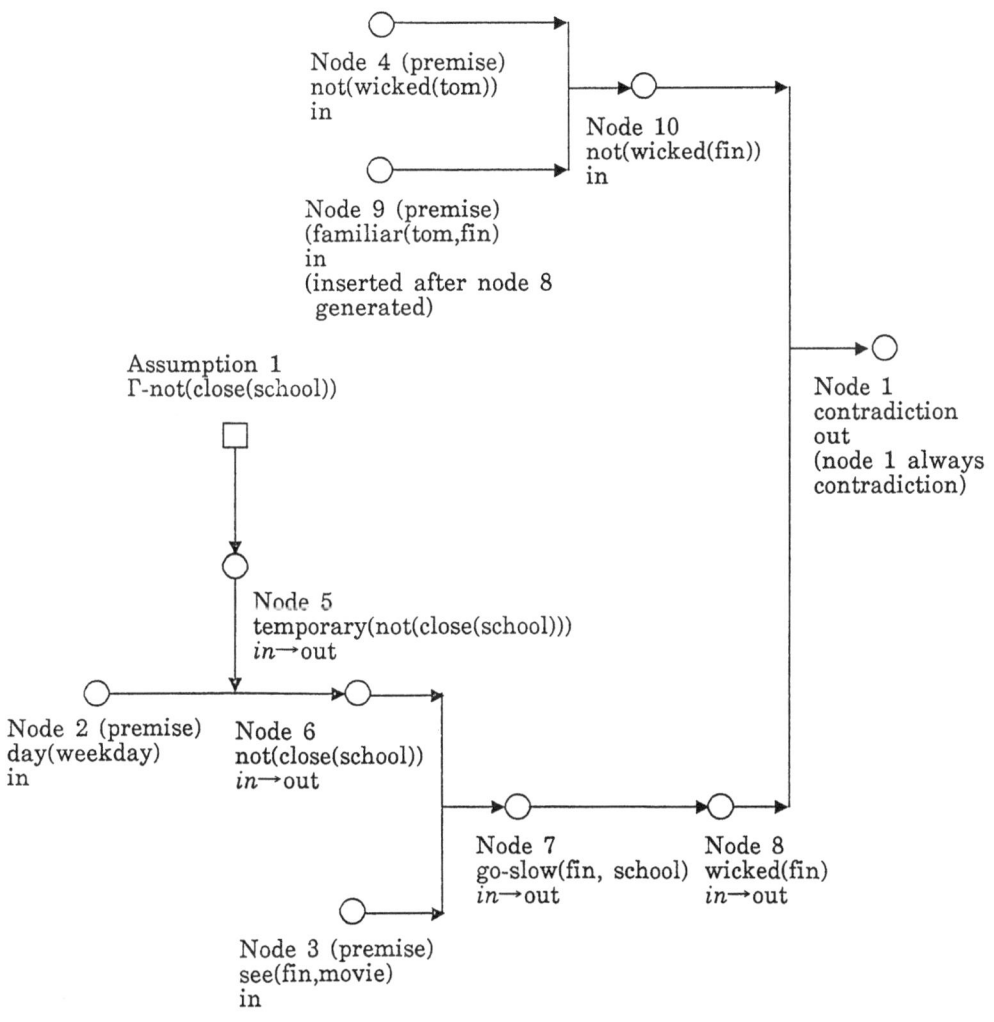

Fig. 4.2 Huckleberry Finn justification network

```
rule4:: go_slow(X,school) -> wicked(X).
        %People skipping school are juvenile
        delinquents.

rule5:: familiar(Man1,Man2),not(
        wicked(Man1))->not(wicked(Man2)).
        %Man not a delinquent, so his friend not a
        delinquent.
```

4.3.2 Inference Rules for Natural Deduction

Production rules, with which inference is executed through Modus Ponens, have been conventionally used in heuristic rule description. With this framework alone, handling more logical structures such as circuits leads to a situation where logical completeness cannot be assured. If logical inference rule descriptions are expressed by the AIE rules, it becomes possible to describe And Elimination, Or Elimination, Modus Tollens, and so on.

4.3.3 Handling Constraints

One of the uses of the ATMS in constraint-based problem solving is *constraint satisfaction*, where solutions satisfy the set of all constraints. This regards assignments of values to variables as assumptions, and determines consistent sets of assumptions that do not violate the constraints to make them solutions. A solver equipped with an assumption generator and a constraint checker can allow the ATMS functions to obtain all solutions. This type of assumption-based problem solving can be applied to combinatorial problems and design problems [Inoue 88].

If some mechanism of *constraint propagation* can be incorporated organically, problem solving becomes even more flexible. The interface between the ATMS and a problem solver handling constraints has been proposed in the form of the *consumer architecture* (CA) [de Kleer 86c] incorporating the data-flow mechanism. In this concept, consumers are unit problem solving steps attached to the corresponding ATMS nodes through an analysis of the set of constraints (called *precompiling*). The consumer generation procedure (precompiling) is as follows. First, consumers are shaped through the data-flow analysis of the set of constraints (input by the user as relational expressions among variables) based on heuristics related to the usage of constraints. Then, the action parts are attached to the ATMS nodes related to each condition part. The consumer execution procedure is as follows. When the ATMS node becomes IN during the inference

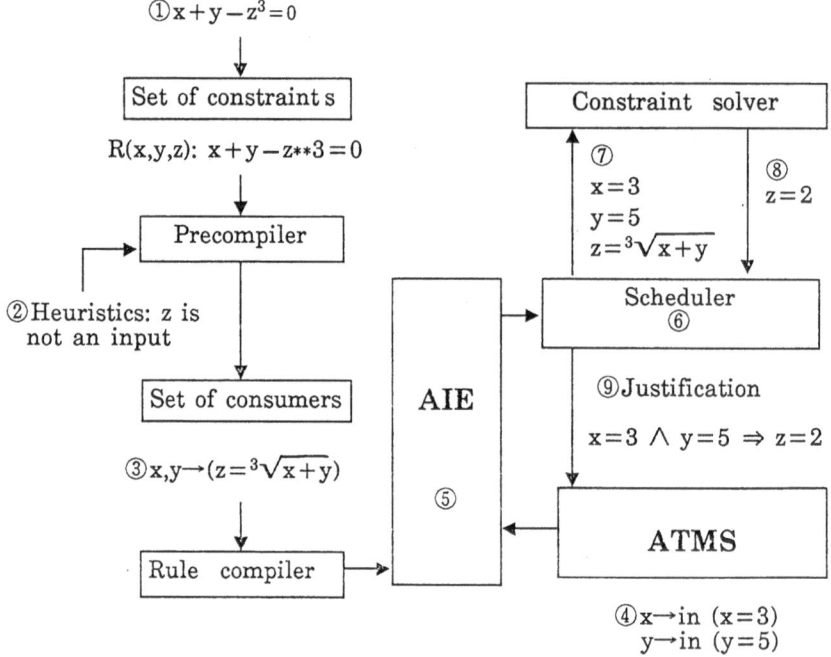

Fig. 4.3   CA by APRICOT/0

process, the attached consumers are passed to the scheduler, and passed to some solver when appropriate, and then the results are passed to the ATMS along with its justification.

The implementation of CA using APRICOT/0 is as follows and as shown in Fig. 4.3. Consumers in [de Kleer 86c] are attached to the ATMS nodes, but here they are converted to AIE rule formats. This enables simultaneous handling of heuristic rules and constraints through the common framework, that is, AIE and a scheduler. In this architecture, if a value of a variable, say "a", is assigned or updated, then the predicate "equal(a, A)" is introduced (indicating that "a" has a value, say λ, and is unified with ESP variable "A"). In AIE, this predicate is interpreted as IN when variable "a" is bound by λ in some context, and so delayed execution of consumers is possible. This means that constraint propagation is possible as a data-driven evaluator, and CA can be implemented.

Example 4.3 (A process of consumer generation and execution (See Fig. 4.3))

(1) Relationship among x, y, z : "$x + y - z^3 = 0$" is input.

(2) In the way of using the constraint, it can be seen that "z" is only used as the output.

(3) Data-flow in the variable set is determined, and the constraint is converted to a rule.

(4) In an inference process, x and y become IN.

(5) Rule conditions are satisfied, and the action part is sent to the scheduler.

(6) The consumer is scheduled to the queue according to a certain strategy.

(7) The consumer is picked up from the queue and passed to the solver when appropriate.

(8) The result given by the solver is returned to the CA.

(9) The CA registers the justification "$x = 3 \wedge y = 5 \Rightarrow z = 2$" in the ATMS.

Example 4.4
The following constraints (and heuristics related to their usages) are converted into AIE rules below, taking constraint analysis into account.

$g = -6*a*a + 0.7*b + c$
(g is only used as an output)
$g > 3*a + b*c$
(this is used as a test after calculating the value of g)
$g < a*b*c$
(this is used as a test after calculating the value of g)

```
rule101::equal(a,X), equal(b,Y), equal(c,Z)
         -> {G is -6*X*X+0. 7*Y+Z},
             equal(g,G).
rule102::equal(a,X), equal(b,Y), equal(c,Z),
          equal(g,G), {G<=3*X+Y*Z} -> [].
```

```
rule103::equal(a,X), equal(b,Y), equal(c,Z),
          equal(g,G), {G>=X*Y*Z} -> [].
```

4.3.4 Scheduling

The knowledge compiling function handles various types of knowledge (such as constraints, heuristic rules, defaults, and logical inference rules) under the common framework, so it is not enough for its implementation merely to convert that knowledge into the single AIE rule representation; it must schedule action parts of invoked rules. This can be accomplished by adding the following functions to the action part queue.

(1) Sort the queued action part list in ascending order of environment size.

(2) If consumer execution causes a contradiction to be detected and then some action parts to be no longer IN, they are removed from the queue. This prevents unnecessary justification generation and consumer execution.

(3) Add some kind of priority as heuristics. For example, higher priority is given to rules introducing contradictions. Set the priority according to types of knowledge and circumstances where to use it.

(4) Incorporate various kinds of search algorithms [Inoue 88a].

4.4 Conclusions and Future Research

This section discussed the architecture of the APRICOT/0 hypothetical reasoning system, composed of the ATMS maintaining concurrent representation of all contexts and the AIE rule-based problem solver, as well as the techniques used to implement knowledge compiling. Application is currently being considered for design and planning problems such as the design problem of the main spindle head in a lathe [Inoue et al. 88] and the problem of automatic generation of the disassembly sequence of machine tool head stocks (see 8.2), as well as distributed cooperative problems such as a delivery planning problem (see 8.3). Future plans include extension and generalization of the ATMS, and parallel implementation of the ATMS and AIE in GHC.

5 DISTRIBUTED COOPERATIVE PROBLEM SOLVING SYSTEM

A cooperative problem solving system solves problems for which optimum solutions are difficult to obtain. A typical model of such a system is the blackboard model. To improve automation system performance, cooperative problem solving functions may be useful particularly in the field of designing. Instance where they are useful are large-scale objects such as LSI circuits, because (1) combinations of constraints must be considered in phases of a design process (including the verification phase) to solve design problems; and (2) a conventional design process is divided into phases which are executed separately; thus it may not be able to produce the best product or design the required production this field. A typical conventional system is the HEARSAY-II system developed in the early '70s by the speech understanding project at CMU.

This system was designed to obtain solutions from ambiguous incomplete data (including noise) and knowledge. The architecture of the system was very promising [Nii 86]. However, it gave rise to difficulties in representing knowledge about inference control and in processing a large volume of data. For this reason, it has been left unused without finding out its full advantages. However, the recent progress in LSI and network technologies is spotlighting this architecture again. The system has turned out to be able to exhibit the originally expected performance if the architecture is expanded to cover a multiprocessing environment. Theoretical researche has also progressed in problem solving with uncertain incomplete data and knowledge. Distributed cooperative problem solving techniques have been developed, mainly by the members of Distributed AI workshops in the United States. Target environments pursued by the members for system models are versatile; they range from an environment for connectionist models (massively parallel machines) to a conventional computer environment [Davis 80, Fehling 83, Gasser 87, Smith 85]. Nevertheless, the environments lack clear basic concepts that serve as criteria or assessing their features. This fact darkens the outlook of the research. We are now trying to clarify the concepts of distributed cooperative problem solving, enumerating technical objectives, and probing possible methods.

5.1 Definition of distributed cooperative problem solving

Distributed cooperative problem solving is defined typically by Smith as follows [Smith 85]. "Distributed cooperative problem solving is cooperative solving of a problem by a group of decentralized and loosely coupled knowledge sources. Knowledge sources here mean knowledge systems described by some knowledge representations in various processors. They are cooperative because none of them has the necessary information or information processing capability to solve the whole problem. They are said to be decentralized if no global control and no global data storage site exist. They are said to be loosely coupled if they spend more time on computation than on communication".

As in above, distributed cooperative problem solving is irrelevant to a specific knowledge representation form and inference method. It stipulates a coarse system architecture for problem solving. It does not determine what sorts of knowledge sources are decentralized or how they are decentralized. Nor does it clarify how knowledge sources cooperate. A distributed AI system like the connectionist model includes tightly coupled problem solvers which are assigned small tasks. However, they are not regarded as distributed cooperative problem solvers [Decker 87].

5.2 Structure of a problem solver

The system consists of multiple problem solvers. It divides a problem, solves subproblems, and synthesizes the solutions. Various architectures can be considered for this system. We present only the structure common to problem solvers making up the system. Each problem solver consists of the following components (Fig. 5.1):

(1) Communicator: Exchanges processing results with other problem solvers.

(2) Controller: Borders retrieval spaces for tasks and performs focus control to reduce communications. Focus control selects the least costly, most efficient subtask when subtasks are connected by OR logic. When subtasks are connected by AND logic, the controller analyzes parallelism.

(3) Reasoner: Performs inference.

(4) Knowledge base: Contains knowledge of experts. Knowledge is dispersed to problem solvers, and no problem solver has the necessary knowledge to solve the whole problem.

(5) Working memory: Stores processing results of tasks.

5.3 Advantages of distributed cooperative problem solving

A distributed cooperative problem solving system improves, as do existing distribution systems, in performance. It heightens its processing speed and reliability. Routine programs have difficulty in performing knowledge processing subtasks. Therefore, if the subtasks were distributed to existing data processing subsystems, communication overhead would increase and thus would the advantage of distribution be offset. Cooperation functions are necessary in an environment where these subtasks can be efficiently distributed. Introduction of cooperation functions also improves the expandability of the system. When the system is expanded, cooperation between modules eliminates the need to change existing system resources. Another advantage of cooperative problem solving is the capability to obtain appropriate solutions. A feature of problems now under discussion is uncertainty. Uncertainty here means lack of data and lack of guarantee for completeness, correctness, and consistency of processing results supplied to a problem solver from others. Cooperative problem solving may obtain justifiable solutions under this uncertainty.

5.4 Features of a distributed cooperative problem solving system

Distributed cooperative problem solving can be regarded as a framework of inference control over multiple problem solvers to solve a problem cooperatively by using inference functions rather than knowledge representations. The optimum framework may depend on problems. An inference control frame has the following facilities:

(1) Integration mechanisms
 Multiple problem solvers in a distributed cooperative problem solving system work in harmony solve a problem. An integration mechanism is thus necessary in the system to integrate the actions of problem solvers.

(2) Communications between problem solvers
 Suitable communications facilities are important resources for a distributed cooperative problem solving system. The facilities may take various forms from the perspectives of: communication paradigms, communication contents, and communication protocols.
 Communication paradigms refer to the following two communication forms:
  (a)Communication through global memory (blackboard model)
  (b)Message passing

 (a) may be asynchronous communication, and (b) synchronous. Synchronous communication lowers processing speed, whereas asynchronous communication makes it difficult to guarantee data compatibility between problem solvers.

5.5 Technical objectives

Advantages of distributed cooperative problem solving can be divided into the following two groups:

(1) Advantages given by distribution processing, that is, ease of system construction, high execution speed, and high reliability

(2) Advantage given by cooperation processing, that is, generation of appropriate solutions by using limited data, knowledge, and processing time

In a distributed cooperative problem solving system, tasks and intermediate solutions are exchanged through communications. The communication speed is generally slower than computation speeds in problem solvers. Nevertheless, working towards a better solution increases communication frequency and quantity. Therefore, improvement in efficiency of communications is a major technical objective. How to obtain appropriate solutions through cooperative processing is another major technical objective. To achieve these objectives, we are now studying the following techniques:

(1) Efficient communication in a distribution environment
 In a distributed problem solving environment, each problem solver assumes self-control over its inference function. In this environment, problem solvers share tasks, processing results, or resources, and thus must be coordinated functionally. A technique for satisfying this requirement is the inference control technique proposed by Durfee and Lesser, called partial global plans [Durfee & Lesser 87]. This technique makes each problem solver create tactics for

solving a problem, which arises in the whole network but is viewed from the local standpoint, and exchange the tactics with other problem solvers. Whether one problem solver should employ tactics offered by another depends on evaluation standards implemented by the problem solver. The above technique may be a meta-communication technique. Another technique for efficient communication is the expectation-driven communication, which is performed by anticipating the actions of partner problem solvers. For one problem solver to anticipate the action of another, it must know the intention and action plan of the latter. The situation theory may be used to find out the intention action plan. This theory was first used by SRI to devise a cooperative work plan for multiple robots. Concerning this plan, Georgeff proposed an action theory, and Konolige presented a belief mode[Konolige 85].

(2) Cooperation for obtaining an appropriate solution
 A problem solving technique used in an environment where applicable knowledge and input data fall short is inference based on evidence. Human beings copy flexibly with problems by assuming the presence of exceptions in incomplete knowledge about the real world. The knowledge assuming exceptions are called default knowledge. Inference based on evidence uses default knowledge and instances supporting the correctness of default knowledge. When an inference process encounters conflicting assumptions, it selects an appropriate one based on supporting values[Shastri 85]. Through the above studies and analyses, we will propose a framework of distributed cooperative problem solving.

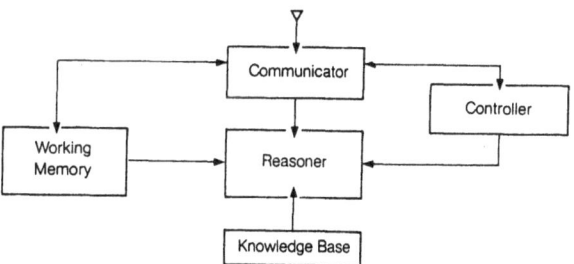

Fig. 5.1 Structure of a problem solver

6 USE OF DEEP KNOWLEDGE AND QUALITATIVE REASONING

6.1 Use of Deep Knowledge and Its Effects

One problem with conventional expert systems involves the complete inability of the system to solve a problem if it does not have inference rules for the problem, Because the basic ability of the conventional expert systems for solving a problem is based on the range of the inference rules in the problem domain. Moreover, as the expert system does not in essence understand the knowledge in problem domain, there are limitations in the intelligent problem solving and the explanation of reasoning processes. As one solution to overcome this problem, reasoning using deep knowledge (deep reasoning) has been proposed. Shallow and deep knowledge are defined as follows.

Shallow knowledge: Knowledge directly related to the tasks performed by an human expert.

Deep knowledge: Basic knowledge close to the universal laws or principles in the problem domain, or knowledge of general validity such as representations of the structure and function of the object.

Use of deep reasoning is anticipated to have the following effects.

(1) Completeness of knowledge :
   As each item of deep knowledge is expressed at a more basic level, the range covered by a single piece of knowledge is more broad. Hence, deep knowledge can cope with situations which cannot be predicted in advance on the basis of direct cause-effect relations, such as production rules.

(2) Understanding and explaining causality :
   As the knowledge in the problem domain is in a form which is close to physical laws and principles or the structure of the object, the system is far more capable of explaining the results of reasoning processes.

(3) Automatic generation of shallow knowledge :
   By compiling and storing reasoning results for various situations in a rule format, deep knowledge can be used in the automatic generation of shallow knowledge. General deep knowledge in the domain can be used in the construction of various expert systems for different applications in the domain (for instance, design knowledge can be used to generate diagnostic rules). That is, deep knowledge acquired can be used efficiently. On the other hand, shallow knowledge generated can be used for high-speed inference.

One means to achieve deep reasoning is qualitative reasoning. Its basic procedure is to express physical quantities and constraints existing among them qualitatively, and to reason about the system behavior. Methods for current qualitative reasoning systems (simulators) may be broadly divided into two categories :

(1) Qualitative modeling type :
   In this type of simulator, variables and constraints representing the system dynamics (a set of simultaneous qualitative differential equations) are given and fixed. All of these variables and constraints are used to reason the qualitative behavior of the whole system. An example is QSIM [Kuipers 85].

(2) Qualitative process theory type :
   Basic knowledge representations of this type of simulator are objects and, process or physical rules. Process and physical rules contain the constraints to change the states of

each object. Process or physical rules which are currently active are identified to construct a set of constraints representing the system. System behavior changing over time is reasoned using the constraints. Not only are qualitative states determined, but an understanding of causality is also sought. QPT [Forbus 84] is an example of such a system.

6.2 Qualitative Reasoning Mechanism

The Fifth Research Laboratory is studying qualitative reasoning mechanisms from the following two approaches.

(a) Research and development of Qupras [Ohki 88], a QPT-type qualitative reasoning system, which aims to deal with physical laws in their original form (without qualitative modeling).

(b) Research for improving the efficiency of the reasoning processes of the two types of qualitative reasoning systems mentioned above.

6.2.1 Outline of Qupras

As stated above, QPT is closer to the reasoning using deep knowledge than the approaches oriented to qualitative simulation. However, the QPT framework is in some respects inadequate to express knowledge at the level of general physical laws as basic knowledge. Hence, Qupras (for the qualitative physical reasoning system), a qualitative reasoning system which overcomes these difficulties is under development. As shown in Fig. 6.1, Qupras consists of a knowledge representation supporting subsystem and a reasoning subsystem.

(1) Knowledge representation in Qupras

Knowledge representation in Qupras involves descriptions of the object, physical rules and initial states. Objects are described in terms of (i) attributes (definition of attributes which describe the object), (ii) parts (definition of parts of the object), (iii) conditions (the object becomes active only when these conditions are satisfied), and (iv) relations (relations among physical quantities which are valid when the object is active). Fig. 6.2 is an example of an object describing a boiler class.

Physical rules are expressed in terms of (i) objects (to which the physical rule can be applied), (ii) conditions (conditions under which the physical rules may be applied), and (iii) relations (between the attributes of objects or other quantities). The physical rules are active only when both (i) and (ii) are active. Fig. 6.3 gives an example of a physical rules describing heat flow.

The initial state defines the state of the target system at the beginning of reasoning (that is, instances of objects and definition of facts).

Conditions and relations of objects and physical rules are expressed as equalities (using addition, subtraction, multiplication and division), inequalities, or terms which describe facts such as positions. Further, Qupras is capable of handling these formulas not only qualitatively, but also quantitatively.

Knowledge about objects and physical rules is given in the form of templates. Prior to the inference process, the knowledge representation supporting subsystem of the Qupras applies template knowledge to instances in the initial state, to generate instances of the object and physical rule, then converts them to an intermediate format which the reasoning subsystem can understand.

(2) Qualitative reasoning in Qupras

The qualitative reasoning subsystem in Qupras has the structure shown in Fig. 6.4. Beginning from the given initial state, the succeeding behavior of the target system is reasoned. The qualitative reasoning is performed by two processes, intra-state analysis (propagation) and limit analysis (prediction), in turn.

In intra-state analysis, the reasoning subsystem searches for active objects or physical rules whose conditions are satisfied, and collects constraints in them to construct the simultaneous differential equations describing the target system at that time. The subsystem propagates known attribute values to undetermined attribute values through constraints.

In limit analysis, the reasoning subsystem predicts a qualitative value at the next time for each attribute changing with time. It is selected from the nearest limit points of the present value searching for the equalities and inequalities of conditions of objects and physical rules.

```
object boiler:Boiler
  parts—of
    container—container;
    heat—source—heat—source;
  relations
    on (Container! Boiler, heat—source! Boiler);
    melting—point @ container! Boiler
    < temperature @ heat—source! Boiler;
  end.
```

Fig. 6.2 Definition of a Boiler

(3) Features of Qupras

(a) Knowledge related to physical laws can be represented in a single formulation. (QPT handles dynamic and static phenomena separately.)

(b) Formulas describing physical laws may be represented without qualitative modeling: further, physical quantities may be handled in either a qualitative or a quantitative manner, as the situation demands.

(c) No statements of the partial ordering between the values of varying physical quantities, or of quantity spaces, are required.

(d) Representation and reasoning about states changing of physical variables is possible. In

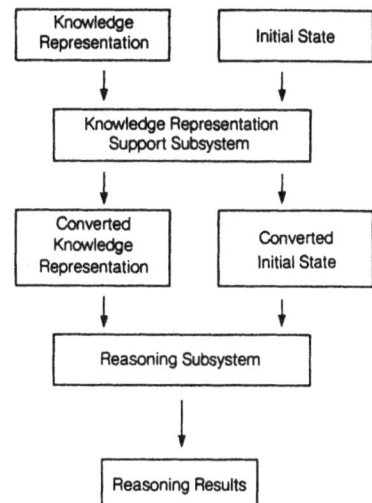

Fig. 6.1 Outiline of Qupras

```
physics heat—flow
  objects
    Heat—source—heat—source;
    Container—container;
  conditions
    on (Container, Heat—source);
    temperature@Heat—source<>temperature@Container;
  relations
    ddt (heat Container) : = :
      temperature@Heat—source—temperature@Container;
  end.
```

Fig. 6.3 Definition of Heat Flow

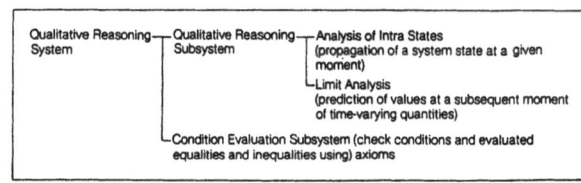

Fig. 6.4 Structure of the Qupras Qualitative Reasoning System

other words, Qupras expresses physical laws in a more primitive form.

(4) Remaining subjects for study

(a) Studies of better primitives for representing such physical laws as the conservation of energy

(b) Improvement of the condition evaluator
We have partially enabled the solution of non-linear simultaneous inequalities by combining the Sup-Inf method for linear simultaneous inequalities [Shostak 77] and the Groebner-base method for non-linear simultaneous equation

98

[Buchberger 83]. We have also enabled control of the sequence of evaluation of equalities and inequalities (freeze function). However, we have to increase the execution speed.

(c) Constructing a hierarchical structure of object definition, and generalizing definitions of physical rules. At present, an improved version, Qupras ver.2,which adopts these functions and features, is under development.

6.2.2 Improvement of Qualitative Reasoning System

One of the problems with the current qualitative reasoning system is that it cannot predict the behavior of large target systems because of the limitations of computation time and memory capacity. Even the QSIM algorithm, which presently performs reasoning at the highest speed of all the qualitative reasoning systems, can handle only a small continuous system. One method to realize a qualitative reasoning system which can reason the behavior of large target system including multiple physical domains is partition of the target system. We propose two methods for partition based on the heuristics with the structure and properties of the target system. We estimate the effect of the partition methods for computational complexity of qualitative reasoning and discuss the applied conditions of the methods.

(1)Partition method of target system based on heuristics with their structure and properties

(a) Method 1 : Partition method of variables according to the independence of each subsystem.
   Assume a target system which consists of many parts that have close interactions between internal components and only weak interactions with external components. Such a target system can be divided into loosely connected subsystems corresponding to the parts. All variables belonging to only one part are assigned to the subsystem as its internal variables. Each external variable (that is. an output from a part and/or an input to the other) is shared by both of these subsystems as a common variable. The behavior of each subsystem can be simulated independently as response to the input state. The simulated results of each subsystem are communicated to others via common variables. They are integrated to constitute the behavior of the whole target system.

(b) Method 2 :Partition method of a system by the field of applicable rules.
   Assume another target system, each of whose components is designed and operated according to the rules of a different physical field (for example, electronic circuit, thermodynamics, electrostatics, and quantum mechanics) to satisfy a different function. In this case, the target system can be partitioned into subsystems. Each subsystem consists of parts whose fields of dominant rules are identical. As the range of rules applicable to each object is limited, the number of objects contained in each subsystem is also reduced. Because the rules of different physical fields have little effect, the target system is divided into independent subsystems. Therefore, the behavior of each subsystem can be simulated independently.

(2)Effect of partition methods on the computational efficiency of Qupras

This section estimates the effects of applying partition methods 1 and 2 to the qualitative reasoning system, Qupras. (For more details, refer to [Sakane 88].)

(a) Effect on propagation process

   Suppose that an object system is partitioned into W subsystems of the same size by partition methods 1 and 2 . We estimate the computational complexity required for simulating the system behavior using the equally partitioned model. Because the number of instance rules generated is reduced to 1/W, the computational complexity required to find active physical rules is also reduced to 1/W. Thus, the computational complexity in the propagation process is reduced to approximately 1/W times under the following conditions:

   (i) application to large target systems without feedback loops consisting of relatively independent subsystems.

   (ii) Expression of each physical rule in a general form.

(b) Effect on prediction process

   The cost required to predict the next value of each variable changing with time is proportional to the number of instance rules generated. The cost is reduced to 1/W times using the equally partitioned model. However, if there are many variables changing with time, all the combinations of their next values must be checked for consistency. The total computational complexity in the prediction process increases sharply as the number of variables changing with time, Y, increases. Then, the computational complexity is not reduced unless Y decreases. To reduce the number of such variables, some knowledge to control the order of changes among variables is needed.
   The partition methods also have advantages in acquiring this kind of knowledge. When the simulator simulates the system behavior as a whole, only the knowledge of the order of changing among variables is available. However, it is very rare in practice that sufficient knowledge is given to specify a variable to be changed first. When the system is partitioned into subsystems by the partition method, the knowledge with the order of variable changes among subsystems is also available. This knowledge is likely to be known, even if the

orders of changing among variables are not known.

(3) Remaining subjects for study

(a) Studies of efficient methods of partition of target systems other than the above two methods

(b) Study of a method of mapping the qualitative time of each subsystem to real time

(c) Dealing with discontinuous change which occurs at the beginning and/or end of the interval of qualitative time in each subsystem.

(d) Controlling reasoning: controlling the order of changes among variables and controlling the order of propagation using the dependency among variables.

6.3 Systems Which Apply Deep Knowledge

The range of application of deep reasoning (and qualitative reasoning in particular) may consist of analytic problems and synthetic problems; here we consider a malfunction diagnostic system employing deep knowledge as an example of an analytical problem. The following two types of use are possible.

(1) Generation of diagnostic rules (knowledge compilation)

Qualitative differential equations of the faulty system are constructed for each candidate of malfunction. Qualitative behavior of the faulty systems is acquired, using the model to obtain malfunction symptoms. By connecting the malfunction to the symptoms, the system generates diagnostic rules in the form of "If (symptom) Then (malfunction)". Because the diagnostic rules are generated for all the malfunction candidates, this method is not efficient with regard to the execution time. Therefore, it is suited to off-line generation of diagnostic rules.

(2) Identifying faults based on symptoms

First, the qualitative value of the variable representing the malfunction symptom is propagated to other variables through the constraints. When propagated qualitative values contradict at a certain variable, the variable is considered to be the point where the malfunction causes. In this method, contradiction may be detected at many variables. Therefore, it is necessary to eliminate secondary symptoms by some knowledge and select only the direct cause of malfunction. Because only a set of differential equations must be considered, this method is suited for on-line use with respect to the execution efficiency.

7 KNOWLEDGE ACQUISITION SUPPORT SYSTEMS

A major problem which tends to arise when constructing knowledge-base systems concerns bottlenecks at the knowledge acquisition stage.

Knowledge acquisition involves the collection of knowledge from human experts, arrangement and systematization of this information, and construction of a knowledge base for use in a knowledge-base system. At present, this task is performed by knowledge engineers (KEs); that is, knowledge acquisition relies entirely on human efforts. And, since systematic methods of knowledge acquisition have not yet been established, the process of knowledge acquisition is an extremely troublesome one for the knowledge engineer. Our goal is to improve such bottlenecks. Somewhat more concretely, we are responsible for the clarification of the types and structures of knowledge possessed by human experts, and with the establishment of effective methods for the extraction and organization of expert knowledge. In considering knowledge acquisition support systems, we may analyze the work of the knowledge engineer in the following four broad phases.

(1) Problem analysis:
In this phase, the tasks of system to be developed are determined, and the system feasibility and significance of development are analyzed.

(2) Expert model building:
The technical terminology, task procedures (problem-solving strategies) and conceptual structure used by human experts are clarified, and the methods and environments of expert system use are determined.

(3) Expert model instantiation:
Expert knowledge is elicited and organized in the form of the expert model, and the knowledge base is built.

(4) Knowledge-base management:
The knowledge base is modified, added to, or deleted to correct any contradictions, redundancies, deficiencies, or unnecessary (isolated) data.

Knowledge acquisition support systems capable of supporting each of these phases are required. Below, we discuss the basic technology required for such knowledge acquisition support systems, and briefly sketch some systems (CATS and EPSILON/One) which are now being researched.

7.1 Basic Technology for Knowledge Acquisition Support Systems

Knowledge acquisition support systems are hybrid systems, consisting of a number of basic technologies. We list some of these here.

(1) Knowledge acquisition interface (interface with knowledge source)
Interfaces for knowledge acquisition are divided into interpretive and interactive interfaces, according to the manner in which information is exchanged with the knowledge source. In interactive interfaces, knowledge is obtained directly from human experts through that interaction. Conversational representations

employ symbols, numbers, or. words, etc.), tables (spread-sheets, for instance) and other means of expression. Interpretive interfaces, such as those used in protocol analysis and text analysis, on the other hand, involve the direct one-way flow of information from the knowledge source to the knowledge acquisition support system. Here, techniques for interpreting knowledge representations used by the knowledge source (i.e. techniques for natural language understanding) are required.

(2) Interviewing techniques

In interactive knowledge acquisition, only the necessary information must be extracted from the human expert if the acquisition process is to be efficient. Further, knowledge which is to be acquired must be educed through association. Methods for prompting associations include pairwise comparison, personal construct theory (used with CATS, discussed below) and the pre-post method (used with EPSILON/One, below).

(3) Building of conceptual structures (domain models, expert models and knowledge representation)

In general, the knowledge representation supported by expert shells is extremely basic (for instance, rules and frames). Because of this, it is difficult for experts to express their specialized knowledge. Knowledge acquisition support systems can facilitate the extraction of knowledge, by supporting knowledge representation in specialized operations or tasks. Such representation may take the form of domain models (basic conceptions of the objects with which the expert deals, and relations between objects) or of expert models (expressions of the task performed by the expert in terms of basic operations; used with EPSILON/One).

(4) Refinement of task models (expert and domain models)

During the process of acquisition, acquired knowledge contains deficiencies, redundancies and contradictions. A refinement method appropriate to the model structure is thus used to perfect the task model.

(5) Knowledge base evaluation The acquired knowledge (task representation knowledge) is translated to the knowledge representation of an expert shell, and the inference engine of the expert shell is used to evaluate the extent to which the system is capable of the intellectual activity of the expert.

7.2 Classified Task Acquisition Support (CTAS) System

CTAS [Yamazaki et al. 87] is a knowledge acquisition support system which builds an initial knowledge base for classification-type problems. Knowledge-base systems may be broadly classified into a synthetic class and an analytical class; of these, CTAS is applied to the analytical class. In general, problem solving for the analytical class consists of a hierarchical classification task and an ordering task. The hierarchical classification task classifies the elements (items to be classified) on the basis of broad, clear traits. The ordering task, on the other hand, classifies elements that can no longer be classified by clearly distinguishable traits, according to the strength of correlations between traits and elements. CTAS enables the acquisition of knowledge bases in which these two tasks are done using knowledge acquisition methods based on George Kelly's Personal Construct Theory. Using the elements, traits by which elements are classified, and scaled ratings(a scaled rating is the correlation between elements and traits), CTAS generates production rules with a certainty factor. CTAS consultation consists of five stages – elicitation, arrangement, refinement, rule generation, and testing. In the elicitation process, elements for classification, traits and scaled rating are elicited; the arrangement stage involves making graphs and tables using the elicited information so that the acquired knowledge can be perceived visually. The refinement process comprises refinement of elements, traits and scaled ratings, while the rule generation process is concerned with the generation of production rules. In the testing process, the rules thus generated are evaluated. Consultation for each of these processes is explained below. In the elicitation process, support of hierarchical classification task and ordering tasks relies on the elicitation of classification elements, traits, and scaled ratings. In hierarchical classification tasks, traits which can be used to classify elements into hierarchical levels are elicited, and elements are thereby organized into groups; this process may be performed either top-down or bottom-up. In top-down classification, division into hierarchical levels is first performed; this method is effective when experts have already organized elements (into a hierarchy). In bottom-up classification, classification is performed after elicitation of elements; this method is advantageous when elements have not been organized, or have not been organized throughly, by experts. An ordering task involves the elicitation of traits, and scaled ratings between elements and traits for every group. Four types of graphs and a table are prepared in the arrangement process - hierarchical trees, rating grids, implication graphs, and cluster trees. All except hierarchical trees are prepared for each group in a hierarchy. The hierarchical tree indicates the hierarchical relationship between groups of classified elements. A rating grid indicates, in table form, the elements, traits and scaled ratings contained in a group. An implication graph shows the implication relationships between traits in a group. A cluster tree is prepared for each of the elements and traits contained in a group. Each cluster tree indicates the similarity of relationships between items (classification elements and traits). The graphs and table facilitate visual inspection and verification of elicited knowledge by human experts. In refinement processes, several types of refinement methods based on the Personal Construct Theory are used in the refinement of elements, traits and scaled ratings. Additions, deletion, integration and renaming are performed for the different items (elements and traits). Scaled ratings are also corrected. In the rule generation process, three types of production rules - hierarchical rules, conclusion rules and intermediate rules - are generated. Hierarchical rules are used for hierarchical classification, and express the hierarchical relationships between elements. Conclusion and intermediate rules are used for the ordering tasks; and the correlations between traits and elements contained in a group are expressed using the certainty factor. In the testing process, rules thus generated are evaluated through use. In this process, the hierarchical rules are invoked, and groups of elements which are to be assessed are determined. Then the conclusion rules and intermediate rules are first invoked, and result in classified elements which are displayed in order of the certainty factor. The advantage of CTAS lies in its support of knowledge acquisition focusing on the structure of tasks which the knowledge-base systems perform. Also, the graphs and table enable efficient refinement of the acquired knowledge base. By using the CTAS system, a high-quality knowledge base for classification-type problems can be obtained, and the knowledge base can be refined efficiently. Possible applications of CTAS lie in classification tasks in the various areas of diagnostics and planning. CTAS was developed using ESP running on the PSI, and knowledge bases thus acquired are performed using the CTAS inference engine.

7.3 Knowledge Acquisition Support System Based on Expert Model (EPSILON/One)

The EPSILON/One [Tsubaki et al. 88] [Ohsaki et al. 88] is a knowledge acquisition support system which gathers intelligent expert work in small units called operations and builds a knowledge base. We designed an expert model [Taki et al. 87] to represent a knowledge base consisting of these operations. We also developed the pre-post method as a means of acquiring knowledge for the expert mode. Fig. 7.1 shows the configuration of the EPSILON/One. The knowledge acquisition strategy of the pre-post method acquires knowledge through the knowledge acquisition interface and builds an expert model. In addition, as a knowledge representation model of structural information, the structural information knowledge representation construction module acquires structural information knowledge through the knowledge acquisition interface. Then, the refinement module refines the expert model based on structural information knowledge. The expert model and structural information knowledge are converted into a knowledge base for expert shells by the knowledge representation translator. In the following, we discuss the basic concepts employed in expert models, representations of the structure and functions of the expert model, and pre-post method.

7.3.1 Basic concepts of the expert model

We propose an expert model based on two different ideas - a simplified expert task model, and analysis and grouping of diagnostic expert knowledge for production expressions.

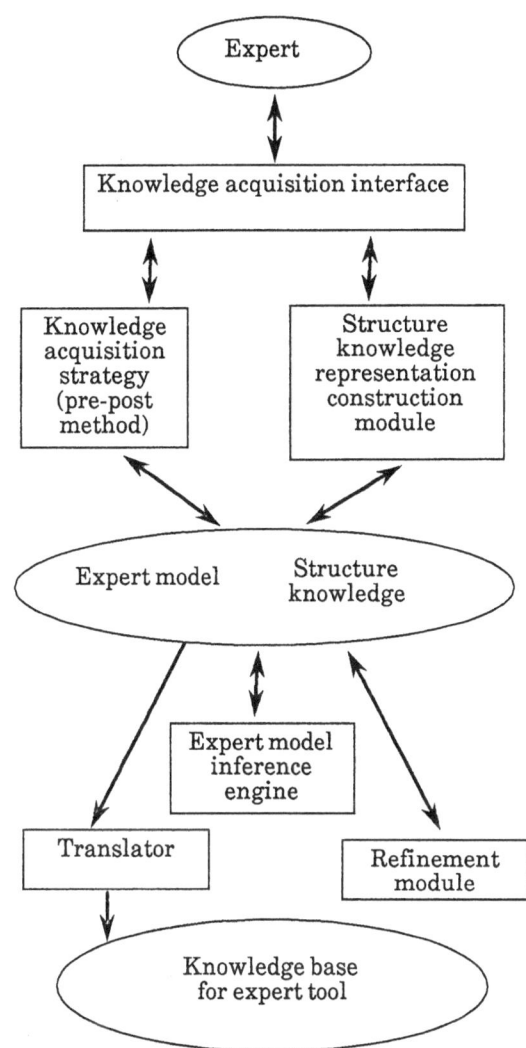

Fig. 7.1 EPSILON/One overview

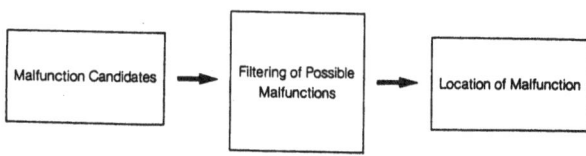

Fig. 7.2 Simplified diagnostic task model

(1) Simplified expert task model
The operations performed by an expert system may be divided into a number of task types, such as diagnostics, design and control. We attempted to represent these task types using simple models. We show this approach because simplified expert

tasks allow us to provide images of expert system operations to human experts, to enable them to give expression to their own knowledge. We here present one example of this (Fig. 7.2). On studying simplified expert task models, we found that such models (that is, operations) could be conceived to consist of the object (source element group), processing (evaluator), and processing results (destination element group).

(2) Rule analysis in diagnostic expert systems
Production rules are the general means of representing knowledge in expert systems. The knowledge engineer must possess knowledge representation techniques having a production rule form. We assumed that such techniques appear in rule forms, and discovered the following seven description forms in sets of production rules: selection, classification, sort, combination, translation, input and output forms. The result of combining these two ideas is generic operation.

7.3.2　Structure of expert models

As just explained, expert models consist of types of operations and the relations between operations. These operation relations contain information on the order of execution of operations. Next, as an example of an operation, we consider a classification into types (Fig. 7.4). In the figure, group animals-1 is the source element group, while animals-2, animals-3 and animals-4 are destination element groups. Suppose that the evaluator's task is to divide the elements into three groups according to size. In this example, the elements are dog, cat, wolf, porpoise, rat, whale, elephant, and the size of each animal is its attribute.

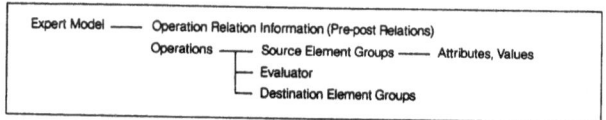

Fig. 7.3 Expert model structure

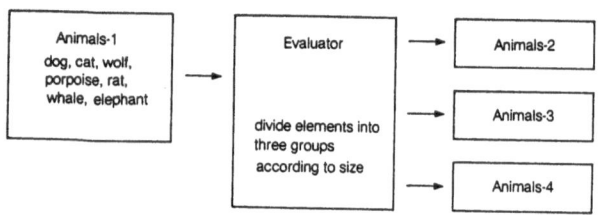

Fig. 7.4 Example of an operation type
(classification)

7.3.3　Method of knowledge acquisition (pre-post method)

The main strategy of the pre-post method stimulated the expert to remember the associative operations before and after (pre- and post-) a given operation. It is relatively easy for the expert to state what operations are necessary before and after a given operation. For instance, when a car will not run, if a human is asked "What should be done before checking the engine?", it is easy to answer "Check if there's gasoline in the tank" or "Check the battery". Further, in the pre-post method, the details of operations are determined, and the operation management structure (meta-script) is configured. The knowledge acquisition process by the pre-post method proceeds as follows.

(1) Collection of operations serving as the starting-point of knowledge acquisition Arbitrary operations are extracted from the expert. (An example is the "engine check" just mentioned.)

(2) Extraction pre- and post- operations
Extraction of operations preceding and following each of the above operations (in the above example, "Check the gasoline" and "Check the battery").

(3) Checking of pre-post relations
Graphic illustration of the operations preceding and following each operation, and checks for differences in these relations.

(4) Determination of operation types
Types are assigned to operations; when assignments cannot be made, operations are further divided into smaller units. Operation types are chosen from among seven types, such as selection and sort.

(5) Operation merging operations in which the same processing is performed are merged.

(6) Evaluator determination
By extracting the necessary information for operation types, the details of the evaluator are decided. (When the type of operation is selection, selection criteria are extracted.)

(7) Determination of source element groups
The elements to be processed by the evaluator are determined. (When the type is selection, objects for selection are extracted.)

(8) Determination of element attributes and values
The attributes and attribute values for each element, to be evaluated by the evaluator, are determined.

(9) Grouping of operations into blocks
Operations which rely on identical reasoning methods are combined.

(10)　Determination of reasoning method
The operation reasoning method is determined sequential or parallel, full-solution or partial-solution search.

7.3.4 Refinement method by using different knowledge representation models

Human knowledge consists of a variety of domain knowledge. Accordingly, it is desirable that each piece of knowledge should be acquired in a format suited to its representation. However, a knowledge base of a single knowledge representation must be refined from many points of view. Besides the expert model of the EPSILON/One, there is a knowledge representation model which can hierarchically represent the structural information of the system. It seems useful to refine the expert model by comparing this knowledge representation model to the expert model, so we are presently studying this method.

7.3.5 Future reseach

We have introduced an expert model derived from analysis of production rules in diagnostic expert systems and the simplified expert task model, and acquisition method (pre-post method) for this model. We are developing the EPSILON/One by ESP on the PSI. At present, it is equipped with a sequential inference engine for the expert model. The expert model is a framework which can represent parallel operation knowledge, so we will have to study the possibility of applying it to knowledge acquisition suited to parallel inference. Moreover, we will have to develop parallel inference engines for the expert model.

8 EXPERIMENTAL EXPERT SYSTEMS

8.1 Expert System for VLSI Logic Circuit Design

A cooperative expert system for logic circuit design, called co-LODEX, accepts input of the VLSI behavioral algorithm specifications, datapath structure and constraints to support automatic design of CMOS standard cells. Constraints on gate count (or more precisely, basic cell count) and constraints on delay time can also be input. As indicated in Fig. 8.1.1, co-LODEX performs overall design through cooperation between the agents designing the finite-state machine and control circuit, and those implementing the datapath structures (registers and multipliers) in the CMOS standard cell. Cooperative operation is handled by requesting one agent to alter something when an other agent prevents the constraints from being satisfied. For example, if a datapath satisfying the constraints cannot be implemented under the controls generated by the control design agent, the data path design agent request changes the control of the control system design agent. In design work, there are cases where redesign is unavoidable. Especially in cooperative systems, where changes may be requested from the outside, efficient redesign is essential. In co-LODEX the problem is resolved through assumption-based reasoning.

(1) Alternatives occurring in design are regarded as assumptions, and change is managed through use/non-use of assumptions in redesign.

(2) Violation of constraints is a contradiction, and redesign cancels the contradiction.

(3) Constraints can also be treated as assumptions, considering that design may be repeated while changing constraints.

(4) Redesign must be handled through operations on the conjunction of delay time conditions, conditions related to basic cell count, and assumptions expressing the cause of the violation of constraints.

8.2 An Expert System for Automatic Determination of Disassembly Sequence of a Head Stock

This system aims at studying efficient inference control mechanisms. To accomplish the aim, problems in automatic generation of disassembly sequence of machine tool head stocks are employed as specific examples. An example of machine tool head stocks is shown in Fig. 8.2.1. This example consists of 80 components, which are represented by the connective relations based on a fitting tolerances and by three-dimensional data using generalized cylinder expression. This system generates the disassembly sequence with the connective relations and from (1) knowledge to extract candidate components for disassembly, (2) knowledge to select the component to be disassembled from the list of candidates, (3) knowledge to evaluate the disassembly cost and to check the inter-component interference, and (4) knowledge to update connective relations. The processing sequence is given in Fig. 8.2.2. The disassembly sequence is generated as follows. First, extraction knowledge is applied to connective relations, and components that can be disassembled are listed. Next, selection knowledge is used to determine the component in the list that is the easiest to disassemble. Selection knowledge is given a priority and ordered, based on ease of disassembly derived from connective relations. Components with the same disassembly priority are evaluated by disassembly cost and checked by inter-component interference knowledge. When a component is removed, connective relations are renewed by knowledge to update connective relations. This process is repeated until all components are disassembled. Even with evaluation knowledge, the sequence will have alternatives because ease of disassembly and cost are equivalent for multiple components. The sequence will also be forced to change by inter-component interference. To solve these problems, this system employed the following approach.

(1) Alternatives of disassembly sequence are handled as multiple contexts.

(2) A hypothetical reasoning mechanism is applied, assuming that alternatives of disassembly sequences are hypotheses, and the evidence for disassembly sequences being inappropriate as shown by the cost evaluation and inter-component interference check is a contradiction.

This research is based on research performed in cooperation with the Mechanical Engineering

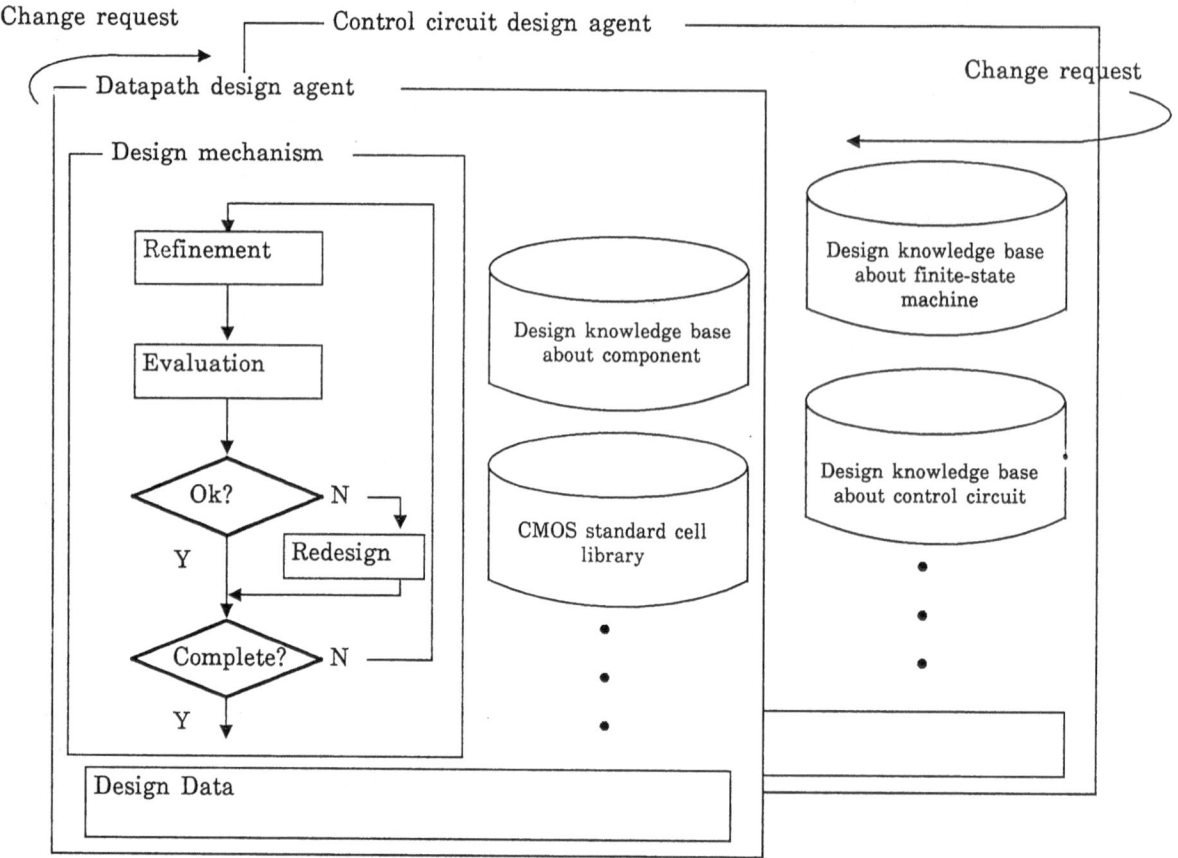

Fig. 8.1.1 System Structure

Laboratory, Agency of Industrial Science and Technology, Ministry of International Trade and Industry [Sekiguchi 83], [Sekiguchi 87].

8.3 Delivery planning

The delivery planning support system supports the assignment of trucks and drivers, and the selection of routes. The delivery task is that packages from a distribution center are delivered on multiple trucks to multiple destinations (retailers). This system generates satisfactory plans. This problem has some constraints, for example, they are numbers of trucks and drivers as resources, required visiting time intervals for the destinations, and trucks' capacity. The primary target of this system is a feasibility study for distributed cooperative problem solving systems. First, delivery requests (packages) are divided into groups called areas, through heuristics. This means dividing the problem into subproblems. A delivery plan for each area can be generated autonomously by the distributed problem solver called the area agent, but each generated plan is not complete. Fig. 8.3.1 shows a simple example of area agents and delivery requests. Resources for delivery (trucks and drivers) can be shared between areas, so resources for an area need to be allocated in cooperation with other areas. The flexibility of the generated plans is also enhanced by giving a package to multiple areas and through cooperation between the areas. System input consists of route information, truck and driver information, and delivery orders. System output is the delivery plan for a single day. Fig. 8.3.2 shows a simple delivery plan. Multiple candidates are evaluated by the total cost. This system accepts user input with the guide in the event of loops or dead ends. It has a function to explain the plan generation process.

8.4 Troubleshooting Expert System for Electronic Switching Systems

This system infers the probable cause from the symptoms of an electronic switching system fault. The diagnostic process is as given below.

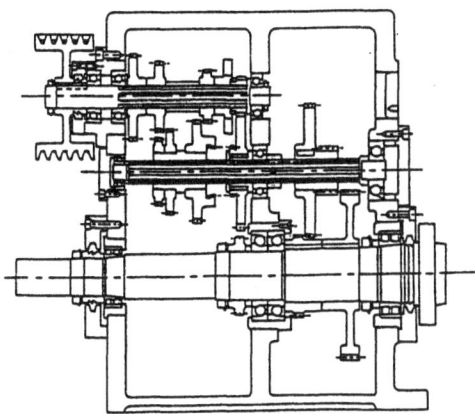

Fig. 8.2.1 Example of a mchine tool headstock

Table 1. Connective relations

Connective relations		Code	Level
Fit	Pressure fit	Pr	↑
	Push fit	Pu	
	Screw fit	Sc	
	Taper fit	Ta	
	Spline fit	Sp	
	Position fit	Po	
	Movable fit	Mo	
	Gear coupling	Ge	
	Ring fit	Ri	
	(Key fit)	Ke	
Contact	Clamp contact	Cl	↑
	Taper contact	Ta	
	Plane contact	Pl	
	External contact	Ex	
	Gear meshing	Ge	
	(Gap plane)	Ga	

(1) Symptom data is analyzed, and the components that could be causing the problem (suspects) determined.

(2) The suspects are represented as a group of functional blocks.

(3) Effective tests are selected for each suspect and executed. The number of suspects is reduced from the results. This process is repeated.

(4) Finally, the remaining suspect is replaced, and a check made to see if the fault disappears.

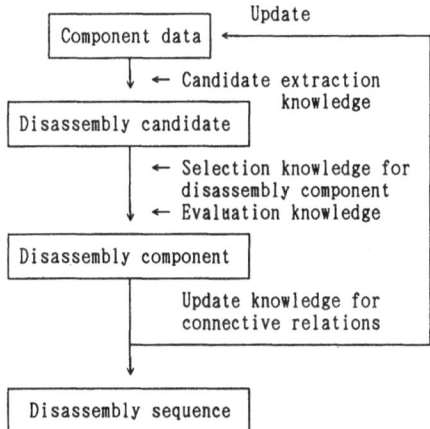

Fig. 8.2.2   Processing procedure

Inferences in narrowing down suspected components by test results are frequently indeterminate. In inferences of this type, the final indicated suspect is in error through errors in judgment. If the suspected component is replaced and the fault is still present, it indicates an error (contradiction) in a judgment made up to that point, so that judgment is deleted and a different conclusion is reasoned (a different suspect is selected). A truth maintenance technique such as an ATMS is incorporated in order to realize this kind of indeterminate inference. An ATMS can handle multiple contexts simultaneously. In this case, restrictions on the number of environments handled simultaneously were imposed to prevent a drop in processing efficiency. As an example of an imprecise judgement, it can be assumed that the power supply is normal is the power supply alarm is not active, but if the power supply alarm indicator lamp is broken, there will be no alarm even if the power supply is abnormal. In this situation, the assumption that the power supply is normal is made.
The rule may be expressed as:

if power_supply_lamp_not_on ,

  asm_alarm_ok % power supply alarm is normal
then power_supply_is_normal (cause is other than power supply)

In this rule asm_alarm_ok is an assumption. If the truth of this assumption becomes doubtful, a test is executed. If no contradiction is generated, then the test may be omitted, which is an advantage in system performance.

8.5 Computer Layout

This system aims at a feasibility study of parallel processing in problem-solving, using the problem of laying out geometrical shapes within a limited space (that is, computer layout). ESP is used, and the pilot system is implemented on the PSI. The basic configuration of ESP objects is given in Fig. 8.5.1, and the following hierarchical problem-solving approach is tried, taking parallel processing into consideration. The parallel problem-solving object invoked by user request requires an upper-level processing object. The upper-level processing object divides given equipment into groups, and the room into zones so that the problem can be reduced to subproblems by allocating each group to an appropriate zone. Through pseudo-parallel processing realized by the above problem division, a layout satisfying semantical constraint conditions (that is, equipment maintenance areas and pillars may not overlap) is obtained. Pseudo-parallel processing and the reduction of possible answer sets by semantical constraint conditions makes the search for an answer more efficient. Constraint conditions imposed between parallel processes consist of constraints to align the front of units of equipment, and limitations on distances between specified equipment pairs. These are relatively weak constraints, so parallel processing is extremely efficient. However, if there are strong constraints such as the requirement for the front of one zone to be aligned with that of another zone, interference between parallel processes often reduces parallel processing efficiency. Future research is required on the allocation of information acquisition rights to minimize inter-process interference.

8.6 Intelligent secretary

The most common method of building a knowledge base for expert systems is for a knowledge engineer (KE) to interview a domain expert and extract his/her knowledge. In this method, however, a new expert (the KE) is required, and there are not enough KEs to spread expert systems. Much of the knowledge of experts is already available in printed form, in various forms as dissertations and books. As human beings acquire knowledge, they acquire vast quantities of knowledge already arranged systematically through books, and experts and KEs can also form knowledge bases for expert systems from such basic knowledge and experience. If it were possible to convert the natural language found in such documentation into a knowledge base suitable for an expert system, it would be extremely easy to develop expert systems. The goal of this research is to establish methods for converting knowledge expressed in natural language into knowledge bases for expert systems. The field is limited to secretarial work, primarily scheduling, and we present a knowledge acquisition method by using the text knowledge primitive (SKIP) to be problem solution elicited from documentation. A knowledge acquisition method using SKIP requires a function to draw concrete actions from general concepts, and a function to systematize text using multiple jargon and expressions in a single form suitable for a system. These are called the expression systematization function and the structural systematization function. We are studying and developing a knowledge compiler which links these functions. The overall structure of the knowledge acquisition support tool prototype, including the intelligent scheduling system, is shown in Fig. 8.6.1. Current knowledge acquisition support tools process documentation in SKIP format (which restricts scheduling) into a knowledge base for scheduling

systems, and then its knowledge base is used for intelligent scheduling.

8.7 Plant Control

This study aims to demonstrate the potential of a logic programming language for application to the plant control domain. A prototype plant control system was constructed and applied to a steam power plant as an example of a control object. Knowledge representation techniques were investigated for describing the structural and dynamic characteristics of the plant in the control domain. Basic functions needed for controlling the power plant are:

(1) Monitoring the states of the plant;

(2) Selecting and/or determining the timing and amount of control action;

(3) Planning the sequence of control actions responding to malfunctions detected or aiming to improve the control performance;

(4) predicting the transition of the states of the plant by simulation.

Here, (3) and (4) were selected as the main subjects of the prototype system.

In the prototype system, the plant model is described in the form of deep knowledge such as physical laws and the structure of the plant. Using deep knowledge, the control system enables control actions to be generated even if an unexpected situation occurs where heuristic control knowledge (shallow knowledge) does not exist. The behavior of the plant responding to the specified control action is predicted. This result is used for evaluating the validity of the sequence of control actions generated.

We employ qualitative reasoning mechanism to realize deep reasoning. In qualitative reasoning, the object plant is modeled qualitatively with the variables and constraints contained in it expressed qualitatively. The behavior of the plant is acquired in the form of the transition of qualitative states. Both of the qualitative reasoning systems based on the methodologies of [Kuipers 86] and [deKleer 84] have been explored and compared. Due to the ambiguity caused by qualitative values, a great number of states are generated which actually never occur. Therefore, neither method can be applied directly to plant control. To avoid combinatorial explosion, pruning the unsuitable candidates of the states based on heuristics proved to be more effective than introducing the full order among the landmarks of different variables.

In future study, the mechanism of generating control actions using deep reasoning must be examined in more detail. Parallel processing and knowledge compilation of the reasoning results are considered to be effective to improve the efficiency of deep reasoning processing.

8.8 Portfolio planning support system

This system is designed to support portfolio planning, where a specific amount of capital is divided among multiple investment options. The user inputs the portfolio problem by specifying profit and safety targets, and the portfolio plan is generated and refined by analysis from multiple viewpoints to output the final portfolio plan, The objective is the establishment of cooperation technology which can reach a solution to the overall problem by exchanging planning information between individual agents in a multi-agent problem resolution process. A knowledge base module of this system stores the knowledge essential for problem resolution by a standard portfolio generation module and a portfolio improvement module. For the standard portfolio, agents are structured primarily on investment options, and for portfolio improvements primarily on evaluation viewpoints for generated investment plans or aggressive investment strategies. The knowledge module is implemented on a parallel logic language (FGHC), in the POOL (Parallel Object Oriented Language for cooperative problem solving) parallel object-oriented language. The POOL program is a set of class descriptions defining objects. Class definitions consist of inheritance, slots and default values, methods and local predicates. One-to-one and broadcasting communication functions are supported as message handling functions. Fig. 8.8.1 shows class hierarchical structuring for the investement option agents.

9 CONCLUSIONS

This paper reviewed the current state of research and development on experimental knowledge processing systems. The next steps forwards the final stage will consist of enhancements of functions and technologies, through use and verification of experimental expert systems for individual component technologies. Parallel processing will be introduced, and integration as a next-generation tool will be promoted.

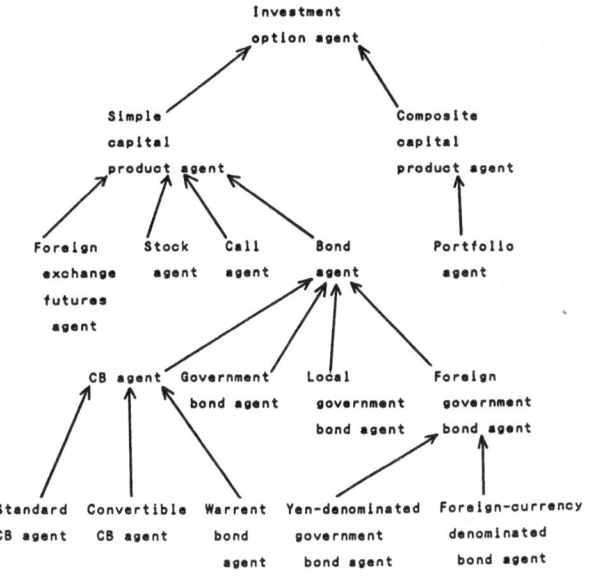

Fig. 8.8.1   Class Hierarchy for Investment Option Agent

REFERENCES

[Araya 87] Araya, A.A. and Mittal, S., "Compiling Design Plans from Descriptions of Artifacts and Problem Solving Heuristics", Proc. of IJCAI 1987, pp.552-558
[Buchberger 83] Buchberger, B., "Groebner Bases: An Algorithmic Method in Polynomial Ideal Theory", TR CAMP-LINTS (1983)
[Chandrasekaran 86] Chandrasekaran, B., "Generic Tasks in Knowledge-Based REasoning: High Level Building Blocks for Expert System Design", IEEE Expert, Vol. 1 (1986), pp. 23-30
[Davis 80]Davis, R., "Report on the Workshop on Distributed AI", SIGART Newsletter, No. 73, October, 1980
[Decker 87]Decker, Keith S., "Distributed Problem-Solving Techniques: A Survey", IEEE Trans. on System, Man, and Cybernetics, Vol.SMC-17, No. 5 Sep./Oct. 1987

[deKleer 84] de Kleer and Brown, "A Qualitative Physics Based on Confluence", Artificial Intelligence Vol. 24 (1984), pp.7-83
[de Kleer 86a] de Kleer, J., "An Assumption-based TMS", Artificial Intelligence 28 (1986), pp.127-162.
[de Kleer 86b] de Kleer, J., "Extending the ATMS", Artificial Intelligence 28 (1986), pp.163-196
[de Kleer 86c] de Kleer, J., "Problem Solving with the ATMS", Artificial Intelligence 28 (1986), pp.197-224
[Doyle 79] Doyle, J., "A Truth Maintenance System", Artificial Intelligence 12 (1979), pp.231-272
[Durfee&Lesser 87]Durfcc, Edmond II. and Lesser, Victor R., "Using Partial Global Plans to Coordinate Distributed Solvers", Proc. of IJCAI 87, pp.875-883
[Fehling 83]Fehling, M., "Report on the Third Annual Workshop on Distributed Artificial Intelligence", SIGART Newsletter, No. 84, April, 1983
[Feldman 88] Feldman, R., "Design of a Depandency-Directed Compiler for Constraint Propagation", Proc. of 1st International Conference on Industrial & Engineering Application of Artificial Intellignece and Expert Systems, IEA/AIE '88, (1988)
[Forbus 84]Forbus, Kenneth D., "Qualitative Process Theory", Artificial Intelligence 24(1984), pp.85-168
[Fujiwara & Inoue 88] Fujiwara, T. and Inoue, K., "A Hypothetical Reasoning System in ESP - ASTRON-"(An ATMS implemented in ESP (Ver. 2)), ICOT Technical Memorandum No. TM-587, ICOT, 1988(in Japanese)
[Gasser 87]Gasser, Les, "The 1985 Workshop on Distributed Artificial Intelligence", AI Magazine, Summer, 1987

[Iijima & Inoue 88] Iijima, K. and Inoue, K., "An ATMS implemented in ESP (Ver. 1), ICOT Technical Memorandum No. TM-467,ICOT, 1988 (in Japanese).

[Inoue 88a] Inoue, K., "Pruning Search Trees in Assumption-based Reasoning", Proc. Avignon '88: The 8th International Workshop on Expert Systems & their Applications (1988), pp.133-151

[Inoue 88b] Inoue, K., "On the Semantics of Hypothetical Reasoning and Truth Maintenance", ICOT Technical Report No. TR-357, ICOT, 1988.

[Inoue 88c] Inoue, K., "Problem Solving with Hypothetical Reasoning", FGCS '88: International Conference on Fifth Generation Computer Systems (1988), in these Proceedings

[Inoue, ed. 88] Inoue, K., (ed.), "Expectations and Images for Hypothetical Reasoning", KSS-WG HYR-SWG Report for 1987, ICOT Technical Memorandum No. TM-487, ICOT, 1988 (in Japanese).

[Inoue et al. 88] Inoue, K., Nagai, Y., Fujii, Y., Imamura, S. and Kojima, T., "Analysis of the Design Process of Machine Tools – Example of a Machine Unit for Lathes –", ICOT Technical Memorandum No. TM-494, ICOT, 1988 (in Japanese)

[Kobayashi 86] Kobayashi, s., "Knowledge Engineering", Shokado, 1986

[Konolige 85] Konolige, Kurt, "Research on distributed artificial intelligence", Stanford Research Institute, AI Center, 1985

[Kuipers 86] Kuipers, B., "Qualitative Simulation", Artificial Intelligence Vol. 29(1986), pp.289-338

[Kuipers 85] Kuipers, B., "Qualitative Simulation of Mechanisms", MIT LCS TM-274, 1985

[Kuipers 87] Kuipers, B., "Abstraction by Time-scale in Qualitative Simulation", Proceedings of AAAI-87(1987), pp.621-625

[Nagai 88a] Nagai, Y., "Towards Desgin Plan Generation for Routine Design using Knowledge Compilation -Forcusing on Constarint Representation and its Application Mechanism for Mecahnical Design-", ICOT Techincal Memorandum, TM-504, (1988)

[Nagai 88b] Nagai, Y. "Towards an Expert System Architecture for Routine Design -Focusing on Constraint Representation and an Application Mechanism for Mechnical Design-", ICOT Technical Memorandum, 1988

[Nii 86] Nii, H.Penny , "Blackboard Systems",Technical Report No. STAN-CS-86-1123, June 1986

[Ohki 88] Ohki, M., "Towards Qualitative Physics", ICOT-TR-221, 1988, (to appear)

[Ohsuga 85] Ohsuga, S. "Conceptual Design of CAD Systems Involving Knowledge Bases", Knowledge Engineering in Computer-Aided Design(Gero, J.S. (ed.)), North-Holland, pp.29-50, 1985

[Oosaki et al. 88] Oosaki, H., Tsubaki, K. and Taki, H., "Knowledge Acquisition Support System EPSILON/One (2)", Proceeding of 8th SICE Knowledge Engineering Symposium, 1988 (in Japanese)

[Poole 88] Poole, D., "A Logical Framework for Default Reasoning", Artificial Intelligence 36 (1988), pp.27-47

[Reiter 80] Reiter, R., "A Logic for Default Reasoning", Artificial Intelligence 13 (1980), pp.81-132

[Sakane 88] Sakane, K., "Methods for Partition of Target Systems in Qualitative Reasoning", Proceedings of FGCS '88 (1988)

[Sekiguchi 83] Sekiguchi, H., Kojima, T. and Inoue, K., "Study on Automatic Determination of Assembly Sequence", Annals of the CIRP, Vol. 32, No. 1 (1983), pp.371-374

[Sekiguchi 87] Sekiguchi, H., Imamura, S., Kojima, T. and Inoue, K., "Method of Developing Part Specifications from Assembly Drawing of Machine Unit (2nd Report) -Automatic Determination of Assembly/Disassembly Sequence-" Journal of the JSPE, Aug.1987, pp.1183-1188 (in Japanese)

[Shastri 85] Shastri, L., "Evidential Reasoning in Semantic Network: A Formal Theory and its Parallel Implimentation", TR166, The University of Rochester,Sept. 1985

[Shostak 77] Shostak, R. E., "On the SUP-INF Method for Proving Presburger Formulas", Journal of ACM, 24 (1977), pp.529-543

[Smith 85]Smith, R.G., "Report on the 1984 Distributed Artificial Intelligence", AI Magazine, Fall, 1985.

[Taki et al. 87] Taki, H., Tsubaki, K. and Iwashita, Y., "EXPERT MODEL for Knowledge Acquisition", IEEE Expert Systems in Government Conference, 1987

[Taki 88] Taki, H., "Knowledge Acquisition by Observation", Proceedings of FGCS '88, 1988

[Tanaka 88] Tanaka, H., "Temporal-hierarchical Qualitative Reasoning and its Application to Medicine", Proceedings of Logic Programming Conference '88, pp.11-17 (1988)

[Terasaki 88] Terasaki, S. Nagai, Y. Yokoyama, T. Inoue, K. Horiuchi, E. and Taki, H., "Mechanical Design Expert System Constructing Tool, MecanICOT", SIG-KBS, JSAI, Oct. 1988 (in Japanese)

[Tomiyama 85] Tomiyama,T. and Yoshikawa,H. "Requirements and Principles for Intelligent CAD Systems" Knowledge Engineering in Computer-Aided Design(Gero,J.S. (ed)), North-Holland, 1985 pp.1-23

[Tsubaki et al. 88] Tsubaki, K., Oosaki,H. and Taki,H., "Knowledge Acquisition Support System EPSILON/One (1)", Proceeding of 8th SICE Knowledge Engineering Symposium, 1988 (in Japanese)

[Yamazaki et al. 87] Yamazaki, T., Taki, H., Tsubaki, K., "Classification Task Acquisition System Based on Generic Tasks CTAS", Proceeding of 1st JSAI Knowledge Base Research Meeting, 1987 (in Japanese)

[Yokoyama 88] Yokoyama, T., "FREEDOM: A Knowledge Representation System for Design Object Modeling"(in Japanese) WGAI, IPSJ, Preprints, 88-60 1988, ICOT Technical Memorandum No. TM-467, ICOT, 1988 (in Japanese)

INVITED LECTURES

PROCEEDINGS OF THE INTERNATIONAL CONFERENCE
ON FIFTH GENERATION COMPUTER SYSTEMS 1988,
edited by ICOT. © ICOT, 1988

PROSPECTS FOR COGNITIVE SCIENCE

Herbert A. Simon

Professor of Computer Science and Psychology
Carnegie-Mellon University
Psychology Department
Pittsburgh, Pennsylvania 15213, U.S.A.

ABSTRACT

From the very beginning, researchers in artificial intelligence and cognitive science have been accused of excessive optimism. I hope we have been guilty of some optimism, and in a field that has moved as far in thirty years as this one has, I deny that there has been excess.

Our understanding of both human intelligence and machine intelligence continues to widen and deepen at a rapid pace, and if there are any limits to the kinds of intelligence that can be represented by computer programs, those limits have not yet made themselves evident. If I have been skeptical that we need anything that is properly described as a "breakthrough" we can proceed further, I am not at all skeptical about the research possibilities for important new ideas and advances.

Mankind has been enthralled by four great questions: the nature of matter, the origins of the universe, the nature of life, and the emergence of mind from matter. It is the privilege of all us in the cognitive sciences to spend our professional lives grappling with the fourth of these questions.

Until the computer was recognized as the general physical symbol system that it is, we had almost no tools for investigating the nature of intelligence and mind. Combining its intelligence with ours, we will continue to move rapidly toward a fuller and clearer conception of the minds of both computers and people.

1 PROSPECTS FOR COGNITIVE SCIENCE

Ten year predictions of the development of a science are rather more feasible than one-day predictions of the stock market. Science and technology do not proceed in instantaneous breakthroughs. Instead, momentous events cast long shadows before them. It was forty years from the recognition of the black body problem to Planck's law, another five years before the significance of the quantum in that law was recognized, another eight before Bohr constructed his theory of atomic structure, and another thirteen before Heisenberg and Schroedinger provided the modern equations of quantum mechanics. While no one (without making the discoveries themselves!) could have predicted these discoveries, much less their exact timing, there was no great problem in predicting where the good research problems lay, and hence, the promising directions of research.

A ten year look ahead to the future of cognitive science does not, therefore, seem too formidable a task - provided that you do not ask me what the precise results of the research will be or just when they will occur. If we wish to sound bold, we can even call this a look into the next century, which is, after all, little more than a decade away. To look ahead in this way, we must first study the shadows that portend the events: We must look briefly at where cognitive science has been, and at where it now is. That is where I will begin.

2 THE ACHIEVEMENTS OF COGNITIVE SCIENCE

In what follows, the terms "cognitive science" and "artificial intelligence" will be used more or less interchangeably. Both domains are concerned with producing intelligent behavior in computers. Cognitive science wishes to do so in order to understand human intelligence, and the programs it writes are intended to use the same kinds of methods that people use in their thinking, speaking, understanding, learning, and so on. AI wishes to produce machine intelligence in order to augment human intelligence, and in the programs it writes, no holds are barred. AI can use machine nanosecond or picosecond speed that is unavailable to the millisecond human brain. But the two fields have worked so closely together since their origin, and have borrowed so freely back and forth, that it is not necessary to consider them separately; the progress of each will continue to depend upon and to support the progress of the other.

2.1 Programming Languages

The very existence of cognitive science depended on having programming languages that allow complex, irregular, constantly changing, unpredictable structures to be stored in memory and processed. The invention of list processing languages, as early as 1956, provided cognitive science and AI with the programming tools it needed and which it has relied upon since. Initially rebuffed and scorned by systems programmers as intolerably slow and wasteful of computer memory, list processing languages turned out to be a major contribution of AI to computer science generally.

Beginning around 1972, LISP, which had become the standard list processing language, was joined by production system languages like OPS5; and more recently by logic programming, as exemplified in PROLOG, has been added to the kit of AI tools. The current interest in connectionism and parallel networks is sure to spawn still another class of programming languages - early examples can already be seen.

2.2 Hardware

The obvious precondition for cognitive science was the existence of computer hardware to support the execution of its programs. The dependence of the research on computers is beyond question or discussion. What is less obvious is whether hardware availability has been a major determinant of the speed at which the research has advanced. Has hardware been the bottleneck, or has it always been available when needed, with the required memory capacities and operation speeds?

One must give a mixed answer to this question. Current systems for visual or auditory pattern recognition, chess programs, and some other expert systems, could not operate at tolerable speeds on the computers available as recently as five or ten years ago. In this sense, the remarkable and continuing advance of hardware has been absolutely essential to the development of AI and cognitive science. We may expect this to continue to be true in the future: we will find needs for even faster computers, with ever larger memory capacities.

But one can ask a different question: Has hardware development been the bottleneck that has limited the rate of progress in cognitive science? Here, the answer is largely negative. The rate at which machine intelligence has been pushed into new domains and new levels of performance has depended mainly on the ingenuity of the researchers. When new ideas have been invented, hardware has usually been available to implement them - not always with the speed and scope that we might wish, but sufficiently well to test the soundness of the ideas. Basic research seldom has to be carried out in real time.

There are exceptions. In designing programs to play chess, machine speed has been of the essence, and much (not all) of the rapid progress of the past five years has come from the availability of special purpose hardware.

Some of us have long believed that computer chess research should put more emphasis on incorporating chess knowledge in the programs, and less on speeding up brute-force search. However, the history of progress in that field does not support our position. Will the future, as chess programs reach grandmaster levels, be different? That spot on my crystal ball is rather foggy.

A few years ago, the idea was popular that AI programming would be greatly facilitated by the availability of special LISP machines or PROLOG machines. Those machines now exist and they achieved a speedup - but only that. They allow us to execute important primitive operations more rapidly, but they still compete with powerful general-purpose hardware, and the verdict is not clear whether the special-purpose machines will be cost effective. At any rate, they represent not a "breakthrough" but just another source, one of many, of speedup in hardware.

In the case both of PROLOG and of languages for connectionist programming, it is widely believed that major problems of execution speed would be solved if we had massively parallel hardware, and much effort is now being devoted to bringing about that result. I am skeptical on two scores: (1) that parallel hardware is the answer to exponential explosion of search (a problem that plagues PROLOG), or (2) that it is, even in principle, feasible to design parallel hardware that has genuine general purpose capabilities.

I will have more to say later on both these points. For the moment, I would simply observe, first, that some impressive special-purpose parallel hardware has already been produced (e.g., array-processors, or the chess machines mentioned earlier); second, that there are no convincing demonstrations of massively parallel general-purpose hardware; third, the newer supercomputers, with only a little parallel capacity, but offering the fastest computing that is available, are used mostly for numerical analysis, and except for connectionist research, have found relatively little application in cognitive science.

The significance of the first observation is that we can, indeed, achieve major speedups (which wound, but do not slay, the dragon of exponential explosion) by parallelism adapted to special uses. The significance of the second is that we do not now know how to bring about several-order-of-magnitude speedups in general-purpose parallel architectures. The significance of the third is that success in designing effective parallel systems may not be the key to progress in cognitive science.

2.3 Programs

For this audience, I do not need to list

the many domains in which computer programs exist that reach or surpass human levels of intelligent behavior, or the many answers we have gained to our questions about how the human mind manipulates symbols in thinking, problem solving, language understanding or learning. I shall only try to summarize some of the common characteristics of these programs, characteristics that seem important to defining the nature of intelligence itself.

First, we do achieve speeds in computer programs that are simply unattainable for people - speed in arithmetic operations being the most striking example. Nevertheless, we have found that speed and brute force, unless combined with heuristics borrowed from our understanding of human cunning, does not go far toward achieving intelligence.

Very early in research on human intelligence, some of the heuristics were discovered that permit people to search very selectively in problem spaces that would otherwise be far too large for human computational capabilities. Even rather simple hill-climbing heuristics, which select the next search step with the aim of increasing some evaluation function, have proved powerful for reducing the necessity for extensive search. More sophisticated, and widely used, is means-ends analysis, which guides search by comparing the current problem state with the goal state, detects differences between them, and takes actions to reduce the differences.

These and other search heuristics were found through research on relatively simple puzzle-like problems, which don't require much real-world knowledge of the solver, but which nevertheless can be quite difficult for people when they first encounter them.

The intelligence of experts, on the other hand, is most often applied to domains that have a large information content. We know today that the human world-class expert (in every one of the dozen or more domains that has been studied intensively) bases his or her expertise on the possession of vast knowledge as well as on the ability to do means-ends analysis or other forms of inference. The expert typically knows 50,000 or more "things" (we call them "chunks") in the domain of expertise. We have evidence that this knowledge is stored in a production-like form, like an indexed encyclopedia. The index enables the expert to recognize key factors (cues, symptoms) in situations in his or her domain, and thereby to access the knowledge stored in the encyclopedia about the significance of those symptoms.

Each of us, expert on our own native language, recognizes while reading any one of 50,000 or 100,000 words in this language, and retrieves immediately from memory our knowledge about the meanings of these words. Doctors do the same with medical symptoms, chess masters with visible features of the chess board, and so on. We know (because we have done it) that we can build expert systems, capable of performing at the level of human experts, by constructing such encyclopedias in the form of production systems and endowing them with a little capability to do means-ends reasoning or other inference.

Today, we also know that those responses of human experts that we call "intuitive" or judgmental," or even "creative," are precisely acts of recognition, based on the 50,000 chunks held in memory. As Pasteur put it, "Accidents happen to the prepared mind." Knowing that, we have pushed our computer explorations into the domain of ill-structured problems and creativity. Programs have been constructed and tested, like EURISKO, BACON, and KEKADA, that are capable of creating new concepts out of old, and scientific laws from raw data, and which can plan, intelligently, sequences of experiments for achieving a research goal.

Most of the accomplishments of cognitive science up to the present time relate to the programming of relatively well structured tasks, where the goals and admissible operators are fairly clearly defined. More recent successes with programs that do scientific discovery - and in quite a different realm, with programs that compose music and make creative drawings - raise our aspirations for the field. The tasks performed by such programs involve vaguely defined goals and no clear boundaries for the legality of "moves." There are no longer, if there ever have been, clear limits to the kinds of human cognition that can be analyzed by the methods of cognitive science.

When cognitive science began, I suppose most of us thought it would be easiest to write programs to do ordinary everyday things - observing, recognizing, making physical movements - while it would be very hard to simulate the "higher" flights of the human mind into scientific and professional activity. It turned out exactly the opposite. Professors, engineers, and businessmen have been much easier to simulate than bulldozer drivers. Building systems to match the human eyes and ears, and their control over the fingers and hands, has proved to be the most difficult of all our research challenges.

We should have predicted that. (We didn't.) The mammalian sensory and motor systems have been evolving for nearly a half billion years. There has been plenty of time for natural selection to hone them into complex and finely-tuned devices. The new brain, which distinguishes us from the rest of the mammals, has been developing for less than a million years. With such a short period of shaping, it is probably still a very simple and crude device - indeed that is exactly what our cognitive science research and expert systems have been revealing to us. For this reason, the hardest problems ahead are still those of understanding and simulating the sensory and motor systems.

From the very beginning, cognitive science has been fascinated with the processes of learning, but fascination has not always been accompanied by rapid progress. In the early years, we had one spectacular success, Samuel's program for learning to play checkers. But we also had disappointments, for example in our experiences with Perceptrons and other schemes for self-organizing networks.

In the past decade, however, research in learning has taken off again, and much has been accomplished. One of the most significant accomplishments is the understanding we have gained about how people can learn by examining worked-out examples, and then "re-programming" themselves to retain the skills employed in working the examples - skills that then can be transfered to other problems.

The computer counterparts of schemes for learning from examples and learning by doing (i.e., by solving problems) are adaptive production systems. Adaptive production systems are simply production systems that can form new productions and add them to memory. Beginning with the work of Neves a decade ago, it has been demonstrated convincingly that such systems can be built for learning subjects, like algebra and geometry, at high school level.

The insights we have gained from adaptive production systems that learn from examples have already been applied in several research studies to the improvement of human teaching and learning. For example, in a study carried out with Chinese colleagues in a Beijing public school, we have shown that the entire three-year algebra and geometry curriculum can be taught from examples and problem-solving practice, without lectures or textbooks. Moreover, the new methods are more efficient in terms of student time and level of learning than the standard classroom methods.

2.4 Applications

I have already mentioned some of the main areas of application of cognitive science today. Most of them we bundle together under the heading of "expert systems," but that label covers a vast and growing collection of different kinds of programs, as the recent book by Feigenbaum, McCorduck, and Nii demonstrates.

Other real-world applications are barely on stage, or remain in the wings. Robotics has had much visibility, but most robots working in factories today have their basis in classical control theory rather than artificial intelligence. Developing robots that incorporate genuine AI techniques will depend on our pro-

gress in making sensory and motor devices, a topic that was mentioned earlier.

We now understand how humans manipulate natural language and extract meaning from it (or put meaning into it). As a result of that understanding, we now know what the REAL problem is of achieving effective and practical language understanding and language translation by computer. The real problem is that a language translator must itself have a great deal of semantic knowledge about the subjects it is translating. Applications in this domain will be paced by progress in building large semantic memories that are organized so that relevant information can readily be found and accessed as needed.

Clearly, these potential fields of application of cognitive science depend for their realization on progress in basic research. It is time for me to turn now to a discussion of the frontiers and prospects of such research.

3 RESEARCH FRONTIERS

My discussion of where we are today in cognitive science provides the basis for my forward view from the frontiers, and enables me to be relatively brief in describing the prospects that I see from there. I will look successively at some of the areas that I have already identified as critical; then I will say something about our needs for software and hardware supporting systems, and our prospects for meeting these needs.

3.1 Task Domains

The topics on which I wish to comment are robotics, language, expert systems, learning, and representation. All but the last of these has already been discussed briefly.

3.1.1 Robotics

Earlier, I identified the development of sensors and effectors as the key to progress in robotics. These hard problems are attracting much research attention today, and there is not much I can say about them that cannot be said better by the researchers. Progress is slow, but there is definite movement. We should expect it to continue and to accelerate, but we should not look for a sudden "breakthrough" that will dissolve all of our difficulties. My crystal ball shows no breakthrough on the horizon.

Clearly, the sensory domain - visual and auditory pattern recognition - is the area where connectionist ideas could make their earliest and most important contribution. The evidence is very strong that most of the human "higher" mental functions are carried out in a serial, one-at-a-time fashion, all passing through the narrow bottleneck of attention.

The difficulties we experience in carrying on a serious conversation while driving a car in heavy traffic is just one of the evidences that, while we may have some time-sharing capabilities, we are not, at this level, parallel processors.

The evidence is equally clear that the eye and the ear, and to a lesser extent the motor system, are parallel devices. It is here where the main connectionist research effort needs to be focused. Some connectionists are more sanguine. They think the whole of cognitive science can be handled with their models, without the need for a separate symbolic level. Time will tell (obviously I don't agree with them).

Finally, there is more to robotics than sensory and motor systems. There must be a thinking and planning system to connect them. Much of the basic equipment and organization for it is in place (as witness systems like STRIPS), derived from the research on problem solving. But the problem that needs more attention, and is just beginning to receive it, is how a planning system, using a very gross and inexact model of the real world outside, guides a robot that has to survive and operate in that real world. This need presents problems of correction and feedback of planning models, problems that are surely solvable, but that need to be addressed.

3.1.2 Language

The long shadow that predicts the main direction of language research is, as I have already explained, the shadow of semantics. Already, Lenat and his colleagues in Texas are engaged in building an information base of encyclopedic dimensions that can be used to test the use of semantic knowledge in informing and guiding language understanding and translation systems. I would expect to see more enterprises of this kind, guided by what we already know about large expert systems, production systems, and data base architectures.

If there are any fundamentally new ideas that have to be invented before progress can be made, they are not visible to me. Undoubtedly, new ideas will emerge as the work progresses - intelligent empirical work always produces them - but what is needed right now and in the near future is large-scale experimentation with data bases.

3.1.3 Expert Systems

Development work on expert systems hardly needs encouragement or guidance. The demonstrations of commerical value are sufficiently numerous and convincing to support vigorous continuing work. The expansion of expert systems to new domains will depend, however, primarily on the progress that is made in the other

dimensions of research I have been discussing: especially sensory systems, robotics, language, learning, and (a topic not yet discussed) representation.

3.1.4 Learning

There are two or three main foci of learning research today. I have already mentioned the two that seem to me most promising. One is connectionist research for the learning of visual and auditory patterns. The other is research on adaptive production systems that learn from examples. I am fairly sure that these two do not cover the whole range of mechanisms the human brain uses to improve its performance, but they seem to be among the most important, and we understand enough about them so that research can progress rapidly.

An intriguing question, on which one can find many opinions but little evidence, is when one should choose learning and when one should choose programming as the preferred method for giving new knowledge to an expert system. Human experts gain all their knowledge by learning, but that is perhaps because we don't know how to open the box and stuff the program in. Would we program people, instead of teaching them, if we could? This is a question that is bound to attract attention as we gain increasing ability to build learning systems, then seek to incorporate these learning capabilities in expert systems.

3.1.5 Representation

Information has to be taken out of Plato's abstract world of ideas and provided with some concrete form of representation before it can be processed by computers or brains. The typical representations we use in cognitive science today include list structures, and schemas constructed from them (alias descriptions, scripts, frames), productions, and declarative statements. All of these are good for stating propositions, or can be made to look as though they were.

There is a great deal of evidence, however, that people use pictures and diagram-like structures as preferred representations in much of their thinking. Einstein was always adamant in insisting that he did not think in words, and many other scientists and mathematicians have endorsed his view. We are just beginning to ask what these non-propositional representations might be, and how they can be implemented in computer systems, and simulated for cognitive research.

Novak's ISAAC program, which understood physics problems stated in words, then wrote the equations and solved them, is an important landmark in our understanding of pictorial representations. For ISAAC understood the words by transforming them into a picture (actually, a list-structure schema) in computer memory. It was easier to form equations from the picture than from the verbal statement of the problem.

It is sometimes said that "a problem well represented is a problem half solved." Certainly, we know problems that are almost impossible to solve as presented, but which become quite easy when a good representation is found. The mutilated checkerboard problem, introduced into AI by John McCarthy, is an example. What we are now learning about diagrammatic representations provides a foundation for substantial progress during the next decade, both in widening the range of representations we can employ, and in building systems that have some capability for finding good representations for the problems that confront them.

4 SUPPORTING SYSTEMS

Having described a number of directions for the future of cognitive science, something needs to be said about the hardware and software supporting systems that will permit the research to go forward - or better yet, that will facilitate it. I will arrange my discussion around four important issues, that have already been raised in our examination of the present state of affairs: serial and parallel architecture, connectionism, logic programming, and non-verbal representations.

4.1 Serial versus Parallel

The brain is a vast network of neurons, whose number has variously been estimated 10^9 or $10+(12)$. The dendrites are themselves branching structures, so that the total number of connections in the brain may be of the order of $10+(15)$. In the face of this architecture, it is quite natural to think that intelligence must require parallel computation. Why else would the processes of evolution have created this vast potential for simultaneous activity?

But the matter is not quite this simple. First, our computers also have vast memories holding information in parallel. Of course, these memories are passive structures, not active computing devices. But neurophysiologists have not yet discovered to what extent the neurons are also essentially passive memory structures, and to what extent they carry on active computation that goes beyond self-maintenance.

Second, as pointed out earlier, the human thinking process contains a narrow bottleneck, the bottleneck of attention, which severely limits the number of thoughts that can be entertained at one time. At least at the level of conscious activity, the brain is demonstrably a serial, one-at-a-time system, rather than a parallel one. It is also a very slow system (by computer standards), for even a simple act of recognition takes the better part of a second.

Its slowness and seriality have made it possible to simulate such activities as problem solving and language understanding in considerable detail using general purpose serial computers. Even recognition processes, after features have been extracted from the stimulus, are easily accomplished in real time by serial discrimination nets like EPAM.

But we have already seen that, if conscious thought is demonstrably serial, seeing and hearing are demonstrably parallel. In terms of any evidence we have today, the most prudent conjecture, perhaps, is that the brain has both parallel and serial components, and that a complete computational theory of intelligence must accommodate both. There is no need to take an either-or attitude on the serial-parallel debate, in fact the empirical evidence argues against such an extreme resolution of the issue in either direction. ·

I have already argued that the strongest case for parallelism, especially in connectionist form, lies in the realm of visual and auditory pattern recognition, and to a somewhat lesser extent in the control of motor activity. Since these have turned out to be some of the most refractory aspects of intelligence, offering very stubborn resistance to our attempts to understand and simulate them, progress of research on sensory and motor functions would be greatly facilitated if we could provide the researchers with the right kind of parallel hardware. What "right kind" means is subject to considerable uncertainty.

As anyone who has attempted it will testify, achieving massive parallelism in computation is extremely difficult, except where hardware is custom designed to handle certain special kinds of precisely defined tasks (e.g., array processors). "General purpose" parallel processors like ILLIAC IV, and its ancestors and descendants, have proved very hard to program except for tasks whose precedence requirements matched closely the hardware design. A typical expecttation for an architecture, on tasks not closely matched to it, is to achieve a speedup by a factor of three to five with the use of 30 processors.

There is no reason to believe that someone will invent a clever idea that will suddenly make general-purpose parallelism feasible. The difficulties are not superficial, but fundamental. Basically, parallelism is constrained by the precedence requirements of the subtasks of any complex task. When there is little connection among tasks, a great deal of parallelism is attainable; when connections are dense and rigid, a large part of the potential capacity of the parallel machine goes unused while tasks await the completion of their predecessors (and while knowledge of that completion is communicated).

Nature itself is constrained from full parallelism by the informational complexity it creates. The dominant architecture of natural systems is hierarchical - with each component at a given level interacting intensively with only a few other components at that level - the protons and neutrons in an atom, the atoms in a molecule, the molecules in a cellular microstructure, and so on.

I have speculated elsewhere as to why natural structures should have evolved mainly into hierarchies. The evolutionary lesson is one that designers of computer architectures might examine closely and consider imitating. Of course we have already had considerable experience with the hierarchical organization of memories, but much less with hierarchies of active processors. Computer networks can also teach us something about hierarchization.

The conclusion I would draw is that we will continue to make progress toward the design of effective parallel systems, but probably without a sudden burst of illumination that will make that progress speedy. Moreover, parallel architectures designed with particular applications in mind are likely to advance more rapidly and to reach more satisfactory levels than attempts at general-purpose massive parallelism. As we learn more about the brain, perhaps we will gain useful ideas for parallel design from that knowledge. Meanwhile, the design of hierarchical systems deserves more attention than it has received.

4.2 Connectionism

I have stated my reasons for thinking that connectionist systems may play a large role, perhaps a decisive one, in modeling sensory and motor systems. Some connectionists, in their enthusiasm, believe that there is no longer any need for serial symbolic systems - that they will soon be replaced by connectionist nets. This seems to me exceedingly unlikely. Again, I would appeal to the evidences of hierarchy in nature as a reason for thinking that the mind is arranged in levels - that there is a level of neuronal organization, and that these neuronal systems, in turn, implement the primitive structures and operators of the symbolic systems at the next level above.

The analogy to the relation between hardware and languages, or between assembly languages and higher-level languages in computers seems quite plausible here. The argument can be stated a little more quantitatively. At the neuronal level, we are concerned with events with durations from one to ten milliseconds, while at the symbolic level, we are concerned with events enduring from hundreds of milliseconds to tens of seconds and longer.

As far as research programs are concerned, a good philosophy is to "let a hundred flowers bloom." Both connectionist and symbolic directions of research hold out great promise, and there is no great urgency now to draw exact boundaries between their respective spheres of applicability. But in particular, connectionists should be encouraged to give high priority to the problems of processing sensory stimuli.

4.3 Logic Programming

The analogy between computing and logical inference, and the consequent notion of modeling programming languages on systems of logic has a long and interesting history. Of course, it started the other way around: Aristotle modeled logic on human reasoning, and Turing modeled it on a computing machine. I will not elaborate on this history, but take up the question of logic programming as exemplified by such languages as PROLOG. I am treading on dangerous ground, for there are many persons present here who know a great deal more about PROLOG and logic programming than I do.

Simply put, the idea behind logic programming is that reasoning should be logical, and that programming languages should incorporate from logic the principles and insights that make logic a powerful and rigorous form of reasoning. Underlying any inferential system are principles, some of which are expressed in declarative form, others in procedural form. The former are called axioms, the latter, inference rules. It is an ideal of logic that both axioms and inference rules should be independent of subject matter; that they should give valid results for all possible worlds. When the logic is applied to a particular domain, additional axioms (domain-specific axioms) are supplied to specify what is known about that domain.

Because formal logic has historically been closely connected with questions of rigor in reasoning, systems of logic are usually designed to make verification of proofs as clear and transparent as possible. This is accomplished, first, by separating logical axioms from domain-specific axioms, as already explained, and second, by severely restricting the inference rules (e.g., in the system of Whitehead and Russell they include only substitution and modus ponens.)

A heavy price is paid for adhering to these principles: the reasoning proceeds by tiny steps, huge numbers of which are needed for even the simplest proofs. Whitehead and Russell paid that price (as attested by the thickness of the volumes of PRINCIPIA MATHE-MATICA) because rigor was the name of the game they were playing. But there are many other games that intelligence plays and that we want to play on computers. They do not all have the same requirements.

The slow, and to some of us, disappointing,

progress in computer theorem proving provides evidence of the cost of adhering to the principles of logic at the expense of alternative possibilities. Only grudgingly did the authors of early theorem proving programs admit inference procedures for equality, commutativity, and transitivity, instead of axiomatizing them. Today, single rules of inference like resolution and its derivatives are still generally preferred over systems with multiple rules. (I would point to the work of Woody Bledsoe and his associates in Austin, Texas, to illustrate what can be accomplished when, departing from this preference, heuristic principles are used freely to supplement the limited procedures of logic in building theorem proving programs.)

When we examine human reasoning, especially as it is applied to substantive affairs, it proceeds in quite a different way. There are not just a few inference procedures but many; and these are not all logical rules, but generally incorporate important domain-specific knowledge. If we watch a good student solving a problem in kinematics, we find the law of uniform acceleration is being used not as an axiom but as a computational procedure for inferring, say, distance from time and acceleration. The human processes in situations like these are readily modeled by production systems with relatively little use of declarative knowledge.

Human reasoning is a mixed bag which serves many purposes. It is used to a much greater extent to discover than to verify, and we know that discovery often requires heuristic search, taking long jumps at the expense of guarantees either of completeness or validity. The lack of these guarantees is not a virtue - it is the price we pay for living in a world where completeness and guaranteed correctness of search are computationally infeasible. Better to find an answer sometimes than to be assured that you will eventually find it (in eons?), and that if you do, it will not be a mirage. Better to check AFTER you have found a candidate than to refuse to hazard possibly false steps.

The principles I have just announced are not laws of logic, but empirical generalizations from human experience. In most real-life situations, human reasoning is, and must be, heuristic search. If powerful inference rules, even vulnerable ones, can be incorporated in the search, it will be more likely to reach its goal in a tolerable time.

Now there is no reason why logic programming cannot be carried on in the spirit of these principles, just as there is no reason why a language like PROLOG cannot be extended to equivalence with a Turing machine. But if the principles are followed, then logic programming loses its special rationale and claim to preference. Contrary to the underlying justification for logic programming, procedures will then be substituted for declarative statements, and flexible best-first search control will replace depth-first backtrack search.

My problem is not with a programming language. My problem is with what seems to me a misconception of the central principles that underlie intelligence, and that should guide the design of intelligent programs for AI and cognitive science. Among those central principles is the idea that problem solving is heuristic search.

One of the oldest issues in cognitive science, along with the competition between seriality and parallelism, is the issue of whether knowledge should be represented declaratively or procedurally. I suspect that here, as in the serial/parallel issue, the answer is "both." There is probably good reason to believe that much of our knowledge of the world is stored in declarative form, but that much of our capability for using that knowledge is stored procedurally, as sets of productions. We need to be suspicious of proposals to place the whole of intelligence, or nearly the whole, in one or the other of these forms of representation.

4.4 Nonverbal Representation

In my plea for a balance between declarative and procedural knowledge, I have defined the latter in terms of productions, but haven't said exactly what I mean by the former. "Declarative" should not be equated with "propositional." One important form of declarative representation, widely used in AI, consists of list structures and description lists (property list) structures - often called schemas, scripts, or frames.

Of course, such structures can be interpreted as sets of interrelated propositions. But though list structures and propositions may be logically equivalent, they are not computationally equivalent. In propositional representations, variables play the role that is played by common linked nodes in list structures. List structures can be used to build representations that are computationally equivalent to diagrams (see Novak, and Larkin and Simon), allowing in many cases far more efficient computation than can be achieved with sets of propositions.

List structures are not the only form of storage of picture-like information. One important alternative is the raster of pixel arrays. The computational convenience and power of such rasters of course depends heavily on the hardware and software processes that are available for manipulating them and reading information from them. The same is true of other representations, which describe figures in terms of the equations of their boundaries, or the like.

If it is true, as seems probable, that much human reasoning uses picture-like and diagram-like mental and external representations, then research on computer hardware and software for implementing such representations will be of great value. There has been substantial research activity of this kind in connection with CAD, but to the best of my knowledge, it has not been closely linked with research in artificial intelligence or cognitive science. A closer linkage could lead to very interesting and useful ideas about how to represent knowledge that is declarative, but not explicitly propositional.

PROCEEDINGS OF THE INTERNATIONAL CONFERENCE
ON FIFTH GENERATION COMPUTER SYSTEMS 1988,
edited by ICOT. © ICOT, 1988

Logic Programming Schemes

Keith L. Clark

Department of Computing
Imperial College
180 Queens Gate
London SW7 2BZ

Abstract

This paper offers a tutorial but incomplete survey of a succession of proposed logic programming language schemes all of which can be considered variants or descendants of the original Kowalski scheme. Semantic properties and implementation issues are discussed.

1 Introduction

It is now 14 years since Kowalski(1974) described his scheme for logic programming based on a backward chaining resolution inference system for Horn clause programs and 15 years since the first implementation of Prolog (Battani & Meloni 1973), a language which is an instance of that scheme. Since, many extensions of the Kowalski scheme have been proposed, and many successors of Prolog have been implemented. This paper is a tutorial introduction to a succession of logic language schemes starting with the Kowalski scheme and ending with the CLP scheme of Joxan and Lassez (1987).

The schemes are presented using a common framework derived from Colmerauer(1982). The semantic properties are discussed using concepts from (Clark 1979,1982). This was the first formulation that focussed on the semantics of the answer substitutions returned by the Kowalski scheme, interpreting them as conjunctions of equalities denoting relations over the Herbrand universe. This is the formulation that best relates the Kowalski scheme to the other schemes, which compute descriptions of relations represented by conjunctions of more general formulas, possibly over other domains.

Schemes not based on first order classical logic, such as lambda-Prolog (Miller and Nadathur 1986) and schemes based on bottom up evaluation (Ramakrishnan 1988) (see also Bancilhon & Ramakrishnan 1986) are not covered.

2 Units of computation

The unit of computation of many logic programming schemes is the unification of one or more pairs of terms. Terms are constructed from countably infinite disjoint alphabets F, V of *functors* and *variables*. Each functor has an associated arity. Functors with arity 0 are *constants*. A *term* is a variable, a constant, or of the form $f(t1,..,tk)$, $k \geq 1$, where f is a k-adic functor. $t(F,V)$ is the set of all terms and $t(F)$ is the set of ground (variable free) terms.

An *assignment* is a set A of equations $\{X1=t1,..,Xn=tn\}$ where Xi are distinct variables and ti are terms (which may contain variables). ti is called the *binding* for Xi. A *substitution* S is an assignment where no Xi occurs in any ti. A *unifier* Ø of a pair of terms t,t' is a substitution such that t{Ø} is identical to t'{Ø}. t{Ø} is t with any variable bound by S is replaced by its binding. We give below an algorithm for computing a unifier of a set of pairs of terms given as a set of equations. The algorithm actually returns a most general unifier (mgu). See (Robinson 1979) or (Lassez et al 1987) for a more formal definition of unifier and mgu.

The difference between an assignment and a substitution is important. Let (E)S denote the existential closure of S, the existential quantification of all its variables. (E)S is true no matter what interpretation I is given to the functors. Such an interpretation is a pair $<D,A>$ where D is a non-empty domain and A is a function mapping each k-adic functor into a k-adic function from D^k to D. Let M be a function mapping the variables $Y1,..,Yk$, of the binding terms in S to elements $e1,..,ek$ of D. Letting $Xi = v(ti)$, the value of ti for interpretation A,M gives a tuple of values $X1=v(t1),..,Xn=v(tn),Y1=e1,..,Yk=ek$ which trivially satisfies the equations S.

If S is just an assignment, (E)S is not always true for every I. Consider the assignment $\{X=f(X)\}$. $(EX)\{X=f(X)\}$ is true only if f has a fixed point.

Herbrand interpretation

An interpretation for which $(EX)\{X=f(X)\}$ is false is the free or Herbrand interpretation HI. The domain is the set the functors has a special role in logic programming. A substitution denotes a non-empty relation for any interpretation because it denotes a non-empty relation in the Herbrand interpretation.

Unification algorithm

The following algorithm finds a unifier of a set of pairs of terms expressed as set of equations E={t1=t'1,..,tk=t'k}. The algorithm terminates with a substitution S (a success termination) or it terminates with a set of equations containing **false**, (a fail termination).

(a) Replace any equation of the form f(t1,..,tk)=f(t'1,..,t'k) by the k equations t1=t'1,..,t=t'k.

(b) Delete any equation of the form X=X.

(c) Replace any equation of the form t=X, t a non-variable, by X=t.

(d) Select any equation of the form X=t, where X occurs in some other equation and X≠t.
   (i) If X occurs in t (the occur check), terminate replacing the equation by **false**.
   (ii) Otherwise, replace X by t in all other equations. X=t i is not deleted .

(e) If there is an equation f(...)=g(...), where f and g are different, terminate replacing the equation by **false**.

The above algorithm always terminates. If it fails, the original set of equations E has no unifier. If it terminates with success then S is a substitution which is an mgu of E. A proof is in (Martelli and Montanari 1982). The algorithm is essentially Herbrand's original algorithm for checking whether or not a set of equations has a solution for the Herbrand interpretation (HI) of its functors.

Rule d(ii) can be modified to the instruction: replace X by t in some of the other equations. The rule can then be reapplied, possibly to a different binding equation X=t' for X, until X does not appear in any other equation. This is a modification of the algorithm used in the some of the parallel languages we shall discuss in section 4.

Let us call an equation of the form X=t to which d(ii) applies a binding equation. Applying d(ii), is *communicating* or *broadcasting* the binding. Applying the substitution to every equation is *global* broadcasting, applying it to only some equations in which X appears, is *local* broadcasting. In an implementation in which a variable is a pointer to a single memory location, from which any binding is automatically retrieved, global broadcasting is achieved by simply assigning the value t of a binding equation X=t to the location for X. Local broadcasting must be implemented by having multiple locations for X, or by explicitly copying and substituting for X in those equations covered by the local broadcast.

An implementation that stores bindings instead of substituting in equations corresponds to the following modification of rule (d).

(d') Select any equation of the form X=t.
If there is a broadcasted equation X=t' for X, replace X=t by t'=t. Otherwise,
   (i) If X occurs in t (the occur check), terminate replace the equation by **false**.
   (ii) Otherwise, make X=t the broadcasted equation for X.

Local broadcasting to some subset of equations is the further modification of this rule to incorporate the idea of a broadcast equation restricted to certain other equations. The test then checks for a broadcast equation for this eqaution.

We can also allow simultaneous selection of several equations, each to be handled by application of the appropriate rule, providing we impose some restrictions. If we have global broadcasting, only one binding equation can be selected for any variable. If we have local broadcasting, we can select multiple binding equations providing each is not included in the broadcast range of any other.

Unification as a special form of equation solving

Let X1,..,Xk be the variables of the original set of equations E. E can be be viewed as defining a relation R_E={<X1,..,Xk>:E} given some interpretation I. An empty set of equations defines {<>:**true**}, or equivalently just the logical constant **true**. The equations have a solution for I iff R_E is not empty for I. The final set S produced by the unification algorithm is such that R_S is contained in RE for any interpretation I. If S is a substitution, this tells us that R_E is non-empty, hence that the equations have a solution, for any interpretation I. If S contains **false**, R_S is the empty relation **false**. We cannot conclude that R_E=**false** for any I, but we can conclude that is empty for the interpretation HI. This is because each of the equation rewrites preserves equivalence for HI. The free interpretation of the functors is reflected in rules (a), d(i) and (e).

Unification as inference from a theory of the functors

The following axioms, from (Clark 1978), characterise the Herbrand interpretation.

(F1) for every functor

f(X1,..,Xk) = f(Y1,..,Yk) -> X1=Y1,..,Xk=Yk

(F2) for every pair of distinct functors f,g

    $f(X1,..,Xk) \neq g(Y1,..,Yn)$

(F3) for every non variable term t(X) containing some variable X, $X \neq t(X)$

These axioms, together with the normal reflexive, symmetric, transitive and substitution axioms for =, comprise the Herbrand equality theory HET. Each step of the unification algorithm is a particular use of one of the axioms of the equality theory. This relationship is formalised in the result (Clark 1978):

(R2.1)   HET $\models$ $R_E = R_S$, or equivalently $V(E <-> S)$
           where **V** denotes universal closure.

That E <- S only needs the general equality axioms, which establishes that R_E contains R_S for all interpretations. That E -> S needs the freeness axioms.

As corollaries of (R2.1) we have

(R2.2)   S=**false** iff HET $\models$ R_E=**false**

(R2.3)   S is a substitution iff $R_E \neq$**false** for any I

Thus S is equivalent to E for theory HET and a simple test on the syntactic form of S tells us whether or not E has a solution. S is a *solution form* for equations E for the theory HET.

Solving equations for other theories of the functors

The unification process can be viewed as a special case of a more general process of checking whether or not a set of equations has a solution for some other equality theory. (Colmerauer 1982) is an example of a logic programming scheme in which equations are solved for a different theory, an equality theory of infinite rational trees.

Checking solvability of more general equality formulas

Viewed as a description of a relation, a set of equations is a just a special case of a first order formula using only the predicate =. Unification could be replaced by a process of checking whether or not some more general equality formula is satisfiable (denotes a non-empty relation) for some interpretation of the functors. Colmerauer's (1986) scheme is an example of this. In this scheme, the formulas are conjunctions of equalities and negated equalities reduced to solution form for a theory of infinite rational trees.

Checking solvability of constraint formulas

The final generalization, is to allow other predicates in the formulas for which we need to determine satisfiability.

The key logical requirement is that there is some theory T of the functors and predicates that appear in the formulas which is *satisfaction complete* for the formulas. That is, for any formula it determines whether or not the formula denotes a non-empty relation. Checking this property for some formula F, is this generalization of unification of Jaffer and Lassez's(1987) scheme for constraint logic programming.

Pragmatic requirements

Testing satisfiability of a set of equations using unification is suitable unit of computation for a logic programming language because it is algorithmic, it produces an equivalent solution form and the algorithm is incremental. To reduce a larger set $E \cup E'$ to solution form we can apply the algorithm to $S \cup E'$ where S is the solution form for E. Moreover, the solution form form for $S \cup E'$ it is expressible as an extension $S \cup S'$ of S if rule (d') is used instead of rule (d). This incremental nature of the algorithm is essential for efficient implementation. This is because a unification based logic program computation is essentially the process of reducing to solved form progressively larger sets of equations.

In the non-unification based schemes, we must also have 'algorithmic' and incremental reducibilty to solved form if we are to justify the *programming* label.

3 Schemes based on unification

3.1 SLD resolution - the Kowalski scheme

The first schematic framework for logic programming languages was given by Kowalski (1974). This scheme is actually LUSH resolution (Hill 1974), now referred to as SLD-resolution. Programs comprise rules of the form

    A <- A1,..,An   for n≥0

where A, A1,..,An are atoms. An *atom* is of the form p(t1,..,tn), n≥0, where the ti are terms and p is a n-adic predicate taken from some countably infinite set *P* of predicate names disjoint from *F* and *V*. A is the clause *head* and A1,..,An are *calls* comprising the clause *body*. It is a clause *about* r, if r is the predicate of A. Each variable in the clause is implicitly universally quantified.

A computation is invoked by a conjunction G of calls. If X1,..,Xk are all the variables of G, it is a request to a description of one or more instances of the relation $R_G = \{<X1,..,Xk>:G\}$ for any interpretation which is a model of the program.

A state of the computation is a pair $<G,S>$ where G is a conjunction of calls $B_1,..,B_m$ and S is a substitution or it contains **false**. In the initial state S is the empty substitution $\{\}$. A unit of computation is the unification of some call $B_i = r(t'1,..,t'k)$, selected by a *computation rule* CR, with the head $A = r(t1,..,tk)$ of a clause variant $A < -A_1,..,A_n$ (a clause with variables renamed so as to have no variables in common with G) in the binding environment represented by S. This is the application of the above unification algorithm to $S_U\{t1 = t'1,..,tk = t'k\}$, or equivalently to $S_U\{t1 = t'1,..,tk = t'k\}\{S\}$ to produce a solution form S'. A next state of the computation is

$<\textbf{true},S'>$ if $m=1,n=0$,otherwise

$<B_1,..,B_{i-1},A_1,...,A_n,B_{i+1},..,B_m,S'>$.

The alternative states that can be derived using different clauses for the predicate of the selected atom represent branch points for the computation. The *computation tree* for a goal G and computation rule CR is a finitely branching tree routed at $<G,\{\}>$ labelled with states. The offsprings of a node in the tree are all the alternative states that can be generated using all the clauses about the predicate of the selected call.

A branch of the computation tree terminates with *success* if its end node is labelled by a state $<\textbf{true},S>$ where S is a substitution. A computation path terminates with *failure* if its end node is labelled with a state $<G,S>$, S contains **false**. A branch may be infinite.

The strategy for constructing the computation tree is the *search* strategy. The strategy is *fair* if it does not indefinitely postpone the construction of some branch of the search tree.

The answer computed by a success branch on a tree for computation rule CR is the substitution S restricted to bindings $X_1,..,X_k$ for the variables of the original goal clause G. (If rule unification rule d' is used instead of d, S must also be applied to the bindings for $X_1,...,X_k$.) The answer S' can be interpreted as denoting a k-adic answer relation $R_{S^\wedge} = \{<X_1,..,X_k> : S'^\wedge\}$, where $S'^\wedge$ is the existential quantification of S' with respect to all the variables in the binding terms. Important theoretical results, strengthening the soundness and completeness results of (Hill 1974), were proved in (Clark 1979). They are:

(R3.1.1) *Soundness*

For every CR-computed answer substitution S,

$\quad P |= R_G$ contains $R_{S^\wedge}$

Since for a substitution, $R_{S^\wedge} \neq \textbf{false}$ for any I, this result implies the usual but weaker soundness result :

If there is a success computation path then $P|=(E)G$

(R3.1.2) *Independence of the computation rule*

For each CR-computed answer S there is an CR'-computed answer S' such that $R_{S^\wedge} = R_{S'^\wedge}$ for every I.

(R3.1.3) *Strong completeness*

For every substitution S' such that $P |= R_G$ contains $R_{S'^\wedge}$ there is an CR-computed answer S such that $R_{S^\wedge}$ contains $R_{S'^\wedge}$ for every I.

Proof of (R3.1.3) uses the fact that the unification algorithm returns an mgu but I believe it can be proved using only (R2.1).

The Kowalski scheme allows for or-parallel search down the alternative evaluation paths but only and-sequential evaluation. At each computation step only one call is being unified. A trivial extension, is to allow concurrent evaluation of any sequence of k steps from state $<G,S>$ that select atoms which can be independently unified with heads of clauses in the context S. The condition that guarantees this is that each pair of atoms B, B' of the sequence of selected atoms are such that $B\{S\}$ has no variables in common with $B'\{S\}$. This is *independent and-parallelism*.

Another simple extension, is to allow the return of qualified answers. Suppose the original goal has been reduced to a state $<G',S'>$ where S' is a substitution but $G' \neq \textbf{true}$. Let S be the subset of bindings in S' that bind variables in G. A qualified answer (Vasey 1986) for that computation path is S, G' . A simple generalization of (R3.1.1) tells us that

$\quad P |= R_G$ contains $R_{(S,G')^\wedge}$

Of course, $R_{(S,G')^\wedge} \neq \textbf{false}$ only if $P |= (E)G'$

Types of computation rule

A rule that always selects one of the introduced calls $A_1,..,A_n$ if there is one, is a *depth first* rule. The rule that always selects the leftmost introduced call, or the next call in the goal conjunction if there are no introduced calls, is the *leftmost call* rule. A rule that does not always select an introduced call is a *coroutining rule*. With a coroutining rule the computation can alternate between the evaluation of different calls. With a depth first rule calls are always completely evaluated once selected but the calls are not necessarily selected in the order in which they appear in the goal and in the body of clauses.

Implementations of the Kowalski scheme

The first implementation was Prolog (Battoni and Meloni 1973), which actually predated the publication of the

Kowalski scheme. Prolog uses the leftmost call computation rule. It also uses a depth first backtracking search strategy trying the clauses in the fixed order in which they are entered.

IC-Prolog (Clark and McCabe 1979, Clark et al. 1982) was the first implementation to allow more general computation rules specified by program annotations. Like Prolog it uses depth first backtracking search. The default rule is the leftmost call rule but a different order of the calls in the body of a clause can be specified for different modes of use, causing the calls to be introduced into the goal in different orders for different modes. A mode of use is a restriction of the unification with the head of the clause which specifies certain argument terms as input or output. Suppose that we successfully unify a call $r(t1,..,tk)$ in in state $<G,S>$ with a head $r(t'1,..,t'k)$. The input restriction on $t'i$ is satisfied if all the bindings that result from rewriting equation $ti\{S\}=t'i$ are for variables in $t'i$. The output restriction on $t'j$ is satisfied if tj is a variable that is not bound in S.

A coroutining rule in IC-Prolog is specified by annotations on variables in calls. A ? annotation on a variable V in a call, B, specifies B as a eager consumer of the binding for V. Suppose the leftmost call rule selects a call A to the left of B and the unification with the next clause for the atom results in the broadcasting of a non-variable binding t for V. The body atoms for the clause are introduced into the goal but call B is moved from its position in the current goal conjunction G to the leftmost position. The evaluation then continues with a depth first evaluaton of B. However, no call B', which is a descendant of B, is allowed to broadcast a non-variable binding for a variable in t. If the unification of such a call B', would result in the broadcasting of such a binding, the call is not selected. Instead, the conjunction of all the current descendants $B1,..,Bj$ of B are moved back to the position that B occupied in goal G. The computation continues with the new leftmost call. The descendants of B are moved to the front of the goal if a non-variable binding for any variable in t is computed and back again to the position they occupied if the selection of one of the descendants would result in the broadcasting of a non-variable binding for a variable in t'. The switching forward and back continues until there are no descendants of B. The consumer annotation has no effect if no call to the left of B tries to bind V. A dual notion, that of an lazy producer, is specified by the annotation ^ on a variable in a call B. Strict one step alternation between the depth first evaluation of two or more calls can also be specified, giving pseudo parallel evaluation.

A weaker form of the eager consumer concept of IC-Prolog, which is easier to implement, was independently devised by Colmerauer and colleagues and implemented in Prolog II (Colmerauer 1982b). This is the freeze call. Instead of annotating the variable V in a call B with ^, the call is written freeze(V,B). Suppose now that the leftmost call computation rule selects freeze(V,B). If V is bound to a non-variable in the current environment S, the evaluation continues as though the call was B. If V is unbound, B is temporarily removed from the goal conjunction of the current state and linked with V. Other freeze calls can add to the number of frozen calls linked with V, as can binding V to some other variable U that has linked frozen calls. Now suppose that a non-variable binding for V is broadcast by the unification of some call B' with the head of a clause A<- A1,..,An. B and all other frozen calls linked with V are reintroduced into the goal in front of the body atoms A1,..,An. The freeze condition is not inherited, a descendant of B will resuspend only if it is contained inside another freeze call.

If V is never bound to a non-variable, B and any other frozen calls linked with V will never be re-introduced into the computation. So this implementation computes qualified answers, the qualification being the conjunction of all frozen calls that are not reintroduced. IC-Prolog does not compute qualified answers because all calls always remain in some position in the goal.

In MU-Prolog (Naish 1985) coroutining is also implemented by temporarily removing the leftmost call from the goal. Here, the suspension condition is not specified by the form of call, but by the specification of allowed modes of use of clauses. With each predicate r a set of modes of use is specified by a set of *wait* statements. A *wait* statement specifies a subset of argument positions that are allowed output positions for the unification of any call for r with the head of each clause for r. When the left most call B is for a predicate with *wait* statements, the call is suspended if the unification with the next clause for r would result in the broadcasting of bindings not allowed by any *wait* statement for r . Let U1,..,Uj be those variables for which bindings cannot be broadcast without violating some *wait* statement. The call B is removed from the goal but reintroduced at the front of the goal as as soon as a non-varible binding is broadcast for any of these variables. The call may resuspend.

In Chapter 3 of Naish (1985) an algorithm for automatically generating *wait* statements is given. These have the effect of suspending any call for which a depthfirst evaluation would result in an infinite computation branch.

In NU-Prolog (Thom and Zobel 1887), *wait* statements are replaced by *when* statements which give conditions under which a call can be selected rather than conditions for suspension. The *when* declaration is dummy clause for a predicate that must succeed before any call to the predicate can be selected. Its role is to check that certain arguments are of a particular form, or are non-variable, or are ground terms. As in MU-Prolog, they can cause a call to be temporarily removed until one or more variables are bound to non-variable terms.

(Ciepielewski & Haridi 1984) and (Moto-Oka et al 1984) are designs for or-parallel implementation of SLD with a leftmost call rule. (Conery 1987) has or-parallelism, restricted and-parallelism and dynamic re-ordering of the body calls depending upon which variables in the body are bound by the head unification. (Degroot 1984) is a proposal to allow restricted and-parallelism in an otherwise sequential leftmost call implementation with compile time analysis used to simplify the runtime test for independence of calls. Warren (1987) is a survey of current work on the or-parallel implementations of Prolog.

3.2 Heterogeneous SLD - the Naish scheme

An interesting variation of the SLD, called Heterogeneous SLD, has been proposed by Naish(1984) as a more suitable model for a coroutining implementation. In this variant, it is still the case that only a single call is unified and replaced by the body atoms of some clause during a computation step, but the successor states do not all have to be produced by replacing the same selected call. Some of them can be produced by selecting another call and using only *some* of the clauses for the predicate of that call. The computation rule applied to a state returns a sequence of <call,clause> pairs to be used in generating the successor states, although the sequence order does not constrain the order in which some search strategy generates the successor states. A state of the computation also records the clauses that can be still used to unify with a particular call. Suppose the computation rule returns a sequence <Bi,C>,<Bj,C'>,.. for the state <G,S>, and <Gi,Si> is the successor generated by unifying Bi with the head of C and <Gj,Sj> is the successor obtained by unifying Bj with the head of C'. Then, C' will appear in the list of clauses that can be used to unify with the occurrence of Bj in Gi, but clause C will not appear in the list that can be used for Bi in Gj.

Naish proves that providing the sequence returned by the computation rule includes all the (to be used) clauses for at least one call, the scheme computes the same set of answers as SLD. Operationally, it allows a backtracking implementation which has discovered that all computation paths that result from using clause C to try to solve call Bi in <G,S> ends in failure, to backtrack to <G,S>, select another call Bj in G, and subsequently to try to solve Bi without needing to reconstruct the failure subtree generated by using C. This is because C will have been deleted from the clause set associated with Bi down the new branch routed at <G,S>. Naish also points out that it justifies the following form of intelligent backtracking: once a call has been found to fail, on backtracking to the parent state, retry the failed call if it is in the goal rather than the previously selected call. Repeat this until the call succeeds or until it is no longer in the backtrack goal.

IC-Prolog and MU-Prolog are implementations of this scheme. This is because the attempted unification which causes a call B to be delayed may be an attempted unification with the second or later clause for B. When B is resumed, the previous clauses are not retried.

3.3 SLDNF - the Clark scheme

In (Clark 1978) an extension of SLD was proposed to allow negated atoms in queries and the bodies of rules. Programs are now expressed as implications of the form

A <- L1,...,Lk

where A is an atom and each Li is a literal : an atom B or its negation ~B. Goals are conjunctions of literals. Each variable in a rule is still implicitly universally quantified.

States of the computation are as in SLD except that the goal component is a conjunction of literals and it may contain **false**. The computation rule SR can select any positive call or any negative call ~B in <G,S> such that B{S} is ground (variable free). Following (Lloyd and Topor 1986) we shall call such a rule *safe*. If the selected call is positive, this is a normal call, and is handled as in SLD.

If the selected call is a negative call ~B then the query evaluation process is recursively entered with the ground query B{S}. If every computation path ends in failure, ~B is assumed to succeed and is deleted from the current goal to give the new goal. If some computation branch for B{S} ends in success, ~B is replaced by **false**, giving a failure termination. This is the *negation as failure* rule.

A computation branch *flounders* if a state is generated

which only has an unground negative calls.

Prolog is an SLDNF systems but without the safety constraint on the computation rule. It is left to the programmer to make sure the negated calls come after positive calls that can be used to generate ground bindings for their variables. MU-Prolog and NU-Prolog have safe computation rules. IC-Prolog has an unsafe rule but raises an error if the evaluation of a negated call tries to broadcast a binding for a variable in B{S}.

The answers computed by SLDNF are not logical consequences of the program. Firstly, failure to unify is interpreted as proof of falsity, which is only valid for the Herbrand interpretation. Secondly, there is an implicit assumption that the given clauses somehow constitute a complete definition for each relation.

Program completion

(a) $r(t1,..,kn) <- L1,..,Lk$

is a program clause. The *guarded form* of the clause is

(b) $r(X1,..,Xn) <- X1=t1,..,Xn=tn : L1,..,Lk$

and the *general form* is

(c) $r(X1,..,Xn) <- (EY1,..,Yj)$

$\qquad\qquad\qquad (X1=t1,..,Xn=tn : L1,..,Lk)$

$X1,..Xn$ are new variables not in (a) and $(EY1,..,Yj)$ is the existential quantification of all the variables in (a). The ':' is just a conjunction connective like ','.

Remember that unification between a selected call $r(t'1,..,t'n)$ and the clause head $r(t1,..,tn)$, is the unification of $E_U\{t'1=t1,...,t'n=tn\}$. This is equivalent to the unification of $E_U\{X1=t'1,..,Xn=t'n\}_U X1=t1,..,Xn=tn\}$. If we revised our definition of a computation step, so that all guard equations are also added to E before it is reduced to solution form, computation using the guarded form of the clause is exactly the same as computation using the original clauses. Let

$\quad r(X1,..,Xn) <- E1$

$\quad r(X1,..,Xn) <- E2$

$\quad r(X1,..,Xn) <- Em$

be the general forms of all the clauses for r .

The *completed* definition for r is:

$r(X1,..,Xk) <-> E1 \lor E2 \lor .. \lor Em.$

Program completion

completed(P) comprises:

(i) the completed definition for every predicate that appears in the head of a clause in P,

(ii) the definitions

$\quad Q(X1,..,Xk) <-> false \quad k\geq o$

for every k-adic predicate for which there are no program clauses.

$comp(P) = completed(P)_U HET$

Soundness results for SLNDF (Clark 1978)

(R3.3.1) For every SR computed answer S for goal G,

$\quad comp(P) |= R_G$ contains $R_S\land$

(R3.3.2) If for some safe computation rule every branch of the computation tree for G ends in failure then $comp(P) |= \sim(E)G$

(R3.3.3) If the SR-computation tree routed at G is finite and $S1,..,Sn, n\geq 0$, are all the answers computed by the success branches, then

$\quad comp(P) |= R_G = R_{S1}\land U ...... U R_{Sn}\land$, equivalently

$\quad comp(P) |= (V)[G <-> S1\land \lor .....\lor Sn\land]$

Allowing unshared local variables in the negated call

(R3.3.2) will allow us to generalize SLDNF programs to have negated conjunctions $\sim C$, not just negated calls. We can liberalise the safety condition and allow $\sim C$ to be selected if C{S} does not share a variable with any other call in G{S}. These local variables are then implicitly existentially quantified inside the negation because a completely failed computation is a proof of $\sim(E)C\{S\}$. This is what happens in the Prolog implementation of negation as failure. We can have a rule

maths_major(X)<-

$\quad$ student(X),$\sim$(maths_course(Y),$\sim$takes(X,Y))

The evaluation of maths_course(Y),$\sim$takes(X,Y), with X=p, , will be a proof of

$\sim(EY)(maths\_course(Y),\sim takes(p,Y))$

if it fails. Unfortunatly, this relaxation does effect the simple rule that all variables of a clause are implicitly universally quantified and it is better to insist that the negated condition is explicitly existentially quantified in the rule as in NU-Prolog (Naish 1986). NU-Prolog(Naish 1986) enforces the generalized safety check that all unquantified variables of such a negation (its *global* variables) are bound to non-variables before it can be selected. The quantified variables are its *local* variables.

Suspending evaluation of negated call

Another extension of the negation as failure rule would be to allow selection of a quantified conjunction $\sim(EV_L)C$, with unbound global variables V_G, but to suspend any branch of the computation of $C\{S\}$ that tries to broadcast a non-variable binding for any of these variables. The branch is resumed when a binding for the variable is broadcast. The evaluation will coroutine between the recursively entered goal $C\{S\}$ and the evaluation of the original goal G. Suppose there is a successful evaluation of $C\{S\}$ that succeeds without binding *any* global variable, we can replace $\sim(EV_L)C$ by **false**. For we have established $(VV_G)(EV_L)C\{S\}$ and hence $\sim(EV_G)\sim(EV_L)C\{S\}$. No matter what ground bindings are given to the variables in V_G, $C\{S\}$ will succeed. IC-Prolog has this generalization of the rule, but it raises an error instead of suspending if there is an attempt to bind a global variable.

Allowing generation of values for global variables

(R3.3.3) will allow a negation as failure rule which generates answers. Suppose we allow any negated condition $\sim C$ to be selected and that we always try to construct the complete computation free for $C\{S\}$. If there is a success branch that does not result in any bindings for variables in $C\{S\}$, we can replace $C\{S\}$ by **false**. If all branches fail, we can delete it. If $S1,..Sn$ are all the answer bindings for variables in $C\{S\}$, then result (R3.3.3) tells us that $\sim C$ can be replaced by the conjunction $\sim S1^\wedge,...,\sim Sn^\wedge$. Distributing the negation will give us quantifed negated equalities. To handle these, we need to extend the SLDNF scheme so that unification is replaced by the process of checking that such inequalities are consistent with the binding equations returned as answers to other calls. We shall return to this in section 6.

Constructive proof

As pointed out in (Clark 1978), SLDNF requires each negated atom to be constructively proven, it does not allow case analysis proofs. Thus, q is a consequence of the completion of the program

p <- p   q <- p   q<- ~ p

but the evaluation of q will not terminate under any computation rule. This is because the evaluation cannot make use of the law of the excluded middle, $p \vee \sim p$, hence it cannot show that q is true no matter what the the truth of p is.

Completeness results

Unfortunately there is no simple completeness result. The problems are threefold. Firstly, there is no guarantee that for an arbitrary program that the computation will not flounder, terminate with only non-ground negated calls in the goal. Secondly, it must be the case that everything that can be inferred from comp(P) can be inferred 'constructively', without using the law of excluded middle. Thirdly, when there is a 'constructive' proof of $\sim B\{S\}$ from comp(P), we must be able to generate a finite failure tree. The first two conditions force us to put extra constraints on the syntactic form of P. The last one requires that the computation rule be *fair* as well as safe.

A *fair* computation rule is a concept introduced into logic programming by Lassez and Maher. It is a computation rule which does not indefinitely postpone the selection of any call. No depth first computation rule is fair, a fair rule must be a coroutining rule. The following program from (Clark 1978) is an example of a program and goal that require a fair computation rule:

p(X) <- q(Y),r(Y)
q(h(Y)) <- q(Y)
r(g(Y))

With Prolog's leftmost call rule a single branch infinite computation tree is generated for call p(a). With any fair rule it is finite.

Hierarchical programs

Consider the directed graph representing the relation *refers to* for the predicates of P. There is a +(-) labelled edge in the graph between predicates p and q if q appears in a positive(negative) atom in some clause for p. A edge can be labelled with both + and -. In a *hierarchical* program, there can be no cycles in this graph. Note that this rules out recursion. In (Clark 1978) there was some informal discussion of completeness for *hierarchical* programs. The key result concerning hierarchical programs was later given by Sherpherdson (1985):

(R3.3.4) If the program is hierarchical, every variable in a clause occurs in a positive literal in the body, and every variable in a negative literal in a goal G occurs in a positive literal, then for every SLDNF answer S' such that comp(P) $\models R_G$ contains $R_{S'^\wedge}$ there is an SR-computable answer S such that HET $\models R_{S^\wedge}$ contains $R_{S'^\wedge}$

The conditions concerning variables ensure that the evaluation will not flounder and the hierarchical condition ensures that every call generates a finite computation tree, hence that everything can be inferred from comp(P) constructively.

As (Lloyd and Topur 1986) showed, the syntactic condition of program clauses can be slightly relaxed for predicates that are only used in negated calls. For the clauses for these predicates only the local variables of the body of the clause have to appear in positive atoms, it is not necessary for variables in the head to appear in a positive atom. Programs and goals that satisfy the Lloyd and Topur conditions are called *allowed*. For allowed programs and goals every computed answer is a set of ground bindings for the variables of the goal.

Completeness for negation free programs

A completeness result that is of considerable importance, even though it is only the base case of a general result, was given by Jaffer et al (1983):
(R3.3.5) For pure definite clause programs (i.e. programs that do no contain negated atoms in the bodies of clauses), when comp(P) |= ~B for some ground atom B then for every fair computation rule every branch of the computation tree for B ends in failure.

One might hope to use this result to allow negated calls in allowed programs which are calls to predicates defined by negation free clauses. But as soon as we allow this, we can have non-constructive proofs from comp(P). It allows the program

p <- p   q <- p   q <- ~p

which has the negated call ~p defined by a negation free program.

Completeness for strict programs

A completeness result that constrains P so that there *cannot* be a non-constructive proof from comp(P) is given by Kunen(1988b) for *strict* programs. A program is not *strict* (Apt et al. 1988) iff in its *refers to* graph there are is a pair of relations p,q such that there is a path from p to q which contains an even (possibly 0) number of - labelled edges and a path from p to q that contains an odd number of - labelled edges. In a strict program a predicate p cannot be defined directly or indirectly in terms of positive and negative atoms for some predicate q. The Kunen result is:
(R3.3.7) Suppose P and G are allowed and P is strict. If comp(P) |= GS for some ground substitution S, then S is an SLDNF computable answer. If comp(P) |= ~EG, then there is a finitely failed SLDNF tree for G.

Sherpherdson (1988) and Kunen(1988) are both excellent recent surveys of many other results concerning the semantics, soundness and completeness of negation as failure, for the concept seems to have aroused a lot of interest.

4 Parallel unification based schemes

4.1 GLD resolution -Wolfram, Maher, Lassez scheme

The first scheme to allow unrestricted and-parallel evaluation - the concurrent unification of two or more calls with shared variables is the (Wolfram et al. 1984) GLD scheme. Programs and goals are as in SLD but a state of the computation is a pair $<G,S>$ where G is a multiset of calls. As in SLD, S is a substitution or contains **false**. The computation rule selects $n \geq 1$ calls $\{B1,..,Bn\}$ from G. If $\{A1<-G1,..,An<-Gn\}$ are variants of n program clauses (with no variables in common with G) where Bi and Ai have the same predicates, then a next state of the computation is

$<G \cup G1 \cup ... \cup Gn, S'>$

where S' is the unification solution form of

$S \cup \{B1=A1,..,Bn=An\}$.

(We assume that the unification algorithm is trivially extended to handle the rewriting of $r(t1,..,tk)=r(t'1,..,t'k)$ using rule (a) where r is a predicate.)

Asynchronous GLD

In the GLD scheme, the scope for parallelism is limited because the entire unification must terminate before goals can be selected for the next step. The reduction of each selected goal to the body of a clause is a synchronized step. The following generalization of GLD, implicitly described by Wolfram at al, allows for asynchronous reduction of calls on different processors.

Asynchronous GLD (AGLD) has states $<G,E>$ where G is a multiset of calls and E is a multiset of equations which may contain **false**. The computation rule selects $k \geq 0$ calls $B1,..,Bk$ from G and $n \geq 0$ equations from E, $k+n \neq 0$, where each equation is such that one of the unification rules applies. Each selected equation is handled using the appropriate rule. Let E' be the rewritten set of equations. Let $A1<-G1,..,Ak<-Gk$ be k variants of clauses for the predicates of the selected calls. Let S be the subset of E' that are bindings that have been, in this or a previous step, globally broadcast to all other equations in E. Then

$<G \cup G1 \cup ... \cup Gk, E' \cup \{B1\{S\}=A1,..,Bk\{S\}=Ak\}>$

is a next state of the computation. The definitions of success and failure and computed answer are as for SLD and the results of the Wolfram et al. paper show that the computed answers are exactly the same as SLD for every computation rule.

Types of computation rule

GLD is AGLD with a computation rule that always selects only equations to rewrite until the E component of the state has been reduced to solution form. At the other extreme, we can have a computation rule that only selects equations when the goal component of the state is **true**, delaying all unification until the end of the computation. Wolfram et al. use this rule to prove the independence of the computation rule, which is now just a way of collecting together the final set of equations to be reduced to solution form.

Consider the intermediary computation rule which allows selection of atoms along with equations but which delays the selection of any of the introduced atoms Gi from the body of the i'th clause until $Bi\{S\}=Ai$ has been reduced to a set of binding equations Si, and which only locally broadcasts these bindings to equations descended from $Bi\{S\}=Ai$. That is, bindings for shared variables of Bi are not initially communicated to the other concurrently selected calls. Moreover, body calls in Gi are then unified relative to the locally extended $S \cup Si$. This corresponds to an implementation in which each call is evaluated as in SLD with the computed bindings for shared variables of concurrently selected calls being compared (by global broadcasting of the bindings) only when each call has been reduce to **true**. The Epilog system of (Wise 1986) and the Prism system of (Kasif at al 1983) are or-parallel versions of AGLD with this computation rule.

A sequential AGLD rule is one which at each step selects a single equation or a single atom to replace. If it always selects equations until E is in solution form, this is the same as SLD. An intermediary sequential rule generalizes SLD because it allows coroutining implementations to do partial unification, which is not undone, before switching to another atom. For example, a call Bi that is not allowed to generate a non-variable binding for X can be selected and the unification rewrite of $Bi\{S\}=Ai$ pursued until a binding X=t is generated. This binding is retained, but not broadcast. The next call, or the designated producer of X is then selected in order to generate a binding X=t' which is broadcast. The unification rewrite of the $Bi\{S\}=Ai$ can then continue with t'=t in place of X=t.

Absys (Foster & Elcock 1969), which can with justification be considered the first logic programming language (see Foster 1988), is essentially an implementation of AGLD with a sequential rule. Terms are restricted to variables, constants and lists and programs are entered in a syntactic variant of the completed definitions of 3.3. The computation rule never selects an equation of the form X=Y, X and Y distinct, for application of rule d(ii). Such variable/variable equations remain as qualifications to computed answers if no other equation rewrite generates a non-variable binding for X or Y. Absys also implemented the negation as failure rule but without the safety check.

Data flow parallel rules

The generalization of a sequential coroutining rule that selects another atom when a binding equation for some *input* variable of the call is generated, is a parallel rule which delays the selection of any call in the body Gi of the clause $Ai \leftarrow Gi$, until $Bi\{S\}=Ai$ has been reduced to a set of *allowed* bindings, bindings that can be globally broadcast. Any binding X=t made for some designated *input* variable X of the call, is not an allowed binding. Such a binding cannot be broadcast. The handling of X=t is suspended until a binding equation X=t' is otherwise generated and broadcast to the equation X=t.

If need be, we can distinguish between occurrences of variables, preventing broadcasting of a binding equation only if it is generated by rewriting some particular term in Bi. Let us call such variable occurrences, however specified, *input variable occurrences* for the call Bi. Only binding equations generated for non-input variables of Bi are allowed, and can be globally broadcast.

Delaying the global broadcast of allowed bindings

Allowed bindings generated by the rewrite of $Bi\{S\}=Ai$ do not need to be broadcast immediately they are generated. Data flow rules are used to delay the evaluation of the call until certain bindings have been broadcast to it because the appropriate clause to use for the evaluation of the call is to be determined by the form of the received bindings. This is why we delay the selection of any call in Gi until the unification of $Bi\{S\}=Ai$, in the context of all the extra broadcasted bindings it receives, succeeds. If we delay broadcasting any allowed binding until $Bi\{S\}=Ai$ has been completely reduced to allowed bindings, an attempted unification that fails will have no effect on the evaluation of any other call. We can with impunity substitute for the clause $Ai \leftarrow Gi$ some other clause $A'i \leftarrow G'i$ such that $Bi\{S\}=A'i$ does reduce to a set of allowed bindings. We will usually need to locally broadcast allowed bindings to other equations descended from $B_i\{S\}=A_i$, for example to check for incompatible bindings for variables in the clause head, but we can delay the global broadcasting to all other equations in the environment E. Note that delaying the global broadcasting of some allowed binding $Y=t$ for a variable means that $Y=t$ may be transformed into $t'=t$ if some allowed binding for Y generated by another call is globally broadcast. The unification rewrite of $B_i\{S\}=A_i$ only terminates when all its allowed bindings have been globally broadcast.

Atomic unification

Suppose there is a state of the AGLD computation in which $B_i\{S\}=A_i$ has been completely reduced to a set of allowed bindings S_i (possibly after the receipt of globally broadcast bindings for some variables in $B_i\{S\}$ generated by other unifications). If the computation rule is constrained so that if it selects one of the bindings from S_i for global broadcasting, it must select them all, the rule implements *atomic unification*. (As remarked in section 2, we must already constrain the rule so that it selects only one binding for any variable for global broadcast.)

If, in addition, no call in G_i is selected before all the allowed bindings generated from $B_i\{S\}=A_i$ have been selected for global broadcasting, the rule implements *atomic test unification*.

In a multiprocessor implementation, atomic unification requires synchronization of the global broadcasting of variables bindings. A given processor must get binding permission from all other processors that might generate an alternative allowed binding for each of the variables bound in S_i before broadcasting the bindings. It must be prepared to relinquish the binding permissions given if it cannot get binding permission on them all. A quite complex interprocess protocol is therefore needed to implement atomic unification on a multiprocessor.

Specifying the allowed bindings for a call

The analogue of the freeze call of Prolog II is some sort of annotation in call B_i on the input variable occurrences. Concurrent Prolog (Shapiro 1983) does this by annotating the input occurrences with ?. As with the freeze call, the restriction is not inherited. Occurrences of variables in a binding t' received for an ? annotated variable of a call B_i are not also input variables of B_i, unless they are also annotated with a ?. If the input variable property was automatically inherited, and in addition applied to all calls

descended from B_i, this would be the analogue of the IC-Prolog eager consumer.

An alternative way to determine the allowed bindings for the unification of the call $B_i\{S\}$ with some clause head A_i, is to associate a allowed mode of use with the clause, as in MU-Prolog.

In the Relational Language and Parlog(Clark & Gregory, 1981,1986), this is done by specifying for each argument for each k-adic predicate r an input ? or output ^ mode. Let $r(t'1,..,t'k)$ be the head of the clause being tried and $r(t1,..,tk)$ the call. If i is in an input argument position, then only bindings generated for variables in clause head term $t'i$ are allowed bindings for the unification of $ti\{S\}=t'i$. If the unification rewrite generates an equation $V=t$ for any other variable, this is treated as an input occurrence and the binding cannot be broadcast. If j is an output argument position, all bindings generated by the unification of $tj\{S\}=t'j$ are allowed. The rewriting of the equations for the output argument terms is started only after all the input argument equations have been reduced to allowed bindings. Note that this means that all bindings broadcast to a suspended equation $V=t$ for input variable V must be generated by the unification of other calls. It also means that all variables in the input argument term $ti\{S\}$, and all variables in bindings for these variables globally broadcast before $t'i=ti\{S\}$ is reduced to only allowed bindings, are input variables of the call. The input property is inherited.

In GHC (Ueda 1985), for the whole unification of $B_i\{S\}=A_i$ only bindings for variables in the clause are allowed. In Parlog terms, every argument position is input. All output in GHC is done by explicit equality calls in the body of the clause.

Guard calls

The global broadcasting of allowed bindings for the unification $B_i\{S\}=A_i$ is always delayed until there are no disallowed bindings. In addition, we could further delay their global broadcasting until some *guard* subset $G'i$ of the body calls in G_i have been reduced to **true**. Note that during the evaluation of the guard subset we must also prevent global broadcasting of allowed bindings, having only local broadcasting to equations generated by the evaluation of the guard calls and the rewrite of $B_i\{S\}=A_i$. In GHC this is done by inheriting the input variable restriction, all input variables of the call are input variables for the all the calls in $G'i$ and their descendants. In Concurrent Prolog, only local broadcasting of call variables is allowed until the guard successfully terminates. In Parlog, only calls that cannot generate allowed bindings for the input variables of the call can appear in the guard. Such a guard is called *safe*. In the *flat* versions of all three languages, only calls to primitives are allowed in the guard set G'i. Evaluating these calls can then be implemented as an extension of the unification with the clause head.

Note that this holding back of the broadcasting of allowed bindings for call variables means that we can in parallel unify with the clause heads and evaluate the guard calls of all the clauses for Bi. These parallel evaluations will not compete for the broadcasting of bindings. It also means that we can commence the guard calls as we commence the rewrite of Bi{S}=Ai.

Committed choice

Suppose that there is a state of the computation in which Bi{S}=Ai and evaluation of all the guard calls G'i have successfully terminated producing a set of allowed bindings Si. In the Relational language (the first committed choice language) and in Parlog and GHC, there is a commitment to use the clause Ai <- Gi for call Bi. All competing parallel unifications and guard evaluations using other clauses for the call are aborted, immediately, or on termination of the unification and the guard calls. Calls in Gi-G'i can be selected, and, in the Relational Language and Parlog, the rewriting of the equations t'j{S'}=tj{S} for the output argument terms is commenced. The broadcasting of the allowed bindings generated by these rewrites is not atomic, they can be broadcast independently as and when they are generated. In GHC, selection of equations in Gi-G'i will generate these allowed bindings for call variables, which are also not atomically broadcast.

In Concurrent Prolog, there is no commitment to the clause Ai <- Gi and no call in Gi-G'i is selected, before all allowed bindings generated for call variables during the rewrite of Bi{S}=Ai and the evaluation of the guard calls are atomically globally broadcast.

In Parlog and GHC one must program in such a way that only one call will generate a binding for each shared variable, with all other calls suspending until that binding is broadcast. In Concurrent Prolog, one can allow calls to compete, with the atomic test unification making sure that only one binding is globally broadcast *and* that calls are forced to test the broadcast value before committing to a clause. The disadvantage is the complexity of the implementation of atomic unification.

(Burt & Ringwood 1988) have recently proposed a simpler notion of atomic test broadcasting of a single allowed binding as an extension to Flat Parlog. A single

allowed binding for a call variable is designated as the test binding. The computation rule must select this designated allowed binding and globally broadcast it before trying to globally broadcast any other binding or select a Gi-G'i call.

A recently proposed successor of Flat Concurrent Prolog, the language FCP(|,:,?) (Klinger at al 1988), borrowing ideas from (Saraswat 1988), divides the guard calls into an *ask* component and a *tell* component. Only the *tell* component can generate allowed bindings for variables not in the clause, for the unification of the call with the head of the clause and the evaluation of the *ask* component only bindings for clause variables are allowed. The *tell* component has a role similar to the unification with the output argument terms in Parlog, for no allowed binding generated by the *tell* component is broadcast to the head unification or the *ask* calls. The difference is that in FCP(|,:,?), there is no committment to the clause until the head unification and the guard succeed *and* all the allowed bindings of the *tell* component have been atomically broadcast.

(Takeuchi and Furakawa 1986) and (Shapiro 1988) both survey the family of committed choice concurrent logic languages based on the AGLD scheme, with examples of programming techniques.

Suspending until only one clause will unify

An alternative computation rule, is to select any call Bi for which there is only one clause with a head Ai which will unify with Bi{S}. To implement this, the different clauses must be tried with local broadcasting of bindings. If more than one call/head unification has been reduced to a set of bindings, the call is suspended until bindings are broadcast from elsewhere which cause all but one unification to fail. All the bindings generated by that unification can then be broadcast. P-Prolog (Yang & Aiso 1986) has has such a suspension rule.

Parallel selection until all calls suspend

In any language which has suspension of calls waiting for variable bindings to be broadcast, deadlock can arise. One can break the deadlock, by picking a single call and ignoring the suspension rules.

In Andorra Prolog (Brand et al 1988), deadlock is broken in just this way. The computation rule selects any number of calls providing there is only one candidate clause for the call, calls suspend when there is more than one clause. A candidate clause for a call is one for which the head unification succeeds generating only allowed bindings and some set of guard calls to primitives successfully

132

terminates. The allowed bindings for a call are specified by *wait* declarations similar to the *when* statements of NU-Prolog. A commit operator can make a clause the only candidate clause clause, as in the committed choice languages. No binding is globally broadcast until a single clause remains as candidate. The language has atomic test unification. If all calls are suspended, due to wait declarations, or because there is more than one candidate clause for each call, a single call is selected and alternative new states of the computation are generated for each candidate clause to be pursued as or-parallel computations. The language combines the search capability of the SLD scheme with the concurrency of AGLD with committed choice. The penalty is a more complex implementation than is required by either extreme.

P-Prolog also has both or-parallel and and-parallel evaluation but the or-parallel forking does not delay until all the and-parallel calls suspend. It has uncommitted and-parallelism with parallel evaluation of the alternative computation paths.

The CP language of Saraswat (1987) has committed and uncommitted and-parallelism with the concept of a call block. A call block limits the broadcasting of bindings to calls and their descendants in the block. The bindings are broadcast between sibling blocks only when each call in the block successfully terminates. Putting each call in its own block, gives the communication on termination computation rule we mentioned above that is used in Epilog and Prism. Saraswat's language also allows both parallel and sequential (backtracking) search of the alternative evaluation paths.

Parallelised NU-Prolog(Naish 1988) and ANDOR-II(Takeuchi et al 1987) are other recent proposals for mixing committed choice and-parallelism with uncommitted exploration of alternative evaluation paths. (Clark and Gregory 1987) is a discussion of ways in which Prolog and Parlog might be combined.

5 Schemes based on general equation solving

5.1 Removing the occur check - Colmerauer's equation solving over rational trees

Nearly all the implementations of the SLD or SLDNF schemes do not implement the occur check, rule d(i), of the unification algorithm. In (Colmerauer 1982) this 'bug' was turned into a feature. In his scheme, the *rational tree* scheme RTS, programs and goals are as in SLD but

answers are assignments and states of the computation are pairs <G,A> of goals and assignments. Remember that in an assignment we can have an equation X=f(a,X) which is not allowed in a substitution.

Colmerauer's equation solving algorithm

Rules (a),(b), (c) and (e) are the same as in the unification algorithm. Rule (d)(i) is deleted, as we would expect. Rule d(ii) becomes two rules, which distinguish two cases covered by d(ii):

(di1) Select any equation of the form X=Y where X and Y are distinct variables. If X occurs in other equations, replace all other occurrences of X by Y. X=Y is not deleted.

(dii2) Replace any pair of equations of the form X=t1,X=t2, where X is a variable and t1,t2 are not variables and $|t1| \leq |t2|$, by the pair X=t1,t1=t2. $|t|$ is the number of occurrences of elements from $F \cup V$ in t.

Rule (dii2) limits the application of the replacement of a variable by its non-variable binding. This is necessary to ensure termination. With the old formulation of d(ii), we would not terminate when the system contains a pair of equations such as X=f(Y),Y=g(X) because of the absence of d(i).

What is the relationship of the solved form A produced by this algorithm to the original set E. For the unification algorithm we have the result (R2.1). For Colmerauer's algorithm we must delete (F3) from the freeness axioms in HET to produce the rational tree equational theory RTET. We then have:

(R5.1.1) RTET $|= R_E=R_A$

Hence

(R5.1.2) A=**false** iff RTET $|= R_E = $ **false**

However, we cannot also conclude

A is a assignment iff RTET $|= R_E \neq$ **false**

because an assignment does not denote a non-empty relation for every interpretation. We must strengthen RTET with axioms that tell us that every assignment does denote a non-empty relation. Following (van Emden and Lloyd 1984), the simple way to do this is to add the axiom scheme (E)A , A any assignment, to RTET to give a set of axioms IRTET. IRTET is a first order theory of the infinite rational trees described in Colmerauer (1982). Such a tree contains a finite number of sub-trees but some of the sub-trees can be infinite. In this domain, the assignment X=f(a,X) has a solution, which is the infinite rational tree f(a,f(a,f(a,.....))). We have:

(R5.1.3) A is a assignment iff IRTET $\models R_E \neq$**false**

Correctness of the Colmerauer scheme
(R5.1.4) (van Emden and Lloyd 1984)
For every RTS computed assignment A for goal G,
  IRTET,P $\models R_G$ contains R_A, $R_A \neq$**false**
Independence of the computation rule and a result analogous to the strong completeness result for SLD should also apply.

Extending RTS to include the negation as failure rule for safe computation rules is straightforward. Since the proofs of (Clark 1978) rely only on the use of the completed definitions and the analogue of (R5.1.1), they should with slight modification apply to RTS. In the soundness results we replace Comp(P) by RTET$_U$completed(P). Appropriate versions of the completeness results of section 3.3 should also apply.

5.2 Equation reduction using an general equality theory

Jaffer et al (1986) present a general scheme in which the set of equations introduced at each computation step are reduced to a substitution using an inference from a general equality theory E. The scheme is a generalization of GLD, which we shall call GLDE. Instead of unification using the Herbrand unification algorithm, the unit of computation is finding an E-unifier of a set of equations E. The analogue of property (R2.1) of unification is a property they call *unification completeness* that E must satisfy.

Let t and t' be two terms. They are E-unifiable if there is a substitution S such that $E \models V(S \to t = t')$. Generally, there will be many E unifiers, possibly an infinite number. There may or may not be maximally general unifiers, the analogue of the mgu. Even if there are, there may be more than one maximally general unifier. The equivalent of (R2.1) for a general equality theory E is that

  $E \models V(t=t1 \iff S1_V......_V Si_V......)$

where $S1_V......_V Si_V......$ is a disjunction of all the E-unifiers of t,t'. The <- follows by definition of an E-unifier. The -> is the condition of interest. If this condition holds, E is said to be *unification complete*. When there are no E-unifiers, unification completeness tells us that

  $E \models t \neq t'$

the property we need to justify negation as failure.

In GLDE, program clauses are implications of the form

  A <- E:B

where E is a conjunction of equality atoms and the B is a conjunction of non-equality atoms. A is a non-equality atom. A goal is the same form as a clause body.

A state of the computation is a three-tuple of multisets <E,B,S> where each E is a multiset of equality atoms, B is a multiset of a non-equality atoms and S is a substitution or **false**. The computation rule selects a subset E'={e1,..,em} of E, a subset B'={A1,..,An} of B, m+n≠0. Let

  A'1 <- E1:B1 .... A'n <- En:Bn

be n variants of program clauses. Let S' be an E-unifier of E$_U$(A1{S}=A'1,..,An{S}=A'n). That is,

  $E \models V(S' \to E_U\{A1\{S\}=A'1,..,An\{S\}=A'n\})$

A next state of the computation is

  <E-E'$_U$E1$_U$..$_U$En, B-B'$_U$B1$_U$..$_U$Bn,S{S'}$_U$S'>

If there is no such S', the next state has **false** in place of the substitution component. A computation branch terminates in success when E,B are both empty and S is a substitution. As Jaffer et al remark, in any instance of the scheme, maximally generally unifiers should be used if they exist.

Taking E to be the empty equality theory, we get GLD as an instance of this scheme. S' is then the mgu that can be generated by the unification algorithm. Jaffer et al. (1986) prove the following soundness and completeness result:
(R5.2.1) If A is a ground atom, P,$E \models$ A iff there is a successful computation for goal A using any computation rule.
(R5.2.2) If A is a ground atom, completed(P),$E \models \sim$ A iff for a fair computation rule every branch of the computation ends in failure.

Note that the second result is not the exact analogue of (R3.3.5) because the failure computation tree can be infinite. This is because there can be an infinite number maximally general unifiers of a set of terms, and so the computation tree may not be finitely branching. If we know that there are always only a finite number of maximally general E-unifiers, it is the analogue of (R3.3.5).

The importance of the scheme is that it is a very general framework in which two crucial properties of a logic programming language, (R5.2.1) and (R5.2.2), have been shown to hold. Any instance of the scheme, proposed as a *programming* language, must also have extra computational properties. There must be an algorithm that can be applied to the set of equations

  S$_U$E$_U$(A1=A'1,..,An=A'n)

that returns a finite set of maximally general E-unifiers.

6 Schemes based on testing solvability of more general equality formulas

6.1 Prolog II - Colmerauer's equation, inequation scheme for rational trees

In (Colmerauer 84) the equational solving algorithm for the RTS scheme was extended to apply to sets EI of equations and inequations. An inequation is a negated equality $t \neq t'$. The algorithm divides EI into the set E of equations and the set I of inequations. E is reduced to an assignment $A=\{X1=t1,..,Xn=tn\}$ or **false** using the algorithm of the RTS scheme. If an assignment is generated, for each inequation $t \neq s$ in E the algorithm is reapplied to the $A \cup \{t=s\}$. If this produces **false**, the inequality $t \neq s$ is discarded (because it is satisfied by assignment A). If the algorithm successfully terminates without generating any bindings for variables, $t \neq s$ is replaced by **false** (because the absence of bindings for variables Y1,..,Yk in $t=s$ shows that $t=s$ is satisfied for assignment A for all rational tree values for Y1,..,Yk, hence that there is no rational tree assignment for these variables that will satisfy $t \neq s$ and equations A). If $s=t$ is reduced to a set of bindings Y1=t'1,..,Ym=t'm for variables in $t=t'$, then $t \neq t'$ is replaced by the the inequation one(Y1,..,Ym) $\neq$ one(t'1,..,t'm) (because one(Y1,..,Ym) $\neq$ one(t'1,..,t'm) iff for some i Yi$\neq$t'i iff $t \neq t'$). The result of the algorithm is therefore either **false** or $A \cup I'$ where I' is a set of reduced inequations. Note that no variable bound in A will appear on the left hand side of an inequation in I'. The theory RTET justifies this algorithm, we have:

(R6.1.1) RTET $|= R_{EI} = R_{A,I'}$

If neither A nor I' reduce to **false**, $A \cup S'$ is what Colmerauer calls a *reduced form* set of equations. He shows that a reduced from set of equations always has a solution in the domain of infinite rational trees.

In Colmerauer (1986) this extended algorithm replaced the unification step of a scheme that is the theoretic model for Prolog II. Programs essentially comprise implications of the form

H <- E,I : G

where H is an atom, G is a conjunction of atoms and E is conjunction of equations and I a conjunction of inequations. The rule is still read as universally quantified for every variable. A goal, has the form of a clause body.

A state of the computation is a triple <G,A,I> where G is a conjunction of atoms, and $A \cup I$ is a reduced form set of equations and inequations, or contains **false**.

The first step of a computation is the reduction of the E,I of the goal to solution form, i.e. to reduced form or **false**. Thereafter, a computation step is the selection of some atom Bi in G using the computation rule. If H<-E'',I'':G'' is a clause for the predicate of the selected atom Bi, a next state of the computation is <G',A',I'> where G' is G with Bi replaced by the conjunction G'', A is the solution form of $A \cup E'' \cup \{Bi=H\}$ and I' is the reduced set of inequations produced by applying the above algorithm to each inequation in $I \cup I''$ using the new assignment A'. The computation terminates in failure if either A or I become **false**. It terminates in success, if G=**true**, and neither A nor I contains **false**. A,I is the computed answer, it will be a reduced form set of equations and inequations.

The theory IIRTET, which is RTET augmented with an axiom scheme (E)A,I , A,I any reduced form set of equations and inequations, gives us the correctness result:
(R6.1.2) If $A \cup I$ is a computed answer for goal E,I,G and program P then P,IIRTET $|= R_{E,I,G}$ contains $R_{A,I}$ and IIRTET $|= R_{A,I} \neq$ **false**

In an implementation of the scheme, the inequations can actually be handled by a special negation as failure rule that returns bindings. After the assignment A' for the new state has been generated, only the new inequations in I'', and any inequations in I for which the left hand side variable Y has become bound in A', need be tested. For each such inequation, $s \neq t$, an attempt is made to establish $s \neq t$ by trying to show that $s=t$ fails in the environment A'. If $s=t$ fails, $s \neq t$ is deleted. If $s=t$ succeeds, without binding any variables in s or t, $s \neq t$ is **false**. If it succeeds generating bindings Y1=t'1,..,Ym=t'm for variables in the equation. We have proved that, for theory RTET,

A' -> [s=t <-> (Y1=t'1,..,Ym=t'm)]

The Yi bindings are undone (locations assigned to Y1,..,Ym have there values reset to undefined) and

one(Y1,...,Ym) $\neq$ one (t'1,..,t'm)

is returned as the 'answer' for the negated call $s \neq t$. This is a single inequation representing the disjunction Y1$\neq$t'1 $\vee$...$\vee$ Ym$\neq$t'm which we have proved to be equivalent to $s \neq t$ in the environment A'.

6.2 SLDCNF - the Chan Scheme

In 3.3 we hinted that result (R3.3.3) could be used to allow negated calls to return answers. The handling of inequations in the above scheme is a special case of this. The SLDCNF scheme of (Chan 1988) handles answers returned any negated call of a SLDNF style program.

As in the above Prolog II scheme, a computation step involves checking whether a set of equations and inequations has a solution, but for the theory HET underlying normal unification. Inequations can be universally quantified for some or all their variables. As with Prolog II, the inequations are checked for solvability by applying a specialized negation as failure rule. An inequation $(VL)s{\neq}t$ is **true**, and deleted from the current set of inequations, if $s{=}t$ fails in the environment of the current binding equations. It is replaced by **false**, if it succeeds without binding global variables (variables not in L). (This is one of the extensions to the negation as failure rule we discussed in 3.3.) Unlike Prolog II, the inequation is not reduced to another inequation if $s{=}t$ succeeds. In this case, $(VL)s{\neq}t$ is considered a *primitive* inequation and left unchanged.

Program rules and goals are as in Prolog II except that the inequations can be universally quantified for some (or all) of the variables in the inequation and body calls can be negated as in SLDNF. A state of the computation is of the form <G,E,QI> where G is a conjunction of calls, E is a set of equations and QI is a set of quantified inequations. E or QI can contain **false**. As with AGLD, we let S be the substitution subset of E of globally broadcast bindings.

A computation terminates in success when G=**true**, E is a substitution S, and QI is a set of primitive inequations PI. Since each primitive inequation is satisfiable in the environment of the substitution S, the set S,PI denotes a non-empty relation for theory HET. The computed answer is a *normalised* form for S',PI, where S' is S restricted to variables in the goal G. S',PI is normalised by a two step transformation to produce an HET equivalent answer. Essentially, this process removes irrelevant inequalities (see Chan 1988). In a normalised form each variable in an equation, and each free variable in an inequation, is either in G or it appears inside a constructed term of some binding term in an equation. So, where there are no function symbols in the bindings, every variable in a normalised answer is a variable from G.

Chan also gives a procedure which converts the negation of a normalised answer N into a disjunction $E1\lor....\lor En$,

where each Ei is a conjunction of equations and quantified inequations. This is needed to handle the answers returned by a negated call ~B. The negation as failure rule of SLDCNF, recursively evaluates B{S} even if it contains unbound global variables. If every computation path is finite, a finite set {N1,...,Nk} of normalised answers is returned. By an extension of (R3.3.3), the evaluation has shown that $B\{S\} <\text{-}> N1^\wedge \lor...\lor Nk^\wedge$, so $\sim B\{S\} <\text{-}> \sim N1^\wedge,...,\sim Nk^\wedge$. Each Ni is converted into a disjunction $E1\lor....\lor En$ and then the whole conjunction for ~B is converted into disjunctive normal form. The result is an equivalence $\sim B <\text{-}> BE1\lor...\lor BEn$ where each BEi is a conjunction of equations and quantified inequations.

The computation rule for SLDNF can select any call Bi in the goal G, any equation in E to which a rule of the unification algorithm applies, or any inequation in QI of state <G,E,QI>. The rule does not need to be safe.

A selected inequation is tested to see if it is **true** or **false** in the environment S by the special negation as failure rule described above. If neither, it is left in QI.

If a positive call Bi is selected, let $A <\text{-} E'',QI'':G''$ be a clause for its predicate. A next state of the computation is $<G',E',QI\cup QI>$ where E' is the set of equations produced by applying the rules of unification algorithm to $E\cup E''\cup\{Bi=A\}$ until $Bi\{S\}{=}Ai$ has been reduced to a set of bindings or **false**. In this step, no equation in $E\cup E''$ is selected, but it might be changed by the broadcasting of bindings produced from $Bi\{S\}{=}Ai$.

If a negative call ~B is selected from G, a recursive computation for goal B{S} is commenced. If every path is finite, a set of normalised answers {N1..,Nk} is returned. This is negated and converted into an HET equivalent set of {BE1,...,BEn} representing the set of answers to ~B consistent with the bindings S. Suppose BEi is of the form Ei,Qi where Ei is a set of equations. A next state of the computation is $<G',E\cup Ei,QI\cup QIi>$.

The correctness result given by Chan is:
(R6.2.1) If every branch of the computation tree is finite, and N1,..,Nk are the set of normalised answers for its success terminating branches, then $comp(P) \models (V)[G <\text{-}> N1^\wedge\lor...Nk^\wedge]$.

He gives no completeness results. It should be possible to prove completeness for restricted classes of programs as for SLDNF. Certainly completeness should obtain for hierarchical programs.

(Kunen 1987) gives an alternative approach to allowing negated calls to return answers based on the manipulation of

136

what he calls *elementary* sets. But at the time of writing I could not see how to present his scheme as an extension of SLD.

7 Constraint schemes

7.1 The CLP scheme - Joxan and Lassez

Joxan and Lassez (1987) present the most general scheme yet proposed that is an extension of SLD. It is a generalization of the scheme we discussed in 5.2. The equality theory E becomes a constraint theory C and the unification completeness property of E becomes a *satisfaction completeness* property of C. The following is a slight generalization of the variant of the CLP scheme given in (Maher 1986), which better fits the framework of this paper. SLD, AGLD, AGLDE and Prolog II are special cases of this CLP scheme.

The theory C is a theory for a set of constraint predicates P_C (disjoint from the set of program predicates P) which includes =. A primitive constraint is an atom with a predicate from P_C. An allowed constraint is some subset of all the first order formulas that can constructed from the primitive constraints which minimally contains all equations and is closed under conjunction. For SLD, C is HET and only conjunctions of equations are allowed constraints. For Prolog II, C is IIRTET, and conjunctions of equations and inequations are allowed constraints.

Theory C must be *satisfaction complete* for the allowed set of constraints. That is, for every allowed constraint C, we have

$C \models (E)C$ or $C \models \sim(E)C$

This is the generalization of properties (R2.2) (R2.3) of HET. IIRTET has this property for the allowed constraints of Prolog II.

Programs comprise implications of the form A <- C : G where C is an allowed constraint, A is a program atom, G is a conjunction of program atoms - atoms with predicates from P. A goal is a conjunction of program atoms. The lack of an allowed constraint in the goal is no handicap. We can instead have an extra 0-adic atom A in the goal with a single rule A <- C : true.

A state of the computation is a pair <G,S,C> where G is a multisets of program atoms, S is a satisfiable multiset of allowed constraints, and C is a multiset of constraints. The computation rule selects some multisubset G'={B1,..,Bk} of atoms from G, and some multisubset of C' of the constraints in C. Let

A1 <- C1: G1, ... ,Ak <- Ck: Gk

be variants of k clauses for the predicates of the selected atoms. A next state of the computation is

<G-G'$\cup$G1$\cup$..$\cup$Gk, S',

C-C'$\cup$C1$\cup$..$\cup$Ck$\cup${B1=A1,..,Bk=Ak}>

where S' is S$\cup$C' if $C \models$ (E)S,C', **false** if $C \models \sim$(E)S,C'. A computation terminates in success if G=**true**, C={} with the computed answer the subset of the satisfiable constraints S *related* to G. It terminates in failure, if S = **false**. The constraints related to G are those constraints that share a free variable with G or some other constraint related to G.

The following soundness and completeness results apply to any instance of this scheme (Maher 1987).

(R7.1.1) *Soundness*

If G has a computed answer C' then $C, P \models (V)[C' \to G]$

(R7.1.1) *Strong completeness*

If P, $C \models (V)[C \to G]$ for some constraint C then for any computation rule, G has a k successful derivations with final constraints C1,..,Ck such that $C \models (V) [C \to C1^\wedge \vee ... \vee Ck^\wedge]$ where Ci^ is the existential quantification of Ci with respect to all variables not in C.

As an example of this result, Maher gives the example of the program

p(a,b)

p(X,b) <- X≠a:true

where C is HET. For the constraint Y=b and goal p(X,Y), we have

P,HET $\models$ (VX,Y)[Y=b -> p(X,Y)]

but we need both the computable constraint answers Y=b,X=a and Y=b,X≠a to cover the constraint Y=b. We have

HET $\models$ (VX,Y)[Y=b -> Y=b,X=a $\vee$ Y=b,X≠a]

When the constraints are limited to conjunctions of equations, then k =1 in the above result because of the strong compactness of sets of equations (Lassez et al 1988).

(R7.1.3) *Soundness and completeness of negation as failure*

For goal G, comp(P),$C \models \sim$(E)G iff for a fair computation rule every branch of the computation tree for G is terminates in failure.

This is the generalization of result (R3.3.5) for negation as failure. If C includes the normal axioms for equality, the stronger form of this result should hold (I have not checked the details):

(R7.1.4) For goal G, if every branch of the computation tree terminates and C1,....,Cn are the answers for the success branches, then comp(P),C |= (V)[G <-> C1^ ∨...∨ Cn^].

If the allowed constraints are closed under existential quantification and negation, we can use this result to allow negated atoms to return answers as in the SLDCNF scheme.

Maher (1986) extends the above scheme to incorporate the notion of committed choice with the concept of suspension until some subset GC of the allowed constraints of a clause is *valid* for the current environment of satisfied constraints S, or is the only satisfiable constraint of the alternative clauses. GC is *valid* if it can be satisfied for all values that satisfy S. The unifications with the input argument terms and the evalaution of the guard calls in Parlog and GHC meet this validity condition. The satisfiability condition is similar to the commit rule of P-Prolog.

Saraswat (1988) further refines this scheme to include an *ask* component which must be valid and a *tell* component which must be satisfied, atomically or eventually. In our presentation of the CLP scheme, all constraints are satisfied eventually.

Instances of the scheme

In any instance of the CLP scheme, checking whether or not some multiset of constraints is satisfiable for theory C must be implemented as an algorithm. We cannot have the unit of computation be an inference from some first order theory. As Jaffer and Lassez (1987b) remark, checking solvability should also be *incremental* - when the computation rule selects extra constraints C' to be checked with the existing solvable constraints S, it should not be necessary to recheck S. Also, solvable sets of constraints should have a *canonical form*, an equivalent simplified representation using a minimal number of constraints. This would be used for presenting answers and, ideally, it would also be used for the incremental checking of solvability. This may not always be possible, or the the minimal representation suitable for presenting answers may be different from that needed to check solvability. For SLD

and AGLD, this canonical form is a substitution, for Prolog II it is a reduced set of equations and inequations. As with the *E*-unifiability scheme, the great strength of the CLP scheme is that it provides a logical framework for extensions and modifications of the unification based SLD. We simply need to ensure that the algorithms that replace unification when applied to some expression C correctly determines whether or not C |= (E)C for some consistent first order theory C of the constraint predicates. We then know that the above logical properties hold of the the computed answers. If the algorithm reduces C to a solution form S, we also need to establish that C |= (V)[C <-> S].

Prolog III (Colmerauer 1987) is an extension of Prolog II where the constraints are equations and inequations over terms, inequalities and linear equations of a special form over rational numbers, and boolean expressions over truth values. There is one non-free term constructor . for list concatenation enabling constraint equations such as X.Y.X= [1,2,3,4,1] to be used and solved. The constraint language is restricted to allow algorithmic reducibilty to solution form of any allowed constraint.

CLP(R) (Jaffer & Michaylov 1987) has equations over t(F,V), and inequalities and equations of arithmetic expressions over the real numbers. The implementation only checks the solvability of the term equations, arithmetic inequalities and linear equations. Non-linear equations are stored and checked only if the other constraints determine values for some of the variables that make them linear. If this does not happen, the non-linear equations remain as a qualification on the answer returned.

CIL (Mukai 1985), CS-Prolog (Kawamura et al 1987), CAL (Akiro et al 1988) and CHIP (Dincbas et al 1988) are other constraint languages.

8 Concluding remarks

What does the future hold regarding logic languages. I anticipate much activity in the area of algorithms for checking solvability of richer and richer and sets of constraints, extending the application of logic programming into new areas.

The committed choice languages will be further refined and will further converge to become powerful system building languages for multiprocessor machines.

Finally, I expect considerable impact from the recent developement of languages incorporating committed choice and parallelism and either or=parallel or or sequential search.

References

Akiro, A., Sakia, K., Sato, Y., Hawley, D., Hasegawa, R. (1988) Constraint logic programming language CAL, FGCS88, ICOT.

Apt., K.R., Blair, H., Walker, A., (1988), Towards a theory of declarative knowledge, in (Minker 1988).

Battani, G and Meloni, H. (1973) Interpreteur du Language de Programmation PROLOG, Groupe Intelligence Artificielle, Université Aix-Marseille II.

Bancilon, F., Ramakrishnan, R., An Amateur's introduction to recursive query processing strategies, ACM Int. Conf. on Management of Data, 1986.

Brand,P.,Haridi,S.,Warren,D.H.D. (1988) Andorra Prolog - the language and application in distributed simulation, FGCS88,ICOT

Burt, A., Ringwood, G.A., (1988), The binding conflict problem in concurrent logic languages, Research Report, Parlog Group, Department of Computing, Imperial College.

Chan, D., (1988), Constructive negation based on the completed data base, ICLP5, MIT Press.

Ciepielewski, A., Haridi, S., (1984), A formal model for OR-parallel execution of logic programs; IFIP 84, North-Holland.

Clark, K.L., (1978), Negation as failure, in Logic and Data Bases (eds. Gallaire, H. and Minker, J.), Plenum Press.

Clark, K.L., (1979), Predicate logic as a computational formulism, Research report, Logic Programming Group, Department of Computing, Imperial College.

Clark, K. L., Gregory, S., (1981), A relational language for parallel programming, ACM Conf. on Functional Languages and Computer Architecture.

Clark, K.L., Gregory, S., (1986), PARLOG: parallel programming in logic, ACM Toplas 8(1).

Clark, K. L., Gregory, S., (1987) Parlog amd Prolog United, ICLP4, MIT Press.

Clark, K.L., McCabe, F.G., The Control facilities of IC-Prolog, in Expert Systems in the micro-electronic age (ed. D. Michie), Edinburgh University Press.

Clark, K.L., McCabe, F.G., Gregory, S., (1982), IC-PROLOG language features in in (Clark and Tarnlund 1982)

Clark, K.L., Tarnlund, S-A., (1982), Logic Programming, Academic Press.

Colmerauer, A., (1982), Prolog and infinite trees, in (Clark and Tarnlund 1982)

Colmerauer, A., (1982b), Prolog II Reference manual, Groupe Intelligence Artificielle, Universite Aix-Marseille II.

Colmerauer, A., (1984), Equations and inequations on finite and infinite trees, FGCS84, ICOT

Colmerauer, A., (1986), Theoretical Model of Prolog II, in Logic Programming and its applications (ed. Caneghan, M. V. & Warren, D. H. D.), Ablex.

Colmerauer, A. (1987) Opening the Prolog III universe, Byte August 1987.

Conery, J.S., (1987), Parallel execution of Logic Programs, Kluwer Academic Publishers.

Degroot, D., (1984), Restricted and-parallelism, FGCS 84, ICOT

Dincbas,M.,van Hentenryck, P., Simonis,H., Aggoun,A., Graf,T., Berthier,F.(1988) The constraint logic programming language CHIP, FGCS88, ICOT.

Elcock, E. W., (1988), Absys: The First Logic Programming Language - A retrospective and a commentary, to appear in JLP.

van Emden, M.H., Lloyd, J.W., (1984), A logical reconstruction of Prolog II, ICLP3, Upsalla University.

Foster, E.M., Elcock, E.W., (1969), Absys 1: an incremental compiler for assertions, in Machine Intelligence 4 (ed. Michie, D.), Edinburgh University Press.

Hill, R., (1974), LUSH-resolution and its completeness, DCL Memo 78, Department of Artificial Intelligence, Edinburgh University.

Jaffar, J., Lassez, J-L., Lloyd, J.W., (1983), Completeness of Negation as failure rule, IJCAI-83.

Jaffer, J., Lassez, J-L., Maher, M.J., (1986), A Logic Programming Language Scheme, in Logic Programming Functions, Relations and Equations (ed. Degroot, D. & Lindstrom, G.). Prentice-Hall.

Jaffer, J., Michaylov, S. (1987) Methodology and implementation of a CLP system, ICLP4, MIT Press

Joxan, J., Lassez, J-L., (1987), Constraint Logic Programming, POPL, ACM.

Jaffer, J., Lassez, J-L., (1987b), From unification to constraints, in Logic Programming 87, LNCS 315, Springer-Verlag.

Kasif, S., Kohli, M., Minker, J., (1983), Prism: a parallel inference system for problem solving, IJCAI 83.

Kawamura, T., Ohwada, H., Mizoguchi, F., (1987), CS-Prolog: A generalised constraint solver, in Logic Programming 87, LNCS 315, Springer Verlag.

Kliger, S., Yardeni, E., Kahn, K., Shapiro, S., (1988), The Language FCP(!,:,?), FGCS 1988, ICOT

Kowalski, R. A., (1974), Predicate logic as a programming language, IFIP.

Kunen, K., (1987), Answer sets and negation as failure, ICLP-4, Melbourne, MIT Press.

Kunen, K., (1988), Some remarks on completed data bases, ICLP5, MIT Press.

Kunen, K., (1988b) Signed data dependencies in logic programs, to appear in JLP.

Lassez, J. L., Maher, M.J., Marriot, K.L., (1988), Unification revisited, in Foundations of deductive data bases and logic programming (ed. Minker, J.), Morgan Kaufmann.

Lloyd, J.W., Topor, R.W., (1986), A basis for deductive data base systems II, JLP 3(1).

Maher, M.J., (1986), Logic semantics of a class of committed choice programs, in ICLP 4, MIT Press.

Martelli, A., Montanari, U., (1982), An efficient unification algorithm, ACM Toplas, 4(2).

Miller, D., Nadathur, G. (1986) Higher order logic programming, ICLP3, LNCS 225, Springer-Verlag.

Minker, J., (1988), Foundations of deductive data bases and logic programming, Morgan Kaufmann.

Moto-Oka, T., Tanaka, H., Aida, H., Hirata, K., Maruyama, T., (1984), The architecture of a parallel inference machine - PIE, FGCS 84, North Holland.

Mukai, K., (1985), Unification over complex indeterminates in Prolog, TR-113, ICOT

Naish, L., (1984), Heterogeneous SLD Resolution, JLP 1(4).

Naish, L., (1985), Negation and Control in Prolog, LNCS 238, Springer-Verlag.

Naish, L., (1986), Negation and quantifiers in NU-Prolog, ICLP3, Springer-Verlag.

Naish, L (1988), Parallelizing NU-Prolog, ICLP5, MIT Press.

Pollard, S. H., Parallel execution of Horn clause programs, Ph.D., Thesis, Imperial College, London.

Ramakrishnan, R., (1988), Magic Templates: A spellbinding approach to logic programs, ICLP5, MIT Press, 1988.

Robinson, J.A., (1979), Logic: Form and function, Edinburgh University Press.

Saraswat, V. J., (1987), The concurrent logic programming language cp: definition and operational semantics, POPL, ACM.

Saraswat, V. J., (1988), A somewhat Logical Formulation of CLP Synchronisation Primitives, ICLP5, MIT Press.

Shapiro, E., (1986), Concurrent prolog, a progress report, IEEE Computer 19(8).

Shapiro, E. (1988) The family of concurrent logic programming languages, to appear in ACM Computing Surveys.

Shepherdson, J.C. (1984), Negation as failure: a comparison of Clark's completed data base and Reiters closed world assumption, JLP1(1).

Shepherdson, J.C. (1985), Negation as Failure II, JLP2(3).

Shepherdson, J.C. (1988), Negation in Logic Programming, in (Minker 1988).

Takeuchi, A., Furakawa, K. (1986) Parallel logic programming languages, ICLP3, LNCS 225, Springer-Verlag.

Takeuchi, A.,Takahashi,K.,Shimuzu,H.(1987) A description language with and/or parallelism for concurrency systems and its stream based realisation, ICOT TR-229.

Thorn, J.A., Zobel, J., (1987), NU-Prolog Reference Manual, Department of Computing Science, Melbourne University.

Ueda, K., (1985), Guarded Horn clauses, in Logic Programing, LNCS 221, Springer-Verlag.

Vasey, P., (1986) Qualified answers and their application to transformation, ICLP 3, LNCS 225, Springer-Verlag.

Warren, D.H.D. (1987), OR-Parallel execution models of Prolog, in Tapsoft 87, LNCS 250, Springer-Verlag.

Wise, M., (1986), Prolog multiprocessors, Prentice-Hall.

Wolfram, D.A., Maher, M.J., Lassez, J-L., (1984), A unified treatment of resolution strategies for logic programs, ICLP2, Upsalla University.

Yang, R., Aiso,H. (1986) P-Prolog: parallel language based on exclusive relation, ICLP3, Springer-Verlag.

PANEL DISCUSSIONS

PROCEEDINGS OF THE INTERNATIONAL CONFERENCE
ON FIFTH GENERATION COMPUTER SYSTEMS 1988,
edited by ICOT. © ICOT, 1988

SOCIAL IMPACT OF INFORMATION TECHNOLOGY AND INTERNATIONAL COLLABORATION

Hajime Karatsu

Professor
Institute of Research & Development
Tokai University
Tokyo, Japan

Strong creative imagination is required to forecast the social impact of newly developed and innovative technology. There is a natural tendency to extrapolate past experience when predicting the future, but this when we do so, we are inevitably surprised. And these surprises bring with them much comedy and tragedy occurred. The steam locomotive invented by Trevithic had to be guided by a man waving a red flag to meet the safety regulations.

Concerning the Fifth Generation Computer, unexpected misunderstandings and wrong conclusions would result from projecting the past into the future.

The basic difference between the traditional computer and its Fifth Generation descendant is that the former is for information processing and latter for achieving knowledge processing. The Fifth Generation Computer is expected to make possible easy man-machine conversation, and to "user friendly" and offer "easy programming." In a word, the goal of the Fifth Generation is "popularization" of the computer.

According to a computer white paper by the Japan government, only 2% of the population of Japan uses a computer today. However, the number of computer users may jump up into double digits very soon. At the beginning of the automobile's development, only a man specially trained as a driver could use it. But today the car is involved in our society as a tool that can be easily used by anyone. Without the car, nearly all social activities would grind to a halt. Modern society can fittingly be called a "motorized society".

From the above considerations, we may conclude that technological conditions necessary to creating a computerized society will be realized by the Fifth Generation Computer.

The computerized society of the Fifth Generation will not be like world of "1984" envisioned by George Orwell, but will be the product of a fresh vision created in the coming era in which computing power is not concentrated in one hand but distributed and handled daily by every person.

At the FGCS '81 conference held in Tokyo, I pointed out five issues in Japan to be improved by introducing the Fifth Generation Computer to such areas as follows:

1. Application to low productivity fields.
2. Internationalization of Japanese society.
3. Ways to cope with a highly educated, aging society.
4. Limited natural resources and energy.
5. Individuals self development and fulfillment.

Issues of 1, 3 and 4 are concerned with improving the productivity of our industrial and social activity by utilizing the intellectual processing ability of the Fifth Generation Computer. Item 2 is concerned with machine translation and mutual collaboration between different cultures brought through bilateral dialogues.

In connection with the improvement of productivity, you might raise the question of unemployment. These machines could be installed at job sites to eliminate workers or clerks, and you might think, then, that unemployment will be created.

I am a member of the rationalization committee of Tokyo metropolitan government, serving as chairman of subcommittee for Office Automation. At the end of last year, a plan for OA was sent to the municipal session as a subject for discussion. A member of the session asked me, "What do you think about firing clerks when OA works well?"

I answered, "Of course, OA machines eliminate many kinds of jobs in the office, but there is no need to discharge any personnel." Today, Tokyo city has many institutions for the general public welfare. Libraries, athletic sports houses, museums, homes for the aged, etc. However, all institutions close at 5 p.m. each day and are closed on Sundays and holidays.

A library with a closed door is not a library but a vacant building. According city authorities, we cannot open the doors because of a shortage of personnel.

Public welfare, then, cannot be increased without office automation, and a shift of personnel from clerical work to libraries, museums, sport centers, and so on. This way of thinking and approach is quite important for predicting the nature of the computerized society.

To transfer personnel to a new work place, flexibility in job assignments must be prepared for before such an innovation is carried out. Some may hesitate to discuss it, but you must recognize that our social environment is under the rule of free competition. When robots were first introduced on the production shop floor, almost all scholars and statesmen were afraid of a harmful rise in the jobless rate.

In Japan, on the contrary, we made an effort to use robots to overcome a shortage of workers caused by the rapid economic growth, which lasted until the oil crisis of 1974. And again, robotization was accelerated to increase productivity as a means of survival in the economic squeeze brought about by the rapid appreciation of the yen since 1985.

We can conclude that Japan kept its jobless rate at a low level by attaining high productivity through the use of robots.

The significance of this conclusion can be understood if you imagine what would have happened had Japan not utilized robots: Japan would have lost competitive power of its industries and an enormous number of workers would have lost their jobs.

Recently, most nations have made efforts to introduce automatic machines to the production floor and office in an attempt to reinforce their competitive entrepreneural power. To respond to the job rotation boom expected in the near future, the efficiency of education and training must be improved by using Fifth Generation computers.

It is my judgement that this improvement can be achieved in the preparation of a flexible job assignment structure in our society.

By the way, some of you may have the suspicion that nothing will be left to be done by human beings when the Fifth Generation is permeates in our social activity. Even medical diagnosis by doctors is said to have a lower rate of misdiagnosis rate when done with the aid of a computer.

However, a good answer to that question was brought up by our study at an airline company. An authority of the company said that most aircraft accidents are caused by pilot error. For example, when a plane approaches the airport, the runway is under the assault of a thunderstorm. The pilot must decide whether to stay airborne or to attempt a landing. The fate of the plane rests with a judgement made in a few seconds. In this critical state, the computer may play a dependable role as a machine for decision consultation, acting as a stand-in for an impetuous pilot. The computer never loses its head.

Basically, I think that the computer cannot exceed the ability of human beings. However, sometimes a human being loses his presence of mind, while a computer always works well without getting excited.

So far, I have talked about the target of the Fifth Generation project and the possibilities of its application.

However, these expectations can be achieved only after we prepare a framework for society to implement the Fifth Generation computer; this preparation includes new laws, regulations, culture and educational levels, etc. As we say, "New wine needs a new bottle".

PROCEEDINGS OF THE INTERNATIONAL CONFERENCE
ON FIFTH GENERATION COMPUTER SYSTEMS 1988,
edited by ICOT. © ICOT, 1988

ARTIFICIAL INTELLIGENCE: PERSPECTIVES AND PREDICTIONS

(Extended Abstract)

Jörg H. Siekmann

Department of Computer Science
University of Kaiserslautern
Postfach 30 49
6750 Kaiserslautern
West Germany

> At the end of the century, the use of words and general educated opinion will have changed so much that one is able to speak of "machines thinking" without expecting to be contradicted.
>
> A. Turing, 1950

PERSPECTIVES

A multitude of human activities, such as planning a combined journey by coach and rail, understanding spoken language, proving mathematical theorems, making a medical diagnosis, and seeing and recognizing scenes and objects, clearly require intelligence, irrespective of how one defines this term. Artificial Intelligence or AI to give it its popular acronym, involves the scientific investigation of such cognitive activities using computers. It is a striking feature of this research that it has extensive potential for industrial applications as is now well attested to by the extensive world-wide investment it has attracted.

Until recently AI has been regarded as a sub-field of computer science, not least because of its implications for the future use and design of computers. However though much of this research lies firmly within computer science, there is reason to believe that AI may soon develop into an autonomous scientific discipline, and in doing so will eventually sever the umbilical cord to computer science.

The most significant technological impact of AI (and computer science for that matter) is becoming apparent in two main areas of society - administration and manufacturing. In administration, the "paperless" automated office will become the norm, initially based on standard data processing technology and then increasingly influenced by AI technology. In manufacturing, the production of goods will be characterized by ever increasing automation and the use of robots eventually resulting in the fully automated factory.

This may well have farreaching social consequences. For example just as the mechanization of farming methods has led to a situation where, in highly industrialized countries, only 8-10% of the population produce a country's food supplies (as compared with 50-90% in developing countries), the proportion of the population employed in administration and manufacturing, currently more than 50% in most industrialized countries, will fall to a much smaller percentage, possibly approaching that currently engaged in agriculture. This will mark a significant change in the nature of our society - a change from a society in which the majority of people have to work in order to satisfy their basic needs, to one in which a considerably smaller fraction of the population will have to work in order to meet the basic needs of all.

AI is developing into a scientific field, and though still young, the sheer amount of AI research already carried out is such that it can no longer be completely mastered by any one person. Of course this has been the case for at least a century in older disciplines such as chemistry, mathematics and physics. AI is a field which, together with the biological sciences such as genetics and the neurosciences, will be among the most important sciences of this century, fields which could dominate the end of the 20th century just as physics and chemistry dominated the end of the previous century and the beginning of the present.

In the first part of this paper a brief elementary introduction is given to Artificial Intelligence which is intended for a general audience. In the second part, predictions are made about future developments in each of what are arguably the five major subfields of AI (Natural Language Processing, Expert Systems, Automated Deduction Systems, Robotics, Computer Vision). These predictions evolved over a timespan of about two years. Initial versions of them drawn from the literature and elsewhere, were distributed to a number of experts working in the various subfields, revised following their criticisms and suggestions, distributed again, and so on for a number of iterations. Not surprisingly, no clear consensus emerged and thus we are solely responsible for the final form they take. The second part also takes up some broad questions concerning the future economic significance of these developments and the likely social changes they will bring about.

The paper is based on a report called "Künstliche Intelligenz" commissioned by the German Ministry of Science and Technology in 1984. A translation was edited, substantially revised and rewritten by Michael A. McRobbie and Jörg. H. Siekmann, while Michael McRobbie was a Visiting Professor at the University of Kaiserslautern, funded under DFG (Sonderforschungsbereich 314). The paper appeared as a joint departmental report of the Computer Science Department, University of Kaiserslautern, West Germany as well as of the Center for Information Science Research, Australian National University, Canberra, Australia. The full and final version is to appear in the European Journal "AI Communications", Michael A. McRobbie, Jörg H. Siekmann; "Artificial Intelligence: Perspectives and Predictions", (1988)

PROCEEDINGS OF THE INTERNATIONAL CONFERENCE
ON FIFTH GENERATION COMPUTER SYSTEMS 1988,
edited by ICOT. © ICOT, 1988

INTERNATIONAL COLLABORATION IN IT

TIMOTHY WALKER

Information Engineering Directorate
United Kingdom

ABSTRACT

This paper reviews the social implications for the IT community of greater international collaboration, concentrating on UK and European programmes. It sets out some preliminary criteria for choosing between national and international programmes and advocates cooperation between the different programmes.

The topic of this session is the social impact of information technology and international collaboration. This is a very large subject and in the 20 minutes which Professor Karatsu has given me I can only touch on a small part of it, although one which is, I believe, of most interest to this audience, that is pre-competitive R&D. I speak from some personal experience, having started as an academic scientist, but having, within Government, both run a national programme, helped to run a European one, and been involved in other international cooperation, including with Japan. I shall use this talk to review this experience briefly and then ask some further questions which may stimulate discussion.

I should start by admitting that I have never been able to find a satisfactory definition of pre-competitive R&D, although I think most of us can recognise it when we come across it. My predecessor, Brian Oakley, used to say that it was "any research on which people wanted to collaborate". I doubt myself whether any research is really "precompetitive". My memory of the academic world is that it displays all the hallmarks of extreme competition. Moreover most (although not all) collaboration involves cooperation with a restricted set of partners and thus implies some degree of competition with others, either nationally or internationally.

I suppose that there are two chief elements to precompetitive research, cooperation between companies, and cooperation between industry and academia. The second of these has usually been regarded as common in the US but less so in Europe and in Japan. The first has become identified with Japan, largely through the MITI sponsored programmes and indeed many argue that it was the Fifth Generation Programme that itself stimulated (some say hastened) Europe and America to start similar programmes, although reflecting the particular cultural and business background of the countries concerned.

Before going on to the social aspects of cooperation, it may be worth speculating a little on the reasons for this rush into collaborative R&D. It is of course not new; there has been collaboration between companies for many years, both in cartels and between users and suppliers. This has however not usually been organised by, or under the auspices of Government; nor have the arrangements had a particularly high public profile. They have also tended to concentrate on joint ventures or production agreements rather than R&D. I think there is a clear reason for the growth of collaborative R&D. It stems from the increasingly global nature of the IT market coupled with the nature of that market, a shorter product life cycle with increasing scale and risk of the necessary R&D and the tendency - especially in the IT/electronics area, for product development to be influenced heavily by recent scientific results. This provides an obvious pressure to reduce the risks, both of R&D expenditure and any subsequent investment whether in plant or marketing. This pressure is often increased further by the absence of internationally accepted standards. For some time therefore business school texts have included sections on collaboration as an element of corporate strategy.

Now is not the time for a detailed study of the more technical aspects of this collaboration; no doubt the rest of this conference will report on that. I will confine myself to a personal review of the social implications for those involved, whether as researchers or as managers. This is, I admit, a fairly restricted interpretation of the title of this session, but it is one that is only rarely explored and one where I suspect that there are large differences between countries. It is however one well worth the time since many companies are now spending up to 20% of their budget for longer term R&D on collaborative projects. This is bound to mean a greater mutual dependence as well as a tendency to greater specialisation.

The first social change as a result of cooperative programmes in Europe is the much greater contact between executives of the various companies. My understanding is that when V Davignon called together the Chief Executives of the top 12 European IT companies to create the Round Table, it was the first time that they had met. Now they know each other well.

Moreover the fact that researchers from their companies collaborate on projects means that not only there will be contact at this level, but as those industrial research workers move up their companies, the big change is that they will already know their opposite numbers. By the time they become Chief Executives, they will have known their peers in other European firms for twenty or thirty years. This will normally make cooperation much easier; it will certainly improve their knowledge of what is going on in Europe.

This greater degree of contact is of particular importance in Europe where for too long the firms in individual countries have had insufficient contact with, or knowledge of, each other. Working together on R&D also provides a means for building up relationships in other areas, often closer to the market. Indeed this is one of the major ways in which Esprit - and other similar programmes - support the development of the single European market. It is these commercial considerations rather than solely a desire to do more research that provides the motivation for the involvement of many of the companies and underlies their approach to the formation of the collaborative teams.

The same is true of the national programmes in the UK which have also brought together representatives of the IT supplier companies as well as shared users and suppliers closer together. It is possible, indeed, that this may have contributed to at least some of the takeovers and rationalisations which have taken place in the last year or so. Many industrialists

have told me that one of the aspects of collaborative programmes which they value most highly is the means to meet their peers, to get to know them better, and to be able to discuss issues of the day with them in a neutral forum. The fact that a Government run collaborative programme is necessary to achieve this may come as some surprise, particularly to our Japanese colleagues since, if the myths are to be believed, there is constant contact between the different Japanese companies. It is also different from the US where, prior to initiatives such as MCC and the recent relaxation of anti-trust legislation, there was a danger that the Justice Department would assume that a meeting of chief executives of computing companies could have taken place only for the purpose of arranging an illegal cartel! Nevertheless there does seem to be, at least in the UK, considerable advantages from Government organisations holding the ring for these kind of discussions.

In the same way the Alvey programme has also developed the relations between UK industry and the academic world. Five years ago there was, with notable exceptions on both sides, there was too little contact and too little understanding of what the other had to offer. Now industrialists have a greater appreciation of the relevance of academic research while academics recognise the considerable intellectual content of industrial research. This has a significant impact on teaching; not only do students see their professors working with industry but course material starts to use examples taken from industrial experience. Within the UK the research community is now much better developed in a number of areas and provides scope for much better communication over a wider range of interests. It has also stimulated greater mobility of researchers which is perhaps the best way of securing technology transfer. I believe there have been similar developments as a result of other national programmes in Europe, and that the US programmes have also stimulated greater contact.

The social effects depend somewhat on the geographical nature of the co-operation. The UK has normally preferred to have collaborative projects arranged on a distributed basis with researchers remaining in their parent organisation. While this may be because we recognise our lack of success in winding up laboratories which have fulfilled their usefulness, it does have the advantage of facilitating technology transfer back to the participating organisations. On the other hand MITI has often chosen to establish a central laboratory such as ICOT for the Fifth Generation Programme or optoelectronics to which the partners second staff. MCC and Sematech have taken a similar line in the USA. However one of the most interesting examples is in Europe with the formation of the ECRC by Siemens, ICL and Bull. This is a joint research laboratory for the three companies located in Germany, with a French Director – Herve Gallaire – and whose working language is English!

There have therefore been substantial social results within the IT community as a result of these programmes. I suspect that the largest changes have taken place in Europe where the fragmentation of the community between the different countries has been reduced. There has also been greater contact with Japan, particularly on the part of European academic workers, and contact with the US has been at least maintained, although this traditionally has involved very little direct Government involvement on either side. The economic and commercial pressures are likely to result in a continuation of this increased contact between different parts of the community. Within Europe I believe there will be an increasing concentration of the industrial structure, particularly in the software field, and that this will be facilitated by the greater social contact that has developed over the last few years. In time, the more that companies become genuinely European, rather than regarding themselves as from a particular country, the more we can expect increased interchange between the European IT research community. This will also be helped by the free movement of researchers and the mutual recognition of professional qualifications which has recently been agreed.

However, there are a number of issues that arise from these developments. The first, and perhaps the most crucial, relates to whether these programmes are part of a movement to carry out IT R&D on a genuinely international basis or whether they are part of what might be characterised as "intellectual protectionism". Most of the cooperative programmes are concentrated on a particular country, or, in the case of the European programmes, on a group of countries. Whilst most academic programmes remain international, only some of the more industrially oriented programmes welcome – or acquiesce in – the involvement of "foreign multinationals". Some have been prepared to develop relationships with other programmes; others have not. One might argue that since the reason for the programmes in the first place was to develop

(or protect) a commercial advantage for the organising country, it would make no sense to collaborate with other programmes.

Alternatively, the structure of a programme will have been drawn up to reflect the particular needs or position of the industry in that country and these may make it more difficult to accept foreign participants. Both of these are understandable arguments, but to my mind it would be a pity if they resulted in a collection of programmes which were too inward looking. After all no one can seriously believe that that one country, or group of countries, can do all the R&D necessary for its IT development.

To some extent the need for at least a degree of openness is being recognised. Esprit has allowed the participation of companies from non-EEC European countries and, together with some other European national programmes permits the involvement of multinationals, provided the research is carried out in the country concerned. There are also links between ICOT and other countries. But I must still admit to some unease about the dangers of the research equivalent of a trade war. I hope I am wrong and it would be interesting to hear the comments of other delegates.

Perhaps it would be helpful to illustrate these issues, and the opportunities they provide, by looking at two of the decisions that will have to be taken in Europe. At the moment, many Esprit projects contain universities in one country and firms in another and there is undoubtedly significant cooperation between them. However most industry/academic cooperation still tends to be within the same country and universities are usually brought into a consortium on this basis. However after 1992, when the single market comes into force, it may be more appropriate to think in terms of European companies and universities. Thus the UK may want to encourage its companies to collaborate with the best European university, not just the best UK institution, and correspondingly for universities. This would have considerable implications for the way the UK operates its support for research at universities in IT since it would be important to make sure that enough of our universities were of European stature. At the same time our companies would need to become more aware of the European academic world than they are at the moment. And of course I would expect our French, German and Greek colleagues to be doing exactly the same. This could have a significant effect on the structure of collaboration and hence for the development of a genuinely European IT community.

The second example is the industrial analogue of the first, but is also a key question for Governments in Europe. It is, 'How does one decide what kind of project should be done in a national programme and which in a European programme?' At present there are few clear answers, although my research. In the UK we have been giving some thought to this issue and have been able to produce some initial criteria for making this chance. These are:

EUROPE

a. projects whose exploitation will require very substantial investment in production or marketing, eg VLSI whole processes, parallel processing

b. development of standards, eg PCTE, ANSA

c. projects where European collaboration already exists or is particularly favoured by UK participants.

NATIONAL

a. work becoming interdisciplinary for first time

b. longer term speculative research, often preparing UK for future European programmes, or preliminary work on standards

c. small scale additions to work in category (a) European work

d. areas where UK already has comparative advantage - eg natural language, particularly use of English.

While these do not provide a complete answer to the problem, they are a starting point and allow us to begin to understand the relationship between the two programmes, and hence between the two research communities.

I must admit that we have only just started to think about issues such as these and are by no means clear where they will lead. It would be a pity if the variety of initiatives within the Community was to make Europe inward looking and I hope that we will be able to maintain and develop links with programmes in countries outside Europe as well as with individual companies and institutions.

It is however clear that we need to develop answers to the questions of how a company, university or Government decides whether to pursue particular research topics within its own country; within a programme such as Esprit which involves a defined group of countries; bilaterally with another European country; bilaterally with Japan, the USA or another country outside Europe; or by collaboration between different international programmes. This an embarrassing range of possibilities but the answers we produce and the choices all of us make will define not just the social structure of the IT research community but will also be of great significance for the commercial structure of the industry. It is perhaps too much to hope that we will get the answers right; but I hope we can avoid being too wrong!

PROCEEDINGS OF THE INTERNATIONAL CONFERENCE
ON FIFTH GENERATION COMPUTER SYSTEMS 1988,
edited by ICOT. © ICOT, 1988

SOCIAL IMPACTS OF ADVANCED COMPUTERS

Fred W. Weingarten

Program Manager
Communication and Information Technologies
Office of Technology Assessment
U.S. Congress, U.S.A.

All societies, form the most advanced to the most primitive, are information societies. They all depend on information flows to define their nature and to organize the activities of their members, whether the information exists in electronic form, on paper, or in human memory through an oral tradition. Hence, it is not unreasonable to expect that major changes in the technology of information flows can produce major effects on societies and the individuals in them -- effects that hold out both promise and danger. The principal dilemma presented by advanced computer systems, as well as by other information technologies, will be to capture the enormous opportunities they present while protecting basic and enduring human values.

When analyzing the social implications of advanced generations of computers, it is important to understand first that particular technologies exist in two contexts -- the other related technologies with which they interact in the form of systems and the social structures and institutions that choose the applications that are to be developed and diffused. So it is with computers, in which modern computers form an important part -- but only a part -- of much larger, complex electronic information systems. The way computers are used as well as their social impacts depends on how they are incorporated in this broader

Five major trends form the context for advanced computing applications: (1) widespread distribution of machine intelligence; (2) the worldwide digital communication network; (3) the global electronic library of all human knowledge; (4) the humanized machine interface; and (5) the changing industry and regulatory structure of the industry.

These trends will create great social change and provoke important decisions in a number of areas. Although many could be suggested; I propose the following as among the most important for the person.

1. The nature of work -- The changing role of the person in work, skills and relationships with the employer.

2. The nature of national life -- The changing relationship of the person with the state and of the state with the rest of the world.

3. The nature of human life -- Opportunities and conflicts that emerge as persons are empowered by distributed information systems.

PROCEEDINGS OF THE INTERNATIONAL CONFERENCE
ON FIFTH GENERATION COMPUTER SYSTEMS 1988,
edited by ICOT. © ICOT, 1988

The Panel on Theory and Practice of Concurrent Systems

Ehud Shapiro
The Weizmann Institute of Science
Rehovot 76100, Israel

September 14, 1988

The panel on theory and practice of concurrent systems brings together researchers who approach the problems of concurrency from radically different angles. It is my hope that by exposing and confronting the different perspectives of the penalists all of us will enhance our understanding of what are the problems, concepts, current research directions, and the long term visions of this area of investigation.

In this short note I will attempt to outline the perspectives represented by the penalist. This presentation does not attempt to convey the present ideas and positions of the penalists; these will be presented in the accompanying position papers, written concurrently with this note. Rather, it represents my subjective impressions of the research directions pursued by the panelists. The description is necessarily rough and terse, and since it was not screened by the other panelists, may contain impressions which are either wrong or not up to date. Specifically, the panelists may present a position different than the one ascribed to them in this note.

William Dally represents a research direction that begins with architectural considerations and ends in system and language design. Like the dataflow people a decade ago, hardware architects such as Dally and Chuck Seitz find computational models based on fine grain concurrency to be the best match for parallel computer architectures. At the time, dataflow research faced an immature hardware technology and hardware development tools and, more importantly, the lack of abstract computational models and programming languages suitable for their purposes. This required the development of dataflow languages based on single-assignment (or write-once) variables.

Presently, there are an abundance of models and languages to choose from. The differences between the object-oriented models Dally and colleagues are investigating and early dataflow models is primarily the grain-size: each unit of sequential execution consists of tens or hundreds of the equivalent of conventional machines instructions, compared to one or few instructions in early dataflow models. This makes practical the use of the well-understood and highly optimized

von Newman processor as the building block of the concurrent computer. The research effort is invested mainly in the interconnection network, the communication protocols, resource management, and efficient message handling.

Goeffrey Fox represents the practitioners of concurrent computing. While many are still contemplating whether there is enough concurrency in real-life problems to justify large scale concurrent computers, Fox and his colleagues, working closely with Seitz since the days of the Cosmic Cube, have demonstrated that many computational problems encountered in Physics and Chemistry are amenable to efficient solution on concurrent computers. They have found many "embarrassingly parallel" problems, that is problems amenable to concurrent solution with almost no intellectual effort, and with relatively little implementation efforts. They have also found many other problems that are amenable to efficient parallel implementation using more sophisticated algorithms. They have demonstrated, contrary to what many computer scientists haunted by FORTRAN want to believe, that FORTRAN augmented with *send* and *receive* primitives can go a long way on non-shared memory concurrent computers.

Carl Hewitt represents the object-oriented approach to concurrent systems. This approach suggests that a concurrent system be structured as a collection of communicating objects. The basic operations of an object are receiving and sending messages, changing state, and creating new objects.

Although the object-oriented approach to concurrency was quite radical when first suggested, its ideas have by now penetrated almost all other approaches to concurrency, including the architecture-oriented approach to concurrency mentioned above, the theoretical message-passing models of concurrency, as well as the concurrent logic programming approach, mentioned below.

Related to the object-oriented approach are open systems concerns. In a world of ever-expanding computer communication networks, the concept of a computer system being a closed entity with a fixed set of entities to interact with is no longer valid. Computational objects may join a network, cease to exist, or even change their protocols of interaction dynamically. The goals of research in open systems is to devise techniques and languages that can be used to specify computational objects and systems that can survive in such a dynamic open world. It is stipulated that the object-oriented approach to concurrency may offer a foundation for such open systems.

Robin Milner represents the approach of studying concurrency via abstract calculi such as CCS, CSP, temporal logic, and, more recently, UNITY. This approach devises mathematical models of concurrency and studies them with the goal of increasing our understanding of the fundamental properties and problems of concurrent systems.

Within an abstract setting it is easier to address questions such as program equivalence, compositionality and equivalence of program parts, and fairness, as well as the superposition of algorithms for detecting properties of process networks.

Sometimes, as in the case of CSP and OCCAM, an abstract model gives rise to a concrete programming language that preserves many of its ancestor's properties. However, often there is an undesirable gap between the theoretical and experimental investigations of concurrency. One example is research in semantics. The dominant theoretical message-passing models are synchronous, whereas the majority of concrete models are asynchronous (including object-oriented languages, logic languages, and FORTRAN + send/receive, excluding OCCAM). Another example is research in complexity, where the dominant model used in studies of parallel complexity and parallel algorithms is the synchronous shared memory PRAM. However, most successful experimental work on parallel algorithm was carried out on non-shared-memory asynchronous parallel computers.

It is my hope that the interdisciplinary nature of this conference in general and of this panel in particular will help to bridge this gap between the theory and practice of concurrent systems.

Kazunori Ueda represents the "middle-out" approach to the study of concurrent systems, taken by ICOT and related research groups. In this approach an abstract computational model, with associated programming languages, serve as the starting point for both top-down and bottom-up investigations. The goal of these investigations is the construction of a comprehensive parallel computer system based on this model. ICOT has chosen the concurrent logic programming model and the languages GHC and FGHC as the basis for their investigations.

In the top-down investigation implementation questions are considered: what are suitable architectures for the computational model, and how to implement the language efficiently on target architectures. In the bottom-up investigations the use of the languages, as well as its properties, are investigated. Useful programming techniques are identified, methods for implementing both system programs and application programs in the language are studied, and questions of program developments, program analysis and transformation, including semantics and program equivalence, are pursued.

The integrity of such a broad-spectrums investigation is maintained by adhering to the principle that the abstract computational model is a strict layer of abstraction. This layer of abstraction serves as the platform from which both the top-down and the bottom-up investigations begin, and a meeting point for those who maps the abstract computational model on a concrete architecture, and for those who use the computational model.

David H.D. Warren represents the research aimed at harnessing concurrent computers by parallelizing "conventional" languages. Such research aims at providing better cost/performance ratios by exploiting concurrency without changing language semantics. This research efforts were carried out for FORTRAN and more recently by Warren and colleagues, for Prolog. The philosophy behind this research direction is that concurrent languages (i.e. languages that can express concurrency) are harder to use, and don't have a large software base. Consequently, one should offer programmers a language they know and like (e.g. FORTRAN or Prolog) which does not contain explicit constructs for expressing and controlling concurrency (and in this sense may be higher-level). The task of mapping such a language effectively on a concurrent computer resides with the compiler and runtime system, and not with the programmer.

Such research is often torn between two conflicting goals: one is to provide the programmer with a high-level notation that can be parallelized effectively. The other is to preserve the original, sequential, semantics of a known programming language, which often has constructs that hinder parallel execution without having other clear benefits.

This dilemma suggests defining novel high-level languages that still shelter the programmer from the complexities of concurrency, but differ from their sequential ancestors in being "cleaner" and better amenable to parallel execution. An example of such a language is Andorra, developed by Warren and colleagues.

PROCEEDINGS OF THE INTERNATIONAL CONFERENCE
ON FIFTH GENERATION COMPUTER SYSTEMS 1988,
edited by ICOT. © ICOT, 1988

MECHANISMS FOR CONCURRENT COMPUTING

William J. Dally

Artificial Intelligence Laboratory and
Laboratory for Computer Science
Massachusetts Institute of Technology
Cambridge, Massachusetts

ABSTRACT

Concurrent computing is fundamentally different than
sequential computing. Task size is orders of magnitude
smaller making synchronization and scheduling major concerns, the critical resources are communication and memory, and programs distribute tasks rather than looping.
Conventional hardware and operating system mechanisms
are highly evolved for sequential computing and are not
appropriate for concurrent systems. This position paper
examines the mechanisms required by concurrent systems
and the structure of a system incorporating these mechanisms.

1 FUNDAMENTAL PROBLEMS

1.1 Primitive Mechanisms

A fundamental hardware problem is to identify a set of
primitive mechanisms that efficiently support a broad
range of concurrent execution models. Sequential machines have evolved stacks for memory allocation, pag-
ing for memory management, and program counters for
instruction sequencing. Concurrent machines have very
different demands in each of these areas; the sequential
mechanisms are no longer appropriate. However, no concurrent mechanisms have yet evolved to take their places.
Today's concurrent computers either interpret their execution model using sequential mechanisms or are hard-
wired for a single execution model.

The message-driven processor (MDP) [4] [6] is designed
to evaluate concurrent execution mechanisms for communication, synchronization, and naming. A SEND instruction and hardware message reception and buffering
allow efficient communication of short messages across a
high-speed network [7]. Synchronization is supported by
a dispatch mechanism that creates a new process to handle a message in a single clock cycle. A general purpose
translation mechanism supports naming. These mechanisms provide the primitive support required by many
concurrent models of computation including dataflow [9],
actors[1], and communicating processes [11].

1.2 Resource Management

At the operating system level, a key problem is to develop
resource management techniques suitable for concurrent
systems. In a concurrent system, communication bandwidth and memory capacity are the limiting resources;
processor cycles are almost free. This situation is the
opposite of the sequential case where processor cycles
are considered the critical resource and communication is
not a consideration. To complicate the situation the resources are physically distributed. Objects and processes
must be placed in a manner that balances memory and
processor use across the machine and reduces communication. The JOSS operating system [14] [15] is designed
to satisfy these unconventional requirements.

Methods must also be developed to regulate concurrency.
Many programs have too much parallelism and thus generate more tasks than can be accommodated in the available memory. To avoid the resulting deadlock, the system must regulate programs allowing them to generate
sufficient concurrency to make use of all available processors, but reverting to more sequential execution before exhausting memory. Examples of regulation include
controlled unrolling of loops [2] and adaptive (FIFO vs
LIFO) scheduling [10].

To make efficient use of the communication resources,
memory and tasks must be allocated in a manner that exploits locality. Placing objects near each other to improve
locality is often at odds with the need to distribute objects for load balancing. Also there are some cases where
communication bandwidth can be increased by spreading out a computation to make more channels available.
For static computations min-cut placement techniques
similar to those used to place electronic components [12]
work well. Dynamic computations rely heavily on heuristics (e.g., placing an object near the object that created
it) supplemented by reactive load balancing.

1.3 Overhead

To make use of a computer with thousands of processors,

a program must be decomposed into many small tasks. Each task consists of only a few instructions. In conventional systems, however, the overhead of scheduling, synchronization, and communication is many hundreds of instructions per task. This overhead restricts conventional multicomputers to operating at a very coarse grain size – thousands of instructions per task. Concurrency is reduced because there are fewer large tasks. Also, the resource management problems become harder as resources are allocated in larger chunks.

Overhead can be reduced to just a few instructions per task. The JOSS operating system, using the primitive mechanisms provided by the MDP, can create, suspend, resume, or destroy a task in fewer than ten instructions [15]. This efficient management of fine-grain tasks is achieved without sacrificing protection. Each task executes in its own naming environment.

2 CONCURRENT COMPUTER ORGANIZATION

To make the most efficient use of projected VLSI technology, general purpose concurrent computers will be constructed from a number of fine-grain processing nodes [5] connected by a low-latency, wire-efficient interconnection network [3].

2.1 Fine-Grain Processing Nodes

The *grain size* of a machine refers to the physical size and the amount of memory in one processing node. A coarse-grain processing node requires hundreds of chips (several boards) and has $\approx 10^7$ bytes of memory while fine-grain node fits on a single chip and has $\approx 10^4$ bytes of memory. Fine-grain nodes cost less and have less memory than coarse-grain nodes, however, because so little silicon area is required to build a fast processor, they need not have slower processors than coarse-grain nodes.

VLSI technology makes it possible to build small, powerful processing elements. A 1M-bit DRAM chip has an area of $256M\lambda^2$ (λ is half the minimum line width [13].). In the same area we can build a single chip processing node containing:

A 32-bit processor	$16M\lambda^2$
A floating-point unit	$32M\lambda^2$
A communication controller	$8M\lambda^2$
512Kbits RAM	$128M\lambda^2$

Such a single-chip processing node would have the same processing power as a board-sized node but significantly less memory per node. The memory capacity of the entire machine is comparable to that of a coarse-grained machine. We refer to a machine built from these nodes as a *jellybean machine* as it is built with commodity part (jellybean) technology [8].

A fine-grain processing node has two major advantages: density and memory bandwidth. Several hundred single-chip nodes can be packaged on a single printed circuit board permitting us to exploit hundreds of times the concurrency of machines with board-sized nodes. With on-chip memory we can read an entire row of memory (128 or 256 bits) in a single cycle without incurring the delay of several chip crossings. This high memory bandwidth allows the memory to simultaneously buffer messages from a high bandwidth network and provide the processor with instructions and data.

Fine grain machines are area efficient. Area efficiency is given by $e_A = A_1 T_1 / A_N T_N$ (where A_i is the area of i processors, T_i is execution time on i processors and N is the number of processors). Many researchers have measured their machines effectiveness in terms of node efficiency, $e_N = T_1 / N T_N$ Proponents of coarse-grain machines argue that a machine constructed from several thousand single-chip nodes would be inefficient because many of the processing nodes will be idle. N is large, hence e_N is small. A user, however, is not concerned with N, but rather with machine cost, A_N, and how long it takes to solve a problem, T. Fine-grain machines have a very high e_A because they are able to exploit more concurrency in a smaller area.

2.2 Wire-Efficient Communication Networks

VLSI systems are wire limited. The cost of these systems is predominantly that of connecting devices, and the performance is limited by the delay of these interconnections. Thus, an interconnection network must make efficient use of the available wire. The topology of the network must map into the three physical dimensions so that messages are not required to *double back* on themselves, and in a way that allows messages to use all of the available bandwidth along their path. Also, the topology and routing algorithm must be simple so the network switches will be sufficiently fast to avoid leaving the wires idle while making routing decisions. Our recent findings suggest that low-dimensional k-ary n-cube interconnection networks [3] are capable of providing the performance required by fine-grain concurrent architectures.

3 TRANSITION TO MAINSTREAM CONCURRENT COMPUTING

Select areas of mainstream computing will switch to concurrent computers when (1) concurrent software has matured to the point that it can support a large evolving application and (2) the performance advantage of these machines is sufficient to justify an investment in new software. Concurrent machines are appropriate for applications that are (1) limited by CPU performance (e.g., sci-

156

entific computing and signal processing) and (2) limited by memory system bandwidth (e.g., transaction processing). It is also expected that the availability of these machines will create new applications that were not previously possible.

REFERENCES

References

[1] Agha, Gul A., *Actors: A Model of Concurrent Computation in Distributed Systems*, MIT Press, Cambridge, MA, 1986.

[2] Arvind, and Culler, D., "Managing Resources in a Parallel Machine", Massachusetts Institute of Technology Laboratory for Computer Science CSG Memo 257, 1985.

[3] Dally, William J. "Wire Efficient VLSI Multiprocessor Communication Networks," *Proceedings Stanford Conference on Advanced Research in VLSI,* Paul Losleben, Ed., MIT Press, Cambridge, MA, March 1987, pp. 391-415.

[4] Dally, W.J. et.al, "Architecture of a Message-Driven Processor," *Proc. 14th ACM/IEEE Symposium On Computer Architecture,* 1987, pp. 189-196.

[5] Dally, W.J., "Fine-Grain Concurrent Computers", *Proc. 3rd Symposium on Hypercube Concurrent Computers and Applications,* 1988.

[6] Dally, W.J. et.al, *Message Driven Processor Architecture, Version 11,* MIT VLSI Memo, 1988.

[7] Dally, W.J., "Performance Analysis of k-ary n-cube Interconnection Networks," *IEEE Transactions on Computers,* To appear.

[8] Dally, W.J., "The J-Machine", to appear.

[9] Dennis, Jack B., "Data Flow Supercomputers," *IEEE Computer,* Vol. 13, No. 11, Nov. 1980, pp. 48-56.

[10] Halstead, R., "Parallel Symbolic Computation," *IEEE Computer,* Vol. 19, No. 8, Aug. 1986, pp. 35-43.

[11] Hoare, C.A.R., "Communicating Sequential Processes," *Comm. ACM,* Vol. 21, No. 8, August 1978, pp. 666-677.

[12] Kernighan B.W. and Lin, S., "An Efficient Heuristic Procedure for Partitioning Graphs," *Bell System Technical Journal,* Vol. 49, No. 2, Feb. 1970, pp. 291-307.

[13] Mead, Carver A. and Conway, Lynn A., *Introduction to VLSI Systems,* Addison-Wesley, Reading, Mass., 1980.

[14] Totty, B.K., *An Operating Environment for the Jellybean Machine,* MIT AI-Memo, 1988.

[15] Totty, B.K., and Dally, W.J., "JOSS: The Jellybean Operating System Software," to appear.

PROCEEDINGS OF THE INTERNATIONAL CONFERENCE
ON FIFTH GENERATION COMPUTER SYSTEMS 1988,
edited by ICOT. © ICOT, 1988

Theory and Practice of Concurrent Systems

Geoffrey Fox

California Institute of Technology

Pasadena, CA 91125

August 17, 1988

What are Fundamental Problems in Constructing and Using Concurrent Systems?

We can consider the issues in three categories: (i) Hardware, (ii) Systems Software and Programming Environment, (iii) Application Software.

(i) It appears to me that basic principles of the hardware architecture and construction are understood. One has a collection of nodes connected by some sort of switch or router to a collection of memories. Such machines can be built although there are several important questions.

    (a) Are the nodes powerful or wimpy? Is the Teraflop processor 20,000 twenty nanosec nodes or 1000 one nanosec nodes?

    (b) What is the nature of switch and correct tradeoff between latency, bandwidth and dependence on routing distance?

    (c) Should one build "smart" memories or switches?

    (d) Should control be SIMD or MIMD?

In each case, there will be an inevitable favoring of local data references and varying penalties for access to shared or non-local memories.

There are other architectures to be explored and discovered (using neural networks, dataflow, etc.) but currently known general principles seem to be sufficient to build high performance general purpose concurrent computers.

(iii) Experience such as that gained at Caltech [Angus 89, Fox 87f, Fox 88a, Fox 88b, Fox 88c,] have shown that a broad range of applications - including the majority of those running on current sequential supercomputers - perform well on concurrent computers with speed ups that are typically at least 80% of the number of nodes.

(ii) However, this experience was gained with unusually talented users who rethought problems and rewrote codes from scratch. Further, the resultant programs were quite small (500-5000 lines). In principle, this experience is directly applicable to large industrial and government (defense, national laboratories) applications which use "essentially" the same algorithms. However, these applications involve much larger codes (100,000 lines or more) and it is often impractical to rewrite code - especially for today's concurrent computers where software productivity is low. We need to develop the programming environment to allow semi-automatic (user + compiler) parallelization of existing code and to make it easier to develop new code. This will require both better tools and perhaps new languages. I see little consensus as to the appropriate approach to this issue and not convincing evidence that a good solution will exist in the near term. Thus, I consider that the development of a productive programming environment as the key problem in concurrent computing.

What are fundamental differences between sequential and concurrent systems? Should differences be exposed and hidden and at what level should they be addressed?

Parallel algorithms are usually quite natural e.g. one is often simulating the physical world - a well known parallel system. So in this sense, concurrent computers are natural and are not fundamentally different. However, current programming environments - especially languages such as C and FORTRAN - do not naturally support parallelism. In this sense, there is a fundamental difference between today's sequential systems (hardware + environment) and concurrent systems.

At Caltech, essentially all hypercube applications have addressed concurrency at the application program level. Users decompose data, and write the programs to control the different parts of the decomposed domain. This was the correct approach to quickly show that "parallel processing works" but it is certainly rather tedious and not very portable between concurrent machines of different architectures. Currently, I view the operating system as not getting involved at the level of concurrency within an application program. It should typically view a given application - consisting of many processes on many nodes - as a single entity. Concurrency should be handled at the level of system utilities (e.g. for load balancing [Fox 86f, Fox 88e]), compiler (e.g. for parallelization and vectorizing FORTRAN code) and novel languages. I see several approaches to concurrency at this level for example [Arvind 87, Allen 87, Callahan 88, Chen 88, Fox 85d, Kuck 86, Mirchandaney 88, Rose 87, Taylor 88, Wilson 87, Zima 88,] but I do not yet have a good feeling as to the status and promise of these very different methods.

Will there be a transition in mainstream computing from sequential to concurrent computing?

I certainly hope that such a transition occurs but I fear that, rather, we will evolve from sequential to concurrent computing. Consider Fig. 1 which plots computer performance as a function of time. Messina and I have adapted a plot due to Buzbee [Buzbee 87] to separate sequential and concurrent performance. Current "conventional supercomputers" are already parallel machines with up to 8 heads (ETA-10, CRAY-YMP) and several pipes (functional units) per head. In three years, we can expect this technology to lead to 64 processor machines. We have plotted current distributed memory MIMD machines scaling the number of nodes and hence performance to a large machine with a price tag around $20M - we can define a supercomputer as what you can do for this price. Even with this scaling, the parallel machines are not of significantly higher performance than their commercial "sequential" competition. Thus, we expect the "conventional" (IBM, ETA, CRAY in the U.S.A.) approach to dominate high performance computers in the near term. This approach offers competitive cost-performance and typically better software environment than the "massively-parallel" machines. This assertion assumes that conventional supercomputers use their different heads to run different jobs and do not multitask within a job. Parallelism is achieved by the compiler by using the several pipes on a given head. This conventional approach will lead to concurrent computing with 64 nodes in the early 1990's and 1024 in the later part of the decade. Thus, we have a natural commercial evolution to concurrent computing with the conventional approach eventually needing the programming environment advances discussed above to decompose over 64-1024 heads. A sharp transition to parallel processing, rather than an evolution is possible but it needs development of "massively-parallel" hardware that is clearly more cost-effective than the conventional competition. It also needs the productive software environment already discussed. These are challenges to the parallel computing industry and the computer science research community.

Is there a difference between parallel and distributed systems?

This is partly semantics! Let us interpret parallel to mean tightly coupled cooperating processes such as those involved in domain decomposition of a scientific computation. Let us define distributed to mean more loosely coupled processes such as those occurring in a functional decomposition - say of servers for an operating system or controllers of different parts of an automobile. Then these systems can clearly be approached from a common point of view but this may have limited value. In my terminology [Fox 88a, Fox 88b] parallel systems require substantial interprocess communication in a loosely synchronous fashion; distributed systems often need less communication and are naturally asynchronous. I suspect that it may be crucial to build these characteristics into the support environment to achieve an efficient productive system. For instance, distributed systems are perhaps naturally approached in an object-oriented fashion; parallel systems by a language like C* or CPC [Felten 88a, Rose 87].

What is the structure of future general purpose concurrent computer hardware?

As discussed above, several of today's architectures naturally scale to large machines and are essentially general purpose e.g., can tackle all large scientific computations [Fox 85c, Fox 88b, Gustafson 88]. Examples are the hypercube, transputer arrays and their relations; Butterfly, RP3, Ultracomputer and the SIMD Connection Machine. The latter can naturally address about 50% of major computations on today's supercomputers [Fox 88b].

It is important to improve the cost performance of future machines to compete more favorably with conventional computers.

Is concurrency an artificial nuisance inflicted on us by the deficiences of VLSI techniques?

No, computation is the modelling of one complex system (the problem) by another (the computer). The essential task is to map these systems on to each other. Both systems are naturally parallel and in neither case is the parallelism artificial. Today's nuisance is caused by the available tools and is not intrinsic.

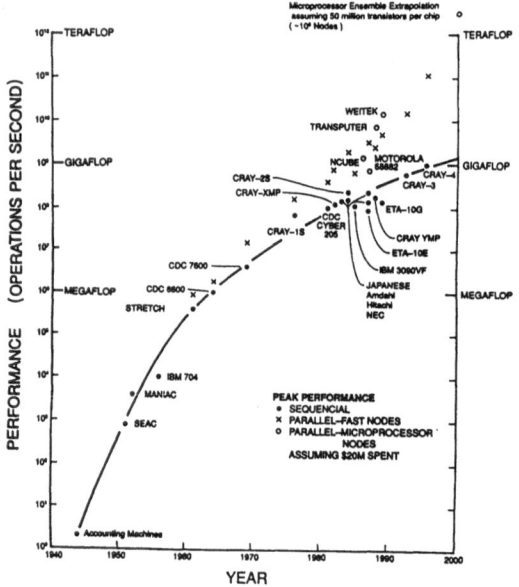

References

[Allen 87]   Allen R., Callahan D., Kennedy K., "Automatic Decomposition of Scientific Programs for Parallel Execution", in proceedings of "14th ACM Symposium on the Principles of Programming Languages", Jan. 87, ACM, New York, N. Y.

[Angus 89]   Angus, I., Fox, G., Kim, J. and Walker, D. "Solving Problems on Concurrent Processors - Software Supplement," to be published by Prentice Hall 1989.

[Arvind 87]   Arvind and Nikhil, R. S., "Executing a program on the MIT tagged-token dataflow architecture," PARLE Conference, in *Lecture Notes in Computer Science, 259* edited by G. Goos and J. Hartmanis, Springer-Verlag, New York (1987), 1.

[Buzbee 87]   Buzbee, B., "Supercomputers: values and trends," *Int. Journal of Supercomputer Applications 1* (1987) 100.

[Callahan 88]   Callahan, D., Kennedy, D. 1988 "Compiling Programs for Distributed-Memory Multiprocessors," in proceedings of "1988 Workshop on Programming Languages and Compilers for Parallel Computing," Cornell, August 2-5, 1988.

[Chen 88]   Chen, M., Choo, Y., Li, J., "Crystal: From Functional Description to efficient Parallel Code" in proceedings of the Third Conference on Hypercube Concurrent Computers and Applications, edited by G. C. Fox, published by ACM, New York, N. Y., [Fox 88c]

[Felten 88a]   Felten, E. and Otto, S. W. 1988 "Coherent Parallel C," in proceedings of the Third Conference on Hypercube Concurrent Computers and Applications, edited by G. C. Fox, published by ACM, New York, N.Y., [Fox 88c], Caltech report C^3P-527.

[Fox 85c]   Fox, G., "The performance of the Caltech hypercube in scientific calculations: A preliminary analysis" in *Supercomputers-Algorithms, Architectures, and Scientific Computation*, edited by F. A. Matsen and T. Tajima, University of Texas Press (1987), Caltech report C^3P-161.

[Fox 85d]   Fox, G. "Use of the Caltech Hypercube": IEEE Software, Vol. 2, p. 73 (July 1985), Caltech report C^3P-162.

[Fox 86f]   Fox, G. C., "A Review of Automatic Load Balancing and Decomposition Methods for the Hypercube," November 1986. The Proceedings for the Workshop on Numerical Algorithms for Modern Parallel Computer Architectures, held at the IMA in November 1985, published as Volume 13 in the IMA Volumes in Mathematics and Its Applications, *Numerical Algorithms for Modern Parallel Computer Architectures*, (Springer-Verlag), New York, Caltech report C^3P-385.

[Fox 87f]   Fox, G. and Frey, A. 1987 "High Performance Parallel Supercomputing Application, Hardware, and Software Issues for a Teraflop Computer," Caltech report C^3P-451b.

[Fox 88a]   Fox, G. C., Johnson, M. A., Lyzenga, G. A., Otto, S. W., Salmon, J. K., and Walker, D. 1988 "Solving Problems on Concurrent Processors," published by Prentice Hall 1988.

[Fox 88b]   Fox, G. C. 1988 "What Have We Learnt from Using Real Parallel Machines to Solve Real Problems?" Invited talk at the Third Conference on Hypercube Concurrent Computers and Applications, sponsored by the Jet Propulsion Laboratory, Pasadena, CA, Jan. 19-20, 1988, in proceedings of the Third Conference on Hypercube Concurrent Computers and Applications, edited by G. C. Fox, published by ACM, New York, N.Y., Caltech report C^3P-522.

[Fox 88c]   Proceedings of Third Conference on Hypercube Concurrent Computers and Applications, edited by G. C. Fox, published by ACM, New York, N.Y.

[Fox 88e]   Fox, G. C, and Furmanski, W. 1988 "Load Balancing Loosely Synchronous Problems with a Neural Network," in proceedings of the Third Conference on Hypercube Concurrent Computers and Applications, edited by G. C. Fox, published by ACM, New York, N.Y., [Fox 88c], Caltech report C^3P-363b.

[Gustafson 88]   Gustafson, J. L., Montry, G. R., Benner, R. E. 1988 "Development of Parallel Methods for a 1024-Processor Hypercube," SIAM journal on Scientific and Statistical Computing.

[Kuck 86]   Kuck, D. J., Davidson, E. S., Lawrie, D. H., Sameh, A. H., "Parallel supercomputing today and the Cedar approach." *Science 231*, (1986), 967.

160

[Mirchandaney 88]   Mirchandaney R., Saltz J. H., Smith R. M., Nicol D. M., Crowley K., "Principles of Runtime Support for Parallel Processors", in proceedings of "1988 International Conference on Supercomputing", St. Malo, July, 1988, published by ACM, New York, N. Y.

[Rose 87]   Rose, J., Steele G. 1987 "C*: An extended C Language for Data Parallel Programming", Thinking Machines Corporation.

[Taylor 88]   Taylor, S., Shapiro, R. and Shapiro, E. 1988 "FCP: A Summary of Performance Results," in proceedings of the Third Conference on Hypercube Concurrent Computers and Applications, edited by G. C. Fox, published by ACM, New York, N.Y., [Fox 88c].

[Wilson 87]   K. Wilson, "The Gibbs Project" in Supercomputers - Algorithms, Architectures and Scientific Computation", edited by F.A. Matsen and T. Tajima, University of Texas Press (1987).

[Zima 88]   Zima, H. P., Bast, H-J., Gerndt, M., "SUPERB: A tool for semi-automatic MIMD/SIMD parallelization," Parallel Computing 6, 1 (1988).

PROCEEDINGS OF THE INTERNATIONAL CONFERENCE
ON FIFTH GENERATION COMPUTER SYSTEMS 1988,
edited by ICOT. © ICOT, 1988

Knowledge Processing

Carl Hewitt
Artificial Intelligence Laboratory
Laboratory for Computer Science
Massachusetts Institute of Technology
Cambridge, MA 02139

Knowledge processing is a new approach to understanding open information systems—an approach which is informed by the social sciences (as opposed to artificial intelligence and cognitive science, which have been principally based on psychological and brain sciences). In this talk, I will outline some of the discoveries and methods in knowledge processing. I will highlight topics that are ripe material for intrepid souls in search of adventure, fun, challenge, and a thesis.

In order to work on large scale tasks—such as going to the moon, building the Golden Gate bridge, or designing earthquake-proof buildings—we need to build open-system, human/computer organizations that can conduct the information processing that is essential to effective performance. Just as organizations can accomplish tasks that individual humans cannot, we are interested in designing computer systems that can be scaled up to take on tasks of similar scope and magnitude.

This talk presents an approach for developing organizational information systems that can operate more effectively and intelligently with human organizations. In this regard, we will study *organizational information systems*—namely, all of the information processing done to coordinate all of an organization's work—with the exception of direct manipulation of physical objects. (Our vision of an *organization* includes humans, computers, and their interaction.)

Conflict is a fundamental aspect of all large-scale intelligent systems, and occurs whenever different forces are pulling in different directions. Conflict is the direct and natural result of differing perspectives and commitments.

Commitments have been discussed by Winograd and Flores in the context of Hermenuetics, and by Richard Fikes in the context of contract nets as developed by Reid Smith and Randy Davis. In this paper we are particularly concerned with organizational conflict, i.e., conflict between specialized components of an organization. Negotiation of conflict can strengthen organizational effectiveness. An organizational ideology that says "We are all in agreement here" denies the existence of internal conflicts. Since such conflicts are denied, they cannot be dealt with explicitly, and organizational performance suffers.

As we shall see, conflict is ubiquitous, inevitable, and must be dealt with in any complex organization. In general, conflicting parties must find ways of negotiating their differences in order to deal effectively with conflict. In the course of negotiations, one party often will deliberately contradict statements made by another party in order to sway organizational behavior.

Consider a meeting between a representative of Marketing and a representative of Development to negotiate whether the company should distribute another company's product or manufacture its own. Each party can present material on its view of the issue, the commitments that intersect the issue, and options for dealing with the issue. It is important to understand that these presentations are seldom ready-made. Instead, each party to the negotiation generates new material to fit the circumstances at hand. Contradictory statements are often generated as a natural way of bringing conflicting commitments to the attention of other parties.

Our goal is to construct a scientific and engineering discipline that supports the design, construction, and management of large-scale, open-system, human/computer organizations. Our challenge is to develop a knowledge processing architecture that supports robustness in open system environments.

The robustness of an organization's know-how is fundamental to its ability to accomplish a task in the face of "normal, everyday" contingencies. For example, the know-how of manufacturing integrated circuit chips means that in spite of various difficulties that arise during the operation of a plant—defective materials, delayed shipments, employee illness, and so on—the operators of the plant can continue production.

Since human organizations have evolved methods of dealing with indeterminacy and conflict—and have made them into strengths rather than weaknesses—adaptation of these methods can help create a foundation for robustness in a computer organization.

The development of a knowledge processing architecture for the design of concurrent computer information systems would have two important potential payoffs.

First, a knowledge processing architecture would have significant advantages in scalability and robustness. By creating a framework for dealing with conflict, knowledge processing makes human organizations both robust and scaleable. This is practical evidence for believing we can achieve the same results for computer organizations. Since conflict is ubiquitous to organizational life, our computer systems must be able to use conflict—and the contradictions that result—as a source of strength rather than weakness.

Second, a knowledge processing architecture will provide a better interface between the humans and the machines. If both organizations work by the same kinds of principles, then people will understand the computers more easily and intuitively—and the computers will also have a compatible model of how decisions are made in the human organization. Such compatibility holds the promise of better interaction between them. We are currently exploring the possibility of basing computer processes on human organizational principles.

Knowledge processing also shows that more formal modes of reasoning can be derived as a natural progression from the needs of organizations in dealing with conflict. As the parties to the conflict negotiate their differences, they generate justifications to support their position. When these justifications are generalized and decontextualized by the parties so that they can decide mechanically whether a given step is in accordance with a rule, then they have developed a microtheory. Since these microtheories are decontextualized, they can be carried from place to place and used to seek additional leverage in many different negotiations. Thus, microtheories and logical deduction can be seen as a natural kind of specialized development that often occurs in the negotiation of conflict.

Negotiation of conflict is a source of creativity and robustness. It allows an organization to consider and explore its alternatives in a way that takes other organizational commitments into account.

PROCEEDINGS OF THE INTERNATIONAL CONFERENCE
ON FIFTH GENERATION COMPUTER SYSTEMS 1988,
edited by ICOT. © ICOT, 1988

Some directions in concurrency theory
(Statement for panel on "Theory and Practice in Concurrency").

Robin Milner

Department of Computer Science, Edinburgh University
King's Buildings, Mayfield Road, Edinburgh EH9 3JZ, U.K.

I want to comment on two aspects in which a theory of concurrent computing is different from a theory of sequential computing. In both aspects, we see the same difference: namely, that the former is about the whole of computation, while the latter is only about a slice of it.

The first aspect is to do with the computer-in-context, as opposed to the computer by itself. There used to be, and largely still is, a strong division among three types of description. First, a sequential program was a high-level description of what can occur in a computer loaded in a certain way. (If you don't like calling a program a 'description' then consider how else, other than just by presenting the program, you could describe the possible sequences of memory transfers that a sequential program can perform.) Second, automata theory or engineers' diagrams described what can go on in the same machine at a *lower level*, and this certainly isn't sequential. Third, narrative prose – or any scientific notation suitable to the applications – described what may occur *outside* the same machine between, or during, program executions; this, too, is only rarely sequential. It took some time – thanks to von Newmann's bottleneck (which, however, got computing off the ground) – before we thought that the same descriptive medium might serve all three purposes. Carl Petri is primarily responsible, via Net Theory, for giving us hope for a unified theory in which to describe and analyse *all* aspects of the computer-in-context (computer + program + aircraft, or computer + program + banking staff) rather than just the computer itself, or just the program itself. This has to be a theory of concurrency, because of the three ingredients *at most* one – the program – is sequential!

The subject matter for such a theory is vast – all discrete dynamic systems – and it is natural to expect specialised theories, with special notations, for particular classes of system. Not all these theories are the concern of the computer scientist; but there is a distinct challenge for computer scientists – namely that they must contribute on two levels. At the lower level they must build the specialised theory for those subsystems which happen to be computers or programs. At the upper level they must provide the global theory, the general theory of concurrency into which all the specialist theories must fit; there must be a theoretical framework which can embrace special theory of information-flow among banking staff, the special theory of programs, and all the other special theories. But it would be untidy and unfortunate if these two levels were fundamentally different! Since a significant part of the general theory must be a tractable descriptive notation, and since we have already classified programs as descriptions, one hopes that concurrent programming languages will be nothing more than a part of the descriptive machinery of a general theory of concurrency. My point is that the barrier to this unification is removed as soon as programs are not forced to be sequential, and we must exploit this freedom.

The second aspect in which concurrency is about the whole of computation is in its concern with structure. A proper theory of concurrency must explain the structure (division into processes) of a program, as well as the structure (division into processors) of a computer, and the relationship between the two. Sometimes – perhaps in solving partial differential equations, or in some large physics calculations, or in weather-forecasting programs – the process structure of the programs can be fixed and simple (e.g. grid-like) and there can be a fixed allocation of processes to processors. Other applications – much more interesting to a computer scientist – are not like that; for example, an operating system program together with all the programs it runs, or the description of architectures such as the ALICE machine which aim at parallel execution of declarative programs. For these applications, if we wish to analyse them thoroughly, we have to find tractable descriptive methods and in which both the virtual (program) and the real (machine) processes are written in the same terms, and in which two kinds of mobility can be reflected: the changing population and linkage of the virtual processes, and their shifting allocation to the processors. It seems only with concurrency that we arrive at, and wish to tackle, this very subtle problem of relating two distinct ways of structuring the behaviour of a complex system.

It is true that some people – including Hewitt, and Kennaway and Sleep – have given notations in which a significant amount of this mobility can be written down. The big challenge, though, remains to find the right mathematics in which to analyse these descriptions; I think that this needs great innovation.

In this second aspect, just as in the first, we can take advantage of the idea that programs are descriptions. When we have found a good mathematical means to describe the mobile structure among processes and their changing association with processors, we shall almost certainly find that we can enrich our concurrent programming languages by absorbing the new descriptive notations into them. It is in this way that programming has become richer in the past, by absorbing the descriptive notations of logical and of functional processes, and I see no reason why it should not happen, even more excitingly, with the notations of various aspects of concurrent processes. I therefore see concurrency theory as a means of coming to understand, through structure, processes (both built by us and naturally existing) which have previously been beyond our grasp.

PROCEEDINGS OF THE INTERNATIONAL CONFERENCE
ON FIFTH GENERATION COMPUTER SYSTEMS 1988,
edited by ICOT. © ICOT, 1988

THEORY AND PRACTICE OF CONCURRENT SYSTEMS
—THE ROLE OF KERNEL LANGUAGE IN THE FGCS PROJECT—

Kazunori Ueda

Institute for New Generation Computer Technology
4-28, Mita 1-chome, Minato-ku, Tokyo 108, Japan

1 INTRODUCTION

An outstanding feature of the Fifth Generation Computer Project is the idea of designing a novel kernel language that links parallel hardware and application software. KL1 (Chikayama et al. 1988), the kernel language for the Multi-PSI (Taki 1988) and the Parallel Inference Machine (PIM) (Goto et al. 1988), is based on the inherently parallel language GHC (Ueda 1988). This means that we chose to expose parallelism to software people and involve them in forming the culture of parallelism, rather than to hide parallelism from them. This paper will describe why we took this approach and will answer the questions of Ehud Shapiro in the light of our methodology.

2 LANGUAGE ISSUES IN CONCURRENT SYSTEMS

The key to the success of concurrent systems lies in how to construct and accumulate parallel software.

It is often claimed that parallel programming is difficult, but the fact is that we have never made as much effort toward creating parallel software as toward creating sequential software. We are too much accustomed to sequential programming of von Neumann computers to change our programming style. It is very important to overcome these non-technical problems and concentrate more research on parallel programming by steadily finding solutions or clues to individual technical problems.

Technical problems include language issues, with which I have been involved for years. There are two candidates for an easy-to-use parallel language: augmenting a sequential language with simple primitives (like Occam) and designing an inherently parallel language. The former might enable smoother transition from sequentiality to parallelism, but our project chose the latter approach for the following reasons:

(1) The existence of sequencing tends to make control overspecific. We wanted to distinguish between the sequentiality essential for the correctness of the algorithm and the other kinds of sequentiality.

(2) We wanted the kernel language to express any potential parallelism of a program independently of the granularity of the hardware we would design.

(3) Parallel programming will require the change of our way of programming and thinking from the von Neumann style. An inherently parallel language will better encourage it.

Another alternative might be to raise the level of the kernel language to where programmers are not bothered by control. However, we do require a parallel language with explicit control when implementing such a high-level declarative language and, more importantly, when describing the communication between a program and the outside world.

It is the attention to communication that characterizes concurrent systems both in theory and in practice. In theory, communication gives the most abstract view of a whole program and its fragments, concurrent processes. In practice, communication is the primary source of bottleneck.

The reason why control is necessary for specifying communication is that communication is a directed, irreversible activity. A language without explicit control is usually considered to be at a higher level than a language with explicit control, but the presence or absence of control is more a matter of formalism than a matter of the level of abstraction. A language without control can be used only in the fragments of a program in which communication is not made or need not be specified.

We chose to expose parallelism to software people by adopting an abstract kernel language with explicit control. It provides software people with an appropriately abstract model of parallel computation, and yet it is amenable to reasonably efficient parallel implementation. Our choice does not necessarily mean that all applications programmers must care about control issues; we could hide parallelism by implementing higher-level languages (like constraint programming languages) on top of the kernel language. The point is that *applications programmers should have explicit access to par-*

allelism if they want. The development of concurrent systems should be supported by many people at various layers from hardware to applications. Our choice allows enterprising applications programmers to consider good use of parallelism for their applications, which can be spread in the form of a programming paradigm or an embedded language whose object codes embody that paradigm.

3 FUTURE RESEARCH

Much research remains to be done on concurrent systems. Making a good parallel implementation of the kernel language will not be sufficient to motivate applications people to write parallel programs. We must show them parallel programming methodologies. We have found that although it is not very difficult to write parallel programs, it is difficult to write *good* parallel programs. We must take two more things into account: the locality of communication and load balancing.

In sequential programming, we rely so much on the flat storage structure. Large and flat memory space has made programming easy by not letting programmers think much about locality. To make full use of a parallel computer with the processing power distributed over the storage, however, we must consider storage and processing at the same time and keep the locality of communication. The notion of constant-time access is by no means scalable.

Parallel programming requires theoretical support, too. We do not yet have a practical computational model with which to argue the real efficiency of parallel algorithms running on, say, the Multi-PSI. Previous theories of parallel computation were concerned mainly with whether parallelism improves time complexity. However, the computers we are building are intended to improve *time* and not time *complexity*.

Some applications programs may have irregular structures that are too difficult to analyze statically. Such programs require a mechanism for keeping the load balance and the locality automatically. In general, a future concurrent system will be supported by a lot of techniques whose basic ideas may be discovered on the analogy of what we do in the real world as members of some community. The actual implementation of those techniques will necessitate statistical analysis.

We must also continue language and implementation research to create a more expressive and more efficient language. As for expressiveness, we must consider how to introduce meta-level operations gracefully. By meta-level operations I mean the operations that refer to and/or modify the "current" status of computation (including physical configurations and time). GHC deliberately excluded meta-level operations to reveal the essence of concurrent logic programming. It is expressive enough for ordinary programs, but is too weak for an operating system like PIMOS (Chikayama et al. 1988). Accordingly, KL1 has featured necessary meta-level operations to describe PIMOS, but we have yet to clarify their semantics by developing an appropriate model of the parallel computers running KL1 programs. Research on reflection in parallel computation (Tanaka 1988) will be helpful in the design of meta-level features.

As for efficiency, we have two directions of research: the simplification of the kernel language (without loss of expressiveness) and the development of high-level optimization techniques. The purpose of the simplification is to make processes and streams more efficient by tuning KL1 for programming with many small communicating processes. It is my consistent view that GHC is a base language from which an appropriate subset should be made. A good subset will be found through the research on sophisticated optimization that employs techniques such as abstract interpretation.

An efficient implementation of processes and streams will better support user languages such as *A'UM* (Yoshida and Chikayama 1988). It will also enable us to use processes as building blocks of a database that allows concurrent access. However, such storage-intensive use of processes requires a new kind of optimization. While most of the current implementations of KL1 are tuned for computation-intensive programs that do not suspend so often, now we need optimization techniques for processes that are almost always dormant.

REFERENCES

Chikayama, T. et al. (1988) Overview of the Parallel Inference Machine Operating System (PIMOS), in this volume.

Goto, A. et al. (1988) Overview of the Parallel Inference Machine Architecture (PIM), in this volume.

Taki, K. (1988) The Parallel Software Research and Development Tool: Multi-PSI System, in *Programming of Future Generation Computers*, Fuchi, K. and Nivat, M. (eds.), North-Holland, 1988, pp. 411–426.

Tanaka, J. (1988) Meta-Interpreters and Reflective Operations in GHC, in this volume.

Ueda, K. (1988) Guarded Horn Clauses: A Parallel Logic Programming Language with the Concept of a Guard, in *Programming of Future Generation Computers*, Fuchi, K. and Nivat, M. (eds.), North-Holland, 1988, pp. 441–456.

Yoshida, K. and Chikayama, T. (1988) *A'UM* — A Stream-Based Concurrent Object-Oriented Language, in this volume.

PROCEEDINGS OF THE INTERNATIONAL CONFERENCE
ON FIFTH GENERATION COMPUTER SYSTEMS 1988,
edited by ICOT. © ICOT, 1988

THEORY AND PRACTICE OF CONCURRENT SYSTEMS
–A POSITION PAPER

David H. D. Warren

Department of Computer Science

University of Bristol
Bristol BS8 1TR, U.K.

What do we mean by concurrent systems?

We have to be careful what we mean by a concurrent system. Computer systems are built in levels one on top of another, for example an application on top of a high-level language emulator on top of microcode on top of hardware. Concurrency at one level does not necessarily imply concurrency at another. For example, a pipelined processor has concurrency that manifests itself at the microcode level, but is irrelevant and invisible to the higher levels. Equally, there may be concurrency at a higher level but no concurrency at a lower level. For example, an operating system running on a sequential machine supports concurrent activities at a high level without there being any parallelism at the machine level. In this case, the concurrency at the high level is apparent rather than actual. There is no true parallelism in the sense that operations are in fact performed simultaneously leading to an increase in speed. In this paper, I shall reserve the word "parallelism" for concurrency in this more restricted sense, and use "concurrency" as the more general term. The two concepts are often confused.

I shall call a system a concurrent system only if there is concurrent activity apparent at the highest level. Thus an application should not be regarded as a concurrent system simply because it is running on a parallel computer.

Is concurrency irrelevant to the real problems we wish to solve with computers?

Some applications are intrinsically concurrent (e.g. an operating system or an airport simulation), and are best expressed in a concurrent programming language. However most problems that we want to solve on a computer are not intrinsically concurrent, and do not require a concurrent programming language. Thus concurrency is indeed irrelevant to most (but by no means all) real problems.

Of course, we would like our applications to run faster, and parallel computers are one very promising way to achieve this. However we should not confuse parallelism with concurrency and feel obliged to reprogram our application in a concurrent programming language. Parallelism is best exploited at a lower level, and concurrency should then only be of concern to the implementor of that lower level.

What are the fundamental differences between sequential and parallel systems? Should these differences be exposed or hidden?

The only fundamental difference between a sequential and a parallel system should be that the parallel system runs faster! Any other differences should be hidden. If I ask a builder to build me a house, it shouldn't concern me whether he uses one workman or many. Equally, if I want a computation performed, it shouldn't concern me whether the computer has one processor or many.

Do you envisage a transition in mainstream computing from sequential to parallel systems? Can you specify preconditions and milestones for such a transition?

I believe parallel computers will only gain widespread use when parallelism can be exploited invisibly to the normal programmer (or user). Computers are hard enough to use, and applications are difficult enough to program, without introducing a further dimension of complexity. Parallel computers will only supplant sequential ones when they can be treated as "black boxes" that happen to run faster.

This is very difficult to achieve with conventional programming languages. Conventional languages have a notion of time and change of state built into them, and depend on assignment as the basic operation. They can be classified into sequential languages (e.g. Fortran) and parallel languages (e.g. Occam). It is difficult for the language implementor to extract parallelism from a sequential language because the semantics of the language is so much bound up with a particular order of execution. This has led to the development of parallel languages. In these languages parallelism can be exploited, but only at the expense of making it very visible to the programmer.

To exploit parallelism invisibly, I believe the most promising approach is to switch our attention to declarative languages (e.g. Prolog and other logic programming languages). Declarative languages define a computation through a declarative description of the problem, plus some control information which serves to shape the computation of a solution. Declarative languages have two big advantages. Because the language is declarative, it is easier to produce correct programs to solve complex problems. Because the language is not based on assignment, and doesn't force any particular execution order, it is easier to exploit parallelism.

Prolog is often viewed–wrongly in my opinion–as a sequential language, probably because the original implemntations were sequential, and because the language's operational meaning is generally explained in sequential terms. However, I would argue that the Prolog control information (goal ordering, clause ordering and cut) serves only to define the size and shape of the computation that is to be carried out, and leaves largely unspecified the order of operations. Thus in the Aurora system which we have implemented (and is described in this Proceedings), the computation tree is constructed in or-parallel fashion while supporting the full Prolog language. This idea can be extended to encompass and-parallelism as well as or-parallelism while preserving the same language semantics and abstract view of a computation. This we have called the Andorra model (partially described as part of a paper in this Proceedings by my colleague Seif Haridi, and implemented in prototype form by my colleague Rong Yang).

Thus declarative languages are in general neither sequential nor parallel, but should be viewed as neutral towards parallelism. Control information is also ideally largely neutral towards parallelism, although certain language features tend to force a sequential view (e.g. side effect predicates in Prolog), and certain language features tend to force a parallel view (e.g. read-only variable annotations in Concurrent Prolog).

Can you envisage the structure of future general purpose parallel computing systems?

I believe parallel computers of the future must be truly general purpose, and must allow multiple processors to treat all data as shared and uniformly accessible. This implies shared virtual memory but does not necessarily imply shared physical memory. Our proposal for a scalable multiprocessor with these properties, called the data diffusion machine, is described elsewhere in these Proceedings. The machine is completely general purpose in that it can potentially support any kind of application in any kind of language. However it was motivated by the desire to exploit parallelism transparently through declarative language systems such as Aurora and Andorra.

Is concurrency a nuisance inflicted upon us by hardware capabilities? Or is it a blessing that will lead us to better ways of thinking about problems?

Parallelism is in some sense a nuisance that we must endure if we want our applications to run faster. However, hopefully it is a nuisance that need only concern the implementors of the lower levels of a computer system.

Concurrency, as I have mentioned, is an essential feature of certain kinds of applications, and demands new kinds of programming language. It has led to the development of an important new family of declarative languages, the committed choice languages (Parlog, Concurrent Prolog, GHC). These languages are better able to express applications where concurrency is intrinsic. However, in other respects they are more restrictive than Prolog and not so widely applicable. The Andorra model gives Prolog much of the capability of committed choice languages, and it is my belief that the advantages of Prolog and committed choice languages can be combined in a single language, which I will call Andorra Prolog. Ideas in this direction are still emerging; Seif Haridi presents one approach in this proceedings.

SPECIAL SESSION

ADVANCED INFORMATION PROCESSING IN ESPRIT - STATUS AND PLANS

Jean-Marie Cadiou

Director - ESPRIT
DG XIII (Telecommunications, Information Industries and Innovation)
Commission of the European Communities
200 rue de la Loi
B-1049 Brussels

1. INTRODUCTION

1.1 ESPRIT

The European Strategic Programme for Research and Development in Information Technology was launched (1) as a 10 year programme of precompetitive R & D in 1984 with three main objectives:

- to promote European industrial cooperation in IT;
- to provide European IT industry with the basic technologies it needs to meet the competitive requirements of the nineties;
- to contribute to the development of internationally accepted standards.

For the first five-year phase of the programme, an overall effort of 1.5 billion ECUs[1] was undertaken, 50% of which was borne by the research budget of the European Community, while the participants provided the other half. The programme is implemented by means of public calls for proposals, each of which is based upon a regularly updated workprogramme (2) adopted by the Council.

The areas of research covered during the first phase of ESPRIT were Microelectronics, Software Technology, Advanced Information Processing, Office Systems and Computer Integrated Manufacturing. In these areas, a total of some 230 projects have been launched involving more than 420 different industrial, academic and research organisations. Advanced Information Processing has been the label for a broad range of projects covering Artificial Intelligence, Computer Architecture and External Interfaces.

1.2 Advanced Information Processing (AIP)

40 projects are currently supported by the ESPRIT AIP involving 193 European organisations. Because of the rapid progress being made in AIP, the requirements of research are continuously changing. To ensure that work within ESPRIT is directed into the most appropriate areas regular reassessments of the workprogramme are carried out.

Assessment of the needs of the next generation of AIP systems showed that developments are needed in the following areas:

- applicable knowledge engineering techniques;

- new computer architectures for symbolic and numeric processing and fault tolerant systems;

- advanced system interfaces.

Each of these areas has been addressed within the AIP part of the ESPRIT Programme. Below follows a survey of the work carried out as well as a discussion of plans for building upon this work during the second phase of the programme from 1988 to 1992.

2. CURRENT STATUS

2.1 The Development and Application of Knowledge Engineering

The objective of the work in this domain is to accelerate the successful introduction of knowledge-based systems to a wide variety of application domains within industry. Maximum benefit is thus gained from the use of the fast maturing knowledge engineering techniques both in end-products and in the design, manufacture and maintenance phases of the product lifecycle.

---

[1] $ 1.8 billion (June 1988 exchange rate : 1.2 $/ECU)

The approach adopted has been to:

- develop the methods and techniques for knowledge acquisition and knowledge representation;

- develop domain specific systems;

- develop application independent knowledge-based system "shells", supporting languages and user interfaces;

- evaluate knowledge-based systems in the industrial environment.

The main target for recent work has been to encourage wider industrial use of the knowledge-based system shells developed within the programme. This was tackled through a number of actions aimed at evaluating the use of the systems in specific application domains. The domains chosen included disease diagnosis of agricultural crops (project 1063 - INSTIL), financial investment advice (project 316 - ESTEAM), the control and diagnosis of faults in advanced telecommunication switching systems, and the control of electrical power distribution networks (project 387 - KRITIC).

2.1.1 *Knowledge Acquisition and Knowledge Representation*

Of the two main approaches to know-ledge acquisition, the more established one is based on interviews with experts. The second is to derive principles from an analysis of case studies and examples.

ESPRIT projects cover both of these approaches. A system for knowledge acquisition by interview was developed in an early ESPRIT project (304), by two industrial partners, STC (UK) and SCS (D), together with the University of Amsterdam (NL) and the University of the South Bank (UK). The system, named Knowledge Acquisition and Structuring or KADS, helps the Knowledge Based System (KBS) designer to structure the interview process, and, by using protocols of expert consultation, to elicit the requisite expertise. The results of the original KADS system have been incorporated by the partners together with a software company, Scicon (UK), into the Process Control Engineering KBS tool kit which was first demonstrated in late '87. KADS is being used within a major German funded national programme, and has supported the analysis phase of KBS development in several commercial projects undertaken by the project partners.

The second approach to knowledge acquisition develops a set of rules from an analysis of relevant examples. GEC (UK), Cognitech (F) and the University of Paris Sud, the three partners of project 1063 (INSTIL), are currently making an industrial evaluation of tools they have developed to support this process. The integrated learning system which forms the kernel of the system is being strengthened by the inclusion of methods for dealing with incomplete problem descriptors and noise. The ability to generate a knowledge base is being tested by a trial application to disease diagnosis in agriculture. The rules that are emerging are being evaluated by experts in this domain.

The target of the knowledge representation work is to bring computer representation of knowledge closer to conceptualisation and expression by systems designers.

The problem is one of representing concepts (and their defining characteristics) and the relationships between them, in a form that allows the application of reasoning processes. Semantic networks, and logic combined with an object-oriented approach, are two knowledge representation formalisms being examined as the basis of possible solutions to the problem of knowledge representation.

Several variants of semantic networks are explored in ESPRIT projects. Project 280 (EUROHELP) has developed a type of semantic network called a generic graph to represent user and information system modules; such models evolve as they adjust to growing expertise on the part of the user, reflecting the system's experience of the interaction and the current usage of the system. A prototype system to provide both instruction and help to users of the UNIX ^{tm} mail system has been demonstrated. The first prototype of a generic help system will be available in the Spring of 1988.

Another form of semantic network representation to cope with a more dynamic modification of knowledge, has been studied by Delphi (I), CGE (F) and the Free University of Brussels (B) in project 440 (MADS). This has been partially implemented in the OMEGA expert systems shell now on the market. During 1987 the Knowledge Representation System (KRS) also developed in project 440 was taken to the market by Knowledge Technologies, a small company associated with the Free University of Brussels.

The results gained by the partners CISE (I) and Framentec (F) in project 256 on the representation of qualitative or functional models of complex physical systems, such as power plants, are now the basis of an application-oriented project. This project (820) was launched to design a KBS architecture and tool kit for real-time process control applications and the original partners have been joined by Nea-Lindberg (DK), CAP (F), Ansaldo Impianti (I), and the Heriot Watt University (UK). Prototype applications are in the course of development for three areas: a thermal power plant, a cement manufacturing plant and operator support in the control room of a geostationary satellite.

2.1.2 The Development of Domain-specific Knowledge-based Systems

Here we are concerned with systems for specific types of application, viz. manufacturing scheduling, real-time control, and medical diagnosis. Each project combines the application of domain-specific systems with the development of new tools. Some examples are as follows:

A flexible tool package for job shop scheduling is being created by Battelle (D), Aeritalia (I), Italcad (I) and Elsag (I) in project 865. A demonstrator for this project is being used by the aircraft production planners of Aeritalia for operational scheduling of a manufacturing system.

An expert system shell with features to handle the stream of real-time input and output data that arise in the control cycle, has been built on project 857 (GRADIENT) by Computer Resources International (DK), Brown Boveri (D), and the Universities of Kassel (I), Stratchclyde (UK) and Leuven (B).

In project 599, a prototype system has been constructed to assist the consultant in electromyographical diagnosis from the analysis of bioelectrical signals from muscle and nerve tissue. It also advises on the test procedures to be performed. The novel approach adopted combines both causal and probabilistic models for diagnostic purposes, in a single network. Furthermore, it is well-integrated with the equipment and other aspects of the diagnostic system. The team of medical and software partners has successfully taken into account such aspects as user considerations and professional acceptance in the design of the knowledge-based expert system. This system was successfully demonstrated in the Autumn of 1987. One of the partners, Dansk Medico Elektronik (Judex), a computer engineering company working on real-time systems, is incorporating the design of the user interface and the knowledge-based system into its range of medical equipment.

2.1.3 The Development of Application Independent Knowledge-based System Shells, Support Languages and User Interfaces

The majority of knowledge-based systems consist of an inference engine, a set of rules, and a database containing domain specific information. For any particular application it is necessary to develop the set of rules and provide the domain specific data. Clearly it would significantly reduce the cost of developing a particular knowledge-based system if a kernel system was available which could be tailored to any specific application domain simply by providing the necessary rules and domain specific information. Knowledge-based system "shells" provide such a kernel, and because of their potential regarding the reduction in development costs of knowledge-based systems they have been given major emphasis within the programme. Two particular systems developed within the programme are already available. The OMEGA shell from project 440 is being marketed by Delphi (I) in Europe, the US and Japan. It is being hosted onto the currently available Portable Common Tool Environment (PCTE)[1], which will be a very useful facility for industrial users.

A second system, the Expert System Builder (ESB) developed in project 96, which provides a complete environment, compares very favourably with the current market leading shells produced in the US.

The efficient implementation of knowledge-based systems has required the development of logic-based programming languages. In Europe the Prolog language has played a prominent role, and the enhancement of Prolog and its integration into appropriate development support environments is of strategic importance to the effective development of knowledge-based systems.

Throughout 1987, steps were taken to achieve a European-wide consensus on a common definition of Prolog and, in parallel with this action, an ISO working group was officially formed.

Prolog III which extends Prolog by the addition of powerful numerical capabilities, has been fully specified in project 1106 by Prof. Colmerauer, the inventor of Prolog, and his team, and a com-

[1] PCTE : a standard set of Software Tool interfaces coming out of the ESPRIT Software Technology area.

plete implementation is available. It is being used in the development of an expert system for the diagnosis of failures in an automobile engine component by Daimler Benz and Bosch.

A further enhancement of Prolog to provide an interface to the international graphics standard, GKS, has been completed in the ACORD project (393) and the impacts of successors to GKS are being taken into account. The aim is to provide a Prolog graphics capability and natural language parsers are being implemented using the enhanced Prolog.

The development of a new logic programming environment consisting of advanced tools (e.g. a rational debugger, a language-oriented editor and a graphics interface) is being undertaken in project 973 (ALPES). Prototype versions have been demonstrated, and their integration is now in progress. Exploitation prospects are being evaluated by the prime contractor, CRIL (F).

Because of the very large amounts of data required in many industrial applications of knowledge engineering techniques it is very important that efficient interfaces are developed which will support effective interaction between the inference engines and the databases.

Within the project 311 (ADKMS), Bull, Nixdorf and Olivetti together with four universities have implemented an interface representation of two natural language parsers with a hybrid knowledge representation system called BACK. One parser is rule-based. The other is based on a linguistic theory which is being implemented in a computer system for the first time.

Techniques that combine rules and relational algebraic expressions are being developed in project 530 (EPSILON). A prototype workstation has been produced which demonstrates the feasibility of using commercially available software tools, in this case UNIX ^{tm} based Prolog, and a commercially available relational database. In a second work package, a prototype has been developed that connects the database management workstations into an integrated KBMS.

2.2 The Development of New Computer Architectures

The need for high performance computers capable of processing symbolic and numerical information will increase significantly over the next few years as the results of the knowledge engineering work

and the advanced man-machine interfaces become embedded into a wide range of applications, eg CAD, office systems. The decision was taken at the outset of the ESPRIT programme to concentrate on the development of highly parallel architecture machines, and the appropriate software, to achieve the performance levels required. The use of parallelism also gives the additional potential benefit of providing flexible architectures suitable for a large range of system performance. To ensure that a sound basis was provided for the development of these machines one of the first ESPRIT projects (415, PALAVDA) was launched to study the performance of the different approaches to symbolic processing on parallel architecture computers.

The results to date include :

The design of the architecture for parallel object-oriented systems has been completed, and the operating system, the POOL 2 language and its compiler are now available.

The first prototype of a logic machine, based on a Virtual Inference Machine, is now available.

An implementation of a functional parallel programming language (FP 2) is now running, and has been used as a programming language for a parallel inference machine based upon the connection method.

A wide European forum on parallel computing has been established through the organisation of an international conference on parallel architectures and languages.

A particularly important objective in the computer architecture area was to develop a low cost, high performance parallel computing capability. The partners of the Supernode project (1085), Royal Signals and Radar Establishment (UK), Thorn-Emi (UK), APSIS (F), TELMAT (F), INMOS (UK) and the Universities of Grenoble (F) and Southampton (UK), have achieved spectacular results towards this objective, making substantial progress in four key areas:

The basic processing element: a floating point version of the transputer - the T800-20 with 350,000 transistors, and capable of 1.5 MFLOPS - is now commercially available from INMOS.

The interconnection architecture and a non-blocking switch element: a highly modular architecture interconnecting nodes of 20 transputers each, has been designed. The architecture is fully reconfigurable with a project target of up to 64 nodes through the use of software controlled VLSI switches.

Input/output interface components: components are being designed capable of handling data at a rate of 100 Mbytes/sec through a number of 20MHz channels. This allows on-line, real-time handling of high resolution image information, and many other data intensive applications.

System Software: Supernode is currently programmed using OCCAM and versions of the OCCAM support system, TDS. IDRIS, a proprietary version of the emerging standard operating system, POSIX, is also supported. FORTRAN, PASCAL and C are also available. The development of a UNIX ^{tm} based operating system and a range of application software to support CAD, numerical applications, etc. is now underway.

This work has already resulted in products available on the market today. In addition to the floating point transputer already mentioned, two lines of minisupercomputer products are now available: the T.NODE series marketed by TELMAT, and the SN1000 series marketed by PARSYS, an off-shoot of THORN-EMI set up for that purpose. Full user compatibility is ensured between these two product lines. That performance ranges from 25 MFLOPS to 400 MFLOPS and their prices from $ 60 000 to $ 600 000. The performance/price ratio for these machines appear to be superior to any currently available similar machine by a factor of at least 3. Further enhancements of these machines are planned, up to 1.5 GFLOPS in 1989.

In addition, the Supernode project has investigated applications in domains such as CAD and image processing. One of the partners, APSIS, has developed the Lucky Log simulator for computer aided design which is currently undergoing industrial field trials prior to general release.

A further important aspect of system architecture development is in the field of fault tolerant computing tackled in project 818 (DELTA-4). This project has developed a technique to give a distributed computer system protection against local station failures. The technique involves the addition of a plug-in module developed within the project, which can be added to any machine, whose inputs/outputs ports conform to the ISO/OSI specifications. A distributed system employing these modules can then

automatically reconfigure to overcome individual node failures. A multicast communication system implemented on a LAN was demonstrated in early 1987. Demonstrators of a real time UNIX ^{tm} prototype and a Remote Service Request prototype have been developed, and work is under way on a Delta-4 system architecture and computational model.

2.3 Development of Advanced System Interfaces

The prime objective of this part of the programme is to achieve computer understanding of the environment from external sensors. The work has concentrated primarily on image processing, natural language understanding and speech processing. Furthermore, the topic of multisensor operation has been added recently to complement the ongoing work, however it is too early to report significant progress from the projects in this field.

2.3.1 Image Processing

The initial aim is to develop systems capable of analysing and understanding 2-dimensional and 3-dimensional scenes and sequences of pictures (four-dimensional scenes).

The analysis by computer systems of static 2-dimensional and 3-dimensional scenes and of moving scenes is already finding application in domains such as stress analysis, robotics for computer controlled manufacturing systems and security systems. In the area of 2-dimensional image processing a set of algorithms for the processing of medical X-ray images has been produced in project 26 (SIP). These algorithms are now being implemented in a prototype system which uses an explicit model of the scene (the organisation of the blood vessels) together with knowledge-based reasoning techniques to control the different processing levels. In the areas of 3-dimensional scene analysis and motion the following results are particularly interesting for industrial exploitation :

A portable interactive software environment called VIS to generate or interrogate multiple representations of images or image sequences. The VIS system is currently being evaluated prior to full exploitation.

A low-cost (using off the shelf components) prototype system for depth computation of objects in an industrial scene.

A very fast stereo image processor which is currently being extended into an integrated depth and motion analysis system.

2.3.2 *Natural Language Understanding and Speech Processing*

The most significant results achieved to date have been in the areas of natural language dialogue and the development of speech systems. The feasibility of developing an effective interface between text analysis and speech has been shown by the availability of the functional description of a system and its components providing man-machine dialogue for reference to "yellow pages" directories. This result was achieved within project 1015 (PALABRE) completed in 1987.

In the domain of natural language, two universities within the ACORD project (393), have produced parsers for the French, English and German languages. These parsers together with the deduction component produced within the project are capable of handling complex sentences, e.g. sentences which require pronoun resolution.

The availability of systems capable of understanding continuous speech in noisy environments is a requirement for many application domains. This is a longer-term goal for the programme but already significant progress has been made within restricted domains and controlled environments. Within project 26 (SIP) a stand-alone acoustic front-end is under development, an early prototype of which provides lexical access to a very large vocabulary and is capable of recognising continuous utterances under restricted conditions. Sentence recognition at a speed close to real-time is expected from the system by the end of 1988. This front-end sub-system is currently being connected to a sentence understanding sub-system which uses knowledge-based techniques. The understanding sub-system is being implemented on a parallel machine based on the transputer.

3. PLANS

3.1 Objectives

An independent assessment (3) of the first phase of the ESPRIT programme was carried out. This supported the basic ESPRIT concept of collaborative precompetitive research and suggested new areas of emphasis in information processing. In addition, the review of the workplan involving extensive consultation with industry and academia yielded new insights and recommendations. In particular, it was suggested to combine the two areas of Software Technology and Advanced Information Processing into one in order to better bring out the synergies between the two.

In April 1988 the second phase of the ESPRIT programme was adopted. The total volume of effort planned is 3.2 Billion ECU's[2] , half of which financed from the Community's budget in the years up to 1992, the other half being provided by the participants. About one third of this budget is to be directed towards Information Processing Systems work, the combination of the two previous ST and AIP areas. Such a significant effort is justified and indeed necessary in view of the importance it has to the overall ESPRIT objectives.

The programme of work defined within the Information Processing Systems (IPS) area for the second phase of ESPRIT is aimed at:

- The management and control of systems complexity.

- A reduction in system development and operational costs.

- An improvement in system quality and reliability.

- An increase in system performance.

Four key areas have been identified under which the corresponding work will be implemented :

- System Design

- Knowledge Engineering

- Advanced Systems Architectures

- Speech and Image Understanding and Multi-sensorial Systems

These four areas will now be considered in turn in greater depth to highlight the most important features.

3.2   System Design

The progress made in the first phase of ESPRIT on the development of software engineering environments (notably PCTE) and advanced design methods identified the need for greater emphasis to be given to the support of the development of systems

---

[2] $ 3.84 Billion at June 1988 exchange rate

incorporating hardware, software and knowledge-based components. This requirement was evident from the experience which showed that many of the problems associated with complex IT products were due to industry's inability to adequately describe the system requirements and to validate the higher levels of design. Work will now be targeted to future generations of IT products which will require levels of complexity which are far greater than those available today. This increase in complexity will be evident in the functonality of the systems, their size, performance and connectivity.

3.2.1 System Development

This work is expected to involve nearly all the major industrial concerns in Europe with expertise in this field. The opportunity will be taken to develop strong links between related Community and other European projects. The use of knowledge engineering (KE) techniques to support the development of complex systems will receive special consideration as will the development of an advanced system engineering environment providing the technical infrastructure for the integration of hardware, software and knowledge-based computer aided design tools.

3.2.2 System Enhancement/Maintenance and Component Reusability

The main objective of work under this heading is the reduction of costs associated with the post delivery phases of a product lifecycle, increase in product quality and increase in design productivity. An important and related objective of this part of the work is the capability to reuse existing, tested, system components.

3.2.3 Evaluation and Management

To enable fast transfer of system design and maintenance/enhancement methods and tools into product divisions of industry, results emerging from the pre-competitive projects will be fully evaluated within industrial environments. The evaluation work started in the first phase of the programme will be reinforced as the programme matures.

3.3 Knowledge Engineering

The central role that Knowledge Engineering is beginning to have in both support activities and end products puts even greater emphasis on the need for European industry to have a good command of the use of this technology. Through the first phase of ESPRIT and some national initiatives, European industry now has access to good Intelligent Knowledge-Based System (IKBS) development tools and some early results of the use of Knowledge-Based systems in the industrial environment. The technology transfer activities will now be reinforced which will require both further evaluation trials and further development of the technology for use in real-time applications and in ever more complex target systems.

Particular emphasis will be given at this stage to a number of topics which are considered in more detail below.

3.3.1 Real-time and Cooperating Knowledge-based Systems

Work will be carried out in Knowledge-Based techniques for real-time applications and the ability for Knowledge-Based Systems (KBS) to cooperate to solve complex problems in order to open up a broad area of application domains and to stimulate further advancement of Knowledge Engineering methods. In particular, further work will be carried out to develop techniques and tools for real-time KBS including KBS applied to signal understanding.

3.3.2 Industrialisation of Knowledge-based Systems

The aim of the work in this area is the development of means by which industry will be able to build large, efficient and reliable knowledge-based systems. The main topics to be covered are:

- KBS lifecycle;

- Performance evaluation of KBS;

- Man-machine interface for KBS;

- Development, maintenance and use of large knowledge bases.

- Enhancement of existing, more conventional, systems with knowledge-based components, eg. for "intelligent" access to large databases.

3.3.3 Topics for Directed Research

Four topics have been identified for further study to assist in the industrial development and exploitation of KBS. These areas are:

- Explanation facilities;

- Time-dependent reasoning;

- Machine learning;

- Knowledge elicitation and aquisition.

3.4 Advanced System Architectures

Given that the availability of high performance computers to European industry is a central requirement to the development of a strong IT industry in Europe, the work on advanced system architectures will be given particular emphasis in the second phase of ESPRIT.

Emphasis is given to the development of highly parallel machine architectures and exploitation of concurrency generally. Further development of the Supernode architecture and the develpoment of appropriate operating systems, PCTE-based development support environments for a range of programming languages and application software will be addressed. The exploitation of parallelism will be a central theme.

3.4.1 High Performance Computing

The goal is to enable the European computer industry to operate successfully in the market for supply of high-performance low cost computers.

The recognition that the next generation of machines will need to support efficiently both symbolic and numerical applications provides an opportunity for European suppliers to enter into the world market for high-performance, low-cost, computers, which in the past, has been driven by the major US computer suppliers. For these high-performance low-cost machines Europe now has the technology to forge a strong position of its own, with the intention of bringing the basic cost per MFLOPS (or equivalent) down by a factor of ten.

3.4.2 Support for Parallel Architecture Computers

Wide industrial acceptance and use of parallel architecture computers will be critically dependent upon the range of system and application software available to the application developers and end users. Consequently, within this area of the ESPRIT programme, the techniques and tools will be developed to fully exploit the hardware architecture to achieve the highest possible performance and reliability for a range of diverse application domains. The workprogramme has been defined so as to identify the developments in the operating systems to efficiently manage the resources of the highly parallel machines, the development of the design support methods and tools and appropriate environments, and, where necessary, the further development of high level languages.

3.4.3 Fault Tolerant Architectures

The capability of computing systems to operate correctly in the presence of errors and faults is a pre-requisite in many safety critical and other domains. The work on advanced system architectures for current and future generation computing systems will therefore take fully into account the fault tolerance requirements. To achieve these requirements work will be carried out on the target machine architectures themselves as well as the appropriate techniques and tools to be used during the system design phase.

3.4.4 Neural Computing

Interest in this new field of computing is rising strongly and a pilot programme of work is being considered to:

- Assess the maturity of neural computing for industrial applicatons;

- Develop the technical foundations for a more strategic action in the future.

3.5 Speech and Image Understanding and Multi-sensorial Systems

The main aim of the work in this domain is the development of the concept and design tools for use in meeting the substantial industrial demand for complex signal processing and control systems.

In the longer term the requirement will be for more generic speech and image processing and multi-sensorial techniques which are not constrained by particular application domain factors. However, in the shorter-term work will be focused on the design and development of signal analysis systems for speech, vision and muti-sensor signals which can operate effectively in the fields of robotics, manufacturing, process control, medecine, etc. These current signal analysis systems are primarily application specific and of low complexity compared to the needs of the next generation systems. The longer term work will proceed via the integration of a number of technologies to provide powerful numerical computation capabilities, symbolic processing and reasoning capabilities.

This part of the Information Processing Systems sector of the ESPRIT programme provides the opportunity to pull-through much of the technology work underway in the rest of the sector. Speech, vision, and multi-sensorial systems require not just the development of a single technology, but also the effective integration of all of the technologies covered by the programme.

3.5.1 *Speech*

The main objectives of this part of the workprogramme are the development of continuous speech understanding systems, speaker indepenNdent recognition of a medium size vocabulary and the development of dialogue workstations for industrial use.

3.5.2 *Image Understanding*

The emphasis in the second phase of ESPRIT will be placed on the development of versatile, flexible, vision systems; versatility in regard to the interpretation of fast changing image scenes and flexibility to ensure that the user is able to adapt the system to a range of different tasks. Also the movement from low and medium level vision processing to a high level image understanding in two and three dimensions will be specifically addressed.

In the shorter term the objective of utilising the already available algorithms and processing technology to realise complete vision systems will be addressed. In the longer term techniques for handling moving senes in real-time will be developed, and the necessary projects to provide methods and tools to develop systems capable of operating in real-time will be launched in time for use in later phases of the programme.

3.5.3 *Multi-sensorial Systems*

The main goal of the work in muti-sensorial systems is the develpoment of the approNpriate methodology and support tools for the design of a wide range of application independent muti-sensorial signal processing systems. In particular the work will cover:

- The development of methods, tools and archigtectures;

- The development of tools for the fusion of information flow from numerous heterogeneous signal channels;

- The definition of models for information extraction;

- The development of a methodology for knowledge base generation.

4. CONCLUSION

The first phase of ESPRIT has demonstrated the feasibility and importance of industrial cooperation across borders in the European context. Such a cooperation in precompetitive R&D, augmented by a substantial element of academic participation, is having a profound effect on how the Information Technology Community in Europe is viewing its future. These cooperations are already providing building blocks in several areas, notably expert systems and paralNlel architectures.

In the years that lie ahead, the European IT industry will need to build on these foundations and integrate the results already obtained in order to meet the competitive requirements of the 1990's.

5. REFERENCES

(1) Official Journal of the European Communities L69 9.3 1984, page 54.

(2) ESPRIT Workprogramme, CEC, 22 July 1987.

(3) The Mid-Term Review of ESPRIT, CEC, 15 October 1985.

(4) ESPRIT; the First Phase: Progress and Results; EUR 10940; CEC 1987.

(5) ESPRIT Annual Report 87.

(6) Proceedings of the 3rd Annual ESPRIT Conference 1986 - Results and Achievements, North Holland, 1987

(7) Proceedings of the 4th Annual ESPRIT Conference 1987 - Achievements and Impact, North Holland, 1987

PROCEEDINGS OF THE INTERNATIONAL CONFERENCE
ON FIFTH GENERATION COMPUTER SYSTEMS 1988,
edited by ICOT. © ICOT, 1988

A REVIEW OF MCC'S ACCOMPLISHMENTS
AND STRATEGIC OUTLOOK FOR KNOWLEDGE–BASED SYSTEMS

Edited by **Eugene Lowenthal, Vice President,**

Microelectronics and Computer Technology Corporation, Austin,Tx.

ABSTRACT

MCC's Advanced Computer Architecture (ACA) program is divided into three large laboratories and one small one. The large labs are tasked with continually assessing user/industry needs on the 5–to–10 year horizon and providing science and technology responsive to emerging requirements. In the most general terms, the Artificial Intelligence Laboratory is charged with advancing the **functionality** of Knowledge–based Sytems (KBS), while the mission of the Human Interface Laboratory is to enhance the **usability** of KBS, and that of the Systems Technology Laboratory is to provide KBS platforms with superior **performance and capacity**. In addition there is a recently formed laboratory called Experimental Systems which represents MCC's first publicly (DARPA) funded project. This is a three–year effort aimed at tools for rapid prototyping of alternative hardware architectural designs.

The ACA project managers summarize the current projects and past accomplishments of each of the laboratories. Finally, there is a brief description of an effort to establish new long range goals for the next decade.

1. Editor's Introduction

The organizers of FGCS'88 were very kind to invite me to submit a paper. Unlike the other papers offered to the Conference, however, this is not a scholarly contribution. Rather it is a manager's (admittedly proud) chronicle of the accomplishments and aspirations of a very talented ensemble of computer scientists — they take the credit for everything reported here.

I am director of a research program called Advanced Computer Architecture (ACA) which has been in business about five years. The name of our program (the largest of five at MCC) reflects the original charter which was to compete head–on with the ICOT–sponsored effort in fifth generation computer systems. As the program took shape and evolved over the past several years, however, it is clear that our "center of gravity" is now not so much

computer architecture as knowledge–based systems. Certainly there is a strong overlap with the original charter, but we are emphasizing innovation in software much more than in hardware. Thus, for example, less energy is being put into novel parallel hardware and more into the language and software technologies required to exploit current and anticipated commercial offerings in parallel hardware.

The program's concentration on knowledge–based systems (KBS) should not be construed as an exclusive focus on artificial intelligence. On the contrary, we start from the notion that most software systems ("intelligent" or otherwise) should be knowledge–based, that a wide variety of benefits derive from extracting the logic of an application and representing it declaratively in a knowledge base. A clear example of how knowledge bases can be leveraged is our approach to human interfaces, which is described later. Throughout ACA we are concerned with knowledge representation — expressive languages with efficient compilation and execution.

ACA is divided into three large laboratories and one small one. The large labs are tasked with continually assessing user/industry needs on the 5–to–10 year horizon and providing science and technology responsive to emerging requirements.[1] In the most general terms, the Artificial Intelligence Laboratory is charged with advancing the **functionality** of KBS, while the mission of the Human Interface Laboratory is to enhance the **usability** of KBS, and that of the Systems Technology Laboratory is to provide KBS platforms with superior **performance and capacity**.

All of this work is jointly sponsored by member companies of the MCC research consortium; that is, the research is privately funded. In addition there is a recently formed laboratory called Experimental

---

[1] Nearer term, less risky research remains the province of MCC's industrial partners, as does "productization" of MCC–developed technology. Nonetheless, since MCC's inception there have been many commercially valuable results and there is now a steady pipeline of technology being transferred to the sponsoring companies.

Systems which represents MCC's first publicly (DARPA) funded project. This is a three-year effort aimed at tools for rapid prototyping of alternative hardware architectural designs.

The remaining sections summarize the current projects and past accomplishments of each of the laboratories. The final section deals with the difficult task of looking to the end of the century to establish new goals for ACA's long range research. From this point forward I have acted much more in the capacity of an editor than author. The substantive content of what follows was extracted from the annual plans and progress reports of ACA's outstanding research leadership team:

AI Laboratory: Douglas Lenat and Charles Petrie

Human Interface Laboratory: James Hollan and Elaine Rich

Systems Technology Laboratory: Haran Boral, Won Kim and Carlo Zaniolo

Experimental Systems Laboratory: Robert Smith.

2. Artificial Intelligence Laboratory

CYC: The goal of this ambitious, intensive effort is to encode a very large knowledge base of interrelated concepts encompassing the "common-sense" knowledge shared by modern humans. The potential impact of CYC is too great to detail in an overview paper. Suffice it to say that success (which is by no means assured) would have profound effects on progress in natural language processing, machine learning, and expert systems technology. It can be effectively argued that we are at a "plateau" in AI research and that a concentrated effort such as CYC to develop a common-sense knowledge base is an absolute prerequisite for moving to a significantly higher plateau.

Among the key problems facing CYC are: the development of an appropriate knowledge representation language for common-sense knowledge; determination of CYC's ontology — the fundamental structure of knowledge; and the creation of tools that will allow many individuals to introduce new knowledge in an efficient and coordinated manner.

The CYC project has made excellent progress on all these fronts, essentially staying on the original 10-year schedule laid down in 1984. A substantial core of common-sense knowledge, the basic foundation upon which the structure will grow, has been put in place. There now exist powerful editing and visual browsing tools geared to keeping multiple "knowledge enterers" productive while operating from the common ontological model.

A new knowledge representation language called CYCL, has emerged, not as a theory-driven effort, but as a function of the very difficult task of encoding common-sense knowledge in all of its richness. In addition to typical reasoning and representation features, CYCL/CYC necessarily addresses issues of time, space, causality, hypothetical worlds, beliefs/contradictions, guessing, plausibility, introspection (meta-level reasoning), causality, and much more. As CYCL has begun to stabilize, it is finding use in other parts of ACA and in carefully selected collaborative efforts outside of MCC.

The main thrust for the future is a progressively accelerating effort to manually encode more and more knowledge in the context of what has already been stored. In theory, if CYC is successful, it will ultimately learn how to acquire and incorporate new knowledge on its own, thereby eliminating our current dependence on hand-coding.

Throughout the project we will be evaluating CYC as it grows, to see if it gets better at disambiguating natural language segments, removing the "brittleness" from complex expert systems, facilitating cooperation among separately developed expert systems, and other anticipated uses.

Proteus: The Proteus expert system development tool was among the first technologies to be transferred to MCC shareholders, and it is the first one to result in a commercial product (viz. the NCR Design Advisor).

Proteus began in 1984 with two observations:

- The importance of defeasible reasoning in general, and default reasoning in particular, had been almost completely ignored.

- Among traditional expert system development environments, there was a severe trade-off between efficiency and conceptual simplicity, on the one hand, and expressiveness and functionality, on the other.

A key decision, based on the first observation above, was that a *truth maintenance system* (TMS) should be a cornerstone in the design of a knowledge-based application development system. This provides a mechanism for defeasible reasoning, the importance of which has been recognized for constructive tasks, especially design, which involves heuristic choices subject to iterative revision.

Proteus contains three major advances in truth maintenance technology: A *complete* algorithm for belief status labeling --- if a solution is possible, Proteus will find it; A unique integration with rules and frames, including inheritance; and a novel method of representing domain knowledge to control dependency-directed backtracking.

Our approach to addressing the simplicity/expressiveness issue has been to accommodate multiple paradigms within a single system and language. However we are committed to the view that these paradigms must be integrated at the architectural level, rather than merely combined in a "toolkit". The design of Proteus includes a number of established reasoning and representation techniques: nonmonotonic truth maintenance with backtracking, restricted predicate logic, frames with multiple inheritance and metaclasses, forward and backward inference, and Lisp s-expressions.

Future releases of Proteus will introduce enhancements to the system's functionality, human interface, and especially performance. Work in progress includes a complete nonmonotonic TMS, support for multiple inheritance and metaclasses, temporal reasoning, hypothetical worlds, a graphics-oriented development environment, metareasoning to facilitate intelligent control of inference, and dramatic speedups for backward and forward inference. With respect to the latter, we have recently developed a rule compiler that achieves over 100K LIPS on a 68020-based Unix system, and we will be porting this technology to Proteus.

One of the interesting offshoots of Proteus was *Argo*, a modest effort carried out in cooperation with MCC's VLSI CAD project. Argo introduced basic learning and analogical reasoning techniques to Proteus. These capabilities were successfully demonstrated in a small circuit design application in which new rules were learned from training examples resulting in substantially faster execution times and improved design quality for similar circuit specifications subsequently presented to Argo.

Antares: Two of the major problems confronting the developers of KBS are that independently developed expert systems cannot in general be interconnected to work together and that there is no established means for several experts to develop an expert system jointly. Antares, (a new project) will utilize principles of distributed KBS to solve these problems. The result will be a set of methods for interconnecting separately developed KBS to enable them to cooperate in solving problems beyond the capabilities of any one of the KBS. This proposed system can be viewed as a new type of "shell" for the modular development of KBS. It will use the common-sense knowledge in CYC to provide a basis for globally consistent semantics among the KBS, but will not require globally consistent beliefs.

Among the advances required to achieve the Antares objective are: mechanisms for control that enable cooperative problem solving behavior among a set of KBS; representation of principles of "self-interest" within CYC that can be the basis of negotiation and cooperation among agents; and implementation of a general expert system whose expertise is the control and enforcement of cooperation among other expert systems.

Planning and Decision Making: The primary characteristic of current decision support tools is that they are numeric. They are typically based on utility theory and require significant quantification of variables by the user. This quantification task can be difficult or even meaningless. Only recently has work been done to derive appropriate numbers through user-supplied partial orderings. But knowledge acquisition is not the overwhelming disadvantage of the numeric approach. The real problem is that conclusions are not the result of symbolic reasoning.

Decision support methods based on symbolic reasoning are flexible, explicable, and can be revised intelligently. Numeric approaches are not. The semantics behind numeric methods are compiled and encoded into efficient but obscure algorithms. It is difficult to employ alternative computations or modify existing ones to fit the semantics of the problem. Explanations supporting decisions, including rejection of alternatives, are difficult to generate and usually not satisfactory. The traditional numeric approach is weakest in supporting revision of decisions and conclusions. But it is our hypothesis that *revision is a fundamental paradigm* for decision making. This is especially true for complex planning.

Planning and Decision Making is a new project which will build up the experience gained with defeasible reasoning in the Proteus project. The goal is to build complex tools which assist in the design of plans by allowing incremental development and revision of plans. Such systems will be "logical spreadsheets" that allow a user to minimally revise a plan given new data or hypothetical situation changes. The system will also allow users to interactively construct plans using simplifying assumptions and to support reasoned retraction of such assumptions when constraints are violated. Finally, the system should provide explanations for the current plan state.

It is unlikely that we will gain the requisite insights into understanding drafting and revising plans by armchair contemplation or by building toy problems. Our approach is to design a model of planning by iterative revision based on reasonably complex applications. We will work on a series of increasingly difficult planning systems. By intimately understanding each system, we will be able to derive the requisite insight to improve our model for use on the succeeding problem.

3. Human Interface Laboratory

Our work in the HI Lab is largely motivated by the belief that interfaces of the future will increasingly be to KBS and will themselves be knowledge–based. This belief is based both on industry trends in KBS development and on the realization that the key to increasing people's productivity lies primarily in making interfaces more collaborative and allowing people to work closer to their conception of the task rather than requiring them to learn details irrelevant to the accomplishment of their real goals. The only way to provide users with this higher–level flexible access and to enable interfaces to be more cooperative and adaptive is to *represent* the user's task, the language of interaction, the application, and the user. This and the expected continued increase in the development of KBS motivates our focus on knowledge–based interfaces.

HITS: Because many powerful interfaces must rely on several interface capabilities, it is important that our various tools for providing these individual capabilities be designed to function in concert to produce a single, integrated, knowledge–based interface. As a result, we are working on the development of HITS (Human Interface Tools), which is an integration of the tools we are building throughout the laboratory. Our work on HITS as an integrated set of tools is intended both to guarantee that the integration of our tools is possible and to provide us a way of experimenting with such a toolset in order to refine our design. We will release versions of HITS each year. Each such release will incorporate both new results in the overall structure of HITS and new results from our work on the individual pieces of HITS. We expect it to evolve over time, providing shareholders with prototypes and demonstrations of concepts and serving us internally as an experimental vehicle for grounding, motivating, and coordinating our scientific and technological efforts.

Although the idea of a coordinated system for building interfaces is by now widely accepted (such systems are often called User Interface Management Systems), HITS is unique in that: it supports the construction of interfaces to KBS, for which it is often not possible to design unambiguous, humanly learnable input and output languages; the component tools of HITS are themselves knowledge–based; HITS fully supports the construction of integrated multimedia interfaces.

The various components of HITS are discussed in the following sections.

Graphical Interfaces: The approach we are taking in graphics is exemplified in our work on Pogo, a declarative representation system for graphics. We expect that future graphics systems will consist of two components: high–level declarative graphical descriptions and hardware specific interpreters of those descriptions. Separation into these two components has many advantages. Chief among them

are the increased portability of code, the speed that will come from an increasing realization of specific interpreters in hardware and the ability to make use of specialized computational hardware, and the facility to efficiently provide views on multiple displays and form multiple conceptual perspectives.

Our plan, in keeping with our overall knowledge–based approach, is to work on the higher semantic levels of graphical representation and try to build on top of existing efforts for the lower levels of graphical representation. This has led us to focus our graphics work in three areas: high–level tools for graphical interface development, representation of graphical and design knowledge, and exploration of a novel interactive work surface interface paradigm.

The major problems that are being attacked are how to provide users with natural methods for specifying behaviors for new dynamic icons, how to have graphical editors automatically represent substantial portions of the knowledge needed to enable integrated multimodal interfaces and to make it possible for the tools to critique interfaces being constructed in terms of graphic design principles, and how to support paper and pencil kinds of interactions on an interactive worksurface.

Recent accomplishments include implementation of a number of experimental graphics tools such as the Pogo representation system and an editor for constructing "dynamic icons", i.e. their form and behavior. Excellent progress has been made on the Interactive Worksurface, the software and hardware for a system with a flat stylus – sensitive display that uses neural net technology to recognize sketches or annotations that are hand–drawn on the surface. Experimental versions of the IWS are now demonstrable.

Natural Language Interfaces: Our approach to the problem of providing natural language interfaces is to design, build, and evaluate a series of natural language understanding and generation programs that can be incorporated into HITS. Our goal is to produce systems that can be effective as components of complete interfaces even though the general problem of natural language use in unconstrained environments will likely remain intractable for decades.

There are three key problems that exist with current natural language systems and to which we are trying to find solutions in our work. The first such problem is that the linguistic knowledge in most existing systems is not portable and must be reconstructed for each natural language interface. Our work is attempting to represent this knowledge in a portable way. Rather than trying to approximate this knowledge in *ad hoc* structures, as is often done in natural language interfaces, we are attempting to ensure portability by exploiting a linguistically sound theory of morphology and grammar.

A second problem is that rules that translate a natural language sentence into structures interpretable by application programs must be reconstructed for each interface. Although there is no way to avoid this reconstruction entirely, two approaches are being pursued to minimize this effort. The first is to exploit as much as possible the knowledge in the application program itself. Secondly, we are providing powerful tools so that the interface specific knowledge can be built as efficiently as possible.

A third problem with existing natural language interfaces is that they are often superficial in the sense that they do not build on detailed knowledge either about the task that is being performed or about the dialogue that is taking place. As a result, many sentences cannot be interpreted at all and many others are interpreted incorrectly. Our work is attempting to improve this situation by tying the natural language system more closely into the knowledge base of the application program and by providing a deeper analysis of the entire discourse as more than just a sequence of sentences.

The project has produced a series (Lucy) of increasingly sophisticated natural language understanding systems together with an editor (Luke) which can be used to associate linguistic information with domain objects in an application knowledge base.

Intelligent User Assistance: Although an important goal of the HI Laboratory's overall efforts is the design and implementation of interfaces that make the correct use of an application program as obvious to users as possible, in the foreseeable future we will not be able to build interfaces that make the complete functionality of the application and its interface immediately knowable. The goal of the Intelligent User Assistance (IUA) project is to support the development of advising and coaching systems by providing three key capabilities: a generalized architecture for advising and coaching; a knowledge base of advising and coaching strategies that can be exploited within the generalized architecture; and a set of tools for building the application-specific knowledge that each instance of the generalized architecture must also exploit.

Having conducted empirical studies of people performing tasks and of advisors helping them to do so, we have begun developing a series of prototype advisors for specific domains and to construct a set of tools that are useful in doing so. We have in mind a sequence of systems that range from intellectual amplifiers that themselves do relatively little problem solving (but that effectively augment the problem-solving abilities of their users) to intelligent assistants that can be given high-level problem

descriptions and drive the collaboration required to reach a solution to that problem. There are several more specific dimensions that form the basis of this evolution. One is the extent to which it is necessary to incorporate a general purpose planning system. We are getting promising results from a restricted planning system in which solutions to individual problems are generated by referring to a hierarchical model of the way that experts solve problems in this domain.

Another dimension along which we can increase the power of our systems is the flexibility of the interface between the user and the advisor. One powerful idea is that of the *advice object*. Each advice object corresponds to an entity in the interface, such as the screen objects representing the application's data structures or procedures, or a piece of advice. Associated with each such object is a set of strategies and knowledge structures that can be accessed by the user by clicking on the object in the interface.

A third dimension is the locus of control. Control may reside entirely with the user who must ask specific questions to get advice. Alternatively, control may reside with the system, which may be able to volunteer advice under appropriate circumstances. We are exploring both of these approaches.

Last year we transferred the initial version of an experimental Interactive Development Environment for Advising (IDEA). IDEA allows developers to implement domain-independent and domain-specific advisory strategies which can be invoked either by the user on request, or by the system itself when it detects a situation that calls for advising. At run-time IDEA maintains a history of user interactions with the system at various levels of abstraction. It is able to compare this trace with an ideal model of the use of the application (as provided at development time by an expert) to produce efficient, cognitively appropriate advice.

4. Systems Technology Laboratory

The mission of the Systems Technology Laboratory is to develop system architectures and associated technologies that are commensurate with projected improvements in the functionality and usability of future computer applications. Within the broad charter of investigating high performance, high capacity platforms for symbolic computing, we are:

- covering both conventional (sequential) and parallel execution environments
- paying particular attention to the problem of providing very high speed access to, and manipulation of, very large knowledgebases.

Both the computational and data management demands of symbolic applications must be successfully addressed.

Logic-based Programming Languages: In the next two decades, the market for symbolic applications will experience a tremendous growth largely as a result of knowledge-based applications and expert system applications becoming widespread in the business world. Since these new applications will be based upon and extend the functionality of existing management information systems, there will be an acute need for programming languages and systems that are effective in both the domain of knowledge-based applications and in that of the more traditional applications, such as database management and retrieval.

The Logic Data Language (LDL) is designed to amalgamate the functionalities and enabling technologies of relational databases with the general purpose symbolic application development capabilities of logic programming. Thus, the LDL system supports rule based programming, pattern matching and inferencing, as in Prolog, along with the transaction management, recovery, integrity and schema based data definition facilities of relational databases. We are pursuing two experimental implementations of LDL: one is for a highly parallel database machine (Bubba), the other is for a single processor workstation environment. By the end of 1988 we will transfer a version of LDL running on Unix workstations, which will provide a highly portable and efficient demonstration vehicle for LDL. The execution speed of LDL is expected to be competitive with that of current procedural languages. The compiler includes an optimizer that automatically generates efficient execution plans for queries.

LIFE (a Logic of Inheritance, Functions and Equations) tackles the problem of extending logic programming with knowledge representation primitives such as generalization and inheritance. Moreover, it merges key features from functional programming and object oriented programming and also embeds functional and relational constraints and residuation. Performance is obtained by wiring-in the inheritance mechanisms in the unification algorithm. Our experience with LIFE applications suggests that the language represents a powerful tool for the development of ambitious symbolic applications such as CAD expert systems and natural language parsing. Furthermore, the LIFE experiment is teaching us important lessons on how to integrate different declarative languages, and to add knowledge representation primitives to such languages in a clean and efficient fashion. The LIFE interpreter is nearly completed and within a year we will have a compiler.

Future plans center on building upon the experience gained in LDL and LIFE to develop a single advanced language that combines their strengths and in addition can be used by non-programmers through visual programming techniques.

Bubba: Bubba is a highly parallel database machine designed to support a large mix of transactions and query programs of varying complexity all running concurrently against a large database. The market motivation for Bubba is the trend, brought about by relational technology, towards high-level interactive interfaces to operational databases. We believe this trend will lead to the need for large "information servers" providing support for:

- a large volume of transaction classes requiring immediate response and simple update transactions
- complex update transactions, representing a shift from batch processing to interactive processing
- a large number of query programs representing a spectrum of information needs -- from simple requests for stored information to requests that derive new information by applying complex transformations to the stored data (including deductive database management)

The goal of the Bubba project is the design of a dedicated scalable architecture that is dramatically superior in cost/performance compared to a mainframe-based system providing similar functionality in the early 1990s time frame. We envision using Bubba to support a variety of application classes.

The project began in 1984 and is currently in the midst of experimental implementation and modeling activities. Most of the research issues have already been addressed and resolved. The purpose of the implementation and modeling activities is to demonstrate our ideas and validate them with high confidence.

Bubba is undergoing implementation on a commercially available 40-node multiprocessor. We are collaborating with the Languages project to insure that LDL object code will execute efficiently on Bubba, as a demonstration of Bubba's ability to effectively support deductive database management as well as relational and transaction processing demands.

A series of working prototypes will be completed and transferred throughout the coming year. Beyond this the plan is to shift emphasis from parallel database management to parallel architectures for advanced KBS of the variety envisioned by the AI and HI Laboratories.

Orion: The increasing use of object-oriented languages and concepts has exposed the need for augmenting object–oriented programming and application systems with database capabilities. At a minimum, object–oriented programming systems require objects to be persistent and sharable, so that objects generated during the execution of a program will be accessible to the subsequent invocation of the program, and they may further be accessible to a number of concurrently executing programs. Beyond this, within the application domains to which the object–oriented approach is well–suited (including CAD and AI), a number of complex tasks which application programmers have traditionally had to program should be offloaded to the database system; such tasks include version control, change notification, and long–duration transactions.

There were thus a number of major research problems that had to be solved. The impact of object–oriented concepts on the database system had to be fully understood (and vice-versa). The Orion database project was initiated in 1985 to address these research issues and to develop a database system that was well–matched to the unique requirements of object–oriented systems. A non–distributed version of Orion (Orion-1) was released in May of 1987. Since then we been focused on research, design, and prototyping of the Orion-2 homogeneous distributed object–oriented database system. In Orion-2, each workstation will have a full–function Orion which manages a private database. Further, each workstation Orion will participate in the access and management of a common shared database.

After Orion-2 is transferred to shareholders the emphasis of the project will shift to support for distributed heterogeneous databases, perhaps starting with a bridge between logic–oriented (LDL) systems and object–oriented (Orion) systems.

CODE: In conventional object–oriented languages and systems, objects are 'passive', in that they respond only to messages. However, message passing in these systems assumes a synchronous protocol, i.e., the sender of a message is blocked until receiving a reply from the receiver of the message. In contrast, concurrent objects are 'active' with a high degree of autonomous control, i.e., they have more knowledge and responsibility than passive objects to activate themselves and interact with other objects. Concurrent objects may be activated by any type of event, including messages, timer interrupts, and user–specified trigger conditions. The high degree of autonomy in concurrent objects implies an asynchronous communication among objects, and makes concurrent objects well–suited to modeling concurrent or distributed applications such as the scheduling and simulation in computer–integrated manufacturing. Further, successful execution of such applications on parallel/distributed hardware has the potential for dramatic improvement in performance.

CODE (Concurrent Object–oriented Design Environment) is a new project focused on fully exploiting the concurrent object concept. Among the research goals are:

- formalization of a model of concurrency (communication) which will allow maximum exploitation of parallelism in an application

- unification of a selected model of concurrency with the abstract object model

- augmentation of concurrent object–oriented programming with database support (building on the Orion experience)

Neural Networks: This is a brand new project whose long term goal is to develop a theory and practice of neural computation to enable its widespread use as a computing technology. Activities will include: examination of scaling properties of NN learning algorithms, and development of new learning algorithms; development of the mathematics and language to describe adaptive systems; investigation of the properties of the individual neuron as well as collections of neurons working together in biological systems; incorporation of time as a variable in neural computational models; and investigation of heterogeneous neural network models (i.e. incorporating several problem–solving methods, each specialized for a class of sub–problem).

Optical Computing: MCC got involved in optical computing in a small way a few years ago and we are now considering gearing up a significantly larger effort in this interesting technological domain. The past work was centered on investigating the potential of photorefractive crystals as a medium for mass storage, somewhere between RAM and disk in the storage hierarchy.

Our results have been sufficiently encouraging that we anticipate increasing our investment in this line of research. The proposal includes new work in such topics as optical switching networks and optical neural nets. Some of this work is funded by DARPA.

5. Experimental Systems Laboratory (DARPA-funded)

Rapid advancement of leading edge computing system technology requires a balanced mix of theoretical, analytical and experimental research. It is likely that recent thrusts into high performance parallel computation will require increasing emphasis on experimentation. Indeed, there is a clear worldwide trend toward exploratory prototyping of systems that embody innovations in hardware, system software and application technologies.

The recently launched MCC Experimental System Kit (ES-Kit) project may be viewed as a source of

1989-93 timeframe, related research is expected to evolve in directions that place more emphasis on exploitation of ES-Kits to conduct important experimental research at MCC. One could thus view the near-term work as foundation-building, with a longer term objective being use of ES-Kits to rapidly advance computing systems technology.

Two distinct research directions appear to be likely. The first will be software-oriented, typically involving the emulation of new systems layered onto ES-Kit configurations that in effect provide scalable and unusually configurable high performance parallel host systems that are impractical to obtain as commercial products.

The second major thrust will emphasize the development of experimental VLSI and subsystem hardware incorporating innovations that are impractical in some sense to study via software. The emergence of affordable rapid hardware prototyping technologies will tend to naturally accelerate the evolution of high performance hardware in most technical as well as business sectors of shareholder interest. It is therefore important to be near the leading edge of experimental hardware research.

A basic set of ES-Kit hardware and software building blocks are being developed during 1988-1989. Later research is expected to produce a sequence of more advanced hardware and software prototyping modules, which exploit emerging new technologies offering increased performance, capacity and functionality.

Collaboration with other research groups is expected to promote development of specialized modules and support tools, which are compatible with and further expand the applicable domain of ES-Kits. (Given vigorous government and industrial support, it is possible that within two or three years, the majority of the module types available to ES-Kit users could be developed elsewhere.)

Substantial research and development beyond the scope of the initial ES-Kit contract is expected to be launched in future years. Some of this work will undoubtedly involve task-specific development of modules, tools and related capabilities, under sponsorship of follow-on government contracts. Other experimental systems work producing proprietary technology could be sponsored by MCC shareholders.

6. ACA's Next Steps

Most of the research undertaken by ACA has been motivated by a mission and goals established at the time of MCC's inception. Even as we continue to work towards fulfillment of these goals, it is clear that new research must be motivated by an updated perspective on future competitive pressures. Thus we

have found it appropriate to define new long range "beacons" predicated upon a collective vision of how people and institutions will use computers at the turn of the century. The task is to intersect that vision with an assessment of ACA's technical strengths and weaknesses to determine how the research agenda should evolve and how the organization must evolve to meet the challenge.

We are midstream in this exciting, difficult process, starting from the simple notion that information systems of the future – including very large, complex systems – will be knowledge-based. From the vantage point of the computer scientist this may seem to be a mundane prediction by now, but in practice there are myriad technical and organizational problems inhibiting implementation. But if we are moderately optimistic about the march of technology, and if we assume that the practical barriers are eventually overcome, then we can speculate about a powerful spectrum of systems whose end points are characterized by the two research directions shown in Figure 1.

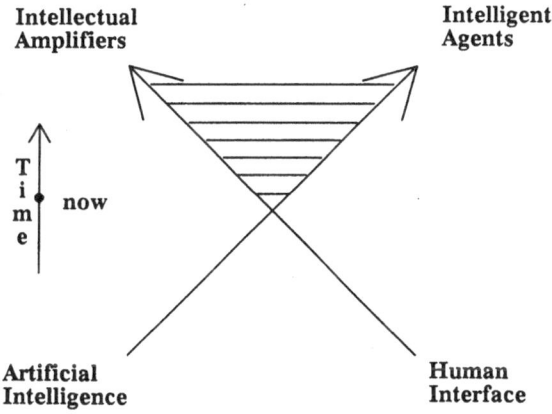

Figure 1: Directions for the Future

The first is towards the development of smarter and smarter systems. This direction has as its ultimate goal the creation of an *intelligent agent* similar to a person. Such an agent would be given a problem to solve. It would then solve it, with only minimal interaction with its user, and report back its result. The second direction is towards the development of *intellectual amplifiers*: systems that allow people to function in smarter ways by augmenting their perceptual, memory retrieval, and reasoning processes. These systems do not solve large problems autonomously. Instead, they interact with their users as the users solve the problems. The first of these directions is supported by the evolving body of research in artificial intelligence; the second by the work in human interface techniques and cognitive science.

In their extreme forms, these goals are different and some of the technologies required to support them are different. But, as the figure attempts to convey by the shaded region between the two lines, there is actually substantial overlap between these two directions, both in the goals and in the necessary technologies.

Intellectual amplifiers can be more and more helpful as they become able to take on more and more complex tasks. Intelligent agents are only intelligent if they interact with their users when that is the best way to acquire the information that they need. Further, some of the best ways for amplifiers to interact, such as through natural language and image recognition, require substantial intelligence in their implementations. This overlap means that we can, by following a single, broadly based research strategy, provide to our shareholders the necessary technology for the creation of both classes of systems. This technology will be derived both from the continued progression of work in artificial intelligence and in human interface technology, as well as from research into the systems problems that must be solved in order to provide the platform upon which these other techniques can be delivered effectively to users.

We are now in the process of identifying some specific regions in the shaded area of figure 1 for further refinement and (eventually) development. Although we naturally want our research results to be as generically applicable as possible, we are interested in selecting a few particular targets to motivate our research, focus the work, and communicate its potential commercial benefits. The challenge is to choose opportunities that are at once intuitively profound in their market impact, feasible in the 10-year outlook, and yet well beyond the reach of today's technology.

Bibliography

Artificial Intelligence Laboratory

Lenat, D. and E. Feigenbaum, "The Knowledge Principle and the Breadth Hypothesis", *Proceedings IJCAI 87, Foundations of AI Workshop*, MIT.

Lenat, D., "CYC: Using Common Sense Knowledge to Overcome Brittleness and Knowledge Acquisition Bottlenecks", *AI Magazine*, Vol. VI, No. 4, Winter 1986.

Ballou, N., H. Chou, F. Garza, W. Kim, C. Petrie, D. Russinoff, D. Steiner, and D. Woelk, "Coupling An Expert System Shell with an Object-Oriented Database System", *The Journal of Object-Oriented Programming*, SIGS Publications, Vol. 1, No. 2, June/July 1988.

Huhns, M. and R. Acosta, "Argo: A System for Design by Analogy", *IEEE Conference on AI Applications*, Summer 1988.

Huhns, M., L. Stephens, and D. Lenat, "Cooperation for DAI through Common Sense Knowledge", *Proceedings of the 8th Workshop on Distributed Artificial Intelligence*, May 1988.

Petrie, C., D. Russinoff, and D. Steiner, "PROTEUS: A Default Reasoning Perspective, *Proceedings of Fifth Generation Systems*, National Institute of Software, 1986.

Human Interface Laboratory

Tarleton, P. Nong and M. Tarleton, "POGO: A Declarative Representation for Graphics", to appear in *Object-Oriented Concepts, Applications, and Databases*, W. Kim and F. Lochovsky, editors, Addison-Wesley, 1988.

Avery, J., "Interactive Worksurface: An Interface Paradigm for Sketchable Things", *Telematics Workshop*, May 1988.

Rich, E. and S. Luper-Foy, "An Architecture for Anaphora Resolution", *Proceedings, Second Conference on Applied Natural Language Processing*, February 1988.

Wroblewski, D. and E. Rich, "Luke: An Experiment in the Early Integration of Natural Language Processing", *Proceedings, Second Conference on Applied Natural Language Processing*, February 1988.

McKendree, J. and J. Zaback, "Planning for Advising", *Proceedings of CHI 1988*, May 1988.

Systems Technology Laboratory

Zaniolo, C., "Design and Implementation of a Logic Based Language for Data Intensive Applications", invited paper, *Proceedings, 5th International Conference/Symposium on Logic Programming*, August, 1988

Boral, H., "Parallelism and Data Management", *Proceedings, 3rd International Israeli Conference on Data and Knowledge Bases*, June 1988.

Copeland, G., W. Alexander, E. Boughter and T. Keller, "Data Placement in Bubba", *Proceedings, SIGMOD '88*, June 1988.

Kim, W., N. Ballou, J. Banerjee, H. Chou, J. Garza and D. Woelk, "Integrating an Object-Oriented Programming System with a Database System", To appear in *Proceedings, 3rd Annual Conference on Object-Oriented Programming Systems, Languages and Applications (OOPSLA)*, September 1988.

Peterson, C. and J. Anderson, "A Mean Field Theory Learning Algorithm for Neural Networks", Published in *Complex Systems I*, 1987.

UK IKBS PROGRAMMES

Timothy Walker

Information Engineering Directorate
United Kingdom

ABSTRACT

This paper reviews the progress of
previous UK programmes in IKBS and describes
the new programmes which have recently been
started.

I am sure that all of us here have found
this conference a fascinating experience.
The quality and range of the papers, and of
the discussion, has demonstrated the results
of work in this area from around the world.
As well as reports on the progress of the
Fifth Generation Programme, the immediately
preceding papers have brought you up to date
with plans for the European programmes
ESPRIT and for the MCC in the US. My talk
reports on UK programmes, both Alvey and its
successor.

Indeed it may be worth stressing that
there is a successor to Alvey and a
substantial one at that. We have new
organisational arrangements which have
brought together for the first time
virtually all Government funding for
research in IT R&D, covering support for
long term basic research in universities,
for collaborative research between industry
and academia, for Government support for
industrial research and awareness and for
higher education and training in IT. This
allows us to take an overview of all
Government activity of this kind in IT and
to produce a more coherent and balanced
programme than might otherwise be possible.
I am glad to say that at least one member of
the committee overseeing these programmes,
Professor Robin Milner, is playing a
prominent role in this conference.

I would however like to start by
commenting on the names of the various
programmes and the way that they have
changed over the years. It was, I think,
Alan Turing in his paper "Computing
Machinery and Intelligence" who first
proposed a definition and test for "machine
intelligence" but the term "Artificial
Intelligence" was coined by John McCarthy in

1956. A considerable effort was
devoted to developing computers which could
play games, particularly chess, but the term
artificial intelligence obviously has a
wider application. In turn it has captured
the imagination and incited hostility.
While it is, I know, supposed to be unlucky
to quote Shakespeare's Macbeth, I am
reminded of Macbeth's question of the
witches ``say from whence you owe this
strange intelligence.''

It has provided a continuing subject for
science fiction from the original
intelligent computer novel by Olaf Stapleton
in 1930 to Asimov's robots in the 1950s,
Arthur Clarke's 2001 and most recently C3PO
in Star Wars. At the same time the
sometimes overstated claims of its
protagonists have encouraged others to argue
that artificial intelligence is a
contradiction in terms. The philosopher
John Searle is perhaps the most recent,
although I have to confess that I found his
argument tended to knock down straw men
rather than those of more substance.

It is perhaps not surprising therefore
that more recent programmes have avoided the
term "artificial intelligence". In Japan
the term "Fifth Generation Programme" was
chosen and it is interesting that while the
titles for papers at this conference often
include the words "intelligent",
"reasoning", "knowledge" (and even
"ignorance"!) none of them refer to
"artificial intelligence". The terms used
now by practitioners tend to be less
grandiose; Professor Aiso describes Fifth
Generation Technology as "the nucleus of
knowledge information processing"; ESPRIT I
used the term "Advanced Information
Processing" but its successor ESPRIT II has
dropped the "advanced" to use "Information
Processing Systems`. In the UK we have used
"Intelligent Knowledge Based Systems" or
IKBS for short.

Some of you may feel that dwelling on the names of these programmes is an irrelevance but I am not so sure. I am certain that there has been a deliberate attempt to distance the community from the more exaggerated claims of the proponents of artificial intelligence. I believe also that the names recognise that the new techniques are much less likely than had been supposed to replace humans, rather they will be used to assist human decision taking. It is from this change in emphasis that the new names have been formulated, most of which concentrate on the processing of knowledge or information.

Certainly this was the thinking that underlay the Alvey report and the programme in IKBS which stemmed from it. An IKBS was defined as a system which uses inference to apply knowledge to perform a task and the Alvey report and the subsequent strategy set out the research that was needed to develop such systems. At that stage, like the Fifth Generation Project, it was seen as a 10 year programme but unlike the Fifth Generation Project, the Alvey programme was not tied to specific goals for hardware or software. It concentrated on tools and methods, sometimes described as enabling technologies, that is those technologies that could then be applied by companies for the development of specific products.

Of course the UK had to start from where we were. At that time almost all the expertise was in universities so much of the development of the IKBS part of the Alvey programme had been done in universities. However the arguments about the nature of artifical intelligence and the usefulness of research in this area which followed the Lighthill report had led to a somewhat demoralised academic community.

Funds had been reduced and some of the most distinguished UK academics had left to work in the US or elsewhere. The overall aims of the IKBS part of the programme were first to revitalise and strengthen the academic groups in the UK and second to achieve some technology transfer into industry. This has been characterised in a recent review of the programme (by Erik Arnold of the Science Policy Research Unit of the University of Sussex) as a science policy rather than an industrial policy. While this has some basis, it neglects the industrial relevance of technology transfer.

The overall strategy of the Alvey IKBS programme therefore had three elements. These comprised a research and development element, an awareness and promotional element and a general support element.

These were set out in 1983 as follows;

The Research and Development Programme

- "Show Me" projects providing immediate industrial demonstrations of existing IKBS technology.

- Short Term Development projects aimed at producing marketable products within 3-4 years based on low risk developments from current technology.

- Demonstrator projects involving industry-led collaborative R&D aimed at building complete prototypes of possible future systems requiring substantial R&D progress.

- Research Themes involving medium to long term directed research by collaborating teams on a limited number of carefully chosen topics likely to be crucial to success in building advanced IKBS.

- General Research accelerated progress in the directed part of the R&D programme will only be possible against a background of a well balanced portfolio of high quality, speculative research into all the important aspects of IKBS and related topics such as software technology and man-machine interaction.

The Awareness and Marketing Programme

In parallel with the R&D activities, this programme is aimed at educating and informing a wide range of possible users of IKBS about their potential, to create an informed marketplace for the products their potential, to create an informed marketplace for the products of the R&D programme as they develop.

In particular, the awareness programme will begin by addressing UK industries where IKBS could have significant impact on productivity, quality and performance in the near term, and will solicit the involvement of selected firms in the definition and implementation of particular demonstrator projects in the R&D programme.

The Infrastructure and Support Programme

- provision and support of common computing hardware for IKBS researchers in industry and academia

- development of common frameworks and standards for interchange of software, including:

- communications network facilities
- software libraries
- software quality assurance
- updating and distributing catalogues of relevant software available from other countries
- an expanded education and training activity to increase the flow of high quality people available for IKBS research, development and production elsewhere which may be relevant to the UK IKBS community

The achievements of Alvey IKBS have been considerable. Significant progress has been made towards reinforcing existing centres of research excellence and a number of key individuals have been encouraged to return from the UK or have decided not to leave in the first place. Industrial interest and capability in AI has been raised; the number of people in industry with relevant experience has risen dramatically. Links between the universities and industry have been improved and academics have a better sense of industrial needs and the intellectual challenge of scaling up laboratory techniques into useable industrial systems. At the peak, about 350 researchers were employed on Alvey projects in addition to existing members of University faculties.

It may be worth saying a little more about the Research Clubs since these have stimulated very considerable industrial interest in expert systems. There were nine in all covering a wide range of activities:

ALFEX	Alvey Financial Expert Systems
ARIES	Insurance Community
DAPES	Data Processing
EMEX	The Econometric Model Building
PLANIT	The Planning IKBS Club
QSES	Quantity Surveying
RESCU	Real Time Expert Systems
TRACE	Transport and Travel
WEISC	Water Industry

In each case membership cost only a few thousand pounds and allowed members to specify an expert system for use in their own industry and to observe its evolution and development in parallel with others with a similar interest. They also have the right to use the resulting software without further payment. Most of these users had no previous experience of expert systems and therefore it provided very useful experience for them in de-mystifying the technology as well as learning how to deal with specification and use. Altogether the nine

have more than 180 member firms and have spread awareness of expert systems through a significant proportion of UK industry and commerce. Many of the clubs are now continuing without Government support.

Another successful initiative was the Journeyman scheme whereby individual industrial workers were seconded into university teams for a few months in order to deveop their own understanding of IKBS techniques to a stage where they could develop industrial projects. Many people have passed through this scheme and this has been a key factor in extending the range and numbers of industrial researchers knowledgeable about IKBS.

At the same time, and perhaps surprisingly for so long term a research programme, there have been significant commercial outputs from the research, not just in expert systems but also in the IKBS aspects of speech and image processing. I have also been struck by the increased interest being shown in industry in natural language, although it is still clearly some time before computers will be able to deal quickly with anything other than a fairly restricted set of language.

In considering the success of Alvey, my own experience gives me a useful perspective. As some of you will know, although I helped to start both the Alvey and the Esprit programmes and worked on them during their first two years, I then moved to other work before returning as Director of the new programme. It is perhaps easier therefore for me to notice changes in the field of IKBS than for those who have been associated with it during the whole period. And indeed I have noticed a number of changes.

The first is that expectations of what might be achieved have been lowered. This has been emphasised by the development of expert systems many of which are now in use commercially as a result partly of the stimulus provided by the Alvey Clubs. But despite this growth, they are put to less ambitious uses than perhaps had been imagined a few years ago. In most cases they are used chiefly to store the knowledge or know how of experts in a form easily recalled by those less expert. This seems to me an eminently sensible use and one that should not be interpreted in any way as second best. I am conscious that I may well be using "knowledge" in a rather loose way but to define it here would take the rest of my paper at least. I am content to rely on

Dr Jowett, the Master of Balliol College, Oxford, during part of the 19 century. An apocryphal verse runs:

First came I: my name is Doctor Jowett
There is no knowledge but I know it
I am the Master of this college
What I don't know, isn't knowledge

Second, in the same way that expectations of IKBS have been reduced, it is becoming increasingly recognised that it is one tool, to be used with others. When I first became involved with Alvey, I was conscious of fierce arguments between the proponents of IKBS and the software engineers about the best way to produce software. Each side regarded the other as misguided and either irrelevant, incompetent or clinging to the past. I was struck by the relative absence of these arguments when I returned to the area. There was a much greater recognition that both approaches had real advantages – and disadvantages – and that the way forward was to devise ways of combining the two approaches. Thus most IPSEs now aim to provide an environment that can support both kinds of activity. I see a similar situation in the proponents of LISP and PROLOG, who now seem also more interested in working together than pointing out the faults in the other approach.

Third, the area of human computer interface (HCI) is receiving much more attention and in a more systematic way. Five years ago it was recognised as important but no one really knew what to do about it. Now we accept that there is no point in devising means to store and process knowledge if we do not have effective techniques for extracting that knowledge from the experts. HCI is becoming an integral part of many different technical areas.

This also leads me on to one of the other major developments in the Alvey Programme, that of systems architectures. Computer architecture has, of course, always had an important part to play in computer science, but has become of increasing importance with the advent of parallel processing and distributed systems. Architectures also need to be more flexible – dare I say more intelligent – and to be able to relate to the system or organisation with which they are dealing. It is interesting that the Alvey Report hardly mentions architectures but that within 18 months the Alvey Directorate found it necessary to create it as a topic in its own right. While the research was naturally concerned at first principally with theoretical studies, it has now moved on to working with systems or

subsystems. One of the most innovative projects, and indeed the only Alvey project where the collaborators all worked at the same location, was ANSA, Advanced Network System Architecture. Although this started as a communications project it has become possibly the single largest driving force behind the ISO model for "open distributed processing". Interestingly it too has become involved in issues such as requirements elicitation and organisational structure. Like many of the Alvey projects ANSA is moving into Europe and will, having taken on other collaborators, become an Esprit project.

All these factors have influenced the new UK programme in terms of both structure and content. The new programme is structured less around individual technologies and more by function. Thus instead of IKBS, software engineering, MMI and so on, we have one area devoted to systems architecture and another to systems engineering, the latter of which contains both IKBS and software engineering as well as human factors. There is of course some overlap between systems engineering and systems architecture but this would be inevitable wherever the boundaries were drawn.

Some of the work will of course be carried out in the European programme, ESPRIT. My paper earlier this week explained the criteria we use for deciding whether a project is more appropriate for a European or national programme and I will not repeat them here but will confine my comments to what is proposed for the national programme.

The major themes of the programme are:

the industrialisation of the techniques developed over the last few years, in Alvey, Esprit and elsewhere;

the promotion of interdisciplinary work; and

the integration of IKBS into the generality of approaches to the building of complex systems.

Thus while containing substantial element of academic research, the programme has clear industrial objectives. In particular it is designed to capitalise on the achievements of previous programmes. Conversely, those areas such as expert systems which are being exploited commercially, are not included in the programme. There will however be scope for more advanced work on particular classes of expert systems, for example these dealing with real time or cooperating or distributed expert systems.

What then does the new IED programme concentrate on? The first point to note of course is that we do not have a IKBS programme as such. One of my first acts on taking over Director was to ask the three people in charge of the IKBS, software engineering and HCI parts of the Alvey programme to produce a joint strategy for the new programme rather than three separate ones. Despite some initial misgivings they did this and it has been welcomed by the community. I will however concentrate in this talk on those aspects of new programme that would normally be recognised as IKBS.

Like Alvey, it concentrates on basic science, methods and tools and in demonstrating their use in practical industrial environments. There are no specific hardware goals. The basic science will concentrate on cognitive science, particularly on inference and reasoning mechanisms and deep knowledge representation, and on recent developments in logic, including those necessary to deal with more advanced systems needed for concurrent system design or for real time and predictably reliable systems. Models also need to be developed for the entire life cycle of software and for simulation of human users.

The theme of bringing software engineering and IKBS together continues in the new programme's work on IPSEs. The Alvey programme supported the development of both second generation IPSEs and the Poplog environment, all of which are now commercial products.

However it is clear that more advanced IPSEs require very substantial investment and must provide acceptable migration paths for new users or those used to different approaches. Our work will emphasise the development of a better balance between the knowledge based and conventional elements, we need to incorporate the results of research conventional elements, we need to incorporate the results of research into life cycle models, project management and development methodologies into the next generation of knowledge based tools. A further area where this kind of interdisciplinary work is needed is in the combination of formal methods and declarative languages.

The more techniques are used which allow a system implementation directly from specification, the more important becomes the development of that specification and the requirements capture which precedes it.

This is closely related to the knowledge elicitation and knowledge representation necessary for IKBS programme. Indeed it can be argued that requirements capture is the elicitation of user knowledge about the desired solution and that system design is the bringing together of that knowledge with a designer's knowledge about the design options available in a suitable knowledge representation framework.

Despite these similarities, there has been relatively little overlap between the two approaches although the use of formally based specification languages and automated reduction systems to reason about characteristics of the specification or to infer realisation of the specified system is common ground. These techniques will need to exploit the potential of massively parallel computing engines and therefore provide a natural link to the systems architecture part of our programme. We hope in the new programme to bring the various communities together to make use of the insights which each of them have gained in the process.

This leads one to another very important problem, that of validation. Traditionally this has been addressed in the software engineering programmes and rather less so in those dealing with IKBS. Yet there are some very fundamental problems which have significant commercial and legal implications. This is already pressing for expert systems. Indeed, as far as I am aware, there is still no way of establishing unambiguously that the contents of the system do indeed represent accurately the knowledge of the expert(s) concerned. (It is interesting to notice that there was a paper on this subject yesterday). The problems that stem from this relate to responsibility for errors produced by the expert system; are these due to inadequacies in the expert's knowledge; in the way the expert system has dealt with them; or in the use to which the system has been put? It is possible to argue that this is not really different from the arguments about whether faults arise from an inadequate specification rather than an inadequate implementation in a conventional piece of software, but the involvement of the expert, often from neither the buyer's or vendor's organisation, does cause extra difficulties. No doubt it will give lucrative employment to lawyers for a long time to come yet!

The final topic I would like to deal with is that of human factors. Although there have been few, if any, papers directly on this subject during this conference, the area is almost always in the background, particularly when dealing with knowledge elicitation or, of course, natural language. There are constant arguments between those who regard human computer interaction as an independent subject and those who feel that it can only be investigated as part of other related topics. The new UK programme tends towards the second view, but not exclusively. Certainly we have chosen to produce a workplan which seeks to integrate HCI with IKBS and software engineering, but which does suggest some topics on HCI alone.

This is one change from Alvey; the other is the increased emphasis on HCI at a organisational level rather than with individual people. This reflects a recognition at a specification level of Donne's phrase "no man is an island" and is of particular importance in knowledge based approaches where much of what is called "knowledge" includes assumptions about how other people in an organisation will react. I am sure that we need to do more work on the effects on organisational structure of the continued increase in the automation of information processing.

To sum up therefore, the new UK programme for IKBS has deliberately attempted to integrate these techniques both with software engineering and with human factors and to accelerate the industrialisation of these methods. It recognises explicitly that these techniques will be used to help and not replace human beings, It will also continue to build up the pool of skilled manpower in this area.

We look forward to reporting the results at future Fifth Generation Programme Conferences.

ICOT RESEARCH
TOPICS

PROCEEDINGS OF THE INTERNATIONAL CONFERENCE
ON FIFTH GENERATION COMPUTER SYSTEMS 1988,
edited by ICOT. © ICOT, 1988

Overview of Knowledge Base Mechanism

Shigeki Shibayama, Hiroshi Sakai, Toshiaki Takewaki

Toshiba Research and Development Center

1, Komukai-Toshiba-cho, Saiwai-ku, Kawasaki, 210, Japan

Hidetoshi Monoi, Yukihiro Morita, Hidenori Itoh

Institute for New Generation Computer Technology

4-28, Mita 1-Chome, Minato-ku, Tokyo, 108, Japan

ABSTRACT

This paper describes an experimental knowledge base system, which is one of the knowledge base mechanism research efforts carried out in the intermediate stage of the Japan's Fifth Generation Computer Project. The system employs the relational knowledge model, an extension of the relational data model, which allows a "term" data type.

The hardware adopted a hybrid shared memory multiprocessor architecture. The processing elements shares a conventional shared memory and a multiport page-memory, a page-based conflict-free memory. Dedicated knowledge base management software was built on the hardware. The efficiency of the software and the effectiveness of the architecture are shown in the preliminary evaluation.

1 INTRODUCTION

In this paper, we will describe a parallel knowledge base machine research effort carried out in the intermediate stage of the Japan's Fifth Generation Computer Project. In another article [Itoh 88] interrelation among the four research efforts, including this one, within the knowledge base mechanism research is given.

In the initial stage of the FGCS project, a relational database machine Delta was built as a first step toward a knowledge base machine [Kakuta 85], [Shibayama 84]. Though Delta was operational, it was recognized that the strict relational model adopted in Delta was not sufficient for the basis of the further knowledge base machine research [Shibayama 85]. The modification of Delta's software was considered to be difficult because of the large amount of software. The quantity came from the fact that there was software for processors which were specialized to different purposes. Also, the amount of parallelism in Delta was limited (four engines) for carrying out research into parallel knowledge base processing.

With the introduction of the relational knowledge model [Yokota 86], we thought that this model was appropriate for a basis of the interface between logic programming languages and knowledge base systems. This is because the model enhanced the relational data model to allow terms as a data primitive and enabled a kind of deduction without the aid of inference machines. The parallel processing method on special hardware was investigated [Morita 87].

However, a simulation study [Sakai 87] disclosed that the deduction was not so attractive in terms of processing speed. This is mainly because there are many repeated relation transfers in the deduction process. Even dedicated hardware (unification engines and a multiport page-memory [Tanaka 84]) did not remedy the situation.

With these intermediate results, we shifted the research direction to implement a backend knowledge base machine. In the course of the simulation study, an experimental parallel machine was being built. Originally it was aimed to be used for the hardware version of the simulation. The architecture proposed in [Yokota 86] incorporated hardware unification engines as the processing element core. The experimental hardware, however, did not incorporate unification engines. It was because at the outset of its development the unification engine design was considered to be premature and the hardware amount was predicted to be too much. This experimental machine was not used for the further simulation but was used for the implementation of the knowledge base management software.

The knowledge model we adopted was still the relational knowledge model. We were more concerned with the incorporation of the relational-algebra-like primitive operations and unification-based query language as an interface to host PSI machines than the deduction capability with the model though it is possible to do that if we do not care much for the processing time.

The hardware was completed by the end of 1986 fiscal year. The knowledge base management software's work has been carried out since 1987.

In the context described above, we have been engaged in the design and implementation of an experimental knowledge base system, named Mu-X. The knowledge base is defined as a collection of term relations, that is,

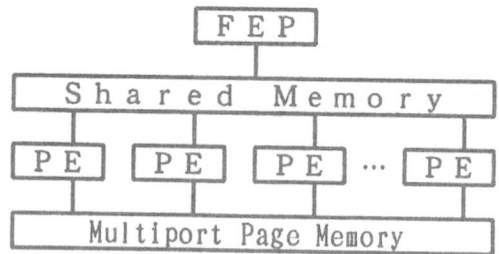

Figure 1. Hardware Configuration

relations extended with attributes that have structured items and variables. Conventional attributes such as integer and character data types are also supported.

In section 2, the hardware of the system is briefly described. In section 3, the software of the system is described somewhat in detail. In section 4, preliminary performance evaluation results are given and discussed. In section 5, discussions are presented on the system architecture and possible improvements. Section 6 introduces a sample information retrieval system developed using the interface set up for the PSI connection. Section 7 is the conclusion.

2 HARDWARE

Mu-X adopted a shared memory multiprocessor architecture. Mu-X mainly consists of eight processing elements (PEs), a conventional shared memory and a multiport page-memory (Figure 1). Each PE consists of a general-purpose microprocessor, a moving-head disk, a local memory and a multiport page-memory interface. There is no special-purpose hardware for functional distribution of database tasks [Shibayama 87].

The multiport page-memory [Tanaka 84] is a conflict-free memory system shared through the ports it provides. The multiport page-memory consists of a set of memory banks, a switching network for interchanging the multiple ports and memory banks, port controllers attached to each port and a main controller. By cyclically interchanging the network and appropriately reading/writing the proper part of memory banks, simultaneous access from each port to arbitrary memory pages is realized. This is illustrated in Figure 2. In our implementation, the port count is equal to the PE count, i.e. eight. Each PE is connected to a port of the multiport page-memory. For the switching network, we used multiplexor between the memory banks and the ports to make the hardware simple. More highly parallel implementation would require, for example, a multistage network.

Hence Mu-X has two types of memory systems. The multiport page-memory and the shared memory both

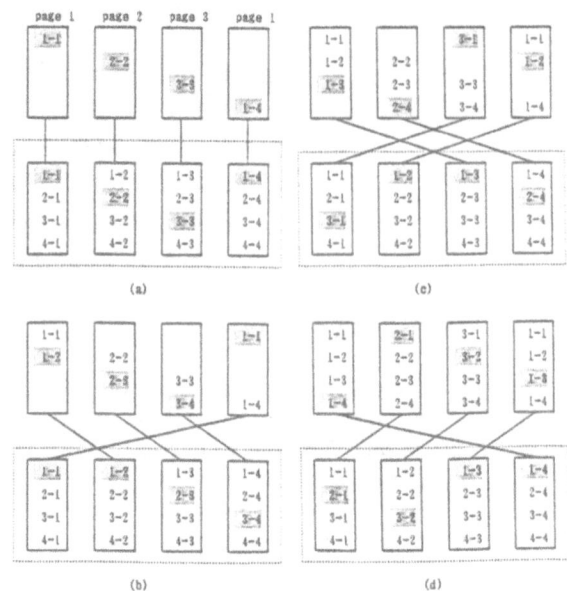

Figure 2. Multiport Page-Memory Principle

provide capability for exchange of information among the PEs. The conventional shared memory and the multiport page-memory have the following characteristics.

(1) For conventional shared memory, the unit of access is typically a word, while for multiport page-memory data is accessed on page basis.

(2) Conventional shared memory has potential access conflict among multiple PEs, while for multiport page-memory no access conflict occurs.

(3) For shared memory, access (when there is no memory access conflict) is quick, typically one or a few microsecond, while there is at least a page transfer time overhead for the multiport page-memory page access.

These characteristics are taken into account in the software implementation.

To complete the machine quickly, we used off-the-shelf components for the processor, local memory, shared memory, disk controller and disk unit. The multiport page-memory, its interface within each PE, and the shared memory arbiter are newly designed and fabricated. The hardware consists of two cabinets. In one cabinet eight processing elements and the conventional shared memory are installed and in another cabinet the multiport page-memory is installed. The front end processor is an off-the-shelf personal computer (VME-10),

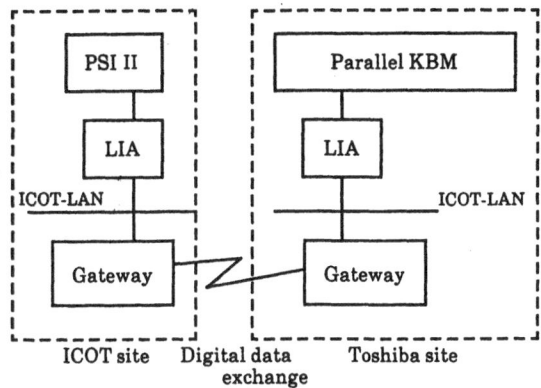

Figure 3. Network Connection

Table 1. Hardware Specifications

PE count	8
PE processor	MC68020 at 12.5MHz
Local memory	2MB/PE
Shared memory	2MB
Multiport page-memory	8 ports
	64MB with 512-byte pages
	5MB/sec/port transfer speed
Multiport page-memory Buffer	12KB
Disk Unit Capacity	47MB, formatted

placed adjacent to Mu-X and connected to the conventional shared memory. The hardware's specification is summarized in table 1.

For the connection to PSI-II machines, Mu-X is connected to the PSI-Net. Mu-X is located at the Toshiba Research and Development Center in Kawasaki City adjacent to Tokyo. Mu-X is connected to ICOT's local PSI-Net via gateways (Figure 3).

3 SOFTWARE

3.1 Design Goals

FUNCTIONALITY

(1) Term data support

As the system is based on the relational knowledge model, capability of manipulation of terms is essential. Additional operations to normal comparison operations are required. The unification operation is the most basic operation associated with terms; the operations such as list membership check must also be supported if we try to use terms in a database context. Figure 4 shows an example of the internal representation of a term.

We also adopted the term representation in various system data structure. For example, in the data dic-

salad(tomato(2),lettace(1))

0111	000000001000
00000010	"s"
"a"	"l"
"a"	"d"
0111	000000001010
00000010	"t"
"o"	"m"
"a"	"t"
"o"	00000000
0000	000000000010
0111	000000001010
00000001	"l"
"e"	"t"
"t"	"a"
"c"	"e"
0000	000000000001

Figure 4. An Example of a Term

tionaries the information about a relation is stored in a tuple and the information about its attributes is stored in an attribute using the term structure. The messages exchanged with a host machine are also represented using the term structure.

(2) Variable-length record support

This is also a derivation from the term data support. The attribute length of a term attribute cannot be defined at the schema definition time. This is because the length of a term may drastically change when a unification is performed. The data structure is determined so that the variable-length records can be manipulated with the least loss of efficiency.

(3) Multitransaction support

Considering the environment that this machine is used, an efficient realization of multitransaction facilities is pursued.

EFFICIENCY

(1) Parallel processing

Parallel processing algorithms on multiprocessor database machine have been extensively studied and implemented [Boral 82], [Hanson 87], [Nakamura 87], [Wilkinson 87], [Bitton 83a], [Kitsuregawa 84], [Shapiro 86]. The algorithms are for the most part aimed at improving the response time of a query. In our parallel processing scheme, we are not only interested in the response time but also the throughput of the system.

200

(2) Minimizing software overhead

The motivation behind this goal is that the conventional operating systems are not suited for the construction of special-purpose software, in particular database or knowledge base machine implementation. The management software is designed and coded with this strongly in mind.

(3) Effective use of the hardware architecture

As is described in the previous section, a feature of the hardware is that it has the hybrid shared memory systems of different nature. The management software aimed to make most of the memory systems. Care is also taken to preserve the scalability as much as possible. Hardware having the same architecture with more PEs could run the software with increased performance.

3.2 Basic Design

DECENTRALIZATION OF FUNCTIONS

Most of the multiprocessor database systems have a control processor and a number of data processors or PEs [Su 88]. The control processor is usually responsible for general and miscellaneous management tasks such as transaction management, data dictionary management, query compilation, parallel execution control and response generation. The PEs are responsible, on the other hand, for database operation execution.

The configuration, in a multi-transaction environment, has the disadvantage that the processing power of the control processor is not enough for managing the many PEs and becomes a performance bottleneck.

Some systems such as DBC/1012 adopt multiple control processors approach to eliminate this bottleneck. Conversely, the processing power of the control processors are not used for the processing of queries. To solve this problem, we assigned both the control processor functions and the data processor functions to each PE. Each PE is in charge of at most one transaction for the control processor tasks. When a host computer issues a transaction, the front end processor seeks an idle PE to be responsible for it. The PE becomes the "transaction master" of that transaction and takes care of the transaction until the end of the transaction. The front end processor is only responsible for the manipulation of network protocols.

CONFIGURATION OF THE PE SOFTWARE

Since each PE has to work on the control processor and data processor tasks concurrently, the execution of each task should be interchanged with little software overhead. We decided not to use the task

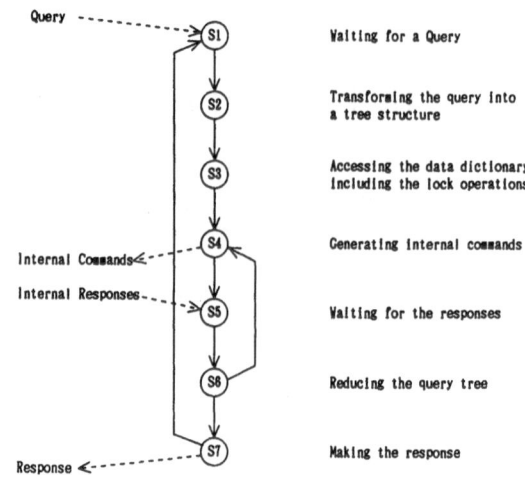

Figure 5. Program Main Flow

switch mechanism provided by the residing operating system. Our solution was that the software consist of two modules, the transaction management module and command processing module, and let the transaction management module call the command processing module at certain program states. Thus the two modules actually comprise a single control flow program where the transaction management program is the main program with the command processing module subroutine. The flowchart of the main program is shown in Figure 5. The following is a brief explanation of the chart.

State S1: idle (waiting for the arrival of a query)

State S2: query transformation to a query tree

State S3: data dictionary consultation and relation locking, if necessary

State S4: internal command(s) generation

State S5: idle (waiting for the responses of the internal command(s))

State S6: reduces the query tree and go to S4 if there remains query tree to be processed

State S7: return response to host, go to S1

The transaction management module calls the command processing module at states S1, S3 (only if the lock operation is suspended), and S5. The command processing module, when called, seeks the internal commands which the PE can, or is supposed, to process. (See the internal command description for details.)

When there is no such internal commands, the control is returned to the management module.

The transaction management module generates and dispatches the internal commands step by step as it reduces the query tree. Optimizations in query processing can be better applied in the process than in the case where internal commands are generated in batch before the query processing, because the temporary relations' sizes are exactly known after a tree reduction. The size information can be used to determine the algorithm for successive operations.

We adopted a single control flow program approach mainly to eliminate task switching overhead between transaction management task and command processing task. The other advantage is that the multiport page-memory interface memory, which is the I/O buffer of the multiport page-memory, can be fully utilized by the current task since the execution is exclusive.

3.3 Internal commands for parallel processing

Internal commands are specifications of relational algebra level operations that PEs should process in parallel. According to the nature of the commands, they are classified into two types, PE specific and PE nonspecific commands.

(1) PE Specific and Nonspecific Commands

A PE specific command is concerned with accessing a portion of a relation stored in the disk. It must be processed by the PE(s) which owns the data in the disk. Therefore a PE specific command has an assignment mask, a bit array which specifies which PE(s) should process it.

A PE nonspecific command is concerned with only those relations stored in the multiport page-memory. In this case it can be processed by any PE. Idle PEs are responsible for processing such commands, which helps balance the processing load among the PEs. Note that both PE specific and nonspecific commands are shared by PEs. This requires a synchronization mechanism as described below.

(2) Assignment, Participation and Completion Masks

These mask fields are provided within the internal command used for synchronization. As the nature of parallel processing, it is not obvious to know when an internal command is finished. For example, as for a PE specific command, there may be a case where some of the PEs have already finished the processing while the others have not even started it yet.

A PE specific command is associated with an assignment mask and a completion mask. The setting of the assignment mask bit indicates that the corresponding PE must process the PE specific command. The completion mask bit is set by a PE that finished the command. If those coincide, it indicates the completion of the command. Similarly, the PE nonspecific command is associated with a participation mask and a completion mask. The participation mask bit is set when a PE participates in the PE nonspecific command processing. The meaning of the completion mask is the same as in the PE specific command. If those coincide, the PE nonspecific command is known to be completed. Using these masks, PEs can suspend the execution of an internal command, which helps to prevent the average response time from getting long in bad situations. In other words, this is part of a mechanism that substitutes the multi-tasking mechanism in a conventional operating system. There is a limit time for a PE to continue the processing of one internal command. If the time exceeds the limit, the PE looks for a queued PE specific command related to itself. If such a command is found, the PE begins the processing of the new command by leaving the completion mask of the current command unchanged.

(3) Object Counter

There is a counter field called the object counter within a PE nonspecific internal command. This is used to specify the current object (page) number ready for processing. For example, in a selection operation which requires the scan of a relation within the multiport page-memory, each page of the relation must be processed only once by an arbitrary PE. In this case, the object counter is initialized to the first page number. Each PE tries to get the content of the object counter (i.e. the page number to be processed next) and to increment it by one in a critical section of its program.

3.4 Data Objects

It is crucial to high performance to effectively use the hybrid memory systems, namely, conventional shared memory and the multiport page-memory.

The multiport page-memory behaves very much like a disk-cache for data stored in the disks; however, strictly speaking, it is not a disk cache. Rather, it is used as a large-capacity buffer. This means that the replacement is under control of the control software at any time. In the following, the major data objects in the system are described with a focus on where they are stored.

(1) Temporary Relation

A temporary relation is created typically by a retrieval operation. It is stored in a "multiport page-memory file", MPPM file for short, which is a sequence of pages allocated within the multiport page-memory.

Control tables are used to get the required page location within the multiport page-memory from the logical page number of the MPPM file. They are stored in the shared memory so that an MPPM file can be accessed by any PE. An MPPM file could be used to store a permanent relation. Thus, the locking protocols and the version management on each page of the MPPM file are also realized in the control tables. There are 256 MPPM files available in the current implementation.

(2) Permanent Relation

A permanent relation is horizontally divided and stored across the disks. Hash-based or round-robin partitioning can be specified at the relation schema definition time. Within a PE, the partitioned portion of a permanent relation is stored in a "disk file". A disk file is basically a sequence of fixed-size pages within a disk device.

In an update operation, the new version of a page data is created and stored in a new page of the multiport page-memory. When the transaction is committed, the new version of the page data is actually stored in the disk device.

(3) Temporary Cluster

A set of temporary clusters are generated in a dynamic clustering operation. Each cluster is stored in a "bucket file". A bucket file is stored in the multiport page-memory like the MPPM file. The control tables, however, are simpler than that of the MPPM file, because their use is limited.

(4) Data Dictionaries

There are two types of data dictionaries, the local data dictionary and the global data dictionary.

(a) Local Data Dictionary

A local data dictionary is associated with a transaction and mainly keeps the information about temporary relations such as the data type, the name of each attribute, and the number of tuples. It is stored in the local memory of the PE responsible for the transaction.

(b) Global Data Dictionary

The global data dictionary mainly keeps the information about the permanent relations. It is a special permanent relation, partitioned across the disks as other permanent relations, and loaded into the multiport page-memory at the system startup time. To process a query which requires access to the global data dictionary, the related portion of the global data dictionary is further copied to the shared memory and is used. The shared memory works as a cache for the global data dictionary. So, once a portion is copied to the shared memory, successive access to the portion goes to the shared memory. This can be determined by examining a hash table. The updates to the global data dictionary are reflected to the cached portion in the shared memory, if it exists, and to the copy in the multiport page-memory.

In summary, we have designed and been implementing the software that we believe is appropriate for knowledge base or database purposes. For the recovery facilities, the transaction recovery mechanism is included. We took into consideration the logging facilities for system recovery, however, it is not included in the implementation.

4 PERFORMANCE EVALUATION

We have done a preliminary performance evaluation using the Wisconsin Benchmark database [Bitton 83b]. According to our data storage scheme, the fixed-length database is stored using variable-length record format though the variable-length field is never used. A record header is attached to each record, while some attributes are stored using a two-byte short integer format against the original four-byte field.

The size of the relation we used is one thousand tuples (Thoustup relation). This is because we used the database that is also used for debugging. The Thoustup relation is stored in 112 2K-byte pages. Each page contains 9 tuples except for the last one.

The evaluation is done without any indexing scheme. That is, the values are all "nonindexed". A full scan of a relation is performed in the selection case and a paged nested-loop algorithm is used in the join case. In all the cases the processing times are measured assuming "cache hit", in other words, assuming that the relation already resides in the multiport page-memory. The evaluation was done in a single-user environment.

We measured the execution times of three queries as shown below. Two of them are selections and one is a join. The join is performed between the copies of the same Thoustup relation. The temporary relation is formed in the multiport page-memory. The values include processing times of all tasks required to execute a query within *Mu-X*, such as query compilation, communication and synchronization. The query transfer time from PSI-II and result transfer time are not included.

Query 1 (1% selection)
```
insert into temp select * from Thoustup
where unique2 between 101 and 110
```

Query 2 (10% selection)

Table 2. Evaluation Results

query	PE count	1	2	4	8
1	total	197ms	110ms	68ms	49ms
	manage.	24ms	24ms	24ms	25ms
	proc.	173ms	86ms	44ms	24ms
2	total	255ms	139ms	83ms	57ms
	manage.	24ms	24ms	24ms	25ms
	proc.	231ms	115ms	59ms	32ms
3	total	85.2s	43.1s	21.2s	10.9s
	manage.	44ms	44ms	44ms	46ms
	proc.	85.1s	43.0s	21.1s	10.9s

Table 3. PE Performance

Processors (All CPUs are 68020s.)	Dhrystone loops/sec
PE 12.5MHz, no cache, off-board memory	925
Sun3/50 15MHz, no cache, on-board memory	2437
Sun3/160 16.7MHz, no cache, on-board memory	3083

```
insert into temp select * from Thoustup
where unique2 between 101 and 200
```

Query 3 (join)
```
insert into temp
select Thoustup1.*, Thoustup2.*
from Thoustup1, Thoustup2
where Thoustup1.unique1 = Thoustup2.unique1
```

Table 2 shows the evaluation results. The total execution time, management task time and net processing time for each case are given. As the used relation size is small, the management task times are comparable to the processing times in the selection cases. According to our nonindexed selection processing scheme, much of the transaction management task done by the transaction master PE remains the same regardless of the size of the target relation. So we can extrapolate the selection processing time to the larger target relation sizes as long as the disk buffer (multiport page-memory) size is reasonably larger than the size of the target relation. We can predict, then, the processing times of 0.27 second for 1% selectivity selection and 0.35 second for 10% selectivity selection against the ten-thousand-tuple (TenKtup) benchmark relation.

OBSERVATIONS

To give the reader the idea of the basic processor speed, the Dhrystone benchmark result of the PE is shown in table 3 in comparison with other processors.[1] The PE is by no means the fastest hardware to the today's standard. If the PEs were replaced with faster hardware of the day, substantial speedup could be obtained for the processor-intensive portion of the processing times.

Still, we think these values are satisfactory for the nonindexed selections. For the join query, because a

nested-loop algorithm is used, the processing time is not as small as other latest evaluation values. However, we think that the values are quite reasonable with respect to the algorithm used and we are expecting a considerable speedup when the bucket-wise hash-join algorithm [Kitsuregawa 83] is completed.

In this evaluation we omitted the disk access times. In the nonindexed cases, we estimate that the disk access time for the TenKtup relation is about 0.6 to 0.7 second in the eight processors case. In the current implementation, as the processing time and disk access time are serialized, the 10% selection time against the TenKtup relation will be about one second. In the join query there will be little effect on the evaluation result because we can store the whole relation in the buffer (multiport page-memory) after the first accesses to the relation.

In summary of this section, though there are only a few evaluation results available now, they show encouraging performance potential of the machine. This will be made further evident after more detailed and exhaustive evaluations.

5 DISCUSSIONS

SYSTEM ARCHITECTURE

Mu-X can be thought to have an architecture that has dynamic processor-memory assignment capability. This is because the portions of the shared memories (both the conventional shared memory and the multiport page-memory) can be used by any PE without explicitly transferring data. In this class of architectures, if the PEs cannot access the data at a rate that matches the PE's processing speed, the performance will become poor. If only the conventional shared memory is shared among PEs, the shared memory and the memory bus should have the bandwidth that pace the processing speed of multiple PEs.

This is considered to be a challenge to the memory system since the clock cycle of processors are becoming faster at a greater rate than the memory chips and memory bus speedup. Even single processor systems'

---

[1] The values are shown for the relative comparison in our environment and not for comparison with the reported values elsewhere.

memory bus often does not have enough bandwidth for the processor's speed. The situation is worse in the multiprocessor case. Generally, cache memories are the solution to the problem; however, it is still questionable if the database processing manifests good memory access locality.

The multiport page-memory is a cost-effective solution to the memory-bandwidth enhancement. The cost-effectiveness results from the separation of ports while a common bus has to shorten the cycle time of bus transfers for high bandwidth. For example, assume that there is a shared bus N-processor multiprocessor with B memory banks each having T bytes/sec transfer capability. For each processor to read a page of K bytes in a buffer it requires $(K \times N)/(T \times B)$ time, provided that the shared bus has enough bandwidth. If N is equal to B, obviously the time is K/T. If the multiport page-memory is used, the time will be also K/T.[2] However, the bandwidth of the shared bus must be more than $T \times B$ bytes/sec to fulfill this. In other words, the shared bus must have the technology that enables $T \times B$ bytes/sec transfer. While the multiport page-memory's port and the switching network must only have T bytes/sec technology.

In the current implementation, the multiport page-memory has eight 16-bit ports each having 5MB/sec transfer capability. Thus in total the bandwidth is 40MB/sec. This is a figure that cannot be achieved using the same class of technology as was adopted to implement the experimental machine.

Overall, the architecture of Mu-X is similar to that of DIRECT [DeWitt 79], [Boral 82] with respect to the processor memory interconnection. The similarity is even stronger when compared to the DIRECT implementation; DIRECT used multiport memory instead of original crossbar connection of the CCD modules and the query processors (or PEs).

The difference with the hardware is the PE configuration. The PEs of Mu-X are provided with separate disks that the PEs can access in parallel. We did not include disk access times in the evaluation, so it is too early to claim the advantage that the parallel disks will bring. However, we are certain that the parallel disks will reduce the I/O bottleneck [Agrawal 84] and can be used effectively in (1) nonindexed query processing and

(2) multiuser query processing.

The difference in software is that (1) Mu-X does not have a centralized control processor and (2) neither conventional operating system nor modules of existing database system are used. The effectiveness of the former is not yet proven in the single-user evaluations. The effectiveness of the latter, on the other hand, is shown in the evaluation values.

POSSIBLE IMPROVEMENTS

Though we are not through with the full implementation of the software and evaluations, we can point out some improvements to the machine architecture and software design. For hardware, it is matter of course that the processing speed would be faster if we used a processor board with a processor cache. To do this, care must be taken for the shared memory caching to keep the coherency of the data as in the case of usual shared memory multiprocessors. One simple way to do this is to avoid caching the shared memory. For the local memory within a PE, information is never shared among PEs; so no coherency problem occurs. We will not discuss this further because the discussion may be too general to be done here.

Another possible improvement is the multiport page-memory buffer allocation in the PE memory space. In the current implementation, in each PE there is a separate memory (multiport page-memory interface memory) for the input/output buffer use. The memory is implemented with dual-port RAMs for enabling the simultaneous access from both PE processor and multiport page-memory port. As a multiport page-memory is an electronically rotating device, the interference of its rotation causes data loss. The usage of dual-port RAMs was a simple solution to the problem. However, the software has come to be responsible for the data page transfer from the dual-port RAM buffer to the local memory for further processing. This transfer is a source of performance degradation.

To remedy this, it is possible to provide hardware which takes care of the buffering of multiport page-memory port data. In that case, a destination buffer in the local memory can be assigned as the destination of multiport page-memory page transfer. When the page transfer begins, the hardware temporarily buffers the data sent from the multiport page-memory port and forwards it to the destination buffer on the fly. The data loss probability can be made reasonably low by appropriately designing the hardware's buffering capability.

The software leaves room for optimization for query processing algorithms. There is a plan of incorporating some of the sophisticated algorithms found in the literature. For example, the bucket-wise hash-join algorithm

---

[2]For the processor connected to a multiport page-memory, K/T is the time that the processor must wait for a page to be filled in a buffer. While the processor connected to a shared bus does not have to wait for a buffer to be filled if the processor's program directly accesses the page in shared memory. In this case, if P is the time for a processor to process a page, then $K/T + P$ is the time for the processor connected to the multiport page-memory to finish the processing of a page. For a processor connected to shared memory, P is the time to finish the processing of a page. For multiple-page processing, double buffering can be used to make the overhead (K/T) effectively negligible.

·[Kitsuregawa 83] is being implemented. The scheme will also be used for operations such as projection and set difference. Other algorithms will be incorporated that help increasing the processing efficiency.

For indexes, a hash-based primary index is being implemented. User-specifiable secondary indexes will also be implemented.

For the basic control mechanism described in section 3.2, there are some points where there is room for further optimizations. For example, currently, disk access specified by PE specific command and internal command processing specified by PE nonspecific command are serialized. This is done because we did not want to run the residing operating system's interrupt routine which is very slow, and we suspected that it would make the software too complex.

6   A SAMPLE INFORMATION RETRIEVAL SYSTEM

To evaluate performance in a real environment and to verify the effectiveness of the unification-based query language [Monoi 88], we used a sample information retrieval system. The knowledge base we built is a technical report database. A QBE-like user-interface is used on the PSI-II using the multi-window facility.

The technical report database contains technical reports from overseas research institutes, which were sent to ICOT on an exchange basis. The database consists of report(author, title, institute_name, keywords, report_no, date_of_issue, received_date, reference),   reference(author, title, institute_name, report_no, date_of_issue), and institute(institute_name, address, research_topic, members). Some of the attributes that have multiple instances, for example, author, keywords, reference, are represented using list structure.

First the user selects the relation(s) concerned with the query. The schema(s) of the relation(s) appear with attribute names. A simple qualification condition such as selection to a value can be specified in the schema window. The inter-relation relationship is specified by means of common variables (specifying unification-join) or by assigning separate variables and relating them in the condition window. For example, to check if a keyword is contained in the keyword list attribute the variable for the keyword (Keyword) and the keyword list (Keyword_list) are related by writing a membership predicate "member(Keyword, Keyword_list)". The output attributes are specified in the result window. The query is generally constructed using the mouse.

In the query example shown in Figure 6, a query is specified that retrieves the author list, title and re-

port number of reports that contain "database" in the keywords and that are issued by institutes that research artificial intelligence. The variable numbers such as Z101_1 are computer-generated because these attributes are specified (mouse-clicked) to be the result relation attributes without explicitly given names by the user. In Figure 6, the query language form of the query is shown in the execution window. This translated query is sent to Mu-X via the knowledge base machine interface classes. The result relation is obtained in the Mu-X and successive "get" commands retrieve the result relation into the PSI-II machine and display it.

Throughout the experience, though this is only a prototyped system, we could see that the query language is powerful enough for the implementation of an application system. Actually, the transformation of the QBE-like query to the query language was quite straightforward; it took only a week to complete that part of the system.

7   CONCLUSION

We have described the hardware, software and evaluation of an experimental parallel knowledge base machine. This can be thought of a parallel relational database machine with an extended data type. The hardware employed a hybrid shared memory multiprocessor architecture. With the software dedicated to the parallel knowledge base operations, the system exhibits a good potential for knowledge/database operations. The effectiveness of the multiport page-memory has been shown by the almost linear speedup in the net processing times of queries.

However, as is mentioned in the foregoing sections, the machine is, at the time of this writing, still under development. The more detailed and thorough evaluations are needed to examine the pros and cons of the system.

References

[Agrawal 84] Agrawal, R., DeWitt, D. J., "Whither hundreds of processors in a Database Machine?", *Proc. Int'l Workshop on High-Level Architectures*, Los Angeles, 1984.

[Bitton 83a] Bitton, D., Boral, H., DeWitt, D. J., Wilkinson, W. K., "Parallel Algorithms for the Execution of Relational Database Operations", *ACM Transactions on Database Systems*, Vol. 8, No. 3, pp. 324-454.

[Bitton 83b] Bitton, D., DeWitt, D. J., Turbyfill, C., "Benchmarking Database Systems: A Systematic

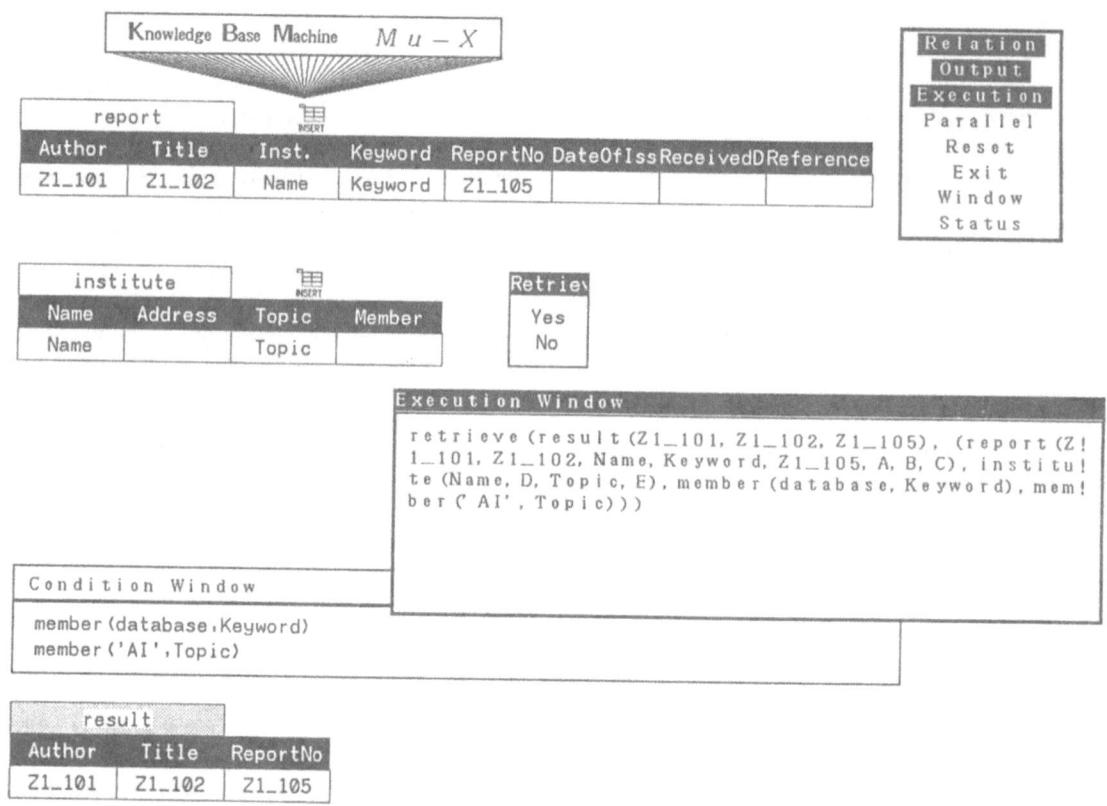

Figure 6. A query example

Approach", *Proc. VLDB*, 1983.

[Boral 82] Boral, H., DeWitt, D. J., Friedland, D., Jarrel, N., Wilkinson, W. K., "Implementation of the database machine DIRECT", *IEEE Trans. on Software Engineering*, vol. SE-8, no. 6, Nov., 1982.

[DeWitt 79] DeWitt, D. J., "DIRECT - A Multiprocessor Organization for Supporting Relational Database Management Systems", *IEEE Trans. on Computers*, vol. C-28, June, 1979.

[DeWitt 86] DeWitt, D. J., Gerber, R. H., Graefe, G., Heytens, M. L., Kumar, K. B., Muralikrishna, M., "GAMMA: A High Performance Dataflow Database Machine", *Proc. 12th VLDB*, Kyoto, 1986.

[Hanson 87] Hanson, J. G., Orooji, A., "Experiments with Data Access and Data Placement Strategies for Multi-computer Database Systems", *Proc. Fifth International Workshop on Database Machines*, pp.597-610, 1987.

[Itoh 88] Itoh, H., Monoi, H., Shibayama, S., Miyazaki, N., Yokota, H., Konagaya, A., "Knowledge Base Subsystem Based on Logic Programming", *Proc. FGCS'88*, Tokyo, 1988.

[Kakuta 85] Kakuta, T., Miyazaki, N., Shibayama, S., Yokota, H., Murakami, K., "The Design and Implementation of Relational Database Machine Delta", *Proc. Fourth International Workshop on Database Machines*, 1985.

[Khoshafian 87] Khoshafian, S., Valduriez, P., "Parallel Execution Strategies for Declustered Databases", *Proc. Fifth International Workshop on Database Machines*, pp.626-639, 1987.

[Kitsuregawa 83] Kitsuregawa, M., Tanaka, H., Motooka, T., "Application of Hash to Data Base Machine and Its Architecture", *New Generation Computing*, vol. 1, no. 1, 1983.

[Kitsuregawa 84] Kitsuregawa, M., Tanaka, H., Motooka, T., "Architecture and Performance of the Relational Algebra Machine GRACE", *Proc. International Conference on Parallel Processing*, 1984.

[Monoi 88] Monoi, H., Morita, Y., Itoh, H., Takewaki, T., Sakai, H., Shibayama, S., "Unification-Based Query Language for Relational Knowledge

Bases and Its Parallel Execution", *Proc. FGCS'88*, Tokyo, 1988.

[Morita 86] Morita, Y., Yokota, H., Nishida, K., Itoh, H., "Retrieval-by-Unification Operation on a Relational Knowledge Base", *Proc. 12th VLDB*, Kyoto, 1986.

[Morita 87] Morita, Y., Oguro, M., Sakai, H., Shibayama, S., Itoh, H., "Performance Evaluation of a Unification Engine for a Knowledge Base Machine", *ICOT Technical Report*, TR-240, 1987.

[Nakamura 87] Nakamura, S., Minemura, H., Minohara, T., Itakura, K., "A High Speed Database Machine - HDM", *Proc. Fifth International Workshop on Database Machines*, Karuizawa, 1987.

[Sakai 87] Sakai, H., Shibayama, S., Monoi, H., Morita, Y., Itoh, H., "A Simulation Study of a Knowledge Base Machine Architecture", *Proc. Fifth International Workshop on Database Machines*, Karuizawa, 1987.

[Shibayama 84] Shibayama, S., Kakuta, T., Miyazaki, N., Yokota, H., Murakami, K., "A Relational Database Machine with Large Semiconductor Disk and Hardware Relational Algebra Processor", *New Generation Computing*, Vol. 2, No. 2, 1984.

[Shibayama 85] Shibayama, S., Sakai, H., Iwata, K., "A Knowledge Base Architecture and its Experimental Hardware", *Proc. IFIP TC-10 Working Conference on Fifth Generation Computer Architectures*, Manchester, 1985.

[Shibayama 87] Shibayama, S., Sakai, H., Monoi, H., Morita, Y., Itoh, H., "Mu-X: An Experimental Knowledge Base Machine with Unification-Based Retrieval Capability", *Proc. 2nd France-Japan Computer Science and Artificial Intelligence Symposium*, Cannes, 1987.

[Shapiro 86] Shapiro, D. L., "Join Processing in Database Systems with Large Main Memories", *ACM Transactions on Database Systems*, Vol. 11, No. 3, pp. 239-264.

[Su 88] Su, S. Y. W., *Database Computers Principles, Architectures and Techniques*, McGraw-Hill, 1988.

[Tanaka 84] Tanaka, Y., "A multiport Page-Memory Architecture and a Multiport Disk-Cache System", *New Generation Computing*, Vol.2, No.3, pp.241-260, 1984.

[Wilkinson 87] Wilkinson, W. K., Boral, H., "KEV - A Kernel for Bubba", *Proc. Fifth International Workshop on Database Machines*, pp.29-42, 1987.

[Yokota 86] Yokota, H., Itoh, H., "A Model and an Architecture for a Relational Knowledge Base", *Proc. 13th International Symposium on Computer Architecture*, Tokyo, 1986.

PROCEEDINGS OF THE INTERNATIONAL CONFERENCE
ON FIFTH GENERATION COMPUTER SYSTEMS 1988,
edited by ICOT. © ICOT, 1988

OVERVIEW OF
THE PARALLEL INFERENCE MACHINE ARCHITECTURE
(PIM)

Atsuhiro Goto   Masatoshi Sato   Katsuto Nakajima
Kazuo Taki   Akira Matsumoto

Institute for New Generation Computer Technology
4-28, Mita-1, Minato-ku, Tokyo 108, Japan

ABSTRACT

As part of the FGCS project, we are developing parallel inference machine (PIM) systems based on a logic programming framework. The PIM systems include the kernel language (KL1), the parallel operating system (PIMOS) and the PIM hardware architectures.

KL1 has been designed with its parallel implementation techniques. We used the characteristics of KL1 to solve the KL1 parallel implementation issues, such as distributed resource management, goal scheduling and distribution, memory management, and distributed unification. They have been condensed into the abstract machine instruction set, KL1-B.

In designing the hardware architecture of the PIM pilot machine, we aimed at a total effective performance of 10 to 20 Mrps. We introduced a hierarchical configuration to connect more than one hundred processing elements. We provided a new instruction architecture for KL1 for the processing elements. We designed a coherent cache protocol to make high-performance clusters, each of which includes eight processing elements connected with shared memory. We designed a multiple hypercube network to connect these clusters.

1   INTRODUCTION

The research and development (R&D) of the parallel inference machine (PIM) system is one of the most important targets in the FGCS project. The PIM systems will be the pioneer of parallel processing in knowledge information processing system (KIPS) application fields (Murakami et al. 1985).

During the initial stage (1982 to 1984) of the FGCS project, the elementary mechanisms of PIM were studied from various standpoints (Murakami et al. 1985, Goto and Uchida 1985, Goto and Uchida 1986). The R&D of the current PIM system started in 1985. It includes the design and implementation of the kernel language (KL1), the PIM operating system (PIMOS), and the PIM hardware architecture as shown in Figure 1. We

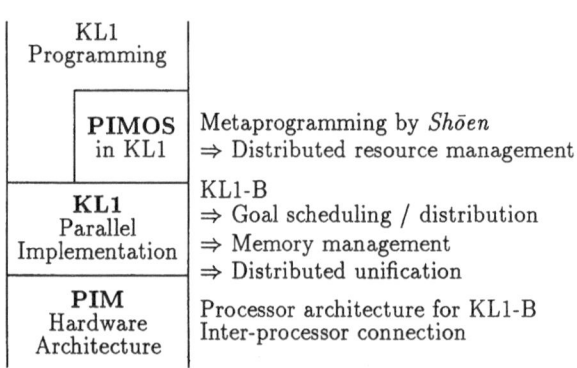

Figure 1: Parallel Inference Machine System Overview

set the following goals for the R&D of the PIM system.

1.1   Research Goals

One of our most important policies in the R&D of the PIM system is to build up a total system based on logic programming, so that the system designers of the PIM can easily look through all levels of the system in a logic programming framework. This is an important way to solve the so-called *semantic gap* argument: application and implementation are closer, therefore execution is faster.

KL1, the kernel language of the PIM system, was designed based on GHC (Ueda 1986a). The major reasons for choosing GHC as the basis for KL1 are as follows. GHC has clear and simple semantics as a concurrent logic programming language, by which programmers can express important concepts in parallel programming, such as inter-process communication and synchronization. In addition, GHC is an efficient language, in the sense that we can specify the machine level language (Goto 1987).

We hope to realize very high execution performance for the logic programming in KL1. We believe that more than one hundred times the performance of current machines will be necessary to enhance the logic programming application research. Parallel machine architecture research to date has explored many new technologies (Hwang and Briggs 1984), but there remain many unsolved problems. To achieve this performance goal, both software and hardware architectures have been studied.

Next, we aimed to build practical systems that would be available as research tools in the next stage of the project. This is essential for the application research. In addition, the development of total and practical systems stresses the importance of memory management and program control in parallel processing systems, and it also reveals the hidden problems in parallel processing.

Finally we tried to build the PIM system by KL1. The PIM operating system, PIMOS (Chikayama et al. 1988), is written in KL1 as a *self-contained* operating system. In addition, the language features of KL1 are fully used in the parallel architecture design.

1.2 Issues in the Following Sections

This report describes the parallel execution mechanism of KL1 and the hardware architecture of the PIM pilot machine. The major issues are as follows.

Distributed management for KL1 programs: The first issue in the KL1 parallel implementation is how to control the KL1 programs in distributed environments. The meta-programming capability by the *shōen* (Chikayama et al. 1988) facility was introduced to KL1 to manage KL1 programs by PIMOS written also in KL1. The next section describes how to realize the shōen facility: more precisely, the shōen and foster-parent scheme with weighted message protocol is discussed.

Scheduling/distribution: Scheduling and distribution of KL1 goals are the key issues for the efficient implementation of KL1. Section 3 describes the non-busy waiting goal scheduling mechanism, as well as the priority goal scheduling. It also shows two kinds of goal distribution mechanisms: for tightly coupled multiprocessors with shared memory, and for loosely coupled multiprocessors.

Memory management: An essential role for logic programming is to free programmers from having to perform the memory management. In other words, the KL1 implementation has to include efficient memory management schemes. Section 4 shows the incremental garbage collection mechanism embedded in the parallel KL1 implementation.

Distributed unification: We have designed the principal operation (unification) in distributed environments. Section 5 discusses how to reduce the communication cost in distributed unification.

KL1-B: The above schemes for the KL1 parallel implementation are condensed into the abstract instruction set, called KL1-B (Kimura and Chikayama 1987).

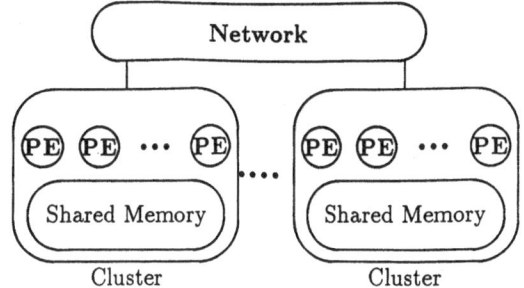

Figure 2: Abstract PIM Configuration

KL1-B interfaces PIMs and KL1, just as WAM (Warren 1983) interfaces Prolog and sequential machines. In other words, KL1-B represents the abstract architecture of PIM. Section 6 overviews the KL1-B features.

Hardware architecture of the PIM pilot machine: The hardware architecture of the PIM pilot machine is shown in section 7. We introduced a hierarchical configuration into the PIM hardware architecture (shown in Figure 2), which is assumed in the above discussions about KL1 parallel implementation. Each processing element (PE) has a tagged architecture. Several PEs form a *cluster*. All PEs in a cluster can share a memory space which is local to each cluster. These clusters are interconnected by a communication network. A shared memory in each cluster works as a local memory for inter-cluster parallel processing. In other words, intra- and inter-cluster addressing systems are separated.

The Multi-PSI (Taki 1986) system has been built to enhance the research for the KL1 parallel implementation and the PIMOS design. The Multi-PSI is a collection of the PSI machines (Nakashima and Nakajima 1987) connected by the fast mesh network (Takeda et al. 1988). From the KL1 implementation viewpoints, each processing element in the Multi-PSI can be seen as a cluster of one processor. Most of the KL1 implementation issues in distributed environments have been studied through the design of the Multi-PSI system (Ichiyoshi et al. 1987).

2 RESOURCE MANAGEMENT BY SHŌEN

KL1 was initially specified as flat GHC (Ueda 1986a, Ueda 1986b), taking efficient implementation into consideration. Flat GHC is a subset of GHC, which allows only built-in predicates as guard goals. This restriction makes language implementation more efficient while retaining most of GHC's descriptive power. Starting from flat GHC, KL1 has been extended so that it has become a practical language with the features required for the PIMOS design[1].

---

[1]Chikayama et al. (1988) describe the system programming features in KL1. Also Miyazaki (1988) in Japanese.

210

2.1 Metaprogramming by Shōen

In GHC or flat GHC, all goals compose a logical conjunction, so that the failure of a certain goal causes a global failure. However, the relation between the operating system and user programs must be that of a meta-level program and object-level programs, where the meta-level program controls or monitors the object-level programs. Therefore, it is necessary to introduce a metaprogramming capability into KL1.

The metaprogramming capability of KL1 is realized by the *shōen* facility. While tail-recursively executed goals look like small-grain threads of control (*processes*), a shōen defines a larger-grain computational unit, that is, the concept of a *job* or a *task*. It deals with execution control of programs, resource management and exception handling.

A shōen may include child shōens, so that we can see KL1 goals form a tree-like structure (shōen tree) whose nodes are shōens and whose leaves are KL1 goals. In this case, when the execution in an outside (or parent) shōen stops, all execution in an inside (child) shōen stops automatically. When the outside execution is restarted, inside execution is also restarted.

Computing resources can be managed in each shōen to avoid, for example, infinite execution of user programs. The management of computing resources is roughly implemented as how many goal reductions can be done within a shōen. The inside shōen can consume the computing resources within the amount of the resources that the outside shōen has.

A shōen is created by a call to the built-in predicate *execute/6*:

$$execute(Goal, Control, Report, Min, Max, Mask)$$

Goal specifies the initial goal, that is, the predicate name and its arguments, to execute in the shōen. All forked goals from the given *Goal* belong to the same shōen. *Min* and *Max* are minimum and maximum possible priorities of goal scheduling allowed in the shōen. (See section 3.3.)

Control and *Report* are the control and the report streams. The control stream is used to start, stop or abort the shōen from outside. The monitoring process can be informed of events within a shōen such as the end of execution and exceptions through the report stream. Exceptions that have occurred in the shōen or are delegated from one of the child shōens are reported as a message to the report stream. *Mask* is a bit pattern for determining which exceptions should be handled in this shōen. The monitoring process can substitute a new goal for the goal that has given rise to the exception. An important thing to note is that there is no failure in a shōen. Any kind of failure is treated as an exception. The logical conjunction between KL1 goals is maintained within each shōen. In other words, goals in a shōen do

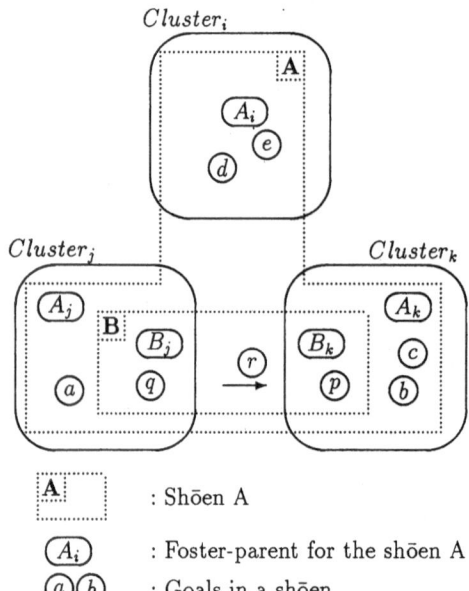

Figure 3: Shōen and Foster-parents

not form a conjunction with goals outside the shōen.

2.2 Distributed Resource Management by Foster-Parents

The main role of a shōen is to control the execution under the shōen, that is, the shōen status is checked in each goal reduction Within a cluster, processing elements can share the shōen status, so that the hardware mechanism (a coherent cache, see section 7.4) can reduce the cost of checking the shōen status in every goal reduction. In inter-cluster parallel processing, the shōen tree crosses memory space boundaries of clusters. If we simply represented a link of a shōen tree using an external reference link, the rate of inter-cluster operations could be very high and the synchronization would be very complicated. We provided a *shōen and foster-parent scheme* to avoid this (Ichiyoshi et al. 1987).

In the shōen and foster-parent scheme, a foster-parent for a certain shōen is created, if necessary, in a cluster. The foster-parent works as a branch of the shōen within the cluster. The foster-parent manages the child shōens or goals belonging to the shōen in that cluster, that is, it may start, stop and abort its children. By this scheme, most communication between the child shōens or goals and the parent shōen can be done by the communication between the children and the foster-parent within a cluster, so that the inter-cluster communication traffic can be reduced.

Figure 3 shows the following situation. A shōen A has a child shōen B and several child goals in clusters, $Cluster_i$, $Cluster_j$ and $Cluster_k$. Therefore, each cluster includes a foster-parent (A_i, A_j or A_k). The shōen

B has its child goals, p, q and r. They were created at $Cluster_j$ and were linked to the foster-parent B_j. When one goal p is thrown to another cluster, $Cluster_k$, a new foster-parent, B_k, is created, and the goal p is linked to it.

2.3 Weighted Throw Count

Termination detection of all or some processes is one of the principal functions in any systems. The end of a KL1 program execution corresponds to the end of the shōen. When all goals in a shōen or descendant shōens are reduced to null, the execution of the shōen finishes.

When all goals under a foster-parent have been reduced to null, the foster-parent sends a termination message to the shōen and disappears. The shōen seems to be able to detect the termination when it receives termination messages from all foster-parents. However, there may be goals in transit as the goal r in Figure 3.

The weighted throw count (WTC) method was provided to solve this problem (Rokusawa et al. 1988), where certain weight is assigned for the shōen, its foster-parents, and messages. The WTC can be seen as an application of the so-called weighted reference counting (Watson and Watson 1987, Bevan 1987).

In the WTC scheme, a shōen has a certain weight of negative value, and all its foster-parents and messages will have a positive weight. The following condition is kept during their execution:

$$W_{shoen} + \sum (W_{fosterparent}) + \sum (W_{message}) = 0$$

For example, when a foster-parent sends a goal to another foster-parent, the sender assigns a certain weight from its own to the goal, then sends the goal with the weight. The receiver adds the weight sent with the goal into its own weight. When a foster-parent disappears, it sends a termination message to the shōen with its weight. When the weight of the shōen becomes zero by adding the weight of the message, the termination of all goals in the shōen is detectable.

3 GOAL SCHEDULING

3.1 Goal Reduction by Register Machines

While any unifications of KL1 can be done in parallel under the semantics of GHC (Ueda 1985), we did not adopt this fine-grained parallelism, but the parallelism between goal reductions. This is because: (1) unifications are granules that are too small to implement in parallel, and (2) we can extract enough parallelism between goal reductions.

A set of candidate clauses for the same predicate is compiled into KL1-B code as shown in section 6, executed by single thread of control from guard to body. No parallelism is expected within each goal reduction.

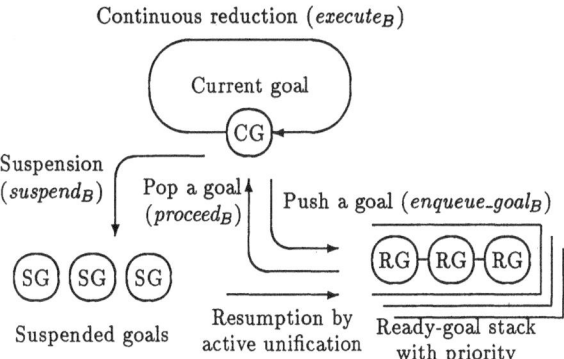

Figure 4: Goal State Transition and KL1-B Instructions

Each passive and active unification can be done by discrete KL1-B instructions as register-memory or register-register operations, so that we can expect optimization by the compiler such as in register allocation.

3.2 Non-Busy Waiting Goal Scheduling

A goal can be a *ready goal* (RG), a *suspended goal* (SG) or a *current goal* (CG), as shown in Figure 4. The *ready* goals are linked into a list forming a *ready-goal-stack*. In principle, a current goal is popped up from the ready-goal-stack, then the goal reduction is performed by KL1-B code corresponding to the goal predicate.

When any unification suspends, the goal is linked as a suspended goal from the variable which caused the suspension (Ichiyoshi et al. 1987, Sato et al. 1987). Here, the *non-busy waiting* method has been adopted. That is, the suspended goal is not scheduled until the variable will be instantiated. When a suspended goal is resumed, it is linked to the ready-goal-stack again.

3.3 Priority Goal Scheduling and Pragmas

Depth-first scheduling is, in principle, adopted for body goals. A left most body goal can be executed without pushing it to the ready-goal-stack (see Figure 4), while other body goals are linked to the ready-goal-stack.

The priority of goal scheduling can be controlled by specifying pragmas (Shapiro 1984). While each shōen is created with the maximum and minimum priority (see section 2.1), the pragmas can specify the relative priority within the range allowed for the shōen. The ready-goal-stack is managed with the priority of goals. The forked goal specified with priority is linked to the specified position. Otherwise, the same priority as with the current goal is adopted.

3.4 Goal Distribution within a Cluster

How to keep the processing load well-balanced is a key issue in making the best use of parallel processing resources. Although several ideas for load distribution

212

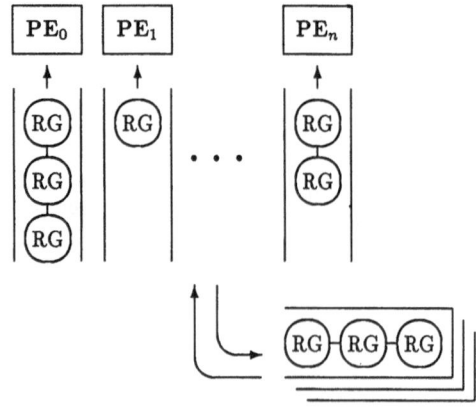

Common ready-goal-stack with priority

Figure 5: Goal Scheduling within a Cluster

have been proposed so far (Chikayama 1986, Takeda et al. 1988, Shapiro 1984), we should continue to study how to distribute the processing load. Currently the following strategies are provided in the KL1 implementation on PIM.

In a cluster, we provided an individual ready-goal-stack for the goals with highest priority on each processing element, as shown in Figure 5, to avoid conflicts of access to the common goal-stack (Sato et al. 1987). The highest-priority goals are distributed to keep the processor loads in good balance. We found *on-demand* distribution to be an effective way to realize a good balance within a cluster while reducing the amount of wasteful communication among processors (Sato and Goto 1988). In the on-demand scheme, an idle processor sends a request to a busy processor. On receiving the request, the busy processor sends the goal from its cache in the ready-goal-stack to the idle processor. These communication should be done efficiently within a cluster, so that we designed a coherent cache and an inter-processor signaling by *slit-checking* for the PIM pilot machines. (See section 7.2.)

New ready goals with higher priority than the current highest priority are possibly born in a cluster, or sent from other clusters. These higher priority goals are distributed gradually, saving the goals in each ready-goal-stack into the common ready-goal-stack.

3.5 Inter-cluster Goal Distribution

The load distribution among clusters should be done carefully because the communication cost is more expensive than within a cluster. Therefore, we provided pragmas by which users can give the indication for load distribution.

The pragmas for load distribution have the form: $goal@node(CL)$, attached to body goals as suffixes, and throw KL1 goals to a certain cluster. A body goal:

$goal@node(CL)$ is thrown by a message *%throw* to a cluster CL when the clause containing the body goal is committed to. The semantics of programs with pragmas is the same as that without them. The node (more precisely, a certain processing element in the cluster CL) that received the *%throw* message links the goal to its ready-goal-stack as well as to the foster-parent. If there is no foster-parent, one will be created on the spot. In the future, we plan to implement a dynamic load-balancing mechanism.

4 MEMORY MANAGEMENT BY MRB

4.1 Importance of Efficient Garbage Collection

While KL1 can describe synchronization and communication between parallel processes without side-effects, naive implementations of KL1 as well as other concurrent logic programming languages (Clark and Gregory 1984, Shapiro 1983, Ueda 1986b) consume memory area very rapidly. For example, whole array elements must simply be copied when only one element is updated because destructive assignment is not allowed. As a result, garbage collection (GC) occurs very frequently. In addition, the locality of memory references is not good during GC by widely used methods, so that cache misses and memory faults occur often. In sequential Prolog (Warren 1983), this problem is not very serious because of the backtracking feature. However, since concurrent logic programming languages have no backtracking, an efficient incremental GC method is important in their implementations.

4.2 Incremental Garbage Collection by MRB

Reference counting (Cohen 1981) is one method by which to recognize incrementally when a certain storage area has become inaccessible from the program. However, in reference counting, each word cell must have a reference counter field for the whole memory space. In addition, the cost of updating the reference counter is high, because data objects must always be accessed.

Several methods were proposed to reduce these overheads relying on the fact that data objects are not used very many times, and most are used only once (Deutsch and Bobrow 1976). Multiple reference bit (MRB) method was proposed as an incremental GC method for concurrent logic programming languages[2] (Chikayama and Kimura 1987).

The MRB method maintains one-bit information in pointers indicating whether the pointed data object has multiple references to it or not. This multiple reference information makes it possible to reclaim storage areas that are no longer used. By keeping information

---

[2]Another incremental GC method called lazy reference counting (LRC) (Goto et al. 1988) was designed. LRC uses two-word indirect pointers with a reference counter.

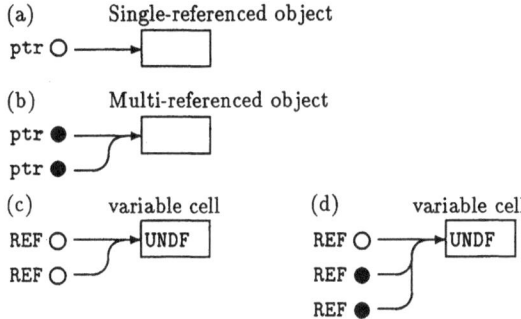

(a) Single-referenced object

ptr

(b) Multi-referenced object

ptr
ptr

(c) variable cell   (d) variable cell

REF —→ UNDF   REF —→ UNDF
REF   REF
                   REF

Figure 6: References in the MRB Scheme

in the pointers rather than in the pointed objects, no extra memory access is required for reference information maintenance.

Figure 6 shows the data representation in the MRB scheme. A single-referenced object (a) and a multi-referenced object (b) can be distinguished by the MRB flag on pointers, *off-MRB* by ○ and *on-MRB* by ●. Because of the single assignment nature of KL1, an unbound variable cell usually has one reference path for instantiating and one or more reference paths for referencing its value. Therefore, an unbound variable cell with only two reference paths is pointed by off-MRB, as in Figure 6(c). On the other hand, an unbound variable with more than two reference paths has only one or no pointer with off-MRB, as in Figure 6(d).

The MRB information on variables or structure pointers is maintained through their unification. When a unification consumes a reference path to a single-referenced data object, the storage area can be reclaimed after the unification. For example, the goal reduction by a clause:

$$p([X|Y]) :- true \mid q(X, Y).$$

is committed when the argument of the goal p is the pointer to a cons cell. Its elements are retrieved as the arguments X and Y of the body goal q, consuming one reference path to the cons cell. If the pointer to the cons cell shows *off-MRB*, the storage area for the cons cell can be reclaimed during the goal reduction.

Although the MRB scheme gives up the storage reclamation for the data objects that were once multi-referenced, the MRB scheme can greatly reduce the memory consumption rate with small run-time overheads. The MRB scheme also makes available several optimization techniques, such as destructive array element update without using the method in Barklund and Millroth (1987).

4.3 Garbage Collection within a Cluster

Data structures or variables in KL1 are stored as shared data in each cluster memory. The MRB scheme enables

storage reclamation for these data structures. Thus, free lists for data structures and variable cells are maintained. Storage allocation and reclamation are very frequent operations. So each processing element has a set of free lists for frequently used cells, enabling each free list access to be done independently in each processing element.

We use another garbage collection that is done locally within a cluster accompanied with the incremental garbage collection by MRB. This is because the MRB scheme leaves some garbages. We first implemented a simple garbage collection of so-called *copying* scheme on our experimental KL1 system.

We designed the parallel mechanism to collect garbages by all processing elements in a cluster. When a certain processing element finds the shortage of memory space during its goal reduction, it informs this event to other processing elements, after it finishes the current goal reduction. This is because garbage collection is difficult to start during a goal reduction. So, the shortage of memory space should be detected before all memory area is used up. After all processing elements stop their goal reductions, they start the copying operations tracing all active cells in a shared memory of a cluster. Here, the copying roots are the ready goals in ready-goal-stacks[3].

We also studied garbage collection schemes tailored to the KL1 parallel processing, and designed a new scheme called *Piling* garbage collection (Nakajima 1988). The piling scheme has the feature of *life-time* (Lieberman and Hewitt 1983). The piling scheme can be used with the MRB scheme, as well as can be done in parallel by all processing elements in a cluster.

5 DISTRIBUTED UNIFICATION

5.1 Export/Import Tables

A goal is thrown by the *%throw* message between the clusters. The *%throw* message includes the following encoded information: the code of the predicate of the goal, the arguments of the goal, and the shōen to which the goal belongs. The encoding of arguments (or any KL1 data) is called *exportation*; decoding is called *importation*.

In the KL1 parallel implementation a reference can be *external* or *internal*. An external reference is a reference to a non-local data. The external reference is identified by the pair ⟨*node, ent*⟩, where *node* is the cluster number in which the referenced data resides, and *ent* is the unique identification number of location of the data in that cluster.

We did not choose to take the memory location directly as the unique identification number, *ent*, because

---

[3]Export tables in section 5 are also the roots of copying operations.

that would make it very difficult to do garbage collections locally within one cluster. Ordinary garbage collections by marking or moving schemes are sometimes required even if the MRB incremental garbage collection is adopted. If the locations of data have moved as the result of these garbage collections, it must be announced to all clusters that may reference the data. Instead, each cluster maintains an *export table* to register all locations that are referenced from other clusters (Ichiyoshi et al. 1987). Each externally referenced cell is pointed to by an entry in the table, and the entry number is used as the unique identification number. When the externally referenced cells are moved as the result of a local garbage collection, the pointers from the export table entries are updated to reflect the movements.

Also, each cluster maintains an *import table* to register all imported external references. All references in a cluster to the same external reference are represented by internal references to the same *external reference cell*. The external reference cell points the import table entry and vice versa. Export and import tables are shown in Figure 7, where an external reference cell is indicated by EX cell[4].

5.2 Avoiding Duplicated Exportation/ Importation

When there are multi-referenced data objects in a cluster, they may be exported more than once. In such cases, each exportation tends to use export table entries. In addition, if a cluster imports the same data structure more than once, the cluster has to allocate its memory for the same data structure.

As multiple references are managed by the MRB scheme in each cluster, each exportation can find the possibility of multiple exportation for each data objects. Single-referenced data objects may not be exported more than once. Therefore, we introduce two kinds of export and import tables, each for single-referenced objects and multi-referenced objects. Slightly complicated procedures are introduced for multi-referenced objects to save export table entries and to avoid duplicated importations, while a simpler external reference mechanism is used for single-referenced objects.

A hash table is attached to the export table for multi-referenced objects. In case a multi-referenced object is exported more than once the same export table entry can be retrieved from the object address and used in the second and later exportations. There is also a hashing mechanism for retrieving an import table entry for multi-referenced objects from an external reference, so that even if a cluster imports the same external reference more than once, only one external reference cell is allocated.

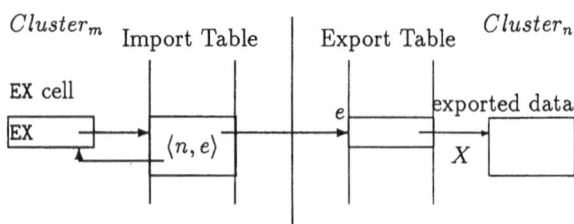

Figure 7: Export Table and Import Table

The introduction of export and import tables help reduce the number of inter-cluster read requests as follows. Suppose $Cluster_n$ exports the same data X twice to $Cluster_m$ as an argument to goals p and q. Since X is exported with the same external reference in the two exportations (by export table mechanism with hashing), $Cluster_m$ allocates only one external reference cell to X (by import table mechanism with hashing). Even if both p and q attempt to read X, only one read request message is sent to $Cluster_n$, because the first read attempt is remembered by the external reference cell and the second attempt only waits for the return of the value. This mechanism also prevents $Cluster_m$ from making duplicate copies of the same external data.

5.3 Unification Messages

In passive unification, the two terms to be unified are read and compared. To read an external reference (EX) cell to X, a read request is made by sending a *%read* message to the referenced cluster.

$$\%read(X, ReturnAddress)$$

Where X is the external reference $\langle n, e \rangle$ in Figure 7, and *ReturnAddress* is a newly created export table entry $\langle m, i \rangle$ for returning the value[5].

If the referenced cell has a concrete value V, it is returned by the *%answer_value* message:

$$\%answer\_value(ReturnAddress, V)$$

If the referenced cell is an unbound variable, the read request is suspended until the variable is instantiated. If it is an EX cell, a *%read* message is passed to the cluster that it references. When the *%answer_value* message returns, the EX cell identified by *ReturnAddress* is overwritten by the value, and the import table entry corresponding to the EX cell can be freed. This is why the cell and the entry are separate.

When an active unification tries to unify an external reference cell X with a term Y:

---

[4]EX cell is either an EXREF cell or an EXVAL cell. The data referenced by an EXVAL cell is known to have a concrete value.

[5]The *%read* and *%answer_value* messages correspond to the *%read_value* and *%return_value* messages in Ichiyoshi et al. (1987).

%unify(X, Y)

is sent to the referenced cluster. It is a request to unify the data referenced by X with a term Y. The cluster that receives the above message does the active unification after translating the two terms into internal representations. Care must be taken with the unifications between two unbound variables in different clusters, because they may make reference loops between clusters. This problem can be solved by: first compare the two cluster identifier, then make reference pointers always in the same direction, in descending order (or ascending order) of cluster identifier (Ichiyoshi et al. 1988).

5.4 Distributed Garbage Collection by WEC

Since export table entries for multi-referenced data objects cannot be freed by a local garbage collection within a cluster written in section 4.3, there must be an inter-cluster garbage collection mechanism to free those entries that have become garbage.

One way of realizing inter-cluster garbage collection is by a *global garbage collection*. We are designing a parallel mark-and-collect type global garbage collection. A serious problem with global garbage collection is that it will take a very long time.

Another is an incremental inter-cluster garbage collection. The merit of such a garbage collection scheme is that it keeps intact the locality of data access in the program. A naive implementation of the standard reference counting scheme, however, does not work correctly in a distributed environment.

Unlike the standard reference counting which assigns reference counts to only referenced data, the weighted export counting (WEC) scheme assigns reference counts, or weighted export counts (*wec*), to references (pointers) as well as to referenced data (Ichiyoshi et al. 1988). More precisely, positive values are assigned to external references (import table entries and references encoded in messages), and negative values are assigned to export table entries, so that the following invariant is kept true for every export table entry E (See Figure 8.):

$$(weight\ of\ E) + \sum_{x:reference\ to\ E} (weight\ of\ x) = 0$$

The weight of E will become zero only when there is no reference to E. As a result, export table entries can be incrementally reclaimed through the message operation with *wec*.

The WEC technique has been used in functional language implementations on multiprocessors (Watson and Watson 1987, Bevan 1987), but we introduced it for the incremental garbage collection of export table entries.

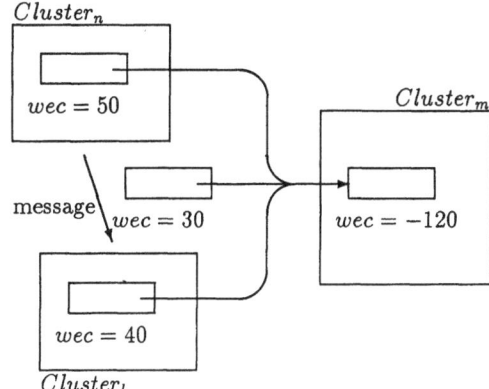

Figure 8: WEC Invariant

6 ABSTRACT INSTRUCTION SET: KL1-B

To build an efficient parallel inference machine, execution on each processing element must be as efficient as possible. Therefore, KL1-B was designed first based on sequential execution[6]. It was extended for parallel execution.

The role of KL1-B is similar to that of WAM (Warren 1983). The major differences are:

- Passive unification instructions will be suspended when instantiation of variables is required to accomplish the unification.

- The guard part is compiled so that argument registers are never destroyed before commitment.

- Instructions are arranged so that reference paths to data objects can be maintained correctly in terms of the MRB scheme.

Most instructions in KL1-B include run-time data type checks. The actions that follow the run-time type check are very different.

6.1 Data Type and Goal Record

All the memory words and all the argument/temporary registers can hold tagged words of the form:

$$\langle tag(MRB, type), value \rangle.$$

The *MRB* in each tag is maintained to show the multiple reference information. The *type* shows the data type information such as:

UNDF : Undefined variable.

---

[6]An explanation of each KL1-B instruction can be found in Chikayama and Kimura (1987), and Kimura and Chikayama (1987).

$Label_1:$ Code for the first clause
       ⟨ Head and guard part: ⟩
          passive unification instructions
          (commit)
          garbage collection instructions
       ⟨ Body part: ⟩
          active unification instructions
          argument preparation instructions
          goal fork instructions
$Label_2:$ Code for the second clause
       · · ·

       · · ·
$Label_n:$ Code for the last clause
       · · ·
$Label_{n+1}:$ $suspend_B$ pred

Figure 9: A Form of Compiled Codes in KL1-B

HOOK: Undefined variable, some goals are waiting for instantiation of this variable. The value is the pointer to these goals.

REF : Indirect pointer or reference pointer to an undefined variable cell.

INT : Integer.

ATOM: Symbolic atom.

LIST: List cell.

EX: External reference pointer.

A data structure called a *goal-record* is used for representing a goal. A goal-record consists of its argument list, a pointer to the compiled code corresponding to its predicate name, and some control information. The argument list includes atomic values or pointers to variables or structure bodies in the heap.

6.2   Compiled Code in KL1-B

A set of candidate clauses for a predicate is compiled into a sequence of KL1-B instructions[7] as in Figure 9. A goal reduction is initiated by a KL1-B instruction[8], $proceed_B$, popping up a goal as a current goal from the ready-goal-stack. Here, we assume that the arguments of a current goal are located in argument registers (Ais). For the current goal, candidate clauses are tested sequentially by head unification and guard execution to choose one clause whose body goals will be executed.

---

[7]The actual compiled code has a different form when indexing instructions are used.

[8]In this article, each KL1-B instruction is written with postfix B, for example: $proceed_B$.

Table 1: Passive Unification Instructions

KL1-B Instruction	Comment
⟨ For goal arguments ⟩	
$wait\_value_B \; Ai, Aj$	Unify two instantiated terms.
$wait\_const_B \; Ai, Const$	Wait a constant $Const$ in Ai.
$wait\_list_B \; Ai$	Wait a list in Ai.
$wait\_vect_B \; Ai, Arity$	Wait an $Arity$ vector in Ai.
⟨ For structure elements ⟩	
$read\_car_B \quad Ai, Aj$	Read car of a list Ai into Aj.
$read\_cdr_B \quad Ai, Aj$	Read cdr of a list Ai into Aj.
$read\_element_B \quad Ai, N, Aj$	
Read the N-th element of a vector Ai into Aj.	
⟨ Indexing ⟩	
$switch\_on\_type_B \quad Ai, Label_{Const}, Label_{List}, \ldots$	
$branch\_on\_const_B \quad Ai, Entry\_Table$	
⟨ Suspension and labels ⟩	
$try\_me\_else_B \quad Label$	Set a branch label $Label$.
$suspend_B \quad Goal$	Suspend $Goal$.

Note: Ai and Aj are the argument registers.

$wait\_const_B \; Ai, Const$:
     put the dereferenced result of Ai to Ai
     check the equality between Ai and $Const$
     if they are equal **then** proceed to the next code
     else if Ai is uninstantiated
                 or an external reference
              then push Ai to the suspension stack
          jump to $Label$

Figure 10: A KL1-B Instruction: $wait\_const_B$

A KL1-B code for a set of candidate clauses includes passive unification instructions for head and guard part, active unification instructions, argument preparation instructions and goal fork instruction for body part, and garbage collection instructions.

6.3   Passive Unification

Table 1 shows typical passive unification instructions and a suspension instruction in KL1-B. They include the instructions for goal arguments ($wait\_XXX_B$), and for structure elements ($read\_XXX_B$). The indexing instructions are also used to avoid duplicated operations between the head and guard part execution of candidate clauses.

Figure 10 shows the action of a passive unification instruction, $wait\_const_B$. $Wait\_const_B$ corresponds to a passive unification between a current goal argument, Ai, and a constant value, $Const$. $Label$, indicated by the preceding $try\_me\_else_B$, is a branch address when the passive unification is suspended or failed.

Dereferencing is required at the beginning of passive and active unification instructions. The data type of an argument register is first tested to see whether its

Table 2: Garbage Collection Instructions

KL1-B Instruction	Comment
$mark_B$ Ai	Set MRB of Ai on.
$collect\_value_B$ Ai	Reclaim along the reference from Ai.
$collect\_list_B$ Ai	Reclaim a list cell Ai.
$collect\_vect_B$ Ai	Reclaim a vector Ai.

content is an indirect pointer or not. If it is an indirect pointer, the pointed cell is dereferenced until some instantiated value, an unbound variable cell, or an external reference is reached.

If the instantiation of a variable (including an external reference) is required during the execution of the passive part, the test for this clause is abandoned. The variable that caused the suspension is saved in a suspension stack, then execution proceeds to the next candidate clause.

The %read message is not sent, in principle, in the passive unification instructions even when the value of a certain external reference cell is required, instead such a message will be sent in the $suspend_B$ instruction. This is because other candidate clauses may be committed.

6.4 Suspension

If no clause is selected for the current goal, $suspend_B$ instruction finally tests the suspension stack. If there is no variable, an exception of failure occurs at the shoen. Otherwise, the current goal becomes a suspended goal. First, variables that cause the suspension are popped up from the suspension stack. Then, the current goal is linked to these variables, setting the tag of the variable by HOOK, to realize a non-busy waiting synchronization mechanism between KL1 goals.

When an external reference is found in the suspension stack, %read message is sent to the node where the exported data resides (see Figure 7). The goal waits for the %answer_value message as a suspended goal.

The processing element that received %read message returns the value of the exported data by %answer_value message. However, the exported data may be an unbound variable cell. In this case, the action of replying the %read message is suspended by linking a reply_record to the unbound variable cell. The reply-record can be seen as a special goal record to reply %answer_value message.

6.5 MRB Maintenance and Garbage Collection

Active unification may produce a chain of variable cells pointed by indirect pointers. These variable cells pointed by an indirect pointer with off-MRB can be reclaimed during the deferencing. Therefore, each dereferencing operation includes the MRB test and, possibly, reclamation operation.

The MRB is maintained in each KL1-B instruction.

$collect\_list_B$ Ai:
    if MRB of Ai is *off*
        then reclaim the cons cell pointed by Ai
        else proceed to the next instruction.

Figure 11: A KL1-B Instruction: $collect\_list_B$

put_list_B	Aj	% allocate a cons cell
$write\_car\_const_B$	Aj, foo	% write the car part
$write\_cdr\_variable_B$	Aj, Ak	% allocate a new variable
$get\_list\_value_B$	Ai, Aj	% active unification

Figure 12: An Active Unification Example

In addition, several garbage collection instructions are introduced to KL1-B. (See Table 2.) The compiler detects candidate places where reference paths are added. In this case, $mark_B$ is used to set MRB on[9]. When the compiler finds a unification in which a reference path to a data object is consumed, it inserts a $collect\_XXX_B$ instruction at an appropriate place. $Collect\_list_B$ in Figure 11 is a typical KL1-B instruction which corresponds to the goal reduction by, for example, the clause:

$$p([X|Y]) : - true \mid q(X, Y).$$

This clause unifies the goal argument with a cons cell, then retrieves its elements X and Y. In this case, one reference path to the cons cell is consumed, if the clause is committed. Therefore, the garbage collection instruction, $collect\_list_B$, is executed after the head and guard part execution ends successfully. The $collect\_list_B$ reclaims the cons cell if it is a single-referenced cell (off-MRB).

6.6 Active Unification and Resumption

If a clause is selected, the body part of that clause is executed. Execution of the body part includes two kinds of operations, *active unification* and *body goal fork*. The KL1-B instructions in Table 3 and 4 are provided for them. Figure 12 shows the typical compiled code for the active unification in such a clause as:

$$\ldots \mid X = [foo|Y], \ldots$$

The structures for the active unifications or the arguments for body goals are prepared by argument preparation instructions, put_XXX_B, $write\_XXX_B$, and set_XXX_B. New variable cells or structures, such as the right-hand-side of the above unification, may be allocated from free lists or in free memory area by these instructions. (See Figure 12.) Unlike the original WAM, structure elements should not be used directly as undefined variable cells to avoid fragmentation. This is because the incremental garbage collection by MRB may

---

[9] $Mark_B$ is merged with the argument preparation instructions in Table 3.

Table 3: Active Unification Instructions

KL1-B Instruction	Comment
⟨ Active unification ⟩	
get_value_B Ai, Aj	Unify Ai and Aj.
get_const_B $Ai, Const$	Unify Ai and $Const$.
$get\_list\_value_B$ Ai, Aj	Unify Ai and a list (Aj).
$get\_vect\_value_B$ Ai, Aj	Unify Ai and a vector (Aj).
⟨ Argument preparation ⟩	
$put\_variable_B$ Ai, Aj	
	Make a new variable pointed by Ai and Aj.
put_value_B Ai, Aj	Move a variable from Ai to Aj.
put_const_B $Ai, Const$	Write $Const$ in Ai.
put_list_B Ai	Allocate a list cell in Ai.
put_vect_B $Ai, Arity$	Allocate an $Arity$ vector in Ai.
⟨ Argument preparation in a forked goal ⟩	
$set\_variable_B$ Gi, Aj	
	Gi is the i-th argument of a forked goal.
set_value_B Gi, Aj	
set_const_B $Gi, Const$	
set_list_B Gi	
set_vect_B $Gi, Arity$	
⟨ For structure elements ⟩	
$write\_car/cdr\_variable_B$ Ai, Aj	
$write\_element\_variable_B$ Ai, N, Aj	
	N: the element position in a vector.
$write\_car/cdr\_value_B$ Ai, Aj	
$write\_element\_value_B$ Ai, N, Aj	
$write\_car/cdr\_const_B$ $Ai, Const$	
$write\_element\_const_B$ $Ai, N, Const$	

$get\_list\_value_B\ Ai, Aj$:
    put the dereferenced result of Ai to Ai
    if Ai is uninstantiated
        then if Ai is linked by suspended goals
            then resume suspended goals
                $Ai := Aj$ and proceed to the next code
        else if Ai is an external reference
            then send %*unify* message
            else if Ai is list
                then do general unification
                    between Aj and Ai
                else *Failure*

Figure 13: A KL1-B Instruction: $get\_list\_value_B$

Table 4: Goal Fork Instructions

$proceed_B$	
$execute_B$	$Goal$
$enqueue\_goal_B$	$Goal$
$enqueue\_with\_priority_B$	$Goal, Priority$
$enqueue\_to\_processor_B$	$Goal, Node$

reclaim a structure body and its elements at different timing. Thus, when a structure element should be initiated as a new variable, the new variable cell is allocated separately from the structure body, and a pointer to the cell is stored inside the body.

The last instruction in Figure 12, $get\_list\_value_B$, is a typical KL1-B instruction for active unification. This instruction has one of four kinds of actions, selected by checking the data type, as in Figure 13.

When Ai is an uninstantiated variable without suspended goals, that is, the tag of Ai is UNDF, Aj (a pointer to a cons cell made by the first instruction in Figure 12) is assigned into the variable cell. Note that unbound variables are located in shared memory. Thus, the instantiation of unbound variables is done by locking and unlocking the variable cells (Sato et al. 1987). Here, it is important to shorten the period fo locking the unbound variable. Therefore, the compiler generates the compiled code as in Figure 12, where the right-hand-side structure is created first. As a result, the unbound variable is locked only within $get\_list\_value_B$ instruction.

If Ai is an uninstantiated variable with suspended goals, that is, the tag is HOOK, these suspended goals are resumed by moving the goal-records linked from the variable to the ready-goal-stack again before instantiating to Aj. (See Figure 4.) When reply_records are linked to that variable, the %*answer_value* messages for each reply_record are sent to the cluster which is waiting for the instantiated value.

Ai may be an external reference: the tag is EX. In this case, the %*unify* message is sent to the node which exported the variable. The node which received the *unify* message performs active unification on the behalf of the sender processor.

When Ai is a pointer to a list cell, general unification is performed. Otherwise, the unification fails and an exception occurs.

6.7 Goal Fork and Slit-checking

Several goal fork instructions are provided to push and pop a goal-record to and from a ready-goal-stack, or to execute goal reductions repeatedly. (See Table 4.) As in Figure 4, a KL1-B instruction $proceed_B$ pops up a goal record (a current goal) from the ready-goal-stack when the previous goal reduction did not fork any body goals. The KL1-B code corresponding to the goal predicate is executed. Assume that there are two body goals in a KL1 clause as:

$$p : - \langle guard \rangle \mid q, r.$$

the reduction of the left most body goal, q, will continue just after the current goal reduction, while other goal(s), r, is pushed into the ready-goal-stack. The KL1-B code for the above clause will be as follows.

> Head and guard execution for p.
> ...(commit)...
> Arguments preparation for a goal record r.
> $enqueue\_goal_B$ r
> Arguments preparation in registers for q.
> $execute_B$ q

The KL1-B instruction $execute_B$ q is a jump operation to the top of KL1-B code for the goal q.

Other body goals are pushed by $enqueue\_goal_B$ instructions. When scheduling priority was specified by the pragmas, the KL1 compiler generates a KL1-B instruction, $enqueue\_with\_priority_B$. When the pragmas for load distribution were specified in a KL1 program, KL1-B instructions $enqueue\_to\_processor_B$ are used. This instruction sends a message, %throw to the specified cluster instead of enqueuing its own ready-goal-stack.

The following events incidentally happen in KL1 execution: a garbage collection requirement (section 4.3), an inter-processor communication request, and a goal fork with the highest priority (section 3.4. These events are only detected by *slit-checking* in $execute_B$, $proceed_B$ and $suspend_B$ instructions, that is, the actions corresponding to these events are delayed until a certain goal reduction finishes, even if the event occurred during a goal reduction. This is because garbage collection is difficult to start during a goal reduction. In inter-processor communication or for a goal fork with highest priority, the corresponding actions do not have to be performed immediately. So, they may be delayed until after the goal reduction finishes.

As in section 2.2, a foster-parent in a cluster holds the shōenstatus as well as the information about the computing resources assigned for the foster-parent. Before $execute_B$, $proceed_B$ or $suspend_B$ start a goal reduction, they check the shōenstatus of a current goal, and the computing resources left in that foster-parent.

7 HARDWARE ARCHITECTURE OF PIM

7.1 Targets of the PIM Hardware Architecture

Our performance target in the R&D of PIM hardware architecture was to execute KL1 programs with more than one hundred times higher performance than conventional machines. To achieve this goal, we studied new processing element architectures as well as new parallel architectures to connect more than one hundred processing elements. The target processing element performance is 200K to 500K RPS[10], so that 10 to 20M RPS is expected to be the total performance for practical applications.

Several pilot machines are now being developed for the PIM research for the final stage of the FGCS project. The PIM/p is one of the PIM pilot machines, which is planned to include 128 processing elements. In the following, we would like to focus on the hardware architecture of the PIM/p.

7.2 The Pilot Machine: PIM/p

7.2.1 Hierarchical Structure in PIM/p

In the parallel architecture design for the PIM/p, we aimed to build a parallel processing architecture where the locality in communication cost can easily be used from software. We introduced a hierarchical structure, as shown in Figure 14. Eight processing elements (PEs) form a cluster with shared memory. The PIM/p consists of 16 clusters connected by inter-cluster network.

7.2.2 Processing Element Design Issues

The PIM/p processing element is newly designed for the efficient implementation of KL1. The design started by analyzing the behavior of the KL1-B instructions (Shinogi et al. 1988).

As discussed in section 6, run-time data type checks are essential for KL1-B instructions. So we introduced the tagged-architecture to the CPU design. The next issue is how to implement the polymorphic functions in KL1-B[11], because most KL1-B instructions include very different actions that follow the run-time data type check. The RISC-like instruction set can be executed using short pipeline cycles and has advantages in hardware design cost. However, considering the naive expansion of KL1-B using RISC-like instructions, the static code size of compiled programs will be very large. This problem can be solved by incorporating the features of microprogrammable processors such as PSI (Nakashima and Nakajima 1987). Therefore, we designed the RISC-like instructions with the conditional macro-call instructions for the PIM/p processing elements, so that both the advantages in the RISC-like instructions and microprogrammable processors are available in the KL1-B implementation on the PIM/p.

The principal operations such as the incremental garbage collection by MRB and dereferencing are supported by the dedicated RISC-like instructions. Section 7.6 discusses the instruction set and corresponding KL1 features. To shorten the machine cycles, the CPU was designed to execute the RISC-like instructions by four-stage pipeline. The processing element performance estimated from the compiled code is over 600 K

---

[10]RPS: KL1 goal reductions per second
[11]The detailed discussion can be found in Shinogi et al. (1988).

220

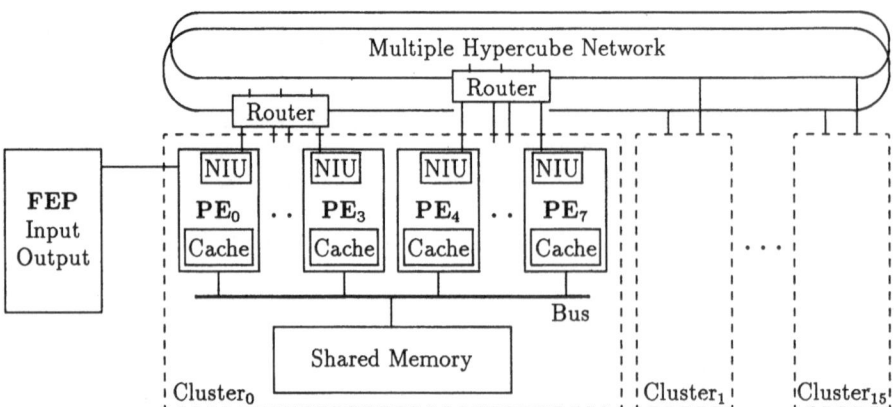

Figure 14: The Pilot Machine: PIM/p

RPS for the append program. Note that the estimated performance includes the incremental garbage collection cost using MRB. The detail configuration of the PIM/p processing elements is shown in section 7.3.

In addition to the KL1-oriented instructions, the PIM/p processing element includes the functions for the KL1 parallel implementation: an interrupt mechanism for the slit-checking, a coherent local cache tailored to the characteristics of KL1, and the network interface for inter-cluster parallel processing.

7.2.3 Design Issues for Cluster

Processing elements within each cluster share one address space. Focusing on KL1 parallel execution in each cluster, quick and exclusive access to shared data is a key issue. We designed a local coherent cache protocol for the KL1 parallel processing. Each processing element in the PIM/p has a coherent cache memory designed specifically for KL1 parallel execution (Matsumoto et al. 1987). The cache mechanism increases not only the efficiency of local execution on each processing element, but enables high-speed communication within a cluster. It is also necessary to provide an efficient mechanism to access shared data exclusively. The exclusive memory access can be obtained at a low cost by using the cache block status of the coherent cache memory. (See section 7.4.)

7.2.4 Design Issues for Inter-Cluster Network

As discussed in section 5 and 6, inter-cluster communication will possibly be required during a unification instruction of KL1-B on each processing element. That communication may include various kinds of messages. We aimed at the followings in the design the inter-cluster network:

- Enough performance for both short and long message packets.

- Inter-cluster processing where it is required.

The hyper-cube structure is introduced to connect clusters in PIM/p, placing each cluster on the hyper-cube node. This is because the hyper-cube structure enables us to shorten the inter-cluster distance with reasonable hardware costs. Each processing element has a network communication port to send and receive messages between clusters, so that inter-cluster communication operations can be done on the spot. The network router and the network interface unit on each processing element are written in section 7.5.

7.3 PIM/p Processing Element

A PIM/p processing element is implemented on a single board with about 20 static RAMs and several custom CMOS LSIs as shown in Figure 15. The target of the basic machine cycle is 50 nanoseconds.

The processing element includes two caches: an instruction cache and a data cache. The contents of both cache memories are identical. They are provided to enable the CPU to fetch both data and instructions every machine cycle. The cache memory redundancy can be useful to detect a cache memory error, because ECC is not adopted in the cache. The cache controller units (CCU) manage both the instruction cache and the data cache. The cache address array would be updated by both commands from the CPU and a common bus. To avoid the access conflict, the CCUs include two cache address arrays with cache block status.

The CPU has two instruction streams, one is from the instruction cache, and the other is from the internal instruction memory (IIM). The IIM is similar to a writable microprogram store. Hopefully, the CPU will execute an instruction at every 50 nanoseconds using a four-stage pipeline in most cases. The CPU has two co-processors: a network interface unit (NIU) and a floating point processor unit (FPU). The CPU has a common protocol to use both co-processors.

64-bit data path

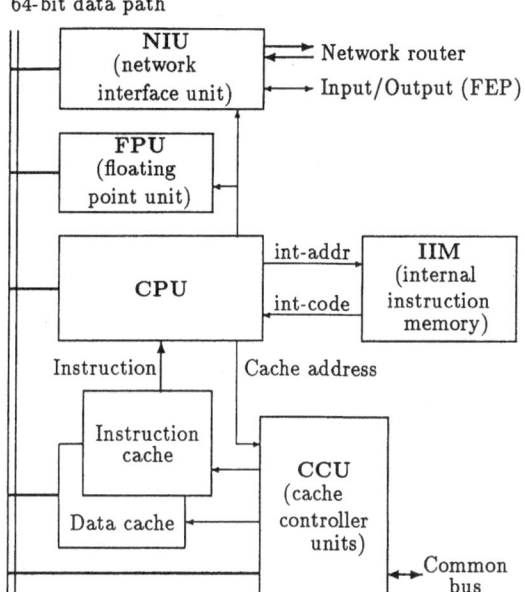

Figure 15: PIM/p Processing Element Configuration

```
63  55        31           0
┌───┬──────┬────────────┐
│Tag│ free │    Data    │
└───┴──────┴────────────┘
```

Figure 16: KL1 Tagged Data Representation

7.3.1 Memory Model

The PIM/p has a 4G-byte global virtual address space on each cluster. Taking practical KL1 implementation into consideration, 40-bit KL1 data (an 8-bit tag and 32-bit data) is necessary. However, we decided not to build a complete 40-bit system, because: (1) it may be difficult to use an off-the-shelf memory system as shared memory; and (2) instructions should not necessarily be placed on the 40-bit boundary. Although KL1 data density will be low in the PIM/p memory system[12], this will not cause performance degradation. Normal KL1 data is placed by 40-bit KL1 tagged data in aligned 64-bit words in the PIM/p memory system, as shown in Figure 16. Instructions and some data structures, such as strings or floating point numbers, are placed on a byte boundary.

7.3.2 CPU Execution Pipeline

A PIM/p processing element has two kinds of instructions, external and internal, but most of them are common. *External instructions* are used to represent compiled codes of user programs. They include KL1 support

---

[12]As an alternative to MRB garbage collection, LRC(lazy reference counting) (Goto et al. 1988) is now being examined. In LRC method, the free three bytes in each tagged data will be used as a reference count field.

Table 5: Pipeline Stage and its Operation

	Operation
D	Decode / Address register read
A	Address calculation
T	Data register read / Cache address access
B	ALU / Cache data access / Register write

instructions as well as simple RISC-like instructions. *Internal instructions* are stored in the internal instruction memory (IIM) of each processor, in the same way as in the microprogrammable processor. Small programs in IIM can specify the complex actions of KL1-B instructions. They are invoked by external macro-call instructions.

The processing element uses an instruction buffer and a four-stage pipeline, **D A T B**, to attempt to issue and complete an external instruction every cycle. External instructions are either four, six or eight bytes long, so that the instruction buffer has a hardware aligner. Each internal instruction requires two additional stages, preceding stage **D**, to set the internal instruction address (stage **S**) and to fetch the instruction (stage **C**).

Table 5 shows the pipeline stages in both ALU and memory access instructions. General-purpose registers are updated only at the last **B** stage, thereby avoiding write conflicts. Internal forwarding is done by hardware so that the result of a register-to-register instruction can be used by the next instruction even though that result has not yet been written to the general registers.

In a branch instruction to an external instruction, the branch target instruction is fetched at stage **B** in the same way as memory read instructions. Therefore, ordinary branch instructions may cost three additional cycles to branch. Delayed branch instructions can avoid the three cycles by executing other effective instructions.

Most tag branch instructions test their condition at stage **B**. However, macro-call instructions and some internal branch instructions test their condition at stage **A**. Figure 17 shows the macro-call instruction pipeline. A macro-call instruction initiates the internal instruction fetch (stage **S**) at its stage **D**, then tests its condition at stage **A**. Therefore, even if the branch is taken, a macro-call instruction costs only one additional cycle to invoke a subroutine in the IIM. In addition, delayed macro-call instructions are provided to avoid the penalty. Return from macro-call, that is, return from internal instructions to external instructions, can be indicated by a one-bit flag: *eoi*. The internal instruction memory has an *eoi* field for each instruction, so that the execution of the macro body will finish at any internal instruction except for branch instructions. (See Figure 17.)

When the condition is true:

```
D  A  (condition test at A)  : macro-call instruction
   D  (canceled)             : next external instruction
S  C  D  A  T  B             : first internal instruction
   S  C  D  A  T  B          : second internal instruction
```

When the condition is false:

```
D  A  (condition test at A)  : macro-call instruction
   D  A  T  B                : next external instruction
      D  A  T  B             : external instruction
```

End of macro body:

```
S  C  D  A  T  B             : internal instruction eoi
   S  C  (canceled)          : internal instruction
      S  (canceled)          : internal instruction
         D  A  T  B          : next external instruction
```

Figure 17: Macro-call Instruction Pipeline

7.3.3 Registers

The processing element includes 32 general-purpose registers with some dedicated registers. These registers are specified by a 6-bit register specifier in most instructions. Each general-purpose register has an 8-bit tag and 32-bit data.

The dedicated registers include: a condition code register for the result of ALU execution, a slit-check register (see sections 6.7 and 7.3.4), and a tag mask register to mask tag fields in conditional branch instructions. Most flags, such as the condition code, are placed in the tag part of the dedicated registers. Therefore, these flags can be tested by the tag-branch instructions. (See section 7.6.5)

Internal instructions can use virtual registers, called indirect registers, in addition to the above registers. Through the indirect registers, internal instructions can handle the operands of a macro-call instruction that has just invoked the internal program code. In other words, each indirect register corresponds to the operand position of the macro-call instruction. It can represent either the immediate value or the contents of a register specified in the operand of the macro-call instruction.

In addition to the above registers, the processing element has co-processor registers, which are handled only by co-processor interface instructions.

7.3.4 Slit-check and Interrupt

A hardware mechanism for *slit-checking* (see section 6.7) is incorporated into the processing element of PIM/p. A normal hardware interrupt causes automatic save of program status, however, slit-checking does not. Each processing element has a dedicated register, each bit of which can keep an individual event. The slit-checking mechanism has an additional one-bit flag to show whether any events happened or not, which can be tested by one conditional branch instruction. On

Table 6: Basic CPU Commands to the Cache

CPU command	Comment
Read	Ordinary memory read.
Write	Ordinary memory write.
Read_Invalidate	When cache-to-cache transfer occurs, the source cache block is invalidated. Otherwise, same as Read.
Read_Purge	After CPU reads, the cache block is purged. The shared blocks in other caches are also purged.
Direct_Write	If cache misses at block boundary, write data into cache without fetching from memory. Otherwise, ordinary memory write.
Lock_Read	Lock address, then memory read.
Write_Unlock	Memory write, followed by unlock.
Unlock	Unlock address.

general purpose computers, the slit-checking might be implemented using normal interrupt mask/unmask operations and cumbersome interrupt handler. It would cost too much for the KL1 system. By incorporating the hardware slit-checkinf mechanism, the processing element can avoid frequent mask/unmask operations and interrupt handling overhead.

7.4 Cache System

The design of a local coherent cache is a key issue to increase the efficiency of local execution on each processing element, and it enables high-speed communication within a cluster. Several coherent cache protocols have been proposed so far (Archibald and Baer 1986, Goodman 1983, Bitar and Despain 1986, Papamarcos and Patel 1984). Here, reducing common bus traffic is a more important design issue than reducing cache miss ratio (Goodman 1983).

We aimed to design a cache protocol for KL1 parallel execution. We developed a coherent cache simulator with a KL1 experimental system. The local coherent cache for PIM/p is designed based on the simulation result (Matsumoto et al. 1987). The simulation results have shown that KL1 programs require more write accesses than conventional languages. Therefore, we chose a write-back protocol which can reduce common bus traffic more than a write-through protocol. When a cache block is updated, the consistency with other cache is kept by invalidating the shared cache blocks in other caches. In addition, we extended some cache functions from ordinary cache protocols using the characteristics of the KL1 parallel execution. Table 6 shows the basic CPU commands to the cache.

7.4.1 Cache Commands for KL1 Support

In parallel implementation of KL1, some data structures can be known when they are not accessible. A typical example is an explicit communication between processing elements. First, a sender processor creates a message in its own cache. The message is sent to a receiver processor as a *cache-to-cache* data transfer. Although the message in the sender processor is useless after message transfer, it remains as shared cache blocks between both processors' caches. So, when the receiver processor makes a message in the same area, cache invalidation of another cache will occur. The CPU command, *Read_Invalidate*, is provided to avoid such invalidation by invalidating at cache-to-cache data transfer.

In normal write operations, *fetch-on-write* is used. However, when new data structures are created in an unused memory area, it may not be necessary to fetch-on-write. This is because the memory contents have no meaning, and because new data structure is not shared by other processors. The *Direct_Write* command is introduced to avoid useless cache block fetch from shared memory. The *Read_Purge* command invalidates the own cache block just after CPU reads the last cache block word, so that *Direct_Write* command can be used for already-used memory area.

7.4.2 Hardware Lock

Lock operations are essential for implementing KL1 in the shared memory multiprocessor. This is because exclusive memory access is required to instantiate variables in active unifications (see section 6.6) or to link suspended goals to them (see section 6.3). Although lock conflicts seldom occur, lock latency is high in KL1 execution. The simulation results in Matsumoto et al. (1987) shows that th *Read_Lock* frequency is about 7 % for data access, so a *lightweight* lock operation is required.

The PIM/p cache enables a *lightweight* lock and unlock operation by using the cache block status, lock address registers, and busy-wait locking scheme. When the CCU receives a *Lock_Read* command from CPU, the CCU checks the corresponding address tag and status tag. If the address hits and its status is *exclusive*, the address can be locked without using the common bus. The locked address is held in a lock address register.

7.4.3 Cache Configuration

The capacity of both the instruction and data caches is 64K bytes. In general, a larger cache is necessary to maintain a high hit-ratio. However, it is preferable to give up forming a large cache by enlarging the cache block size. This is because our software simulation results have found that a cache block larger than four tagged words causes an increase in shared blocks between caches in parallel execution of KL1, so that mutual cache invalidation may increase (Matsumoto et al. 1987). On the other hand, the size of the cache address array is restricted by the LSI capacity of the cache controller unit (CCU). Therefore, the CCU has a block

status tag for each 32-byte (four tagged words) block, and an address tag for each two blocks, that is, every 64 bytes. Our simulation result also shows that that scheme does not decrease the performance so much compared to a full 32-byte block cache of the same capacity.

7.5 Hyper-Cube Network and Network Interface Unit

The hyper-cube structure (Broomell and Heath 1983) is introduced to connect clusters in PIM/p, placing each cluster on the hyper-cube node. This is because the hyper-cube structure enables us to shorten the inter-cluster distance with reasonable hardware costs. In addition, the network router can be distributedly implemented on each cluster.

The network was designed aiming at the inter-cluster communication throughput of 40 M bytes/second. We chose the following configuration considering the limitations in hardware implementations. A network router was designed for six-dimension hyper-cube connection. While four dimensions are enough to connect 128 processing elements (16 clusters), the router switch will be available for the future extension. Each communication path has the throughput of a 20 M bytes/second, one byte every 50 nanoseconds, in both directions. To enable the 40 M bytes/second throughput, the inter-cluster network is doubled. Therefore, two network routers are provided for each cluster, one for four processing elements.

Each processing element has a network interface unit (NIU) as a co-processor of the CPU. The NIU has two packet buffers, one for each direction, whose contents can be transferred to and from CPU registers. A packet is sent to the other processing element from the NIU by the CPU requests. The buffer status in a NIU, full or empty, can be informed to the CPU by slit-checking mechanism. Therefore, these message handling operations can be done on each processing element.

7.6 PIM/p Instructions and Corresponding KL1 Features

This section focuses on the PIM/p instruction set and several important points in its design. Table 7 lists the notation for instruction operands.

7.6.1 Basic Memory Access and Tag Handling

Table 8 shows the basic memory access instructions. Each memory access instruction reads data to a destination register from a memory location whose address is specified by a register and immediate offset, and vice versa. The transferred data width can be 8, 16, 32 bits, 32 bits with an 8-bit tag, or 64 bits. 64-bit data is loaded to (or stored from) two neighboring registers. The memory access instructions for 64-bit data are useful to load

Table 8: Memory Access Instructions

Instruction	Operands	Comment
Read	Rd, Ra, ofst	Read tag and 4-byte data
ReadB/HW/W/DW	Rd, Ra, ofst	Read 1, 2, 4, 8-byte data
Write	Rs, Ra, ofst	Write tag and 4-byte data
WriteB/HW/W/DW	Rs, Ra, ofst	Write 1, 2, 4, 8-byte data
WritewTag	Rs, Ra, ofst, imtg	Write 4-byte data giving a new tag
PUSH	Rs, Ra, ofst	Push data into a free list
PUSHwTag	Rs, Ra, ofst, imtg	Push data giving a new tag
POP	Rd, Ra, ofst	Pop up data from a free list
POPwTag	Rd, Ra, ofst, imtg	Pop up data giving a new tag
MRBorRead	Rd, Ra, ofst	Read data with mrb OR
DEREF	Rd, Ra, ofst	Pop up data with mrb OR
DirectWrite/B/HW/W/DW	Rs, Ra, ofst	Write data in Direct_Write cache mode
ReadPurge	Rd, Ra, ofst	Read data, followed by cache purge
ReadInvalidate	Rd, Ra, ofst	Read data, invalidating other cache
ExclusiveRead	Rd, Ra, ofst	For the last cache block word: ReadPurge For other words: ReadInvalidate
LockRead	Rd, Ra, ofst	Lock address and read data
WriteUnlock	Rs, Ra, ofst	Write data and unlock address
Unlock	Ra, ofst	Unlock address

Table 7: Notation for Instruction Operands

Six-bit register specifier	
Rs,Rs1,Rs2	Source registers
Rd	Destination register
Ra	Base address register
Rt1,Rt2	Register for testing tag
R,R1,R2,..R5	Argument for macro-call
Immediate value	
imm(8/32/40)	Immediate constant
imtg(8)	Eight-bit immediate tag
ofst(8/16/24/32)	Immediate address offset
retofst(8)	Offset for return address
iaddr(16)	Internal memory address

and store the execution environment to and from a goal-record in $proceed_B$ or $suspend_B$.

The tag part in a KL1 variable cell can be implicitly loaded and stored with the data part by using basic memory access instructions. In addition, a new tag can be given in memory access instructions and ALU computation, as follows.

```
WritewTag Rs, Ra, offset, immTag;
          M[Ra+offset] ← data(Rs),
          M[Ra+offset+7] ← immTag
```

The memory access giving a new tag is a primitive operation in argument preparation instructions of KL1-B. Instructions to move the tag part of a register to the data part of another register, and vice versa, are provided as *register move* instructions in Table 9.

7.6.2 Support for Dereference and MRB Garbage Collection

In MRB incremental garbage collection, each variable cell or structure is allocated from a free list. When reclaimed, its memory area is linked to a free list. To support these free list operations, the PUSH and POP instructions listed in Table 8 are used. PUSH can link a variable cell or a structure to the free list, and POP can allocate it from the free list, in one machine cycle.

Their actions are specified as follows.

```
PUSH  Rs, Ra, offset: M[Ra+offset]←Rs,
                      Rs←Ra;
POP   Rd, Ra, offset: Rd←Ra,
                      Ra←M[Ra+offset];
```

Here, imagine ft to be the free list top pointer register:

```
POP r1, ft, -
```

allocates a cell to r1 from the free list pointed by ft, and:

```
PUSH ft, r1, -
```

links a cell to the free list pointed by ft from r1. The following POPwTag instruction is used to give a new tag.

```
POPwTag Rd, Ra, ofst, imtg
```

The POPwTag instruction is used to put a new tag in the register that has a pointer to a structure just allocated from a free list. For example, the KL1-B instruction, put_list_B, can be expressed as:

put_list_B : POPwTag r1, ft, -, LIST

The MRB of each pointer and data object has to be maintained correctly in all unification instructions. Here, the most primitive operation is MRB maintenance during dereferencing. In dereferencing, the MRB of the dereferenced result should be *off* if and only if MRBs of both the pointer and the cell are *off*. In this case, the indirect word cell can be reclaimed immediately because the indirect word cell has no other reference paths to it. Two dedicated instructions, MRBorRead and DEREF, support this operation. MRBorRead accumulates both the address register's MRB and the destination register's MRB, then sets the result in the destination register. DEREF performs MRB accumulation along with the POP operation. The DEREF instruction acts as follows. Here, r1 is an argument register, and ptr is used to refer to an indirect word cell.

$$DEREF\ r1,\ ptr :$$
$$ptr \leftarrow r1,\ r1 \leftarrow M[r1],$$
$$mrb(r1) \leftarrow mrb(ptr)\ or\ mrb(r1).$$

7.6.3 Memory Access with Coherent Cache Control

As stated in section 7.4, the coherent cache of the processing element has the extended functions for KL1 parallel execution. The instruction set includes memory access instructions corresponding to each cache function: DirectWrite, ReadPurge ,ReadInvalidate, and ExclusiveRead, as shown in Table 8. Exclusive memory access instructions, LockRead and WriteUnlock, are also provided. Incorrect use of these instructions may cause fatal errors. Therefore, the use of these instructions will be limited to internal instructions.

7.6.4 ALU Instructions

Table 9 shows the instructions for data and tag computations. All ALU instructions have two source registers and one destination register. These instructions can be classified into three kinds: 32-bit data computation, 8-bit tag computation, and 40-bit computation. Although logical operations are available for both the tag and data, arithmetic operations and shift operations are limited to the data part.

7.6.5 Tag Branch Instructions

Table 10 shows branch instructions. Each external branch address is specified by the instruction pointer with address offset (ofst). The internal branch address is specified by the absolute address of the internal instruction memory.

The run-time test of the type tag is a primitive operation to implement KL1. As discussed in section 6, most unification includes a multi-way branch for the

$wait\_list_B$ Ai, (Label):

> **if** tag(Ai) is LIST **then** proceed to the next code
>   **elseif** tag(Ai) is REF
>   **then** put the dereference result of Ai to Ai
>   **if** tag(Ai) is LIST
>   **then** proceed to the next code
>   **elseif** Ai is uninstantiated
>   **then** push Ai to the suspension stack
>   and jump to *Label*
>   **else** jump to *Label*
>   **else** jump to *Label*

Figure 18: A KL1-B Instruction: $wait\_list_B$

goal argument type. Some Prolog machines, such as the PSI (Nakashima and Nakajima 1987), have a hardware-supported multi-way branch function. However, the processing element of PIM/p does not have such hardware. This is because: (1) it is difficult to adopt a hardware-supported multi-way branch to a pipeline processor; and (2) branches taken in run-time are biased. Even a normal two-way branch can be useful enough by selecting an appropriate branch condition. Therefore, the PIM/p instruction set has only two-way branch instructions, but various tag conditions can be specified in them.

A branch condition can be specified as a logical operation between two register tags, or between a register tag and an immediate tag. In addition, a tag-mask register is used to mask logical operation (see XorMask, NotXorMask in Table 10). To avoid frequent update of the tag mask register, some branch instructions have an immediate tag mask in their operands, such as Jump$Cond$ImmMask.

In the processing element of PIM/p, various hardware flags, such as the condition code of ALU operation and an interrupt flag, can be accessed as the tag of dedicated registers. Therefore, most conditional branch operations are performed as tag branch operations.

7.6.6 High-Level Instructions Using Macro-Call

Macro-call instructions in Table 10 invoke small programs in the internal instruction memory (IIM) depending on given conditions. They are introduced to implement high-level KL1-B instructions. A macro-call instruction can be regarded as a *lightweight* subroutine call or as a high-level instruction realized by microprogram. For example, the KL1-B instruction $wait\_list_B$ in Figure 18 first tests the data type of a given argument. If the data type is the expected LIST, this instruction finishes. Otherwise, it selects the operation in Figure 18 according to the data type. A macro-call instruction corresponding to $wait\_list_B$ is written as follows, where LIST is an immediate tag value and acp is an alternative

226

Table 9: ALU Instructions

Instruction	Operands	Comment
Dop	Rs1, Rs2/imm, Rd	Normal ALU operation
Dop40	Rs1, Rs2/imm, Rd	40-bit ALU operation
Shift	Rs, R/imm, Rd	Shift operation
AddwTag/SubwTag	Rs1, Rs2/imm, Rd, imtg	ALU operation giving a new tag
AddImm/LoadImm	Rsd, imm(32)	Add or load long immediate constant
SextB/HW	Rs, Rd	Sign extension
Top	Rs1, Rs2/imm, Rd	Tag computation
PEC	Rs, Rd	Priority encode
Move	Rs, Rd	Tag and data transfer
MoveTD	Rs, Rd	Move tag to data transfer
MoveDT	Rs, Rd	Move data to tag transfer

Note: *Dop*: Add, AddCarry, Subtract, SubtractCarry, AND, Or, Xor, NOT
Dop40: AND40, Or40, Xor40, XorMask40
Shift: ShiftLeft, ShiftRight, ShiftLeftDouble, ShiftRightDouble
Top : TagAnd, TagOr, TagXor, TagXorMask

Table 10: Branch Instructions

Instruction	Operands	Comment
External branch		
(Delay) Jump*Cond*	Rt1, Rt2/imtg, ofst	(Delay) Tag jump
(Delay) Jump*Cond*ImmMask	Rt1, Rt2/imtg, imtg, ofst	(Delay) Tag jump under immediate mask
(Delay) Jump*Cond*40	Rt1, Rt2, ofst	(Delay) 40-bit compare jump
sKip*Cond*	Rt1, Rt2/imtg, imm	Conditional skip
(Delay) Jump	Ra, ofst(32)	(Delay) Jump
(Delay) JAL	Ra, ofst(24), retofst	(Delay) Jump and link
Internal branch		
(Delay) MJump*Cond*	Rt1, Rt2/imtg, iaddr	(Delay) Tag jump
(Delay) MJump*Cond*A	Rt1, Rt2/imtg, iaddr	(Delay) Tag jump at A-stage
(Delay) MJump*Cond*ImmMask	Rt1, Rt2/imtg, imtg, iaddr	(Delay) Tag jump under immediate mask
(Delay) MJump*Cond*40	Rt1, Rt2, iaddr	(Delay) 40-bit compare jump
(Delay) MJump*Cond*40A	R1, R2, iaddr	(Delay) 40-bit compare jump at A-stage
MsKip*Cond*	Rt1, Rt2/imtg	Conditional skip
(Delay) MJAL	R, iaddr	(Delay) Jump and link
(Delay) MJump	iaddr	(Delay) Jump
Conditional macro call		
(Delay) MacroCall*Cond*	Rt1,Rt2/imtg,[R3,R4,R5] iaddr	(Delay) Macro call
(Delay) MacroCall	R1,[R2,R3,R4,R5,] iaddr	(Delay) Unconditional macro call

Note: *Cond* : And, NotAnd, Or, NotOr, Xor, NotXor, XorMask, NotXorMask

```
wait_type:  JumpNotXor @r0, REF, @r2;
            DEREF ptr, @r0;
            MJumpNotAnd @r0, UNB, case_unbound;
            MJumpNotAnd @r0, MRP, case_mrp;
            PUSH fr1, ptr;
            MJumpNotXorMask @r0, @d1, wait_type;
            Nop (eoi);
            . . . . . . . . . .
```

Figure 19: *Wait_list$_B$* and Internal Instructions

clause pointer register for *Label*.

```
MacroCallNotXorMask Ai, LIST, acp, wait_type;
```

The data type tag of register Ai is tested first. If the register Ai has a value with the LIST type, this macro-call instruction simply finishes. Otherwise, this macro-call instruction invokes an internal routine whose entry address is specified as *wait_type*. Figure 19 shows the internal instructions corresponding to *wait_list$_B$*. Here, @r0 and @r2 are indirect registers corresponding to arguments Ai and acp in the macro-call instruction. @d1 is also an indirect register to show the immediate value in the second argument of the macro-call, namely, an immediate tag LIST. The first internal instruction, JumpNotXor, tests the tag of @r0, namely Ai. When the tag is REF, it proceeds to the next instruction for dereference. Otherwise, it jumps out to the external instruction specified by @r2, namely acp.

8 SUMMARY

We have described an overview of the parallel inference machine architecture. The KL1 parallel implementation issues, such as distributed resource management, goal scheduling and distribution, memory management, and distributed unification, were discussed based on the logic programming framework. These issues are implemented on the parallel software workbench, the Multi-PSI systems. We showed the design of the PIM pilot machine hardware, including its processing element instruction set. The LSIs are now being implemented.

ACKNOWLEDGEMENT

All the parallel inference machine systems research has been performed with the collaboration of all PIM and Multi-PSI research members in the FGCS project. Most ideas for the KL1 parallel implementations were born from the accumulation of their discussions.

We wish to thank all research members of the participant companies in the PIM R&D project: Fujitsu Limited, Mitsubishi Electric Corporation, Hitachi Ltd., and Oki Electric Industry Co. Ltd. One of the PIM pilot machines, PIM/p, shown in this report was designed and implemented by the cooperative work with Mr. A. Hattori, Mr. T. Shinogi, Mr. K. Kumon and all of their colleagues at Fujitsu Limited. We also wish to thank the general manager of the Information Processing Division in Fujitsu Laboratories, Mr. J. Tanahashi, and the manager of the Artificial Intelligence Laboratory in Fujitsu Laboratories, Mr. H. Hayashi, for their useful comments.

Finally, we would like to thank ICOT Director, Dr. K. Fuchi, and the chief of the fourth research section, Dr. S. Uchida, for their valuable suggestions and guidance.

REFERENCES

(Archibald and Baer 1986) J. Archibald and J. Baer. Cache Coherence Protocols: Evaluation using a multiprocessor simulation model. *ACM Transaction of Computer Systems*, 4(4):273–298, 1986.

(Barklund and Millroth 1987) J. Barklund and H. Millroth. Hash Tables in Logic Programming. In *Proceedings of the Fourth International Conference on Logic Programming*, pages 411–427, 1987.

(Bevan 1987) D.I. Bevan. Distributed Garbage Collection using Reference Counting. In *Proceedings of Parallel Architectures and Languages Europe*, pages 176–187, June 1987.

(Bitar and Despain 1986) P. Bitar and A.M. Despain. Multiprocessor Cache Synchronization. In *Proc. of the 13th Annual International Symposium on Computer Architecture*, pages 424–433, June 1986.

(Broomell and Heath 1983) G. Broomell and J.R. Heath. Classification Categories and Historical Development of Circuit switching topologies. *ACM Computing Surveys*, 15(2):95–133, 1983.

(Chikayama 1986) T. Chikayama. Load Balancing in a Very Large Scale Multi-processor System. In *Proceedings of Fourth Japanese-Swedish Workshop on Fifth Generation Computer Systems*. SICS, 1986.

(Chikayama and Kimura 1987) T. Chikayama and Y. Kimura. Multiple Reference Management in Flat GHC. In *Proceedings of the Fourth International Conference on Logic Programming*, pages 276–293, 1987.

(Chikayama et al. 1988) T. Chikayama, H. Sato, and T. Miyazaki. Overview of the Parallel Inference Machine Operating System (PIMOS). In *Proc. of the International Conference On Fifth Generation Computing Systems 1988*, Tokyo, November 1988.

(Clark and Gregory 1984) K. Clark and S. Gregory. Notes on Systems Programming in PARLOG. In

Proc. of the International Conference on Fifth Generation Computer Systems, pages 299–306, Tokyo, 1984.

(Cohen 1981) J. Cohen. Garbage Collection of Linked Data Structures. *ACM Computing Surveys*, 13(3):341–367, Sept. 1981.

(Deutsch and Bobrow 1976) L.P. Deutsch and D.G. Bobrow. An Efficient, Incremental, Automatic Garbage Collector. *CACM*, 19(9):522–526, Sept. 1976.

(Goodman 1983) J.R. Goodman. Using Cache Memory to Reduce Processor-memory Traffic. In *Proc. of the 10th Annual International Symposium on Computer Architecture*, pages 124–131, 1983.

(Goto and Uchida 1985) A. Goto and S. Uchida. Current Research Status of PIM: Parallel Inference Machine. TM 140, ICOT, 1985. (Third Japan-Sweden workshop on Logic Programming, Tokyo).

(Goto and Uchida 1986) A. Goto and S. Uchida. Toward a High Performance Parallel Inference Machine –the Intermediate Stage Plan of PIM–. In *Future Parallel Computers*, pages 299–320. LNCS 272, Springer-Verlag, 1986.

(Goto 1987) A. Goto. Parallel Inference Machine Research in FGCS Project. In *US-Japan AI Symposium 87*, pages 21–36, Nov. 1987.

(Goto et al. 1988) A. Goto et al. Lazy Reference Counting: An Incremental Garbage Collection Method for Parallel Inference Machines. In *Proc. of the Joint Fifth International Logic Programming Conference and Fifth Logic Programming Symposium*, Seattle, WA, August 1988.

(Hwang and Briggs 1984) K. Hwang and F.A. Briggs. *Computer Architecture and Parallel Processing*. McGraw-Hill, 1984.

(Ichiyoshi et al. 1987) N. Ichiyoshi, T. Miyazaki, and K. Taki. A distributed implementation of flat GHC on the Multi-PSI. In *Proceedings of the Fourth International Conference on Logic Programming*, 1987.

(Ichiyoshi et al. 1988) N. Ichiyoshi, K. Rokusawa, K. Nakajima, and Y. Inamura. A New External Reference Management and Distributed Unification for KL1. In *Proc. of the International Conference On Fifth Generation Computing Systems 1988*, Tokyo, November 1988.

(Kimura and Chikayama 1987) Y. Kimura and T. Chikayama. An Abstract KL1 Machine and its Instruction Set. In *Proceedings of the 1987 Symposium on Logic Programming*, pages 468–477, 1987.

(Lieberman and Hewitt 1983) H. Lieberman and C. Hewitt. A Real-Time Garbage Collector Base on the Lifetimes of Objects. *CACM*, 26(6):419–429, June 1983.

(Matsumoto et al. 1987) A. Matsumoto et al. Locally Parallel Cache Designed Based on KL1 Memory Access Characterstics. TR 327, ICOT, 1987.

(Miyazaki 1988) T. Miyazaki. Parallel Logic Programming Language KL1 – Its Implementation and an Operating System in It –. Transactions of the Institute of Electronics Information and Communication Engineers, J71-D(8), pages 1423–1432, August 1988 (In Japanese).

(Murakami et al. 1985) K. Murakami, K. Kakuta, R. Onai, and N. Ito. Research on Parallel Machine Architecture for Fifth-Generation Computer Systems. *IEEE Computer*, 18(6), June 1985.

(Nakajima 1988) K. Nakajima. Piling GC – Efficient Garbage Collection for AI Languages –. In *Proceedings of IFIP Working Conference on Parallel Processing*, Pisa, Italy, April 1988.

(Nakashima and Nakajima 1987) H. Nakashima and K. Nakajima. Hardware Architecture of the Sequential Inference Machine: PSI-II. In *Proceedings of 1987 Symposium on Logic Programming*, pages 104–113, San Francisco, 1987.

(Papamarcos and Patel 1984) M.S. Papamarcos and J.H. Patel. A Low-overhead Coherence Solution for Multiprocessors with Private Cache Memories. In *Proceedings of the 11th Annual International Symposium on Computer Architecture*, pages 348–354, 1984.

(Rokusawa et al. 1988) K. Rokusawa, N. Ichiyoshi, T. Chikayama, and H. Nakashima. An Efficient Termination Detection and Abortion Algorithm for Distributed Processing Systems. In *Proceedings of the 1988 International Conference on Parallel Processing*, volume 1 Architecture, pages 18–22, August 1988.

(Sato et al. 1987) M. Sato, A. Goto, et al. KL1 Execution Model for PIM Cluster with Shared Memory. In *Proceedings of the Fourth International Conference on Logic Programming*, pages 338–355, 1987.

(Sato and Goto 1988) M. Sato and A. Goto. Evaluation of the KL1 Parallel System on a Shared Memory Multiprocessor. In *Proceedings of IFIP Working Conference on Parallel Processing*, Pisa, Italy, April 1988.

(Shapiro 1983) E.Y. Shapiro. A subset of Concurrent Prolog and Its Interpreter. TR 003, ICOT, 1983.

(Shapiro 1984) E.Y. Shapiro. Systolic Programming: A Paradigm of Parallel Processing. In *Proceedings of the International Conference on Fifth Generation Computer Systems*, pages 458–470, 1984.

(Shinogi et al. 1988) T. Shinogi, K. Kumon, A. Hattori, A. Goto, Y. Kimura, and T. Chikayama. Macro-call Instruction for the Efficient KL1 Implementation on PIM. In *Proc. of the International Conference On Fifth Generation Computing Systems 1988*, Tokyo, November 1988.

(Takeda et al. 1988) Y. Takeda, H. Nakashima, K. Masuda, T. Chikayama, and K. Taki. A Load Balancing Mechanism for Large Scale Multiprocessor Systems and its Implementation. In *Proc. of the International Conference On Fifth Generation Computing Systems 1988*, Tokyo, November 1988.

(Taki 1986) K. Taki. The parallel software research and development tool : Multi-PSI system. In *France-Japan Artificial Intelligence and Computer Science Symposium 86*, pages 365–381, October 1986.

(Ueda 1985) K. Ueda. Guarded Horn Clauses. TR 103, ICOT, 1985.

(Ueda 1986a) K. Ueda. Guarded Horn Clauses: A Parallel Logic Programming Language with the Concept of a Guard. TR 208, ICOT, 1986. (Also in Programming of Future Generation Computers, North-Holland, Amsterdam, 1987.).

(Ueda 1986b) K. Ueda. Introduction to Guarded Horn Clauses. TR 209, ICOT, 1986.

(Veen 1986) A.H. Veen. Dataflow Machine Architecture. *ACM Computing Surveys*, 18(4):365–396, December 1986.

(Warren 1983) D.H.D. Warren. An Abstract Prolog Instruction Set. Technical Note 309, Artificial Intelligence Center, SRI, 1983.

(Watson and Watson 1987) P. Watson and I. Watson. An Efficient Garbage Collection Scheme for Parallel Computer Architecture. In *Proceedings of Parallel Architectures and Languages Europe*, pages 432–443, June 1987.

PROCEEDINGS OF THE INTERNATIONAL CONFERENCE
ON FIFTH GENERATION COMPUTER SYSTEMS 1988,
edited by ICOT. © ICOT, 1988

OVERVIEW OF THE PARALLEL INFERENCE MACHINE
OPERATING SYSTEM (PIMOS)

Takashi Chikayama   Hiroyuki Sato

Institute for New Generation Computer Technology
4-28, Mita 1-chome, Minato-ku,
Tokyo 108, Japan

Toshihiko Miyazaki

Oki Electric Industry Corporation
11-22, Shibaura 4-chome, Minato-ku,
Tokyo, 108, Japan

ABSTRACT

The parallel inference machines are being developed in
the Japanese FGCS project to provide the computational power required for constructing high performance
knowledge information processing systems. To fully exploit the power of parallel inference machines, an operating system tuned to control highly parallel programs
effectively is inevitable. The parallel inference machine
operating system, PIMOS, is designed for this purpose.
This paper describes an overview of the design of the
PIMOS.

The description language of the PIMOS, KL1, is based
on a concurrent logic programming language, Flat GHC.
To obtain the functionality required for writing a complicated system such as an operating system, the KL1
language made numerous extensions to the original GHC
language, mainly for efficient meta-control.

Based on the features provided by the KL1 language,
the PIMOS is designed to be an efficient, robust and
flexible operating system tuned to the parallel inference
systems. Through its development, implementing an operating system in a concurrent logic programming language has been proved to be not only feasible but also
advantageous.

1 INTRODUCTION

1.1 Objective

The parallel inference machines, PIM's (Goto *et al.*
1988), are being developed in the Japanese FGCS
project to provide the computational power required for
high performance knowledge information processing systems. A prototype parallel inference machine, Multi-PSI
(Takeda *et al.* 1988) has also been developed to promote
parallel software research and development. These systems consist of multiple (up to around 1000) processors
for attaining the required processing power.

To fully exploit the power of such parallel inference
machines, an operating system tuned to control highly
parallel programs effectively is inevitable. The system
should also be user-friendly and robust enough to be
used practically and extensively in parallel software re-

search. The parallel inference machine operating system,
PIMOS, is designed to fulfill this requirement.

1.2 Related Works

The possibility and advantages of writing a complete operating system in a concurrent logic programming language are suggested by Shapiro (1984). Based on this
principle but with much improvements in various aspects, several experimental systems such as the Logix
system (Hircsh *et al.* 1987) and the Parlog Programming
System (PPS) (Foster 1987) are actually implemented.

The PIMOS resembles PPS in many aspects. This resemblance is partly due to the resemblance of the implementation languages (KL1 and Parlog) and partly due
to intimate cooperation of two research groups.

A notable difference between the PIMOS and other
above-mentioned systems is in the underlying language
implementations. The PIMOS is designed for hardware
specially devised for parallel inference systems with very
high performance, while other systems are built upon
commercially available software and hardware. This af-
fects the execution efficiency of various language primitives differently, changing design trade-offs considerably.

1.3 Characteristics of the Hardware Systems

The hardware systems for which the PIMOS is designed
have the following characteristics in common.

Stand-Alone Systems: The parallel inference machines are designed to be stand-alone systems; not
as back-end processors of established host systems.

Multiple Processors: The parallel inference machines
have many processors that can execute different
programs in parallel. All processors have the same
functions; any processor can take any part of the
system. Job allocation is left to the software.

Loosely Coupled Processors: In the Multi-PSI system, all the processors are connected loosely via a
specially devised communication network. In certain PIM systems, several processors are connected
tightly, sharing a common bus and memory, forming

a *cluster*. Clusters, however, are interconnected via a communication network. As the inference mechanism itself is highly optimized, communication between processors (or clusters) through the network is relatively costly, and the software must take more care of keeping locality of computation. Especially, the highest cost is in the fixed per communication overhead.

Changing Parameters: We do not have much experience with highly parallel inference systems yet. Although all the parallel inference machines are based on the same design principles, various parameters of the systems may differ depending on our knowledge on such systems available at the time of their design. Also, even for one model, parameters may change in time as the system is gradually tuned up. The same applies to the implementation technique of the KL1 language. Such parameters may considerably affect trade-offs in the software design.

The PIMOS is designed keeping these characteristics of the hardware in mind.

1.4 Requirements

The following items are required for an operating system for systems built upon the hardware with the characteristics described above.

Robustness: As the PIMOS is a stand-alone system, the robustness of the system is more important than in systems based and depending upon another established system.

Parallelism: The ultimate objective of the PIMOS is, as stated above, to provide features that fully exploits the power of parallel inference hardware. Various computations required in such an operating system should also be executed in parallel. Otherwise, the operating system will be the bottleneck of the whole system.

Low Communication Frequency: As the processors or clusters are loosely connected, communication between them are much more costly compared with communication within one processor. Thus, frequency of communication between processors should be kept as low as possible.

Flexibility: As the hardware parameters are expected to change, the system should have enough flexibility to be tuned to the given parameters. When tuning by changing parameters of the operating system becomes insufficient, non-trivial re-design of the system may be required. Thus, a system is desirable on which improvement of the system itself is easy. Features enabling construction of so-called *virtual machine operating systems* are required from this viewpoint.

1.5 Organization of the Paper

The rest of this paper is organized as follows.

Section 2 describes the implementation language of the system, KL1. Many of the features of the operating system PIMOS is based upon the primitives of the KL1 language provided as its meta-level control features. Thus the design of the KL1 language, especially extensions made to its base language GHC, should be considered to be a part of the design of the PIMOS.

Section 3 describes how physical input and output devices are modeled in KL1, what kind of logical interface is provided to the user, and how they are realized.

Section 4 describes how executable programs of the KL1 language are stored and used for execution in the PIMOS.

Section 5 describes how various resources are controlled in the PIMOS.

Section 6 describes how the user programs and the PIMOS can communicate to each other, and how the communication is made in a fail-safe way to protect the PIMOS from accidental or intentional errors of user programs.

Section 7 describes the environment prepared for the development of the PIMOS and other parallel application software.

Finally, in the last section 8, a conclusion and plans for future research and development directions are stated.

2 THE KL1 LANGUAGE

The implementation language of the PIMOS is called KL1, the common kernel language for parallel inference systems in the FGCS project, based on the GHC language (Ueda 1986). GHC is a concurrent logic programming language akin to Concurrent Prolog (Shapiro 1983) or Parlog (Clark and Gregory 1986).

The merit of using a concurrent logic programming language is in its implicit concurrency and synchronization feature. Without explicitly specifying in the program, concurrency of the program is exploited and data-flow synchronization is made automatically in and under the language implementation level. Especially advantageous is the implicit data-flow synchronization mechanism which eliminates almost all the synchronization errors. In a procedural language, required data-flow synchronization must be converted to control-flow synchronization by the system program, which is one of the largest sources of programming errors in operating systems.

KL1 is actually based on a subset of GHC called *Flat* GHC, or FGHC in short. The difference of *flat* version of GHC and its *full* version is that only unification and calls to certain built-in predicates are allowed in the guard

231

part of a clause. This makes efficient implementation considerably easier, without losing essential descriptive power of the language.

However, the GHC language itself does not have enough power for efficient implementation of operating systems or application programs that require sophisticated control mechanism. Thus, several extensions are made to the language, mainly for enabling *meta-level* execution control. This section describes why such extensions are required, what sort of extensions are made, and how they are supposed to be used.

2.1 Requirements

For describing large scale programs requiring complicated execution control, a reasonable structure should be introduced to the program. One of the reasons of the requirement of such a structure is to keep each level of the structure small enough to be comprehended easily at a time. Another reason is to map the structure of the problem directly to the the structure of the program, which also helps easier comprehension.

One way to introduce such a structure to programs is by dividing the program into modules statically. Development of the languages such as Vulcan (Kahn *et al.* 1986) or A'UM (Yoshida and Chikayama 1988) are to build modular programming languages based on the object-oriented notion upon concurrent logic programming languages. This approach is known to be effective for solving many problems and the KL1 language does provide a simple modular program structure also, but unfortunately it is not enough by itself for describing an operating system.

In operating systems, *not* all objects are created equal. The operating system should be able to control the execution of the application programs, and the reverse should not hold. The program that controls the execution of a program is called its *meta-program*; an operating system is a meta-program of the application programs. This meta/object structure is not a structure straightforwardly expressed in modular programming languages.

The simplest and probably the most elegant way to implement the meta-programming feature may be providing an interpreter of a programming language (Shapiro 1984). If the operating system should interpret the application programs under its supervision, any kind of meta-control could have been implemented easily. Such an implementation, however, has an obvious drawback in execution efficiency.

The same sort of meta-control feature required in operating systems is also required for certain kinds of application programs. For example, the command interpreter shell is the meta-program of programs run under it. Programs controlling several solvers with different algorithms for the same problem is the meta-program of the solvers. The operating system is no more than an instance of programs requiring meta/object program structures.

Thus, the layers of meta-control can be nested arbitrarily many times. If the execution efficiency should be reduced to $1/r$ by using the interpreter scheme, the efficiency of a program within n levels of meta-control layers will be r^n times as slow as when it is executed directly by the machine. The partial evaluation technique can solve the problem partly, lowering the overhead of interpretation considerably. Nevertheless, it can only lower the constant factor r and cannot (with currently available technology, at least) make it very close to 1 either when powerful meta-control is required (Hircsh *et al.* 1987). Thus, to encourage meta-level control, a mechanism allowing object-level and meta-level programs to run on the same basis with the same efficiency is required.

The following features should be available in such a meta-programming mechanism.

Preventing Propagation of Failure: In FGHC, all the goals in the system form one large logical conjunction. Thus, failure of one goal in the system means the failure of the whole system. If the meta-level program and supervised object-level programs are to be run this way, failure in an object-level program will cause failure of the whole system including the meta-level program, which is never acceptable. Thus, propagation of the failure should be limited somehow to the object-level, to prevent the failure of the meta-level program.

Meta-Control: The meta-level program should be able to control the execution of the object-level programs. For example, a user should be able to stop his job from the command interpreter shell, when one of his jobs went into a meaningless infinite iteration.

Monitoring: The meta-level program should be notified of exceptional events (arithmetical overflow, for example) raised in the object-level and be able to determine what to do with such events. In general, the meta-level program should be able to monitor the execution of the object-level programs at any time, to be able to control object-level programs based on the monitored information.

2.2 The "Shōen" Feature

For introducing the meta-programming feature, an appropriate program structure should be introduced to the FGHC language to distinguish the meta-level and the object-level. The feature of *Shōen*[1], similar to the meta-call primitive in Parlog (Clark and Gregory 1984), is introduced for this purpose as a language primitive.

---

[1]The word "shōen" (or " 荘園 ") is a Japanese word that means "manor" in English.

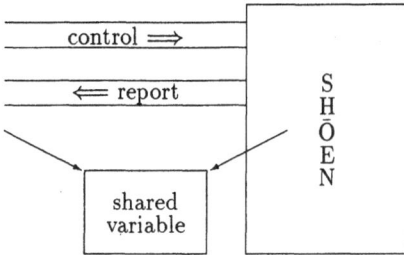

Figure 1: Shōen

The shōen mechanism can be considered to be an interpreter of the KL1 language. Although it is not actually written in KL1 but is implemented by lower level primitives, its semantics is designed so as to preserve the nature of a meta-level interpreter.

2.2.1 Creation of Shōen

A shōen is created by the following primitive.

execute(Goal, Control, Report)

This can be considered to be a call of the top-level predicate of the interpreter. Here, each argument means the following.

Goal: The goal to be executed in the shōen.[2]

Control: A stream from outside of the shōen to the shōen interpreter, through which commands for controlling the execution of the interpreter are sent.

Report: A stream from the shōen interpreter to outside of the shōen, through which various messages are sent from the shōen interpreter to report status of the computation.

Here, the word *stream* actually means a list structure used for stream-like communication between processes (Shapiro and Takeuchi 1983). Each argument will be described further in detail below.[3]

The goals derived from the original goal given to a shōen on its creation form a logical conjunction independent of the goals outside the shōen. Once a shōen is created, its execution is controlled through the *control* stream. Status of the execution of the shōen is notified from the *report* stream. Thus, as far as execution control is concerned, a shōen is a blackbox with one input stream and one output stream.

The original goal given at the creation of a shōen, however, can have variables shared with goals outside of shōen as its arguments. Goals in the shōen can instantiate such variables, thus sending information out; goals out of the shōen may also instantiate such variables, thus sending information into the shōen. In terms of virtual interpreter assumption, this means that the variables in the interpreted program is represented by the variables of the language in which the interpreter is written, as is usually the case with Prolog interpreters.[4]

2.2.2 Controlling the Execution

Execution of a shōen virtual interpreter can be controlled by sending the following messages to the *control* stream of the shōen.

Start: Start (or restart) the execution of the shōen. After its creation, the execution of the shōen is suspended until this message is first received. The same message resumes the execution of the shōen suspended by a *stop* message described below.

Stop: Stop the execution of the shōen. The execution is suspended until a *start* message is received. To allow efficient implementation, the language allows arbitrarily long (but finite) delay until the execution is actually stopped.

Abort: Abort the execution of the shōen. The execution is aborted and (unlike in the case of the *stop* message) can never be resumed afterwards. Again, arbitrary finite delay is allowed here.

In addition to those listed above, commands for resource management are also sent through the same stream (see 2.5).

2.2.3 Reporting Status

The status of the shōen are reported through the *report* stream by the following messages.

Started: Reports the reception of a *start* command.

Stopped: Reports the reception of a *stop* command.

Aborted: Reports the reception of a *abort* command.

Terminated: Reports the termination of the execution. The termination takes place when all the goals in the shōen are reduced. Alternatively, the shōen may have been forced to terminate by an *abort* message.

---

[2]In the actual implementation, it is represented by 2 arguments: a pointer to the executable code and an argument vector. See 2.6.2 for this design choice.

[3]Actually, the *execute* primitive has several more arguments, which also will be described below.

[4]Using this efficient but simple mechanism, however, unexpected instantiation of variables in the object-level may cause failure in the meta-level. In the PIMOS, it is solved by the protection filter technique described in 6.4 with the help of the unification order rules described in 2.2.5.

The first three in the above list are used for deciding the order of commands reception and other internal events. For example, when a *terminated* report is made after an *abort* message is sent to a shōen, there may be two cases: when the execution is aborted by the command, and, when all goals in the shōen has been reduced successfully *before* receiving the *abort* message. These two cases can be distinguished by the order of the *aborted* and *terminated* messages in the report stream.

In addition to those listed above, messages to report exceptions and resource consumption status are also sent to the the report stream (see 2.3 and 2.5).

Note that *failure* is not included in the above list. In KL1, failure is treated as a kind of exception (similar to arithmetical overflow). The meta-level program decides whether to abort the execution (by sending an *abort* message) or try to make it recover from the failure (see 2.3).

2.2.4 Nested Shōens

To allow flexible meta-programming, shōens can nest by arbitrarily many levels.

As the semantic model of a shōen is a virtual interpreter, the semantics of nested shōens is the same as when an interpreter is interpreted by another interpreter. It may be naturally understood that suspending the outer shōen also suspends the inner shōen; stopping the outer shōen is stopping the interpreter that interpretively executes the inner interpreter. Resuming the outer shōen will also resume the inner shōen. Similarly, aborting the execution of one shōen also aborts the execution of its offspring shōens.

With this semantics, the meta-level program can supervise object-level programs without being aware of any lower meta/object layers.

2.2.5 Order of Unifications

No order between distinct unifications is defined in the original GHC language. For example, consider the following KL1 program.

```
p :- q(a).
q(X) :- X = b.
```

Naively considering, when the predicate p is called, the unification X = b in the predicate q will fail. However, The first clause is considered to be equivalent to the following clause in the definition of original GHC.

```
p :- X = a, q(X).
```

The order of the unification "X = a" and the invocation of the predicate q is not defined. Thus, the unification "X = b" may be executed prior to the unification "X = a" in the predicate p, which will fail if this is the case.

This theoretically clean semantics brings in a problem in protecting the meta-level using the shōen mechanism. The same failure may occur even when the predicate q is called wrapped up in a shōen construct as in the following clause.

```
p :- execute(q(a), ...).
```

To avoid the above and similar problems, the following order of unification is assumed in the KL1 language.

- When there are two or more occurrences of the *same* variable, for example, several occurrences of a variable X, in one clause, they are *unified* before the body goals are invoked.

- What are passed as arguments to a body goal are the arguments as written in the program, rather than variables which will be unified with the written arguments later.

- When a structure appears in the body part, its elements are initiated with the values written in the program, rather than variables which will be unified with the written ones later.

Fortunately, there seem to be no reasons for an optimized implementation to violate these rules.

2.3 Exception Handling

Exceptional events during the execution is reported to the *report* stream of one of the surrounding shōens.

2.3.1 Causes of Exceptions

Typical causes of exceptions are the following.

- When invalid arguments are given to a built-in predicates in the body part of a clause. For example, giving non-numerical arguments to arithmetical built-in predicates, giving arguments that cause arithmetical overflow,[5] giving an index value that is out of the range of the given structure, etc., fall into this category.

- When the guards of all the candidate clauses for a goal are known to fail.

- When an active unification[6] fails.

Built-in predicates appearing in the guard of a clause will never cause exceptions. Instead, when a built-in predicate, say addition, is given an invalid argument,

---

[5]Arguments which cause arithmetical overflow are considered to be *invalid* here.

[6]*Active* unification is one appearing in the body part of a clause, which can instantiate unbound variables. *Passive* unification appearing in the head or the guard part of a clause will never give values to variables.

say an atom, it simply fails rather than generating an exception. Built-in predicates appearing in the guard part are considered to be abbreviations of unification patterns. For example, consider the following clause.

```
p(X, Y) :- X > Y | q(X).
```

This is considered to be an abbreviation of the following infinitely many clauses.

```
p(1, 0) :- q(1).
p(2, 0) :- q(2).
...
p(2, 1) :- q(2).
p(3, 2) :- q(3).
...
```

2.3.2 Reporting Exceptions

When an exceptional event is found, a message as shown below is sent to the *report* stream of one of the shōens surrounding the goal that caused the exception.

exception(Info, Goal, NewGoal)

Each argument of the exception information has the following meaning.

Info: The reason of the exception.

Goal: Information on the goal which caused the exception.[7]

NewGoal: A variable to specify a goal that will be executed in place of the original goal that caused the exception.[8]

There may be any number of shōens surrounding the goal that caused the exception, but only one of them receives the exception message. Exceptions are classified into several categories and each category is associated with some *tag* (one word bit pattern). On the other hand, every shōen also has a *tag*, which is specified on its creation by an additional argument to the *execute* primitive. The exception is reported to the innermost shōen whose tag *matches* the tag of the exception. Two tags match when their bit-wise conjunction yields non-zero. Using this mechanism, one shōen monitor can handle only certain kinds of exceptions, leaving others handled by the monitors of outer shōens.

2.3.3 Recovering from an Exception

When an exception report is generated, the execution of the goal that caused the exception (a built-in predicate goal or a failed goal) is replaced by a new goal. That goal waits for the instantiation of *NewGoal* in the exception report message and, after its instantiation, executes it. As this new goal belongs to the same shōen as the original goal, the execution of the shōen will not terminate successfully before the *NewGoal* argument is instantiated.[9]

The semantics of the language can be partly customized by specifying an appropriate *NewGoal* in the shōen monitor program. The semantics of unification can be extended, for example, by giving user-defined unification routine as the *NewGoal* for a unification failure exception.

Even when an exception is reported to the report stream of a surrounding shōen, the execution of other goals in the shōen will *not* be suspended. Whether to stop the execution or not is determined by the monitor program of the shōen via the control stream of the shōen. In parallel implementation of the language, it is practically impossible in anyway to stop the execution immediately.

2.3.4 Deliberate Generation of Exceptions

An exception report can be intentionally generated using the following primitive.

raise(Info, Data, Tag)

Each argument has the following meaning.

Info: Any data identifying the exception. The generation of the exception is deferred until this argument is instantiated completely to a ground term.[10]

Data: Any data. This argument may be instantiated, uninstantiated or partly instantiated.

Tag: An integer to specify the tag of the exception, which, in turn, specifies the shōen whose monitor handles the exception.

When an object-level program sends some information to its meta-level, the part of the data that is inspected by the meta-level should be guaranteed to be instantiated. Otherwise, the object-level program may fail to instantiate it, causing the meta-level program wait for it forever. The argument *Info* is used for this kind of information.

On the other hand, the argument *Data* is used to pass data that are *not* inspected by the meta-level program.

---

[7]In the actual implementation, it is given by two terms; a code pointer and an argument vector.

[8]Like the *goal* information, two variables for a code pointer and an argument vector are used in the actual implementation.

[9]Abortion is possible at any time.

[10]In the actual implementation, the mechanism of deferring the exception report is implemented by a KL1 predicate. However, it is a language feature from the users' point of view.

They are usually passed directly to the goal that is executed in place of the goal *raise*, by including it in the term unified with the *NewGoal* argument of the exception report. As the substitute goal is executed in the object-level, the problem of deadlock in the meta-level will not appear.

A typical usage of this feature is for establishing a communication path from a user program to the PIM-OS, described in section 6.2.

2.3.5 Implicit Stream Argument

The exception mechanism of KL1 can be explained by assuming one additional implicit stream argument to each goal. This implicit argument is unified with [] when the clause has no body goals. When it has body goals, an implicit merger goal is inserted in the body which merges as many streams as the number of body goals to the implicit stream argument, and pass one merged-in stream to each of the body goals as their implicit stream arguments.

For example, a clause such as:

```
p(X,Z) :- q(X,Y), r(Y,Z).
```

is considered to represent a clause:

```
p(X,Z,S) :-
    q(X,Y,S1), r(Y,Z,S2), merge(S1,S2,S).
```

The same rule applies also to built-in predicates in the clause body. This implicit stream is virtually merged into the report stream of the shōen, through which exceptions are reported.

2.4 Priority Management

For specifying sophisticated problem solving strategy that can fully utilize the available computational resources in an effective manner, it is essential to introduce the notion of *priority* between *goals* that can be executed in parallel and between *clauses* that can be chosen non-deterministically.

2.4.1 Requirements

In the original GHC language, the execution order of two goals can be either of the following two.

- The order is not specified. The order is left to the implementation, and the implementation may sequentially execute one after the other, or may execute them in parallel.

- The order is determined by data dependency. One can be executed only after the other makes some data available.

These two may be enough as far as there is no limit in the available resource, because, in that case, everything that can run in terms of data dependency can really proceed. However, in an actual implementation where only limited resource must be fully utilized, the following strategy is often desirable.

- The two goals may be executed in parallel, as far as both can be.

- If there is not enough computational resource (processors, for example), execution of one should have priority to the other.

Consider, for example, the alpha-beta tree search algorithm. It is essential in the algorithm to search one branch thoroughly as early as possible, to utilize its result for pruning other branches. If the search should have been made in the breadth-first order, no pruning procedure would be possible.

When programmed in sequential programming languages, strict depth-first search order is specified. The same kind of strict sequentiality can also be specified in GHC using data dependency, in which case, however, the algorithm cannot make use of otherwise available idle processors.

To solve the problem, more flexible notion of *execution priority* is required, in addition to the strict ordering enforced by data dependency. When there are several computations ready to be executed in terms of data dependency but with different priorities, and the computational resource is available only for some of them, ones with higher priority will be executed first. The essential difference with the strict ordering is that all the computation may be tried in parallel if abundant resource is available.

Priority is not something to be obeyed strictly but merely a guideline suggested to the implementation to determine the execution order of goals. Thus, goals with lower priority *may* be executed even when there exist goals with higher priority ready to be executed. How much the priority is respected determines how good the implementation is, and not whether the implementation is correct or not. Programs that won't be executed correctly without the priority specification are incorrect KL1 programs.

If priority specification should be strictly obeyed in a parallel implementation, the whole system must be inspected in each execution step to ensure that there exist no goals with higher priority. If this should have been done, the locality of computation would be totally lost.

2.4.2 Priority Specification

Two levels of priority specification are provided in KL1: Shōen by shōen coarse specification and goal by goal

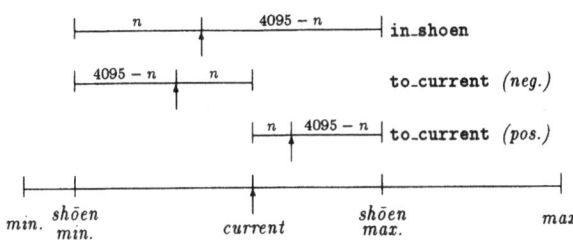

Figure 2: Priority Pragma

finer specification.

When a meta-level program controls the priority of object-level programs (for example, when the operating system specifies the priority of user programs), shōen by shōen specification is the recommended way. Priority of the shōen is specified as the minimum and the maximum priority allowed for goals and children shōens in it. They are given as additional arguments of the *execute* primitive when the shōen is created[11].

When the object-level program controls the execution of itself depending on detailed object-level knowledge (for example, when heuristics are used), goal by goal specification may be appropriate. The priority of a goal can be specified by affixing a priority pragma to the invocation of the goal (see below for details). When no priority pragma is given, the priority of the parent goal is used as the default value. When a new shōen is created, its top level goal will have the maximum priority allowed in the shōen.

In both types of specification, the priority is specified relative to the priority minimum and maximum of the immediately surrounding shōen and the *current* priority (the priority of the goal currently being reduced). There are two ways in this relative specification.

- Specifying by ratio in the range of priority minimum and maximum of the surrounding shōen.

- Specifying by ratio in the range of the *current* priority and the maximum (or the minimum, when a negative value is specified) priority of the surrounding shōen.

The ratios are given by an integer n, where $n/4095$ is the actual value of the ratio[12].

For example, priority pragma for goals is given as follows.

---

[11]In the current implementation, once a shōen is created, its priority range cannot be changed afterwards. An alternative implementation which allows it is being investigated.

[12]It is better understood as representing a fixed-point real number.

```
p(X,W) :-
    q(X,Y)@priority_in_shoen(4095),
    r(Y,Z)@priority_to_current(-16),
    s(Z,W).
```

Here, the goal q(X,Y) will have the highest priority allowed in the shōen, and the goal r(Y,Z) will have the priority somewhat lower than the current priority, i.e., that of the parent goal p(X,W). As s(Z,W) has no priority pragma, it will have the same priority as the parent goal.

Specifying priorities relatively, rather than absolutely, has the following merits.

- Local relative priority specifications are properly respected without any change when the program is run in a shōen with more global priority specification.

- Different implementations may have different physical priority ranges. Relative priority specification can be free from such implementation dependency.

2.4.3 Implicit Fairness?

In an implementation of a parallel language with limited computational resources, execution of object-level programs may make the meta-level program wait for at least a while. In a naive implementation, even if the meta-level program is about to stop the object-level program, the meta-level may not be executed forever, waiting for an infinite loop in the object-level program to terminate and yield the required resources back.

A simple method to solve this problem is to introduce implicit *fairness* to the scheduling strategy. A *fair* scheduling here means, any goals that are ready to be executed will be reduced at least by one step sometime in a finite time period. To implement this, breadth-first scheduling or introducing depth limit to depth-first scheduling has been proposed.

On the other hand, the problem can also be solved by the priority mechanism, by specifying the priority of object-level programs explicitly not to become higher than the meta-level program. Implicit fairness is not required in this case. An important merit of not adopting implicit fairness is that, when all the ready goals have the same priority (that means almost all the time when a simple application program is running without much communicating with the operating system), the implementation is allowed to choose the most efficient scheduling, fully utilizing the locality between goals. Fortunately, simple depth-first scheduling is known to yield the best results usually.

To assure that the meta-level program can stop infinite loops of the object-level programs, the priority must be respected at least a little by the implementation. What is requested is that a goal with the highest priority should be reduced at least by one step within a finite time period.

2.4.4 Priority Between Clauses

In the original GHC, when multiple clauses can be used for reduction of a goal, the implementation is allowed to choose whichever clauses for the reduction. This semantics allows the implementation to choose the most efficient reduction strategy. Consider, for example, the following two clauses.

```
m([W|X], Y, WZ) :-
    WZ = [W|Z], m(X, Y, Z).
m(X, [W|Y], WZ) :-
    WZ = [W|Z], m(X, Y, Z).
```

When the first argument is on a remote processor and the second argument is already known to be instantiated to a list cell on the currently executing processor, the implementation is allowed to choose the second clause without even trying to access the first argument.

With this mechanism, however, preference between clauses cannot be specified in the program. For example, again in an alpha-beta search program, when a new maximum (or minimum) value is found by a child node, that data should be used to control other children nodes more efficiently. If that value is not yet available, the goal will continue with the already known maximum (or minimum). In this case, the clause waiting for the report of new maximum/minimum values should have priority to other clauses.

Specification of priority between multiple candidate clauses are thus introduced to the KL1 language. For example, the above merger program will become a priority merger by adding priority specification between clauses as follows.

```
m([W|X], Y, WZ) :-
    WZ = [W|Z], m(X, Y, Z).
alternatively.
m(X, [W|Y], WZ) :-
    WZ = [W|Z], m(X, Y, Z).
```

Note that the second clause is tried not only when the first clause fails but also when it *suspends*. Thus, it is *not* something like the sequential OR feature seen in Parlog or the *otherwise* feature in Concurrent Prolog.[13]

Similar to priority between goals, the implementation does not have to fully obey the priority specification. In the above example of the priority merger, the second

clause *may* be chosen even after the first argument is already instantiated to a list cell. Execution efficiency will be considerably lost in implementations on parallel hardware if the specification must be obeyed perfectly. What is requested is that the first clause will be chosen sometime within a finite time period even when the second clause can be chosen for infinitely many times.

In the implementation level, the clause with priority will always be used for the reduction as far as all the required data are available within the processor reducing the goal. Otherwise, the second clause may be used but fetching of the data required for reduction by the first clause from remote processors is initiated, even though it is not required for this particular reduction. It will eventually make the first clause ready to be chosen.

2.5 Quantitative Control

As described above, information such as the termination of the computation or emergence of exceptions are notified to the meta-level through the report stream of the shōen. Execution control of shōens to suspend, resume or abort the execution of a shōen is also provided through the control stream.

These features are *qualitative* in that the controlled shōen either can proceed or not. To control the meta-level behavior of the object-level program more into its detail, features to *quantitatively* control the object-level computation are required, in addition to the qualitative control features. Quantitative control is to control meta-level quantities of computation, such as *how much* computation should be allowed for a shōen.

The quantitative control features cannot be efficiently realized easily without certain language level support. The KL1 language thus provides not only the qualitative meta-control, but also quantitative meta-control features as its language primitives.

2.5.1 Principles

The shōen, which is the unit for qualitative execution control, is also used as the unit for quantitative control. Using the same shōen mechanism is profitable in making additional overhead smaller.

Although each program runs differently depending on the problem and the algorithm, lower level notions such as how much processing time or how much memory area the computation consumes can be reasonable common measures for all kinds of programs. Thus, such lower level quantities are controlled by the feature.

The simplest method may be to report each execution step in the object-level to the meta-level. This method, however, requires large a amount of communication between two levels. In KL1, the meta-level sets some limit to the resource consumption of the object-level program, and the object-level only reports the *resource_low* status

---

[13]The KL1 language also provides the sequential OR feature. The sequential OR and *otherwise* directives can, however, be replaced by writing negation of the guard parts of all the preceding clauses. Thus, although such language constructs are quite useful, they merely provide a syntactic convention without extending the essential descriptive power of the language.

to the meta-level when the allowed amount of resource has *almost* been consumed up. If the resource consumption actually reaches the limit, then the execution is suspended until the limit is raised by the meta-level program.

Receiving the *resource_low* report, the meta-level program can choose from the following.

- Add some more to the limit to make the object-level computation continue.

- Abort the object-level computation by sending an *abort* message to the control stream.

- Suspend that computation but freeze the computation status as it is (by simply *not* adding any more to the limit), until possible future resumption.

When the computation should be continued, the meta-level program will add some more amount to the resource consumption limit. However, there may be some delay due to computation required for such a decision or for communication between processors. Thus, the report is made somewhat before the given resource is completely exhausted. This allows pipelined resource supply.

Setting small resource consumption limit and adding to it a small amount frequently, more accurate resource consumption control is possible. However, it may require more resource handling overhead. The accuracy of resource management is a parameter of the system that can be defined by the meta-level program considering this trade-off.

2.5.2 Nested Resource Management

The resource management principle of KL1 is also based on the assumption that shōen is a machine-level interpreter. The virtual interpreter is assumed to be counting the resource consumption.

The virtual interpreter is considered to be made so efficient that interpretation of a program consumes only the same amount of the resource as when the interpreted program is executed directly.

When shōens are nested, the inner interpreter is interpreted by the outer interpreter. If the outer interpreter detects that the resource consumption limit has been reached, it will suspend interpretation until some more resource consumption is allowed. Naturally, the inner interpreter is forced to stop there.

With this semantics, the meta-level program can control resource consumption of the object-level programs without being aware of lower level meta/object layers.

2.5.3 Controlled Quantities

The following are the candidates of resources controlled by the mechanism.

Time: How much CPU time can be used for the execution of the shōen.

Space: How much memory can be used for the execution of the shōen.

In stead of measuring the CPU time, the current implementation counts the number of reductions as its estimate. The current implementation does not count the memory consumption.

For about memory consumption, the garbage collection mechanism makes fair management difficult. As the same memory area can be made available again by garbage collections, such reuse should not be counted as *consumption*. However, a data structure created in one shōen may be passed to another and then garbage-collected. Memorizing all such data transfer has too much overhead. In addition, notifying garbage collector of the affinity of memory blocks to shōens will be quite costly.

Another difficulty is in unbalanced resource consumption. When multiple processors are available, one program may consume much memory on one processor but not on others. To cope with such cases, memory consumption management in terms of total amount of allocated memory is never enough; some amount of memory consumption in one processor is not equivalent to that amount of consumption in another processor. This problem is left over as a further research theme.

2.5.4 Resource Management Messages

Communication required for resource management is effected through the control and report streams of shōen.

When the resource consumption limit is reaching in a shōen, a *resource_low* message is sent to the report stream. Adding some amount to the resource limit of a shoen is effected by sending an *add_resource(Amount)* message. In response to this message, a *resource_added* message is sent to the report stream. Watching the order of this message and a *resource_low* message, it is possible to know whether resource left is found to be low *before* the resource addition is made or it became low even *after* the addition.

To query the resource consumption status, the control message *statistics* can be used. As a direct response to this message, the *statistics_started* message is sent back from the report stream. Sometime after that, a *statistics(Status)* is sent to the report stream, bringing the resource consumption statistics in its argument. The reported resource consumption status is that of sometime in between the two time points at which these messages are issued.

2.6 Executable Code

To be a self-contained computer system, programs in the system must be handled by the system itself. The KL1 language thus provides features to handle executable codes as data.

2.6.1 Module and Code Data Types

A block of object code for KL1 programs can be handled as a data object of type *module*. One module may contain executable codes for several predicates. Predicates declared to be *public* in the source program are registered in a certain table in the corresponding module data object, which can be accessed using a built-in predicate. Such predicates entries can be handled as a data object of type *code*. Other predicates are local and can be invoked only from inside of the module.

Module and code data objects are treated basically the same as data objects of other types; they can be passed as arguments, stored in structures, garbage-collected if no access path remains to them, etc.

A module data structure consists of two parts: *GC part* where pointers to other data are stored and *non-GC part* where only atomic data, mainly executable KL1-B code (Kimura and Chikayama 1987), are stored. All accesses to data outside of a module is made via pointers stored in the GC part. The GC part can contain pointers to uninstantiated variables. Thus, when created, modules can contain an invocation of a module that is not defined yet. Accesses to such a module before its definition will be simply suspended. Later instantiation of the variable will make it proceed. It is along the principle that executable codes should be treated the same as other data objects.

The non-GC part of modules contains lower-level machine code. Thus, if module data objects can be arbitrarily created, any protection mechanism above the KL1 language level may be violated. To avoid this, the built-in predicate for creation of modules is not made available to user programs. This is realized simply by not including it in the built-in predicate table of the compiler when it is in the application program compilation mode. User programs can only create module data objects by asking the PIMOS for compilation of source programs, which will never generate problematic codes.

Creation of a module is suspended until all of the elements of its non-GC part becomes instantiated, and they are fully dereferenced during the creation; the low-level execution mechanism can safely assume that executable machine code is already there.

2.6.2 Higher Order Mechanism

The code object can be used for execution by the built-in predicate *apply*. The *apply* predicate takes two arguments: The code for a predicate and a vector of arguments. When either one of these are still uninstantiated on an invocation of *apply*, it is suspended until both get instantiated.

The *apply* built-in predicate is a higher order extension to the language. The shōen feature described above also takes this higher order approach for treating executable code. Some other concurrent logic programming languages adopt meta-level mechanism, in which usual data structures such as p(X) are treated as executable code (Clark and Gregory 1986). This approach, however, assumes that the mapping from predicate name (the atom p) to the corresponding executable code is available completely in the language implementation level.

When the higher order invocation mechanism is available, the meta-level feature can be implemented in the software, allowing full flexibility in name/code mapping to the software. Section 4 describes how such mapping is implemented in the PIMOS.

2.7 Other Extensions

In addition to the extensions required for meta-level programming, several other extensions to the original GHC language are made in the KL1 language. They are mainly for providing efficient primitives, which, however, affected the design of the PIMOS considerably.

2.7.1 Random Access Structures

Many of the implementation level optimization of the KL1 language are based on the low-level mechanism that distinguishes multiple and single reference paths to data objects. Such information is kept in pointers using one bit tag called the multiple reference bit (MRB) (Chikayama and Kimura 1988). At the implementation level, the information is used mainly for incremental garbage collection. When the sole reference path to an object is known to be required no longer, that object can be reclaimed.

This single reference information can be utilized to implement efficient random access structures. The KL1 language has one-dimensional array structure data type called *vector*.[14] Updating an element of a vector can be effected by the following built-in predicate.

set_vector_element(OldV, N, OldE, NewE, NewV)

The arguments have the following meaning.

OldV: The original vector structure.

N: Index of the element to be updated.

OldE: The *N*th element of the original vector.

---

[14]Usual functor structures such as "f(X)" are also represented using the vector structures such as "{f, X}".

NewE: The Nth element of the newly created vector.

NewV: The newly created vector with the same length and elements as the original vector, except that the Nth element is replaced with *NewE*.

As far as the semantics is concerned, this predicate has no side-effects. It allocates a copy of the original vector with Nth element altered to *NewE*. A naive faithful implementation of this, however, requires time and space proportional to the size of the vector. When the reference path to the original vector is known to be the last one, that data structure can be destructively updated in constant time with no memory allocation, without disturbing the pure semantics.

The semantics of the language is not affected by the existence of such an optimization. However, when such an operation is known to be efficient, use of random access structures is strongly encouraged and the programming style of KL1 may become drastically different.

There exist sequentiality between element accesses to (physically) the same (but logically different) vector. The updated vector can be accessed only after the update procedure is completed. The execution of the *set_vector_element* predicate is automatically suspended until its first and second arguments become instantiated. Note, however, that the *NewE* argument need not be instantiated on update. The corresponding element of the new vector will simply become that uninstantiated variable. Consider, for example, the following process-like program.

```
table([update(N,X)|S], OV) :-
    set_vector_element(OV, N, OE, NE, NV),
    compute(OE, X, NE),
    table(S, NV).
```

The `compute` predicate computes the new element value from its previous value and the data supplied with the message. In a parallel implementation, the call of `compute` and the recursive call of `table` can be executed in parallel. If the next message is updating the same element, it will be suspended naturally because data required for `compute` is not available yet. If it is updating a different element, however, `compute` for that message can be executed in parallel with the first one.

2.7.2 Merger

As stream-like communication using list structures is a frequently used programming technique (Shapiro and Takeuchi 1983), the efficiency of stream merge operation can be a key of the overall efficiency of the system. Thus, a stream merging mechanism is built into the system. Again, it does not affect the semantics of the language but does affect the programming style considerably.

A merger process is created by the following built-in predicate.

merge(In, Out)

Immediately after the invocation, the merger is merging only one input stream to the output stream (this, of course, is not a merger yet). Its semantics can given by the following clauses.

```
merge([],      O ) :- O = [].
merge([X|I], XO) :- XO = [X|O], merge(I, O).
```

More input streams can be added by unifying the input stream argument to a vector structure whose elements are streams to be merged in. This feature can be described by the following additional (infinite number of) clauses (curly brackets are used to denote *vector* structures).

```
merge({},         O) :- O = [].
merge({I},        O) :- merge(I, O).
merge({I1,I2},    O) :- merge(I1, I2, O).
merge({I1,I2,I3}, O) :- merge(I1, I2, I3, O).
...
```

The `merge` predicates with three or more arguments also have clauses for increasing the number of merged streams, in addition to the clauses for actual merging.

This description in the KL1 language gives the semantics but the actual implementation is of course quite different. It is highly optimized using the MRB information.

For increasing the number of input streams, the vector structure is used directly as the argument of merge.[15] This scheme is advantageous to the scheme using a special message for that purpose (Ueda and Chikayama 1984) in that no reserved *message* is used; addition of merged streams is specified by the argument itself rather than the *car* part of the list structure, where a message should be. Uninstantiated messages can go through the merger, because, although being uninstantiated, they are known to be a message that goes through the merger and not something controlling the merger. The basic mechanism of the stream communication using list structures is that, communication control is done by the *cdr* part which is a list cell or nil, and the *car* part brings a message. The scheme adopted in KL1 keeps this principle of using only the *cdr* part for controlling the communication.

3   INPUT AND OUTPUT

This section describes how physical I/O devices are modeled in KL1, what kind of logical I/O interface the PIM-OS provides to the user, and how they are realized.

---

[15] Any structures other than lists could have been used here. The vector structure is used only because it is the most efficiently handled structure.

242

3.1 Model of Physical Devices

I/O devices can be modeled by processes of KL1. In a certain layer of the PIMOS, I/O devices behaves the same as KL1 processes.

A one-line display device can be modeled by the following KL1 clauses.

```
line_display([display(S)|R], E, _) :-
    wait(S) |
    line_display(R, E, S).
alternatively.
  line_display(R, E, S) :-
    E = [photons(S)|E1],
    line_display(R, E1, S).
```

The device is always radiating `photons` messages describing the string displayed to the *ether* (via the stream E in the program). The displayed string can be changed by receiving a request `display` from the host (via the stream R) with its argument being a new string.

A character input device can be modeled by the following KL1 clause.

```
char_input(O, [stroke(C)|K]) :-
    O = [C|O1],
    char_input(O1, K).
```

Unlike in the case of output devices, the communication stream (O in this case) flows from the device to the host. The device simply sends all the characters typed in to its output stream. Buffering is implicitly effected by the output stream.

An explicitly buffered character input device can be modeled by the following KL1 clauses.

```
char_input(R, [stroke(C)|K], B, T) :-
    T = [C|T1],
    char_input(R, K, B, T1).
  char_input([get(X)|R], K, [C|B], T) :-
    X = C,
    char_input(R, K, B, T).
```

In this model, direction of the stream is from the host to the device. Characters typed in are buffered in this process, using the third and the fourth arguments as a difference list representing the buffer. They are sent to the host on `get` request by unifying the argument of the partially instantiated request message.

Among the above two models for input devices, the PIMOS employs the latter, mainly because devices for input, output and both can all be handled uniformly. The request stream from the host to the device is called the *device control stream*.

3.2 Device Control Scheme

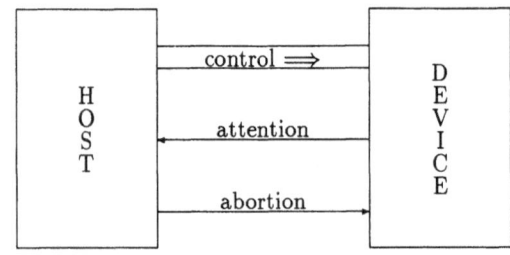

Figure 3: Communication Paths to a Physical Device

3.2.1 Completion Status

All the I/O command messages sent to a device control stream have an argument to which the device process unifies a value indicating whether the command was normally completed or not. This argument is called the *completion status* of the command. Synchronization with the completion of a command can also be possible by waiting instantiation of this argument.

3.2.2 Interrupt

With only the control stream, there is no way to send information actively from the device process to the host. Besides the control stream, a reverse direction communication path called the *attention line* is provided. The attention line is actually a shared variable among the host process and the device. The device may instantiate it when asynchronous communication to the host is required.

3.2.3 Command Abortion

Sometimes, cancellation of commands already sent to the control stream is desired. In the PIMOS, all the I/O devices have an additional communication path from the host to the device, called the *abortion line*, which is actually a shared variable among the host process and the device. When the host instantiates this variable, the device aborts the execution of the command under execution and skips any subsequent commands in the device control stream until a *reset* message appears in the stream. The completion status of the aborted and skipped commands will become *aborted*.

A reset message has the following arguments.

Abort: New abort line.

Attention: New attention line.

Status: Completion status of the *reset* command.

After the reset message is received, subsequent commands are processed normally using the new abort and attention lines specified in the message.

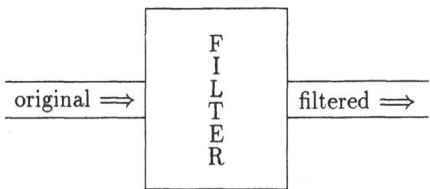

Figure 4: Filter

3.3 Lower Level Implementation

In the current implementation on the Multi-PSI version 2, the above-described communication protocol (based upon the model of physical devices as KL1 processes) is almost faithfully realized by the I/O front-end processors. The KL1 language implementation is not aware of the existence of such specialized front-end processors; the front-end and the host communicate to each other using the same protocols used in the communication between two processors of the host. In this scheme, the message handling mechanism for KL1 language implementation must be implemented also on the front-end processor. The merit of the scheme is that it makes the language implementation simpler, which was quite important in this prototype implementation.

In other implementations in the future, realizing lower levels on the host machine and making I/O processor simpler may become advantageous. In that case, a lower level model of devices with clean semantics will be required.

3.4 Logical Devices

Logical devices are provided by the processes called *device drivers* of the PIMOS. A higher level abortion mechanism which allows retrying of once aborted commands is provided here.

The device driver is a kind of *filter*. Filters are processes that receive messages from its input stream, process them somehow depending on the nature of the filter, and send the processed message to the output stream.

The device driver remembers aborted I/O commands. They can be sent again to the physical device by a *resend* command. Alternatively, that memory can be cleared by a *cancel* command. This decision can be delayed arbitrarily long, even until after another abortion. Thus, multiple such memories for multiple groups of aborted commands are required. The *reset* message in this level has an additional argument *ID* to which the identifier of the immediately preceding aborted command group is returned. This identifier is used in *resend* or *cancel* commands to identify an aborted command group.

This feature is quite useful in programs where two or more tasks share one device. For example, programs running under a command interpreter shell often share a display window with the shell itself for standard input/output. When such a program is suspended by an interruption, there may be multiple I/O requests already sent to the window logical device but not processed yet. In such a case, the shell *aborts* the processing (through the abortion line) and sends a *reset* messages to the window device driver, and then uses the window normally for its own purpose. All the I/O requests of the suspended program are also suspended and remembered in the device driver process, rather than being discarded. When the suspended program is to proceed again, sending a *resend* message to the device driver will continue the processing of the suspended I/O requests. When it is to be killed, a *cancel* message is sent instead.

3.5 Buffering

The I/O commands can be designed to send one command for each character or similar small units, which may be convenient for most application programs. Applying that fine-grained protocol to all the communication channels in the system, however, the communication overhead may become problematic. Where there is a considerable per-message overhead for communication, for example, in communication between the host machine and the I/O devices, one message should bring as much data as possible, as far as communication delay will not become a problem, to attain higher throughput. To realize this without changing the end-user interface, the well-known technique of *buffering* is widely used in conventional operating systems. Simply by buffering n characters, the per-message communication overhead can be reduced to $1/n$.

The PIMOS provides the buffering mechanism in the process called *I/O utility filter*, which is a filter placed between the device driver and the user program.[16] Thus, the command protocol of this buffer is the only one that casual users are concerned. Buffering can be made quite efficient using updatable random access structures (in this case, updatable character strings).

The size of the buffer is a parameter of the system which should be determined depending on the hardware parameters. In addition to the buffering feature, this filter also provides parsing and unparsing features for operator precedence grammars.

4 MANAGEMENT OF PROGRAMS

In the KL1 language level, atoms do not have any association with their name strings nor any other properties such as executable codes. They are merely *identifiers* in its original meaning. It is the PIMOS that associates atoms and their name strings or any other correspond-

---

[16]There are other filters in between the device driver and the I/O utility filter, which will be explained below.

ing properties. This section describes the databases the PIMOS provides for storing such information and how they are used.

4.1 Atom Name Database

Atoms and their names (character strings) are associated by the *atom name database* provided by the PIMOS. This database is accessed when such an association is required; for example, on Prolog-like read or write operations. The database is implemented as a KL1 process, which maintains two hash tables: One for mapping names to atoms and the other for the reverse. These two tables are always kept consistent. Hash tables can be quite efficiently implemented using the randomly accessible and updatable array structures described in 2.7.1.

If this single database is used by all the programs running under the PIMOS each time they need the information, the process realizing the database can be a performance bottleneck of the system. Fortunately, the atom name database is monotonic; new atom/name pairs may be added to the database but there is no deletion nor update. Thus caching of the atom name database is quite easy.

A cache database is created as an empty database. When a query is made to a cache, the query is sent further to the central atom name database (or another cache database) and the answer is remembered in the cache. Any subsequent queries made on the same atom can be answered without accessing the central database. No other synchronization is required.

Note that the association of atoms and their names are provided solely by the software, rather than the language implementation. Thus, the atom/name association provided by the PIMOS is merely the *standard* and not the only possible one. Users can use their own database for specific applications. It is also possible to create unique atoms not associated with any names, if only *identity* is of interest.

4.2 Module Database

As described in 2.6.1, a block of object code for KL1 programs is handled as a data object of type *module*. The *module database* provided by the PIMOS associates module names (atoms rather than name strings, actually) with the corresponding module data objects.

Caching the module database is not as easy as that of the atom name database, because modules may be updated. Non-deterministic parallelism makes keeping of consistency difficult. Fortunately, access frequency is considered to be much lower in this case. Thus, the PIMOS currently does not provide any caching mechanism for the module database.

A module which is not defined yet can also be registered to the module database. Such a module is represented by an uninstantiated variable. When a query to obtain such a module is made, that variable is returned. Accesses to such a module will be simply suspended, as described in 2.6.1.

Note that the association of modules and names provided by the module database of the PIMOS is merely a *standard* also and not the only one, as in the case of atom/name association. When, for example, a higher level language system is to be built upon the PIMOS, it may or may not use the standard association.

When the number of users concurrently using the PIMOS increases, the module database may become a performance bottleneck. In such a case, providing a private module database for each user may be advantageous. Commonly used modules, such as those provided by the PIMOS, should be stored in a common database which does not allow any update, to enable caching in personal module databases. The look-up mechanism will be similar to the *package* system provided by Common Lisp (Steele 1984).

4.3 Linking Modules

There are two types of linkage between modules.

The basic linkage mechanism is *fixed* linkage provided by the language system. When linkage is made this way, a module containing a invocation of a predicate in another module has a pointer to the invoked module object.[17] This is the most efficient mechanism provided for invocation of a predicate in a foreign module.

A drawback of this efficiency is that modules cannot be updated independently. For example, when a module A calls another module B, updating the module B to B' will not make the module A call the new module B'. The newly created module B' is merely replacing B in the module database, without changing already existing pointers to the module B elsewhere. In such cases, the module A must be linked again with B'.

In the more flexible linkage mechanism implemented in KL1 software, modules are not directly referenced but designated by their *names*. Each time an invocation is made using this linkage scheme, a query to the module database is made. When this *soft* linkage is used, each module can be updated independently. Efficiency drawback, of course, is not small.

Fixed linkage is normally used. Name linkage is used in cases where programs are in anyway invoked by their names. For example, the command interpreter shell uses this on invoking programs that run under it. Name linkage may be profitable also in the program development phase, where linkage efficiency may be more important than execution efficiency.

---

[17]There can be many copies of one module on different processors, but they all are logically equivalent.

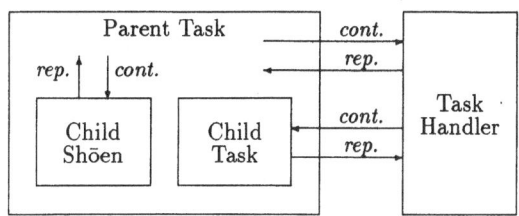

Figure 5: Task and Shōen

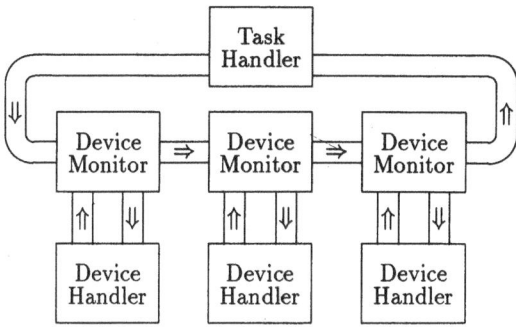

Figure 6: Resource Loop

5 RESOURCE TREE

Controlling computational resource is the most important role of an operating system. Using the shōen feature, consumption of basic resources such as execution time can be controlled. There are, however, other resources, such as I/O devices, which are not controlled by the language primitives and should be controlled by the operating system.

This section describes how management of such resources is realized in the PIMOS. The most crucial part of the resource management is in releasing resources allocated during some computation on abortion of that computation.

5.1 Resources

The shōen feature provided by the KL1 language is capable of controlling basic resources such as execution time. The kinds of resources controlled by the shōen feature is called *language-defined resources*. On the other hand, other resources such as I/O devices cannot be controlled only by the shōen feature. Such resources are called *OS-defined resources*.

5.2 Tasks

Tasks are units of resource management in the PIMOS. Tasks are a shōen specially recognized as a task by the PIMOS.

As the shōen feature is provided by the language, shōens can be arbitrarily created at any time by any program. Tasks, on the other hand, can only be created by asking the PIMOS, because it is the only way a shōen can be recognized as a task by the PIMOS.

The control and report streams of a usual shōen are directly connected to its creator, while those of a task are connected to a PIMOS process corresponding to the task, called *task handler*. The creator of the task can only indirectly control the task and receive reports of the task through streams connected to the task handler process.

5.3 Resource Loop

When a task is aborted, all the OS-defined resources allocated to the task are freed. This is essential to allow abortion of tasks safely without disturbing subsequent processing.

To realize this, all the OS-defined resources allocated to the task must be remembered somehow. All accesses to OS-defined resources from user programs are made through a stream that is connected to a process in the PIMOS, called *device handler*. The device handler process is a filter, through which various requests are sent to the device driver. This handler processes can thus control users' accesses to the OS-resources.

All the OS-defined resources are associated with another PIMOS process called *device monitor*. The monitor processes for resources allocated in a task are connected by a stream in a loop structure called *resource loop*.[18] The monitor process and the handler process have communication streams in both ways. Resources allocated in a task can be released on its termination by sending a message notifying the termination via the resource loop to the monitors, and then to each corresponding handlers. Handlers will close their output streams when when the message is received. When a resource is released individually (when a file is closed, for example), that resource can be eliminated from the loop using the well-known short-circuit technique (Hircsh *et al.* 1987). Queries on the resource allocation status can also be processed along the same path.

A monitor and the corresponding handler are made as distinct processes in the current implementation for keeping the modularity of the system; all the monitors are identical but the handlers depend on the device they handle. It may be possible, however, to merge these two processes.

5.4 Resource Tree

[18]A loop structure similar to the resource loop of PIMOS can also be found in the Logix operating system (Hircsh *et al.* 1987) for controlling user programs. In case of Logix, however, the unit of control is each goal to be reduced, as there is no notion of goal groups such as shōen in the language level.

246

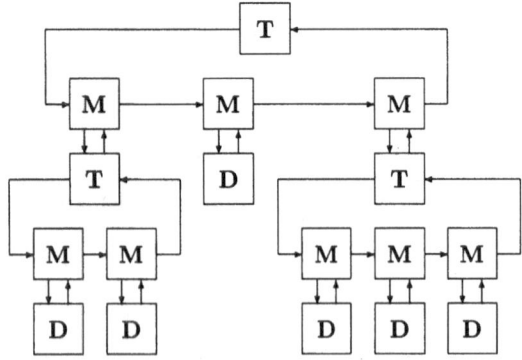

T: Task Handler; **M:** Resource Monitor; **D:** Device Handler

Figure 7: Resource Tree

In the PIMOS, tasks are also considered to be OS-defined resources. A task handler is a kind of device handler whose corresponding device happens to be a shōen. Tasks are different from other devices in that they may have children resources.

As children resources of a task can be tasks again, all the device monitors and handlers form a tree of resources. This is called the *resource tree*. All the resource management of the PIMOS is through this resource tree.

6 COMMUNICATION MECHANISM

As there is only one variable binding environment, the operating system PIMOS and user programs can share variables. Communication between the PIMOS and user programs is made through such shared variables. The user program instantiates a shared variable to a data structure for making a request to the PIMOS, and the PIMOS instantiates certain elements of the structure to return values to the user program.

This section describes how such communication is made, how the communication path is initially established, and how the communication is made in a fail-safe way to protect the PIMOS from accidental or intentional errors of application programs.

6.1 Basic Communication Mechanism

The communication mechanism between the PIMOS and the user programs is based on the scheme proposed in (Shapiro and Takeuchi 1983).

The structure of the top level of the PIMOS may be as follows.

```
boot :-
  pimos(S),
  execute(user(S), ...).
```

The variable S is shared between the user program and the PIMOS and used as a *stream* for communication between the user program and the PIMOS.

For simplicity, we assume here that the PIMOS provides only one device: A character input device. In this case, the clause in a predicate of PIMOS for handling one character input requests may be defined as follows.

```
pimos([get(C)|S]) :-
  read_keyboard(C1),
  C = C1,
  pimos(S).
```

Here, the **read_keyboard** predicate is assumed to do the physical input procedure and unifies the typed-in character with its argument. When a message **get** is received, physical input operation is performed and the typed-in character is unified with the argument of the **get** message.

In the above program, the user program may be as follows.

```
user(S) :-
  S = [get(C)|S1],
  user1(C),
  ...
user1(0'a) :- ...
user1(0'b) :- ...
  ...
```

The user program sends a partially defined **get** request message to the operating system, and then determines its further processing depending upon the result. The predicate **user1** implicitly waits for instantiation of the variable to which the operating system is returning a value by unification.

The order of the commands sent to one message stream is kept in the stream, for it is determined by the data structure, not by the order of operation.[19] This guarantees, for example, two messages to be displayed are displayed in the desired order.

Accesses to databases provided by the PIMOS are also made in the same manner. In this case, the stream obtained by request the PIMOS is an access path to a database, in which commands are ordered.[20]

6.2 Establishing Communication Paths

For communication using the above-described method, the part of the user program which requires some service of the PIMOS must have a stream connected to the PIMOS (or one that merges into it). As there is no notion of

---

[19]When mergers are inserted, the order of messages from originally different streams becomes non-deterministic.

[20]When two or more access paths are created, synchronization of two access paths should be made by the completion status argument of command messages.

global variable in the language, such a stream must be passed all through the chain of invocations from the top level to where actual communication is required. This overhead may be too large if communication is needed only in rare exceptional cases; only in case of error reports, for example.

The PIMOS provides an alternative way of establishing a communication path to the PIMOS. This can be done by deliberately generating an exception using the *raise* primitive (see section 2.3.4). By specifying an appropriate *tag* in this this *raise*, the exception report indicating the request goes directly to the report stream of the shōen used for realizing a *task*. The report stream of a task shōen is monitored by the task handler process of the PIMOS, and there, the request is processed. Thus, shōens in user programs can nest arbitrary number of levels without losing the direct availability of the services of the PIMOS.

It is also possible for a user program to create a shōen specifying a tag corresponding to some requests to the PIMOS. This way, all or part of the requests to the PIMOS can be caught by the program monitoring the report stream of such a shōen. If the monitor program emulates the PIMOS, the program in the shōen runs exactly the same as when it is directly run under the PIMOS. This is the way virtual machine operating systems are implemented under the PIMOS.

There are three layers of communication streams between user programs and the PIMOS.

Device Level: This is the lowest level where concrete I/O command messages are sent.[21]

Device Request Level: This is the level where command messages to obtain device level streams are sent. For example, a file request stream accepts messages asking to open files and return the device level stream connected to the file.

General Request Level: This is the top level where command messages to obtain device request streams are sent.

What is directly obtained by *raising* an exception is a general request stream. All the services provided by the PIMOS are available through this general request stream.

6.3 Protection Problems

With the simple mechanism described above, however, intentional or accidental error in user programs may cause a system failure. This section describes the problems in shared variable communication between user programs and the operating system.

6.3.1 Multiple Writer Problem

As far as the user program is properly written as described above, there will be no problems. If, however, an erroneous user program such as follows is executed, a system failure may take place.

```
user(S) :-
    S = [get(C)|S1],
    user1(C),
    ...
user1(C) :-
    C = O'a,
    ...
```

Here, the user program unifies the variable C. If this happens *before* the unification "C = C1" in the PIMOS, the unification in the PIMOS may fail. Even if it were possible to check that the variable C is uninstantiated *immediately* preceding the unification[22], the unification in the user program can be executed in between the check and the unification in a parallel system.

The Parlog Programming System (PPS) provides a simple solution to this problem (Foster 1987). The problem arises because the value-returning unification is executed in the PIMOS. The PPS solution is to make the unification done in a metacall (a mechanism similar to shōen). Using this scheme, the code for the PIMOS will be as shown below.

```
pimos([get(C)|S]) :-
    read_keyboard(C1),
    wait_and_unify(C1, C),
    pimos(S).
wait_and_unify(C1, C) :- wait(C1) |
    execute(C = C1, ...).
```

Waiting the value of C1 is essential because otherwise the order of the invocation of the predicate **read_keyboard** and the execution of the shōen will not be defined in the language, and thus, without waiting for the value of C1, the unification in the shōen can be executed *before* the invocation of the **read_keyboard** predicate. This solution is simple but requires frequent metacall invocation; one metacall per one communication from the operating system to the user is required. The metacall mechanism cannot be optimized easily by compilation and other optimization efforts. Thus, this solution may be reasonable for interpretive implementations of the language where the metacall mechanism is relatively inexpensive, but may not be the best when the reduction mechanism is highly optimized.

The problem may also be solved by introducing the *atomic commitment* mechanism provided by Concurrent

---

[21]Some devices may also accept commands which creates a new device. For example, a file directory device can create a file device.

[22]The KL1 language does not provide a built-in predicate for variable check, such as *var* in Prolog. Such a predicate can only guarantee that its argument was not instantiated sometime before in parallel implementations.

Prolog (Shapiro 1983). Implementation with atomic commitment mechanism, however, may be not as efficient as one without it. The problem is that the cost of atomic commitment mechanism is not only in the communication with the operating system but also in every goal reduction in the system where such mechanism is not required.

6.3.2 Forsaken Reader Problem

Another problem appears when the user program fails to instantiate a shared variable inspected by the PIMOS. For example, consider the following clause.

```
user(S) :- S = [_|S1], ...
```

As the message to the PIMOS is not instantiated, the PIMOS process will wait for it to be instantiated forever. When the message has an argument which specifies more details of the request (a character code to be output, for example), the same problem may occur in the argument level, too. A similar situation also arises when the execution of the user program is aborted using the shōen mechanism described above, even if the user program is properly written.

This problem cannot be solved using the shōen mechanism nor the atomic commitment mechanism.

6.4 Protection Filter

To solve the above-described problems, a filtering process called the *protection filter* is inserted in the stream between user programs and the PIMOS. This filter is executed in the user shōen rather than in the PIMOS.

The user sends messages to the protection filter stream, not directly to the PIMOS. The protection filter translates the user messages into a different form which does not cause failure in the PIMOS, and sends it to the PIMOS.

The concrete functions of the protection filter are as follows.

- It waits for instantiation of variables which the user should instantiate. The message is sent to the PIMOS only after that. Thus, when a message is sent to the PIMOS, the values of these variables are guaranteed be instantiated. For structures, it waits for instantiation of only certain elements of it which are required to be instantiated, allowing partially defined messages to pass through the filter.

- It replaces variables which the PIMOS should instantiate with new unbound variables. It also initiates processes each of which waits for instantiation of one of the newly created variables, and then unifies ·the corresponding original variable with it. Thus, all value-returning unifications in the PIMOS

will always be with unbound variables, which will never fail.

The protection filter for the above example will be as follows.

```
filter([get(C)|S], OS) :-
  OS = [get(C1)|OS1],
  wait_and_unify(C1, C),
  filter(S, OS1).
wait_and_unify(OSV, UserV) :-
  wait(OSV) |
  UserV = OSV.
```

The filter process will not proceed until the message becomes instantiated to the form get(C1); the wait_and_unify predicate unifies the variable supplied by the user program (UserV) with the variable to which the operating system returns the result (OSV) only after its instantiation.

The key point here is that the protection filter process is in the shōen of the user and thus the unification "UserV = OSV" is executed in the user shōen. Its failure can be safely handled by the shōen mechanism.

The top level of the PIMOS with this protection filter mechanism will be as follows.

```
boot :-
  pimos(OS),
  execute((user(S), filter(S,OS)), ...).
```

As the protection filter is inserted automatically, the user program may not be aware of the existence of such a filter, as far as it is properly using the communication stream.

Note that, the two occurrences of the variable S in the above program must be unified prior to the invocation of the shōen. Otherwise, this unification may fail. The proper unification order is guaranteed by the rules described in 2.2.5.

6.5 Protocol Compiler

A disadvantage of the protection filter scheme is that the filter must know all the details of the message protocol. It may be common in conventional operating systems that the interfacing code knows all the details of the communication protocol. It may, however, make the system maintenance cost considerably higher because the code of the protection filters for various devices may be lengthy, taking a large part of the PIMOS which is relatively compact.

Fortunately, given the communication protocol of the PIMOS and the user programs, the code for the protection filters can be generated automatically. This generator program is called the *protocol compiler*. Using the

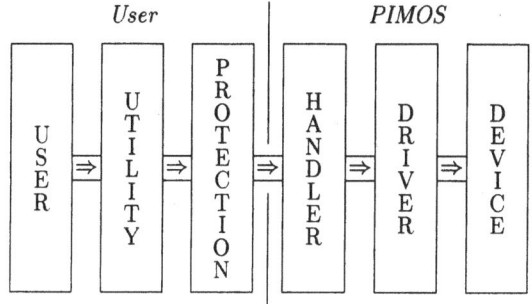

Figure 8: Communication Filters

protocol compiler, a compact specification of the communication protocol with fair readability can be used as the source code of the PIMOS. It is also possible to generate the device handler code using the same technique.[23]

6.6 Summary of Communication

The communication path from a user program to a physical device is summarized in the figure 8. Although I/O messages goes through several filters as shown in the figure, I/O requests are buffered at the utility filter which comes the first, keeping the communication cost to a reasonable level. Also note that all the filters can be executed in a pipelined manner.

6.7 Allocation of Filters

The current version of the PIMOS lets the user determine all the job allocation. All the filters in the communication path from the end user to the device driver are allocated initially to the processor where the user program first requested for the communication path. This makes the communication cost minimum as far as the user program stays in the same processor. The user program can make filters migrate to other processors by sending a reallocation message to the stream afterwards. Filters will not migrate automatically following the user process, for it may not be desirable. The user program may move among processors often but actual I/O may be required only after many migrations, in which case only one migration of filters before massive I/O requests is desirable.

Allocation problem of the processes of the PIMOS should be solved someday with the general load balancing problem, which is one of the most important research topic in the future.

---

[23]In the version of the PIMOS available when this document is being prepared, all the protection filter and device handler codes are hand-written yet.

7 DEVELOPMENT ENVIRONMENT

This section describes the programming environment provided for the development of PIMOS. Some of the utilities described here may be also useful in development of application programs.

7.1 PDSS and Micro-PIMOS

Prior to the development of the KL1 language implementations on parallel inference machines, an implementation of the language for conventional computers was made in the language C. In addition to the language implementation, a primitive operating system is also built upon it. The system is called the PIMOS Development Support System, or PDSS in short, and the operating system is called the Micro-PIMOS (Miyazaki et al. 1988). The primary objective of the development of the PDSS was to provide a program development environment for the KL1 language that enables the development of the PIMOS in parallel with the development of the parallel inference machines.

The PDSS is a pseudo-parallel implementation of the language. Although real parallelism is not in the implementation, all other essential features of the KL1 language are provided by the system. The PDSS implementation thus also played a role of a prototype for implementations on the parallel inference systems. Many of the compilation and other fundamental implementation ideas developed for the KL1 language were verified through this implementation.

The KL1 extensions to the FGHC language were actually utilized in the Micro-PIMOS. For example, the shōen feature and the priority management feature were extensively used in the Micro-PIMOS and have been proved to be effective. The same applies to the various optimizations in the implementation level.

The PDSS system provides various debugging features including the following.

- Reduction by reduction stepwise execution with symbolic trace output. Selective tracing somewhat similar to Prolog debuggers including the *spying* feature is also provided.

- Deadlock detection feature during program execution based upon multiple reference management and during garbage collection. A goal is recognized as deadlocked when it is found to be waiting for a variable to which no other goals have access paths.

- Execution profiling feature counting numbers of invocations of predicates. Useful for program tuning.

- Static program checkers such as void variable detection and predicate dependency analysis.

The system has been revised many times on need adding new features during the development of the PIMOS. These debugging features accelerated the development considerably.

As the parallelism, the only crucial difference between the PDSS and parallel implementations, is implicit on principle in the KL1 language, transporting of the PIMOS from PDSS to the Multi-PSI implementation was extremely easy. As was expected, almost no software synchronization problem was found. This was the greatest merit of writing the system in a logic-based concurrent programming language.

7.2 KL1 Compiler

The compiler for the KL1 language was also written first for the PDSS. As the PDSS implementation and implementations for real parallel machines are both based on the KL1-B abstract machine (Kimura and Chikayama 1987), basically the same compiler could be used for both of them. For parallel implementations, several features were added for enabling parallel execution, but it was quite easy.

7.3 Pseudo Multi-PSI

The Pseudo Multi-PSI is an implementation of the KL1 language on single-processor PSI-II machines (Nakashima and Nakajima 1987). The PSI-II machine is a logic programming workstation, developed earlier in the FGCS project, which is also used as the front-end processor for the Multi-PSI and probably for other parallel inference systems. The processor of the PSI-II is also used as the processors of the Multi-PSI machine.

A pseudo-parallel system for the KL1 language is implemented on the PSI-II by storing two distinct set of microcodes in the microprogram storage: One required for KL1 and the other for KL0, which is the machine language for a sequential logic programming language ESP (Chikayama 1984), originally used in the PSI machine.[24] As the same hardware and the firmware are used, the pseudo Multi-PSI attains almost the same performance as the Multi-PSI system consisting of only one processor.

One *processor* of the Multi-PSI is emulated by one *process* on the *pseudo* version. Pseudo processors are switched when given number of reductions are completed. The scheduler can specify arbitrary scheduling, including random ones. An advantage of pseudo-parallel implementations to real parallel implementations is that the same execution sequence is reproducible. Even if the scheduling is random, it is only pseudo-random; giving the same seed, the same random number sequence can be obtained. This makes bug locating much easier. Symbolic tracing feature of the PDSS was also made available on the pseudo and real Multi-PSI.

---

[24]In the actual implementation, two versions of the microcodes are overlayed due to lack of storage capacity.

The PIMOS was first transported from the PDSS to this Pseudo Multi-PSI and then to the *real* Multi-PSI. As the PSI-II hardware is much more compact and inexpensive than the Multi-PSI, debugging of many parts of the PIMOS and, more importantly, debugging of the firmware could be carried out in parallel. The same would apply to future improvements of the PIMOS and the language implementation, and also to development of application programs.

8 CONCLUSION AND FUTURE RESEARCH PLANS

The development of the PIMOS showed not only the feasibility but also advantages of using concurrent logic programming languages as the basis of operating systems.

As we already experienced during the development of the SIMPOS (the operating system for the logic programming workstation PSI) in a earlier stage of the project, there are various merits in using a symbolic programming language for description of an operating system (Chikayama 1988). The same merits were observed also during the development the PIMOS. The source programs could be written in a quite readable form. An interactive symbolic debugger was made available from the earliest stage of the development, providing trace output quite easily compared with the source program; without this symbolic trace, the development would have been much more toilsome.

The most notable observation made during the development of the PIMOS was that almost no synchronization problem was found in the debugging phase. Using conventional procedural languages, data-flow synchronization must be transformed into control-flow synchronization by the programmers, which is the largest source of bugs in development of operating systems. Using a concurrent logic programming language, the system designers have to be aware only of the flow of data and almost nothing of synchronization, as data-flow synchronization is implicit in the language. This was the largest merit of using the KL1 language.

There are several problems which are yet to be solved in future research.

One of the most important problems left unsolved is balancing computational load of processors. In the current version of the PIMOS, load balancing is specified by the user programs and the PIMOS merely faithfully obeys that (see section 6.7). A semi-automatic load balancing scheme was proposed (Chikayama 1986) and the basic hardware mechanism required for the scheme was provided (Takeda *et al.* 1988), but it is not utilized in the current version of the PIMOS and its effectiveness has yet to be evaluated.

Another problem left is in the memory management.

The garbage collection mechanism and the quantitative memory management scheme proposed in this paper do not necessarily go together well. A new model of memory consumption may be required here.

In the current version of the PIMOS on the Multi-PSI machine, the front-end processor provides a high-level I/O interface. This scheme gives clean semantics to the physical I/O, but it may be laying too much burden on the back of the front-end processor. A decent model of lower-level I/O operations, which also can be implemented more efficiently, is desirable.

Tuning of various parameters of the PIMOS, communication buffer size or resource management accuracy, for example, are not carried out yet. Such parameters should be determined through future experiences with the system and parallel application software.

ACKNOWLEDGMENTS

Many researchers of ICOT and other related research groups, too numerous to be listed here, participated in the design and implementation of the the KL1 language, the operating system itself and the development tools. We would also like to express our thanks to Dr. S. Uchida, the manager of the fourth research laboratory of ICOT, and Dr. K. Fuchi, the director of the ICOT research center, for their valuable suggestions and encouragement.

REFERENCES

(Chikayama 1984) T. Chikayama. Unique Features of ESP. In *Proceedings of FGCS'84*, pages 292–298. ICOT, Tokyo, 1984.

(Chikayama 1986) T. Chikayama. Load balancing in a very large scale multi-processor system. In *Proceedings of Fourth Japanese-Swedish Workshop on Fifth Generation Computer Systems* SICS, Stockholm, 1986. Also as ICOT Technical Memorandum, TM-276, ICOT, 1986.

(Chikayama 1988) T. Chikayama. Programming in ESP — experiences with SIMPOS. In K. Fuchi and M. Nivat, editor, *Programming of Future Generation Computers*, pages 75–86. North-Holland, New York, New York, 1988.

(Chikayama and Kimura 1988) T. Chikayama and Y. Kimura. Multiple reference management in flat GHC. In *Proceedings of Fourth International Conference on Logic Programming*, volume 2, pages 276–293. The MIT Press, Cambridge, Massachusetts, 1987.

(Clark and Gregory 1984) K. Clark and S. Gregory. Notes on systems programming in Parlog. In *Proceedings of FGCS'84*, pages 299–306. ICOT, Tokyo, 1984.

(Clark and Gregory 1986) K. L. Clark and S. Gregory. Parlog: A parallel logic programming language. *ACM Transaction on Programming Languages and Systems*, 8(1), 1986.

(Foster 1987) I. Foster. Logic operating systems: Design issues. *Proceedings of the Fourth International Conference on Logic Programming*, volume 2, pages 910–926. The MIT Press, Cambridge, Massachusetts, 1987.

(Foster 1988) I. Foster. Parlog as a systems programming language. *Ph. D. Thesis*, Imperial College, London, 1988.

(Goto et al. 1988) A. Goto et al.. Overview of the parallel inference machine architecture (PIM). In *Proceedings of FGCS'88*. ICOT, Tokyo, 1988.

(Hircsh et al. 1987) M. Hircsh et al.. Computation control and protection in the Logix system. In E. Shapiro, editor, *Concurrent Prolog: Collected Papers*, volume 2, pages 28–45. The MIT Press, Cambridge, Massachusetts, 1987.

(Kahn et al. 1986) K. Kahn et al.. Objects in concurrent logic programming languages. *Sigplan Notices*, 21(11):242–257, 1986.

(Kimura and Chikayama 1987) Y. Kimura and T. Chikayama. An abstract KL1 machine and its instruction set. In *Proceedings of 1987 Symposium on Logic Programming*, pages 468–477. Computer Society Press of the IEEE, Washingon, D.C., 1987.

(Miyazaki 1988) T. Miyazaki. Parallel logic programming language KL1 — Its implementation and an operating system in it —. In *The Transaction of the Institute of Electronics, Information and Communication Engineers*, J71-D(8):1423–1432, 1988. *in Japanese*.

(Miyazaki et al. 1988) T. Miyazaki et al. PDSS Manual. ICOT Technical Memorandum, TM-437, ICOT, 1988. *in Japanese*.

(Nakashima and Nakajima 1987) H. Nakashima and K. Nakajima. Hardware architecture of the sequential inference machine PSI-II. In *Proceedings of 1987 Symposium on Logic Programming*, pages 104–113. Computer Society Press of the IEEE, Washingon, D.C., 1987.

(Shapiro 1983) E. Shapiro. A subset of Concurrent Prolog and its interpreter. ICOT Technical Report TR-003, ICOT, 1983.

(Shapiro 1984) E. Shapiro. Systems programming in Concurrent Prolog. In *Proceedings of the 11th ACM Symposium on Principles of Programming Languages*, 1984.

(Shapiro and Takeuchi 1983) E. Shapiro and A. Takeuchi. Object Oriented Programming in Concurrent Prolog. ICOT Technical Report TR-004, ICOT, 1983. Also in *New Generation Computing*, 1-1, 1983.

(Steele 1984) Guy Steele et al.. *Common Lisp, the Language*. Digital Press, 1984.

(Takeda et al. 1988) Y. Takeda et al.. A load balancing mechanism for large scale multiprocessor systems and its implementation. In *Proceedings of FGCS'88*. ICOT, Tokyo, 1988.

(Ueda 1986) K. Ueda. Guarded horn clauses: A parallel logic programming language with the concept of a guard. ICOT Technical Report TR-208, ICOT, Tokyo, 1986.

(Ueda and Chikayama 1984) K. Ueda and T. Chikayama. Efficient stream/array processing in logic programming languages. In *Proceedings of FGCS'84*, pages 317–326. ICOT, Tokyo, 1984.

(Yoshida and Chikayama 1988) K. Yoshida and T. Chikayama. A'UM — a stream-based concurrent object-oriented language. In *Proceedings of FGCS'88*. ICOT, Tokyo, 1988.

PROCEEDINGS OF THE INTERNATIONAL CONFERENCE
ON FIFTH GENERATION COMPUTER SYSTEMS 1988,
edited by ICOT. © ICOT, 1988

OVERVIEW OF THE KNOWLEDGE BASE MANAGEMENT SYSTEM (KAPPA)

Kazumasa Yokota,* Moto Kawamura, Atsushi Kanaegami

Institute for New Generation Computer Technology (ICOT)

4-28, Mita 1-chome, Minato-ku, Tokyo 108, Japan

ABSTRACT

This is an overview of the knowledge base management system called Kappa, one of the research and development activities performed at ICOT on databases and knowledge bases. The underlying data model is a nested relational model, and some complex data models are constructed and under consideration on the model. Deductive databases are constructed as one of knowledge base mechanisms and further extensions are planned within the framework of deductive and object-oriented databases. In this paper, we overview not only the current status of the system and the project but also their conception and activities related to them, and discuss the framework of deductive and object-oriented databases.

1 INTRODUCTION

Many knowledge information processing systems (KIPSs) have been developed and planned for the target of the Fifth Generation Computer System (FGCS) project. Most of them presuppose smaller or larger databases or knowledge bases, reflecting their own requirements, which are not usually based on traditional data models but on more complex and higher level data (knowledge) models. The term 'knowledge bases' generally means convenient black boxes with some kind of intelligence in each application, but that are located centrally. Unlike 'database', whose meaning is specific, 'knowledge base' is a very general term whose meaning ranges from naive databases to emulation of the human brain, and furthermore tends to depend on specific domains. At ICOT, under the various requirements of KIPSs and their environments, many kinds of research and development on database and knowledge base machines (DBMs and KBMs) and database and knowledge base management systems (DBMSs and KBMSs) have been done from different perspectives [Itoh86, Itoh+88] and will be integrated during the final stage of the FGCS project.

Generally speaking, in our environment, an approach for knowledge bases should be based on database, logic programming and artificial intelligence technologies, and should work towards their integration, regarding efficient performance, modeling power, clear and formal semantics, deductive mechanism, abstraction mechanism and parallel processing. In other words, the approach is a way of direct or declarative representation of objects in each domain of KIPSs and efficient processing of those objects on that level, without translation into the lower level language. As long as there is a problem of quantity, whether knowledge bases are stored in main memory or secondary memory, knowledge bases are not different from databases but are a developed or extended form of them.

The *Kappa* (Knowledge APPlication-oriented Advanced Database and Knowledge Base Management System) project started on September, 1985 as one of the KBMS projects at ICOT. The project was dedicated to the following environments: a personal sequential inference machine (PSI), its programming and operating system (SIMPOS), and a logic programming language (ESP) with 'object' concept; and multi-PSI and parallel inference machine (PIM) [Goto+88], its operating system (PIMOS) [Chik+88] and a parallel language (KL1) based on GHC. Under the first environment, the prototype system called Kappa-I has already worked not only as an experiment of research and development on KBMSs but also as tools for various applications.

This paper is an overview of the activities on KBMS, focusing on the Kappa project. Section 2 explains typical applications at ICOT, the basic policy for the KBMS, reflecting them, and the overall configuration. Section 3 describes some features of the database layer underlying the Kappa system, and briefly explains the architecture and some extensions under consideration. The knowledge base layer of Kappa is being constructed and designed on the database layer in the framework of deductive and object-oriented databases. Section 4 overviews the deductive features and Section 5 discusses the framework of deductive and object-oriented databases. Section 6

---

*e-mail: {enea,inria,kddlab,mit-eddie,ukc}!icot!kyokota;
kyokota%icot.jp@relay.cs.net

outlines the Kappa project and its related projects on the knowledge base systems at ICOT.

2 KNOWLEDGE BASES AT ICOT

Knowledge base facilities play an important role in many KIPSs, and are expected to make each knowledge base easy to create and utilize. From another point of view, it is very difficult to discriminate between data and knowledge, so free access is required for both data and knowledge from knowledge bases. For such purposes, Kappa project was planned to provide experimental environments of databases and knowledge bases for many applications. In that sense, the underlying frameworks or constraints are not independent of KIPSs developed or planned at ICOT, and are also not merely for basic research. In this section, we explain some requirements of KIPSs and the design principles of Kappa based on them.

2.1 Typical Applications

As Kappa presupposes conditions required by some applications, its universality, which reserves the independence of the applications' specific domains, depends on selection of applications from the viewpoints of importance, relevance, prospects and requisition of knowledge bases used by KIPSs. We analyzed many KIPSs in our environments and considered two applications, which are expected to be kernel systems in FGCS project, as typical and decided to address their requirements in the design of Kappa.

The first application is a proof checking system called *computer aided proof* (*CAP*) [Hirose⁺87, Sakai88], which requires various kinds of mathematical knowledge bases. The system has functions of theorem prover, term rewriting system and proof compiler (realizer), and is not only an artificial intelligence system but also expected to be one of the kernels of various problem solving systems. The system is based on Gentzen's natural deduction system (NK) with additional inference rules, and its proof description language (PDL) reflects the inference mechanism. Mathematical knowledge is classified into the form of texts (axioms, definitions, theorems and proofs) written in PDL, and the form of terms (proof trees during proof checking, and inference rules extracted from checked or assumed theorems). The unit of mathematical knowledge is a theory and the knowledge base constitutes a directed acyclic graph by reference relation between theories. There are various kinds of databases and knowledge bases in the system. In particular the inference mechanism, for a forward and backward reasoning mechanism during filling the gap between lines in a proof text, corresponds to query processing in deductive databases.

Another application is natural language processing

systems, which play an important role in many KIPSs. These systems require many large *electronic dictionaries* as indispensable parts [Ishi⁺85, TaYo88]. These dictionaries are under construction and are a big step towards building huge knowledge bases. There are three kinds of dictionary:

- Electronic word dictionaries, each of which has a few hundred thousand words. Each dictionary constitutes a typical nested relation.

- A concept dictionary, which is a classification hierarchy of IS_A relations with several hundred thousand concepts.

- A thesaurus in the form of a semantic network, which is also an intermediate form between a word dictionary and a concept dictionary.

Furthermore, as many natural language processing systems are written in a logic programming language called CIL based on situation semantics [Mukai87], familiarity with CIL is also expected. In this domain, we face a problem of quantity as well as one of complex data structure.

2.2 Design Policy for the Kappa System

Considering the above requirements, a policy for the design of the Kappa system was set up:

- In our environment, knowledge bases should contain databases, and be considered as the database's extension.

- The system consists of three layers: *database*, *knowledge base* and *user interface* layers. Users can define each interface of the layers for their own applications and access any of them, that is, each layer should be extensible.

- The underlying data model of the database layer is a *nested relational model*, and some structured models such as *semantic network* and *classification hierarchy* are supported on nested relations in the layer. Terms expressing rules or structured data should be treated as a data type and be retrieved by unification and pattern matching.

- At least in the database layer, efficient performance for processing a large quantity of data is necessary to provide experimental environments for many KIPSs. Furthermore, as one of our environments consists of many personal workstations (PSIs) connected by a network, the system should be a distributed DBMS and KBMS, which features are different from some features of traditional centralized DBMSs.

254

- The knowledge base layer consists of some knowledge representation languages and various kinds of experimental modules based on them, such as deductive mechanism and object management in the framework of *deductive and object-oriented databases.*

- The user interface layer provides convenient interfaces and experimental features with graphic facilities, a structured editor (shared with CAP), and semi-automatic design tools for various kinds of structured data.

- For software development, we employ *object concept* in the physical and logical design, such as database object, relation object, tuple object and schema object. This is very different from conventional designs of DBMSs.

2.3 Configuration of the KBMS

According to the above policy, the first version of the prototype system (Kappa-I) was implemented in August 1987. The second version called Kappa-II is now being built and will be widely released next April (see Section 6, for details). Furthermore the Kappa system and other systems for DBMS and KBMS will be integrated into one system at the final stage of the FGCS project. The current overall configuration is shown in the following picture:

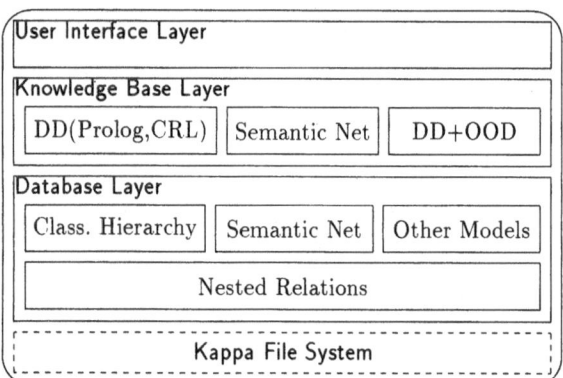

In the picture 'DD' and 'OOD' mean deductive databases and object-oriented databases respectively. In the following sections, we explain the database layer and deductive database in the knowledge base layer, and discuss the conception of deductive and object-oriented databases.

3 DATABASES FOR KNOWLEDGE BASES

The database layer is expected to manage various kinds of structured data and to process them efficiently. To cope with such requirements, we employ some data models in the layer. The underlying one is a nested relational model, and some other models are supported on the model.

3.1 Nested Relations

The advantages of a nested relational model over an ordinary relational model are that it offers more efficient representation and processing. In the ten years since the advantages were pointed out in [Maki77], there have been many works but few implementations [Verso86, Dadam+86, ScWe86, ScSc87, DeGu88]. It is also widely known that a nested relational model is better than a relational model for new applications such as engineering, office and geographical databases; and many commercial DBMSs also employ the idea from a practical point of view. However, as there are some variants of the name, the formal semantics should be made clear.

A nested tuple is defined as a subclass of objects, which notation is according to CRL [Yokota88]: assume a set O of atomic objects, a set A of attribute names, a tuple constructor $[,]$, and a set constructor $\{, \}$. O may contain a special object ω to represent explicitly a void or null object, which is used for partial information of a tuple object. An *object* is defined as follows:

(1) Any atomic object is an object.

(2) If $o_1, \cdots, o_n$ are objects, then $\{o_1, \cdots, o_n\}$ is an object, which is called a *set object*.

(3) If $a_1, \cdots, a_n$ are different attribute names and $o_1, \cdots, o_n$ are objects, $[a_1/o_1, \cdots, a_n/o_n]$ is an object, which is called a *tuple object*. a_i/o_i is called a *tuple element*.

If a set object has only one element, the set brackets are omitted. A tuple object is called a *nested tuple*, if all elements of each set object contained in the tuple object are compatible mutually and the structure of attribute names of a tuple object constitutes a finite tree domain without duplication of attribute names, In the case, an atomic object is rather called an *individual*. A *nested relation* is a set object consisting of nested tuples, each of which has structure compatible with other tuples, and the *schema* is defined as a type (abstract structure) defined in Section 5.2. And a *nested relational database* is a tuple object consisting of pairs of a relation (attribute) name and a nested relation. It is easy to see that these definitions correspond with those of ordinary nested relations.

In this formulation, we can give two kinds of semantics to a set constructor, especially connected with row-nest and row-unnest operations. Assume there are two tuples: $[a/c_1, b/\{c_2, c_3\}]$ and $[a/c_1, b/\{c_3, c_4\}]$. There are two possible tuples after application of a row-nest operation to the given tuples:

$$[a/c_1, b/\{c_2, c_3, c_4\}], \quad \text{or}$$
$$[a/c_1, b/\{\{c_2, c_3\}, \{c_3, c_4\}\}].$$

Each tuple is resulted by a set union or a set-of (set grouping) operation respectively. While an (extended) NF^2 model [Dadam$^+$86, ScWe86] employs the second semantics, Verso model [Verso86] employs the first. LDL [Beeri$^+$87] is also considered as the second case. We take the first, and give the semantics of a nested tuple as a set of only column-nested tuples, which is independent of row-nest and row-unnest operation. Under the semantics, users do not need to be conscious of the structure when they query a database. For example, according to the semantics, all of the following relations

R_1: $\{[a/c_1, b/c_3], [a/c_2, b/c_3], [a/c_2, b/c_4]\}$,
R_2: $\{[a/\{c_1, c_2\}, b/c_3], [a/c_2, b/c_4]\}$, and
R_3: $\{[a/c_1, b/c_3], [a/c_2, b/\{c_3, c_4\}]\}$

have the same meaning, and $[a/\{c_1, c_2\}, b/c_3]$ is implied by each of them. A nested relational model based on such semantics is a natural extension of a relational model, and its characteristics are more efficient representation and more efficient processing performance. The extended relational algebra including nest and unnest operations is reconstructed according to the semantics.

Strictly speaking, such relations are classified into unnormalized relations and nested relations from a structural point of view, depending on whether the relations can be reversible by row-unnest and row-nest operations, and also classified into value-oriented relations and expression-oriented relations from an operational point of view, depending on whether sets have intrinsic meaning or not [Miura87]. Although in this context we do not discriminate the differences explicitly, the system supports the both. From an operational point of view, the extended algebra suppresses treatment of subtuples for selection, set operations, nest and unnest operations if the relations are value-oriented; the algebra manipulates subtuples according to the above semantics if the relations are expression-oriented. From a structural point of view, for nested relations in the strict sense, the system should support some automatic transformation from a given relation to the corresponding 'normal form' by using semantic constraints such as multi-value dependency; this is under consideration.

The actual model has some additional features for practical use: list and bag constructors, term as a data type and its retrieval by unification or pattern matching, and use of a constraint logic programming language CAL [Aiba$^+$88] as generation or integrity rules for algebraic constraints. The extended relational algebra corresponds to such features, and furthermore supports some convenient operators. For example, let R be a nested relation, S be the schema and A be the subschema. In an intuitive notation of the algebra, the following operation

$$(\pi_{S \backslash A} \sigma_{Cond}(R)) \bowtie_{S \backslash A} R$$

is frequently used for some condition $Cond$ that includes a subset of A. The processing of this operation does not need to read tuples if $S \backslash A$ has a key property. Such an operation is supported as one algebraic operator for efficient processing.

Further extensions for nested relations are now under consideration: introduction of set grouping semantics and its corresponding operations, semi-automatic design support by using semantic constraints, parallel processing for Kappa-P (see Section 6), and some more built-in functions both for practical use and for efficient processing.

3.2 For More Structured Data

While a nested relational model is flexible and efficient for structured data used by many KIPSs, it fails to represent semantic relations between entities (objects or tuples). In practice, for the purpose, two data models are supported on nested relations. The first one is a *classification hierarchy* connected by a single link such as IS_A or HAS_A, and the second one is a *semantic network*. They are very useful for a concept dictionary and a thesaurus in natural language processing. This layer gives operations only for data manipulation (including simple inheritance) of nodes and links in hierarchies or networks, although such structures usually need more semantic manipulation along the links. More semantic operations will be supported on the upper knowledge base layer.

Other extensions on nested relations are being considered to provide an integrated environment, especially for a workstation environment: text as a data type and combination with interface facilities such as editors, and interfaces including a usual file interface. In such an environment, a DBMS should contain a usual file interface and provide a common interface to secondary memory. A (nested) term relation [Itoh86] is also considered using terms as a data type. Terms are convenient representations even with complex structure, but the semantics is outside the DBMS and the operations are expensive, so only the restricted form can be considered. In this layer, some more data models would be added, both to be practical and in order to support the above knowledge base layer.

3.3 Some Features of the DBMS

We overview some features of the system of the database layer. The prototype system called Kappa-I already works for various KIPSs and the second version called Kappa-II is under construction. In this subsection, we explain Kappa-II.

The database for nested relations resides in both main and secondary memories. Main memory is used as a cache and as a main memory database accompanying the delayed update process. For access to secondary memory, a new file system was implemented in order to make it possible to assign physical disk pages effectively and schedule physical accesses to them. Briefly, secondary memory for a database is divided physically into control, index, record, temporary, buffer-swap and log areas. The control area has information of database identity and the physical layout of the database. Each nested tuple is encoded into one string and stored in the record area. Data that relate to one relation are put as close together as possible in each of index and record areas. The temporary area is used for storing and manipulating intermediate relations.

One of the unique features of our system is a tuple identifier (TID), which identifies with one nested tuple. As the extended relational algebra can manipulate subtuples in the narrower sense of nested relations, according to the above semantics, a real TID consists of a set of sequences of the original TID and subTIDs identifying to subtuples. Indexes contain such sequences and support such mechanism. Intermediate relations as subsets of the original relation are in the form of a set of such TIDs. While unnest and nest operations are required during set operations to reserve the nest sequence of the schema, it is possible not by reading the corresponding values but by using only subTIDs. For example, assume the following relation with one nested tuple:

$$\{[a/k_1, b/\{d_1, d_2\}, c/\{d_3, d_4\}]\}.$$

For queries $b = d_1$ and $c = d_3$, the resulting relations are as follows:

$$\{[a/k_1, b/d_1, c/\{d_3, d_4\}]\}, \quad \text{and}$$
$$\{[a/k_1, b/\{d_1, d_2\}, c/d_3]\}.$$

If a union operation is applied to these relations, according to the above semantics, the result is

$$\{[a/k_1, b/d_1, c/\{d_3, d_4\}], [a/k_1, b/d_2, c/d_3]\}, \quad \text{or}$$
$$\{[a/k_1, b/\{d_1, d_2\}, c/d_3], [a/k_1, b/d_2, c/d_4]\},$$

where a/k_1 is not a tuple's key but a key of a set of tuples, whereas Verso generates the original relation to reserve the property of a tuple's key. Which relation should be taken depends on the nesting order between a and b, and the processing does not need to read tuples. Such use of identifiers is similar with ANDA [DeGu88], but the index structure is different: in our system, indexes are separate for each attribute, and each index entry contains a set of homogeneous sequences of a TID and subTIDs.

Familiar database facilities such as resource management. concurrency control and user management are

of course equipped. For distributed facility, a server DBMS is assigned in each domain in PSI-network and controls all databases in the domain. Features of a distributed DBMS such as two phase commit and replication are not supported because they are not required so much in a personal workstation environment.

As the system is written in ESP, its object concept is used in the design and the development, and make the system simpler. Various logical elements such as a database, relations, sets, tuples, schemata and so on are all in the form of objects, and are thrown mutually between modules, which are also in the form of objects. An interface between user programs and the system is defined as methods of objects. There are two kinds of methods: system built-in methods such as extended relational algebra, and user-defined methods. Users can define any interface in the form of methods of an object for their applications and register the object to the system.

4 DEDUCTIVE DATABASES

The knowledge base layer consists of some subsystems such as deductive mechanism based on some languages, and inference mechanism of more structured data. Each deductive and inference mechanism is provided according to each knowledge representation language. We focus on the deductive database (DD) mechanism in this section and discuss structured data in next section.

A DD is an extension of a relational database in the light of logic. In other words a DD is the proof-theoretic reconstruction of a relational database [GMN84]. We consider DDs as a first step towards knowledge bases. As mentioned in Section 2, CAP system is one of the applications that needs deductive mechanism during proof checking. We have developed the prototype system based on definite clauses which correspond to relations without a set constructor as a proper subclass of nested relations, and we are now developing query processing based on CRL for a subclass of nested relations.

In the first step, we implemented query processing mechanism based on definite clauses: *sideways information passing* [Ullman85], *generalized magic sets* [BeRa87] and *semi-naive evaluation* [Ban86]. We plan to combine it with the CAP system. Some extensions are now under consideration: query optimization called Horn clauses transformation by restrictor (HCT/R) [Miya+88] in less restricted form than generalized magic sets, query processing by using semantic relations such as equivalence relation [Sakama88], query evaluation for stratified databases under the standard model semantics [Seki88], indefinite answer as a set of constraints combined with CAL [Aiba+88], and integrity constraint for update of DDs.

The next step aims at deductive mechanism on nested relations, for which we proposed a logic programming language called *CRL* [Yokota88]. It uses an attribute-valued notation instead of a predicate notation. Assume a set of variables besides the symbols of the nested tuples, the *term* is defined as follows:

(1) An atomic object o is a term,

(1') A variable X is a term,

(2) If $t_1, \cdots, t_n$ are terms, then $\{t_1, \cdots, t_n\}$ is a term, which is called a *set term*,

(3) If $a_1, \cdots, a_n$ are attribute names and $t_1, \cdots, t_n$ are terms, then $[a_1/t_1, \cdots, a_n/t_n]$ is a term, which is called a *tuple term*.

This attribute-valued notation is an extension of a usual predicate notation by introducing a set of some attribute names.:

$$p(t_1, \cdots, t_n) \Rightarrow [\$0/p, \$1/t_1, \cdots, \$n/t_n],$$

where $\$0, \$1, \cdots, \$n$ are newly introduced attribute names. The advantages are flexibility in the position and the number of arguments, and natural representation of column and row nesting tuples by set and tuple constructors. The same restrictions as nested tuples are also imposed on the terms for nested relations. Furthermore the notation can be used for more structured data (see Section 5.2).

For the semantics of the term, corresponding to the semantics of nested tuples, a term is mapped into a set of *partially tagged trees* (*PTTs*), each of which is defined as a partial function from a set of leaves of a tree domain of attribute names to a set of atomic objects without a void object: for a set M of PTTs, a variable assignment η and a tuple t,

$$[M; \eta] \models t \Leftrightarrow t\eta \in M.$$

While a PTT is given for the semantics of CIL [Mukai87], the term in this case is interpreted as a set of PTTs because of the set constructor. The semantics of the terms reserves the semantics of nested tuples. According to the semantics, row-nest and row-unnest operations correspond to a distributive law under an algebraic structure with tuple and set constructors:

$$\{[a/c_1, b/\{c_2, c_3\}]\} \Leftrightarrow \{[a/c_1, b/c_2], [a/c_1, b/c_3]\}.$$

Hence the syntax of terms is restricted to a multi-valued level so that unification can be made decidable and a logic programming language constructed, although the database with only ground terms (nested tuples) may have more deeply nested tuples. Unification between the terms are defined by merge (overlapping) of tree domains of attribute names, set intersection between subterms of set type, which reduced to non-empty set, and atomic object identity.

A *program clause* is a pair of a tuple term t and a set $\{t_1, \cdots, t_n\}$ of tuple terms. A pair $(t, \{t_1, \cdots, t_n\})$ is written as follows:

$$t \leftarrow t_1, \cdots, t_n.$$

A *CRL program* is a set of clauses. And a *goal* is a set of tuple terms $q_1, \cdots, q_m$, which is written as $\leftarrow q_1, \cdots, q_m$, and a *database query* is a query with one term, which does not mean loss of generality. For example,

$$[par/\{\text{``}mary\text{''}\}, chi/\{\text{``}john\text{''}, \text{``}lisa\text{''}\}],$$
$$[par/\{\text{``}paul\text{''}, \text{``}kate\text{''}\}, chi/\{\text{``}mary\text{''}\}],$$
$$[anc/X, des/Y] \leftarrow [par/X, chi/Y],$$
$$[anc/X, des/Y] \leftarrow [par/X, chi/Z], [anc/Z, des/Y]$$

is a CRL program. A *CRL database* is a CRL program and is divided into an intensional and an extensional databases (an IDB and an EDB), just like a definite clause based DD. An EDB is a set of nested tuples.

For a program or a database P, a non-empty set M of PTTs, which is constructed by PTTs included in P, is called a *model* of P when M satisfies the following condition:

$$\forall q \leftarrow p_1, \cdots, p_n \in P(M \models p_1 \wedge \cdots \wedge p_n \supset M \models q).$$

The definition shows the following properties:

$$q \leftarrow p_1, \cdots, p_n$$
$$\equiv q \leftarrow p_1, \cdots, p_{i-1}, p_{i1}, \cdots, p_{im}, p_{i+1}, \cdots, p_n$$
$$\equiv q_1 \leftarrow p_1, \cdots, p_n \wedge \cdots \wedge q_k \leftarrow p_1, \cdots, p_n,$$

where $p_{i1}, \cdots, p_{im}$ and $q_1, \cdots, q_k$ are 'unnested' results of p_i and q, respectively. The relation guarantees to reserve the declarative and procedural semantics of Prolog. As the extended SLD resolution for the CRL program, set unification (intersection) is applied for an EDB term without being unnesting, and the new goal corresponding to the set difference is generated for an IDB. For example, consider the following goal:

$$\leftarrow G_1, [\cdots, a/S, \cdots], G_2,$$

where S is a set term. If the subgoal $[\cdots, a/S, \cdots]$ can be unified with an EDB term $[\cdots, a/S', \cdots]$ by a unifier θ, the new goal is generated as follows:

$$\leftarrow (G_1, [\cdots, a/(S \setminus S'), \cdots], G_2)\theta,$$

if $S \setminus S'$ is not an empty set.

As for bottom-up evaluation, the least fixpoint semantics like Prolog is also defined, and similar optimization strategies can be applied. For example, for a query $\leftarrow [anc/\{\text{``}paul\text{''}, \text{``}kate\text{''}\}, des/X]$ ($\leftarrow [anc/\text{``}paul\text{''}, des/X], [anc/\text{``}kate\text{''}, des/X]$), the above

CRL database (program) can be transformed into the following form:

$$[par/\{``mary"\}, chi/\{``john", ``lisa"\}].$$
$$[par/\{``paul", ``kate"\}, chi/\{``mary"\}].$$
$$[anc/X, des/Y] \leftarrow [anc^*/X], [par/X, chi/Y].$$
$$[anc/X, des/Y] \leftarrow [anc^*/X], [par/X, chi/Z],$$
$$[anc/Z, des/Y].$$
$$[anc^*/``paul"].$$
$$[anc^*/``kate"].$$
$$[anc^*/Z] \leftarrow [anc^*/X], [par/X, chi/Z].$$

This is an example of HCT/R [Miya+88] for a CRL database.

Current CRL (intensional) databases are restricted to multi-valued nested relations, although the database layer supports unlimited nesting logically. Under the same semantics, looser restrictions are required. Some extensions are considered in addition to the case of definite clauses. The first extension is the introduction of set grouping semantics like LDL [Beeri+87], which corresponds to an extension of the database layer. Another extension is the creation of an attribute system that can compose attribute names, introduced in [Tanaka87], where an initial set of attributes, simply called a vocabulary dictionary, is extended by repeating both composition of attribute names and labeling the result. The introduction of such a dictionary also makes it possible to introduce 'constraints' by attribute composition.

5 TOWARDS DEDUCTIVE AND OBJECT-ORIENTED DATABASES

5.1 Deductive vs. Object-Oriented

In order to cope with wider applications including KIPSs, more complex data models which extend from flat relations to (nearly) direct representation of objects of the real world are required and proposed [BaKh85, Maier86, AbGr88, Lecluse+88, Beeri+88, Beeri88]. These data models includes various elements: data modeling in the database area; data abstraction, type disciplines and object concept in programming language; and type inheritance in knowledge representation language. We set up the direction of knowledge bases in our environment as representation of 'objects' and their processing in the framework of DDs, (as integration of DDs and object-oriented databases (OODs)).

The formalization of nested relations as one of 'objects' is tried or pointed out in various contexts: type inheritance [Ait86], complex objects [BaKh85, AbGr88], objects [Maier86] and logic programming with sets [Beeri+87]. These ways show a framework of formulation common to that of more structured data such as nested relations, complex objects and objects, although each specific object has its

intrinsic operations, such as row-nest and row-unnest operations in nested relations. Such formulation is also related to other areas such as representation of situation in natural language processing [Mukai87]. We generally call such structured data 'objects', which include nested relations and complex objects.

OODs are proposed by stimulation of the success of object-oriented programming languages (OOPs). They are more appropriate for representation of 'objects' of the real world and have many possibilities such as providing the framework of multi-media databases, serving as dissolution of 'impedance mismatch', (filling gaps in data structure and data operation between database and programming languages), or helping to create classification hierarchy. However most of the approaches are rather practical and is not based on logic or mathematics. The concept is still vague and there is no consensus [Ban88].

An OOP is not the same as an OOD even though it would support data persistence, because OODs should support intrinsic objects in a database area, including nested relations and complex objects, and have traditional features of DBMSs as a management system. The term 'object-oriented' has two kinds of meanings: the structural aspect (static objects) such as complex structure, object identity, data abstraction and classification hierarchy; and behavioral aspects (active objects) such as methods, message passing and information encapsulation. OODs except Smalltalk-based databases focus mainly on the first aspect, whereas OOPs focus on the second aspect.

In a database area, an approach for DDs gives logical foundations and perspectives of extensions towards knowledge bases, whereas an approach for OODs gives the framework of 'object' modeling of the real world. Most of advanced applications including KIPSs require new databases (or knowledge bases) which support both powerful inference mechanism and high-level modeling capability. If OODs could be treated based on such formulation as an approach for DDs has proposes, they would serve many KIPSs even without the behavioral aspect, and more with the aspect.

For such purposes, many approaches for integration of DDs and OODs, i.e., a framework called *deductive and object-oriented databases (DOODs)* can be considered. We set up a DOOD as a framework of knowledge bases in our target. We started to take such an approach for a subclass of 'objects' (nested relations), which is also appropriate for many applications in our environments, and being developed a deductive mechanism based on CRL as a first step.

5.2 The Framework of DOOD

As mentioned above, the predicate notation like Prolog lacks flexibility for more structured data. Although it is considered to embed new expression into the predicate notation, it is only convenient but not essential; there seems to be no reason to persist in it. We use objects defined in Section 3.1. Such an object might be called a nested tuple or a complex object with some restrictions according to each domain.

In order to classify objects, a *type* is defined as follows:

(1) A void object ω belongs to a type $\top$ and all other atomic objects belong to a same type **atom**,

(2) If $o_1, \cdots, o_n$ belong to types, $\tau_1, \cdots, \tau_n$ respectively, then a set object $o = \{o_1, \cdots, o_n\}$ belongs to a set type $\{\tau_1, \cdots, \tau_n\}$.

(3) If each of $o_1, \cdots, o_n$ belongs to a type, $\tau_1, \cdots, \tau_n$, then a tuple object $o = [a_1/o_1, \cdots, a_n/o_n]$ belongs to a tuple type $[a_1/\tau_1, \cdots, a_n/\tau_n]$.

Note that atomic objects except ω do not necessarily belong to one type, and might be divided into some atomic types such as **string** and **integer**.

We add another type $\bot$ to a set of types and define a partial order $\preceq$ between types as follows:

(1) For any type τ, $\bot \preceq \tau$ and $\tau \preceq \top$.

(2) For set types $\tau_1 = \{\tau_{11}, \cdots, \tau_{1n}\}$ and $\tau_2 = \{\tau_{21}, \cdots, \tau_{2m}\}$, if $\forall \tau_{1i}, \exists \tau_{2j}(\tau_{1i} \preceq \tau_{2j})$, then $\tau_1 \preceq \tau_2$.

(3) For a tuple type $\tau = [a_1/\tau_1, \cdots, a_n/\tau_n]$, let τ' be a type, obtained by τ, which excludes a_i/τ_i such that $\tau_i = \top$. For tuple types τ_1 and τ_2, let $\tau_1' = [a_{11}/\tau_{11}, \cdots, a_{1n}/\tau_{1n}]$ and $\tau_2' = [a_{21}/\tau_{21}, \cdots, a_{2m}/\tau_{2m}]$. If there exists i such that $\tau_{1i} = \bot$, or $\{a_{11}, \cdots, a_{1n}\} \supseteq \{a_{21}, \cdots, a_{2m}\}$ and $\forall j, \exists i(a_{1i} = a_{2j} \wedge \tau_{1i} \preceq \tau_{2j})$, then $\tau_1 \preceq \tau_2$.

According to the definition, we can obtain the following equivalence relation $\approx$:

$$
\begin{aligned}
\{\tau_1, \tau_2, \cdots, \tau_n\} &\approx \{\tau_2, \cdots, \tau_n\}, \text{ if } \tau_1 \preceq \tau_2, \\
\{\top, \tau_2, \cdots, \tau_n\} &\approx \{\top\}, \\
\{\bot, \tau_2, \cdots, \tau_n\} &\approx \{\tau_2, \cdots, \tau_n\}, \\
[a_1/\top, a_2/\tau_2, \cdots, a_n/\tau_n] &\approx [a_2/\tau_2, \cdots, a_n/\tau_n], \\
[a_1/\bot, a_2/\tau_2, \cdots, a_n/\tau_n] &\approx [a_i/\bot], \text{ for any } i.
\end{aligned}
$$

Note that elements in a set object or a tuple object are commutative. Without loss of generality, we consider an equivalence class modulo $\approx$ and assume that each tuple element of a tuple object does not contain $\top$ or $\bot$, and each element of a set object is not ordered with others. A type τ_1 is *compatible* with a type τ_2 if there exists a type τ such that $\tau \neq \top$, $\tau_1 \preceq \tau$ and $\tau_2 \preceq \tau$. According to the definition, we exclude incompatible (heterogeneous) set objects, some elements of which belong to incompatible types. A type might be called

a schema for nested relations. A set of types including $\top$ and $\bot$ constitutes a lattice, where g.l.b. and l.u.b. between set types correspond to set intersection and union respectively, and g.l.b. and l.u.b. between a set type and a tuple type result in $\bot$ and $\top$ respectively.

We can redefine objects by combining objects and types:

(1) For a null object ω, $\omega : \top$ is an object.

(2) For any atomic object o except ω, $o : $ **atom** is an object.

(3) If $o_1 : \tau_1, \cdots, o_n : \tau_n$ are objects and $\tau_1, \cdots, \tau_n$ are compatible, then $\{o_1 : \tau_1, \cdots, o_n : \tau_n\} : \{\tau_1, \cdots, \tau_n\}$ is a set object.

(4) If $a_1, \cdots, a_n$ are different attribute names and $o_1 : \tau_1, \cdots, o_n : \tau_n$ are objects, $[a_1/o_1 : \tau_1, \cdots, a_n/o_n : \tau_n] : [a_1/\tau_1, \cdots, a_n/\tau_n]$ is a tuple object.

(5) If $o : \tau_1$ is an object and $\tau_1 \preceq \tau_2$, then $o : \tau_2$ is an object.

Even if types are not attached explicitly, they can be inferred from the innermost.

New type symbols are introduced to define structured types and reserve the original ordering. A set type τ_s or a tuple type τ_t is can be redefined as follows:

$$\tau = \tau_s, \text{ or } \tau = \tau_t,$$

where τ is a newly introduced type name. Furthermore, a type can be defined recursively and represent infinite structure, like tags in [Ait86]. For example,

$$\tau = [id/\textbf{integer}, name/\textbf{string}, age/\textbf{integer}, \cdots, des/\{\tau\}].$$

Corresponding to the type, an object can be represented by introducing object identities. For example,

$$
\begin{aligned}
[&id/10, \\
&name/\text{``taro''}, \\
&age/30, \cdots, \\
&des/\{[id/20], [id/30]\} : \{\tau\}] : \tau,
\end{aligned}
$$

where obvious types are omitted and 'id' is an attribute name of an object identity.

In such formulation, various structured data such nested relations, complex objects and classification hierarchy can be developed. For the purpose, specific operations such as row-nest and row-unnest for nested relations, or specific orderings such as HAS_A relation in complex objects [BaKh85] and IS_A relation for classification hierarchy or nested relations with inheritance [Nakano88] should be introduced. We can consider such formulation as a general framework of DOOD, which is independent of specific domains, and construct various structured objects as an instance of

260

the framework by introducing each intrinsic meaning and specific restrictions.

Some of them can be resolved into conjunction of simple forms, pointed out in [Beeri88]:

$$o = [a_1/o_1, \cdots, a_n/o_n] \Leftrightarrow o.a_1 = o_1 \wedge \cdots \wedge o.a_n = o_n.$$

Such translation makes the semantics clear but goes far from our intention such as nearly direct representation of 'objects' of the real world and its inference at the level.

In the above construction, further considerations remain:

- Mathematical structure for a set of objects with each specific domain, and the formal semantics. If their objects constitute a lattice such as [Ait86, BaKh85, Nakano88], the treatment would become easier.

- Restrictions to make up a logic programming language or an IDB in a DD based on such objects, for example, limitation for decidability of unification. Not only a fixpoint semantics such as [Beeri+87, AbGr88] but also a procedural semantics should be given.

- How to relate such objects to more general knowledge representation such as semantic networks and frames. Although knowledge is represented in the form of a rule from a viewpoint of DDs based on definite clauses, it might be represented in another form such as a set of orderings in DOOD. This is also a problem for integration of Kappa and ETA.

- An object itself and a relation between objects can be considered as constraints, and a logic programming language based on them can be within the framework of a constraint logic programming scheme $CLP(X)$ [JaLa87]. If we could consider the scheme of DOOD such as the above formulation, each specific meaning and operation could be given as a constraint solver in each domain.

- Even in the structural aspects of objects, an update problem [Maier86, Beeri88] should be solved for a 'real' extension of traditional databases.

Although we have not discussed the behavioral aspects of objects, there are already some researches such as [Beeri+88, Lecluse+88]. Such aspects can be considered from two viewpoints: uniform framework of interface including dissolution of impedance mismatch; data manipulation depending on kinds of objects such as text, picture or geographical data. There remain problems about how such an aspect fits a framework of DDs or OOPs. This approach also will contribute to many new applications.

6 OVERVIEW OF THE PROJECTS

We have overviewed the knowledge base management system, Kappa, and in this section explain the outline of the project and the other related projects: *ETA* and *PHI* projects. Kappa project started in September, 1985, and is divided into two-year subprojects.

The first subproject called, *Kappa-I*, started in September, 1985 and ended in August, 1987. It intended to make a DBMS that would reflect some requirements of CAP and electronic language dictionaries in its design, provide experimental environments for other KIPSs, and form the grounds for knowledge bases. The underlying data model of the DBMS is a nested relational model in the above sense, and has some advanced features such as terms as a data type. Classification hierarchy is also supported on nested relations. The size of the system consists of about 60,000 lines in ESP. The evaluation test shows that the system works efficiently, and some KIPSs already use the system as the underlying database.

The second subproject called, *Kappa-II*, started in April, 1987, overlapping with Kappa-I, and will end in March, 1989. The targets of the system are further improvement of Kappa-I, especially in processing performance and in management of main memory, introduction of semantic network as one of the basic objects, implementation of various interfaces, and implementation of the prototype of DDs both in definite clauses and CRL. We are now constructing the system; it will be released next April for users who engage in knowledge information processing systems on PSI.

The third subproject, *Kappa-III*, and the fourth subproject, *Kappa-P*, will start in December, 1988, also overlapping with Kappa-II. In Kappa-III, object flavors are added to all layers of Kappa-II, as mentioned in Section 5. More structured data than nested relations are supported, and knowledge bases are considered in the framework of deductive and object-oriented databases. Kappa-P is intended to do research and development on parallel processing of Kappa-II and providing experimental environments of databases and knowledge bases on Multi-PSI and PIM. These subprojects are mutually related: some parallel algorithms devised in the former will be also implemented in the latter.

The ETA is a knowledge object management system, devoted to knowledge representation in the form of semantic network and its intelligence information retrieval mechanism based on abstractive layers of the objects [Koguchi+88]. The prototype system was implemented on PSI, and shows such an approach to be very useful for structured knowledge such as text data. The language for structured data is being refined towards having clear semantics, and realizing deductive and inference mechanisms. The system is being designed to work on Kappa system.

The PHI project is intended to investigate the mechanism of a distributed DD system based on a relational database in PSIs and PSI-network environment [Itoh+88, Miya+88]. The prototype system was implemented on PSI, focusing on the superimposed code scheme for term access, recursive query optimization (HCT), and its distributed processing. Query optimization of stratified databases is under further consideration.

At the final stage of the FGCS project, these systems and various ideas for knowledge base management systems will be integrated, and will provide an experimental environment for many knowledge information processing systems.

7 CONCLUSIONS

Kappa is a software project among the knowledge base projects in ICOT. As the middle-range target of the knowledge base management system, we set up a framework of deductive and object-oriented databases. Although the two approaches for deductive databases and object-oriented databases have been taken almost independently, some work towards their integration has begun recently, and we are working towards integration. Among them the characteristics of our research and development can be summarized as follows:

- Knowledge bases in our environment are taken as an extended form of databases, especially for a deductive approach to structured data including terms, in the framework of deductive and object-oriented databases.

- The underlying data model of our system is a nested relational model because of the efficient internal representation and the efficient processing of structured data; more complex data models are constructed on the nested relational model.

- A deductive approach is taken first for nested relations as a subclass of 'objects', and being further considered for more structured data such as classification hierarchy, complex objects and semantic network.

- Some projects for databases and knowledge bases, such as Kappa, ETA and PHI are in cooperation with each other, and will be integrated with other systems such as PIM, PIMOS and KBM at the final stage of the FGCS project for the target.

Acknowledgments

The research and development described in this article is being done mainly by the members of the KBMS groups both in ICOT and the participating companies. The authors are grateful to Dr. Kazuhiro Fuchi and Dr. Shunichi Uchida for encouraging the projects and providing useful suggestion.

References

[AbGr88] S. Abiteboul and S. Grumbach, "COL: A Logic-Based language for Complex Objects", *EDBT*, in *LNCS*, 303, Springer, 1988

[Aiba+88] Z. Aiba, K. Sakai, Y. Sato, D. Hawley and R. Hasegawa, "Constraint Logic Programming Language CAL", *FGCS*, 1988

[Ait86] H. Ait-Kaci, "An Algebraic Semantics Approach to the Effective Resolution of Type Equations", *TCS*, vol.45, 1986

[BaKh85] F. Bancilhon and S. Khoshahian, "A Calculus for Complex Objects", *ACM PODS*, 1985

[Ban86] F. Bancilhon, "Naive Evaluation of Recursively Defined Relations", in *On Knowledge Base Management Systems*, M.L. Brodie, et al, eds., Springer, 1986

[Ban88] F. Bancilhon, "Object-Oriented Database Systems", *ACM PODS*, 1988

[Beeri88] C. Beeri, "Data Models and Languages for Databases", *ICDT*, 1988

[Beeri+87] C. Beeri, S. Naqvi, O. Shnueli and S. Tsur, "Sets and Negation in a Logic Database Language (LDL)", *ACM PODS*, 1987

[Beeri+88] C. Beeri, R. Nasr and S. Tsur, "Embedding ψ-term in a Horn-clause Logic", in *Proc. of Third Int'l Conf. on Data and Knowledge Bases*, Jersalem, 1988

[BeRa87] C. Beeri and R. Ramakrishnam, "On the Power of Magic", *ACM PODS*, 1987

[Chik+88] T. Chikayama, H. Sato and T. Miyazaki, "Overview of the Parallel Inference Machine Operating System (PIMOS)", *FGCS*, 1988

[Dadam+86] P. Dadam, et al, "A DBMS Prototype to Support Extended NF² Relations: An Integrated View on Flat Tables and Hierarchies", *ACM SIGMOD*, 1986

[DeGu88] A. Deshpande and D. Van Gucht, "An Implementation for Nested Relational Databases", *VLDB*, 1988

[GMN84] H. Gallaire, J. Minker and L.-M. Nicolas, "Logic and Databases: A Deductive Approach", *ACM Computing Surveys*, vol.16, no.2, 1984

[Goto+88] A. Goto, M. Sato, K. Nakajima, K. Taki and A. Matsumoto, "Overview of the Parallel Inference Machine Architecture (PIM)", *FGCS*, 1988

[Hirose+87] K. Hirose, K. Yokota and K. Sakai, "An Approach to Proof Checker", *ICOT-TR*, 224, 1987

[Ishi+85] T. Ishikawa, H. Tanaka, et al, "Basic Specifications of the Machine-Readable Dictionary", *ICOT-TR*, 100, 1985

[Itoh86] H. Itoh, "Research and Development on Knowledge Base Systems at ICOT", *VLDB*, 1986

[Itoh+88] H. Itoh, H. Monoi et al, "Outline of the Knowledge Base Subsystem", *FGCS*, 1988

[JaLa87] J. Jaffer and J.-L Lassez, "Constraint Logic Programming", *IEEE SLP*, 1987

[Koguchi+88] T. Koguchi, H. Kondo, M. Oba and H. Itoh, "Knowledge Representation with Abstractive Layers for Information Retrieval", *FGCS*, 1988

[Lecluse+88] C. Lecluse, P. Richard and F. Velez, "O_2, an Object-Oriented Data Model", *EDBT*, in *LNCS*, 303, Springer, 1988

[Maier86] D. Maier, "A Logic for Objects", in *Preprint of the Workshop on Foundations of Deductive Databases and Logic Programming*, 1986

[Maki77] A. Makinouchi, "A Consideration on Normal Form of Not-Necessarily-Normalized Relation in the Relational Data Model", *VLDB*, 1977

[Miura87] T. Miura, "Theory of Non First Normal Form Relational Databases – A Survey", in *Proc. of Advanced Database Symposium*, IPSJ, Tokyo, Dec., 1987 (in Japanese)

[Miya+88] N. Miyazaki, K. Yokota, H. Haniuda and H. Itoh, "Horn Clause Transformation by Restrictor in Deductive Databases", *ICOT-TR*, 407, 1988

[Mukai87] K. Mukai, "Anadic Tuples in Prolog", *ICOT-TR*, 239, 1987

[Nakano88] R. Nakano, "Frame Lattice Model", in *Special Interest Group Notes of IPSJ*, Sep., 1988 (in Japanese)

[Sakai88] K. Sakai, "Towards Mechanization of Mathematics – Proof Checker and Term Rewriting System", in *Programming of Future Generation Computers*, K. Fuchi and M. Nivat, eds., Elsevier, 1988

[Sakama88] C. Sakama and H. Itoh, "Handling Knowledge by its Representative", *EDS*, 1988

[ScSc87] M.H. Scholl and H.-J. Schek, (eds.), *Theory and Applications of Nested Relations and Complex Objects – An International Workshop, Workshop Material*, 1987

[ScWe86] H.-J. Schek and G. Weikum, "DASDBS: Concepts and Architecture of a Database System for Advanced Applications", *Tech. Univ. of Darmstadt, TR*, DVSI-1986-T1, 1986

[Seki88] H. Seki and H. Itoh, "A Query Evaluation Method for Stratified Programs under the Extended CWA", *LP*, 1988

[Tanaka87] Y. Tanaka, "Roles of a Vocabulary in Knowledge-Based Systems", *IFIP WG 10.1 Workshop*, Gotenba, 1987

[TaYo88] Y. Tanaka and Y. Yoshioka, "Overview of the Dictionary and Lexical Knowledge Base Research", *FGCS*, 1988

[Ullman85] J.D. Ullman, "Implementation of Logical Query languages for Databases", *ACM TODS*, vol.10, no.3, 1985

[Verso86] J. Verso, "VERSO: A Data Base Machine Based on Non 1NF Relations", *INRIA-TR*, 523, 1986

[Yokota88] K. Yokota, "Deductive Approach for Nested Relations", *ICOT-TR*, 1988

Constraint Logic Programming Language CAL

Akira Aiba   Kô Sakai   Yosuke Sato   David J. Hawley

and Ryuzo Hasegawa

Institute for New Generation Computer Technology

4-28, Mita 1-Chome, Minatoku, Tokyo 108 JAPAN

October 6, 1988

Abstract

In this paper, we describe the current state of development of the constraint logic programming language CAL (*Contrainte Avec Logique*), and several future extensions. CAL supports the writing and solving as constraints of linear and non-linear algebraic polynomial equations, boolean equations, and linear inequalities. An implementation currently exists on the PSI machine. In the future, we are aiming to build a very flexible constraint logic programming language by combining multiple constraint solvers in one system.

1 Introduction

Constraint is one of the most important programming paradigms and is discussed in various field of knowledge processing from both the applicational and theoretical points of view. There are many advantages of constraint programming. The most outstanding feature of constraint programming is that it allows the declarative description of problems. That is, a problem is solved by indicating a goal without reference to the method by which it should be established.

In order to solve a problem by computers, we first have to precisely describe the problem. Therefore, in general, we have to determine a field and objects in it. In computer graphics, for example, the field is an Euclidean plane and the objects are points or other geometrical elements in the plane.

The set of objects in a certain field form a system. For example, the positions of points in Euclidean plane and their mutual distances satisfy a set of conditions. In general, these conditions are relations among the objects (or the parameters representing them).

Constraints are formulas representing such relations. The constraint programming paradigm is that conditions which must be satisfied by the objects in a program are described declaratively in terms of constraints [Ste-81],

[Fik-70], [StS-78]. Constraints in a program are evaluated automatically and affect the execution of the program depending on their meaning.

When constraints are incorporated into logic programming, it is natural to call it constraint logic programming (CLP). Jaffar and Lassez were the first advocates of CLP [Jal-86], [JaL-87]. Similar paradigms (or languages) were proposed by Colmerauer [Col-82], [Col-87], and by Dincbas, Simonis, and van Hentenryck [Din-87]. Prolog programs are executed by a mechanism which includes unification as a major component. CLP is an attempt to increase the descriptive power of logic programming by employing constraint solving instead of unification in its execution mechanism. Unification itself is a kind of constraint solving. In this sense, CLP is a generalization of logic programming.

It is in the framework of logic programming that constraints give full play to their ability. In particular, the feature of declarative description, which is also a feature of logic programming, is preserved naturally and completely in CLP. There is other evidence that CLP is a natural extension of logic programming. For example, there is a simple and unified framework for the declarative and operational semantics of CLP. This may not be true for a language in which control is described operationally. However, the operational semantics of CLP can be viewed as a simple generalization of the ordinary goal-reduction technique of logic programming.

Traditional logic programming possesses logical, functional, and operational semantics, which coincide with each other [EmK-76], [ApE-82], [Llo-84]. Jaffar and Lassez showed that CLP is a generalization of traditional logic programming in the sense that it possesses these three semantics [JaL-87]. In addition, they introduced algebraic semantics for CLP.

The execution steps of CLP programs depend upon the decision of whether or not a constraint is satisfiable in a given domain. However, we require more; the canonical forms of constraints should be computed if the constraints are satisfiable. The situation resembles that in ordinary logic programming, where unification decides the satisfiability of a set of equations in the Herbrand universe, and computes the most general unifier if the set is satisfiable. Since equations are typical constraints, the operational model of CLP is clearly an extension of that of logic programming. Moreover, the criteria of decidability of satisfiability, and the existence and computability of a canonical form, clarifies the requirements for constrain solvers in CLP and spurs on research on efficient methods to solve constraints in various domains.

This paper describes the theoretical foundation, implementation, and application of CAL (Contrainte avec Logique), which is the CLP language being developed at ICOT. Section 2 introduces constraint logic programming using $CLP(R)$ as an example. Section 3 describes the semantics of CLP, focusing on the CAL system. Section 4 describes the current status of CAL: the system, language, constraint solver, and example programs. Section 5 discusses applications and future extensions of CAL.

2 Constraint Logic Programming Language

Constraint Logic Programming Languages originated with Prolog-II by Colmerauer [Col-82]. Subsequently, a scheme for constraint logic programming $CLP(\mathbf{X})$ was proposed by Jaffar, Lassez, et. al. [JaL-86], and they gave its semantics in a logical frame-work. This scheme includes Prolog, Prolog-II, Prolog-III [Col-87], and $CLP(\mathcal{R})$ [JaM-85] which was developed at Monash University in Australia as an example of the scheme. In a different approach, Dincbas proposed a constraint logic programming language in [Din-87], based on extended unification.

The difference between these constraint logic programming languages is the sort of constraints which they can handle. For instance, linear algebraic and boolean equations can be written in Prolog-III, while in $CLP(\mathcal{R})$ algebraic equations and inequalities can be expressed, but only linear ones can be solved.

Constraint logic programming languages handle constraints by the following two methods: by extending the unification component of the logic programming language or by introducing a mechanism called the "Constraint Solver". We will discuss the processing of programs under the latter paradigm, which seems at least as general as the former.

Constraints are identified from other predicate-invocations by having a distinguished "constraint symbol", for example the "equality symbol" or "inequality symbol", as their principal functor. The execution model is similar to that for a logic programming language except that constraints are considered to be builtin predicates handled by the constraint solver.

To design a constraint logic programming language, the most important question is the selection of a computation domain and the selection of relations which will be handled as constraints. Dincbas proposed the following criteria to select a computation domain whose equations are embedded into unification [Din-87].

1. Each equation in the domain should be solved in a deterministic way without losing completeness.

2. Efficient equation solving methods should exist within the domain.

3. The computation domain should be used sufficiently often to justify its introduction inside unification.

We propose the following alternate set of criteria for the selection of computation domains over which equations and other constraints may be written [SaA-88]. The first three criteria correspond to those above.

1. Satisfiability (solvability) of constraints should be decidable.

2. An efficient algorithm to determine satisfiability should exist.

3. The computation domain should be used sufficiently often to justify supporting it directly in the language.

4. A canonical form for a constraint should exist if it is satisfiable, and the canonical form should be considered as the answer.

The last criterion has the following meaning. For example, the constraint X+Y=1, X-Y=1 is equivalent to X=1, Y=0. In this case, if the latter can be considered the canonical form, the latter should be computed from the former. Canonical forms are described precisely in the next section.

We now consider an example. The following is a program to compute the product of two complex-numbers. This program is taken from the $CLP(\mathcal{R})$ manual [Hei-86].

```
zmult(c(R1,I1),c(R2,I2),c(R3,I3)) :-
    R3 = R1*R2-I1*I2,
    I3 = R1*I2+R2*I1.
```

This clause means that a multiplication of a complex number c(R1,I1) and c(R2,I2) equals c(R3,I3). Two equations in the body of the above clause are constraints, and the equality symbol indicates a constraint. A characteristic of the processing of this program is that the following three queries can be processed against the above clause.

```
?-zmult(c(1,1),c(1,2),c(R,I)).
?-zmult(c(1,1),c(R,I),c(-1,3)).
?-zmult(c(R,I),c(1,2),c(-1,3)).
```

For example, the processing of the second query proceeds as follows.

1. `?- zmult(c(1,1),c(R,I),c(-1,3)).` is unified against the clause head, and the substitution {R1/1, I1/1, R2/R, I2/I, R3/-1, I3/3} is obtained.

2. This substitution is applied to constraints (equations) in the body of the clause, and the following are obtained.

```
-1 = 1*R-1*I
3  = 1*I+R*1
```

When a new constraint is obtained, the constraint solver adds it to the set of constraints. More precisely, a newly obtained constraint is added to the previously computed constraint, and then computes the canonical form of the resulting constraint. Inconsistency of the new constraint with the previous constraint is treated in the same way as unification failure in a logic programming language.

3. The above system of equations is solved by Gaussian elimination, and the canonical form (solution) R=1, I=2 is obtained.

3 Semantics of CLP

3.1 CLP on Many Sorted Algebra and its declarative semantics

This section presents the basic notions needed to describe the semantics of CLP. The argument in this section is generally along the lines of that by Jaffar and Lassez [JaL-87], but is different in the details.

Let S be a finite set of *sorts*, F a set of *function symbols*, C a set of *constraint symbols*, P a set of *predicate symbols*, and V a set of *variables*. A sort is assigned to each variable and function symbol. A finite (possibly empty) sequence of sorts, called a *signature*, is assigned to each function, predicate, and constraint symbol. We write $v : s$, $f : s_1 s_2 \ldots s_n \to s$, and $p : s_1 s_2 \ldots s_n$ if a variable, v, has a sort, s, if a function symbol, f, has a signature, $s_1 s_2 \ldots s_n$, and a sort, s, and if a predicate or constraint symbol, p, has a signature, $s_1 s_2 \ldots s_n$, respectively.

Terms and their sorts are defined inductively as follows.

1. A variable of sort s is a term of sort s.

2. If f is a function symbol such that $f : s_1 s_2 \ldots s_n \to s$, and $t_1, t_2, \ldots, t_n$ are terms of sorts $s_1, s_2, \ldots, s_n$ respectively, then $f(t_1, t_2, \ldots, t_n)$ is a term of sort s.

Atomic formulae and *atomic constraints* are defined as follows.

3. If p is a predicate symbol such that $p : s_1 s_2 \ldots s_n$, and $t_1, t_2, \ldots, t_n$ are terms of sorts $s_1, s_2, \ldots, s_n$ respectively, then $p(t_1, t_2, \ldots, t_n)$ is an atomic formula.

4. If c is a *constraint* symbol such that $c : s_1 s_2 \ldots s_n$, and $t_1, t_2, \ldots, t_n$ are terms of sorts $s_1, s_2, \ldots, s_n$ respectively, then $c(t_1, t_2, \ldots, t_n)$ is an atomic constraint.

We write $t : s$ if a term t has a sort s. The sets of terms, atomic formulae, and atomic constraints are denoted by $T(F,V)$, $A(P,F,V)$, and $A(C,F,V)$, respectively. A constraint is a finite (possibly empty) set of atomic constraints. Intuitively, a constraint is a finite conjunction of atomic constraints. The empty constraint means **true**.

We assume that for each sort, s, there is a special constraint symbol, $=_s$, of signature ss. For this symbol, we use infix notation, and the suffix s may be omitted if there is no danger of confusion.

A combination D of a class of sets, $\{D(s)|s \in S\}$, a class of functions, $\{D(f)|f \in F\}$, and a class of functions, $\{D(c)|c \in C\}$, satisfying the following conditions is called a *structure*. A structure plays the same role as the Herbrand universe does in the semantics of ordinary Prolog.

1. If f is a function symbol such that $f : s_1 s_2 \ldots s_n \to s$, then $D(f)$ is a function from $D(s_1) \times D(s_2) \times \cdots \times D(s_n)$ to $D(s)$.

2. If c is a constraint symbol such that $c : s_1 s_2 \ldots s_n$, then $D(c)$ is a function from $D(s_1) \times D(s_2) \times \cdots \times D(s_n)$ to $\{$**false**, **true**$\}$.

In what follows, let D be a fixed structure. Suppose that $D(=_s)$, which is a function from $D(s) \times D(s)$ to $\{$**false**, **true**$\}$, satisfies the following condition.

$$D(=_s)(x,y) = \text{if } x = y \text{ then } \textbf{true} \text{ else } \textbf{false}$$

Note that $=_s$ here plays the same role as unification in ordinary Prolog.

A class, I, of functions, $\{I(p)|p \in P\}$, satisfying the following conditions is called an *interpretation*, which plays the same role as an Herbrand interpretation in the semantics of ordinary Prolog.

3. If p is a predicate symbol such that $p : s_1 s_2 \ldots s_n$, then $I(p)$ is a function from $D(s_1) \times D(s_2) \times \cdots \times D(s_n)$ to $\{$**false**, **true**$\}$.

An *assignment* is a function, Θ, from V to $\bigcup_s D(s)$ satisfying the following condition.

4. If $v : s$, then $v\Theta \in D(s)$. (We use the symbol, Θ, in postfix notation as usual.)

An assignment Θ can be naturally extended to be a function over $T(F, V)$ and $A(C, F, V)$. Then $t\Theta \in D(s)$ if t is a term of sort s, and $p\Theta$ is **false** or **true** if p is an atomic constraint. Let C be a constraint. If there exists an assignment, Θ, such that $c\Theta = \textbf{true}$ for every $c \in C$, then C is said to be *satisfiable*, and Θ is called a *solution* of C. Similarly, Θ can be extended to a be function of $A(P, F, V)$ into {**false**, **true**}, denoted ΘI, if an interpretation, I, is given.

A *program clause*, which is an extension of a definite clause, is an expression in the form of $p : -p_1, p_2, \ldots, p_n$ ($n \geq 0$), where p is an atomic formula and each p_i is either an atomic constraint or an atomic formula. A finite set of program clauses is called a (constraint logic) program. Let L be a program. An interpretation is called a model of L if for any program clause $(p : -p_1, p_2, \ldots, p_n) \in L$, and for any assignment, Θ, $p_1\Theta I = p_2\Theta I = \cdots = p_n\Theta I = \textbf{true}$ implies $p\Theta I = \textbf{true}$.

3.2 Functional Interpretation of a Program

First, we extend the function given by van Emden and Kowalski [EmK-76] for CLP. Let there be a program, L. Based on an interpretation, I, we can define another interpretation, J, as follows.

$J(p)(d_1, d_2, \ldots, d_n) =$
    if there is a program clause $p(t_1, t_2, \ldots, t_n) :\!-$
    $p_1, p_2, \ldots, p_m \in L$ and an assignment, Θ,
    such that $p_1\Theta I = p_2\Theta I = \ldots = p_m\Theta I = \textbf{true}$
    and $d_1 = t_1\Theta, d_2 = t_2\Theta, \ldots, d_n = t_n\Theta$
    then **true**
    else **false**

Since interpretation J is dependent on program L and interpretation I, we denote it $T(L, I)$. Then $T(L, \_)$ forms a function which maps one interpretation to another. An interpretation, I, is said to be *less than* another interpretation, J, denoted $I \leq J$, if the following hold. For every predicate symbol $p : s_1 s_2 \ldots s_n$, and for every element $d_1 \in D(s_1), d_2 \in D(s_2), \ldots, d_n \in D(s_n)$, if $I(p)(d_1, d_2, \ldots, d_n) = \textbf{true}$, then $J(p)(d_1, d_2, \ldots, d_n) = \textbf{true}$. Proof of the following proposition is routine.

Proposition 3.1 *The set of all the interpretations forms a complete lattice with respect to $\leq$, and $T(L, \_)$ is continuous on it. That is to say, the following conditions hold.*

1. If $I \leq J$ then $T(L, I) \leq T(L, J)$.

2. If $I_1 \leq I_2 \leq \ldots$, then $\sup T(L, I_i) = T(L, \sup I_i)$.

For any ordinal number, α, interpretations $T \uparrow \alpha$ and $T \downarrow \alpha$ are defined by transfinite induction as follows.

$T \uparrow \alpha =$ if α is a successor ordinal, $\beta + 1$,
    then $T(L, T \uparrow \beta)$ else $\sup\{T \uparrow \beta \mid \beta < \alpha\}$
$T \downarrow \alpha =$ if α is a successor ordinal, $\beta + 1$,
    then $T(L, T \downarrow \beta)$ else $\inf\{T \downarrow \beta \mid \beta < \alpha\}$

The definition after "else" is adopted also when $\alpha = 0$. Thus, $T \uparrow 0$ becomes the least element with respect to $\leq$. That is to say, for every predicate symbol $p : s_1 s_2 \ldots s_n$, and for every element, $d_1 \in D(s_1), d_2 \in D(s_2), \ldots, d_n \in D(s_n)$, $T \uparrow 0(p)(d_1, d_2, \ldots, d_n) = \textbf{false}$. On the other hand, $T \downarrow 0$ becomes the greatest element with respect to $\leq$. That is, for every predicate symbol, $p : s_1, s_2, \ldots, s_n$, and for every element, $d_1 \in D(s_1), d_2 \in D(s_2), \ldots, d_n \in D(s_n)$, $T \downarrow 0(p)(d_1, d_2, \ldots, d_n) = \textbf{true}$.

It is easy to show the following.

$$T \uparrow 0 \leq T \uparrow 1 \leq T \uparrow 2 \leq \cdots$$
$$T \downarrow 0 \geq T \downarrow 1 \geq T \downarrow 2 \geq \cdots$$

From Proposition 3.1 (1) and the fixed-point theorem with respect to order homomorphisms of a complete lattice, $T(L, \_)$ has the least and the greatest fixed-points. We write them lfp(T, L) and gfp(T, L), respectively. Then, for some sufficiently large ordinals, α and β, lfp$(P, T) = T \uparrow \alpha$ and gfp$(T, L) = T \downarrow \beta$. In fact, it is easy to show that lfp$(T, L) = T \uparrow \omega$ from Proposition 3.1 (2). In general, the greatest fixed-point gfp(T, L) is different from $T \downarrow \omega$.

Lemma 3.1 *For any program, L, the following conditions hold.*

1. $T(L, I) \leq I$ if and only if I is a model of L. Especially, the greatest element, $T \downarrow 0$, is the greatest model of L.

2. lfp(T, L) is a model, and for any model, I, lfp$(T, L) \leq I$. Therefore, lfp(T, L) is the least model of L.

Here, we define the syntactical counterpart to the function, $T(L, \_)$. Consider a pair of an atomic formula, p, and a satisfiable constraint, C. For convenience, we denote this pair $p : -C$ and call it a *QA-pair* (question and answer). We denote the set of all QA-pairs **QA**. From a subset, S, of **QA**, another subset, T, is defined as the set of all QA-pairs, $\{p(s_1, s_2, \ldots, s_n) : -C\}$, such that there is a program clause, $p(t_1, t_2, \ldots, t_n) : -p_1, p_2, \ldots, p_m \in L$, and

1. For each p_i, p_i is an atomic formula such that $(p_i : -C_i) \in S$, or an atomic constraint such that $C_i = \{p_i\}$,

2. $C = \{s_1 = t_1, s_2 = t_2, \ldots, s_n = t_n\} \cup C_1 \cup C_2 \cup \ldots \cup C_m$,

3. C is satisfiable.

We denote T, defined above, $Q(L, S)$. Then $Q(L, \_)$ is a function which maps one subset of **QA** to another. Function $Q(L, \_)$ has a similar property to $T(L, \_)$ with respect to the inclusion relation on sets, $\subseteq$.

Proposition 3.2 $Q(L, \_)$ *is continuous with respect to the inclusion relation of sets* $\subseteq$. *That is, the following conditions hold.*

1. If $S \subseteq T$, then $Q(L, S) \subseteq Q(L, T)$.

2. If $S_1 \subseteq S_2 \subseteq \ldots$, then $\bigcup Q(L, S_i) = Q(L, \bigcup S_i)$.

Similarly, $Q \uparrow \alpha$, and $Q \downarrow \alpha$ are defined as follows.

$Q \uparrow \alpha = $ if α is a successor ordinal, $\beta + 1$,
  then $Q(L, Q \uparrow \beta)$ else $\bigcup \{Q \uparrow \beta \mid \beta < \alpha\}$
$Q \downarrow \alpha = $ if α is a successor ordinal, $\beta + 1$,
  then $Q(L, Q \downarrow \beta)$ else $\bigcap \{Q \downarrow \beta \mid \beta < \alpha\}$

In particular, $Q \uparrow 0 = \emptyset$ and $Q \downarrow 0 = \mathbf{QA}$. The following are also routine.

$$Q \uparrow 0 \subseteq Q \uparrow 1 \subseteq Q \uparrow 2 \subseteq \cdots$$
$$Q \downarrow 0 \supseteq Q \downarrow 1 \supseteq Q \downarrow 2 \supseteq \cdots$$

$Q(L, \_)$ has the least fixed-point, $\mathrm{lfp}(Q, L)$, and the greatest fixed-point, $\mathrm{gfp}(Q, L)$. For sufficiently large ordinals, α and β, $\mathrm{lfp}(Q, L) = Q \uparrow \alpha$, and $\mathrm{gfp}(Q, L) = Q \downarrow \beta$. In fact, $\mathrm{lfp}(Q, L) = Q \uparrow \omega$, but $\mathrm{gfp}(Q, L)$ is different from $Q \downarrow \omega$, in general.

For $S \subseteq \mathbf{QA}$, an interpretation, $|S|$, is defined as follows.

$|S|(p) \, (d_1, d_2, \ldots, d_n)$
  if there is a QA-pair $(p(t_1, t_2, \ldots, t_n) : -C) \subseteq S$
  and an assignment, ΘI,
  such that $d_1 = t_1 \Theta, d_2 = t_2 \Theta, \ldots, d_n = t_n \Theta$
  and Θ is a solution of C
  then **true**
  else **false**

Lemma 3.2 *For any program, L, and for any ordinal, α, $T \uparrow \alpha = |Q \uparrow \alpha|$ and $T \downarrow \alpha = |Q \downarrow \alpha|$.*

By the above lemma, $\mathrm{lfp}(T, L) = |\mathrm{lfp}(Q, L)|$ and $\mathrm{gfp}(T, L) = |\mathrm{gfp}(Q, L)|$.

3.3 Operational Interpretation of a Program

This section defines an operational model for CLP. A formula in the form of $p_1, p_2, \ldots, p_n; C$ is called a goal, where each p_i is an atomic constraint or an atomic formula, and C is a satisfiable constraint. When $n = 0$, the goal comprising only a satisfiable constraint is called a *successful* goal. L be a program. The (extended) *SLD-resolution* is the process which obtains a new goal from another goal $p_1, p_2, \ldots, p_n; C$ in the following way.

1. If p_1 is an atomic constraint such that $D = \{p_1\} \cup C$ is satisfiable, then the goal, $p_2, \ldots, p_n; D$, is obtained.

2. If $p_1 = p(s_1, s_2, \ldots, s_m)$ is an atomic formula such that there is a program clause $(p(t_1, t_2, \ldots, t_m) : -q_1, q_2, \ldots, q_k) \in P$ such that $D = \{s_1 = t_1, s_2 = t_2, \ldots, s_m = t_m\} \cup C$ is satisfiable, then the goal, $q_1, q_2, \ldots, q_k, p_2, \ldots, p_n; D$, is obtained.

A sequence of goals, $G_0, G_1, \ldots, G_n$, is called an *SLD-resolution sequence* if each G_{i+1} is obtained from G_i by SLD-resolution. Here, we define a success set, $SS(L)$.

$SS(L) = \{ (p : -C) \in \mathbf{QA} \mid$
    there exists an SLD-resolution sequence which
    begins with the goal, $p; \emptyset$,
    and ends with the successful goal, $C \}$.

Theorem 3.1 *For any program, L, $|\mathrm{lfp}(Q, L)| = |SS(L)|$.*

The reader can easily see that if p is input as a query, a constraint, C, such that $(p : -C) \in SS(L)$, is output as an answer from the system. The above theorem guarantees the correctness of this mechanism.

3.4 Constraint Solving and Canonical Forms

According to the operational model of CLP described in the previous section, decidability of the satisfiability of constraints is necessary and sufficient to execute a program by (extended) SLD-resolution. However, a satisfiable constraint, as it is, may not be a satisfactory form of output from the system. For example, the constraint, $\{x + y = 3, \ x - y = 1\}$, is satisfiable, and is therefore qualified to be output as an answer according to the definition in the previous section. However, the answer that users actually want in many cases is something like $\{x = 2, \ y = 1\}$. In this sense, *constraint solving* should not be a mere decision on the satisfiability of constraints, but a conversion of constraints into another form that users can understand easily.

Two constraints are said to be equivalent if they have the same solutions. We write $C \sim D$ if C and D are equivalent. For example,

$$\{x + y = 3, \ x - y = 1\} \sim \{x = 2, \ y = 1\}$$

Clearly, $\sim$ defines an equivalence relation for constraints. Suppose that for each equivalence class, E, there is a representative, $E \downarrow$. The equivalence class to which C belongs is denoted $[C]$, and the representative, $[C] \downarrow$, is called the canonical form of C. Let us call an algorithm, **a**, satisfying the following conditions, a *constraint solver* with respect to $\downarrow$.

1. **a** decides the satisfiability of an arbitrary constraint.

2. **a** computes the canonical form of an arbitrary satisfiable constraint.

When there is a constraint solver, as defined above, the SLD-resolution in the previous section can be improved to compute the canonical form of the union, D, of constraints instead of merely making the union. Actually, the unification procedure of ordinary logic programming can be seen as computation of the canonical form of equality constraints in the Herbrand universe. Moreover, computation of the canonical forms may make program execution more efficient, if there is an algorithm that solves constraints incrementally based on the canonical forms.

3.5 Examples of Language and Domain

A typical domain of CLP is the field of all the algebraic numbers, of which the formal language, for example, is defined as follows.

$S = \{\mathbf{A}\}$
$F = \{\times : \mathbf{AA} \to \mathbf{A}, + : \mathbf{AA} \to \mathbf{A}\} \cup \{\text{fraction} :\to \mathbf{A}\}$
$C = \{=\}$
$P = \{\text{string starting with a lowercase letter}\}$
$V = \{\text{string starting with an uppercase letter}\}$

We assume that there is only one sort $\mathbf{A}$ of algebraic numbers for simplicity. We define a structure for the above language as follows.

$D(\mathbf{A}) = $ the set of all algebraic numbers
$D(\times) = $ multiplication
$D(+) = $ addition
$D(\text{fraction}) = $ the rational number it denotes

It is clear that we can write polynomial equations as constraints.

The next example is CLP in a Boolean algebra (or more precisely, in a Boolean ring). The language and the structure is defined, for example, as follows.

$S = \{\mathbf{B}\}$
$F = \{\wedge : \mathbf{BB} \to \mathbf{B}, \oplus : \mathbf{BB} \to \mathbf{B}, \bot :\to \mathbf{B}, \top :\to \mathbf{B}\}$
$C = \{=\}$
$P = \{\text{string starting with a lowercase letter}\}$
$V = \{\text{string starting with an uppercase letter}\}$

$D(\mathbf{B}) = $ an arbitrary Boolean algebra
$D(\wedge) = $ conjunction
$D(\oplus) = $ exclusive disjunction
$D(\bot) = $ false
$D(\top) = $ true

Ordinary Prolog can be defined as an CLP language as follows.

$S = \{\mathbf{H}\}$
$F = \{\text{string starting with a lowercase letter}\}$
$C = \{=\}$
$P = \{\text{string starting with a lowercase letter}\}$
$V = \{\text{string starting with an uppercase letter}\}$

$D(\mathbf{H}) = $ Herbrand universe $ = \{\text{ground term}\}$
$D(F) = $ syntactic construction

4 CAL

4.1 The current status of CAL interpreter

The present CAL is not a single language, but a family of languages over different computation domains. Languages within this family are as follows.

On DEC2060, there are three CAL interpreters: Algebraic CAL for algebraic equations, Boolean CAL for boolean equations, and Linear CAL for linear algebraic equations and inequalities. On the PSI, there are: Algebraic CAL, Boolean CAL, and Typed CAL; the last supports constraints in many sorted algebra described in Section 3.

In the actual CAL interpreter, some semantically impure features have been added for the convenience of users, as was done for Prolog. Since we will be discussing the actual CAL interpreter, we will also mention these features where it seems appropriate.

On both DEC 2060 and PSI, each CAL interpreter comprises the following components.

1. Pre-processor

   Translates CAL source program and query into DEC-10 Prolog on DEC 2060, and into ESP on PSI.

2. Constraint solver

   Receives constraints, and computes their canonical form.

4.2 Evaluation of CAL programs

The current CAL implementations are layered on top of Prolog systems using preprocessors. The most significant difference between logic programming languages and constraint logic programming languages is that the former maintains the solution of unifications as bindings, and the latter maintains the canonical form of a constraint (a set of atomic constraints). Both language classes, however, must maintain these partial solutions during both forward (resolution) and backward (backtracking) execution of their programs. The preprocessing of a CAL program is done in similar way to that for a DCG (*Definite Clause Grammar*); namely, a pair of variables is added as the last arguments of each clause, for the input of the old, and the output of the new constraint.

A CAL program

```
zmult(c(R1,I1),c(R2,I2),c(R3,I3)) :-
      R3 = R1*R2-I1*I2,
      I3 = R1*I2+R2*I1.
```

is translated into the following Prolog program.

```
zmult(c(R1,I1),c(R2,I2),c(R3,I3),V0,V2) :-
      constraint(R3 = R1*R2-I1*I2,V0,V1)
      constraint(I3 = R1*I2+R2*I1,V1,V2).
```

The meaning of predicate `constraint/3` is to add a newly obtained constraint, which is passed through its first parameter to the canonical constraint, which is passed through the second parameter, to compute a new canonical constraint, and to unify it to the third parameter.

In the same style, the preprocessor adds two extra variables to all predicates except those built into Prolog. Since the output of the translation is a Prolog program, we only need to provide a predicate `constraint` satisfying the above specification.

4.3 Algorithms for Constraint Solving

As shown in the example in section 2, algorithms for constraint solving should have the ability to solve constraints incrementally. Since constraints are obtained one by one, canonical forms are obtained by transforming former canonical forms and newly obtained constraints.

We now describe the algorithms for the constraint solving component of the following CAL interpreters.

1. Algebraic CAL

2. Boolean CAL

3. Linear CAL

4.3.1 Algebraic CAL

In this section, we describe the algorithm for Algebraic CAL. The Buchberger algorithm for computing Gröbner bases of polynomials, which has been used in recent years in computer algebra and geometrical theorem proving, is utilized as the constraint solving algorithm.

Buchberger introduced the concept of Gröbner bases, and presented the algorithm to compute the bases of input polynomials [Buc-83].

Without loss of generality, we can assume the form of equations to be $p = 0$. Let $E=\{p_1 = 0, p_2 = 0, \ldots, p_n = 0\}$ be a system of polynomial equations, and let I be the ideal generated from $\{p_1, p_2, \ldots, p_n\}$ in the polynomial ring. The following theorem shows the relationship between elements of I and solutions of E.

Theorem 4.1 (Hilbert's zero point theorem)
Let p be a polynomial. Every solution of E is also a solution of $p = 0$, if and only if p^n is an element of I for some integer n [Hil-90].

The next corollary is important for determining the solvability of constraints.

Corollary 4.1
E has no solutions if and only if $1 \in I$.

By the above considerations, the problem of satisfying the polynomial equation $p = 0$ under constraints E can be transformed into the problem of the determination of whether a polynomial p^n belongs to the ideal generated from E or not. Buchberger gave an algorithm to determine whether a polynomial belongs to the ideal or not.

In the system of polynomial equations, each equation can be considered as a rewriting rule which rewrites the maximal monomial to a remaining polynomial under a certain ordering of monomials. When the left-hand sides of an arbitrary pair of rewrite rules are not mutually prime, their least common multiplier can be rewritten to two polynomials by two rules. The pair of these polynomials is called the *critical pair* of these two rules. Among critical pairs, there may be ones whose rewriting are not confluent. This kind of critical pair is called *divergent*.

Let E be a set of given equations, and R be a set of rewriting rules. A Göbner base of E is computed as the final R by the following algorithm:

1. $R \leftarrow \emptyset$

2. For each equation $l - r$ in E, simplify it by rewriting rules in R and arithmetic operations. Let e be an equation resulting from this simplification. If $e \equiv 0$, then this equation is thrown away. Otherwise, replace the original equation $l = r$ in E by $e = 0$.

3. If $E = \emptyset$, then end.

4. Select an equation $e = 0$ in E.

5. Let l' be the maximal monomial in e under a certain monomial ordering. Solve $e = 0$ with respect to l'. Let $l' = r'$ be the result.

6. Add a rule $l' \rightarrow r'$ to R.

7. Add every divergent critical pair of rules in R to E as equations.

8. Go to 2.

The next theorem states the relationship between ideals and Gröbner-bases.

Theorem 4.2 (Buchberger)
Let R be a Gröbner-base of system of equations, $\{p_1 = 0, p_2 = 0, \ldots, p_n = 0\}$, I be an ideal generated from $\{p_1, p_2, \ldots, p_n\}$. Then a polynomial p belongs to I if and only if p can be rewritten into 0 by R.

The next theorem certify the validity of Gröbner-base as canonical form of constraints. Here, irreducible Gröbner-base is the base in which no couple of rules can rewrite each other.

Theorem 4.3
Suppose that the monomial ordering is fixed. Let E and F be systems of equations. If an ideal generated from E is same as that from F, then the irreducible Gröbner-base of E is same as that of F.

In Algebraic CAL, constraints can have "=" and "==" as their constraint symbols. A constraint $f = g$ indicates a so-called active constraint, and the constraint solver computes the new canonical forms by adding this constraint. That is to say, the Gröbner-base is modified to satisfy $f = g$. On the other hand, $f == g$ is a kind of a passive constraint, and the constraint solver checks whether $f = g$ is satisfied or not under the corrected constraints. "Passive" as used above has a different meaning from that used by Dincbas. The meaning here is constraints without modifying Gröbner-base. This is analogous to "==" in Prolog, which does not cause unification. Note that the relationship between constraints and ideal is not complete. For instance, $X = 0$ is satisfied under constraints $\{X^2 = 0\}$, but it does not belong to the ideal generated from $\{X^2 = 0\}$. Therefore, check of the latter constraints needs more careful use of the Gröbner-base than rewriting with it.

This "==" is added to the system for the convenience of users.

4.3.2 Boolean CAL

In this section, we describe the algorithm used in the constraint solver for Boolean CAL. In Boolean CAL, boolean equations can be written, and can be processed as constraints. The typical computation domain is the set of truth-values.

There are many decision procedures for the solvability of boolean equations. Among them, the typical one is *semantic unification* employed by Dincbas [Din-87]. We, in CAL, use the approach of Boolean Gröbner-bases [SaS-87] which is obtained by slight modification of Buchberger algorithm. We think that this method has advantages in the following points:

1. This algorithm computes answer constraints without introducing extra variables. Thus answer constraints can be understood easily.

2. There exist canonical forms for constraints, and their meaning is clear.

In Boolean CAL, given constraints are translated into boolean polynomials, and then the Gröbner-base of them are computed. This is the evaluation of constraints in Boolean CAL.

A boolean equation is a polynomial whose coefficients are 0 or 1. Moreover, we can define it so that degree of each variable in every monomial is 1. That is to say, there are no monomials such as $x^3 y$ in boolean equations. Instead, it must be written as xy. This is caused by the fact that every elements in boolean rings are idempotent.

The most significant difference between boolean equations and ordinary algebraic equations is that the constraint evaluation in the former can be completely described by the ideal.

Corresponding to the theorem 4.1, the next theorem holds.

Theorem 4.4
Let p be a boolean polynomial. Every solution of the system of boolean equations $E = \{p_1 = 0, \ldots p_n = 0\}$ is also a solution of $p=0$ if and only if p is an element of I.[1]

The algorithm to compute boolean Gröbner-bases is almost the same as that for polynomial rings, excepting the following points.

For a boolean polynomial $AX + Z$, $AZ + Z$ is called its *self critical pair*, where A, X, and Z are a variable, a monomial, and a polynomial, respectively, and AX is the maximal monomial in $AX + Z$. In boolean ring, $x + x = 0$ and $xx = x$,

$$AX + Z = 0 \Rightarrow (AX + Z)(A + 1) = AZ + Z = 0,$$

which certify that $AZ + Z$ should be a critical pair.

---

[1] This property holds in arbitrary boolean rings

By using the concept of the self critical pair, the algorithm to compute boolean Gröbner-bases can be obtained by modifying that for Gröbner-bases as follows.

In 7., not only divergent critical pairs but also divergent self critical pairs are added to E as equations.

For boolean Gröbner-bases obtained as the above, Theorem 4.2 and 4.3 are hold as they are. Refer to [SaS-88] for preciseness.

4.3.3 Linear CAL

In this section, we describe constraint solving in Linear CAL. In Linear CAL, linear equations and linear inequalities can be written and processed as constraints. A number of constraint solvers based on either the simplex or Min-Max method have ben proposed for their solution. We are now developing a simplex-method based constraint solver which satisfies our criteria for computation domains.

However, since the canonical form at present is not easily understandable by users, we have to consider the following points:

1. The method of output of answer constraints.

2. Canonical forms of constraints.

3. Constraint solving algorithm.

4.4 Programming Examples

In this section, we describe the description power of CAL by showing programming examples for each of its constraint solvers.

4.4.1 Programming Examples in Algebraic CAL

As we described above, the major characteristic of Algebraic CAL is the ability to solve non-linear equations. The following examples include one on the edges and surfaces of triangles, and several of geometrical theorem proving.

Example 4.1 (Geometrical Theorem Proving)
The following theorem is considered.

Theorem 4.5
Let ABCD be an arbitrary quadrangle, and E, F, G, and H be mid-points of edges AB, BC, CD, and DA, respectively. Then the quadrangle EFGH is a parallelogram.

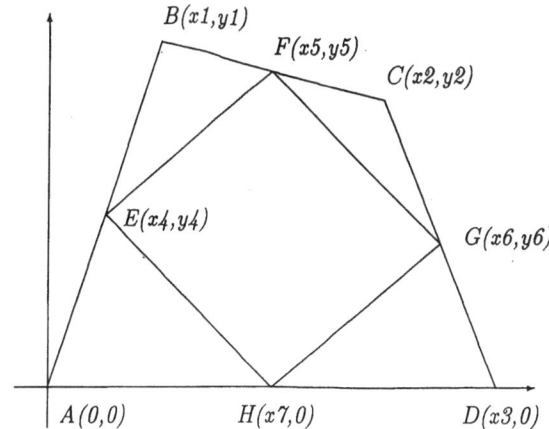

Fig.–1: Geometrical Theorem Proving

To prove the theorem, we transform this geometrical problem to an algebraic problem by introducing Cartesian coordinate system. A mid-point (x_2, y_2) of a segment $(x_1, y_1) - (x_3, y_3)$ can be represented by equations $x_2 = (x_1 + x_3)/2, y_2 = (y_1 + y_3)/2$. The fact that segment $(x_1, y_1) - (x_2, y_2)$ is parallel with segment $(x_3, y_3) - (x_4, y_4)$ can be represented by an equation $(y_2 - y_1)/(x_2 - x_1) = (y_4 - y_3)/(x_4 - x_3)$.

These equations are represented by CAL as follows:

```
mid(X1,Y1,X2,Y2,X3,Y3) :-
        2*X2 = X1+X3,
        2*Y2 = Y1+Y3.
para(X1,Y1,X2,Y2,X3,Y3,X4,Y4) :-
        (X1-X2)*(Y3-Y4)==(Y1-Y2)*(X3-X4).
```

By evaluating the following query against the above program, the given theorem is proven.

```
?-mid(0,0,x4,y4,x1,y1),
  mid(x1,y1,x5,y5,x2,y2),
  mid(x2,y2,x6,y6,x3,0),
  mid(x3,0,x7,0,0,0),
  para(x4,y4,x5,y5,x7,0,x6,y6),
  para(x4,y4,x7,0,x5,y5,x6,y6).
```

The basic idea of this program and query is to certify that the two pairs of segments, whose endpoints are constrained to be the midpoints of the original quadrilateral, are parallel.

As mentioned before, we introduce the constraint symbol "==" in the above program for programming convenience.

Example 4.2 (Heron's formula)
The problem is to obtain the relationship between the length of three edges of a triangle and its surface. For an arbitrary triangle, let l be the length of its base edge,

272

h be its height, and s be its surface. Then the following relation holds: $l * h = 2 * s$, implemented as the predicate sur.

Then, we describe the Pythagorean Theorem by the predicate right. *Let a and b be lengths of edges which are connected to the square corner, and c be the length of the other edge. If $a^2 + b^2 = c^2$, then that triangle is a right triangle. In the following program, $n\char`^m$ means n^m.*

Moreover, the fact that an arbitrary triangle can be divided into two right triangles is described by the predicate tri *(see Fig-2).*

```
sur(L,H,S) :- L*H=2*S.
right(A,B,C) :- A^2+B^2=C^2.
tri(A,B,C,S) :-
        C=CA+CB,
        right(CA,H,A), right(CB,H,B),
        sur(C,H,S).
```

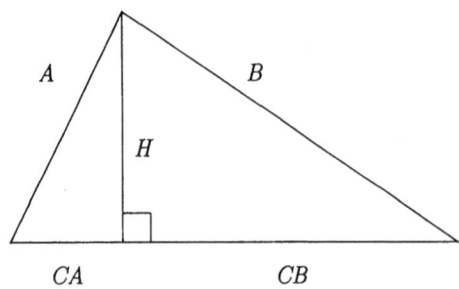

Fig-2: Three edges of a triangle and its surface

When a goal in which all arguments are free tri(a,b,c,s) is given, this program outputs the Gröbner-base with 7 rules. Among them, there is the following rule which contains only a, b, c, and s. This is equivalent to the Heron's formula.

```
c^2 = (-c^4+ -1*a^4+2*(2*b^2*a^2)+ -1*b^4
      +2*(2*c^2*a^2)+2*(2*c^2*b^2))/16
```

This program will also run with instantiated queries. For instance, if a goal tri(3,4,5,s) is given, then s^2=36 is output.

Example 4.3 (Conditional Extremum)
Compute the conditional extremum using Lagrange's method of indeterminate coefficients.

The following CAL program realizes Lagrange's method of indeterminate coefficients.

```
ex(F, Constraint,Vars) :-
            lag(Constraint, Lag),
            difs(Vars, F, Lag).
lag([ ], 0) :- !.
```

```
lag([L=R |Cs], Mult*(L-R)+Lag) :-
            L=R,
            lag(Cs, Lag), !.
difs([ ], _, _) :- !.
difs([Var |Vars], F, Lag) :-
            dif(F, Var)=dif(Lag, Var), !,
            difs(Vars, F, Lag).
```

The first argument for a predicate ex is an objective function whose extremum will be computed, the second argument is a list of conditions on the computation, and the third argument is a list of symbols whose values can be modified (that is to say, this is a list of variables). dif(F,Var) denotes a polynomial obtained by differentiating a polynomial F by a variable Var. This notation is built into the CAL interpreter for the convenience of users.

Strictly speaking, dif(F,Var) is not a polynomial, but a term in the Prolog sense, and so it is misleading to describe it as a constraint. However, we introduce it for programming convenience.

This program can be used to solve the following problem.

Problem 4.1
Divide a circle into two fans by two radial cuts, making two cones. The problem is to obtain the angle between the two radial cuts which maximizes the sum of the volumes of the two cones.

We can assume a circle of radius 1, since the answer doesn't depend on the size of the circle. After making the first cut, make the second one at a distance $\pi + r$ along the circumference, measured in one direction, $\pi - r$ in the other. Suppose the cones have height sA and sB respectively. Then, factoring out constants, we obtain the following query.

```
ex((1/2+r)^2*sA+(1/2-r)^2*sB,
   [sA^2+(1/2+r)^2 = 1, sB^2+(1/2-r)^2 = 1],
   [sA, sB]).
```

This program outputs a Gröbner-base of three rules, among them the following degree-7 polynomial which contains r as its only variable. However, if both sides of this equation are divided by r, then it becomes a cubic over r^2, whose roots can be obtained easily.

```
r^7 = (29/12)*r^5+(-17/48)*r^3+(5/576)*r
```

4.4.2   Programming Example of Boolean CAL

As we mentioned above, Boolean CAL handles boolean equations. Here we present the verification of a logic circuit taken from [Din-87] as an example of its use.

Example 4.4 (Cross Circuit)

The problem is to prove that the following circuit is a cross circuit.

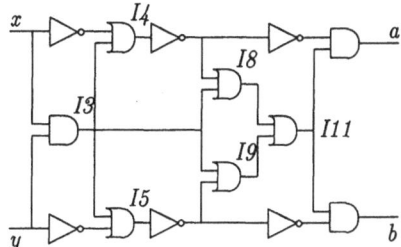

Fig.-3: Cross Circuit

To prove that the circuit is a cross circuit, we must do the following. First of all, we describe the specification of the circuit in terms of boolean equations. Secondly, the relation between input-terminals and output-terminals are described. Accordingly, the following program is obtained.

```
cir(X,Y,A,B) :-
    I4 = ~XVI3, I3 = X∧Y, I5 = ~YVI3,
    I8 = ~I4VI3, I9 = ~I5∧I3,
    A = I4∧I11, I11 = I8VI9, B = I5∧I11.
```

The following query is evaluated against the above program. In the query, all arguments are left free.

```
?- cir(x,y,a,b).
```

The resulting output proves the result.

$$x=b$$

$$y=a$$

5 Extensions of CAL

At present, we have three constraint solvers for CAL. Moreover, we implement Typed CAL in which users can use constraints on several types of objects simultaneously. In this section, we describe Typed CAL, and some future extensions.

5.1 Typed CAL

The basic idea of Typed CAL is to realize constraints in many sorted algebras discussed in Section 3, and thus allow users to use multiple constraint solvers simultaneously. Typing is introduced to indicate the sorts of parameters. In execution of a program, a suitable solver is selected automatically according to the type of each atomic constraint. At the time that we designed Typed CAL, the Buchberger Algorithm to compute Gröbner bases, and the algorithm to compute boolean Gröbner

bases were available. We made an experimental implementation of Typed CAL on the PSI–machine with these two constraint solvers. Recently, a third constraint solver based on linear programming has been implemented, and there are plans to implement another constraint solver for real closed fields. We intend to add two new types corresponding to these new solvers to Typed CAL.

The indication of the type for each constraint will be made as follows. Available types will be:

1. alg (algebraic number – To invoke a constraint solver for Gröbner-bases),

2. bool (To invoke a constraint solver for boolean Gröbner-bases),

3. lin (To invoke a constraint solver for linear equations and linear, and inequalities),

4. real (To invoke a constraint solver for the real closed field),

5. _ (To invoke ordinary unification for ordinary Prolog term)

The type of a constraint is indicated by placing a ":" followed by the appropriate type-name after the constraint.n

To allow users to write formulae in the head of a clause, we will introduce type declarations for predicates. For instance, type declaration :- type p(alg, bool, _). means that the first argument of p is an algebraic constraint to compute Gröbner-bases, the second argument is a boolean constraint, and the third one is an ordinary argument in Prolog. For instance, we may write the following program:

$$p(X+Y, \sim B, C) :- Q .$$

Suppose that we evaluate the following query against the program.

```
p(5, true, a).
```

Unification between the query and clause-head succeeds, and the algebraic constraint X+Y=5, the boolean constraint ~ B = true, and the substitution {C/a} are obtained. This result is brought about by the preprocessing of the above program into the following clause.

```
p(D1, D2, C) :- X+Y=D1:alg, ~ B = D2:bool, Q
```

Thus, the above constraints and substitution are obtained.

By introducing types into predicates, we can implement very similar features to those provided by Dincbas' semantic unification [Din-87].

The following is an example of using type declarations. The next clause solves the *man and horse* problem, using constraint typing, but without predicate type declarations.

```
mah(Man,Horse, Legs, Heads) :-
        Heads = Man+Horse,
        Legs = Man*2+Horse*4.
```

By introducing a predicate type declaration, the above program can be written in the form of a unit clause as follows.

```
:- type mah(_, _, alg, alg).
mah(Man, Horse, Man*2+Horse*4, Man+Horse).
```

5.2 The requirement for CAL from geometry theorem proving

In this section, we discuss geometrical theorem proving, a typical application of CAL. Elementary geometry can be classified into the following hierarchy of classes, arranged in order of increasing size. i) affine geometry, ii) pre-Euclidean geometry, and iii) Euclidean geometry. Example 4.1 belongs to i). In general many theorems in class(i) can be proved by using a simple Gröbner base method. The case of class(ii) is more complicated.

Example 5.1 *Three perpendiculars drawn from three vertices of a triangle converge. Let A,B,C be three vertices of a triangle, D,E be the feet of perpendiculars drawn from A,B respectively, and F be the intersection point of the lines AD and BE.*

We put A=$(u_1, 0)$, B=$(u_2, 0)$, C=$(0, u_3)$, D=(x_1, x_2), E=(x_3, x_4), F=(x_5, x_6). Then the conditions are expressed as follows.

D is on CB	$h_1 = u_2x_2 + u_3x_1 = 0$
$AD \perp CB$	$h_2 = u_3x_2 - u_2x_1 + u_1u_2 = 0$
E is on CA	$h_3 = u_1x_4 + u_3x_3 = 0$
$BE \perp CA$	$h_4 = x_4u_3 - u_3u_1) + u_1u_2$
F is on AC	$h_5 = x_1x_6 - x_2x_5 - u_1x_6 + u_1x_2 = 0$
F is on BE	$h_6 = x_3x_6 - x_4x_5 + u_2x_4 - u_2x_6 = 0$

Convergence of the three perpendiculars is expressed by the next equation.

$$g = x_5 = 0$$

If we evaluate $g = 0$ under the constraint $h_1 = 0, \ldots h_6 = 0$, by a CAL program in the same manner as example 4.1, the system replies "NO". The problem is that when

$$u_1 = u_2 = u_3 = 0,$$

the constraint becomes $x_1x_6 - x_2x_5 = 0, x_3x_6 - x_4x_5$. Clearly $g = 0$ does not obtain under this degenerate condition, where A, B, C are congruent.

For solving this kind of nondegenerate problem, the well-known Ritt's Decomposition Algorithm [Rit-38] is very effective. Not only can we make a complete prover of class(ii) problems using this algorithm, but also it is very powerful for decomposing algebraic constraints. The reason we can make a complete prover of class(ii) problems fairly easily is that it has models over the complex numbers. On the other hand class(iii) has models over the reals.

We are now implementing this algorithm as a constraint solver for CAL.

Example 5.2
Take two squares ACDE, BCFG outside of a given triangle ABC. Let M be the midpoint of AB. Then DF=2CM.

In order to express "outside of" algebraically, we need inequalities over real numbers.

It is well known that we can have a complete prover for class(iii) using Tarski's algorithm or Collins' quantifier elimination algorithm [Col-75]. However these algorithms are not impractical due to their time and memory inefficiency. Implementing efficient algorithms dealing with the real closed field to meet the needs of geometry theorem proving is our future task.

5.3 parallelization of CAL

Parallelization of CAL is still in the stage of preliminary investigation, and we do not have a definite policy under which all researches are conducted. Here, we discuss problems in parallel constraint logic programming based on the current CAL.

Programs in a constraint logic programming language fit into one of the following two cases:

1. There is a definite constraint set (deterministic type). The purpose of computation is to obtain a unique solution. All the examples in this paper are of this type.

2. There are several possible constraint sets (nondeterministic type). Among these, a searching is done for a consistent constraint set. This is a kind of search problem, and is seen in applications like CAD and some kinds of puzzles.

Problems of the former type do not need exhaustive search and, therefore, fit committed-choice type languages like GHC. Those of the latter type definitely depend on the search mechanism povided with logic programming languages, and need "OR-parallel" execution or an equivalent. If an exhaustive search type problem is programmed in GHC, for example, conversion to a committed choice type program or simulation of exhaustive search by an interpreter is necessary. We aim at research into (i) parallelization of Constraint Solver, (ii) parallelization of Inference Engine, and (iii) design of a parallel CLP language. Before researching of (ii) and (iii), however, the characteristic of application programs should be investigated.

If the future parallel CLP language is implemented in GHC, it may be reasonable to change the operational semantic of CLP to fit committed choice execution, though practicality of this approach is highly dependent on application characteristics. If this is the case, the specifications for guards and suspension rules should be similar to those for GHC. Our current opinion is as follows. In a GHC-like CLP language, we can write passive constraints in the guard part of a clause and active constraints in the body part. Committed choice of a clause is caused by satisfaction of all the head unification and all the passive constraints in the guard parts. When they are not satisfied currently but are satisfiable, the execution of the clause is suspended until a new active constraint is obtained. A lot of GHC features are reserved by this CLP version of GHC, and so this approach makes it easy to implement a system for constraint programs of deterministic type.

6   Conclusion

CAL is still under development, and its final shape is not yet clear. However, we can see three future directions for development.

1. implementation new constraint solvers

    For example, a constraint solver of linear inequalities, or specializations of the quantifier elimination algorithm mentioned in section 5.

2. combining constraint solvers for application

    Among the applications of Gröbner bases, the automated theorem prover for elementary geometry is one of the most successful topics of research. We are planning to develop a theorem prover for geometry as a CAL application. Since constraint solvers based on Gröbner bases are not strong enough to support a prover, we have to develop subalgorithms of the quantifier elimination. Furthermore these must be available in a uniform environment, which should be realized by Typed CAL. In this uniform environment, it would be better to make hierarchies of constraint solvers, since a general algorithm is usually less efficient than its specializations.

3. Parallel CAL

The final form of CAL will be a parallel constraint programming language with full functions obtained as the results of the researches described in 1 and 2. In the design of parallel CAL, however, deep consideration of cost-effectiveness is necessary. In particular, the characteristics of algorithms used in application programs should be carefully investigated. For the moment, a few prototype languages will be designed and implemented experimentally according to characteristics, for instance deterministic or non-deterministic, of application fields, through which we can gain our experience in order to unify those prototypes into parallel CAL.

The argument on semantics of CAL [SaS-88] is mainly along the lines of that by Jaffar and Lassez [JaL-87]. Here we summarize the differences. We separated the constraint symbols from the predicate symbols. In general, a CAL programmer knows what function symbols and constraint symbols mean, but does not know how the system solves constraints. In this sense, these symbols are built-in to CAL. On the other hand, a programmer must know all about the predicate symbols because he introduces the symbols. Therefore, the semantics of constraint symbols and function symbols should be given a priori as a structure, while predicate symbols should be defined by the programmer. In this situation, separating the symbols at the beginning enables us to define the semantics naturally. In [JaL-87], the constraints are supposed to go ahead of the other literals in a clause. For flexibility, we did not assume this. We did not discuss *finite definability*, *solution compactness*, or *satisfaction completeness*, since we are not very interested in *negation as failure*, in particular, in constraint logic programming. There are many predicates for which negation as failure is inappropriate. Even if a predicate fits such negation, there is most likely to be a decision procedure for the predicate, and in such a case, it seems to be more natural in constraint logic programming to incorporate the decision procedure into the constraint solver. Instead of these three topics, we discussed the canonical forms of constraints as suitable output from a constraint logic programming system.

Both CAL and CLP(R) can obtain an answer in the form of a relation among parameters, in particular, in the case where many parameters in a goal remain free. This effect is very similar to that of *partial evaluation*, e.g. [TaF-86], or the *unfolding technique* in logic programming, e.g. [TaS-84]. However, the result is more impressive and effective in CAL, since computation of Gröbner bases is much heavier and much more complicated than mere unification.

276

In the present version of Algebraic CAL, the imaginary value of each variable in a constraint is an algebraic number i.e. a complex number which could be a solution of a polynomial equation with integers as its coefficients. If we have a constraint solver over a more restricted domain, the efficiency of solving some problems is drastically improved. For example, when we know a variable x can take only a real number as its value, a constraint like $x^2 + 1 = 0$ leads to a contradiction. On the other hand, we might want to have non-algebraic constraints like $\sin(x) = 1$ or $e^x = \pi$. We might have to extend the domain to all complex numbers. There are many requirements other than these for describing and solving constraints. In order to satisfy these requirements, constraint solvers must be completely changeable by users. We designed the system so that users can define constraint solvers for their own purpose, by making the semantics of the domains precise, and implementing corresponding solvers.

[References]

[**ApE-82**] K. R. Apt, and M. H. van Emden, "Contributions to the Theory of Logic Programming", *JACM*, 29(3), July, 1982, pp.841-862.

[**Buc-83**] B. Buchberger, "Gröbner Bases: an Algebraic method in Polynomial Ideal Theory", Technical Report, CAMP-LINZ, 1983.

[**Col-75**] G. E. Collins, "Quantifier Elimination for Real Closed Fields by Cylindrical Algebraic Decomposition," Lecture Notes In Computer Science 33, 1975.

[**Col-82**] A. Colmerauer, "PROLOG-II – Reference Manual and Theoretical Model", Internal Report, Groupe Intelligence Artificille, Universite Aix-Marseille II, October, 1982.

[**Col-87**] A. Colmerauer, "Introduction to Prolog-III", ESPRIT'87, Achievements and Impact, Proc. of the 4th Annual ESPRIT Conference, Brussels, September 28-29, 1987, North-Holland.

[**Din-87**] M. Dincbas, H. Simonis, and P. van Hentenryck, "Extending Equation Solving and Constraint Handling in Logic Programming", ECRC Internal Report, IR-LP-2203, February, 1987.

[**EmK-76**] M. H. van Emden, and R. A. Kowalski, "The Semantics of Predicate Logic as a Programming Language", *JACM*, 23(4), October, 1976, pp.733-742.

[**Fik-70**] R. E. Fikes, "REF-ARF: A System for Solving Problems stated as Procedures", *Artificial Intelligence*, 1, 1970, 27-120.

[**Hei-86**] N. Heintze, J. Jaffar, C. S. Lim, S. Michaylov, P. Stuckey R. Yap, and C. N. Yee, "The CLP Programmer's Manual – Version 1.0", Department of Computer Science, Monash University, 1986.

[**Hil-90**] D. Hilbert, "Über die Theorie der algebraischen Formen", *Math. Ann.* 36, pp.473-534, 1890.

[**JaL-86**] J. Jaffar, and J-L. Lassez, "Constraint Logic Programming", IBM Thomas J. Watson Research Center, Internal Memo, 1986.

[**JaL-87**] J. Jaffar, and J-L. Lassez, "Constraint Logic Programming",*4th IEEE Symposium on Logic Programming*, 1987.

[**JaM-85**] J. Jaffar, and S. Michaylov, "Methodology and Implementation of a Constraint Logic Programming System", TR 54, Department of Computer Science, Monash University, June, 1985.

[**Llo-84**] J. W. Lloyd, "Foundations of Logic Programming", Springer-Verlag, 1984.

[**Rit-38**] R. F. Ritt, "Differential Equation from Algebraic Standpoint," AMS Colloquium Publications Volume 14, New York, 1938.

[**SaA-88**] K. Sakai, and A. Aiba, "CAL : A Theoretical Background of Constraint Logic Programming and Its Applications (In Japanese)", Information Processing Society of Japan, vol. 88, No. 8, 88-SF-24, pp. 9–17, Feb. 12, 1988.

[**SaS-88**] Y. Sato, and K. Sakai, "Boolean Gröbner Bases", LA-Symposium, February, 1988.

[**Ste-81**] M. Stefik, "Planning with Constraints", *Artificial Intelligence*, 16, 2, 1981.

[**StS-78**] G. L. Steele, and G. J. Sussman, "Constraints", MIT AI Lab Memo 502, Cambridge, Massachusetts, 1978.

[**TaF-86**] A. Takeuchi, and K. Furukawa, "Partial evaluation of Prolog Programs and Its Application to Meta Programming", *Information processing 86*, Dublin, North-Holland, pp. 415–420, 1986.

[**TaS-84**] H. Tamaki, and T. Sato, "Unfold/Fold transformation of Logic Programs", *Second International Logic Programming Conference*, Uppsala, 1984.

PROCEEDINGS OF THE INTERNATIONAL CONFERENCE
ON FIFTH GENERATION COMPUTER SYSTEMS 1988,
edited by ICOT. © ICOT, 1988

Overview of the Dictionary and Lexical Knowledge Base Research

Yuichi Tanaka   Tsutomu Yoshioka

Institute for New Generation Computer Technology

Mita-Kokusai Bldg 21F, 4-28, Mita 1-chome, Minato-ku

Tokyo 108 JAPAN

ABSTRACT

Overview of structure and contents of our dictionary and lexical knowledge base is described in this paper.

There are two main objectives in ICOT's research on natural language processing, *i.e.* experimental research on discourse understanding and development of efficient, general purpose natural language processing system.

Discourse understanding systems based on logic programming have been investigated since 1982 at ICOT. The focus of the research has been mainly on basic mechanisms of discourse understanding, and the parallel algorithms for these mechanisms.

Experimental system called *DUALS* has been developed and to verify the research results.

These results have been put together to form a general purpose software environment for natural language processing named *LTB* (Language Tool Box).

This paper presents an overview of the dictionary and lexical knowledge base for both *DUALS* and *LTB* , and discusses the future research and development direction of lexical knowledge bases.

1 Introduction

It might be said that Natural Language Processing (NLP) has come to a turning point. In the first place, we have come to the situation in which we have to develop new ideas and mechanisms to deal with large amount of data because current NLP, such as machine translation, is involved in the stream of vast data in the real world. Secondly, to qualify the NLP, we need much deeper semantic analysis such as sentence/discourse understanding, inference of speaker's/hearer's mental state, and so on. In other words, we must increase the quantity and quality of NLP to get over today's difficult situation. It has been recognized that large-scale dictionary or lexical database with precise semantic description is indispensable to support NLP of today and further.

In ICOT, research and development of general purpose Japanese language processor (LTB) has made the way of high speed processing of vast amount of actual data, as well as research experience of discourse understanding experiment system (DUALS) has shown clues to establishment of mathematical basis of discourse understanding.

We are developing a dictionary and lexical database for these two purposes. We have developed a dictionary with several thousand entries of Japanese words for the LTB system, and are planning to increase the vocabulary to ten times larger in the near future. At the same time, we have prepared a dictionary for DUALS which includes 2,000 entries with precise semantic description. One of our objectives is to integrate these two dictionaries to produce a semantic dictionary of appropriate size.

2 Common Tool vs World Knowledge

In the very early stage of NLP, researchers developed experimental small dictionaries for their own use. Next, printed dictionary for human use was substituted as a source to reproduce NLP databases, and now large-scale dictionaries for strict computer purposes are developed from scratch again by many institutions in the world. Main reason is that deep semantic analysis in current NLP requires various new information which cannot be extracted from traditional dictionaries, in which complicated description of meaning is, for instance, replaced by example sentence in many cases.

In NLP, highly sophisticated inference based on so called "common sense" or world knowledge is necessary to understand the meaning of sentence/discourse, to analyze sentences with infering speaker's intention, or to generate sentences with guessing hearer's mental state. In order to support this kind of inference, world knowledge must be described in the dictionary.

World knowledge base of this kind can be used as a basic database not only in NLP but also in the variety of knowledge information processing systems. Actually, the trial has been done in which the articles of an encyclopedia are transformed into some terms in a knowledge representation language. Its apparent target is to get over vulnerability of "expert" knowledge information processing without world knowledge. However, in a long period, it aims to acquire further knowledge by learning, and to produce an intelligence by combining its own knowledge.

World knowledge being also indispensable for our research, we must accumulate sufficient knowledge into our dictionary. Distinction between lexical knowledge and world knowledge is a problem here. How to express both knowledge is another problem. We will propose a framework to deal with these problems.

It is difficult to distinguish world knowledge from lexical knowledge because the boundary is vague. We have decided to select following items as lexical knowledge: morphological information, syntactical information, case information, semantic feature and cooccurrence relation. Other items are involved in world knowledge. They are expressed in a constraint style description, which will be shown precisely in the later section.

3   Overview of the Dictionary

We are developing the lexical knowledge base for the both objectives described above. It is necessary to construct two different dictionaries together, each of which is explained in the following subsections.

3.1   The LTB dictionary with lexical knowledge

We have already completed this type of dictionary with 4,000 entries. This is used for *LTB* (general purpose japanese language processor) system, where each subsystem (lexical analyzer, syntax analyzer, sentence generator) transforms this dictionary into its own internal representation. The dictionary includes lexical knowledge such as morphological information, syntactical information, case information and basic semantic information.

The semantic information is expressed in basic *soa* (state of affairs) form, called *infon* in terms of situation theory and situation semantics. The syntax analyzer *SAX* makes use of this information in the way that it composes the semantics of a sentence out of each infons corresponding to each surface morphemes according to the dependency structure of a sentence, at the same time

it solves cooccurrence constraints of the surface words in order to reduce ambiguity.

In our grammar, we established 7 parts of speech listed below:

noun (*meishi*)
Stems for both *sahen-meishi* and *keiyou-doushi* are also included in this category. Prefixes and postfixes are considered to be nouns with complement.

verb (*doushi*)
Words which conjugate and have *u*-ending in present form.

adjective (*keiyoushi*)
Words which conjugate and have *i*-ending in present form.

adverb (*fukushi*)
Words which do not conjugate, do not appear at the end of sentences, and are able to modify verbs and adjectives.

nominal modifier (*rentaishi*)
Words which do not conjugate and modify nouns only.

auxiliary verb (*jodoushi*)
(Our dictionary does not include auxiliary verbs, which are treated by grammar rules instead.)

particle (*joshi*)
(Our dictionary does not include particles, which are treated by grammar rules instead.)

Dictionary format, which will be described in section 4, is designed appropriately for each part of speech.

Currently we are expanding vocabulary up to 100,000 entries. This supplement part contains only morphological information and some items in syntactical information which can be used for *LAX* system.

3.2   DUALS dictionary with world knowledge

We have given the detailed semantic information to 2,000 words within *LTB* dictionary. These words appear in the evaluation text of *DUALS* version 3.

As explained above, world knowledge is described in constraint form. Word meaning consists of two parts, the first of which will be a direct constituent of a sentence meaning called *infon*, the second of which controls validity and applicability of infon called *constraint*.

Specific constraints are described in each entry of semantic dictionary, on the other hand, general constraints are stored in the constraint dictionary. Constraint solver deals with these constraints impartially.

4 Structure and Contents

The dictionary consists of three parts, entry word dictionary, semantic dictionary, and constraint dictionary. In this section, structure and contents of entry word dictionary and semantic dictionary are described.

4.1 Entry Word Dictionary

The structure of entry word dictionary is common to all part of speeches. The entry word dictionary consists of entry word records, shown in Fig. 1, prepared for each word.

Currently over 4,000 records are used by *LAX* and *DUALS* system.

4.2 Semantic Dictionary

The semantic dictionary consists of semantic records, the structure of which is peculiar to each part of speeches. The structure of semantic record of verbs is shown in Fig. 2.

Average number of meaning within an entry being over 4, the number of semantic records is nearly 20,000. These records are compiled together with entry word records, and used by *LAX* and *DUALS* system.

ID : Unique identification number for each word.

Part of speech : Part of speech listed in the previous section.

Conjugation type : For conjugated words (*i.e.* verbs and adjectives), conjugation types are specified. For other words, this slot is omitted.

Surface expression : Surface expression is described in *kanji* and *kana* characters. For conjugated words, expression is divided into stem and ending.

Pronunciation : Pronunciation is described in *kana* characters. Variant pronunciations are also listed.

Semantic index : List of link pointers to the semantic dictionary. For words having more than one meaning, each element of the list points each different meaning. Difference of deep case combination is regarded as defference of meaning.

Figure 1: Format of Entry Word Record

5 Semantic Description

5.1 Classification of Words

In describing semantics of words, it is necessary to classify words into their function class first. We have assumed the following three classes:

ID : Unique identification number for each meaning. The semantic pointer in the entry word record above uses this ID number.

Deep case : Deep case indices of a verb. Optional cases are ignored.

Active surface case : In case of active voice, pairs of deep case index and surface case particle are listed.

Passive surface case : In case of passive voice, list of pairs of deep case index and surface case particle are described. If there are more than one passive voice expressions to active one, alternative lists are also described. If there are no passive voice expression, this slot is omitted.

Arguments : Correspondence between deep case index and argument in the semantic structure is described.

Semantic structure : Semantic structure of verb in an infon style.

Constraints : Constraints for arguments in logical expression.

Thesaurus codes : Thesaurus codes for verb.

Complement : In case of function verbs, which must take verb or noun complement to form the meaning, the complement class are described here.

Voice : Existence of four expressions related with voice, *i.e.* direct passive, indirect passive, causative, giving-receiving expression.

Aspect : Original aspect of the verb alone.

Transitivity : Distinction between transitive and intransitive verb.

Volitivity : Volitional or not.

Figure 2: Format of Semantic Record

Function Words: Auxiliary words, function nouns, function verbs. These words attach to other words to produce new meaning or to transform the original meaning. They have no concrete meaning but transformational function. The semantics of these words can be described in syntactical level.

Basic Words: Adjectives, adverbs, basic nouns, basic verbs. These words have basic and abstract meaning, and are used very widely. Metaphorical usage is available. There being only less than 1000 adjectives in Japanese, the semantics of adjectives are usually abstract and vague. For example, *takai* means high, tall, expensive, etc. Our current objective is to describe the semantics of basic nouns and basic verbs.

Other Words: Words which have concrete and compound meaning. Most nouns and Cino-Japanese verbs are included in this category. However, their syntactic function in sentences is simple. The core of the description of these words is knowledge representation.

Assuming two categories *function nouns* and *function verbs*, we selected words in these categories. Number of function words is several hundred.

There are about 4000 *basic nouns* and *basic verbs* in Japanese. We have classified the meaning of basic words by the thesaurus which was created anew for our purpose. For verbs, we indicate explicitly the relation between surface representation, semantic structure and semantic constraints.

5.2 Function Nouns

Japanese nouns cover very large range of the semantic world. We count as function nouns the nouns which have no correspondence to reality and can express meaning when connecting to other words or phrases. In this definition, we focus on the function of a word in a sentence. For example, the noun *mae* (front) means nothing in the real world, however, it inputs an object to output location if it is used in the form *X no mae* (in front of *X*).

There are so many kind of function nouns, such as *time*, *location*, *order*, *degree*, etc. Examples of function nouns are shown in Fig. 3.

Group	Subgroup	Examples
時間 (Time)	前	前, 以前, 先 (さき), ⋯
	後	後, 以後, 以降, ⋯
	間	間, 合間, 内, ⋯
	最中	最中, 盛り, さなか, ⋯
	始め	始め, 始まり, 当初, 端, ⋯
	終り	終り, 最後, 終局, 終盤, 結び, ⋯
	⋯	⋯
場所 (Location)	上	上, 上側, 上方, 上部, ⋯
	下	下, 下側, 下方, 下部, ⋯
	前	前, 手前, 先 (さき), 表, ⋯
	後	後ろ, 後部, 後方, 背後, ⋯
	間	間, 中, 中間, 区間, ⋯
	⋯	⋯
順序 (Order)	前	前, 先頭, ⋯
	後	後ろ, 後尾, ⋯
	⋯	⋯
程度 (Degree)	上	上, 以上, ⋯
	中	中, 半ば, 中程, ⋯
	下	下, 以下, ⋯
	⋯	⋯

Figure 3: Example of Function Nouns

object

  inanimate object

    artificial object

      · material
        lumber, steel

      · parts
        tile, battery, IC

      · tools [*use*]
        household
        construction
        communication
        medicine
        ...

      · tools [*material*]
        steel
        wood
        plastic
        ...

      · tools [*feature*]
        electric
        blade
        ...

      · *etc.*

Figure 4: Example of Thesaurus

5.3 Thesaurus for Nouns

We have created a thesaurus which expresses *super-sub* relationship among concepts. This thesaurus is used for cooccurrence checking of verbs and nouns, helping to paraphrase texts, selecting appropriate word in sentence generation, and so on. It has a tree-like structure in which each concepts is represented by a node while super-sub relation is represented by an arc. Each node in the thesaurus has a code which represents the location in the tree. The code is assigned for each word in the dictionary.

Generally in thesaurus, super concepts are divided into some lower concepts that should be mutually exclusive. In conventional thesauri, however, lower concepts are not strictly exclusive, but simply collection of words. To make the division clear, we have introduced *axis of division* or *viewpoint*. When we divide a super concept, first we set up an axis of division, along which some values from that viewpoint are taken. For example, taking *material* as an axis, a concept *tools* is divided into *metal-tools*, *wood-tools*, *plastic-tools*, and so on. On the other hand, the same concept is divided into *kitchen-tools*, *carpenters-tools*, etc. when we take *use* as an axis. A concept is, as a result, usually divided in some higher dimensional space in our thesaurus. Our coding reflects the structure of this space.

This thesaurus is used for cooccurrence checking of the surface words, especially verb and noun combination. This is performed with the semantic constraint information of each cases of verbs. Thesaurus code is involved in this semantic constraint.

Finding higher abstract concept, our thesaurus will help to paraphrase text. This is performed by searching the instances of super concept of a given word. Rhetoric expressions could also be analyzed by similar procedure.

And besides, to reduce the searching space of words to be selected in sentence generation, the thesaurus is useful. In other words, it is difficult to find an appropriate word directly from the formal semantic description, however, one can restrict the candidates with going down the tree structure of this thesaurus. In this case, description with viewpoint is also useful.

A part of our thesaurus is shown in Fig. 4.

5.4 Function Verbs

We have defined function verbs that work merely as syntactical elements carrying no substantial meaning. Verbs or nouns combining with function verbs express the meaning, that will be transformed or modified by function verbs. By this definition, there are many function verbs of various levels, where meaninglessness varies from zero to some extent. For example, in sentences

... oto ga suru
sound *subj.* do
(= it sounds ...)

and

kekkon-shiki wo ageru
wedding *obj.* raise
(= to hold a wedding ceremony)

the verbs *suru* and *ageru* are function verbs.

Verbs which express syntactic feature such as voice or aspect are also classified in function verbs by our definition. They are listed in Fig. 5 and Fig. 6.

Voice	Verb	Examples
Mutual	*kawasu* (exchange)	*keiyaku* (contract) *wo kawasu* *aisatsu* (greeting) *wo kawasu* *houyou* (embrace) *wo kawasu*
Basic	*okonau* (do)	*undou* (exercise) *wo okonau* *kouen* (lecture) *wo okonau* *kaiten* (rotation) *wo okonau*
Passive	*koumuru* (suffer)	*higai* (damage) *wo koumuru* *meiwaku* (trouble) *wo koumuru*

Figure 5: Example of Function Verbs (1)

Aspect	Verb	Examples
Inchoative	*hajimaru* *hajimeru* (begin)	*oinori* (prayer) *ga hajimaru* *kenkyuu* (research) *wo hajimeru* *giron* (debate) *wo hajimeru*
Completion	*owaru* *oeru* (finish)	*shokuji* (meal) *ga owaru* *shirabe* (investigation) *wo oeru* *giron* (debate) *wo oeru*
Continuation	*tamotsu* (keep) *tsuduku* *tsudukeru* (continue)	*chinmoku* (silence) *wo tamotsu* *sesshoku* (contact) *wo tamotsu* *sentou* (battle) *ga tsuduku* *kenkyuu* (research) *wo tsudukeru* *susurinaki* (sob) *wo tsudukeru*
Reiteration	*kurikaesu* (repeat)	*hentou* (response) *wo kurikaesu* *jikken* (experiment) *wo kurikaesu*

Figure 6: Example of Function Verbs (2)

5.5 Deep Case System for Verbs

We have prepared a deep case system to describe case relation of predicate. The deep case information is appeared in a dictionary entry as:

1. deep case
   List of deep cases of the verb. Optional cases are omitted.

2. surface case of active voice
   List of pairs of case index and particle of active voice. Correspondence between deep case index and surface case particle is expressed.

3. surface case of passive voice
   List of pairs of case index and particle of passive voice.

4. semantic constraint on nouns
   List of pairs of case index and thesaurus code for nouns. Nouns being able to appear in the case are restricted by thesaurus code.

5. argument of semantic structure
   List of pairs of case index and argument of semantic structure. Semantic structure of the word has some variables in the expression. These variables are linked to deep case indices by this list.

The example of deep case information of verb is shown in Fig. 7.

- surface expression: 与え・る (give)

- pronunciation: あたえる (*ataeru*)

- part of speech: verb

- deep case: (AGT, GOA, OBJ)

- surface case: (AGT: *ga*, GOA: *ni*, OBJ: *wo*)

- passive case: (GOA: *ga*, AGT: *ni*, OBJ: *wo*),
  (OBJ: *ga*, AGT: *niyotte*, GOA: *ni*)

- thesaurus code:
  (AGT: 1.1/1.2.2, GOA: 1.1/1.2.2, OBJ: 1.2)

- argument: (AGT: a, GOA: x, OBJ: y)

Figure 7: Example of Deep Case Information

5.6 Semantic Structure for Words

Semantic structure of a word is expressed with *basic state of affairs* or *infon* in terms of situation theory and situation semantics. Basically speaking, predicate represents some relation among objects in the world, while noun represents a object having some relation between other objects. These relationship can be represented by infons.

An object is not always able to appear in an arbitrary argument place of infons. Infons sometimes have some relation to other infons such as *equivalence*, *involve*, etc. This kind of information is expressed by *constraints* connected to each infons. Constraints such as cooccurrence restriction are described within dictionary entry for each word, while general constraints between infons (*e.g.* "Kissing means touching.") are stored in a constraint dictionary.

6 Conclusion

Current subjects on the dictionary and lexical knowledge base research are as follows:

- Extending vocabulary of dictionary. To make our dictionary useful, we must extend the vocabulary up to a hundred thousand at least. We are planning to develop morphological information of this size.

- Describing more knowledge on our lexical knowledge base. The more knowledge it has, the more knowledge it learns.

- Establishing the framework of formal description of tense and aspect. They must be involved in the semantic structure of words, however, current description is insufficient. This research cannot be performed within dictionary system alone. Cooperative study with logical inference module is indispensable.

- Studying rules or mechanism of change of meaning according to change of aspect. Semantic description and deep case information for each word cannot be independent from aspectuality. Then, data in the dictionary should be modified according to the surface word form when applied to the expression in sentences.

To improve our dictionary and lexical knowledge base in both quality and quantity, they should be evaluated with vast amount of actual data. We will make use of *DUALS* and *LTB* as evaluation systems for our dictionary and lexical knowledge base as well as users of them.

ACKNOWLEDGEMENTS

We would like to thank Professor Hozumi Tanaka at Tokyo Institute of Technology and the members of working group NLU/SG-2 for their intensive discussions and suggestions. We would also like to thank Mr. Oshima, Miss Nagasawa, Mr. Umino and Mrs. Kunieda for their enormous effort of dictionary description and theoretical advice, Dr. Shun-ichi Uchida, the chief, and all the members of the Second Research Laboratory for their valuable discussions. We also wish to express our thanks to Dr. Kazuhiro Fuchi, Director of ICOT Research Center, who, as the pioneer in this research area, provided us with the opportunity to pursue this development in the Fifth Generation Computer Systems Project at ICOT.

References

[1] Barwise, J., and Perry, J. "Situations and Attitudes" MIT Press, Cambridge, 1983.

[2] Barwise, J. "The Situation in Logic-III, — Situations, Sets and the Axiom of Foundation", CLSI Report No. CLSI-85-26, 1985.

[3] Cohen, P. R., *et al.* "Persistence, Intention and Commitment", CLSI Report No. CLSI-87-88, 1987.

[4] Ikeda, T., *et al.* "Sentence Generation in LTB, *in Japanese*", *5th Conference Proceedings of Japan Software Science and Technology*, 1988.

[5] Kimura, K., Sugimura, R., Takizuka, T. and Mukai, K. "Danwa Rikai Jikken System DU-ALS dai 2-han no Sekkei to Jissou (Design and Implementation of Discourse Understanding System DUALS-V2, *in Japanese*)", *Proceedings of the 3rd Conference of Japan Society for Software Science and Technology*, Tokyo, 1986.

[6] Matsumoto, Y. and Sugimura, R. "Koubun Kaiseki System SAX no tameno Bunpô Kijutu Gengo (Grammar Description Language for The SAX Parsing System, *in Japanese*), *5th Conference Proceedings of Japan Society for Software Science and Technology*, Tokyo, 1988.

[7] Morioka, K. "Goi no Keisei (Formation of a vocabulary, *in Japanese*)" *Gendai-go Kenkyuu Series 1*, Meiji-Shoin, 1987.

[8] Mukai, K. "A system of Logic Programming for Linguistic Analysis Based on Situation Semantics", *Proceedings of the workshop on semantic issues in human and computer languages.*, CSLI, 1987.

[9] Muraki, S. "Nihongo no Kinou-doushi Hyougen wo Megutte (On Function Verb Expression in Japanese, *in Japanese*)", *Research Report 2*, National Language Institute, 1980.

[10] Ogino, T. "Nihongo no Imi Bunrui Shian (Proposal on Semantic Classification of Japanese Words, *in Japanese*)", *Proceedings of the 31st Conference of Japanese Association for Metrical Linguistics*, 1987.

[11] Okutsu, K. "Seisei Nihon Bunpou-ron (Theory of Generative Japanese Grammar, *in Japanese*)", Taishuukan-Shoten, 1974.

[12] Sano, H., Akasaka, K., Kubo, Y., and Sugimura, R. "Go-Kousei ni Motoduku Keitaiso Kaiseki (Morphological Analysis with derivation and inflection, *in Japanese*), *Proceedings of the 36th Conference of Information Processing Society of Japan*, 1988.

[13] Sugimura, R., Akasaka, K., Kubo, Y., Sano, H., and Matsumoto, Y. "Ronri-gata Keitaiso Kaiseki LAX (Logic Based Lexical Analyzer LAX, *in Japanese*)", *Proceedings of the Logic Programming Conference '88*, ICOT, 1988 (English version will be appeared in *The Lecture Notes on Computer Science.*)

[14] Sugimura, R. "Ronri-Gata Bunpô ni okeru Seiyaku Kaiseki (Constraint Analysis on Logic Grammars, *in Japanese*)", *Proceedings of the 2nd Annual Conference of Japanese society for Artificial Intelligence*, Tokyo, 1988.

[15] Sugimura, R., Hasida, K., Akasaka, K., Hatano, K., Kubo, Y., Okunishi, T., and Takizuka, T. "A Software Environment for Research into Discourse Understanding Systems", *in this proceedings* FGCS'88, ICOT, 1988.

[16] Takizuka, T., Tanaka, Y., and Sugimura, R. "LTB Master Jisho no Kousei (Configuration of LTB Master Dictionary, *in Japanese*)", *Logic and Natural Language Research Group in Japan Society for Software Science and Technology*, 1988.

[17] Miyoshi, H., Tanaka, Y., Yokoi, T., *et al.* "Basic Specification of the Machine-Readable Dictionary", TR-100, ICOT, 1985.

[18] Tanaka, Y., Oshima, M., and Oshima, R. "LTB Master Jisho no Imi Kijutsu no Kousou (Design of Semantic Description for LTB Master Dictionary, *in Japanese*)", *Logic and Natural Language Research Group* in Japan Society for Software Science and Technology, 1988.

[19] Tanaka, Y., Oshima, M., and Nagasawa, Y. "LTB Master Jisho no Imi Kijutsu (On Semantic Description for LTB Master Dictionary, *in Japanese*)", *Proceedings of the 37th Conference of Information Processing Society of Japan*, 1988.

[20] Tanaka, Y., Umino, B. "LTB Master Jisho no Kouzou to Naiyou (Structure and Contents of LTB Master Dictionary, *in Japanese*)", *Proceedings of the 37th Conference of Information Processing Society of Japan*, 1988.

PROCEEDINGS OF THE INTERNATIONAL CONFERENCE
ON FIFTH GENERATION COMPUTER SYSTEMS 1988,
edited by ICOT. © ICOT, 1988

A Software Environment for Research into Discourse Understanding Systems

Ryôichi Sugimura   Kôiti Hasida   Kouji Akasaka   Kôzi Hatano   Yukihiro Kubo
Toshiyuki Okunishi
Institute for New Generation Computer Technology (ICOT)
Takashi Takizuka
KDD Kamifukuoka R&D Laboratories

ABSTRACT

This paper describes a software environment for research on discourse understanding systems.

Discourse understanding systems based on logic programming have been investigated since 1982 at ICOT. The focus of the research has been mainly on the basic mechanisms of *discourse understanding*, and the *parallel algorithms* for these mechanisms.

Experimental systems called **DUALS-I** and **DUALS-II** were developed to verify the research results.

These results have been put together to form a general purpose software environment for natural language processing named the Language Tool Box **LTB** .

This paper presents an overview of the LTB and discusses its future research and development direction.

1 INTRODUCTION

A natural language understanding system (NLS) must meet many kinds of demands.

As the interface system between computer systems and their users, an NLS should be able to understand not only what users say but also what they intend. An NLS is expected to make the interface more comfortable.

An NLS for researchers of linguistics or computer linguistics should be very flexible. It should enable researchers to input their ideas freely, such as grammars and lexical entries, so that it can be used to verify their research ideas. There should also be some debugging tools to check how a grammar or a lexicon works.

An NLS for software system development should have modularity, high performance, and compatibility with other application software such as an expert system. Maintenance tools should be prepared in the NLS.

The Language Tool Box (LTB) has been developed to meet these demands.

Since the foundation of ICOT in 1982, we have been researching many fundamental issues of natural language. Our basic starting point was logic. We have been focusing our research on complicated phenomena of natural language, using logic and logic programming.

Versions I and II of **DUALS** (Discourse Understanding Aimed at Logic Based Systems) have already been

developed. Many ideas were poured into *DUALS*. Its main goal has been to verify fundamental ideas that arise from our basic research on natural language understanding. In the course of the development of *DUALS*, many kinds of software were developed and evaluated.

The LTB is the NLS developed from a collection of these software systems. The latest version of DUALS, **DUALS-III**, was developed on the LTB as shown in Figure 1.

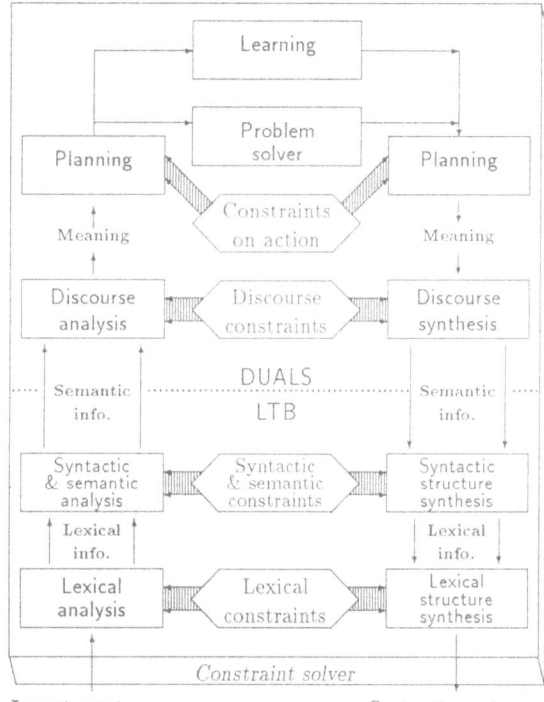

Figure 1: DUALS configuration

Features of the LTB include the following.

- It provides up-to-date logic-based tools for natural language understanding research.

- It accommodates many types of software environments such as debuggers and editors.

- All the tools are written in ESP [6] so that they have high modularity and compatibility with each other.

We believe that a variety of **NLS** could be developed based on the LTB.

2 STRUCTURE OF LTB

As shown in Figure 2, the LTB is constructed from the following component tools.

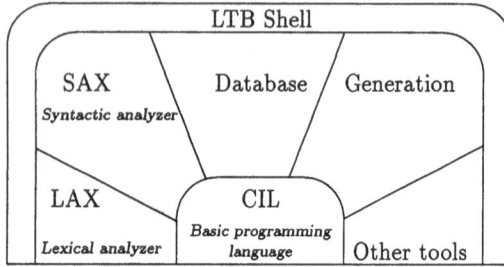

Figure 2: Configuration of the LTB

Shell: The LTB shell [40] facilitates the interaction with tools in the LTB. The shell itself can also be executed in a parallel logic programming language.

Database: The collection of Japanese lexicon, Japanese morphological grammar and syntactic grammars [41].

CIL: The basic programming language of the LTB. Every tool in the LTB has access to CIL and its software environments.

LAX: The morphological and semantic analyzer. The morphological grammars which the LAX looks up are written in a kind of extended regular expression. The LAX can execute analysis both in sequential logic programming languages such as Prolog or ESP, and in parallel logic programming languages such as GHC [44].

SAX: The syntactic and semantic analyzer. The grammar is written in DCG [32]. The SAX [21] can also execute analysis both in sequential and parallel logic programming languages.

Generator: The Japanese sentence generator, whose input is a frame structure written in CIL, outputs Japanese surface sentences.

3 LTB SHELL

The LTB shell has the following features.

- It manages all the communications in the LTB. It controls all the information flow among the user and application tools in the LTB.

- It accommodates the notify function which informs the shell of data communication among processes, so that the shell can measure the execution interval of a process in the LTB.

- It controls all the processes in the LTB.

- It provides a standard window. The window has a multi-lingual menu so that users can use LTB tools in either English or Japanese.

- It provides help instructions.

On parallel machines like PIM, the shell will enable each process to move simultaneously. Communications among the parallel processes in the LTB are performed as shown in figure 3.

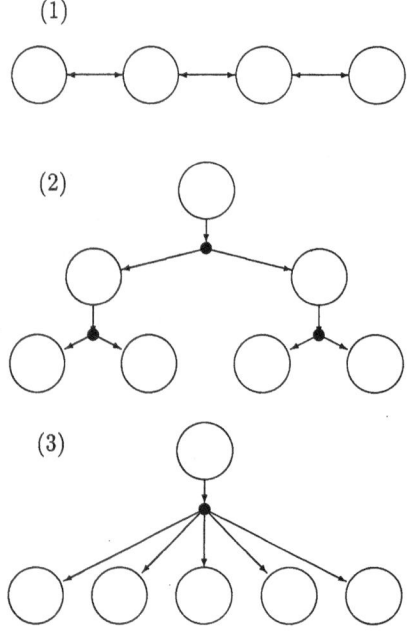

Figure 3: Redirection of stream data

In figure 3, graph (1) shows the data flow through a pipe-line in which there is no need for the data sender to specify the data receiver. Graph (2) enables communication between hierarchical processes in which the data sender should specify the direction, right or left. Graph (3) enables network communication between processes in which the data sender should specify the name of the receiver. We think that these three ways of communication are enough to install natural language processing systems on the LTB.

4   DATABASE

The LTB uses the following three databases for discourse understanding research. See [42] for details.

Japanese Word Dictionary: It provides a master dictionary of 4000 word entries for morphological analysis and synthesis, and a Japanese thesaurus of 800 concepts.

Japanese Grammars: Grammar for morphological analysis and syntactic analysis. Their features are as follows.

Morphological Grammar

1. It is written in a regular grammar.
2. It is based on Morioka grammar [24] along the line of structural linguistics.
3. Its semantics is formulated in situation theory [3] and situation semantics [2].
4. 2,000 lines/1,000 rules for derivations and inflections.
5. 30,000 lines/10,000 rules for word stems.

Syntactic Grammar

1. It is written in DCG.
2. It is based on dependency grammar [45].
3. Its semantics is formulated in situation theory and situation semantics.
4. 1,000 lines/2,000 rules.

Japanese KWIC: A Japanese key word in context (KWIC) has been under development, making it possible to analyse Japanese grammatical features.

5   BASIC PROGRAMMING LANGUAGE

CIL [30], the basic programming language of the LTB, is being developed to make it easy to describe natural language processing systems. An overview of CIL is given. See [25] [26] [27] [28] for further information.

CIL has two augmentations to Prolog (figure 4). One is a record-like structure called a **partially specified term** (PST). The other is the **freeze mechanism**, originating in PrologII [7]. A passive constraint solver is provided as a built-in predicate based on the freeze mechanism.

Currently, CIL is implemented on PSI machines and prepares the entire programming environment. Its debugging environment, which is a full-screen source image tracer based on the extended procedure box model, is customized for all LTB application tools.

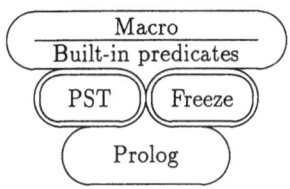

Figure 4: CIL language

5.1   PST

A PST is a record-like structure. [29] demonstrates that a record structure is useful for complicated data representation such as linguistic information, and that many useful data structures can be seen as derived from record structures.

A PST is a set of attribute-value pairs in the form:

$$\{a_1/b_1, ..., a_n/b_n\}$$

where

$$n \geq 0, \quad a_i \neq a_j \quad (i \neq j)$$

The order of pairs whose label is a_i and whose value is b_i can be ignored. For instance, $\{a/1, b/\{c/2, d/3\}\}$ and $\{b/\{d/3, c/2\}, a/1\}$ are identical. They represent a tagged tree in Figure 5.

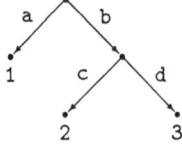

Figure 5: PST as a tagged tree

A value may also be a PST, which may be the parent PST, giving rise to circular data. A PST is designed to represent partial information. Unification of CIL has been extended to deal with this aspect. Pairs of different labels are merged with each other.

```
CIL> {a/{b/2}}={a/{b/3}}.
no
CIL> X={a/1},X={b/2}.
X = {a/1,b/2}
```

A PST can simplify the representation of and operation on data structure. CIL provides various operation predicates for a PST. For example, role(L,P,V) accesses value V with label L in PST P. In t_subpat(P1,P2), P1 is a transitive subpattern of P2.

288

```
CIL> role(a,{a/1,b/2},V).
V = 1
CIL> t_subpat({a/{b/Y}},{b/1,a/{c/2,b/3}}).
yes
```

5.2 Constraint Solver

Freeze can specify constraints that variables must satisfy. These constraints are solved on a lazy evaluation basis. That is, they are executed when the connected variables are instantiated. For instance,

```
CIL> freeze(X,X=2),print(ok),X=1.
ok
no
```

The freeze mechanism is one of the approaches to (passive) constraint solving. CIL has the constr predicate composed from freeze. Arithmetic and propositional constraints can be written in constr. For example,

```
CIL> constr((X=1;Y=:=X+2)),constr((X=3)).
X = 3,
Y = 5
```

While only constraints (not values) are accumulated, however, constr can only wait for a value and yields no solution:

```
CIL> constr((X=1;X=2)),constr((X=2;X=3)).
yes     % X is frozen.
```

For this reason, the constraint solver in CIL is passive. Introduction of an active constraint solver such as a Boolean constraint is being considered.

5.3 Macro and Built-in Predicates

For effective programming with a PST and freeze, CIL supplies a macro function and many built-in predicates, such as role, t_subpat and constr. Users can define their own macro with the following system macros.

$$
\begin{aligned}
p(X:C) &\Rightarrow \texttt{solve}(C), p(X) \\
X!Y &\Rightarrow Z : \texttt{role}(Y, X, Z) \\
X\#Y &\Rightarrow X : X = Y \\
p(X?) &\Rightarrow \texttt{freeze}(X, p(X)) \\
X@p &\Rightarrow X : p(X?)
\end{aligned}
$$

CIL expands the form of the left-hand side of $\Rightarrow$ to that of the right-hand side in the program.

5.4 Programming Environment

Figure 6 shows the configuration of the CIL system.

CIL has extended unification, various extended notations and a freeze mechanism. Therefore, a standard debugger for Prolog cannot give very useful information. *Debug aid* extends the ordinary procedure box model and provides a full-screen source image tracer [1]. The box model is modified for constraint and head unification. The full-screen source image tracer enables the user to debug visually programs executed on a lazy evaluation basis. The *inspector* can inspect a nested PST. A *CIL editor* with a syntax checker is also available. Users can invoke them interactively through the *command interpreter* during program debugging. The *Compiler* translates the CIL program, after debugging, to an ESP program, which is executed efficiently.

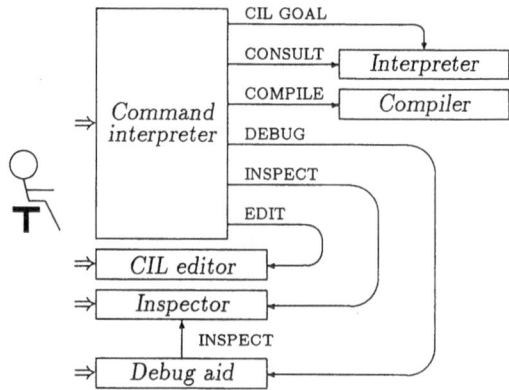

Figure 6: Configuration of the CIL system and user interface

6 APPLICATION TOOLS

This section describes the fundamental application tools in the LTB. The application tools consist of analysis tools and a synthesis tool. Currently, these tools process only Japanese, but can be extended to process other languages by changing the grammars and dictionaries. All application tools have programming environments with multi-window interface facilities.

7 MORPHOLOGICAL AND SEMANTIC ANALYSIS

The *LAX* is a software environment which enables us to develop morphological analysis programs effectively. These programs have an analysis engine and a dictionary which is compiled from a morphological dictionary (the *LAX dictionary*).

Morphological analysis consists of two phases. The first phase is to recognize morphemes from an input sentence that consists of kanji (Chinese characters) and the two kinds of Japanese phonograms, and put them into a sequence of words. The second phase is to construct the meaning of each word from semantic information written in the *LAX dictionary*, and output sequences of nonterminal symbols with semantic structures. This output is used as an input for syntactic analyzer *SAX*.

The *LAX system* supports a sequential LAX analysis algorithm and has two types of development tools called the *LAX inspector* and *LAX dictionary*.

7.1 Morphological Analysis Algorithm

This section briefly explains the features of the LAX analysis algorithm. For details, see [38]. In this method, a morphological dictionary is transformed into sequential logic programming languages such as ESP or Prolog, or into parallel logic programming languages such as GHC. These programs can analyze Japanese sentences without backtracking and output all ambiguities at one time. This algorithm is based on the layered stream technique and can be regarded as a parallel to the method of Earley's algorithm or the bottom-up Chart parsing algorithm applied to regular grammars.

7.2 Morphological Dictionary

Figure 7 shows the format of the *LAX dictionary*. Definitions of morphemes that belong to the same category are written between `begin(Category Name)` and `end(Category Name)`. Three kinds of information are declared for each morpheme. The first is a *left-hand feature* which is the identifier of the morpheme. The second is a *right-hand feature* which indicates what kinds of morphemes can follow that morpheme. The third is a *semantic rule* which is evaluated in the second phase of analysis. These semantic rules are written in CIL, and semantic structures are represented in terms of PSTs. This dictionary describes a regular grammar so that the analyzer can be regarded as a non-deterministic finite state automaton.

```
begin(Category Name)
morpheme ::  Lefthand Feature
         &&  Righthand Feature
         $$  Semantic Rule
          ⋮
end(Category Name)
```

Figure 7: LAX dictionary format

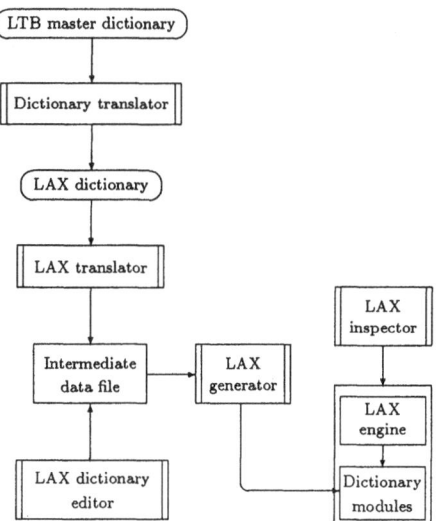

Figure 8: Configuration of the LAX system

7.3 Configuration of LAX Software Environment

Figure 8 shows the configuration of the *LAX system*. The *dictionary translator* transforms the *LTB master dictionary* into the *LAX dictionary*. Using the *LAX translator*, the *LAX dictionary* is transformed into an intermediate data file. The analysis program is generated by the *LAX generator* from this intermediate data file. From the user's point of view, this intermediate data file is identical to the *LAX dictionary*.

To debug the *LAX dictionary*, the *LAX inspector* provides many pieces of useful information. It has two modes: the analysis mode and the inspection mode. In the analysis mode, you can check the results of analysis, looking at the time and the number of ambiguities for each input sentence. If the analysis fails, you can also see which morpheme cannot be connected with its adjoining morpheme. In the inspection mode, you can examine the contents of the dictionary of the morphemes that belong to each adjoining point of input sentences.

We can easily modify the definitions of morphemes and add new entries by using the *LAX dictionary editor*. To modify a definition of a morpheme, we only have to rewrite the left-thand or right-hand features or semantic rule in the edit window after locating the definition. To add new definitions, we may pick up another definition, copy it, and rewrite it.

7.4 Morphological Grammar

Using the *LAX system*, we have been developing a Japanese morphological grammar [35]. We have defined about 2000 morphemes and succeeded in analyzing about 200 sentences. A Japanese morphological grammar can be developed naturally in the *LAX system*.

8 SYNTACTIC AND SEMANTIC ANALYSIS

This section describes the syntactic and semantic analysis part of the LTB, called the SAX system. First, in section 8.1, the grammar syntax and SAX semantics are represented. Then, the SAX is outlined, mainly referring to its relationship with other LTB components. Section 8.3 briefly explains the SAX parsing method. A restricted Definite Clause Grammar is assumed as the grammar description. See [21] for a detailed description. Finally, section 8.4 introduces the debugging tools [46] provided by our system.

8.1 SAX Grammar Rules

Figure 9 shows the SAX grammar rules. Basically, they are rules extended from DCG [32].

$$head \;\rightarrow\; body_1, \{extra_1\} \qquad (1)$$
$$:: \{pref\_rule_1\}, \qquad (2)$$
$$\cdots \qquad (3)$$
$$body_n, \{extra_n\} \qquad (4)$$
$$:: \{pref\_rule_n\}, \qquad (5)$$
$$\& \{delayed\_extra\}, \qquad (6)$$
$$\&\& \{pref\_rule\} \qquad (7)$$

Figure 9: SAX grammar rules

In figure 9, *head* at line (1) and $body_i$ in line (1) or (4) represent grammatical categories. They are presented in the form of Prolog terms which can have optional arguments. $extra_i$ in line (1) or (4) is the extra condition in which an optional Prolog program can be written. *delayed_extra* in line (6) is also an extra condition called the *delayed extra condition*. The optional Prolog program in the *delayed extra condition* is evaluated after completion of the parsing.

SAX executes parsing bottom-up and breadth-first so that there is some limitation on the rules. Firstly, on the left-hand side of $body_1$ in line (1), we cannot write any extra conditions. Secondly, the Prolog variables in $extra_i$ should be instantiated when $extra_i$ is evaluated.

Rules in lines (2), (5), and (7) never fail. They are used to calculate *lexical preference*. Generally, a sentence has more than one interpretation. Disambiguation of the sentence interpretations has been one of the hardest problems in natural language processing. Therefore, many kinds of approaches have been studied, such as disambiguation with local lexical constraints [43], or disambiguation with the discourse [37]. The rules in lines (2), (5), and (7) enable us to calculate one of the local lexical constraints.

The SAX system supplies several items of information related to the calculation of *lexical preference* as follows.

1. In $\{pref\_rule_i\}$ after ::

   pref_cat In $pref\_rule_i$, preference for $body_i$ which is calculated in the rule whose head is $body_i$.

   pref In $pref\_rule_i$, preference for $body_i$ in the rule.

2. In $\{pref\_rule\}$ after &&

   pref_CAT Preference for the *head*.

   prefs(i) *pref* in $pref\_rule_i$.

3. In $\{pref\_rule\}$ after ::, or &&

   super_cat_set The set of grammatical categories which includes the *head* as its partial tree.

   next_pos The grammatical category ahead of the right most leaf node of the tree whose root node is *head*.

Another feature of the SAX is that Gapping Grammar (GG) [8][9] can be written. GG is the grammar formalism in which a discontinuous sequence of grammar categories can be written. It is performed with the expansion of the SAX parsing algorithm[20][22].

Generally, the grammar rules in GG are as follows.

$$\beta \;\rightarrow\; \alpha_1, skip(G_1),$$
$$\cdots$$
$$\alpha_n, skip(G_n), \alpha.$$

In the rules, α and α_i are a sequence of grammatical categories whose length is greater than 0. $skip(G_i)$ is a special symbol in GG. β is a sequence of symbols including some grammatical categories and $skip(G_i)$. In β, every $skip(G_i)$ in the rule body should be included. In the course of the parsing, $skip(G_i)$ can be matched to any grammatical category, and a $skip(G_i)$ in β should represent the same grammatical category of a $skip(G_i)$ in the rule body.

In SAX, rules for GG are analyzed bottom-up so that there are limitations and expansion for the GG rules in the SAX as follows.

- α_1 should not be empty.

- GG rules should not be applied recursively.

- $skip_i$ can be matched with grammatical categories.

- $skip_i$ is represented as follows.
  $skip(i)$ or $skip(i, S)$
  i is a natural number, and S is the set of grammatical categories which *skip* matches or does not match. Specifically, S is either of the following: $+\{a_1, \ldots, a_n\}$ representing *skip* can be matched only with a_1, or, $\ldots$, or a_n, or $-\{body_1, \ldots, body_n\}$ representing *skip* cannot be matched with $body_1$, and, $\ldots$, and $body_n$.

8.2 SAX System

Figure 10 shows the configuration of the SAX. Given grammar rules are translated into a parsing program written in ESP. In these grammar rules, CIL notations are allowed in DCG's extra condition, so that many CIL functions are available. We have developed Japanese grammar rules, using CIL's built-in predicate for describing syntactic and semantic constraints, and for constructing semantic structure.

The translated parsing program receives the results of morphological and semantic analysis and parses at high speed. Semantic representation is constructed simultaneously from the semantic information supplied by lexical semantic processing.

Some other tools, such as the grammar debugger, and graphic display utility, are provided for effective development of the grammar.

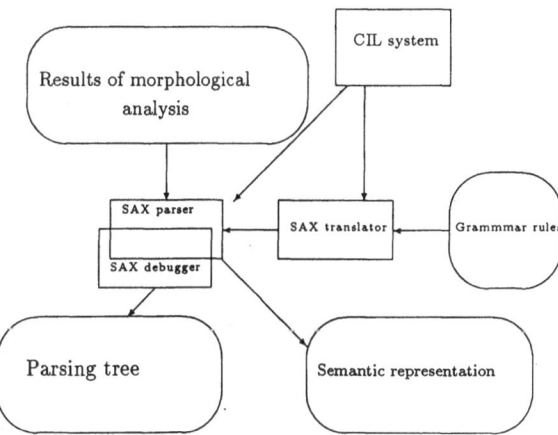

Figure 10: Configuration of the SAX system

8.3 Parsing Method

The SAX parsing algorithm was devised for parrallel parsing [21]. However, it turned out to work efficiently in sequential implementation as well [31].

The system employs bottom-up parsing with top-down prediction. The major advantages of our system are that the system works bottom-up: therefore, the left-recursive rules do not cause problems, and the parsing process does not involve backtracking, which means that there is no redundant construction of syntactic structures.

8.4 Debugging Environment

Grammar debugging tools are indispensable for the development of practical grammar rules. The SAX provides two types of debugging tools.

The first is an interactive tracer, which shows the parsing process, displaying the rules currently being applied. As with the Prolog tracer, the user can control the trace by issuing commands such as "skip" and "leap". However, this kind of debugging tool is not very suitable for the SAX since it is hard to follow the process of parsing breadth-first, and in order to use the tracer, the user needs to know the SAX parsing mechanism.

The second is an algorithmic debugger on DCG. Using this tool, the user interacts with the system and tries to construct the expected parsing tree from input words according to the grammar rules. The user specifies the start point and end point of the sequence of words, and the system parses the sequence. If the parsing succeeds, the system displays the obtained root categories of the resultant trees.

If the user does not find the expected category in them, an error is in the grammar rules that are to be applied when parsing that sequence of words. In this way, the user can narrow the candidates for the wrong rule.

9 JAPANESE GENERATION

The Japanese generation module provides a function for generating sentences, and tools for customizing the module itself. This section describes the basic concept of sentence generation and tools in the module.

9.1 Aim and Features of the Japanese Generation Module

The Japanese synthesis module generates sentences from "intermediate representation". The intermediate representation is basically a syntactic structure and contains all the information needed to generate sentences. The module does not reshape its output using contextual information.

One of the important goals of designing the module is to enable it to be used as an NLS interface in various systems such as expert systems, so the rule definition such as grammar in it must be easy to customize. We made customization easy by introducing the following features.

- Most of the generating process is done by macro expansion.

– Tools for tracing the process and making data are provided.

9.2 Sentence Generation as Macro Expansion

Although the module does not process contextual information, sometimes users may want to input abstract information such as deep structure (or a thematic role). The module allows users to include such information in the intermediate representation, and regards it as a **macro expression** in the syntactic structure.

Figure 11 shows the sentence generation flow. First, the macro expander expands macro expression in the intermediate representation and makes a pure syntactic structure. In this phase, the macro expander uses several macro definitions and a lexicon. Each macro definition is a rule for translating a macro expression to part of the syntactic structure. The lexicon gives lexical information such as the correspondence between thematic roles and case markers. The next phase is to translate the syntactic structure to the output sentence (character string). In this phase, the string synthesizer picks up lexical information in the syntactic structure, applies a morphological rule to it, and inflects each word.

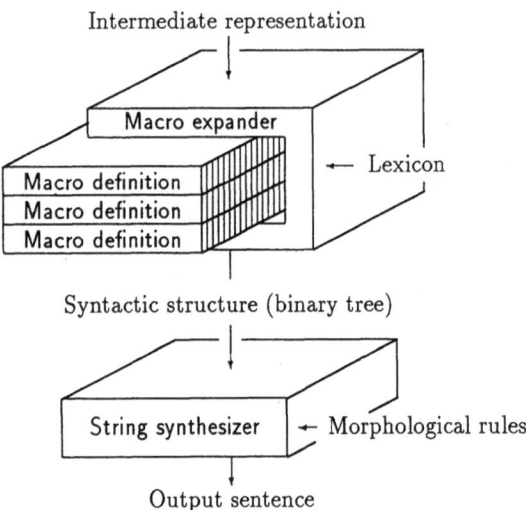

Figure 11: Sentence generation

The advantages of this method are:

– Users can design the intermediate representation that they want, by changing the macro definition.
– By defining macros on another definition, intermediate representation can be constructed hierarchically.

– Users can specify information roughly or precisely in intermediate representation. For example, if they want to specify a strict word order, they may write it in pure syntactic structure, but if they do not need to specify it as exactly, they may write it in terms of a more abstract expression.

It has been said that the syntactic structure of a Japanese sentence is clearly represented by a binary tree [12]. In the Japanese generation module, the syntactic structure is represented in a binary tree. Figure 12 shows a simplified example of the Japanese phrase "Kodomo wo gakkô e ika seru (to make a child go to school)" written in the form of a binary tree.

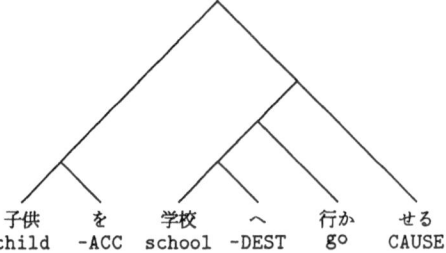

Figure 12: Example of syntactic structure

Although users can define the syntax of intermediate representation, the *standard macros* are already defined in the module [11]. The definition includes several rules, including the following.

– A meaning role may be expanded into a binary tree with a case marker.
– Voice information may change case markers.
– Auxiliaries are added to the tree when aspect, tense, or modality information is given.

Figure 13 shows the intermediate representation of the sentence shown in Figure 12 using standard macros.

9.3 Tools

The configuration of the whole generation module, including the tools, is shown in Figure 14. Thus, the generation module includes the following two parts besides the **generation engine**.

Debugger: Traces the execution of the **generation engine** (macro expander and string synthesizer), switches the rules (lexicon, macro definition, and morphological rule), and reads the input data (intermediate representation).

```
{関係 /{語彙 / 行く},
 rel   lex  go
 ロール /{行為者 /{補語 /{語彙 / 子供}},
 role    agt     comp lex   child
       終点 /{補語 /{語彙 / 学校}}},
       dest comp lex   school
 ヴォイス / 使役}
 voice    causative
```

Figure 13: Example of intermediate representation

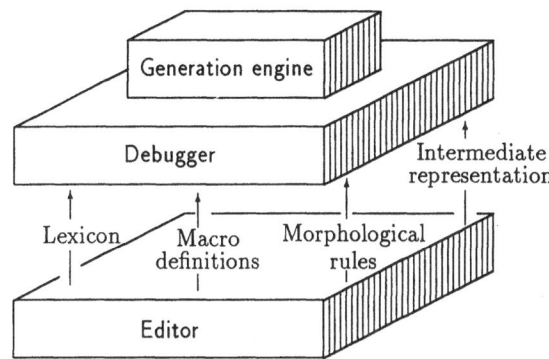

Figure 14: Configuration of the Japanese generation module

Editor: Edits the rules and input data.

These tools have the following features.

- The debugger is built on the CIL debugger. Its window, mouse and key manipulation are the same as those of CIL.

- The editor is built on pmacs [17]. Its key assignments are the same as those of pmacs. It checks and guides the syntax of the data at the users request.

10   CONCLUSION

Current research subjects in the *LTB* are as follows.

- Filling up the more comfortable programming environments such as debugger, inspector, and pretty printer. To improve the programming environments, they should be evaluated in terms of performance and competence by users and developers.

- Building up more convenient linguistic databases and interface facilities for them.

- Installation of the LTB on the parallel logic programming language GHC which runs on the multi-PSI [23] or PIM. Some LTB tools have been installed on the multi-PSI for experiments.

- Supplements of built-in predicates such as constraint unification [13][14][15][16], Boolean Gröbner base [34], type inference [4] [33], and finite domains [10], which execute fundamental inferences for discourse processing.

Current research and development in the LTB are supported by a working group (WG-Sig2) at ICOT which is chaired by Professor Hozumi Tanaka of the Tokyo Institute of Technology.

There is much room for improvements in the LTB. Improvements and evaluations of the LTB will be carried out mainly by ICOT and WG-Sig2 researchers.

To supplement built-in predicates or functions, we need to study implicit rules of discourse [5] [18] [19] [36] [39] in more detail. In discourse analysis, we have not yet found or created explicit rules, which are exemplified by sufficient numbers of experimental results. We should be able to use some general tools such as constraint unification and the Boolean Gröbner base solver, and experimental tools such as the KWIC. These tools will be installed in the LTB.

After finding some rules, we will research basic core constraints and solution mechanisms for them. These mechanisms will then be new tools for the LTB.

ACKNOWLEDGEMENTS

We would like to thank Professor Hozumi Tanaka at Tokyo Institute of Technology and the members of working group Sig-2 for their intensive discussions and suggestions. We would also like to thank Dr. Fuchi, the director of ICOT Research Laboratory, and Dr. Uchida, the chief of the Second Research Laboratory at ICOT, for their encouragement and support for this work.

References

[1] T. Amanuma, T. Suzuki, T. Okunishi, and K. Mukai. CIL Programming kankyô (CIL Programming Environment (*in Japanese*)). In *Proceedings of the 2nd Annual Conference of Japanese Society for Artificial Intelligence*, pages 211–214, 1988.

[2] J. Barwise. Recent Developments in Situation Semantics. In M. Nagao, editor, *Language and Artificial Intelligence*, pages 387–399, Amsterdam, 1987. North-Holland.

294

[3] J. Barwise and J. Perry. *Situations and Attitudes*. MIT Press, Cambridge, 1983.

[4] L. Cardelli. Typechecking Dependent Types and Subtypes. Technical report, DEC Systems Research Center, 1987.

[5] D. Carter. *Interpreting anaphors in natural language texts*. Ellis Horwood Series in Artificial Intelligence. Ellis Horwood, 1987.

[6] T. Chikayama. ESP Reference Manual. Technical Report 044, ICOT, 1984.

[7] A. Colmerauer. Prolog-II: Reference Manual and Theoretical Model. İnternal report, Group Intelligence Artificielle, Université d'Aix-Marseille II, 1982.

[8] V. Dahl. More on Gapping Grammar. In *Proceedings of the International Conference on FGCS '84*, pages 669–677, Tokyo, 1984.

[9] V. Dahl and H. Abramson. On Gapping Grammar. In *Proceedings of 2nd ICLP*, pages 77–88, Sweden, 1984.

[10] M. Dincbas, H. Simonis, and P.V. Hentenryck. Extending equation solving and constraint handling in logic programming. Internal Report IR-LP-2203, ECRC, 1987.

[11] T. Ikeda et al. Sentence generation in LTB (*in Japanese*). In *5th Conference Proceedings of Japan Software Science and Technology*, 1988.

[12] T. Gunji. *Japanese Phrase Structure Grammar*. Dordrecht D. Reidel, 1987.

[13] K. Hasida. Conditioned Unification for Natural Language Processing. In *Proceedings of the 11th COLING*, pages 85–87, 1986.

[14] K. Hasida. Dependency Propagation: A Unified Theory of Sentence Comprehension and Generation. In *Proceedings of the 10th IJCAI*, pages 664–670, 1987.

[15] K. Hasida. Izondenpa (Dependency Propagation (*in Japanese*)). In *Proceedings of the 29th Programming Symposium*, pages 147–158, 1988.

[16] K. Hasida and H. Sirai. Zyôkentsuki tan-itsuka (Conditioned Unification (*in Japanese*)). *Computer Software*, 3:28–38, 1986.

[17] ICOT. PSI/SIMPOS Editor Manual. 1988.

[18] M. Kameyama. *Zero Anaphora : The case of Japanese*. PhD thesis, Stanford University, 1984.

[19] K. Kimura, R. Sugimura, T. Takizuka, and K. Mukai. Danwa Rikai Jikken System DUALS Dai 2-han no Sekkei to Jissô (Design and Implementation of Discourse Understanding System DUALS-v2 (*in Japanese*)). In *3rd

Conference Proceedings of Japan Society for Software Science and Technology*, pages 33–36, Tokyo, 1986.

[20] Y. Matsumoto. Ronri Bunpô no Heiretsu Kôbun Kaiseki (Parallel Analysis of Logic Grammars (*in Japanese*)). *IPSJ*, 29(4):335–341, 1988.

[21] Y. Matsumoto and R. Sugimura. A Parsing System Based on Logic Programming. In *Proceedings of IJCAI 87*, 1987.

[22] Y. Matsumoto and R. Sugimura. Kôbun Kaiseki System SAX no tameno Bunpô Kijutsu Gengo (Grammar Description Language for the SAX Parsing System (*in Japanese*)). In *5th Conference Proceedings of Japan Society for Software Science and Technology*, pages 77–80, Tokyo, 1988.

[23] T. Miyazaki and K. Taki. Multi-PSI ni okeru Flat GHC no Jitsugen Hôshiki (Installation of Flat GHC on Multi-PSI (*in Japanese*)). Technical Report 190, ICOT, 1986.

[24] K. Morioka. Goi no Keisei (Formation of a Vocabulary (*in Japanese*)), volume 1 of *Gendaigo Kenkyuu*. Meiji Shoin, 1987.

[25] K. Mukai. Horn Clause Logic with Parameterized Types for Situation Semantics Programming. Technical Report 101, ICOT, 1985.

[26] K. Mukai. Unification over Complex Indterminates in Prolog. Technical Report 113, ICOT, 1985.

[27] K. Mukai. Anadic Tuples in Prolog. Technical Report 239, ICOT, 1987.

[28] K. Mukai. A System of Logic Programming for Linguistic Analysis based on Situation Semantics. In *Proceedings of the workshop on semantic issues in human and computer languages*. CSLI, 1987.

[29] K. Mukai. Partially Specified Term in Logic Programming for Linguistic Analysis. In *Proceedings of the International Conference on FGCS '88*, 1988.

[30] K. Mukai and H. Yasukawa. *Complex Indeterminates in Prolog and its Application to Discourse Models*, volume 3, pages 441–466. OHMUSHA, ltd. and Spring Verlag, 1985.

[31] T. Okunishi, R. Sugimura, Y. Matsumoto, N. Tamura, T. Kamiwaki, and H. Tanaka. *Comparison of Logic Programming Based Natural Language Parsing Systems*, volume 2, pages 1–14. North-Holland, v. dahl edition, 1988.

[32] F. Pereira and D.H.D. Warren. Definite clause grammars for language analysis – a survey of

the formalism and a comparison with augmented transition networks. *Artificial Intelligence*, 13:231–278, 1980.

[33] J. Reynolds. Three approaches to type structures. *Lecture Note in Computer Science*, volume 185, Springer Verlag, 1985.

[34] K. Sakai and Y. Sato. Boolean Gröbner bases. Technical Memo 488, ICOT, 1988.

[35] H. Sano, K. Akasaka, Y. Kubo, and R. Sugimura. Go-kôsei ni motoduku Keitaiso Kaiseki (Morphological Analysis with Derivation and Inflection (*in Japanese*)). In *Proceedings of the 36th Conference of Information Processing Society of Japan*, 1988.

[36] R. Sugimura. Japanese Honorifics and Stuation Semantics. In *Proceedings of the 11th COLING*, pages 507–510, 1986.

[37] R. Sugimura. Ronri-gata Bunpô ni okeru Seiyaku Kaiseki (Constraint Analysis on Logic Grammars (*in Japanese*)). In *Proceedings of the 2nd Annual Conference of Japanese society for Artificial Intelligence*, pages 427–430. Japanese Society for Artificial Intelligence, 1988. a prize-winning paper.

[38] R. Sugimura, K. Akasaka, Y. Kubo, H. Sano, and Y. Matsumoto. Ronri-gata Keitaiso Kaiseki LAX (Logic Based Lexical Analyzer LAX (*in Japanese*)). In *Proceedings of the Logic Programming Conference '88*, pages 213–222. ICOT, 1988. English version will appear in The Lecture Note on Computer Science.

[39] R. Sugimura, H. Miyoshi, and K K. Mukai. *Constraint Analysis on Japanese Modifying Relations*, volume II, pages 93–106. North-Holland, 1988.

[40] T. Takizuka and R. Sugimura. Ltb Shell no Kôsei (Configurationof LTB Shell (*in Japanese*)). In *Proceedings of the 37th Conference of Information Processing Society of Japan*, pages 1074–1075, 1988.

[41] T. Takizuka, Y. Tanaka, and R. Sugimura. LTB Master Jisho no Kôsei (Configuration of LTB Master Dictionary (*in Japanese*)). In *Proceedings of Logic and Natural Language Conference*. Japan Society for Software Science and Technology, 1987.

[42] Y. Tanaka and T. Yoshioka. Overview of the Dictionary and Lexical Knowledge Base Research. In *Proceedings of the International Conference on FGCS '88*. ICOT, 1988.

[43] J. Tsujii. Bun-kaiseki system KGW+P no seigyo hôsiki (Controlling Methodology of Sentence Analysis System KGW+P (*in Japanese*)). In *4th Conference Proceedings of Japan Society for Software Science and Technology*, pages B-4–3, 1987.

[44] K. Ueda. Guarded Horn Clauses. Technical Report 103, ICOT, 1985.

[45] M. Watanabe. Kokugo kôbun-ron (Syntax of Japanese (*in Japanese*)). Hakama Shobô, 1971.

[46] S. Yamasaki, R. Sugimura, K. Akasaka, and Y. Matsumoto. Kôbun Kaiseki System SAX no Debug Kankyou (Debugging Environment of SAX System (*in Japanese*)). In *Proceedings of the 2nd Annual Conference of Japanese Society for Artificial Intelligence*, pages 411–414, 1988.

PROCEEDINGS OF THE INTERNATIONAL CONFERENCE
ON FIFTH GENERATION COMPUTER SYSTEMS 1988,
edited by ICOT. © ICOT, 1988

EXPERT SYSTEM ARCHITECTURE FOR DESIGN TASKS

Yasuo Nagai, Satoshi Terasaki, Takanori Yokoyama, and Hirokazu Taki

Institute for New Generation Computer Technology

4-28, Mita 1-chome, Minato-ku, Tokyo, 108, Japan

csnet: nagai%icot.jp@relay.cs.net
uucp: {kddlab,mit-eddie,ukc,enea,inria}!icot!nagai

ABSTRACT

Research is being conducted to develop expert systems that solve design problems. The strategy of this research is to research and develop basic software, with emphasis on user needs and application systems. The goals of this research are:

o To clarify the architecture of the expert system for various designs by introducing constraint-based problem solving.

o To propose primitive tasks to realize the architecture.

o To provide an expert system building tool based on the above considerations.

This paper focuses on and specifies constraint-based problem solving in order to consider expert system architecture, including the modeling facility of the design object.

In this case, though the design knowledge must be supported and handled, current expert systems and tools do not always do so, especially for the design object. Therefore, the handling of design object and problem-solving mechanism are considered. Design object representation system, called FREEDOM, is explained. Moreover, a detailed architecture for an expert system building tool, including the knowledge compilation technique for the efficient problem solving, is described. Finally, current state of a design support system, called MECHANICOT, is explained as a practical example of this building tool.

1 INTRODUCTION

Design systems, such as design automation (DA) systems and computer aided design (CAD) systems, have been developed and used in various design fields. More and more of these systems have incorporated expert systems and knowledge-based systems for design problems.

Design systems can be classified as automated design systems or interactive design systems; it depends on whether there is interaction during design [Eastman 81]. Automated design systems require the determination of definition of the design process and the decision-making sequences. Automated design systems do not usually interact with the designer, and they demand vast amounts of data and computation time. Interactive systems are very flexible and open-ended to the designer, who may input multiple descriptions as input specification. They have a decentralized control structure for the design process, while the structure of the non-predetermined decision-making sequence and its control depend on the designer. Most CAD systems are interactive and are applied only to parts of the design process. Furthermore, the structure of the process model and the decision-making sequence for design systems depend on the design area.

Expert systems have two major applications: diagnosis problems and design problems. Expert systems for design problems are being developed and evaluated for various application fields, such as VLSI design [Kowalski and Thomas 83] [Subrahmanyam 86]; mechanical design [Brown and Chandrasekaran 86] [Dixon and Simmons 84] [Mittal et al. 86]; configuration [McDermott 82]; and process planning; [Descotte and Latombe 85] [Eliyahu et al. 87].

The architecture of expert systems for design problems is not yet as explicit as that for diagnosis problems. Design problems can be regarded as complicated problems that contain a synthesis task in addition to analysis and simulation tasks [Medland 86]. The descriptions of objects to be designed are changed and determined dynamically because of the trial and error nature of the synthesis task, and the results from the synthesis task are analyzed and evaluated in the analysis task. In other words, first the models for design objects are selected, modified and determined so that the design specification can be satisfied, then the synthesis and analysis tasks are performed repeatedly according to the model for detailed description of design objects.

However, this modeling facility is not provided explicitly in existing expert systems for design problems, and the relation between the expert system architecture and this modeling function has not been considered. Most expert systems for design problems are formalized as systems that generate detailed descriptions of the design objects as the solution by combining known components, assemblies or parts, then refining them so that the design specification can be satisfied. Moreover, it seems that such systems lack recognition of the modeling concept from the viewpoint of design. Therefore, expert systems for design problems require a sophisticated architecture that considers the design process model, including planning and modeling facilities.

Section 2 is an overview of the design systems in relation to the design process model; it clarifies the relation of the expert system to the design system. When the design process models of the expert system are applied to the design problems for automated design or interactive design, we need to regard these design problems as a well-defined and well-structured problems, and they are defined as routine design. This routine design is classified in more detail, and the design process model for each detailed design, its fundamental design task and the relation between the classified designs and practical design fields are specified.

Section 3 describes the architecture and necessary problem-solving mechanism of the expert system for routine design. First, researches on architectures consisting of primitive tasks for routine design, called *design generic tasks* [Chandrasekaran 86] [Brown and Chandrasekaran 86] [Mittal *et al.* 86] are described as previous works. Next, the architecture and necessary problem-solving mechanism are described considering *generic task* research.

In our research approach, technical issues of considering expert system architecture for *design generic tasks*, especially design knowledge and problem-solving mechanisms for realization of these tasks are investigated.

Section 4 considers design object model. To make an efficient mechanism to solve design problems, we must consider a way to model the design object, which uses knowledge about the design object effectively. At present, frame-based and object-oriented representations are popular knowledge representation for this purpose. In comparison with them, it is not sufficient that the modeling method of the design object handles the dynamic management of constraint. The modeling system of the design object is described according to the above considerations.

Section 5 defines the application mechanisms for constraint representation in routine design expert systems as constraint-based problem solving, and describes them. For this purpose, constraint representation is classified as the general constraints that are needed for routine design or domain-specific con-

straints; application mechanisms are considered according to these kinds of constraint. Modeling of the design object corresponds to the formalization of various descriptions for design knowledge and to the method of handling design knowledge by trial and error.

These constraints are generated, derived, modified, or deleted from modeling during the design process. The constraint-based problem-solving mechanism is described according to the constraint classifications by matching the design process model for a routine design with the design system.

Section 6 describes the architecture for expert systems and expert system building tools based on this architecture, introducing the modeling concept of the design object and focusing on constraint representation. The design support system is proposed as the specialized solution of the expert system building tool. It introduces the design plan generation facility using constraint analysis method, according to the above architecture.

Section 7 explains in detail the architecture and current state of a support environment called MECHAN-ICOT in which the designer can construct design systems easily. This system focuses on mechanical design, using the design of a main spindle head for a lathe as an example.

2 DESIGN SYSTEM

2.1 Necessary Functions

A design system executes the following design activity in an automated or interactive manner. Design is a creative and intelligent human activity that transforms the requirements represented by formalized languages, symbols, and figures, into physical objects. In other words, given requirements, design creates the structure and the form of the design object according to the design object model that satisfies these requirements. Design can also be considered as synthesis and analysis tasks. It is necessary to consider the correspondence between the analysis task and the model of the design object.

Design consists of three phases:

o Conceptual design

o Fundamental design

o Detailed design

The design in each phase creates the model and executes the analysis and evaluation, and modification in the indeterministic manner.

There are various design systems that cover various design levels such as conceptual design, fundamental design and detailed design. Design systems must execute the design activity at each level.

Conceptual design enumerates the requirements for the realized design objects. It focuses on and formalizes the design problem, including the specification definition. This phase begins a creative task that formalizes the concepts and ideas applied to the designed object. Except for parts of the stylized design, conceptual design is not formalized explicitly and is executed according to skills such as the designers' ideas and experience. Designers mull and judge the conceptual models and choose among them. In fact, there are design systems for conceptual design.

Fundamental design analyzes, evaluates, and modifies the models from various viewpoints according to the result of the conceptual design. It does this in order to refine the design objects and to select some models. The methods of analysis and evaluation for each model are predetermined, but when these methods are not established, they are determined by experiment and simulation.

Detailed design refines the components of the design object and relations between components using the selected model, according to the result of the fundamental design. The optimization and evaluation of the result of the design are executed according to this model.

Most design systems are intended for fundamental design and detailed design.

Next, necessary functions for the design systems, considering mechanical and VLSI designs, are described. In mechanical engineering, there are many cases in which design systems such as DA systems and CAD systems are provided for each design object. In fact, the individuality that the design object possesses makes it difficult to abstract, arrange, and use the design systems as the design environment, because the corresponding model and analysis method for this object usually change when the structure of the design object changes. In other words, of all the synthesis and analysis tasks used in DA systems or CAD systems, the analysis tasks for the performance and behavior (function) prediction and evaluation are especially determined and provided based on the model of the design object. This is caused by the fact that a change in the structure of the design object, such as its geometrical characteristics, may result in a change in its functions.

The models of VLSI design for the analysis of the performance and behavior (function) and evaluation are fixed and formalized as the design methodology, because structural changes have little effect on the function and behavior. The hierarchical structure of the VLSI design, especially the nested structure with the function, can be represented by combining the lower level functions so that interactions between sub-structures of the design can be minimized.

2.2 Routine Design

2.2.1 Definition of Routine Design

Routine design determines the structure of the design object by combining predetermined components, given the model of the basic components and structures of the design object and the methods by which they are to be analyzed and evaluated. In routine design, the two levels of design activity, functional level and physical level, are executed. First, functional level design is executed. It includes the functional decomposition of the specification into a functional description such as functional specification, unit, block, or component. Next, physical level design is executed. It contains the decomposition of the functional description into a physical description of the components for implementation. Finally, the physical description can be obtained as the solution of the design.

Routine design satisfies the following items.

1) The functional or behavioral description can be formalized explicitly as the design requirement or specification.

2) The design plans at each phase can be formalized. They consist of a problem decomposition method such as functional or structural decomposition of the specification or problem, a refinement method, an analysis method, and an evaluation method.

Routine design can formalize a design that has been realized as a well-defined and well-structured problem. It is a design that uses the same expertise and problem-solving method in the previous design. The design specification of routine design is well understood. The problem can be solved using the standard problem solving method, and DA systems and semi-DA systems are realized instances of routine design.

Modification or edit design can also be interpreted as typical routine design. They improve the results of previous designs (the explicit specification of the design parameters and their dimensions).

In contrast with these DA systems and semi-DA systems, most CAD systems that conduct drawing, mass property determination, finite-element analysis, or dynamics analysis, provide only basic assistance facilities for the designer. They are not suitable for routine design, which decides whether the design result satisfies the design requirements.

2.2.2 Design Process Model and Fundamental Design Task

This section describes the fundamental tasks in the design process model.

Considering the design process of routine design, the following items are required [Rinderle 87].

1) Interaction between conceptual design, fundamental design, and detailed design

2) Design objects can be structured with minimal or no interaction between conceptual design, fundamental design, and detailed design.

3) The design process can be structured so that the design task at each phase can be executed independently.

Fig. 2.2.2 describes the design process model including design object model. The design process decomposes the design problem into sub-problems, and the design tasks at each abstract level are executed top-down. The design specification given as input must be a well-defined representation, and the design process must be modeled as a well-structured problem.

The fundamental task of the design at each level consists of planning, problem decomposition, refinement, optimization, analysis, and evaluation tasks. It corresponds to repetitive refinement in terms of the execution of these tasks.

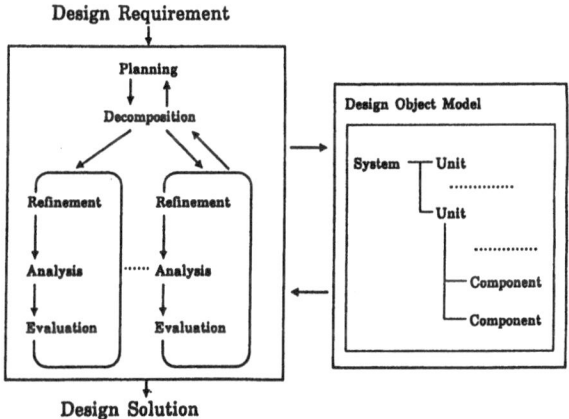

Design Requirement

Design Solution

Fig. 2.2.2 Design Process Model

Especially, we must consider strategies for the decomposition of the problem or specification at each level in order to discuss the design process model for the routine design. The strategies of the problem decomposition must take into account the interactions between functional description and physical description for both circuit and mechanical design. These strategies are not always formalized clearly and applied in the mechanical design, as they are in the VLSI design. In VLSI design, the design process at each level is formalized to make the design task more simple, modular, and easy to apply.

In mechanical design, most interactions are caused by the execution of the constraint representation composed of the function concept, which is based on physical laws, and the feature concept of the form, such as the topology or geometry of the design object at a functional or physical level. The design problem must be dealt with by investigating the degree of decomposition of the problem or specification. The structure of the design object at the functional level is assumed to have already been decided when the above items are examined.

2.2.3 Classification of Routine Design

The design has three levels: new design, combinatory design, and parametric design [Tomiyama and Hagen 87].

New design is executed at each design phase as conceptual design, fundamental design, and detailed design. It is executed from scratch without using results of previous designs. It is a creative activity by the designer and the design process is modeled as an ill-structured problem.

Combinatory design realizes the design objects by combining the basic predetermined components according to the result of the previous design such that the input specification can be satisfied.

Parametric design determines and modifies the attribute parameters of the design objects when their structures can be fixed and the components can be described in the form of the attribute modeling.

Routine design applies to combinatory design and parametric design only. It includes tasks for both combinatory and parametric design.

3 EXPERT SYSTEM ARCHITECTURE FOR DESIGN TASKS

We will begin by discussing important current issues concerning expert systems, focusing on mechanical design and VLSI design. After that, we will describe related works, necessary architecture, and problem-solving mechanisms in order to consider a suitable expert system architecture for design tasks.

In mechanical design, it is difficult to modularize the design object because geometrical information (such as the representation in three dimensions) and manufacturing and assembly information are closely linked with the design object. The behavior of the design object changes as the geometric features change, because the geometric features or form description depend on the functional description or fabrication information. This behavioral change results from the dynamic creation of the model about the components of the design object.

In contrast to the VLSI design, feature description at the functional level has little effect on feature description at the physical level and it is difficult to abstract the components of the design object from their behavior or function. Therefore, given the specifications, it is difficult to determine whether the behavior satisfies the specifications and it is necessary to consider the analysis task.

3.1 Previous Works

The present trend in architecture research for the design tasks can be divided into two types: the problem-solving based approach, and the design object modeling based approach. In research on the design object modeling based approach, the ICAD system are considered as typical example [Phillips and Rosenfeld 87].

In this section, research based on the problem-solving approach, called *generic task*, is described.

Typical research has been conducted on architectures consisting of primitive tasks for routine design, called *design generic tasks*, focusing on the mechanical design.

These architectures provide ways to structure knowledge for the various design descriptions and solve design problems, thus reducing the gaps between functions needed for the task in the design process and functions supported by expert system building tools.

We describe one branch of this research below. The DESI system [McDermott 78] represents an expert system for the design problem at an early stage. This system focuses on the design problem of an analog filter by regarding the design tasks as the problem-solving approach. It is the system that introduces *generic task* concept for the design problem.

Thus, in VEXPERT system [Dixon and Simmons 84, Dixon *et al.* 87], the design task is modeled using the problem-solving approach and is extended, and the design process of this system is regarded and modeled using the design-evaluate-redesign architecture. The redesign task in this design-evaluate-redesign architecture executes the new design according to the new design plan and the systems cannot realize the local modification facility for the analysis and evaluation of the result of the design.

The AIR-CYL system deals with the weak points of the redesign task differently from design-evaluate-redesign architecture based systems such as the VEXPERT system, in that it provides a local modification facility by improving the problem solver. DSPL is a design language supported for building the AIR-CYL system. It supports the ability to describe the design process model in terms of the combination of the problem-solving agents [Brown and Chandrasekaran 86]. It is rather difficult for the designer to build the system using this design language.

The PRIDE system [Mittal *et al.* 86] is the design support system, not for automated use, but for interactive use. In the PRIDE system, the problem-solving agent is described more easily than by using DSPL in the AIR-CYL system, and a local modification facility with multiple context management and a search control facility for the user are added and extended to the problem solver.

The AIR-CYL and PRIDE systems realize local modification facility, but when the form or structure of the design object, and the material for implementation are modified, it is very difficult for these systems to analyze and predict the behavior of the modified design object. Therefore, in this case, the behavior analysis of the design object based on the first principle of the physical environment is required. The PROMPT system [Murthy and Addanki 87] is a tool for design problems which facilitates the behavior analysis of a complicated design object by realizing the simulation mechanism, and by introducing deep knowledge and first principle to the *design generic task* concept.

In design problems, the optimization problem of parameters is especially required. The ENGINIOUS system [Nicklous *et al.* 87] is an automated design system that bases on the same design-evaluate-redesign architecture as VEXPERT system and integrates the simulation facility using the execution of CAE program and sophisticated techniques for optimization.

3.2 Architecture and Problem-Solving Mechanism

An expert system for routine design performs the following four tasks by examining existing systems, especially the mechanical design mentioned above [Nagasawa 87].

1) Determines structures (mechanisms) of the design object

2) Optimizes the attribute parameters for structures of the design object

3) Searches the attribute parameters for structures of the design object

4) Optimizes and transforms structures of the design object

The design for the expert system is applied to routine design only and includes combinatory design and parametric design.

Fig. 3.2 shows a basic structure of expert system for routine design based on the design process model. First, structures of the design object (structural model) are determined by searching the predefined design style of the design object, or by configuring or combining the predefined components. After determining structures of the design object, and refinement of the engineering model is executed. This refinement can be regarded as the optimization of the attribute parameters of structures of the design object and can be regarded as the search of the attribute parameters considering implementation constraints such as resources. Structures of the design object are transformed or modified locally without the changes of the required functional or behavioral specifications by the optimization task, if possible.

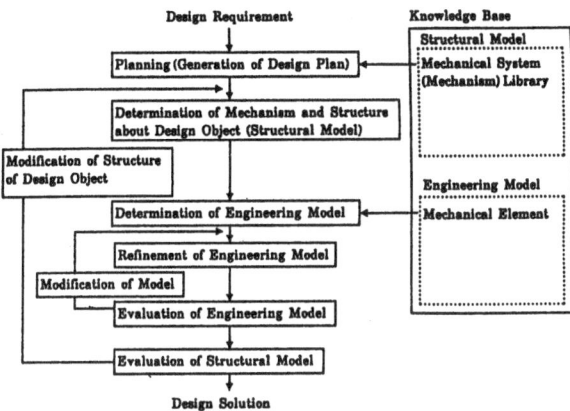

Fig. 3.2 Basic Structure of Expert System for Routine Design

In LSI design, after the structure of the design object is determined by combining the predefined components, the components and their attributes are refined. The structure is then transformed and optimized to resolve the trade-off problem so that the specifications are not violated.

In most mechanical design, structures or mechanisms of the design object are predetermined, and the search and optimization of the structural parameters are executed based on that predetermined structure or mechanism. Design where all the components and relations among them are determined after structures or mechanisms of the design object are determined is called parametric design.

Architectures based on the above *generic task* concept do not support the modeling facility of design knowledge, especially the design object; and when regarding the design knowledge as constraint representation, it seems that the architectures are insufficient for this *generic task* approach and unable to handle the constraint representation. Therefore, an architecture that includes the constraint representation, its application mechanism, and the modeling facility, is required.

This constraint representation is proposed as a new paradigm for knowledge representation, and the application mechanism is proposed as a new paradigm for the architecture of routine design expert systems.

The application mechanisms for constraint representation in routine design expert systems are defined

as constraint-based problem solving. Modeling corresponds to the formalization of various descriptions for design knowledge and the handling of design knowledge by trial and error. Constraints are generated, derived, modified, or deleted from modeling during the design process.

The constraint-based problem-solving mechanism is considered according to the constraint classifications by matching the design process model for a routine design with the design system.

3.3 Technical Issues

There are many issues concerning expert system architecture for design tasks, called *design generic task*. The following items are shown as practical issues [Nagai 88a].

1) Relation of Expert System to Design System

2) Modeling of Design Process

3) Modeling of Design Object

4) Control of Problem Solving during Design Process

5) Improvement of Problem Solving and Knowledge Representation Mechanisms

We will describe our research approach for these items shown in Fig. 3.3.

To resolve the above issues, we focused on and investigated knowledge representation and a problem-solving mechanism to realize design process.

There are various kinds of knowledge in design problems. Two of them are design knowledge, composed of knowledge about the design object and knowledge about the problem solving.

Knowledge about the design object includes knowledge about the structure of functional and physical components. Knowledge about problem solving includes knowledge about ways to refine, analyze, and evaluate the design object.

When considering the expert systems for design task and expert system building tools for design problem, design knowledge, especially knowledge about the design object, must be separated from the problem-solving mechanism to make the architecture clear.

However, this design knowledge is not always classified explicitly and used separately. And current systems and tools do not support and handle the knowledge about the design object, and it is not enough that their problem-solving mechanism handles the design knowledge efficiently.

In Section 4, we investigated the design object model. The design problem requires ways to model the design objects so that we can use the knowledge that have about them. It also requires ways to solve problems by using this knowledge.

302

The FREEDOM system is explained as the modeling system of the design object according to this consideration.

By the way, when we consider the problem-solving mechanism for design knowledge in current systems, there are the problem-solving mechanisms both for knowledge about design object and for knowledge about problem solving, and each mechanism is not integrated into the identical problem solver. Fortunately, each mechanism can be integrated easily by regarding these knowledge as constraint representation.

However, existing expert systems and tools do not support and handle the constraint representation, and it is not enough that their problem-solving mechanism handles the constraint representation efficiently.

In Section 5, we discussed the application mechanism for constraints. By constraint, we means either general constraints necessary for routine design, or constraints that are specific to one.

As described above, the effective utilization of design knowledge and efficient problem solving are required to expert systems for design problems, because various knowledge must be treated.

Knowledge compilation is being investigated for raising of the efficiency of the problem solver in many problem areas, such as diagnostic and machine learning problems [Anderson 86].

This compilation is a technique by which knowledge in declarative form, such as facts and theories, about the domain is stored and this stored knowledge is applied and utilized by interpretive procedures. This technique makes existing paths of processing more efficient rather than enabling new paths of processing.

Therefore, more efficient procedures specific to the task domain can be generated using the knowledge compilation technique.

In our research, this compilation technique is applied to a design problems, especially mechanical design by considering the design knowledge as constraint representation.

Concretely, given the design plan generated by compiling constraint representation, derived from the concept of the design task and design object, and problem-solving heuristics, the design activity corresponds to the interpretation and execution of this design plan and it can be regarded as constraint satisfaction problem. The synthesis and analysis tasks in the design process are interpreted and executed according to this design plan generated by knowledge compilation on the predetermined system architecture. The interpretation and execution of the design plan corresponds to the execution of the design system.

However, at the moment there are many cases where only constraints are given; design plans are not.

Therefore, the environment of this design plan generation using the knowledge compilation technique

and its interpretation and execution are required.

In Section 6, we describe the architecture for expert system and expert system building tool according above considerations.

At present, as various design systems including expert systems, especially for mechanical design, are implemented using a typical procedural language such as Fortran, Pascal and C, and these systems for only specific design problems are provided to designers as individualized systems. Therefore, it is inconvenient and inefficient for designers to use them for design.

In this case, for the designer, the design knowledge must not be represented merely in the form of the procedure. This knowledge must not be described specific with the specific problem solver.

To reduce these inconvenience and inefficiency of existing design systems, it is necessary for the designers to provide a support systems in which the designer can construct design systems easily.

After all, the facility where the designer can build the expert system for design problem by representing the design knowledge, not procedurally, but declaratively, and in the form independent of the problem solver, is required.

Thus, the environment of this design plan generation using knowledge compilation may be considered as support for a CAD system construction environment customizable by the designer.

In Section 7, the expert system building tool, called MECHANICOT, that supports the problem-solving mechanism that suits the design knowledge in the form of the declarative description, by considering their architectures as uniform framework from the viewpoint of constraint-based problem solving, is described.

Expert System Building Tool for Design Problem

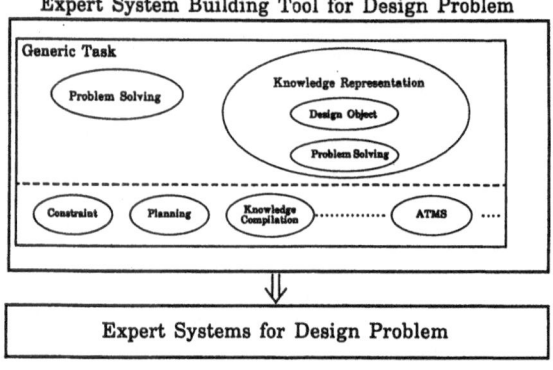

Fig. 3.3 Research Approach

4 DESIGN OBJECT MODEL

4.1 Object Model in the Design Expert System

4.1.1 Role of Design Object Model

Design objects in design systems are represented in the form of model descriptions. A design object model represents information and knowledge about design objects, such as their attributes, shapes, structures, and so on. During a design process, a model that satisfies all requirements is constructed; it represents a solution.

Models used in conventional design systems consist of data structures that are merely static. They need to be interpreted and manipulated in terms of design tasks or procedures. Only the knowledge about design methods is important, and the knowledge about design objects is embedded in model manipulation procedures or design methods. In conventional design systems, it is difficult to make effective use of the knowledge about design objects. Also, high performance design and the establishment of a general methodology by which to build design expert systems may be obstructed because two kinds of knowledge are not identified.

To avoid a combinatorial explosion and to solve design problems effectively, it is important to represent the knowledge about design objects as object models and to put those models to practical use in the design process. A framework must be developed that represents knowledge about design objects that help to make a design process support mechanism that can solve problems.

4.1.2 Frameworks for Representation

A frame system has been used to represent structures and attributes of objects in knowledge systems. Using a frame system, we can represent each element of an object in understandable, and modular form. Recently, an object-oriented paradigm whose concept is similar to frame system has been generally used and also applied to design problems. Though conventional object-oriented languages are suitable for representing structures, attributes and behaviors, they do not provide facilities for representing and using constraints on design objects. Constraints are typical and important knowledge in design problems.

Methods by which to represent knowledge about design objects that introduce constraints have been investigated [Stallman and Sussman 77] [Sussman and Steel 80] [Heintze *et al.* 87]. These provide efficient formalism for knowledge representation in terms of declarative description, but they are not suitable for the representation of large-scaled and complicated objects because they lack structural representation.

Investigations introducing constraints to an object-oriented paradigm have been done [Borning 81, Borning and Duisberg 86] [Harris 86] [Struss 87], and

have made it possible to represent properties of design objects in an understandable form. However, only constraints on numerical attributes (instance variables) can be represented in these systems, and these constraints may be used only to calculate the values of attributes.

Representation of structures of design objects is an important part of solving a design problem, so a function to describe and use structural constraints is needed.

While the object model in an analytical problem such as a diagnose is formalized in a fixed form, one in a design problem takes a variable form because of the nature of the dynamic change. In a design problem, the model handling functions such as selection, modification, and refinement are important in design object modeling, since the designer constructs a object model.

4.1.3 Use of Object Model

The architectures for knowledge systems and expert systems are different according to the way the systems use the object model. We are examining two of these ways. One is to generate a design plan by analyzing and compiling knowledge about the design object model and design methods. We call this knowledge compiling method and will describe it in more detail later. It is suitable for a parametric design.

The second way is to provide a system for supporting design process interpreting knowledge that is described on object models. The system makes it possible to construct only models that satisfy the constraints, and also supports their effective construction.

This second way is suitable for a problem in which the structure of the design object is not given or not fixed. In such a case, the problem must be solved by trial and error or by interaction with users. Currently, the design object system is being developed and is explained in the next section.

4.2 FREEDOM : A Design Object Representation System

4.2.1 Basic Functions

Here, a knowledge representation system for design object modeling, A Framework for REprEsenting Design Object Model (FREEDOM), that facilitates an effective problem-solving mechanism, is presented [Yokoyama 88]. FREEDOM provides the facilities that keep the state of the model for constraint satisfaction and supports design tasks, and currently it is being developed and implemented using ESP language [Chikayamka 84] on a PSI machine [Taki *et al.* 84].

It is useful to distinguish between a model representing a solution and a model representing general and fundamental knowledge about design objects. Here, we call the former an instance model and the latter a template model. For example, in a mechanical design, the fundamental structure of the machine and constraints on attributes are described as a template model, and the values of size and material attributes of parts are described as an instance model.

This system describes a template model and supports the creation of an instance model that satisfies the design requirements. Fig. 4.1 represents the basic structure of a design system that includes the **FREEDOM** system. Knowledge about a design object, namely an object model, is described in this system. Procedures caused by design tasks are positioned outside.

Procedures caused by design tasks correspond to the manipulation of an instance model on this system, modification of elements and values of attributes, addition of constraints, and so on. At this time, the **FREEDOM** system creates an instance model that satisfies the constraints for realization of an effective design.

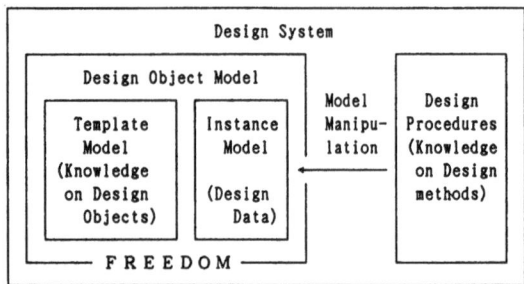

Fig. 4.1 Basic Structure of a Design System with FREEDOM

4.2.2 Knowledge Representation Framework

Knowledge representation provided in the **FREEDOM** system, based on an object-oriented paradigm, makes it possible to describe constraints in declarative form. A template model corresponds to classes in the object-oriented paradigm, and an instance model corresponds to instances. The features of knowledge representation are described below.

(1) Introduction of Constraints to an Object-oriented Paradigm

Constraints play important roles in solving problems in designs. They reduce a combinatorial explosion, and values of attributes and structures of objects can be determined using them. Thus, it is effective to introduce the constraints concept to an object-oriented paradigm. Constraints are described in the form of a predicate.

The whole-part relation, so-called *part-of*, is an important way to represent the structure of objects. The relation is classified into two: the first is that parts are

needed to construct the whole; the second is that parts are not needed to construct the whole. For example, the relation of a rectangle and its four sides corresponds to the former case and the relation of a bookshelf and books in it corresponds to the latter case. The former is called a *consists-of* relation and can be regarded as a structural constraint of an object.

Because constraints may be generated dynamically during a design process, functions for addition or deletion of a constraint on an instance must be provided.

(2) Dynamically Changeable Relation between Class and Instance

In a design process, parts that satisfy the design requirement must be searched and the values of their attributes must be determined.

For example, after the values of attributes of an instance that corresponds to a selected class have already determined, the designer may want to perform an operation that changes the class to another class to which the instance belongs.

In this case, in existing object-oriented languages, we must remove an instance that belongs to old class, create an instance that belongs to new class, copy attributes common between these two classes, and remove the old instance.

Therefore, the **FREEDOM** system handles the relation between class and instance, the *instance-of* relation, which can be changed and maintained dynamically. This makes it possible to design effectively, because it is unnecessary to create a new instance and to copy attributes.

It is inefficient for a realization of a system to admit a dynamic change of class definition with no restriction. Moreover, it is not necessary to change a class definition dynamically because class change is needed when only a part of the corresponding instance is modified.

In general, class change is required because a top-down design is regarded as a refinement from a abstract level to a concrete level. An *is-a* hierarchy of classes which represents relations between an abstract level and a concrete level is applied to a refinement. A dynamic change of a limited class definition is refined according to a hierarchy of *is-a* relations.

(3) Class Hierarchy using *is-a* and *includes* Relations

As discussed before, a refinement is performed according to a hierarchy of *is-a* relations of classes. A class hierarchy with multiple inheritance is not always represented using a relation between an abstract level and a concrete level, but using inclusion relation of function in many object-oriented systems. It also makes a class hierarchy too complex to understand.

Thus, *is-a* relations can be declared only in the case when two classes belong to the same category, and they must be represented in the form of simple tree structures. A refinement in a design process corresponds to the search operation of a class that satisfies design requirements by referring to the *is-a* tree structure.

The multiple inheritance mechanism is useful for representing inclusion of functions, so a definition of this *includes* relation is introduced for representation of the class hierarchy.

Here, a class with an *includes* relation is not applied to the corresponding class, but to the corresponding subclass. Refinement is executed only to a specific class such as *include* class.

Fig. 4.2 represents an example of class hierarchy of plates. Relations, such as the *is-a* relation between *PLATE* and *BOARD*, the *includes* relation between *PLATE* and *METAL*, and the *is-a* relation between *IRON* and *METAL* are described. It is possible to simplify description of class hierarchies using the *includes* relation.

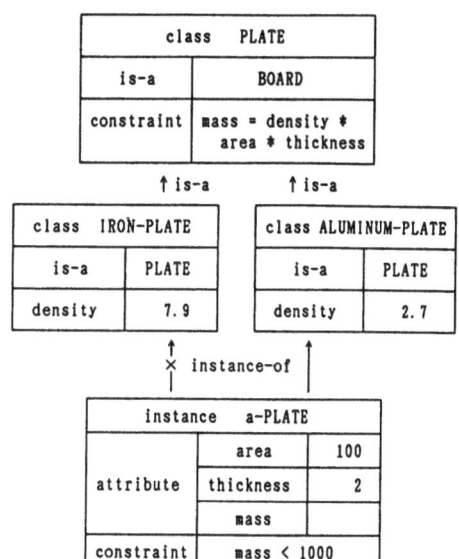

Fig. 4.3 Change of a Class by Constraint Satisfaction

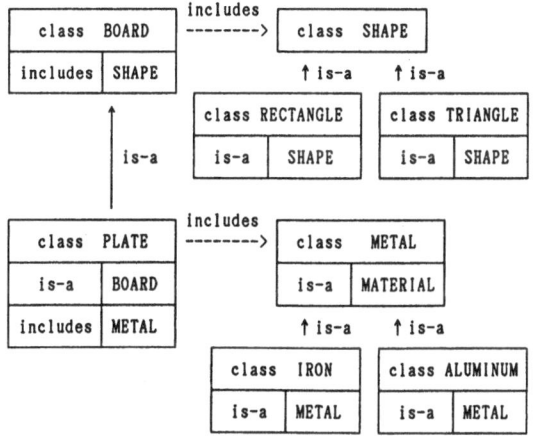

Fig. 4.2 Class Hierarchy with "is-a" and "includes" relations

4.2.3 Functions Required for Supporting the Design Process

FREEDOM provides functions to keep the states of instances. that satisfy constraints. derived from design object model. These functions make it possible to solve design problems effectively. The functions of this system are described below.

(1) Maintenance of a Model that Satisfies Constraints

The attributes of a design object model are represented numerically or symbolically, and their values can be obtained by solving constraints derived from them. For example, when there is the constraint on four attributes shown below, such as mass, density, area and thickness, the value of one attribute is determined if values of other three attributes are given.

$$mass = density * area * thickness$$

In FREEDOM, a definition of a class is regarded as a description of constraints on objects belonging to a certain category. Search for a class that satisfies design requirements is realized using a constraint satisfaction mechanism.

In other words, when a structure or attribute of an instance is modified, if constraint satisfaction cannot be executed in the class to which it belongs, the class may be changed automatically to another class to satisfy the constraints. In this way, it is possible to search for a class that satisfies design requirements by a modification of a corresponding instance.

For example, a problem to determine the kind of a plate is considered. Fig. 4.3 represents a class hierarchy of plates.

Though a *a-PLATE* instance for representation of the solution corresponds to an *IRON-PLATE* instance, where an area and thickness are determined, its class is changed to *ALUMINUM-PLATE* according to the constraint on the mass.

(2) Support of Top-down Design

Generally, designs are executed in a top-down manner, so the main operations consist of refinements of objects. Refinement is executed in two ways: the first way is from the abstract level to the concrete level, and the second way is from the whole to parts. The former corresponds to refinement using *is-a* relations and the latter corresponds to refinement using *includes* and *consists-of* relations in FREEDOM.

Is-a relations are used to select a system structure or a component type, *includes* relations are used to refine parts of an object in parallel from several viewpoints, and *consists-of* relations are used to design some components divided from an object, independently.

A class declared as a part with a *consists-of* relation can be applied to a subclass of a declared class, such as a class with an *includes* relation. Thus, a design process can be considered as follows: first, an instance of an abstract class is created, then it is refined along an *is-a* hierarchy and divided into parts using *includes* and *consists-of* relations, and those divided parts are refined. This cycle is repeated in the design process.

As mentioned above, the FREEDOM system represents not only knowledge on design objects but also supports design tasks.

5 CONSTRAINT-BASED PROBLEM-SOLVING MECHANISMS

5.1 Constraint Representation

Constraints can be defined as certain relations or conditions that may exist between components of the design objects, as relations or conditions between properties of those design objects, and as expressions of laws or rules which must be satisfied (expressed in the form of equalities or inequalities). One example of an explicit constraint is a constraint on the structural information from the modeling representation of the design object. The other examples of constraints are *Kirchhoff's* laws and *Ohm's* law in circuit analysis [Stallman and Sussman 77] [Sussman and Steel 80], the number of resources, costs, operation priorities and dates in job-shop scheduling [Fox 83], and the edge connections that are physically possible in attempting to recognize a line drawing [Clowes 71]. However, the given representation of constraint is not always used effectively in existing systems. The effective use of such constraints should make it possible to restrict searches in the solution space, thus improving efficiency by eliminating unnecessary searches. Not many of the existing tools supporting the construction of expert systems provide an environment that makes it easy to express the constraint concept explicitly. Therefore, the person constructing the system must use the tool development language to attempt to realize mechanisms for applying constraint representations which depend on the design object. Most design problems can be regarded as constraint satisfaction problems. For instance, considering the concept *design generic task*, constraint handling is equivalent to checking the constraints in the test process of the generate and test method. In the step-wise refinement method, constraint handling involves refinement from an abstract level to a more concrete level, and the constraints imposed at each level also change dynamically. In general, when a set of given specifications is refined, it is also usually divided into different sub-problems, and there are often interactions between constraints on different sub-problems as well.

Those functions are required for problem solving according to the classification and effective solving mechanisms of constraints when addressing problems of a synthetic nature, such as in design and scheduling. The purpose of this is to provide the person constructing the system with an environment that enables the convenient representation of constraints.

5.2 Classification of Constraints [Nagai 88b]

(a) General (Domain-independent) Constraints for Routine Design

Constraints are classified according to the following characteristics.

1) Classification According to Generation Method

Constraints may be classified according to whether they are generated statically or dynamically. Static constraints are specified in advance, and are constant and unchanging. Dynamic constraints depend both on interactions with the user and on the system; they tend to change, with their range of applicability varying. Such constraints may be interpreted as incomplete knowledge, and, in order to manage changes in truth in the knowledge base accompanying changes in constraints, the functions of the Truth Maintenance System (TMS) [Doyle 79] and Assumption-Based Truth Maintenance System (ATMS) [deKleer 86] are necessary.

2) Classification According to Importance

Constraints may be classified according to importance into obligatory or requisite constraints, and suggestive constraints. When such a distinction is made, not all the constraints are selected and executed on an equal basis. That is, the importance of a constraint may depend on the context, the time, or another concept. All obligatory constraints must be satisfied, and these are given explicitly. Suggestive constraints are also referred to as weak constraints, and are used as guides in choosing the optimum branch at a node in the search tree. Such constraints may be described in rule form, and are given priorities and other attributes.

3) Classification According to Scope

Constraints may also be classified according to whether they apply locally or globally; this distinction is used in evaluating states in the search space. Local constraints are used to conduct searches when a state changes within a given model, object or process and the scope over which the constraint is valid is limited to within the model or object or process. Global constraints are used when a state is to be evaluated using not only local constraints, but all related constraints, without imposing any limit. For instance, when the solution space is divided and searches performed, this is equivalent to taking into account all those constraints that have been applied to states leading up to the present state, or to evaluating different parts of the solution space relative to each other.

4) Classification According to Propagating Variable Information

Constraints may be classified according to the propagating variable information, that is, depending on whether the variables of constraints propagate over value, or whether the constraint propagates over the interval bound in which the variable can take on a value or values. At present, the constraint logic programming system [Dincbas 86] [Heintze *et al.* 87], CONSTRAINT system [Sussman and Steel 80], and most other constraint systems [Borning 81] handle only constraints in which values are propagated.

Constraints that propagate over interval bounds in which variables can take certain values, are described using inequalities, and the variables of the constraint are not constant; these constraints propagate over the interval bound as a label. Most design problems include sub-problems that can be solved using the method of existing operations research; it is essential that the architecture should enable functions to operate in a unified framework based on constraint propagation in labels with interval bounds [Davis 87].

When considering practical design problems, there are some combinatory possibilities of handling of above classified constraints.

(b) Domain-specific Constraint for Routine Design

There are various domain-specific constraints for routine design. These constraints are related to the simplified design process composed of the conceptual design, fundamental design and detailed design.

In particular, structural constraints should be considered in routine design. Structural constraints are reflected in terms of the design style, and specifications, and requirements at each abstract level of the design, and determine the structural decomposition, partition, and design style at a lower design level. In hierarchical design, it should be noted that the constraints are propagated to a lower design level. The design style constraints decide the structure of the design object and the problem decomposition at a lower design level. Constraints are partitioned through the structure of the design object and decomposition of the design problem. For example, there are the imprementation constraints (technology-dependent constraints at the implementation level).

5.3 Necessary Functions

The functions required for constraint-based problem solving [Nagai 88b] are listed below.

1) Function for Constraint Propagation and its Control

In the process of satisfying constraints, and when values are assigned to variables of the constraint, the values of other constraint variables may be determined by the former variable; this is the mechanism of constraint propagation. Such a mechanism must take into account both cases considering local constraint propagation and cases where the problem cannot be solved by local constraint propagation alone. A typical example of the former is the propagation method using data-flow analysis introduced in the CONSTRAINT system. An example of the latter case is the variable elimination method of simultaneous equations. In particular, when using propagation methods based on data-flow analysis, the trade-off between constraints, such as occur when regarding the TMS as a constraint satisfaction problem (CSP) [Dechter and Pearl 87], may result when the propagation is not always sufficient. Clearly, a strategy for controlling constraint propagation is needed. Interactions between constraints and the least commitment of constraints are also indispensable for realizing the constraint propagation. For instance, in practical design problems, if we consider design by step-wise refinement, interaction between constraints applying to sub-problems that are solved separately is extremely important. One approach to the problem of constraint interactions is to minimize interactions between sub-problems. This approach is the one adopted in the MOLGEN system [Stefik 81a, 81b]. It is referred to as the least commitment; by delaying constraint evaluations as far as possible, refinements according to the design plan are executed, and evaluations are performed when necessary.

2) Constraint Relaxation and Selection

Relaxation and selection are applied to weak constraints. Relaxation of a constraint is equivalent to searching for alternatives to the specified constraint. That is, at the failure stage, when a constraint has not been satisfied, an alternative constraint, at the same or a lower level, is sought. Selection involves the choice of a constraint when there are two or more competing constraints, and is regarded as constraint interpretation. In this way, it is thought that constraint relaxation and selection can be formulated as a planning problem [Descotte and Latombe 85].

3) Preservation and Management of Dependency Relations

In processes where the values of constrained variables are propagated through the execution of constraint propagation mechanisms, when contradictions in variable values arise, the preservation and management of dependency relations among constraints, variables, and constant values are deemed important to resolve such contradictions and to explain the propagating values [Harris 86].

4) Monitoring Mechanism for Constraint Evaluation

A monitoring mechanism for constraint evaluation should not be omitted from any problem-solving mechanism that relies on constraint representations. It manages constraint checks and ensures consistency, and is to some extent realizable using demons or attached procedures.

5.4 Role of this Mechanism to Design Process

This section considers constraint-based problem solving relative to the design process. As discussed previously, the fundamental task at each design level makes the iterative design composed of the problem decomposition and refinement proceed according to the design plan. If a design fails, redesign is executed, and the problem is decomposed and refined again. It backtracks the previous design decisions in the tasks at the higher level or executes local modification at the same level, and executes the iterative design.

Mechanical design that mainly belongs to parametric design can be regarded as the generate and test + failure recovery (+ optimization + analysis and evaluation) paradigm.

Planning decomposes and refines the problem or specification according to the design plan. The design style determined from the design plan (the configurational or architectural knowledge about the design object) is indexed by the requirement or specification of the design, and can be regarded as a constraint. The refinement, optimization, and analysis and evaluation tasks are selected and executed according to this constraint. The decomposition of the requirements or specifications of the design are executed by applying this design style constraint.

Parameters and constraints between the hierarchies of the design are propagated upward or downward or the interactions among the decomposed sub-problems occur when there are constraints among them, so it is necessary to consider the tasks for these types of processing, such as constraint posting and propagation.

Assuming that problem decomposition can transform or map the sub-problem to the component or assembly, there are two ways to decompose a problem. The first way is problem decomposition into sub-problems with interactions; the second way is problem decomposition into independent sub-problems. In the first way, it is important to consider the relations among the compositions at the same level. In the second way, it is important to consider the relations between the components and sub-components.

Refinement transforms the divided specification into structural representation composed of the components and relations among them. These relations among components can be regarded as a constraint. Constraints on the component attributes are particularly important. For example, the propagation mechanism of constraints of the component attributes, in decomposition into interacting sub-problems is different from that in decomposition into independent sub-problems. The former mechanism propagates the interactions among sub-problems as the constraints, and the latter propagates the constraints upward or downward according to the hierarchical representation of the design object when there are no interactions among independent sub-problems.

Optimization modifies the structural representation locally, so that the functions expressed in the specification do not change.

5.5 Constraint-based Problem Solving on Generate and Test (G & T) + Failure Recovery (FR) Paradigm

Tasks for routine mechanical design consist of the determination of structures and structural parameters of the design object, without the optimization and transformation of structures of the design object.

The structure of the design object in routine design is determined by combining the components or is determined according to predefined design styles of the design object. It is determined by retrieving the appropriate design style from the predetermined design plan.

The components are implemented using the standard parts by looking them up in catalogues or by using non-standard parts by the design. Most of the selection strategies of standard or non-standard parts for component implementation are described in the specifications or requirements. They mostly depend on a trade-off of the performance against cost.

The necessary architecture for this design can be formalized as the generate and test + failure recovery (+ optimization + analysis and evaluation) paradigm shown in Fig. 5.5.

The problem-solving primitives are the generator, propagator, tester, and failure recoverer.

The generator assigns values to parameters or assigns functional components to the components for implementation. This parameter can be classified in one of two ways according to the type of the value: one takes the continuous value, and the other takes the discrete value. The former assigns parameters of the attributes by local modification based on the predetermined component. The latter assigns parameters by retrieving the standard parts for implementing components from the catalogue, a table look-up method.

The propagator assigns the values to the parameters by using the active evaluation of the constraint and propagation of constraints.

The tester checks the constraint and can be considered as the passive handler of constraint. In general, the inequality description can be handled by the tester, but in some contexts it can also be considered and handled as the generator.

The failure recoverer modifies the attributes of the components locally using the advice mechanism and replans the problem decomposition. The advice mechanism can be considered as the repair of the partial or local design using the heuristics about the attributes of the components. It uses the above generator and propagator as primitives. In failure recovery handling, the obligatory or suggestive constraints must be handled. The advice mechanism by the selection and evaluation of the constraint is executed to the obligatory constraint. For the suggestive constraints, planning such as a compromising algorithm is required in order to relax and select this constraint. This is a mechanism that satisfies as many constraints as possible, too.

Design knowledge, especially the constraint representation such as the various formulas about the features of the functional or physical environment is compiled and this compiled representation can be considered as the constraint network, when the structure of the design object, configuration of the components, is fixed.

In other words, the constraint-based problem-solving mechanism in the generate and test + failure recovery architecture corresponds to the execution of the representation generated by compiling various kinds of this design knowledge based on the fundamental tasks of the design process such as planning, problem decomposition, and refinement.

6 ARCHITECTURE FOR AN EXPERT SYSTEM BUILDING TOOL

6.1 Knowledge Representation

Designers' knowledge must be easily represented in a building tool, to enable them to build an expert system by themselves. In this section, representation of

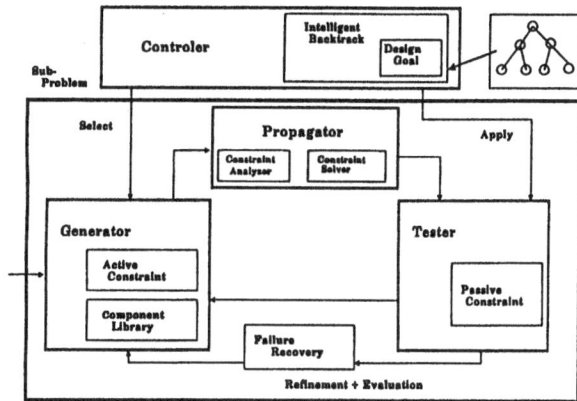

Fig. 5.5 Constraint-based Problem Solving on G & T + FR Paradigm

design knowledge about problem solving is described, since an object model which is knowledge about a design object itself has already been discussed in Section 3.3. Design knowledge about problem solving consists of methods to analyze object models, to evaluate and modify solutions, and plans to design the object and search from candidate solutions.

Methods to analyze object models are regarded as constraints; they are expressed in the form of formulas derived from physical laws or experiments, and are composed of equalities, inequalities and mathematical functions. Methods to search from catalogues, tables, and graphs are also included in this knowledge, in terms of deciding parameters. Knowledge to modify solutions generates alternatives after determining modification scope, if solutions cannot satisfy design requirements. Modification scope is not only locally close within a subproblem, but also globally related to other subproblems. Knowledge to evaluate solutions, often expressed by inequalities, decides whether solutions can satisfy design requirements such as functions, efficiency, and cost performance. Plans to design indicate orders to solve constraints given as analysis methods and requirements, but plans to search restrict the search space when many alternatives exist. Using this

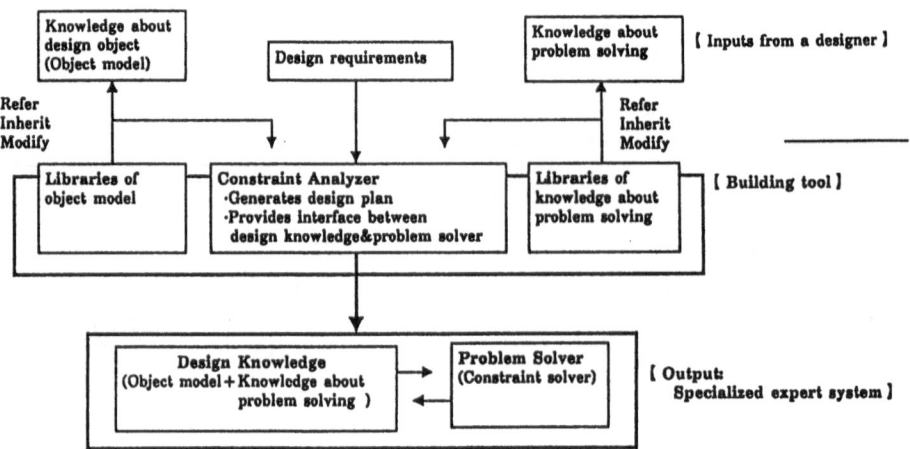

Fig.6.2 Architecture for an Expert System Building Tool

with evaluation knowledge, problem solving is made more efficient. Thus, design knowledge about problem solving has various representation types.

In addition, knowledge that is independent on a design object and heuristics that is closely dependent on a certain design object are mixed. For example, design formulas and searching from catalogues in design knowledge about problem solving, and basic parts and function units in object models are independent from a design object.

Therefore, with the aim of enabling designers to represent this knowledge easily, we employed the approach that those independent kinds of knowledge are prepared as system libraries: sets of design formulas and catalogues in knowledge about design problem solving, and sets of basic parts and function units in object models are prepared respectively. And these knowledge are expressed in object-oriented. Because an object-oriented system has advantages that parts and their attributes are represented naturally as *object* for object models, and knowledge can describe declaratively as *methods* for knowledge about problem solving. Consequently, designers' heuristics can be expressed explicitly, by referring to or by inheriting and modifying libraries.

6.2 Architecture for an Expert System Building Tool

As shown above, we divide design knowledge into object models and knowledge about problem solving. This enables us to maintain knowledge and to modify knowledge flexibly. Viewing knowledge and requirements as constraints, constraint based problem solving is employed.

To build an expert system suitable for a design problem by a designer, we propose a building tool that regards inputs of design knowledge as constraints, generates design plans by analyzing their dependencies,

and provides an interface between design knowledge and a constraint solver.

We used a constraint analyzer to obtain facilities for this building tool. The constraint analyzer, similar to a knowledge compiler [Araya and Mittal 87] [Nagai 88c] and a constraint compiler [Feldman 88], analyzes dependencies among constraints and produces a design plan to solve a problem efficiently. In other words, the constraint analyzer specializes knowledge by combining knowledge independent from a certain design object and designers' heuristics which depend from a certain design object. Fig. 6.2 shows the architecture of the tool.

Inputs to the tool are design requirements, object models, and knowledge about problem solving. They are given by specifying system libraries, or by modifying libraries with referencing or inheriting libraries. Referencing results of previous design and designers' heuristics about searching from alternatives are also represented as knowledge about problem solving.

From these inputs, the tool analyzes dependencies among constraints and parameters, generates a design plan, and provides an interface between design knowledge and the constraint solver. The output from the tool is a specialized expert system including designers' heuristics.

7 MECHANICOT: A SPECIFIC EXPERT SYSTEM BUILDING TOOL

As an example of a specific expert system building tool, MECHANICOT [Terasaki *et al.* 88], which is under development, is described. MECHANICOT is a tool for a mechanical parametric design. It analyzes dependencies between structures of a design object and parameters, produces a design plan, and builds a specialized design expert system.

7.1 Design Problem of Main Spindle Head in a Lathe

The design object is the main spindle head of a lathe, shown in Fig. 7.1. It consists of a main spindle to grip a workpiece and to rotate it, a motor as a power source, V-belts and a pair of pulleys to transmit power from the motor to a pulley-shaft, bearings to support both the main spindle and the pulley-shaft, and two pairs of gears to change the main spindle speed. The problem is to determine the dimensions of each part and find each part number by searching catalogues.

The design requirements must be satisfied:

o Cutting capacity and the maximum diameter of the workpiece
o Maximum rotating speed of the main spindle
o Maximum cutting depth and feeding speed
o Minimum life time of the bearing to be evaluated

This is a parametric design problem in which the structure of the design object is fixed and knowledge about problem solving is well known [Inoue *et al.* 88]. In addition, parameters are discrete values which are decided by searching from catalogues or by adjusting to standard values. Tab. 7.1 shows input requirements and design parameters.

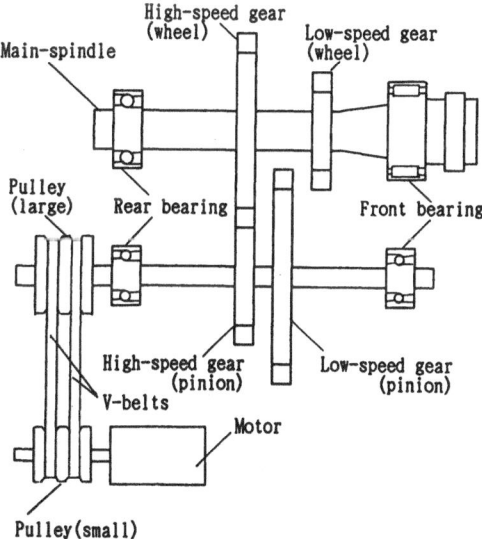

Fig. 7.1 Outline of Design Object
— Main-spindle Head Of Lathe —

Tab. 7.1 Example of Input & Design Parameters

Input parameters

Cutting capacity	Workpiece material Tool material Workpiece diameter (max.) Main-spindle speed (max.) Cutting depth (max.) Feeding speed (max.) Drill diameter (max.) Drill speed (max.)
Evaluation	Life of bearings

Design parameters

Decided by calculation	Main-spindle diameter Pulley-shaft diameter Gears & pulleys ratio Number of gear teeth Gears pitch diameters
Result of previous design	Bearing mount type Bearing span
Search from catalogues or tables	Bearing part number Motor part number V-belt part number Pulleys part number

7.2 Specific Example of an Expert System Building Tool

7.2.1 Input

a) Design Object Models

Design object models consist of the structure of the design object, constraints derived from structural relations, and design parameters. The structure is hierarchically represented: the whole of the design object, function units, and parts which are elements of a function unit are described as *class objects* respectively. Fig. 7.2.1.1 shows this class hierarchy in the case of Fig. 7.1. Description of object models is composed of *consist_of* for component elements in a function unit, *constraint* for constraints from structural relations, and *parameter* for design parameters. Fig. 7.2.1.2 (a) shows the object model definition for a class *pulley_shaft* which is one of the function units in the main spindle head.

b) Knowledge about Problem solving

Description of knowledge about problem solving is shown in Tab. 7.2.1. Equalities and inequalities, and search method from catalogues, tables and results of previous design are included in the form of table, excepts in the form of functions and equalities. There are two types in inequalities: one is used for limiting generating space of alternatives, and the other is used for testing solutions. Searching from catalogues, tables may have alternatives, similar to inequalities which used for restricting search space. To handle such constraints, they are classified into four types: *design_method*, *generator*, *tester*, and *adjust_by*.

312

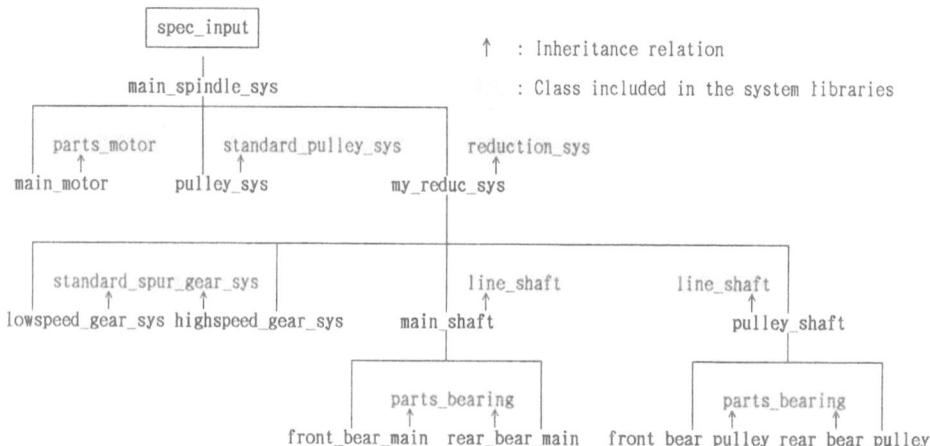

Fig. 7.2.1.1 Hierarchical Class Structure of Main Spindle Head

```
class_name
        pulley_shaft;
inherit_from
        line_shaft;
consist_of
        front_bear_pulley, rear_bear_pulley;
parameter
        front_bearing_type, rear_bearing_type;

constraint
        #front_bear_pulley!shaft_dia := shaft_dia,
    % If 'shaft_dia' is designed, propagates it to 'shaft_dia'
    % in the class 'front_bearing'. This is a constraint to
    % fit a bearing on the pulley shaft.
        #front_bear_pulley!type := front_bearing_type,
        #front_bear_pulley!shaft_rpm := rpm_max,
        #rear_bear_pulley!shaft_dia := shaft_dia,
        #rear_bear_pulley!type := rear_bearing_type,
        #rear_bear_pulley!shaft_rpm := rpm_max;
end.
```

```
class_name
        line_shaft;

parameter
        shaft_dia, hole_dia, material, rpm_max,
        twisting_moment, shearing_strength,
        torsion_angle;
end.
```

Fig. 7.2.1.2 (a) Object Model Definition for the class pulley_shaft

Functions and search method from catalogues or tables which have no alternatives indicated by *design_method*, whereas having alternatives such as inequalities used for restricting search space are expressed by *generator*. And *tester* represents inequalities used for testing solutions led from *generator* or evaluating solutions. To adjust solutions to standard values as a filter is *adjust_by*. Knowledge about design problem solving is presented by specifying a *method_name* and a type of method as described above to a parameter in an object model. Fig. 7.2.1.2 (b) shows an example of the object model definitions including *design_method* description for the class *pulley_shaft*.

Tab. 7.2.1 Description of Knowledge about Problem Solving

Description type	
Functions, equalities (Results of previous design) (Catalogues or tables search)	**design_method** (No alternatives)
Inequalities (Limiting generating scope) Catalogues or tables search Refer from results of previous design	**generator** (Generate alternatives)
Equalities Inequalities	**tester** (Evaluation & test)
Tables search	**adjust_by** (Filter)

c) Design Requirements

Design requirements indicate the design object, parameter names which are given as an input, and relations between design parameters and input parameters. To express the design object, the highest class name in a class structure is given by *design_object*. For instance, the class name for *design_object* is the class *main_spindle_sys* in the case of Fig. 7.2.1.1. Names of

```
class_name
      pulley_shaft;
inherit_from
      line_shaft;
consist_of
      front_bear_pulley, rear_bear_pulley;
parameter
      front_bearing_type, rear_bearing_type;
constraint
      #front_bear_pulley!type := front_bearing_type,

            ~

      #rear_bear_pulley!shaft_rpm := rpm_max;
design_method
      { [front_bearing_type, rear_bearing_type],
      bearing_mount_search(#result_of_previous_design,
      front_bearing_type, rear_bearing_type)
      };
% Parameters 'front_bearing_type' and 'rear_bearing_type'
% are designed by the method 'bearing_mount_search' in the
% class 'result_of_previous_design'.
end.
```

```
class_name
      line_shaft;
parameter
      shaft_dia, hole_dia, material, rpm_max,
      twisting_moment, shearing_strength,
      torsion_angle;
design_method
      { [shaft_dia],
      shaft_dia(#shaft_dia_calc, twisting_moment,
      torsion_angle, shearing_strength,
      hole_dia, shaft_dia)
      },
% Parameter 'shaft_dia' is designed by the method
% 'shaft_dia' in the class 'shaft_dia_calc'.
% And parameters 'twisting_moment','torsion_angle',
% 'shearing_strength' and 'hole_dia' are input for this method.
      { [shearing_strength],
      shearing_strength_search(#material_data_base,
      material, shearing_strength)
      } ;
end.
```

Fig. 7.2.1.2 (b) Adding Design Methods for the class pulley_shaft

input parameters are represented by *parameter*. Note that specific values of input parameters are given when the system which is produced by the tool is actually executed. The relations between input parameters and design parameters are given by *constraints*, indicating which design parameter in a class receives a value from a input parameter.

7.2.2 Design Plan Generation

Design plan generations using the constraint analyzer after being given design knowledge are described below. Generating a design plan, similar to data-flow analysis in a compiler, is accomplished as shown.

1) Subgoals are assigned to *constraint*, *generator*, *tester*, *design_method*, and *adjust_by* in each class. In the case of processing *constraint*, a subgoal is assigned to each constraint statements. Otherwise, a subgoal is given to each methods. Note that the name of each subgoal should be unique. Fig. 7.2.2 (a) shows the assignment of this subgoal.

2) Subgoals are integrated into some goals, based on the input-output dependencies of parameters. The way of giving names to goals is exactly the same as the case of subgoals. Fig. 7.2.2 (b) shows this grouping from subgoals to goals.

3) An execution sequence of goals is determined based on the input-output dependencies of goals. The sequence is managed in a class that is one level higher than the class in which the goal is included. For instance, in the Fig. 7.2.1.1, the sequence of goals in the class *pulley_shaft* is managed by the class *my_reduc_sys*. And goals in the class *main_spindle_sys* are controlled by the class *spec_input*. Fig. 7.2.2 (c) shows the hierarchical control of the calling sequence.

Analyzing dependencies between constraints initiates from the lowest level of the class hierarchy. That is to say, the level including a class *input_shaft* and a class *front_bear_pulley* exist on the start level, in example of Fig. 7.2.1.1. The analysis proceeds towards the highest level class *spec_input*. In the case when inheritance relations are exist, the constraints are not processed along class hierarchy between parent classes and a child class, but are treated as a flat set of the constraints included in both parent classes and their children classes.

The advantage of this constraint analyzer is to analyze the relation between *generator* and *tester* for realization of an efficient execution of generate and test loop.

When G & T loops are included in execution statements, a *generator* corresponding to a *tester* is found by

```
class_name
    pulley_shaft;

        ~

constraint
    #front_bear_pulley!shaft_dia := shaft_dia,
        ⇒ pulley_shaft_subgoal1

        ~

    #rear_bear_pulley!shaft_rpm := rpm_max;
        ⇒ pulley_shaft_subgoal6

design_method
    {[front_bearing_type, rear_bearing_type],
    bearing_mount_search(#result_of_previous_design,
            ...)
    };      ⇒ pulley_shaft_subgoal7
end.



class_name
    line_shaft;

        ~

design_method
    { [shaft_dia],
    shaft_dia(#shaft_dia_calc, twisting_moment,
            ...)
    },      ⇒ line_shaft_subgoal1
    { [shearing_strength],
    shearing_strength_search(#material_data_base,
            ...)
    };      ⇒ line_shaft_ subgoal2
end.
```

Fig. 7.2.2 (a) Subgoals Assignment

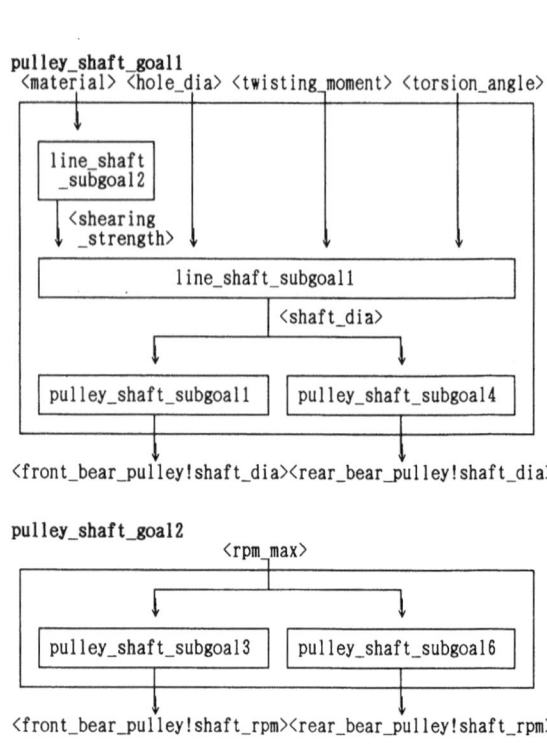

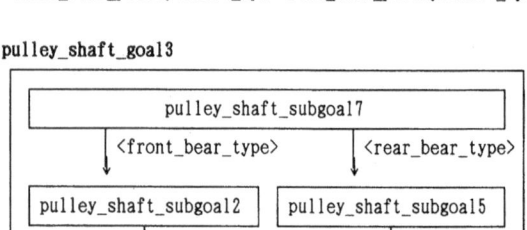

Fig. 7.2.2(b) Grouping of Subgoals as Goals

analyzing dependencies of constraints. It is considered that an execution of those statements is equivalent to a realization of the Dependency-Directed Backtracking (DDB) mechanism.

7.3 Considerations

The MECHANICOT system provides a design support environment where a designer can input and modify design requirements, design knowledge composed of the model of design object and design process easily and where the design plan can be generated using constraints derived from that knowledge.

At present, the MECHANICOT system is being developed and implemented using ESP language on a PSI machine. This system is in the style of an automated system with no user interaction. It receives design requirements and design object representation written in ESP-like language as input, and generates the design plan written in ESP as output. The following items are not provided sufficiently or are missing.

(1) Support of Multiple Context Management

The design object must be modeled and represented from various points of view, as shown in Section 4. These points of view to the design object can be interpreted as the design contexts. A multiple context management mechanism is required for the execution and evaluation of design object models under certain design contexts as alternatives. This is a very effective and important mechanism for design systems.

(2) Improvement of Constraint Analyzer

In this system, only the handling of static con-

```
class spec_input has
design_object block1;

    goal(#spec_input) :-
        spec_input_goal1(#spec_input),
        block1_goal1(#block1),
        block1_goal3(#block1),
        block1_goal2(#block1);

    spec_input_goal1(#spec_input) :-
        spec_input_subgoal1(#spec_input),
        spec_input_subgoal2(#spec_input);
end.
```

```
class block1 has
consist_of parts1;

    block1_goal1(#block1) :-
        block1_subgoal1(#block1),
        block1_subgoal2(#block1);

    block1_goal2(#block1) :-
        block1_subgoal4(#block1),
        block1_subgoal3(#block1);

    block1_goal3(#block1) :-
        parts1_goal1(#parts1),
        parts0_goal1(#parts1),
        parts1_goal2(#parts1);
end.
```

```
class parts1 has
inherit_from parts0;

    parts1_goal1(#parts1) :-
        parts1_subgoal1(#parts1);

    parts1_goal2(#parts1) :-
        parts1_subgoal3(#parts1),
        parts1_subgoal2(#parts1);
end.
```

```
class parts0 has

    parts0_goal1(#parts0) :-
        parts0_subgoal1(#parts0),
        parts0_subgoal2(#parts0);
end.
```

Fig. 7.2.2(C) Hierarchical Control of Calling Sequence

straint and obligatory constraint is considered. For example, because the role of a constraint such as a generator and tester to a constraint-handling mechanism is predetermined, the interpretation of a constraint is fixed.

However, the handling of dynamic constraint, such as addition, deletion and modification of constraints during design process, and suggestive constraint, is not investigated.

Therefore, both static analysis for constraint and dynamic analysis, including constraint relaxation, are required for realization of dynamic constraint handling, considering a current constraint analyzer.

(3) Improvement of Constraint Solver

In this system, a specific mechanism for the constraint-based problem solving shown in section 5, is not realized, and a constraint propagation is performed using unification function in ESP language. Moreover, for the above dynamic constraint handling, constraint solver including constraint propagation and relaxation mechanism, is required.

(4) Improvement of User Interface

Currently, the system does not provide a friendly user interface, where the designer can give knowledge about design requirements and the design object in the form of a schematic description as an input, interacting with the system.

Such a user interface facility linked with a design object modeling facility is required.

The design plan generated using constraint analyzer is executed by an inference mechanism of ESP language, but in future an interpreter for the design plan will be implemented and this design plan description will be interpreted and executed by it.

8 CONCLUSION (FUTURE WORK)

In conclusion, the architecture of expert systems, including the design object modeling facility for routine design, was proposed by focusing on constraint-based problem solving composed of constraint representation and the application mechanism.

For realization of this architecture, the design object representation system, called FREEDOM, and the design support system, called MECHANICOT, were described. Particularly, the MECHANICOT system supports machining tools, specifically a main spindle head of a lathe, a design target.

Our future research is to clarify the architecture of expert systems for various routine designs, such as LSI design, mechanical design, and configuration, by regarding constraint-based problem solving as a new paradigm. In other words, this research is to propose *generic tasks* for various routine designs. We will also propose primitive tasks for the constraint-based problem solving required to realize the architecture of expert systems for various routine designs.

Furthermore, incorporation of knowledge acquisition system, especially for acquisition of design knowledge using design object modeling facility and a sophisticated user interface, and the use of ATMS as a knowledge maintenance system is required in order to realize more effective and practical design system.

316

ACKNOWLEDGMENTS

We would like to thank Mr. Yuichi Fujii, Chief of the Fifth Research Laboratory for encouraging research and to thank Mr. Katsumi Inoue and other members of the Fifth Research Laboratory for helpful comments. We would also like to thank Dr. Isao Nagasawa, Kyushu University, for useful comments on needs of design plan generation for mechanical design. Furthermore, we would also like to thank Mr. Satoshi Imamura and Dr. Toshio Kojima, Mechanical Engineering Laboratory, for technical support to a formalization of the design problem of main spindle head in a lathe. Finally, we would like to express special thanks to Dr. Kazuhiro Fuchi, Director of ICOT Research Center, who has given us the opportunity to carry out research in the Fifth Generation Computer Systems Project.

REFERENCES

[Anderson 86] J.R. Anderson, "Knowledge Compilation: The General Learning Mechanism", Machine Learning, An Artificial Intelligence Approach, Vol. 2, R.S. Micahlski, J.G. Carbonell and T.M. Mitchell (ed.), Morgan Kaufmann Publisher, Inc., 1986

[Araya and Mittal 87] A.A. Araya and S. Mittal, Compiling Design Plans from Descriptions of Artifacts and Problem Solving Heuristics", Proc. of IJCAI-87, 1987

[Borning 81] A. Borning, "The Programming Language Aspects of ThingLab, a Constraint-Oriented Simulation Laboratory", ACM Trans. on Programming Language and System, Vol. 3, 1981

[Borning and Duisberg 86] A. Borning and R. Duisberg, "Constraint- Based Tools for Building User Interfaces", ACM Trans. on Graphics, Vol.5, no.4, pp345-374, 1986

[Brown and Chandrasekaran 86] D.C. Brown and B. Chandrasekaran, "Knowledge and Control for a Mechanical Design Expert System", IEEE COMPUTER, 1986

[Chandrasekaran 86] B. Chandrasekaran, "Generic Tasks in Knowledge-based Reasoning: High-Level Building Blocks for Expert System Design", IEEE expert, 1984

[Chikayama 84] T. Chikayama, "Unique Features of ESP", Proc. of International Conference on Fifth Generation Computer Systems, 1984

[Clowes 71] M. B. Clowes, "On Seeing Things", Artificial Intelligence, Vol. 2, 1971

[Davis 87] E. Davis, "Constraint Propagation with Interval Labels", Artificial Intelligence, 32, 1987

[Dechter and Pearl 87] R. Dechter and J. Pearl, "Network-based heuristics for constraint satisfaction problems", Artificial Intelligence, Vol. 34, 1987

[deKleer 86] J. de Kleer, "An Assumption-Based TMS", Artificial Intelligence, Vol. 28, 1986

[Descotte and Latombe 85] Y. Descotte and J.- C. Latombe, "Making Compromises among Antagonist Constraints in a Planner", Artificial Intelligence, 27, 1985

[Dincbas 86] M. Dincbas, "Constraints, Logic Programming and Deductive Databases", France-Japan Artificial Intelligence and Computer Symposium 86, 1986

[Dixon and Simmons 84] J. R. Dixon and M. K. Simmons, "Expert Systems for Design: Standard V-Belt Drive Design as an Example of the Design-Evaluate-Redesign Architecture", Proc. of ASME Computers in Engineering Conference, 1984

[Dixon et al. 87] J. R. Dixon, A. Howes, P. R. Cohen, and M.K. Simmons, "DOMINIC I: Progress Towards Domain Independence In Design By Iterative Redesign", Proc. of ASME Computers in Engineering Conference, 1987

[Doyle 79] J. Doyle, "A Truth Maintenance System", Artificial Intelligence, Vol. 12, 1979

[Eastman 81] C. M. Eastman, "Recent Developments in Representation in the Science of Design", Proc. of IEEE 18th Design Automation Conference, 1981

[Eliyahu et al. 87] O. Eliyahu, L. Zaidenberg, and M. Ben-Bassat, "CAMEX - An Expert System For Process Planning On CNC Machines", Proc. of AAAI-87, 1987

[Feldman 88] R. Feldman, "Design of a Dependency-Directed Compiler for Constraint Propagation", Proc. of 1st International Conference on Industrial and Engineering Application of Artificial Intelligence and Expert Systems (IEA/AIE-88), 1988

[Fox 83] M. S. Fox, "Constraint-Directed Search: A Case Study of Job-Shop Scheduling", CMU-RI-TR-83-22, 1983

[Harris 86] D. R. Harris, "A Hybrid Structured Object and Constraint Representation Language", Proc. of AAAI-86, 1986

[Heintze et al. 86] N. C. Heintze, J. Jaffar, C. Lassez, J.-C. Lassez, K. McAloon, S. Michaylov, P. J. Stuckey, and R. H. C. Yap, "Constraint Logic Programming: A Reader", Proc. of Fourth IEEE Symposium on Logic Programming, 1987

[Inoue et al. 88] K. Inoue, Y. Nagai, Y. Fujii, S. Imamura, and T. Kojima, "Analysis of the Design Process of Machine Tools - Example of a Machine Unit for Lathes - " (in Japanese), ICOT Technical Memorandum, TM-494, 1988

[Kowalski and Thomas 83] T. J. Kowalski and D. E. Thomas, "The VLSI Design Automation Assistant: Prototype System", Proc. of IEEE 20th Design Automation Conference, 1983

[McDermott 78] D. McDermott, "Circuit Design as Problem Solving", Artificial Intelligence and Pattern Recognition in Computer Aided Design, (ed. J. C. Latombe), North-Holland, 1978

[McDermott 82] J. McDermott, "R1: A Rule-Based Configurer of Computer Systems", Artificial Intelligence, 19, 1982

[Medland 86] A. J. Medland, "The Computer-Based Design Process. 1., Engineering design-data processing I.", Kogan Page Ltd, 1986

[Mittal et al. 86] S. Mittal, C. L. Dym, and M. Morjaria, "A Knowledge-Based Framework for Design", Proc. of AAAI-86, 1986

[Murthy and Addanki 87] S. Murthy and S. Addanki, "PROMPT: An Innovative Design Tool", Proc. of AAAI 87, 1987

[Nagai 88a] Y. Nagai, "Expert System for Design Problems", Proc. of 6th Symposium on Fifth Generation Computer, (in Japanese), 1988

[Nagai 88b] Y. Nagai, "Towards an Expert System Architecture for Routine Design - Focusing on Constraint Representation and an Application Mechanism for Mechanical Design", Proc. of 3rd International Conference on CAD/CAM, Robotics and Factories of the Future (CARS & FOF '88), 1988

[Nagai 88c] Y. Nagai, "Towards Design Plan Generation for Routine Design Using Knowledge Compilation - Focusing on Constraint Representation and Its Application Mechanism for Mechanical Design", ICOT Technical Memorandum, TM-504, 1988

[Nagasawa 87] I. Nagasawa, "Design Expert System", IPSJ, Vol. 28, No. 2, (in Japanese), 1987

[Nicklaus et al. 87] D. J. Nicklaus, S. S. Tong, and C. J. Russo, "ENGENIOUS: A KNOWLEDGE-DIRECTED COMPUTER-AIDED DESIGN SHELL", Proc. of 3rd Conference on Artificial Intelligence Applications, 1987

[Phillips and Rosenfeld 87] R. E. Phillips and L. W. Rosenfeld, "A Knowledge-Based System for Design Automation", ICAD Inc., 1987

[Rinderle 87] J. R. Rinderle, "Implications of Function-Form-Fabrication Relations on Design Decomposition Strategies", Proc. of ASME Computers in Engineering Conference, 1987

[Stallman and Sussman 77] R. M. Stallman and G. L. Sussman, "Forward Reasoning and Dependency-Directed Backtracking in a System for Computer-Aided Circuit Analysis", Artificial Intelligence, Vol. 9, 1977

[Stefik 81a] M. Stefik, "Planning with Constraints (MOLGEN: Part 1)", Artificial Intelligence, Vol. 16, 1981

[Stefik 81b] M. Stefik, "Planning and Meta-Planning (MOLGEN: Part 2)", Artificial Intelligence, Vol. 16, 1981

[Struss 87] P. Struss, "Multiple Representation of Structure and Function", in "Expert Systems in Computer-Aided Design (ed. J. Gero), North-Holland, 1987

[Subrahmanyam 86] P. A. Subrahmanyam, "Synapse: An Expert System for VLSI Design", IEEE Computer, July, 1986

[Sussman and Steel 80] G. J. Sussman and G. L. Steel Jr., "CONSTRAINT - A Language for Expressing Almost-Hierarchical Descriptions", Artificial Intelligence, Vol. 14, 1980

[Taki et al. 84] K. Taki, M. Yokota, A. Yamamoto, H. Nishikawa, S. Uchida, N. Nakajima, and M. Mitsui, "Hardware Design and Implementation of the Personal Sequential Inference Machine (PSI)", Proc. of International Conference on Fifth Generation Computer Systems, 1984

[Terasaki et al. 88] S. Terasaki, Y. Nagai, T. Yokoyama, K. Inoue, E. Horiuchi and H. Taki, "Mechanical Design System Building Tool: MECHANICOT", JSAI, SIG-KBS, (in Japanese), October, 1988, (to-appear)

[Tomiyama and Hagen 87] T. Tomiyama and P. J. W. T. Hagen, "Organizing of Design Knowledge in an Intelligent CAD System", in Expert Systems in Computer-Aided Design (ed. J. Gero), North-Holland, 1987

[Yokoyama 88] T. Yokoyama, "FREEDOM : A Knowledge Representation System for Design Object Modeling", IPSJ, WG-AI, 88-AI-60, (in Japanese), 1988

Authors Index